Second Edition

Criminal Conduct & Substance Abuse Treatment

The Provider's Guide

TO THOSE WITH COMPASSION FOR HUMANKIND

Second Edition

Criminal Conduct & Substance Abuse Treatment

Strategies for Self-Improvement and Change

pathways to responsible living

The Provider's Guide

Kenneth W. Wanberg

Center for Addictions Research and Evaluation, Denver

Harvey B. Milkman

Metropolitan State College of Denver

SAGE Publications

Los Angeles • London • New Delhi • Singapore

The preparation and development of the 2nd edition of the *Provider's Guide* and the *Participant's Workbook of Criminal Conduct and Substance Abuse Treatment, Strategies for Self-Improvement and Change - Pathways to Responsible Living* were funded by: The Center for Addictions Research and Evaluation; The Center for Interdisciplinary Services; Sage Publications, Inc.; and the time and efforts of the authors.

The copyright holders and the authors grant to the State of Colorado, Alcohol and Drug Abuse Division, the rights to reproduce, or otherwise use *Criminal Conduct and Substance Abuse Treatment, Strategies for Self-Improvement and Change, Pathways to Responsible Living - The Provider's Guide* and the *Participant's Workbook* in treatment, probation, judicial, and correctional programs within the State of Colorado.

For information:

Sage Publications, Inc.
2455 Teller Road
Thousand Oaks, California 91320
E-mail: order@sagepub.com

Sage Publications India Pvt. Ltd.
B 1/I 1 Mohan Cooperative Industrial Area
Mathura Road, New Delhi 110 044
India

Sage Publications Ltd.
1 Oliver's Yard
55 City Road
London, EC1Y 1SP
United Kingdom

Sage Publications Asia-Pacific Pte. Ltd.
33 Pekin Street #02-01
Far East Square
Singapore 048763

Printed in the United States of America

Library of Congress Cataloging-in Publication Data

Wanberg, Kenneth W.
Criminal conduct and substance abuse treatment: Strategies for self-improvement and change: Pathways to responsible living-The provider's guide/Kenneth W. Wanberg and Harvey B. Milkman. -- 2nd ed.

p. cm.
Includes bibliographical references and index.

ISBN 978-1-4129-0592-3 (pbk.)

1. Criminals--Mental health. 2. Drug addicts--Treatment. 3. Criminals--Alcohol use. 4. Criminals--Drug use. I. Milkman, Harvey B. II. Title.

Printed on acid-free paper.

RC451.4.P68W36 2008

364.3--dc22   2007032326

08 09 10 11 10 9 8 7 6 5 4 3 2 1

Direct Correspondence should be sent to:

The Center for Addictions Research and Evaluation - CARE   or
P. O. Box 1975
Arvada, CO 80001-1975
303.421.1261
CARE@nilenet.com

The Center for Interdisciplinary Services - CIS
P. O. Box 16745
Golden, CO 80402
303.830.8500
cisdenver@msn.com

Acquiring Editor: Kassie Graves
Editorial Assistant: Veronica Novak
Production Editor: Sarah K. Quesenberry
Layout and Design: Karyn Sader

TABLE OF CONTENTS

PREFACE..xiii

INTRODUCTION...1

Overview of Second Edition..1
Changes in the Workbook...1
Treatment Changes and Enhancements..2
How This Provider's Guide Is Organized..3
The Participant's Workbook..3
Individualized Treatment Plan..4
The *SSC* Provider..5
Adjunct Provider's Guide for Women in Corrections...5
Addressing Diversity...5
Target Groups and Delivery Setting...5
Effectiveness and Efficacy of *SSC*...5
Distinguishing Between Self-Improvement and Change..8
Summary...8

SECTION I: THE TREATMENT PLATFORM...9

CHAPTER 1: Core Strategies and Conceptual Framework for Criminal Conduct and Substance Abuse Treatment............10
    Chapter Outline...10
    Chapter Objectives...10
    Overview..11
    Understanding Treatment, Psychotherapy and Counseling...11
    The Core Strategies of the Treatment Platform..14
    Program Conceptual Framework..22
    Chapter Review..22

CHAPTER 2: The Therapeutic Relationship and Motivational Enhancement.......................................24
    Chapter Outline...24
    Chapter Objectives...24
    Overview..25
    Efficacy of Psychosocial Therapies..25
    Common Determinants of Treatment Outcome..26
    Provider Skills in Integrating Education and Therapy...36
    Correctional-Therapeutic Partnership...37
    Profile of the Effective SA Judicial Client Provider..40
    Provider Cultural Competence: Capitalizing on Strengths of Diversity...42
    Chapter Review..45

CHAPTER 3: Treatment Phases: Facilitating Learning, Growth and Change.......................................46
    Chapter Outline...46
    Chapter Objectives...46
    Overview..47
    Traditional Theories of Learning...47
    A Dynamic Model for Learning and Growth..48
    The Stages of Change and the *SSC* Treatment Structure..51
    Fundamental Issues Regarding Learning and Change..59
    Chapter Review..62

CHAPTER 4: Cognitive-Behavioral Approach as the Platform for Change 63
    Chapter Outline 63
    Chapter Objectives 63
    Overview 64
    Brief Summary of Historical Roots of CB Treatment 64
    Effectiveness of CBT 65
    CB Assumptions Underlying AOD Abuse and CC and Their Treatment 66
    Cognitive Structures That Are the Focus of Treatment 66
    Cognitive Processes That Are the Focus of Treatment 69
    Cognitive-Behavioral Methods Used in *SSC* 72
    Self-Efficacy: A Focal Issue in CB Treatment 75
    The Context of Change 76
    The Emotional Component of CBT 76
    The *SSC* CB Model for Change: The *SSC* Cognitive-Behavioral Map 77
    Chapter Review 79

CHAPTER 5: Relapse and Recidivism Prevention 80
    Chapter Outline 80
    Chapter Objectives 80
    Overview 81
    Relapse Prevention: A Major Paradigm Shift 81
    Addressing Recidivism Prevention 81
    Overview of Marlatt's Relapse Prevention Model 82
    The Relapse and Recidivism Model Used in *SSC* 84
    Chapter Review 94

SECTION II: OPERATIONAL GUIDELINES **96**

CHAPTER 6: Assessment Structure, Process and Instrumentation 97
    Chapter Outline 97
    Chapter Objectives 97
    Overview 98
    The Convergent Validation Model of Assessment 98
    Screening for *SSC*: Discerning Criminal Conduct and AOD Problems 101
    The Assessment Program: The *PACE* Index 105
    PACE Case Example Presentation 111
    Client Self-Assessment During *SSC* 119
    Summary of *PACE* and the Automated *PACE Manager* 120
    Chapter Review 120

CHAPTER 7: Methods and Skills for Effective Program Delivery 123
    Chapter Outline 123
    Chapter Objectives 123
    Overview 124
    Intake and Admission Procedures and Guidelines 124
    Program Agreements and Ground Rules: Expectations of Clients 125
    Expectations of Providers and Group Leaders 126
    Structure and Strategies of Program Delivery 126
    Phase and Program Closure Guidelines 128
    Removal of Client From Program 130
    Manual-Guided Delivery Principles for *SSC* 131

CHAPTER 7: Provider Knowledge and Skills Necessary in *SSC* Delivery...133
    Principles of Effective Group Leadership...137
    The Provider's Many Hats...139
    Reentry and Reintegration..139
    Provider Skill Evaluation and Supervision 140
    Provider Qualifications..140
    Evaluating Session Delivery Efficacy 140
    Chapter Review...140

SECTION III: THE TREATMENT CURRICULUM **143**

INTRODUCTION TO SECTION III..144
    Overview 144
    Goals and Objectives of *SSC*...145
    Key Topics of the Treatment Curriculum...145
    How *Section III* of This Provider's Guide Is Organized..146
    Participant's Workbook 147
    Program Agreements and Ground Rules: Expectations of Clients 147
    Service Delivery Options and Approaches...148
    Intake and In-Depth Assessment...148
    Client Progress and Change Evaluation 148
    Orientation Session 148

PHASE I: CHALLENGE TO CHANGE - BUILDING KNOWLEDGE AND SKILLS FOR RESPONSIBLE LIVING **149**

Introduction to *Phase I*..150
Provider Goals and Objectives for *Phase I* 150

MODULE 1: ORIENTATION: HOW THIS PROGRAM WORKS 151

Session 1: Getting Started: How *SSC* Works and Developing Trust 152
Session 2: Rules, Tools and Targets for Change..155

MODULE 2: COGNITIVE-BEHAVIORAL APPROACH TO CHANGE AND RESPONSIBLE LIVING.........................158

Session 3: How Our Thinking, Attitudes and Beliefs Control Our Actions...159
Session 4: How Behavior Is Learned and Changed...162

MODULE 3: ALCOHOL AND OTHER DRUG (AOD) USE PATTERNS AND OUTCOMES 164

Session 5: Alcohol and Other Drugs: How Do the Facts Fit You?...165
Session 6: Understanding Alcohol or Other Drug Use Patterns: How Do They Fit You?..............................169
Session 7: AOD Impaired Control Cycles: Pathways to Problem Outcomes Addiction................................171
Session 8: AOD Problem Outcomes - Patterns of Misuse and Abuse: How Do They Fit You?......................176

MODULE 4: UNDERSTANDING AND CHANGING CRIMINAL THINKING AND BEHAVIOR 179

Session 9: Prosocial, Antisocial and Criminal Thinking and Behavior 180
Session 10: Thinking Errors and the Criminal Conduct Cycle 183

MODULE 5: SHARING AND LISTENING: COMMUNICATION PATHWAYS TO SELF-AWARENESS AND OTHER-
AWARENESS 185

Session 11: Pathways to Self-Awareness: The Skills of Active Sharing..186
Session 12: Pathways to Other-Awareness: The Skills of Active Listening...192
Session 13: Deeper Sharing of Your AOD Use Problems and Emotions...194
Session 14: Deeper Sharing of Your Criminal Conduct History 196

MODULE 6: UNDERSTANDING AND PREVENTING RELAPSE AND RECIDIVISM...199

Session 15: Pathways to Relapse and Recidivism 205
Session 16: Pathways to Relapse and Recidivism Prevention..208
Session 17: Managing Urges and Cravings and Learning Refusal Skills 211

MODULE 7: STEPS, STAGES AND SKILLS FOR SELF-IMPROVEMENT AND CHANGE 215

Session 18: Stages, Steps and Roadblocks to Change..218
Session 19: Skills for Changing Thinking and Beliefs 220
Session 20: Plan for Change: Your *Master Profile* and *Master Assessment Plan*...224

PHASE I CLOSURE: LOOKING FORWARD AND MAKING A COMMITMENT...226

PHASE II: COMMITMENT TO CHANGE - STRENGTHENING SKILLS FOR SELF-IMPROVEMENT, CHANGE AND RESPONSIBLE LIVING 227

Summary of *Phase I*...228
Provider Skills and Treatment Strategies for *Phase II*...228
Provider Goals and Objectives for *Phase II* 229
Focus on Positive Actions and Outcomes - The STEP Approach...229
Preparation Session for *Phase II*..230

MODULE 8: MENTAL SELF-CONTROL: MANAGING THOUGHTS AND EMOTIONS 231

Session 21: Practicing Mental Self-Control and Change Skills...233
Session 22: Recognizing and Being Aware of Negative Thinking 234
Session 23: Managing and Changing Negative Thinking and Beliefs 237
Session 24: Recognizing and Changing Errors in Thinking 240
Session 25: Understanding Stress: Its Causes and Roots 242
Session 26: Managing Stress and Emotions...246
Session 27: Managing and Regulating Anger...248
Session 28: Managing Guilt and Depression and Increasing Positive Emotions..253

MODULE 9: SOCIAL AND RELATIONSHIP SKILLS BUILDING...257

Session 29: Strengthening Communication Skills...260
Session 30: Starting a Difficult Conversation and Keeping It Going...262
Session 31: Giving and Receiving Praise and Positive Reinforcement..264
Session 32: Skills in Problem Solving..265
Session 33: It's Your Right: Developing Assertiveness Skills 267
Session 34: Managing Anger in Relationships - The Guilt-Anger Cycle..270
Session 35: Developing and Keeping Close and Intimate Relationships 275

MODULE 10: SKILLS IN SOCIAL AND COMMUNITY RESPONSIBILITY..278

Session 36: Strengthening Character and Prosocial Attitudes and Behaviors..281
Session 37: Understanding and Practicing Empathy...283

Session 38: Understanding Aggression, Abuse and Violence 288
Session 39: Preventing Aggression, Abuse and Violence.. 292
Session 40: Settling Conflicts and Getting to a Win-Win 295
Session 41: Values and Morals for Responsible Living: The Moral Dilemma 299
Session 42: Giving to the Community and Driving With Care 302

PHASE II CLOSURE: LOOKING FORWARD AND TAKING OWNERSHIP 304

PHASE III: OWNERSHIP OF CHANGE - LIFESTYLE BALANCE AND HEALTHY LIVING 305

Summary of *Phases I* and *II*.. 306
Provider Skills and Treatment Strategies for *Phase III* 306
Provider Goals and Objectives of *Phase III* 307
Preparation Session for *Phase III* 307

MODULE 11: RELAPSE AND RECIDIVISM PREVENTION: STRATEGIES FOR A BALANCED LIFESTYLE 308

Session 43: Strengthening Your Relapse and Recidivism Prevention Skills 310
Session 44: Strengthening Your Relapse and Recidivism Prevention Plan 311
Session 45: Strengthening R&R Prevention Through Critical Reasoning................................ 315

MODULE 12: STRENGTHENING OWNERSHIP OF CHANGE: SKILLS FOR A HEALTHY LIFESTYLE 318

Session 46: Managing Work, Job and Time... 319
Session 47: Healthy Play and Leisure Time... 323
Session 48: Relaxation Skills for a Healthy Lifestyle.. 325
Session 49: Healthy Eating, Personal Care and Physical Activity 326
Session 50: Receiving and Giving Support for Change and Responsible Living................... 328

PHASE III CLOSURE: CONTINUING YOUR JOURNEY OF RESPONSIBLE LIVING........................ 329

REFERENCES 331
APPENDIX A: INTAKE AND ADMISSION FORMS.. 357
APPENDIX B: DRIVING ASSESSMENT SURVEY.. 365

LIST OF FIGURES

SECTION I

Figure 1.1: Conceptual Framework for the Treatment of Substance Abusing Judicial Clients................. 23
Figure 2.1: Interactive Components of the Treatment Process... 35
Figure 2.2: Collaborative Correctional-Intervention Partnership 40
Figure 2.3: Profile of the Judicial Provider.. 43
Figure 3.1: The Cyclical Process and Change in Treatment 50
Figure 4.1: Model of Cognitive Structures and Processes... 68
Figure 4.2: The Cognitive-Behavioral (CB) Map... 78
Figure 5.1: Marlatt's Relapse Prevention Model... 85
Figure 5.2: Process of Relapse and Recidivism Prevention.. 90
Figure 5.3: Cognitive Behavioral Pathways for Relapse and Recidivism................................. 91
Figure 5.4: Pathways for Relapse and Recidivism Prevention 92

SECTION II

Figure 6.1: Adult Substance Use Survey - Revised (ASUS-R) Profile Summary 115
Figure 6.2: Adult Clinical Assessment Profile Summary 116
Figure 6.3: Adult Self-Assessment Questionnaire (AdSAQ) Profile Summary 117
Figure 6.4: Program Attending Record (PAR) for Client at End of Phase I 117
Figure 6.5: Client Program Response - Client (CPR-C) Global Response Scale 117
Figure 6.6: Client Program Response - Provider (CPR-P) Global Response Scale 118
Figure 6.7: Self-Evaluation Questionnaire (SEQ): Admission Results Compared with *SSC* Three Months Across Six
    Scales 118

SECTION III

Figure 1: *SSC* Goals and Objectives 145
Figure 2: The Cognitive-Behavioral (CB) Map 154
Figure 3: Cognitive-Behavioral Process of Learning and Change 161
Figure 4: Cognitive-Behavioral *STEP Method* 230
Figure 5: Internal Cognitive and Affective Stimulation and Outcomes 232

LIST OF TABLES

SECTION I

Table 3.1: Goal and Objectives for Phase I: Challenge to Change 55
Table 3.2: Goal and Objectives for Phase II: Commitment to Change 57
Table 3.3: Goal and Objectives for Phase III: Ownership of Change 59

SECTION II

Table 6.1: Characteristics of the Antisocial Personality Pattern 102
Table 6.2: DSM-IV Criteria for Substance Abuse 104
Table 6.3: DSM-IV Criteria for Substance Dependence 105
Table 6.4: Tasks and Instruments used in *PACE* 107
Table 6.5: Master Assessment Plan (MAP) 121
Table 7.1: Phase I Review Guide 130
Table 7.2: Provider's Master Knowledge and Skills List 141

SECTION III

Table 1: Examples of Cognitive-Behavioral Responses That Reduce Risk Factors and Criminogenic Needs 182

ACKNOWLEDGMENTS

In the decade since its initial publication, *Criminal Conduct and Substance Abuse Treatment: Strategies for Self-Improvement and Change (SSC)* has been delivered to an estimated 75,000 judicial clients throughout the United States as well as in correctional institutions in Queensland and New South Whales Australia. Treatment settings have included community-based alcohol and drug treatment agencies, probation and parole supervision sites, residential community corrections placements, jails and prisons.

As in the first edition, the authors have drawn upon numerous resources, documents and publications in developing the second edition of this *Provider's Guide*. In addition to reviewing the vast repository of research and literature on criminal conduct and substance abuse treatment that has emerged in the past ten years, the authors have consulted with hundreds of treatment provider's and correctional clients regarding their first-hand experience with SSC facilitation and participation. We extend our heartfelt appreciation for their invaluable suggestions concerning additions and modifications to the first edition.

We also want to recognize major works in the treatment field that have provided guidance for the development of the core strategies and foundational models on which both the first and second edition were built. We acknowledge and extend our appreciation to the importance of the work of Alan Marlatt, George Parks and their associates for their seminal and evolving perspectives on Relapse Prevention (RP). Their contribution provided an invaluable shift in the substance abuse treatment paradigm and has had profound influence on enhancing the efficacy of addictions treatment. Marlatt's RP model provided the basis for the development of the relapse and recidivism prevention foundational model of *SSC*.

The work of Kurt Lewin and Heinz Werner on how individuals grow and develop and the work of James Prochaska, Carlo DiClemente and associates in their ground breaking transtheoretical formulation of stages of change were merged to provided an important basis for the development of the treatment phases and change model of *SSC*. We are indebted to the work of Albert Bandura and Donald Meichenbaum who laid the groundwork for applying social learning theory to clinical practice and to Albert Ellis and Aaron Beck whose works were the primary forces behind the emergence of cognitive-behavioral therapy - the primary foundational model for *SSC*.

Carl Rogers and associates pinpointed the essential components of the client-centered approach and the therapeutic relationship - empathy, genuineness and unconditional positive regard - a core strategy and the connecting thread for the matrix of *SSC*. The work of William Miller and associates provided guideposts for understanding and enhancing client motivation and readiness for treatment, all essential components of the therapeutic relationship.

The development of the core strategy of integrating the therapeutic and correctional within the framework of the *SSC* strategy of moral responsibility to others and the community drew from the work of Don Andrews and Jim Bonta and their associates who explored essential principles and validated the efficacy of correctional treatment; and from the pioneering work of Robert Ross and associates who provided an understanding of the application of cognitive-behavioral approaches and moral reasoning in the treatment of correctional clients. Finally, John Horn, Kenneth Wanberg and their associates are acknowledged for their pioneering work in identifying multiple dimensions and conditions associated with substance use and abuse which provided the basis for the multidimensional and convergent validation model that is used in evaluating substance abusing judicial clients.

The clinical, research, consultation and academic experience of the authors have provided the most substantive basis for this edition. We view the most important impact of our work as implementing a new wave in CBT correctional treatment - *Social Responsibility Therapy* - responding to the ethical mandate for combining effective and humane treatment for judicial clients while holding high standards for accountability and moral development. We are most grateful of the inestimable contributions from social scientists, correctional practitioners, judicial program administrators and judicial clients for having promoted the intent and implementation of this approach.

PREFACE

No man is an island entire of itself; any man's death diminishes me, because I am involved in mankind, and therefore never send to know for whom the bell tolls; it tolls for thee.

JOHN DONNE, 1572-1631

AS THE 20TH century dawned, medicine was confronted with a new type of malady. It was functional or psychologically based. The condition was called "neurosis." Freudian thinking and psychoanalysis defined both the cause and response to this new "illness." Freudian theory concluded that the basis of neurosis was the dominant conscience or superego that repressed freedom of expression and desires (Mowrer, 1963, p. 160).

The Freudian response to this new illness set the stage for 100 years of psychotherapy that was self-oriented and directed at relieving the psychological pain of guilt, depression and anxiety. At the time, this was a therapy that people needed. It was a therapy that saw the "cure" as being free of the constraints and repression of a strong conscience and guilt - of the superego. But it did not provide us with the answer to the problem of moral responsibility towards others and the community and the problem of freedom of choice. Freudian theory was just as deterministic as were the voices of moral suasion, philosophy and theology of the past (Mowrer, 1963).

O. H. Mowrer observed that as the 19th century came to a close, Western society was left with two major dilemmas: the failure of the voices of moral suasion, philosophy and theology to provide us with a reasonable answer to the problem of guilt and moral responsibility and the issue of freedom of choice (1963, 1964). Freudian psychology gave us insight and a therapy that helped to address the problem of neurosis. What was lacking was a clear approach to responsibility towards and caring about others and the issue of freedom of choice. As Mowrer observed, "...to be 'free' in the sense of embracing the doctrine of...irresponsibility is not to be free at all, humanly speaking, but lost" (1963, p. 161).

Behaviorism was a response to the Freudian doctrine. It repudiated the idea that things internal, personal or subjective had anything to do with the outcome of behavior. The stimulus-response model was all that was needed to explain behavior. Yet, behaviorism was just as deterministic as Freudian doctrine. Accountability and choice were removed. As Mowrer (1963) noted, behaviorism ended up "obliterating the whole notion of freedom, choice, responsibility by reducing behavior, absolutely and completely, to S-R connections and reflexes" (p. 163).

At the mid-point of the 20th century, psychotherapy and psychology were still left with the solution to the two major dilemmas:

▶ a need for a theory that was not deterministic, but one that could give the individual the freedom to choose right and wrong, to develop what we might call moral freedom; and

▶ a need to develop a therapeutic method that places the responsibility of behavior on conscious choice; and to challenge individuals to be responsible in their choices.

As a response to the determinism of psychoanalysis and behaviorism, new approaches began to emerge that clearly addressed the dilemma of freedom of choice - or that the disturbances in behavior were not determined by factors and conditions beyond individual choice.

Mowrer's work, *The New Group Therapy* (1964), provided us with some guidelines with respect to resolving the issue of moral freedom and responsibility. He saw some hope in existential psychology, particularly in its firm stand against the determinism of behaviorism and psychoanalysis. He noted the change in behavior theory as it moved away from the simplistic ideas of behaviorism, and began to give credence to the concept of choice and decision as determinants of behavioral outcomes.

He also noted that the emphasis on the unconscious, even within the psychoanalytic school, was giving way to a focus on "ego psychology," "ego strength" and "ego weakness," and a renewed interest in the superego or conscience. He saw psychology moving towards a greater awareness of man being a social creature that needs to be connected, united and that "current therapeutic effort is in the direction of trying to help such individuals recover their sociality, relatedness, community, identity" (1963, p. 166).

Other schools emerged that began to provide some solutions to these issues. Humanistic approaches, and more specifically, the client-centered models of Rogers gave clear guidelines with respect to freedom of choice and self-responsibility. Within this framework, each individual has the capacity to make choices, and to make decisions about his or her own destiny.

The integration of cognitive approaches with behavioral therapy provided greater strides in rendering a model as to how individuals can be responsible for their own behavior. The cognitive-behavioral paradigm that the individual can be in control of the thoughts that produce feelings and behavioral outcomes provided an even clearer resolution of moral freedom and the resolution of the guilt problem.

Yet, all of the new therapies developed within the humanistic, existential and cognitive-behavioral schools were still self-directed or self-focused. These therapies were primarily concerned with alleviating the pain of the client, whether this pain be depression, anxiety, disturbed thinking or substance abuse. The issues of sociality, relatedness and responsibility to others and the community were still to be addressed by mainstream psychotherapy.

The philosophical roots of mainstream psychotherapy are based on the Western view of modernity which sees man as egocentric, puts the individual as supraordinate to social role obligations, and focuses on individualism, freedom and individual expression (O'Hara, 1997). This worldview idealizes and codifies the individual and projects the individual outward. Thus, mainstream psychotherapy is essentially egocentric. O'Hara (1997) sees a need to move beyond the egocentric therapy of Western civilization to a sociocentric, more holistic framework. This is moving towards a connected consciousness and builds on the gains of egocentric psychology. Sociocentric therapy focuses on prosociality, relational awareness and moral responsibility to others and the community.

There was some clear movement in this direction in the last one-third of the 20th century as social systems theory and family therapy impacted on the helping-psychology movement. The effect of the "system" on the individual, relationship building and maintenance and interpersonal theory became important focuses. Success in marriage, in relationships and in the workplace became strong focuses in psychology. The family and interpersonal movements introduced the element of responsibility towards others. Yet, boiled down, the ultimate focus of therapy was still on responsibility to the self, personal growth and change, and the mitigation of psychological pain. The new therapies that emerged to address the determinism of psychoanalysis and behaviorism remained egocentric and still did not fully address the issue of prosociality and moral responsibility towards others, the community and society.

At the close of the 20th century, we were again faced with another malady, one that inundates human service treatment centers and clinics and the helping professions. It is an even more serious malady than that of neurosis since it has a profound effect on society and culture. It is called sociopathy or character pathology. Whereas a strong and restrictive superego and conscience and a repressed id may have been a valid explanation of psychopathology and an important focus in therapy in Freud's day and even during much of the 20th century, it failed to address an epidemic psychopathology - sociopathy. The focus on responsibility to the self, the mitigation of personal psychological pain, personal growth, unbounded self-expression in therapeutic approaches and treatment and in pop psychology may have been at the expense of ignoring the importance of moral development, character building and responsibility towards others and society. This may be what Paul Tillich meant by "the psychic disintegration of the masses" in modern times (from Mowrer, 1964).

In a lecture delivered at a theological seminary in the early 1960's, O. H. Mowrer pointed out that psychology and psychiatry failed to firmly address moral responsibility (Wanberg, 2007). In that lecture, Mowrer, somewhat explicitly, predicted that in the latter part of the 20th century we would see an increase in antisocial behaviors, criminal conduct and the violation of the rights of others, including an increase in violence in American society.

Indeed, in the last quarter of the 20th century, we saw prisons fill faster than we could build them. At the turn of the 21st century, over two million Americans were incarcerated and almost 10 million juveniles and adults were under some kind of criminal justice supervision. Yet, the offender element represents only one component of the new psychopathology. Antisocial behavior, character pathology and violence became major and dominant character expressions and themes in movie and television productions. In the last 20 years of the 20th century, traffic accidents, mostly caused by carelessness and irresponsibility, resulted in an annual average of over 50,000 deaths, hundreds of thousands of injuries and billions of dollars in cost. We have seen the lack of moral responsibility in the workplace, in business practices, and in unscrupulous attitudes and behaviors of management and officers in corporate society. It is represented by the enormous amount of public littering, and the lack of pride and concern towards personal and community property, e.g., graffiti. It is found at all levels of society.

In the last decade of the 20th century, a large percent of the clients in mental health and addiction treatment centers were found to have characterological and antisocial problems. Today, these problems are prominent features among mental health and substance abuse client populations, and in many treatment centers they are found in the majority of the treatment population. Leukefeld and Tims (1992) stated: "...the criminal justice system is awash with drug users." The opposite is just as true. "The mental health and substance abuse treatment system is awash with offenders and clients with characterological and antisocial problems." We acknowledge this. But this is not the main issue.

The main issue is that we have not significantly developed our approaches to psychotherapy in order to address sociopathy. We continue using therapeutic interventions based on the old model of focusing mainly on individual growth and change, enhancing responsibility to the self and easing psychological pain. For a long time, we refused to even offer psychotherapeutic and mental health services to individuals who were labeled "antisocial."

During the 1970's up through the early 1990's,

there was a resistance on the part of adolescent mental health treatment facilities to admit juvenile offenders. Often such requests were met with downright refusal even when a mental health problem was apparent with the offender (Wanberg, 2007). The stock response was, "he's antisocial." Well into the 1990's, psychiatry and psychology often judged individuals with antisocial personality problems or a history of criminal conduct as untreatable.

Even as late as 1999, treatment of the antisocial personality disorder was left out of a text that addressed the treatment of personality disorders (Sperry, 1999). In that work, it was concluded that antisocial personality disorders "are not considered as treatable and are less commonly seen in outpatient settings" (p. xvii). In the 2006 edition of this book, this statement was changed to "are still considered as less treatable..." (p. xxi).

Beck et al. (2004) did include a chapter on the treatment of antisocial personality disorders (APD) in their book *Cognitive Therapy of Personality Disorders.* Acknowledging that therapists view this group of clients as "especially difficult," they clearly state that cognitive therapy of APD can "be conceptualized as improving moral and social behavior through enhancement of cognitive functioning" (p. 168). Such cognitive growth would involve "fostering a transition from concrete operations and self-determination towards more abstract thinking and interpersonal consideration. Moral functioning is regarded as a dimension within the broader context of epistemology, or ways of thinking and knowing" (p. 169).

Today, a large percent of clients in adolescent and adult mental health and substance abuse outpatient and inpatient programs have significant if not serious antisocial problems. In fact, juvenile offenders make up a large proportion of many of these treatment settings across America. But have the mental health and substance abuse treatment institutions risen to the challenge of delivering a sociocentric therapy of moral responsibility and caring towards others and the community?

We are beginning to acknowledge the importance of sociocentric therapies and bringing together the therapeutic and the correctional approaches. Our first work in this field, *Criminal Conduct and Substance Abuse Treatment: Strategies for Self-*

Improvement and Change, made this the key focus in developing an approach in treating the substance abusing offender (Wanberg & Milkman, 1998). Our work in *Criminal Conduct and Substance Abuse Treatment for Adolescents* (Milkman & Wanberg 2005) and the *Education and Treatment of the Impaired Driving Offender* (Wanberg, Milkman & Timken, 2005) expanded on this focus. In our current review of the literature, it is apparent that considerable progress has been made in this area. Yet, further program development and research are needed on what are the most effective approaches in enhancing prosociality, not only with judicial clients, but within society as a whole.

Suffice it to say, if treatment of the judicial client is to be effective, the therapeutic goal of helping clients resolve their psychological problems and pain must be integrated with the correctional goal of helping the client develop thinking and behaviors that demonstrate responsibility towards others and towards society. Even more important, if we are to effectively address the "new" psychopathology of sociopathy found in many clients who are not offenders, then we must merge the egocentric therapeutic paradigm with a sociocentric approach that includes a psychology of caring and social responsibility towards others and the community.

A number of disciplines during the last half of the 20th century did acknowledge the importance of addressing moral and character development, going beyond responsibility to the self and the treatment of personal pain and problems, and focusing on responsible living and responsibility to society. Piaget's work on moral judgment in childhood (1932), Erikson's work on the developmental stages and integrity (1959, 1968, 1975), Kohlberg and Colby's work on moral development and judgment (Colby & Kohlberg, 1987; Kohlberg, 1964, 1981), Bandura's (1977a) work on social learning theory, Hare's work on psychopathy (1970, 1980), Ross and his colleagues' (Ross, Fabiano & Ross, 1986) work on reasoning and rehabilitation; Hoffman's (1984, 1987) studies on the relationship of empathy to prosocial behavior and moral judgment; Little and Robinson's (1986) moral reconation program; and Peterson and Seligman's (2004) work on character strengths and virtue are but a few that should be acknowledged. As well, the emergence of community psychology during the 1960's addresses the importance of the individual's relationship to the community and the society at large.

Alan Wolfe (2001) noted that the 19th century was about gaining economic freedom and the 20th century was about gaining political freedom. He suggests that the 21st century will be about deciding what is moral and what is not moral - or gaining moral freedom. Choosing to live unbounded by moral rules is not a viable option. The higher consciousness of the 21st century will enable us to live with a clear sense of responsibility, not only to oneself, but to others and the community. Wolfe concludes from his interviews that "Americans make a clear distinction between moral choice and unboundedness. The former, they usually insist, is something worth having. The latter, most of them feel, is something worth avoiding" (p. 51).

The underlying assumption of this second edition of *Criminal Conduct and Substance Abuse Treatment, Strategies for Self-Improvement and Change - Pathways to Responsible Living* is that effective intervention and treatment of the judicial client must involve an education and therapeutic model that is centered around responsibility to others and the community. Effective treatment of judicial clients must go beyond the more traditional therapeutic approaches of self-caring and responsibility to the self and make caring about and responsibility to the community and society of equal importance. Thus, we see social responsibility therapy (SRT) as a core element in the treatment of judicial clients.

We hope to provide the judicial client with strategies that will prevent relapsing into problematic AOD use and criminal conduct. However, we strive to do more than prevent the occurrence of these negative behaviors. As conveyed by our second title of this work, *Pathways for Responsible Living,* we also strive to provide judicial clients with the strategies, concepts and skills to bring meaning and responsibility into all facets of their lives.

INTRODUCTION

OVERVIEW OF SECOND EDITION

This second edition of *Criminal Conduct and Substance Abuse Treatment: Strategies for Self-Improvement and Change - Pathways to Responsible Living (SSC)* builds on the basic foundation of the first edition. However, there are some significant enhancements and changes in the *Participant's Workbook (Workbook)* and a restructuring of the *Provider's Guide (Guide)*.

First, the historical perspectives, theoretical and research foundations of criminal conduct and substance abuse treatment covered in *Section I* of the first edition of the *Provider's Guide* are now presented in a separate resource book: *Criminal Conduct and Substance Abuse Treatment: History, Research and Foundational Models, A Resource Guide* (Wanberg & Milkman, 2008). This comprehensive and scholarly work describes historical foundations of the judicial system and the evolution of correctional treatment. Additionally, the resource volume presents research that supports the efficacy of correctional treatment, and a description of several high-quality treatment and rehabilitation programs for judicial clients. Finally, the key foundational strategies that are basic to reputable treatment programs addressing substance abuse and criminal conduct are presented. We will refer to this companion book to the current *SSC Provider's Guide* as *The Resource Guide*.

Second, the current document, *Criminal Conduct and Substance Abuse Treatment: Strategies for Self-Improvement and Change - Pathways to Responsible Living, the Provider's Guide,* referred to from now on as the *Guide,* consists of three sections, each directly relevant to the delivery of the *SSC* curriculum as presented in the *Participant's Workbook (Workbook).* The organization and essential elements of this current work will be summarized later in this *Introduction*.

CHANGES IN THE WORKBOOK

The most important change in the *Workbook* has been to include all of the essential and necessary concepts, skills, and exercises for the delivery of each session. In the first edition, much of the essential delivery content was in the *Provider's Guide.* Although the second edition *Guide* provides enhanced information and adjunct exercises to supplement session delivery, the provider can essentially use what is in the *Workbook* to deliver each session. This prevents having to go back and forth between the *Guide* and the *Workbook* in making sure that all of the necessary information was covered in each session.

This, however, makes the *Workbook* more dense and comprehensive, and initially, this can overwhelm clients. Some clients will not be able to read or digest all of the material in some sessions, particularly those in *Phase I.* Thus, the provider should explain that the essential material will be presented in group, and not to be concerned if all of the material is not read by clients on their own. However, clients should be encouraged to read each session before coming to group.

The *Workbook* has been reorganized. *Phase I* still covers all of the essential skills and concepts that are the primary focus in *SSC.* The two sessions in *Module I* of *Phase I* have been clearly delineated as the *Orientation to SSC.* All clients receive this module, either in their initial group where a closed group model is used, or in an orientation group or individual session where the *SSC* delivery structure uses an open group approach (clients enter *SSC* at certain designated points).

Module 8 of the first edition of the *Workbook,* which was the client in-depth self-assessment and included the *Master Profile (MP)* and the *Master Assessment Plan (MAP),* is now *Session 20* of *Phase I, Module 7.* Clients are asked to complete the *MP* and *MAP* within the first month of *SSC,* or before eight sessions are completed.

There are several reasons for having clients complete a draft of the *MP* and *MAP* during the first month of *SSC,* and then updating it during *SSC.* First, it gives clients and providers a blueprint or plan for change in *Phase I.* Second, when clients update their *MAP* by dating the completion of a treatment objective or resolving a problem, this represents a measure of change. Adding new problems to the *MAP* represents awareness of changes that need to be made. Third, satisfactory development of the *MAP*, which includes a relapse and recidivism prevention plan, represents an important criterion for being admitted into *Phases II* and *III* of *SSC*. For agencies that offer only *Phase I*, and then refer clients to another agency for *Phases II* and *III*, the *MAP* accompanies the client and continues as the *Guide* for change. Finally, the *MAP* can be used by judicial supervisors to guide successful completion of the supervision process.

TREATMENT CHANGES AND ENHANCEMENTS

The *SSC* treatment curriculum has been changed and enhanced in several important ways. First, nine tools for change are specifically identified and introduced in the *Orientation Session* of *Module 1*. Four of the nine are new to the curriculum. These nine tools are:

1. *Cognitive-Behavioral Map Exercise (CB Map Exercise)*;

2. *Autobiography*;

3. *Master Skills List* (*MSL*), *Program Guide 1*, new in the curriculum;

4. *Master Profile* (*MP*), *Program Guide 2*;

5. *Master Assessment Plan* (*MAP*), *Program Guide 3*;

6. *Weekly Thinking and Action Patterns (TAP) Charting, Program Guide 4*, also new in the curriculum;

7. *Thinking Report*;

8. *Re-thinking Report*, a new innovation; and the

9. *SSC Change Scale* which is a self-assessment measure of the client's level of knowledge and skills learned during each session. This is also a new introduction to *SSC*.

Each of these is described in *Section III* of this *Guide* and in *Session 2* of the *Workbook*.

Another important change is the organization of *Phase II*, which is the skills-building stage of *SSC*. It is structured into three cognitive-behavioral (CB) approaches to the treatment of substance abusing (SA) judicial clients:

▶ Cognitive restructuring and self-control, *Module 8*;

▶ Social and interpersonal skills building, *Module 9*; and

▶ Skills to develop a prosocial and harmonious relationship with the community or social responsibility therapy (SRT), *Module 10*.

Another new feature is the *STEP* (**S**ituation - **T**hinking Change - **E**motional Response - **P**ositive Outcomes) *Method*, which helps clients focus on **thinking change** that leads to positive outcomes. This is introduced in *Phase II*. Whereas *Phase I* of treatment uses the *CB Map* to help clients look at how thinking leads to both adaptive or positive outcomes and maladaptive or negative outcomes, *STEP* focuses on how to generate positive outcomes from situations and events.

Phase III enhances the focus on relapse and recidivism and establishing a balanced lifestyle. *Module 12* provides a strong focus on developing healthy lifestyle alternatives to alcohol and other drug (AOD) use and criminal involvement. New features include sessions on relaxation skills, healthy eating and physical activity, and receiving and giving support through mentoring.

Overall, there is an enhancement in the concepts and skills of cognitive restructuring and social skills building with additional and new approaches to these areas of implementing change. There is a much stronger emphasis on learning skills and concepts to establish a positive and harmonious - prosocial and moral responsibility - relationship with others and the community.

The second edition of the *SSC* treatment curriculum builds on and utilizes the vast work and literature found in the general treatment of alcohol and other drug (AOD) problems. It also builds on and utilizes recent developments in the area of assessment and therapeutic interventions, and particularly cognitive-behavioral treatment. In the past 10 years, a fairly extensive corpus of literature on offender and judicial client treatment has emerged. Every effort was made to integrate these more recent developments in the treatment of criminal conduct (CC).

HOW THIS PROVIDER'S GUIDE IS ORGANIZED

This *Guide* has three sections. *Section I* provides the core strategies upon which *SSC* is built. *Chapter 1* outlines the treatment platform and conceptual framework of *SSC*. It provides an overview of the treatment dimensions and principles that represent the connecting threads of the *SSC* program. It also discusses the 10 core strategies that are used in the delivery of *SSC*.

Chapters 2 through *5* discuss five foundational strategies of *SSC*. *Chapter 2* focuses on the core strategy of developing a therapeutic relationship through motivational enhancement and a therapeutic alliance. The essential traits and characteristics of the effective *SSC* provider are outlined. This chapter also addresses the issue of seeing service providers as educators and skills trainers as well as providers in the more traditional counseling and therapy roles.

Chapter 3 focuses on the core strategy of facilitating the phases of learning and growth and a stage of change model upon which the three phases of *SSC* are built. These three *Phases* are: *Challenge to Change, Commitment to Change, and Ownership of Change.*

The cognitive-behavioral (CB) approach is the platform strategy of *SSC*. *Chapter 4* provides a description of a specific CB model developed for *SSC* that provides the basic structure for utilizing the principles of CB change for substance abusing judicial clients.

Chapter 5 focuses on two major treatment goals for substance abusing judicial clients: preventing relapse and recidivism (R&R). Based on the Marlatt relapse prevention model, a model for R&R prevention is presented that provides a basis for integrating the treatment of criminal conduct and substance abuse.

Section II provides the specific methods, procedures and skills for the implementation and delivery of the *SSC* treatment curriculum. *Chapter 6* describes a specific assessment protocol for *SSC*. Effective treatment is based on a comprehensive and accurate assessment of the problems, vulnerabilities and resiliency factors for each judicial client. Multifactorial assessment, conducted in an atmosphere of empathy and concern, provides a basis upon which the client can plan for self-improvement and change. Based on convergent validation and multidimensional approaches, this chapter provides the rationale and methods for screening clients into *SSC*, for doing the in-depth differential assessment, and for evaluating client progress and change.

Chapter 7 outlines the operational procedures and methods of the *SSC* program. It describes the essential skills that the provider must have to deliver the various phases of *SSC* including guidelines for group facilitation. The recommended ground rules for client participation are discussed. It also discusses issues pertaining to client admission, consent for treatment, counselor full disclosure and client confidentiality. This chapter also provides guidelines for the reentry and aftercare plan. Ethical considerations in working with judicial clients are addressed.

Section III provides guidelines for the delivery of the *SSC* modules, the individual treatment sessions, and the *Phase Closure* sessions. Literature and research rationale are provided for each session along with explanations of important concepts and skills used in the *Workbook*. The *Workbook* provides the essential concepts and client activities necessary for the delivery of each session. However, for many sessions, adjunct information, additional exercises, and specific skills that can enhance session delivery are included that are not provided in the *Workbook*.

THE PARTICIPANT'S WORKBOOK

The Participant's Workbook provides detailed content of the session theme or topic. It includes in-session skill development exercises and homework assignments carefully designed to complement each session plan. The *Workbook* has been reviewed to ensure cultural appropriateness, sensitivity and optimal responsivity. The *Workbook* was written to accommodate a seventh-to-eighth grade reading level. Clients with reading levels below grade seven may need assistance in understanding some portions of the *Workbook*. Reading skills can be checked by asking the client in a matter-of-fact and non-threatening manner, to read and explain portions of the *Workbook* text during the *SSC* orientation (*Module 1*) sessions.

The treatment program is delivered primarily in group format and is structured around the three phases of treatment: 1) *Challenge to Change;* 2) *Commitment to Change;* and 3) *Ownership of Change.* Each treatment phase is divided into specific modules built around a particular treatment theme.

Phase I, Challenge to Change, involves the client in a reflective-contemplative process. A series of session experiences are utilized to build a working relationship with clients and to help clients develop motivation to change. Sessions provide information on how people change, how thought and behavior are related to change, and basic information about substance abuse and criminal conduct. A major focus of *Phase I* is helping the client develop self-awareness through self-disclosure and receiving feedback. Clients are confronted with their past problems and then challenged to bring that past into a present change-focus. The goal is to motivate clients to define the specific areas of change and to commit to that change. During *Phase I*, clients complete an in-depth self-assessment using the *MP* and *MAP* and learn to use nine tools to enhance growth and change. *Phase I* is comprised of seven modules and 20 sessions with the two sessions of *Module I* used for orientation.

Phase II, Commitment to Change, involves clients in an active demonstration of implementing and practicing change. Three modules are provided to strengthen basic skills for change and help the client to learn key CB methods for changing thoughts and behaviors that contribute to substance abuse and criminal conduct (CC). These modules are built around specific themes. *Module 8* focuses on cognitive restructuring and self-control; *Module 9* on social and relationship skills building; and *Module 10* on skills in developing a prosocial and harmonious relationship with the community. Perusal of the *Table of Contents* of the *Workbook* provides a good summary of the themes in these three modules.

Phase III, Ownership of Change, represents the stabilization and maintenance phase of treatment. Clients

demonstrate ownership of change over time. This involves treatment experiences designed to reinforce and strengthen commitment to established changes. The focus is on maintaining a balanced lifestyle and presenting alternatives to the lifestyle of AOD and criminal involvement. Change is strengthened through involving clients in a variety of auxiliary methods including mentoring and role modeling, self-help groups and other community-based recovery maintenance resources.

The *Workbook* is the client's handbook for change. A requirement for the delivery of *SSC* is that **each client has the entire *Workbook* at the beginning of the program.** The *Workbook* provides evidence for change, and can be utilized in the judicial supervision process.

The *Progress and Change Evaluation (PACE) Monitor* provides the methods to evaluate client problem areas, treatment needs, and response to treatment. It includes pre-treatment, during-treatment, and treatment outcome instruments and measures. It is designed to monitor change and progress during *SSC*. *PACE* is described in detail in *Chapter 6*.

INDIVIDUALIZED TREATMENT PLAN

The *Individualized Treatment Plan (ITP)* provides guidelines for individualized treatment determined through differential assessment. The *ITP* addresses the individual needs of clients through both in-program resources and outside service providers.

Individualized treatment may include family, relationship and marital treatment sessions provided within the context of cognitive-behavioral techniques. These resources may also include the use of urine and breath analyses in monitoring the client's goals of maintaining drug-free behavior.

Pharmacologic treatments may also be available, depending on the resources of the service provider. These would include antabuse, blocking AOD effects (naltrexone), treating abstinence syndromes, and the use of adjunct pharmacologic treatment for anxiety, mood or thought disorders (e.g., antidepressants, antianxiety and antipsychotic medications).

Most programs will provide opportunity for clients to continue the reinforcement of change through aftercare and maintenance support groups. Most clients will have completed their judicial supervision by the time they complete some if not all of *SSC*. Thus, participation in aftercare maintenance may be voluntary. Opportunities for mentoring should also be made available to those completing the program.

THE *SSC* PROVIDER

We use the term provider in this *Guide* to refer to the individual who directly presents *SSC* to client groups. This could be a therapist or substance abuse counselor experienced in working with judicial clients preferably trained in the delivery of the *SSC* curriculum. When specific *SSC* training is not available, providers should have the knowledge and skills to effectively deliver cognitive-behavioral based treatment to substance abusing correctional clients.

Delivery supervision and support should be available for those starting out in this area and ongoing supervision support should be sought by even the seasoned providers. This *Guide* represents a manual for providers to use for effective *SSC* delivery.

As discussed in several places in this *Guide*, the role of the *SSC* provider is not only counselor and therapist, but also teacher, coach and skills trainer. Most important, effective providers offer judicial clients a role model for prosocial attitudes and behavior and responsible living.

ADJUNCT PROVIDER'S GUIDE FOR WOMEN IN CORRECTIONS

Recognizing that women in corrections have special psychological, social and treatment needs, an adjunct provider's guide is available for *SSC* providers: *Criminal Conduct and Substance Abuse Treatment for Women in Correctional Settings* (Milkman, Wanberg & Gagliardi, 2008). This *Women's Adjunct Guide* provides a comprehensive review of the special concerns and needs of women judicial clients. It also provides supplemental guidelines for tailoring the delivery of the 50 *SSC* sessions to address, where appropriate, the special needs of women judicial clients.

ADDRESSING DIVERSITY

Efforts were made to make *SSC* sensitive to the diverse needs across gender, race, culture and age. Although sessions do not address specific diversity topics, providers should strive to be culturally sensitive and competent and to help clients capitalize on their cultural strengths.

Some guidelines for enhancing cultural competence are provided in *Chapter 2* and this topic is addressed in greater depth in the *Resource Guide* (Wanberg & Milkman, 2008). Providers should address the diversity of judicial clients according to the special needs of individuals and groups. The broad range of topics covered in the treatment curriculum provide ample opportunity to capitalize on the strengths of diversity within clients and the providers themselves.

TARGET GROUPS AND DELIVERY SETTING

This manual is designed to deliver a long-term (nine months to one year) intensive, cognitive-behavioral oriented treatment program to adults in the judicial system with substance abusing problems. The recommended client age is 18 years or above. However, some older adolescents may benefit from portions of the curriculum. *Pathways to Self-Discovery and Change* (Milkman & Wanberg, 2005) is a comparable curriculum for adolescents ages 13 through 17 that is available to providers in the juvenile justice system.

SSC is designed to be delivered in all treatment settings, e.g., regular and intensive outpatient, day treatment and residential programs within the judicial system. A more detailed discussion of delivery settings, approaches and options is provided in *Chapter 7*.

EFFECTIVENESS AND EFFICACY OF *SSC*

An overarching goal guiding the development of *SSC* was to construct a program based on treatment approaches that have empirical support with respect to their value in addressing the treatment needs of substance abusing (SA) judicial clients. We see *SSC* as meeting this standard in several ways.

First, when putting together the programmatic elements of *SSC*, we made every effort to see that it had content validity with respect to addressing individuals with a history of substance abuse and criminal conduct. We did a review of programs designed to provide offender treatment services and included in *SSC* elements considered to be essential and relevant to offender treatment. We consulted with a number of experts in the field - treatment and research specialists - to identify the elements that should be included in such treatment. Also, we received input relative to what works best in the program and what areas might be enhanced to improve the program from about 1000 providers who attended *SSC* staff development and training programs for the first edition of *SSC*. Many attending these trainings were providing treatment services to substance abusing judicial clients, and some had been delivering the *SSC* curriculum.

Using these resources, we endeavored to see that *SSC* had content validity - that its concepts, skills, content, processes and structure are relevant and necessary in addressing individuals with a history of criminal conduct and substance abuse.

Second, in the *Resource Guide* (Wanberg & Milkman, 2008) and in *Section I* of this *Guide*, we provided documentation to show that treatment of judicial clients in general is effective in reducing recidivism and, for those with substance abuse problems, in reducing the probability of relapse. There is strong evidence that punishment does not reduce recidivism, and in fact, may contribute to a slight increase in recidivism across the broad gamut of offenders. Andrews and Bonta (2003) note "that we have been unable to find any review of experimental studies that reveals systematically positive effects of official punishment on recidivism (that is, there is no evidence that official punishment reduces recidivism)" (pp. 92-93). They go on to say that direct treatment services provided under a variety of conditions of judicial sanctioning (e.g., diversion, probation, custody) demonstrate reduced recidivism from 40% to 80%. And, "the mean effect of correctional treatment service, averaged across a number of dispositions, was clearly greater and more positive than that of criminal sanctioning without the delivery of treatment services" (p. 288). Given the

evidence that treatment is effective with offenders, and that *SSC* has content validity with respect to the treatment of substance abuse and criminal conduct, we would expect it to have comparable effects with substance abusing judicial clients.

Third, beyond the expected general treatment effect of *SSC*, we have made every effort to use treatment methods and techniques that are evidence based - that is, there is empirical support that they can bring about positive changes in individuals. The five foundational strategies of *SSC* have support in the literature with respect to having value and being effective in their use with substance abuse clients and more specifically, for those with a co-occurring history of criminal conduct: 1) Multidimensional screening and assessment; 2) enhancing the therapeutic alliance and motivation to change; 3) tailoring treatment objectives and intervention strategies to the clients' stages of change; 4) cognitive-behavioral treatment; and 5) relapse (and recidivism) prevention.

Relapse prevention approaches have strong documentation with respect to their efficacy in reducing relapse among AOD problem clients and recidivism among judicial clients. Cognitive behavioral (CB) therapy also has a robust set of literature supporting its efficacy with disorders and problem behaviors other than substance abuse and criminal conduct. The CB approach is the core foundational mode for *SSC*, delivered in the context of clients' progression through stages of increasing motivation, commitment and ownership of the change process.

Fourth, and more specifically, within the framework of CB treatment approaches, the *SSC* sessions are built on methods and techniques that have empirical support as to their efficacy across a variety of disorders and problem behaviors. These include: cognitive restructuring; communication skills training; social and interpersonal skills training; changing negative thinking; anger management; stress management; relaxation therapies; problem-solving skills; assertiveness training; preventing and replacing aggression; using CB approaches to address antisocial and criminal thinking; conflict resolution; and empathy training. We made every effort to provide documentation regarding the value and empirical support of these methods as they are addressed in various *SSC* sessions in *Section III* of this *Guide*.

We concluded that cognitive-behavioral strategies as the core foundational treatment strategy for *SSC* would meet the responsivity principle of correctional treatment. The responsivity principle (Andrews & Bonta, 2003) refers to "delivering treatment programs in a style and mode that is consistent with the ability and learning style of the offender" (p. 262). Programs that maximize the ability of judicial clients to respond in a positive way meet the responsivity principle. Cognitive-behavioral strategies are seen as being the most promising with respect to maximizing treatment responsivity, and as "being the most powerful influence strategies available" (Andrews & Bonta, 2003, p. 262).

Fifth, to date, the first edition of *SSC* has been delivered to thousands of substance abusing judicial clients across a variety of judicial settings. This suggests that there is a quality of consumer satisfaction on the part of both clients and providers. As well, it lends good support to the validity of delivery feasibility of *SSC* within the judicial system to a variety of judicial clients.

Finally, a study of both provider (N=483) and client (N=360) responses to the first edition of *SSC* provides some preliminary findings regarding delivery feasibility, provider and client consumer satisfaction, and client response to the program (Wanberg & Milkman, 2001). Following is a brief summary of some of the provider and client responses based on instruments generated by both provider ratings and client self-report. The following is a brief summary based on provider ratings of 334 clients at the time of discharge from various phases of *SSC*.

▶ From an analysis of an instrument designed to measure the degree to which providers working with substance abuse clients and clients in the judicial system use specific cognitive-behavioral related approaches and methods, four reliable common factors were found: cognitive restructuring and cognitive self-control; social and interpersonal skills building; recidivism prevention and community responsibility; and relapse prevention. This provides construct validity for the four primary areas of focus in *SSC* training

and that these are reliable and valid components of the treatment of substance abusing offenders.

▶ Around 95% of the providers rated the components of *SSC* to be adequate to very adequate with respect to meeting the treatment needs of judicial clients, and 75% rated themselves as effective to very effective in program delivery.

▶ Almost all providers rated *SSC* as being effective in bringing about changes in clients, and most providers report that clients had a positive to very positive response to the program.

▶ Those providers who see themselves as effective in delivering *SSC* are more apt to rate *SSC* as being effective with clients.

▶ Over 90% of the providers rated clients as having a moderate to very high involvement in homework and reading, and 97% rated clients as having moderate to very high understanding of the program concepts.

▶ All providers rated *SSC* as being of some benefit to clients, and 70% rated *SSC* as being of great benefit.

▶ Successful delivery of *SSC* was reported across the following settings: jail, prison, residential treatment, therapeutic communities and outpatient settings.

▶ Providers report that 70%, 76%, and 80% completed the *SSC* program in the outpatient, prison, and residential care settings, respectively.

▶ Over 85% of the clients were rated as having moderate to very high positive involvement in *SSC*.

A sample of 174 clients was evaluated across a large set of variables at the time of completing *SSC*.

▶ Around 95% of the clients rated as very high their satisfaction of *SSC* delivery, the provider's response to client needs, and clients' comfortability with providers.

▶ Almost 94% of the clients reported they understood the content of the sessions most of the time or all of the time, and almost 92% report they were satisfied with the *SSC* most of the time or all of the time.

- Around 80% of the clients report their cognitive and behavioral control over AOD use and criminal conduct had improved or gotten better during *SSC*.

- Over 93% of the clients report having made changes in their lives while in *SSC*.

- Self-report by outpatients during *SSC* as to **no use** of alcohol, marijuana, and other drugs was 62.8%, 84.6% and 87.2%, respectively. Ratings by providers were lower, with 48% of clients rated as not using alcohol and 56.7% rated as not using other drugs.

- Self-report by incarcerated clients as to not using alcohol, marijuana, and other drugs during *SSC* was 94.8%, 97.9% and 97.9% respectively. Ratings of this group by providers as to no use of alcohol or other drugs were similar.

- About 77% of outpatient clients and 91% of incarcerated clients reported engaging in no behaviors that would be considered to be violating or breaking the law. Provider reports as to whether clients reoffended during *SSC* were essentially the same as client self-reports.

DISTINGUISHING BETWEEN SELF-IMPROVEMENT AND CHANGE

SSC is about self-improvement and change. Improvement as a noun represents a state of condition such as progression, betterment, refinement or recovery. Improvement implies that even though a change has been made, it can be improved or made better. This is the verb or action component of improvement: to make better or to improve on the changes that have been made. Clients may have already made significant changes e.g., no longer use substances, no longer engage in CC, but they can still work on improving the skills and lifestyle that reinforce and maintain these changes. Maintenance is part of this improvement process. Using the word improvement gives clients credit for changes that have been made.

We use change as a verb that means to correct, modify, alter, replace and transform. It is the action process in treatment. It implies changing the state of condition; making that state of condition differ-

ent. Much of *SSC* is directed at change - changing thoughts, emotions, and behaviors that lead to relapse and recidivism. Yet, we can see change as a noun - a state of change, modification, or difference. Thus, once change has taken place, *SSC* is directed at improving and making better those changes.

In this *Guide,* for convenience of not repeating words, we use the word change to include both self-improvement and change. When we refer to a particular change concept or skill, such as cognitive restructuring, it is for the purpose of making both improvement and change.

SUMMARY

Strategies for Self-Improvement and Change (SSC) provides a standardized, structured and well-defined approach to the treatment of substance abusing judicial clients. The efficacy and effectiveness of *SSC* depends on developing a positive relationship between the client and provider. As we show in *Chapter 2,* the therapeutic relationship and alliance is a strong determinant of treatment outcome, regardless of the treatment method or approach. The success of *SSC*, or any comparable program, will depend, in part, on the strength of that relationship.

Also, the unique style and approach of each provider are important variables in effective treatment of co-occurring AOD abuse and CC. Some modifications, changes and enhancements of approach and curricula are to be expected, based on the experiences, skills and training of each provider. However, the effectiveness and efficacy of *SSC* mainly depend on the provider maintaining fidelity to the *SSC* treatment protocol. This is a crucial consideration when evaluating the efficacy of the program.

There are many methods and approaches to the treatment of individuals with substance abuse problems and a history of criminal conduct. No one approach has been shown effective for all judicial clients. Although many approaches were blended in the development of *SSC*, it represents one of a number of approaches that can be used in the treatment of the co-occurring problems of AOD abuse and criminal conduct.

SECTION I

THE TREATMENT PLATFORM

The purpose of *Section I* of this *Provider's Guide* is to delineate the conceptual framework and treatment platform for *Criminal Conduct and Substance Abuse Treatment: Strategies for Self-Improvement and Change (SSC) - Pathways to Responsible Living*. It provides an overview of the treatment dimensions and principles that are the connecting threads of *SSC* and the 10 core strategies that are used in *SSC* delivery. Five of the 10 core *SSC* strategies represent the foundational approaches of *SSC*. These are:

▶ Developing a therapeutic relationship through motivational enhancement and a therapeutic alliance;

▶ The phases of learning and growth and a stage of change model upon which the three phases of *SSC* are built: Challenge to Change, Commitment to Change, and Ownership of Change;

▶ A specific CB model developed for *SSC* that provides the basic structure for the utilization of the principles of CB change for substance abusing judicial clients;

▶ A model for addressing relapse and recidivism prevention.

▶ A multidimensional and convergent validation model for the assessment of the substance abusing judicial client.

This section devotes a chapter to each of the first four of these foundational strategies. The fifth foundational strategy, multidimensional and convergent validation model for assessment, is addressed in *Chapter 6* of *Section II*.

Section I is designed to give the provider a thorough understanding of the major concepts, methods and core strategies upon which *SSC* is based.

I have found it enriching to open channels
whereby others can communicate their feelings,
their private perceptual worlds.
-CARL ROGERS

CHAPTER 1: Core Strategies and Conceptual Framework for Criminal Conduct and Substance Abuse Treatment

CHAPTER OUTLINE

OVERVIEW

UNDERSTANDING TREATMENT, PSYCHOTHERAPY AND COUNSELING

Definition of Treatment
Dimensions of Treatment Services

Treatment structures
Treatment modalities
Treatment strategies
Specific treatment programs

Defining Psychotherapy and Counseling
Shifting the Paradigm for Correctional
    Treatment

THE CORE STRATEGIES OF THE TREATMENT PLAT-FORM

1. Developing a Therapeutic Relationship Through Motivational Enhancement and a Therapeutic Alliance

2. Multidimensional Assessment Based on Convergent Validation

3. Integrating Education and Therapeutic Approaches

    Support for psychoeducation in treatment

    Psychoeducational methods and approaches

    What makes psychoeducational approaches effective

    Two modes of including psychoeducational approaches

    How education differs from psychotherapy/counseling

4. Facilitating Learning and Growth and the Stages of Change

5. Cognitive-Behavioral Approach

6. Relapse and Recidivism Prevention

7. Focusing on Moral Responsibility to Others and the Community

8. Integrating the Therapeutic and Correctional

9. A Cohesive Group That Elicits a Prosocial Identity

10. Reentry and Reintegration Into the Community

PROGRAM CONCEPTUAL FRAMEWORK

CHAPTER REVIEW

CHAPTER OBJECTIVES

◗ Provide working definitions of the principles of psychoeducation, psychotherapy and counseling.

◗ Provide literature support for the importance of the psychoeducation method in *SSC*.

◗ Present the 10 core strategies of *SSC* and identify the five strategies that are foundational to the *SSC* program.

◗ Provide a graphic representation of the conceptual framework of *SSC*.

OVERVIEW

This chapter defines the conceptual framework and the core strategies for the treatment of judicial clients with substance abuse problems and the delivery of *SSC*. The first objective of this chapter is to define the meaning and goals of treatment and to help providers understand how *SSC*, as a specific treatment program, fits into the overall treatment framework. Since *SSC* relies on the principles of psychotherapy and counseling, the meaning and understanding of these terms will be addressed. In this discussion, we make it clear that correctional treatment needs to go beyond the traditional principles of psychotherapy. Second, we look at the core strategies that are used in the delivery of *SSC*. Finally, a conceptual framework will be presented which provides an integration of the process and structure of the treatment skills utilized in implementing the *SSC* curriculum.

UNDERSTANDING TREATMENT, PSYCHOTHERAPY AND COUNSELING

The *SSC* curriculum is a program for the treatment of persons with a combined history of substance abuse (SA) and criminal conduct (CC). However, there is often confusion among the terms treatment, psychotherapy and counseling. Following are some guidelines that help gain a better understanding of these terms as they apply to *SSC*.

Definition of Treatment

One way to understand the meaning of an approach or method is to define its goals. The traditional goal of treatment is to intervene in and change patterns of thinking and behavior that cause or are part of specific disorders and that lead to maladaptive and undesirable outcomes. Treatment is designed to address specific psychological and mental health symptoms that define these disorders. The two target disorders for *SSC* are: substance use problems and antisocial behavior that manifests criminal conduct (CC). We look at how these two disorders are defined and evaluated in *Chapter 6*.

This first goal of treatment is to eliminate or manage problems, or a harm avoidance approach. This is congruent with the medical model: to cure the ailment and eliminate the pain of the patient. However, in psychosocial treatment of substance abusing offenders, the goal is also the relief of pain and suffering of others and of society. Although this may be the goal of social medicine, it is not the primary objective - or even an objective in most cases - of the medical practitioner in the medicine.

The position can also be taken that this treatment goal can be defined as reducing harm or pain. This harm reduction model has been effectively applied to psychosocial and medical problems that impact on society, e.g., HIV/AIDS. This is often the goal of the treatment of an incurable disease. However, with respect to CC (criminal conduct), this is not an objective. Behaviors and disorders associated with CC may be approached from a harm reduction model such as reducing, if not eliminating, criminal thinking, harmful effects of substance use, time with criminal associates and antisocial behaviors associated with CC, but not defined as criminal behavior per se. But the goal of criminal conduct treatment is preventing recidivism (committing another crime).

The goal of *Phase I* of *SSC* is to help judicial clients establish a stable living pattern that is free of SA (substance abuse) problems and CC. It is directed at the first goal of treatment - elimination of the disruptive and maladaptive symptoms and behaviors of AOD (alcohol or other drug) abuse and preventing CC.

The second goal of treatment is to bring about growth and change that lead to positive outcomes and a more meaningful life. With respect to judicial clients, this also involves prosocial and responsible living. Although this may be the by-product of the first objective - elimination of symptoms - it is not a primary goal of that objective.

Within the framework of the medical model, the physician heals the broken bone, but once that is accomplished, the efforts of the practitioner have ended. In psychosocial treatment, the practitioner, in this case, the *SSC* provider (counselor, therapist), sees both goals as primary. The first objective of preventing recidivism must be accomplished in order to meet the second objective. However, when judicial clients begin to experience positive outcomes and a meaningful life, and engage in prosocial actions and responsible living, the probability of achieving and sustaining the first goal of treatment is increased: maintaining a life free of SA problems and CC. *SSC Phases II* and *III* are directed at sustaining the accomplishment of the first goal of treatment and meeting the objectives of the second goal.

Dimensions of Treatment Services

Although there are different ways to conceptualize the taxonomy of treatment, we define treatment as organized across four dimensions as they occur within the judicial system: structures, modalities, specific treatment strategies or approaches, and specific programs. Each of these dimensions can be utilized to address specific types of problem behaviors or disorders, or in the case of this *Guide*, SA and CC.

Treatment structures

There is a broad continuum of treatment structures that operate within various judicial systems.

- Therapeutic community.
- Intensive residential treatment.
- Day treatment.
- Intensive outpatient.
- Regular outpatient.
- Aftercare or continuing care services.

With respect to the judicial system, all of these structures can be offered within an incarcerated setting, community corrections or parole and probation. For example, an outpatient program can operate within an incarcerated setting where inmates attend treatment once or twice a week.

Treatment modalities

There are different treatment modalities offered within these treatment structures. They include: group, individual, family and marital treatment. Also included as treatment modalities are: vocational services; medical services; and psychotropic medica-

tions management. Psychosocial treatment modalities are usually platformed on the basic principles of psychotherapy and counseling. We consider these to be generic principles that are basic to the delivery of treatment and define specific modalities, e.g., individual therapy, group therapy, etc.

Treatment strategies

Various treatment strategies or approaches can be used within the broad domain of treatment. These are based on theory (usually personality) and research that support the efficacy of the approach. Some of these approaches are: behavioral; cognitive-behavioral; psychodynamic; relapse prevention; motivational enhancement; client-centered, etc. Most often, several of these strategies are used in working towards the achievement of treatment goals. For example, cognitive-behavioral therapy will utilize a client-centered approach to establish a working and therapeutic relationship with a client or group. As with treatment methods, the fundamental and common principles of psychotherapy and counseling provide the foundation for all psychosocial therapies. For example, cognitive-behavioral, client-centered, psychodynamic strategies or approaches are built on the common principles of psychotherapy and counseling, to be discussed below.

Specific treatment programs

In the past 40 years, there have emerged specific programs that are directed at addressing specific disorders or problems, e.g., sex-offender, violent offender, anger and aggression management, depression, personality disorders, etc. *SSC* is a specific program directed at addressing individuals with the co-occurring problems of SA and CC. In the *Resource Guide* (Wanberg & Milkman, 2008), we outline a number of programs that are designed to treat judicial clients with or without a SA focus.

Specific treatment programs can be nested within broad judicial structures, such as prison settings, or nested within the various treatment structures outlined above, e.g., a therapeutic community. Or, specific programs can be stand-alone, and represent the treatment structure and modality. For example, *SSC* can be offered within a prison setting, within a therapeutic community, or as a stand-alone out-patient treatment program in and of itself. As with treatment methods and strategies, the common principles of psychotherapy and counseling provide the foundation for specific treatment programs.

Defining Psychotherapy and Counseling

We noted above that the generic principles of psychotherapy and counseling represent the foundation of most treatment methods and approaches. Because of this, and because *SSC* utilizes these principles, it is important that providers have an understanding of these principles. Although much of this discussion is couched in the one-one therapy relationship, it also applies to group treatment.

Psychotherapy has been defined as "a situation where two people interact and try to come to an understanding of one another, with the specific goal of accomplishing something beneficial for the complaining person" (Bruch, 1981, p. 86), achieving personal change and growth (Rogers, 1951, 1980) and changing "...the patient's image of himself from a person who is overwhelmed by his symptoms and problems to one who can master them" (Frank, 1971, p. 357). It can also be defined in terms of its goal: either symptom relief or cure - the prevention of recurrence (Seligman et al., 2001, p. 11).

Patterson, in his seminal work, *Theories of Counseling and Psychotherapy* (1966), defines counseling and psychotherapy as "processes involving a special kind of relationship between a person who asks for help with a psychological problem and a person who is trained to provide that help" (p. 1). Over 30 years later, he (Patterson & Hidore, 1997) gave a similar definition as a psychological relationship between a person (client), whose progress in self-actualization has been blocked or impeded by the absence of good interpersonal relationships, and a person (therapist) who provides that relationship (p. xiii).

Strupp's (1978) definition is commonly accepted by most in the field. He defines psychotherapy as "an interpersonal process designed to bring about modifications of feelings, cognitions, attitudes and behaviors which have proved troublesome to the person seeking help from a trained professional" (p. 3).

Lang (1990) also sees psychotherapy as "a relationship and interaction between an individual with an emotionally founded problem who is seeking help... and an expert who is capable of assisting him or her in effecting its resolution..." (p. 3). He defines the core dimension of psychotherapy as the object relationship between the patient and therapist and the interpersonal interaction that unfolds on the basis of this relatedness (p. 219). Bateman, Brown and Pedder (2000) see psychotherapy as "a conversation that involves listening to and talking with those in trouble with the aim of helping them understand and resolve their predicament" (p. xiii).

Jerome Frank defines psychotherapy as a process through which a socially sanctioned healer works to help individuals to overcome psychological stress and disability based on a theory of the sufferer's difficulties and a theory of the methods to alleviate them. He identifies five features common to all forms of psychotherapy (Frank, 1963, 1974): 1) a trusting and emotional relationship between client and therapist; 2) a therapist genuinely concerned about the sufferer's welfare and is committed to bring about some kind of desirable change; 3) a conceptual framework that explains what has happened and what will happen; 4) methods to bring about change and/or restore health; and 5) the theory, approaches and outcome are linked to the dominant worldview of the client's culture.

This *Guide* treats psychotherapy and counseling as having similar meanings and the terms are used synonymously. However, there has been some debate about whether they are synonymous. The term psychotherapy was first used in the late 1880s (Efran & Clarfield, 1992) when psychological problems came to the forefront in medicine ("psyche" meaning mind, and "therapeia" meaning treatment). Carl Rogers used the term counseling in the 1930s and 1940s to "side-step" the legal restriction that only medical doctors were allowed legally to practice psychotherapy (Dryden & Mytton, 1999).

Most experts in the field see the two as having the same or similar processes and methods. Dryden and Mytton (1999) view the two as having the same meaning, both referring to helping individuals with personal or relationship problems directed at bringing about self-improvement and emotional changes so as to improve personal functioning.

Patterson (1966) concluded that there is no essential difference between the two in terms of the process, methods or techniques, the goals or expected outcomes, the relationship between the client and therapist or the clients involved. The one distinction he notes is that counseling sometimes refers to work with less disturbed clients with special change needs, and psychotherapy may refer to work with the more seriously disturbed persons. Ivey and Simek-Downing (1980) also saw this as a noteworthy distinction: counseling directed at assisting "normal people" to achieve their goals or to function more effectively; and psychotherapy as a longer term process concerned with the implementation of personality change.

George and Cristiani (1981) concluded from their literature review that the distinction is on a continuum, with counseling directed more at aiding growth, focusing on the present, aimed at helping individuals function adequately in appropriate roles, more supportive, situational, problem-solving and short term; whereas psychotherapy is more reconstructive, analytical, focused on past and present, directed at more severe emotional problems and at change in basic character and personality (p. 8).

Another differentiation between counseling and psychotherapy lies in the former lacking in a connection with a theoretical orientation. Most psychotherapies rest on some specific orientation such as psychodynamic, cognitive, behavioral, interpersonal, etc. (Roth & Fonagy, 2005). Counseling does not necessarily represent a unitary theoretical orientation, tends to be defined by the setting in which it takes place, tends to treat the relationship between the client and counselor as one of equals, usually focuses on current problems in a pragmatic manner, and is premised on the client-centered principles of empathy, warmth, and genuineness (Roth & Fonagy, 2005, p. 13).

In summary, the above definitions indicate that both psychotherapy and counseling have several factors in common: 1) there is a trusting and working relationship; 2) an interpersonal context; 3) a trained and professional provider who has concern and empathy for the client's pain and welfare; 4) a theory of psychological and behavioral problems; 5) a method of how to approach those problems; 6) a client who presents with a unique set of problems; and, 7) an expectation of change found within the context of a set of cultural and societal values.

Shifting the Paradigm for Correctional Treatment

All of the above definitions are essentially egocentric. As discussed in the *Preface* to this *Guide,* if treatment is to be effective with correctional clients, traditional therapy, as defined above, needs to shift the paradigm from egocentric approaches to including sociocentric approaches. Thus, correctional therapy is not just concerned about the symptoms, disorder, welfare and healing of the individual client; it also focuses on the client's responsibility to others and the community. This shift in therapy represents one of the core strategies of *SSC* and is discussed below.

THE CORE STRATEGIES OF THE TREATMENT PLATFORM

SSC is built around 10 core strategies. These operationally define the foundation of *SSC*. In this chapter, we provide a summary of all 10 strategies. Five represent foundational strategies for *SSC* and will be briefly summarized in this chapter and then addressed in separate chapters. These are: Developing an effective client-provider relationship; multidimensional and convergent validation assessment; facilitating learning and growth and the stages of change; the cognitive-behavioral model for change; and relapse and recidivism prevention. The other five strategies will also be addressed in this chapter.

1. **Developing a Therapeutic Relationship Through Motivational Enhancement and a Therapeutic Alliance**

The **first core strategy** is building a therapeutic relationship of trust and rapport with clients through developing a therapeutic alliance and motivational enhancement. The therapeutic relationship and motivational enhancement represent a foundational strategy of CC and SA abuse treatment, and are discussed in more detail in *Chapter 2* and in the *Resource Guide* (Wanberg & Milkman, 2008).

Many judicial clients initially present with a considerable degree of defensiveness and resistance to involvement in therapy. They also have considerable distrust of treatment providers and counselors in the judicial system. They often see judicial counselors as "on the side of the system," and see counselors as "in it for the money." Clients with greater character problems and antisocial histories have higher probabilities of dropping out of treatment.

The therapeutic alliance provides the basis for the motivation to change and is a predictor of treatment retention and outcome. Once a therapeutic alliance is forged, self-regulating skills may then be learned through motivational counseling, therapeutic confrontation and reinforcement of responsible and positive behaviors.

There is a great deal of research evidence supporting the efficacy of motivational enhancement as an important component in building the therapist-client relationship and implementing treatment readiness and change in AOD abuse clients. The counselor-client relationship, therapeutic stance and alliance, motivational enhancement and use of reflective acceptance in managing resistance and ambivalence, and counselor cultural competency, as these are related to the treatment of judicial clients, will be discussed in more detail in *Chapter 2*.

2. Multidimensional Assessment Based on Convergent Validation

The **second core strategy** for *SSC* is that screening and evaluation are based on a convergent validation model that involves a multidimensional assessment of the client's condition at admission to *SSC* and the client's progress and change during treatment.

Effective screening and in-depth assessment of the SA judicial client will use self-report and other report in order to converge on the best estimate of the client's past and current life-adjustment problems and motivation and strengths for responsible living and change. Assessment is most effective when it is based on the idea that the origins, expressions and continuation of AOD use and abuse and CC are multidimensional in nature (Wanberg & Horn, 1987). Individuals will vary according to how they fit the different causes and patterns of AOD abuse and CC and different patterns of life-adjustment problems. Effective intervention is based on a comprehensive and accurate assessment of the problems and resiliency factors for each judicial client.

This is another foundational strategy for *SSC*. The *Resource Guide* provides a chapter on exploring these issues. *Chapter 6* in this *Guide* provides specific methods and operational approaches to the differential screening and assessment of the presenting problems of *SSC* clients and their change and outcome in treatment.

3. Integrating Education and Therapeutic Approaches

The **third core strategy** of *SSC* is psychoeducation. This involves building and integrating a knowledge base around key concepts and change skills that are essential in the change process. It lays the groundwork for treatment with education being learner-centered and therapy focusing on the process of cognitive, affective and behavioral change.

We look at the general issues related to this *SSC* strategy. In *Chapter 2*, we look at the provider's role in integrating psychoeducation and therapy, and then how these areas are integrated in the *SSC* curriculum.

Support for psychoeducation in treatment

There is strong support in contemporary treatment literature, particularly that which is CB oriented, for the use of knowledge building, and psychoeducation in the treatment process.

Wright (2004) sees psychoeducation as a shared feature of CBT. "CBT is well known for using psycho-educational procedures to assist patients with learning new patterns of thinking and behaving" (p. 357). Psychoeducation is seen as an important component in the CB treatment of most psychosocial problems including panic disorders and agoraphobia (McCabe

& Antony, 2005), social and general anxiety disorders (Ledley & Heimberg, 2005; Waters & Craske, 2005), obsessive-compulsive disorders (Clark, 2004), the borderline personality disorder (Klosko & Young, 2004), and in treating AOD problems (Washton & Zweben, 2006). In applying the principles of acceptance, mindfulness and cognitive-behavioral therapy to the treatment of anxiety, Orsillo et al. (2004) state that "consistent with traditional cognitive-behavioral approaches, our introduction to treatment includes psychoeducation" (p. 87).

Ross et al. see cognitive approaches that are directed at helping judicial clients modify their antisocial attitudes, correct thinking errors and inappropriate social perceptions as involving more training and education than therapy (Hollin, 1990; Ross et al., 1988). From a cognitive perspective, judicial clients have failed to acquire the necessary reasoning and problem-solving skills to deal with the various cognitive, social, economic, behavioral and situational factors that lead to CC (Foglia, 2000). Education and training are important steps in helping judicial clients acquire these reasoning and problem-solving skills.

Clients learn key concepts and skills through psychoeducation. Washton and Zweben (2006) illustrate the importance of this method in relapse prevention strategies when they state: "...one of the most important strategies is to teach patients how to prevent a slip from developing into a full-blown relapse" (p. 216). They see client education as one of the components of an integrated approach to treatment (p. 73). They stress that educational approaches are of particular value in the precontemplative and early stages of change. "Taking an educative, non-confrontational stance avoids the problems of stimulating defensiveness and getting into power struggles - the primary pitfalls of working with patients in the precontemplative stage" (p. 175).

Judy Beck sees educating patients around core beliefs and coping strategies as an essential component of treatment (2005, p. 270). She stresses that some clients "need additional psychoeducation before they are willing to engage in problem solving" (2005, p. 179).

Most literature sources, then, see psychoeducation as a valuable method to teach clients key concepts around their problem condition as well as key CB concepts and skills to bring about change. It can give clients some reassurance around their particular problems and conditions and can increase motivation for treatment. It can help them understand the process and risks related to relapse and recidivism.

What makes psychoeducation effective

Psychoeducation is more effective when based on cognitive processing and when clients can relate the knowledge and skills to their personal lives and problems (Dees et al., 1991; Farabee & Leukefeld, 2002; Farabee et al., 1995). All sources stress that relevancy is essential, that growth and change result from learned skills and knowledge, and that material should be presented in brief segments (Washton & Zweben, 2006). All warn of the dangers of being too didactic and engaging in lengthy lectures.

As noted, CB therapies rely heavily on psychoeducation. Since there is a robust set of literature to support the efficacy of CB treatment (see *SSC Resource Guide,* Wanberg & Milkman, 2008), we can assume that psychoeducation must provide a measurable contribution to the positive outcomes of CB. To what extent is unknown, and no substantive research was found in this area.

Two modes of including psychoeducation

Psychoeducational approaches are utilized in two ways. First, they can be stand-alone programs where judicial clients are required to complete educational classes or groups as part of treatment (Springer et al., 2003). These are usually didactic sessions that provide information about AOD use and abuse followed by interactive discussion. Although supportive of the use of psychoeducational approaches, Springer et al. (2003) acknowledge that as stand-alone approaches, there is little research as to their efficacy. They do point to a couple of studies that lend support to the stand-alone approach (Pomeroy et al., 2000; Anderson & Reiss, 1994).

A second approach is to integrate psychoeducation into the therapeutic process. This involves combining the presentation of knowledge and information with therapeutic and treatment methods which facilitate change (McNeece & DiNitto, 1994). Facilitator interaction is important, but also includes the interactive methods discussed above with the objectives of: 1) increasing motivation and commitment to treatment; 2) enhancing life-management, communication and relapse prevention skills (Springer et al., 2003).

How education differs from psychotherapy/counseling

As discussed above, psychotherapy and counseling involve basic principles that are used across various treatment dimensions, structures, modalities, approaches and specific programs. However, do counseling and psychotherapy (therapy) differ from psychoeducation?

Patterson (1966) states that most in the field would agree that counseling and psychotherapy "deal with the conative or affective realm - attitudes, feelings, and emotions, and not simply ideas" (p.3). He sees teaching or education as being concerned only with the rational, non-ego-involved solution of problems. "Where there are no affective elements involved, then the process is not counseling, but is probably teaching, information giving, or an intellectual discussion" (p. 3). Patterson clearly indentifies counseling and psychotherapy as not just the giving of information, advice, suggestions or recommendations. He sees them as influencing and facilitating behavior change.

4. Facilitating Learning and Growth and the Stages of Change

The **fourth core strategy** and another foundational approach of *SSC* is facilitating the client's process of learning and growth and structuring treatment around the stages of change. We briefly summarize this strategy here and then address it in greater detail in *Chapter 3*.

This strategy is based on two assumptions: 1) that learning and growth occur in phases; and 2) when people make changes, they go through specific stages of change.

First, with respect to learning and growth, the work of Kurt Lewin (Ham, 1957; Lewin, 1935, 1936, 1951) and Werner's Orthogenetic Principle (1957) identify three phases of responding that formulate the basis of learning and growth: a global, undifferentiated response; a differentiative or sorting out response; and an integration or "putting together" response. Although these phases of growth are seen as natural processes, they are facilitated in treatment by applying three methods of therapeutic communication: 1) getting clients to openly share their problems and concerns or "tell their story"; 2) provide feedback to the clients so that they "hear their story"; and 3) strengthen and reinforce clients' effort to "act on their story."

Second, research has indicated that people go through various stages when making changes in addictive lifestyles. From this research, the transtheoretical model of change was formulated (Connors, Donovan & DiClemente, 2001; Prochaska & DiClemente, 1992; Prochaska, DiClemente & Norcross, 1992).

Building on the three phases of learning and growth, and a three-stage model of change using the findings of the transtheoretical model, the *SSC* treatment protocol is structured into three treatment phases (Wanberg & Milkman, 1998): **Challenge to Change; Commitment to Change;** and **Ownership of Change.**

Challenge to Change represents the pre-contemplative, contemplative and preparation for change stages. The **Commitment to Change** represents both the determination and action states in the transtheoretical model. The **Ownership** stage, representing action and maintenance, occurs when judicial clients live up to their relapse and recidivism prevention goals because they want to do it for themselves and their community.

Judicial client treatment strategies for achieving increased self-regulation for preventing AOD relapse and CC recidivism must fit the client's level of awareness, cognitive development and determination to change patterns of thoughts and behaviors.

Effective treatment will use the right strategies at particular stages of each client's process of change. For example, a person in the comtemplative stage (challenge) may not respond well if initially placed in action-orientated treatment.

5. Cognitive-Behavioral Approach

The **fifth core strategy** and another foundational approach of *SSC* is that the concepts and methods of cognitive-behavioral change provide the basis for the treatment of the substance abusing judicial client. One of the most significant advances in treating individuals with AOD use problems and/or criminal conduct has been in the field of cognitive-behavioral psychology. From a review of the CB literature, summarized in the *Resource Guide* (Wanber & Milkman, 2008), a CB treatment approach specifically designed for *SSC* was developed.

The term cognitive-behavioral therapy (CBT) is used quite broadly to refer to approaches that focus on the interplay between thought, emotion and action in human functioning and in psychopathology (Freeman, Pretzer, Fleming & Simon, 1990). Although there are varying forms of CBT, most would agree with Hollen and Beck (1986) who define cognitive-behavioral therapies as "those approaches that attempt to modify existing or anticipated disorders by virtue of altering cognitive processes" (p. 443).

SSC is built around the two traditional cognitive-behavioral (CB) approaches: cognitive or thought restructuring or helping clients learn the skills of changing thoughts so as to modify or change behavior; and social and interpersonal skill building. However, a third approach has been added to this work that utilizes the basic methods and concept of CBT: moral and community responsibility skill building, or *Social Responsibilty Therapy* (SRT) discussed below. The CB model specifically adapted for *SSC* is addressed in detail in *Chapter 4*.

6. Relapse and Recidivism Prevention

Relapse and recidivism (R&R) prevention is the **sixth core strategy** and another foundational approach of *SSC*. The literature clearly indicates that relapse prevention is an integral component of the treatment of substance abuse. However, clear and concise models for recidivism prevention, with a distinct conceptual framework, are not well identified in the literature.

The principles of relapse prevention as defined by Marlatt (1985a) and adapted by Wanberg and Milkman (1998) are applied to both relapse and recidivism prevention in the *SSC* protocol. Effective judicial client treatment will have separate though linked models for addressing R&R and R&R prevention. R&R prevention is another foundational strategy for *SSC*. It is addressed in *Chapter 5*.

7. Focusing on Moral Responsibility to Others and the Community - SRT

An essential strategy in the treatment of CC is a focus on the moral responsibility to others and the community, the **seventh core strategy.** CC is based on antisocial attitudes and behaviors that have a common outcome: they destroy the basic fabric of a positive and harmonious society; they go against society. Thus, strategies for building moral responsibility towards others and the community are essential elements of CC treatment.

We define moral responsibility as a complex set of attitudes and behaviors directed at respecting the rights of others, being accountable to the laws of society, having positive regard for and caring about the welfare and safety of others, and contributing to the good of the community. In essence, it means engaging in responsible thinking and actions towards others and society.

Traditional psychotherapy, including cognitive-behavioral treatment, is egocentric. It puts the person at the center of its focus, with the goal of relieving the pain and suffering of individuals, e.g., depression, anxiety, stress, disturbed thinking, substance abuse.

Within the framework of egocentric approaches, sociopathy, antisocial disorders, criminal conduct and character pathology were often viewed as not treatable. When traditional egocentric treatment was applied to these groups, the outcomes were poor. This merely reinforced the belief that antisocial patterns and criminal conduct would not respond to treatment.

In order to effectively address and treat antisocial and criminal patterns, we must shift the paradigm and go beyond an egocentric psychology to a sociocentric and holistic framework. This involves moving towards a connected consciousness and relational empathy (O'Hara, 1997). We build on the gains and strengths of egocentric psychology and include a sociocentric approach. We see social responsibility therapy (SRT) as a necessary component of correctional treatment.

Some began advocating the importance of moral and social responsibility in the treatment of antisocial persons in the 1990s. Ross et al. (1986) made this a focus in their *Reasoning and Rehabilitation* treatment program for offenders. Snortum and Berger (1989) early on indicated that the variables of personal morality and social morality are important in impaired driving and other offender deterrence. Wanberg and Milkman (1998) made this a central focus in the first edition of this work and in the education and treatment of impaired driving offenders (Wanberg, Milkman & Timken, 2005).

Mauck and Zagummy (2000) state that the areas of moral and social obligation have been conspicuously absent in the research and treatment of correctional clients. With respect to impaired driving, they found that the level and sense of moral and social obligation on the part of a peer to intervene in drunk driving behavior significantly predicted the success of impaired driving intervention.

It wasn't until the early 2000s that traditional CB psychotherapy saw its importance in treating the antisocial personality disorder. As noted in the *Preface,* Beck et al. (2004) stress the importance of moving antisocial clients towards interpersonal consideration and moral functioning (p. 169) and towards responsibility towards others and a commitment to the guiding principles for the good of society (p. 179).

8. Integrating the Therapeutic and Correctional

Effective treatment of the SA judicial client integrates the principles of therapy with correctional deterrence. Outcome research indicates that effective treatment integrates sanctions with treatment approaches (Andrews & Bonta, 2003). In essence, treatment providers become partners with the judicial system in helping to administer the judicial sentence.

Our review of the literature for this and our previous work (Wanberg & Milkman, 1998) clearly indicates that sanctioning and punishment alone are not effective methods to prevent recidivism (see Andrews & Bonta, 2003). It also indicated that treatment intervention alone is not as effective as when intervention is integrated with the sanctioning process. The **eighth core strategy** of *SSC* is that of integrating the efforts of the sanctioning and judicial system with the efforts of the treatment system.

There are some traditional differences between the treatment of AOD abuse and intervention and treatment of CC. First, alcohol abuse by adults in and of itself does not have legal implications and the treatment of AOD abuse does not necessarily involve sanctions; only certain behaviors associated with AOD use such as impaired driving or the possession of illegal drugs.

Treatment outcomes for AOD abuse can tolerate relapse. Such treatment or education is usually psychotherapeutic and it is client-centered in that treatment starts with the client's goals, needs and expectations. The healing expectations come from the client.

The treatment of judicial clients always involves sanctions: treatment and sanctioning are almost always integrated. The client's referral to treatment is often part of the judicial sentence. Recidivism prevention and goals must take a "zero tolerance" position for criminal conduct. Recidivism is not tolerated and when occurring, the provider and judicial client must engage the correctional and judicial processes. Correctional treatment is both client-centered and society-centered. It is correctional and parenting with a focus on behavior that violates society. The change expectations, at least initially, come from society - from outside the offender.

Thus, when addressing CC recidivism, the focus must be on cognitive, affective and pre-recidivism behavior with these elements being considered as leading to recidivism such as thinking about committing a crime, spending time with criminal associates, and becoming involved in other high-risk situations or high-risk thinking that lead to CC.

The confrontational process is also different. The provider in the correctional role states, "I confront you with me, I represent the external world you have violated and I confront you with the values and laws of society and I expect you to change." The provider or therapist represents society in the intervention process and is the client's "victim" as is any other member of society who is potentially impacted by criminal behavior. The provider has the clear role of helping to administer the judicial sentence along with providing services and treatment to the judicial client. The intervention referral and the sentence are clearly linked.

The provider in the therapeutic role states: "I confront you with you, I confront you with what you say you want and need and the contradictions in your thinking, emotions and behavior that violate your own needs and goals." The provider, in the therapeutic role, always works towards helping clients achieve their agenda and assume responsibility for their own behavior.

What is most important in this integration process is that the provider responds at least initially to the correctional process within the framework of the therapeutic role. For example, when clients violate the terms of their judicial order, such as using illegal drugs, violating the requirements of probation or parole, or admit to breaking the law, the provider first manages this situation from a therapeutic stance. The provider works with the client's thoughts, underlying beliefs and emotions that led to that behavior and helps the client to identify the triggers that led to that behavior. However, the provider has the judicial obligation of engaging and informing the correctional system in sanctioning or correcting the behavior that violates the judicial status of the client. This is done from a therapeutic perspective, and if there is a therapeutic alliance, then many clients will take responsibility to engage and inform the judicial system around their infractions.

This core strategy is also addressed in *Chapter 7, Section II,* with respect to operational guidelines of working with the judicial system and enhance the partnership between the judicial and therapeutic systems.

9. A Cohesive Group That Elicits a Prosocial Identity

The **ninth core strategy** of *SSC* is to build a treatment group that becomes a primary source of therapeutic change and the development of prosocial attitudes and behavior. In order to do this, the provider works at building positive "in group" identity, continually strengthens the prosocial behavior of the group and group members, applies motivational enhancement and therapeutic counseling skills to the group itself, and continues to foster group cohesiveness.

The judicial client's treatment group becomes the laboratory for learning self-control, responsible actions towards others, and learning and practicing prosocial attitudes and behaviors. The cohesive prosocial group becomes a major force in bringing about change in the client. Group membership becomes an important aspect of the client's emerging identity as a responsible, caring, and productive member of society. Methods for developing and enhancing a cohesive group that can become a vehicle for change are discussed in *Chapter 7.*

10. Reentry and Reintegration Into the Community

The **tenth core strategy** of *SSC* is to use all of the possible resources and skills to enhance successful reentry and reintegration of clients into the community. Reentry and reintegration are seen as important focuses in the judicial system and have become a major objective in criminal justice treatment (Knight, Simpson & Hiller, 1999; Wexler, 2004; Wexler, Melnick & Chaple, 2007).

Between 2001 and 2004, the federal government allocated over $100 million to support the development of new reentry programs in all 50 states (Petersilia, 2004). The National Institute of Corrections, the American Probation and Parole Association, the National Governor Association, and State Departments of Corrections have each created special task forces to work on the reentry issue.

There is a robust set of literature that provides cogent evidence that aftercare programs reduce the rates of rearrest and reincarceration (e.g., Knight et al., 1997; Inciardi et al., 1997; Inciardi et al., 2002; Pelissier et al., 1998; Wexler, 1995; Wexler et al., 1999). Aftercare from prison is most effective if it involves a structured program such as a residential treatment program or transitional structured care such as a halfway house. Studies indicate that offenders who participate in these programs were better able to negotiate employment, find a more stable residential arrangement and had lower rates of rearrest following release from prison (Hiller et al., 1999; Knight, Simpson & Hiller, 1999). A summary of the efficacy of continuing care and aftercare programs is provided in the *Resource Guide* (Wanberg & Milkman, 2008).

Seiter and Kadela (2003) defined reentry programs as those that specifically focus on the transition from prison to community; or initiate treatment in a prison setting and link with a community program to provide continuity of care. Parole is the judicial structure that is utilized to manage the reentry and reintegration process. However, the parole system does not meet the treatment needs of judicial clients.

Reentry and reintegration are just as important for those who are not incarcerated, but sentenced to probation. Although these offenders remain in the community, there is a quality of being "removed" from normal community living by virtue of being in the judicial system. Release from community judicial supervision results in identifiable reentry and reintegration needs that must be met in order to capitalize on the efforts of supervision. Unfortunately, few programmatic efforts are made to address reintegration from probation.

Reentry and reintegration must involve more than judicial supervision and include services to address the treatment needs of the judicial client. Ideally, it should start once the offender enters the judicial system. Thus, reintegration begs the necessity of continuing care beginning with the first entry point into the system and ending with an effective aftercare program.

Field (2004) points out that effective continuing care involves services for offenders that are designed to prevent recidivism, and which are found across the continuum from arrest, diversion, conviction, probation, revocation, jail, prison, and parole or post-prison supervision; or, for the probation client, from arrest through the term of probation. He offers the critique that although continuing care may exist in exceptional programs, it is not a common and integral part of the judicial system. In fact, he notes that, with respect to linking together these specific points, "the offender is confronted with and by a system that largely isn't a system in the usual sense" (p. 33-34).

Field (2004) identifies a number of barriers and obstacles to continuing care in offender treatment: segmentation of the judicial system; lack of or poor coordination between corrections and treatment programs; failure to provide offenders post-release structure outside of parole; attenuation of incentives and sanctions at post-release; lack of aftercare services in the community; lack of experience by treatment providers in working with offenders; and the usual crunch - lack of funding.

The reentry and reintegration task is also made difficult because of the cautious and negative attitudes in the community towards persons with a history of criminal conduct, particularly those with violent and sexual offense histories. Many types of employment and many employers screen out persons with a felony history. This only points to the importance of addressing reentry and reintegration.

Continuing care and aftercare involve more than providing offenders with a structured setting in making the transition back to the community, e.g., halfway houses, community corrections facilities. They must also involve a treatment program component. One of the values of programs such as *SSC* is that they go beyond judicial supervision and link the treatment dimension to the reintegration process. In essence, one could conclude that these programs are reentry and reintegration efforts in and of themselves. One of their goals is to enhance the offender's adjustment to normative community living.

Even though we can construe these programs as having the goal of reintegration, at the same time, such programs need to have built-in components and sessions that address specific issues relevant to reentry and reintegration. This would involve connecting clients with community reinforcement programs that continue beyond formal treatment. Support and self-help groups are major components of these programs.

Effective reintegration involves helping clients reestablish supportive and positive relationships with their significant others and their primary social units. These connections are powerful elements in implementing responsible living and change. *Phase III* of the *SSC* curriculum includes sessions that address these issues. *Chapter 7* provides some specific guidelines for implementing the reentry and reintegrating processes.

PROGRAM CONCEPTUAL FRAMEWORK

Utilizing the learning and growth model, the stages of change and approaches to assessment, a conceptual framework for the delivery of *SSC* to judicial clients was developed. This structure involves three phases of intervention which have been described above.

This conceptual framework is provided in *Figure 1.1*. For each phase of treatment, the following are identified and defined:

- types of assessment completed;

- counseling and therapy goals;

- process goals;

- the provider skills that facilitate learning, self-improvement, responsible living and change;

- facilitation methods and techniques;

- treatment and correctional goals and expected experiences;

- treatment strategies;

- transtheoretical stages of change.

CHAPTER REVIEW

Criminal Conduct and Substance Abuse Treatment: Strategies for Self-Improvement and Change (SSC) - Pathways to Responsible Living was developed out of evidence-based treatment approaches directed at changing the cognitive structures that determine antisocial attitudes and behavior upon which criminal conduct is based. In addition to these targets of change, substance abuse patterns that interact with CC are also primary targets.

The principles of psychoeducation, psychotherapy and counseling, which represent the integrating threads of the *SSC* fabric, are defined. Also discussed are the two ways that the *SSC* program can fit into the judicial system: either as a nested program within more comprehensive judicial structures; or as a stand-alone program in a community outpatient setting.

The 10 core strategies of *SSC* which operationally define the underlying assumptions of the program were summarized. The five foundational strategies are addressed in more depth in subsequent chapters: 1) the therapeutic relationship, *Chapter 2*; 2) multidimensional and convergent validation model for assessment, *Chapter 6*; 3) phases of learning and growth and the stages of change, *Chapter 3*; 4) the CB approach as the primary treatment platform, *Chapter 4*; and 5) the strategies of relapse and recidivism prevention, *Chapter 5*.

The other five core strategies, discussed in some detail, are addressed in subsequent chapters as they relate to the five foundational models of *SSC*. The 10 core strategies are integrated into a graphic presentation and conceptual framework of the *SSC* program as presented in *Figure 1.1*.

FIGURE 1.1 Conceptual Framework for the Treatment of the Substance Abusing Judicial Clients

TREATMENT PHASES	CHALLENGE TO CHANGE	COMMITMENT TO CHANGE	TAKING OWNERSHIP FOR CHANGE
CHANGE PROCESS	**UNDIFFERENTIATED**	**DIFFERENTIATED**	**INTEGRATIVE**
ASSESSMENT	Screening/in-depth	Progress and Change	Progress and Change
COUNSELING AND THERAPY GOALS	Clients tell story Unpack thoughts, feelings and problems	Help clients hear their story Sort out, identify thoughts/feelings	Help clients act on their story Putting together Reinforce change
COUNSELING AND THERAPY SKILLS	Responding attentiveness Encouragers to share Reflective acceptance →	Reflection skills Therapeutic confrontation Correctional confrontation Change clarification →	Change Reinforcements
FACILITATION METHODS AND TECHNIQUES	Interactive teaching Interactive work sheets/ journaling Multi-media presentations Role playing Skills rehearsal Group processing →		
TREATMENT AND CORRECTIONAL GOALS	Build trust Caring environment Self-evaluation Self-disclosure Build AOD, CC and CB knowledge base Resolve ambivalence Thinking change MAP R&R prevention R&R prevention plan	Maintain trust Caring environment Self-awareness Apply knowledge Self-control Prosocial attitudes/ behavior Revise/extend →	Maintain trust Caring environment Self-change
TREATMENT STRATEGIES	Psychoeducation Therapy alliance Stages of change Basic CB skills R&R prevention Partnership with judicial system Cognitive behavioral map Phase I Closure	Cognitive restructuring IPR skills *Social Responsibility Therapy* (SRT) CB Map-STEP method → Phase II closure	Balanced lifestyle Healthy lifestyle SSC graduation
TRANSTHEORETICAL STAGES OF CHANGE	Precontemplative Contemplative	Preparation Action	Continued action Maintenance

CHAPTER OUTLINE

OVERVIEW

EFFICACY OF PSYCHOSOCIAL THERAPIES

COMMON DETERMINANTS OF TREATMENT OUTCOME

Provider Personal Characteristics

Empathy as the primary characteristic
Empathy as a skill
Empathy and prosocial behavior
Empathy training

The Counselor-Client Relationship

Therapeutic stance
Therapeutic alliance
Reflective acceptance
Enhancing motivation and interest in change
Therapeutic relationship with judicial clients
Therapeutic alliance with the group

The Client as a Person

PROVIDER SKILLS IN INTEGRATING EDUCATION AND THERAPY

The Adult Learning Model
The Psychoeducational Methods and Approaches
Integrating Psychoeducation and Therapy

THE CORRECTIONAL-THERAPEUTIC PARTNERSHIP

Elements of Effective Correctional Counseling Relationship
Anticriminal Versus Procriminal Expressions
Reinforcing Positive Thoughts and Behaviors
Sanctioning Within the Therapeutic Context

Provider and Client Partnership
Interactive Partners With the Correctional System

PROFILE OF THE EFFECTIVE JUDICIAL PROVIDER

The Personal Dimension
The Professional Dimension
Philosophical Perspectives

PROVIDER CULTURAL COMPETENCE: CAPITALIZING ON THE STRENGTHS OF DIVERSITY

CHAPTER REVIEW

CHAPTER OBJECTIVES

▶ Provide an understanding of the importance of the therapeutic relationship.

▶ Learn the principles of effective judicial counseling and facilitating the correctional-treatment partnership.

▶ Learn the dimensions, skills and characteristics of the effective SA judicial client counselor.

OVERVIEW

The focus of this chapter is one of the foundational strategies of *SSC*: Building a therapeutic relationship of trust and rapport with clients through developing a working alliance and the use of motivational enhancement skills. We first look at the efficacy of psychosocial therapies and the common factors that account for much of the variance contributing to positive treatment outcome. We then look at one of the most important of these factors, the therapeutic relationship. Two important components of this relationship are the provider (counselor) and the client. Thus, we identify the characteristics of the effective counselor and the client's contribution to the therapeutic alliance. We then look at one of the critical roles of the counselor and *SSC* provider: integrating the psychoeducation and therapeutic processes. Pertinent to the treatment of substance abusing (SA) judicial clients, we summarize the elements of effective correctional counseling. Finally, we provide a profile that defines three broad dimensions of the primary characteristics of the counselor or provider working with substance abusing judicial clients. The overall purpose of this chapter is to help providers enhance their effectiveness in working with SA judicial clients.

EFFICACY OF PSYCHOSOCIAL THERAPIES

Evidence provided in the literature indicates there is a general positive effect of psychosocial therapies. Meta-analyses of outcome studies conclude "Psychotherapy is effective at helping people achieve their goals and overcome their psychopathologies at a rate that is faster and more substantial than change that results from the client's natural healing process and supportive elements in the environment" (Lambert & Bergin, 1992, p. 363). Roth and Fonagy (2005), in their critical review of psychotherapy research, provide consistent evidence that a variety of psychotherapies across a variety of conditions and applied to a variety of disorders can be effective in producing positive outcomes.

More specific to the focus of this work, the authors (Milkman & Wanberg, 2007; Wanberg & Milkman, 2008) provide a summary of the efficacy of treatment across a wide variety of conditions and spe-

cific groups within the judicial system. We looked at the efficacy of the therapeutic community, CB approaches, aftercare, outcomes related to specific types of offenders, and outcomes related to specific correctional programs. The general conclusion, both in terms of meta-analyses and individual studies, is that there is strong evidence to support the efficacy of correctional treatment in terms of the reduction of relapse and recidivism. Another conclusion in these reports is that the efficacy of correctional treatments is enhanced by the use of cognitive-behavioral therapy approaches (e.g., Andrews & Bonta, 2003; Lipsey & Landenberger, 2006).

In their summary of *What Works*, Roth and Fonagy (2005) report that certain types of therapies are more effective for different types of disorders and psychological problems. For example, there appears to be evidence of the efficacy of cognitive-behavioral approaches for major depression, general anxiety, panic disorders, posttraumatic stress disorders, and dialectical behavior therapy for personality disorders (Roth & Fonagy, 2005). And, as noted, CBT has been found to be more effective than other approaches in reducing recidivism among judicial clients.

Somewhat contrary to conclusions that specific therapies may be more effective with different types of disorders, Lambert and Bergin (1992) argued that across the general application of various theoretical approaches, no one clinical approach seems to be superior over another; and that different therapeutic approaches, e.g., behavioral, psychodynamic, client-centered, "appear to secure comparable outcomes" (Garfield, 1992, p. 349). Differences in outcome between various forms of treatment are simply not as pronounced as might be expected (Lambert & Bergin, 1992) and "other purportedly unique features of a system may be relatively inconsequential" (Strupp & Howard, 1992, p. 313).

This argument is supported by the findings of Project Match (Project Match Research Group, 1997) which compared three treatment approaches administered on a one-to-one basis to those whose history involved only alcohol abuse using large samples of clients conducted within a random clinical trial design: CBT Coping Skills Therapy; Motivational Enhancement Therapy (Brief Therapy); and 12-Step

Facilitation; all delivered over a period of 12 weeks. Although significant and sustained improvements were achieved across all three treatment groups with respect to drinking outcomes, the outcomes did not differ across the three approaches.

First, what is important from the above discussion and our review of the literature summarized in other documents (Milkman & Wanberg, 2007; Wanberg & Milkman, 2008) is that psychosocial therapies are efficacious in bringing about change and positive outcomes in individuals across a variety of psychosocial problems and that CBT appears to offer greater benefits with selected disorders, e.g., criminal conduct and substance abuse. And, Roth and Fonagy (2005) conclude: "Our interpretation of the evidence is that a variety of techniques in the hands of well-trained and supervised practitioners, operating within a structured and controlled framework, are likely to be both safe and effective" (p. 487).

Second, even though there are somewhat diverse findings regarding the contribution of different theoretical orientations and therapeutic approaches, it is concluded that different therapies embody common factors that are curative but not emphasized by the theory of change central to a particular school (Gurman & Messer, 2003; Wampold, 2001). Besides treatment approach and orientation, what are those common factors that contribute to positive outcomes of psychosocial therapies?

COMMON DETERMINANTS OF TREATMENT OUTCOME

The common determinants of treatment outcome that cut across therapeutic approaches and types are: personal characteristics of the provider; the counselor-client relationship; and the characteristics of the client. Each of these three variables and their interaction contribute significant variance to change in the client and to treatment outcome. *Figure 2.1,* page 35, provides a summary of these three broad variables. Each will be discussed.

Provider Personal Characteristics

One common factor that contributes to the effectiveness of psychosocial therapies is a set of core personal characteristics and features of the treatment provider. Carl Rogers provided the foundation for understanding these core dimensions (1957). He concluded that the communication of **genuine warmth** and **empathy** by the therapist alone is sufficient in producing constructive changes in clients. He was the first to clearly identify in the literature the traits of **warmth, genuineness, respect** and **empathy** as essential in not only establishing a therapeutic relationship with clients, but also in producing the desired therapeutic outcomes.

Early pioneering studies by Truax and Carkuff (Carkhuff, 1969, 1971; Carkhuff & Truax, 1965; Truax, 1963; Truax & Carkhuff, 1967) and others (e.g., Berenson & Carkhuff, 1967; Carkhuff & Berenson, 1977; Rogers, Gendlan, Kiesler & Truax, 1967; Truax & Mitchell, 1971) supported this conclusion. Lazarus (1971) found that the most desirable characteristics that clients found in counselors were sensitivity, honesty and gentleness. And, in more recent work, Ackerman and Hilsenroth (2001, 2003) confirmed the personal characteristics of empathy, warmth and understanding, and perceived trustworthiness as essential contributions to the therapeutic process.

These core characteristics are invariably seen as part of effective substance abuse counseling. George (1990) identifies the personal characteristics of the effective substance abuse counselor as genuineness, ability to form warm and caring relationships, sensitivity and understanding, sense of humor, having realistic levels of aspirations for client change and self-awareness. The characteristics of empathy, warmth, and genuineness are also seen as necessary characteristics of the correctional counselor (e.g., Andrews & Bonta, 1994, 2003; Masters, 2004).

Thus, although interpreted in different ways, these core characteristics of empathic understanding, genuineness or congruence, positive regard and respect, warmth, and concreteness (specificity of expression) are considered basic to the effective helping relationship. It is safe to say that these characteristics are emphasized in virtually every text on therapy and counseling, including texts addressing counseling of substance abuse and criminal justice clients. They are foundational to the therapeutic change process.

Empathy as the primary characteristic

Rogers (1959) defined empathy as an ability to "perceive the internal frame of reference of another with accuracy and with the emotional components and meaning which pertain thereto as an ability if one were the person, but without ever losing the 'as if' condition" (p. 210). It is the ability to enter into another person's subjective world, to put oneself into the place of the other person.

Roger's definition clearly implies that empathy has a cognitive component, e.g., "to perceive." Feshbach (1997) notes that although empathy refers to an emotional response that stems from the emotional state of another person, "it is contingent on cognitive as well as emotional factors" (p. 36). She concludes that the general consensus is that empathy involves both affective and cognitive elements. Thus, the counselor has both an emotional as well as a cognitive response to the client's situation or condition.

Rogers et al. (1967) made the bold statement that through the therapist's warmth and empathy, even the most severely disturbed clients can be helped. What they were saying is that empathy is the **core of the core characteristics** of the effective therapist.

The bulk of the studies of the impact of empathy on treatment outcome were done in the 1960s, 1970s and 1980s. Certainly, the early studies by Rogers, Truax, Carkhuff and associates gave robust support for the efficacy of empathy on the positive outcome of therapy. Bohart and Greenberg (1997) note that since that time, "research on empathy has been sporadic" (p. 15; see pp.17-19 for a summary of studies).

Studies of substance abuse clients not only identify empathy as a significant determinant of their response to treatment, but contributing to the major variance of outcome (Miller & Rollnick, 2002). A series of studies reported that empathy shown by counselors during treatment accounted for two-thirds, one-half, and one-fourth of the variance of drinking outcomes at six months, 12 months and 24 months, respectively (Miller & Rollnick, 2002).

Bohart and Greenberg (1997) note that empathy is often taken too lightly and is often seen as a kindly and supportive posture in treatment. It is more than this. It is ".....central to therapeutic change and far more than just acknowledging the client's perspective and being warm and supportive. It is a major component of the healing process." It "....includes the making of deep and sustained psychological contact with another person" and includes "...deep sustained empathic inquiry or immersing of oneself in the experience of the other" (pp. 4-5). Acknowledging that different writers see different meanings of empathy, they schematize therapeutic empathy as:

- rapport that is kindly, global understanding, being tolerant and accepting of the client's feelings and frame of reference;

- experience near understanding of the client's world, and grasping the "whole of the client's perceived situation"; and

- communicative attunement involving frequent understanding expressions and putting oneself into the client's shoes and communicating in the moment what the client is experiencing.

Empathy as a skill

Describing empathy as a counselor characteristic does not mean that it is a trait that one has or does not have. Although some individuals seem to have greater ability to show empathy than others, we see it as a learned characteristic.

The fact that empathy has important cognitive elements suggests that it is based on operationally defined skill that can be learned. Some of these learned skills are inherent in its definition. Feshbach, through her broad meaning of empathy, implies that the skills of communication is at the core of learned empathy, as she states: "Empathy is a basic form of social communication that can occur in many different social contexts" (1997, p. 33).

For example, communicative attunement is seen as one of these skills (Bohart & Greenberg, 1997). Other skills that operationally define empathy are: listening, verbal and nonverbal attending, and responding.

Empathy and prosocial behavior

There are two important values regarding empathy and *SSC*. First, as established in the above discussion, the utilization of empathic communication is essential in establishing a working relationship with SA judicial clients. Second, empathy is the core of prosocial responding and responsibility towards others. Empathy training in the treatment of judicial clients is a given (recognized early on by Ross et al., 1986). Feshbach's (1997) model describes the prosocial aspects of empathy:

▶ it allows one to discriminate emotional cues in others; and

▶ it involves the more mature cognitive skills that allows others to take the role or perspective of someone (and society).

Others have established the relationship between empathy and prosocial behavior (Eisenberg & Miller, 1987). Bohart and Greenberg (1997) note that "empathy also has motivational properties in that it motivates altruistic and moral behavior" (p. 23).

Feshbach (1997), defining prosocial or moral behavior (she equates the two) as "behavior that reflects caring and concern for others" (p. 45), cites research findings that support the relationship between empathy and prosocial behavior (pp. 45-46).

Other correlates of empathy that have prosocial implications are (studies referenced by Feshbach, p. 48): helping behavior; cooperation; generosity; academic achievement; better adjustment after a social and interpersonal stress experience; and fewer adjustment problems in school. Generally, this suggests that "empathy may function as a coping skill or serve as a protective factor in reactions to stress" (p. 48). This has a bearing on antisocial behavior in that one of the risk factors for relapse and recidivism that we work on in *SSC* is stress - both emotional and interpersonal.

Empathy training

If one important goal in working with judicial clients is to increase prosocial behavior, then empathy training should be part of the treatment process. Feshbach's (1997) discussion of empathy development in children concludes these are interactive. Empathy training can increase prosocial behavior. However, "for prosocial behavior to occur when the child is empathic, the prosocial response must be in the child's repertoire and occur in the situation" (p. 47). Thus, this implies that "empathy training must be accompanied by prosocial behavioral-transaction training" (p. 47).

Some of the skills that can be learned and are part of enhancing empathy and prosocial behavior include (Feshbach, 1997, pp. 49-50):

▶ role-taking and perspective-taking skills enhanced through the therapy techniques of role-reversal and doubling;

▶ perceptual training that focuses on perceptual accuracy and sensitivity;

▶ cognitive analysis training, such as analyzing non-verbal behavior, e.g., meaning of facial expressions; and

▶ mediation and compromising.

Specific techniques to facilitate the learning of empathy include role-playing, modeling, doubling, role-reversal, affective recognition of emotions using pictures and audio-suppressed video, vicarious problem solving (solving someone else's problems), and communication skills training, e.g., practicing active listening (see *Session 37* in the *Workbook* and in *Section III* of this *Guide* for a summary of these techniques).

The Counselor-Client Relationship

One of the robust predictors of treatment retention and outcome is the relationship between the client and the provider, regardless of the therapeutic orientation or treatment approach (Bachelor, 1991, 1995; Barber et al., 2001; Beutler et al., 1994; Connors et al., 1997; Gaston, 1990; Hartley & Strupp, 1983; Horvath, 2006; Horvath & Symonds, 1991; Krupnick et al., 1996; Martin, Garske & Davis, 2000; Raue & Goldfried, 1994; Raue et al., 1997; Roth & Fonagy, 2005; Zuroff et al., 2000). In fact, there is "evidence that the therapeutic relationship is the best predictor of success in psychotherapy" (Bohart & Greenberg, 1997, p. 3). And, as Washton and Zweben (2006) note, "The therapeutic relationship is by far the most important ingredient of the integrated approach and, as in all other forms of effective psychotherapy, it is the primary vehicle for facilitating positive change" (p. 74).

Strupp and Howard (1992) state poignantly: "...the research literature has strongly suggested, generic (or common) relationship factors in all forms of psychotherapy (e.g., empathic understanding, respect, caring, genuineness, warmth) carry most of the weight..." (p. 313). "Reviewers are virtually unanimous in their opinion that the therapist-patient relationship is central to therapeutic change" (Lambert & Bergin, 1992, p. 372; also documented in other references cited above).

The elements of the therapist-client relationship are central to verbal therapies that are premised on acceptance, tolerance, therapeutic alliance, working alliance and support (Lambert, 1983). They are also seen as important elements in cognitive and behavioral therapies "as an essential means for establishing the rapport necessary to motivate clients to complete treatment" (Lambert & Bergin, 1992, p. 371). These are also basic elements of developing motivation in the treatment of the substance abuser (Miller & Rollnick, 1991, 2002).

George and Christiani (1981) contend that the essential elements that promote an effective treatment relationship are trust and acceptance of the client. They outline the following specific characteristics of the effective therapeutic and helping relationship.

- The relationship is affective: it explores emotions and feelings.

- It is intense: the relationship promotes an open sharing of perceptions and reactions between client and worker.

- It involves growth and change: it is dynamic, continually changing.

- It is private and confidential.

- It is supportive: the treatment relationship offers a system of support.

- It is honest: it is based on honest and open and direct communication between the worker and client.

The more specific components or elements of the therapeutic change relationship are best illustrated by the following, as summarized early on by Marmor (1975).

- The relationship promotes a release of tension.

- It involves cognitive learning.

- It involves operant conditioning and reinforcement.

- The client identifies with the counselor.

- It involves reality testing.

Sloane et al. (1975) indicate that successful clients in treatment identify a number of factors important to their change and improvement, several of which are specific relationship factors. These involve the therapist helping them to understand their problems; receiving encouragement to practice facing the issues that bother them; being able to talk to an understanding person; and developing greater understanding from the therapeutic relationship.

There are a number of specific issues that are relevant to understanding and developing the therapeutic relationship. They include: therapeutic stance; the therapeutic alliance; appropriate use of therapeutic confrontation; use of motivational enhancement skills; developing an alliance with judicial clients; and alliance with the group.

Therapeutic stance

The therapeutic stance or position that builds and sustains the therapeutic relationship is based on the core counselor characteristics of: warmth, empathy, genuineness and positive regard (Lambert & Bergin, 1992; Rogers, 1942, 1951, 1957). Judy Beck (2005) sees this stance as involving understanding, caring and competence. Style of relating becomes apparent early in treatment and impacts retention, even in one introductory session. With respect to AOD clients, Miller and Rollnick (1991, 2002) show that successful therapy is predicated upon counselors presenting the therapeutic posture of accurate empathy, non-possessive warmth, and genuineness.

The therapeutic stance also involves the provider's attitude towards clients. This is of particular importance regarding clients whose problem behaviors are repudiated and looked upon in a negative way by the community and society. Providers will have had strong exposure to these negative attitudes long before entering the helping professions. The two problem behaviors most repudiated by society are criminal conduct and substance abuse. The media reports daily the negative aspects of these problem behaviors, particularly when those behaviors cause harm to others and the community.

Given these exposures to sociocultural negativity, judicial counselors must be aware of their own attitudes and biases towards these problem behaviors. It is easy to inculcate society's negative attitudes around these behaviors and society's expectations that SA judicial clients will inevitably relapse or recidivate.

Providers need to be cognizant of their personal attitudes and beliefs around these problem behaviors, and their counter-transference responses to clients who relapse and recidivate (Imhoff, 1995; Kaufman, 1994; Washton & Zweben, 2006). When considering those judicial populations that are strongly castigated by the public, such as the sex and violent offenders, judicial counselors need to have a clear understanding of their own personal attitudes and posture towards these groups.

Washton and Zweben (2006) stress that negative, strong and judgmental attitudes by counselors can "fracture the therapeutic alliance," causing treatment dropout and failure (p. 207). Judicial providers must always keep in mind the seriousness of relapse and recidivism for judicial clients and for the community. Yet, maintaining the therapeutic posture of showing empathy, genuineness and respect is essential even with the most difficult of judicial clients, and under the most difficult of circumstances when the client relapses or recidivates after a period of positive adjustment.

Therapeutic Alliance

Therapeutic alliance builds on but goes beyond the therapeutic stance. Therapeutic alliance involves a collaborative relationship, affective bonding, rapport building, and a mutual understanding and sharing of the intervention goals between the client and the provider (Bordin, 1979; Connors et al, 1997; Raue, Goldfried & Barkham, 1997). It "acts as a moderating variable - a catalytic mode of action that makes treatment more effective" (Roth & Fonagy, 2005, p. 464). It is seen as the therapist's "most powerful tool" (Washton & Zweben, 2006, p. 167).

The importance - viz. necessity - of rapport in the therapeutic relationship and therapeutic alliance has been a construct established very early in psychosocial therapies (Horvath, 2006). Freud made it clear that treatment should proceed when the therapist has effectively established rapport with the client (1913). Such rapport is established when the therapist shows interest in the psychological condition of the patient but also shows personal concern for the patient (Freud, 1893-1895, p. 265). He notes that the initial phase of treatment will go well when the therapist demonstrates concern and interest and "sympathetic understanding" (Freud, 1913, pp. 139-140) and that a "pact" is established where patient and therapist "band" together to work on the problems presented by the outside world (1964). Roth and Fonagy (2005, p. 461) note that Zetzel (1956) coined the term "therapeutic alliance" which involves deliberate collaboration and a rational agreement between therapist and client.

Connors et al.'s (1997) examination of the therapeutic alliance data gathered in Project MATCH (Project MATCH Research Group, 1993, 1997) revealed a consistent positive relationship between therapeutic alliance and treatment participation and positive drinking-related outcomes, regardless of whether the rating was based on client self-report or on therapist report. This finding was consistent across treatment approaches, modalities and different nosological groupings and clearly indicates the crucial importance of this component in the treatment process.

Although, as noted above, most research confirms that the therapeutic alliance is a common underlying factor in treatment outcome, there is some evidence that the therapeutic alliance varies across therapeutic orientations. Roth and Fonagy (2005) cite a number of studies to indicate that client-therapist partnership ratings (by clients), overall alliance ratings, and the association between alliance and outcome tended to be higher for CB approaches when compared to other approaches (pp. 469-470). They conclude that this may result from the fact that part and parcel of the CB approach is clear and explicit collaboration between client and therapist (p. 470).

A variety of studies and literature reviews indicate several important conclusions around therapeutic alliance (Bachelor, 1991, 1995; Barber et al., 1999, 2001; Beutler et al., 1994; Castonguay,, Constantino & Heltforth, 2006; Connors et al., 1997; Gaston, 1990; Hartley & Strupp, 1983; Horvath, 2006; Krupnick et al., 1996; Martin, Garske & Davis, 2000; Raue & Goldfried, 1994; Raue et al., 1997; Roth & Fonagy, 2005; Zuroff et al., 2000):

▶ Client ratings of therapeutic alliance are more predictive of outcome than therapist ratings (Barber et al., 2001);

▶ Therapeutic alliance scores tend to be higher for cognitive-behavioral sessions than for sessions conducted under a psychodynamic-interpersonal orientation;

▶ The efficacy of therapeutic alliance is found across various therapeutic approaches, modalities and intervention methods;

▶ Positive therapeutic alliance developed early in treatment predicts positive outcomes.

Judy Beck (2005) notes that the modification of core beliefs is more likely to be successful when clients have trust in the therapist and for the treatment process, particularly when they discover the process helps and that belief change brings better outcomes (p. 269). She also stresses that the therapeutic alliance is a major vehicle through which the goals of treatment can be met and notes three main strategies to accomplish this (pp. 77-85):

▶ providing positive relationship experiences between therapist and clients;

▶ working through problems that develop between therapist and clients, and in the case of groups, between an individual client and the group;

▶ when positive outcomes of the therapeutic relationship model how the client can establish positive relationships with others and how it generalizes to other relationships.

Beck provides five strategies to build the therapeutic alliance (p. 64):

▶ collaborate with the patient;

▶ demonstrate empathy, caring, understanding;

▶ adapt one's therapeutic style;

▶ alleviate distress; and

▶ elicit feedback at the end of sessions.

Finally, therapeutic alliance is not a simple variable that operates consistently over time in treatment. After reviewing a number of studies of how alliance is affected by symptom change over time, Roth and Fonagy (2005) conclude "at the very least, it seems appropriate to question the assumption that the alliance represents a homogeneous variable" (p. 468). It is multidimensional and represents complex processes, varies across stages of therapy and that at different points in treatment, it acts in different ways (p. 468). Thus, the provider is wise to monitor the therapeutic alliance over time and in relationship to the stage of change that the individual or group might be in at particular points in treatment.

Reflective acceptance in managing resistance and preserving therapeutic alliance

Developing a positive intervention relationship, building rapport and trust, and developing a therapeutic alliance with the client all depend on how client resistance, defensiveness and ambivalence are managed. This management is of particular importance in the early stages of treatment.

We distinguish reflective therapeutic confrontation from the traditional methods of confrontational therapy and coercive intervention in managing resistance and "denial." The traditional methods were previously touted as the treatment choice for substance abuse and often resulted in increasing client resistance and defensiveness. Bill Wilson, one of the co-founders of Alcoholics Anonymous, held that intervention works best on the basis of attraction and support. Wilson advocated that alcoholics be treated with an approach that "would contain no basis for contention or argument. Most of us sense that real tolerance of other people's shortcomings and viewpoints, and a respect for their opinions are attitudes which make us more helpful to others" (Alcoholics Anonymous, 1976, pp. 19-20). These words are of particular relevance to the treatment of judicial clients with substance abuse problems.

According to Miller and Rollnick (1991) research does not support the common belief that people with AOD problems display pathological lying or an abnormal level of self-deception. Nor does self-labeling promote more effective recovery. In fact Sovereign and Miller (1987) found that problem drinkers randomly assigned to confrontational counseling showed a far greater incidence of arguing, denying or changing the topic than those given a more client-oriented motivational intervening approach.

The most effective way to manage client resistance, defensiveness and ambivalence is to **first** encourage the client to share thoughts and feelings of resistance and defensiveness, and **second,** to use reflective-acceptance skills to help clients hear their resistance. These are the two basic steps of the therapeutic change process as described above, and represent the elements of reflective or therapeutic confrontation (Wanberg, 1974, 1983, 1990; Wanberg & Milkman, 1998; Wanberg, Milkman & Timken, 2005).

These are the key components in Miller and Rollnick's motivational interviewing model (Miller & Rollnick, 1991, 2002). This involves fostering an environment of acceptance for clients to share their thoughts and feelings and then reflecting the client's specific statements of anger, resistance and ambivalence. Miller's (Miller & Rollnick, 2002) clinical principles of avoid argumentation, develop discrepancy and roll with resistance underlie the reflective-acceptance approach in dealing with client resistance and defensiveness.

Enhancing Motivation and Interest in Change

Miller states: "Addiction is fundamentally a problem of motivation" (2006a, p. 134). We can say the same for criminal conduct. But motivation cuts both ways. It contributes significantly to the development and maintenance of CC and addiction patterns; it is critical in the change of those patterns.

In the summary of their edited book: *Rethinking Substance Abuse: What the Science Shows, and What We Should Do about It,* Miller and Carroll (2006) include as one of the 10 broad principles of drug use and problems: "Motivation is central to prevention and intention" (p. 296); and the companion recommendation for intervention is that "enhancing motivation for and commitment to change should be an early goal and key component of intervention" (p. 307).

Motivation for change and the therapeutic relationship are interactive. First, there is a great deal of research evidence supporting the efficacy of motivational enhancement as an important component in building the therapist-client relationship and implementing treatment readiness and change in AOD abuse clients (e.g., Miller & Rollnick, 1991, 2002; Project Match Research Group, 1997). On the other hand, a person's strength of motivation for change is strongly influenced by the client-therapist relationship. Thus, therapeutic alliance increases motivation; and motivation strengthens the therapeutic alliance.

Miller points out that the most critical component of motivational enhancement is focusing on the client's own verbalizations and expressions of an intrinsic desire, perceived ability, and need and rationality for committing to change (Miller, 2006a). The critical barrier that this component targets is the ambivalence to change. As Miller and Carroll note, "ambivalence is the resting state, the status quo from which instigation to change begins" (p. 147). The critical step in that change is instigation, which happens when individuals see that their current situation is discrepant from their most important goals and values. And, what influences instigation is the confluence of intrapersonal, interpersonal and contextual factors.

As with the erosion process involving the many links in the chain of relapse (Daley & Marlatt, 1992) and recidivism (Wanberg & Milkman, 1998; Wanberg, Milkman & Timken, 2005), there is a process involving many variables that leads to change. Yet, as Miller (2006a) notes, it seems that there is a time "of reaching a decision, making a commitment as a final common pathway to change" (p. 149). And this "instigation" could be: "something clicks." Or, it could be an insignificant factor that from a linear measurement standpoint has little weight, but the results are geometric as in catastrophe theory (Thom, 1975; see pp. 23-24 in Marlatt & Witkiewitz, 2005; and *Chapter 5* in this *Guide*). Or, there is no identifiable event, not even an "I will change" verbal expression (Miller, 2006a). But what is important, for many substance abuse and judicial clients - it does happen, change does occur.

Research has identified some methods and approaches that are not effective in enhancing motivation to change. These include: punishment; confrontation with the intent to elicit fear, shame, guilt or humiliation; pure education programs that are designed **only** to enlighten clients around the dangers of drugs; and large doses of attention in the form of generic treatment (Miller, 2006a).

Two approaches that work in enhancing motivation to change are: short-term, brief interventions that utilize the FRAMES model described below; and a strong positive reinforcement approach for non-use or the use of alternatives to AOD use (Miller, 2006a).

The necessity for the use of motivational enhancement methods is found in managing client resistance and ambivalence. Most individuals with AOD and CC histories display an ambivalence about changing their lives, or at least, changing the behavior patterns that lead to these problems (e.g., Connors et al., 2001; Miller & Rollnick, 1991, 2002). Resolving ambivalence and resistance to these patterns, and helping clients to develop an internal sense of readiness, openness and responsiveness to treatment are primary objectives of the early phases of treatment.

Motivational strategies are based on the compensatory attribution model of treatment (Brickman et

al., 1982), which sees the client as having the power to influence change and focuses on building client self-efficacy and responsibility in the change process. Motivation is a state of readiness and openness or eagerness to participate in a change process. Miller, Zweben et al. (1994, p. 2) summarized the research on what motivates problem drinkers to change. Their work on Motivational Enhancement Therapy (MET) highlights the effectiveness of relatively brief treatment for problem drinkers. The elements that the authors consider necessary to induce change are summarized by the acronym **FRAMES** (also in Miller, 2006a, p. 146):

▶ **FEEDBACK** of personal risk impairment;

▶ Emphasis on personal **RESPONSIBILITY** for change;

▶ **ADVICE**;

▶ A **MENU** of alternative change options;

▶ Therapist **EMPATHY**;

▶ Facilitation of client **SELF-EFFICACY** or optimism.

Therapeutic interventions containing some or all of these motivational elements have been demonstrated to be effective in "initiating treatment and in reducing long-term alcohol use, alcohol-related problems, and health consequences of drinking" (Miller et al., 1994, p. 2).

Therapeutic relationship with judicial clients

Establishing a working relationship with judicial clients is complex and difficult. As noted, these clients often have great distrust in the "system" and have a difficult time believing and trusting that judicial providers and counselors will advocate for and support their treatment needs.

One problem of developing a working relationship is compounded by the vast differences among offenders, e.g., many different types of offenders and different offender populations. Different approaches will be required for the sex-offender versus the substance abusing offender. Whereas one judicial client may need more compassion and caring at the initial stage of treatment, another may need more structure to control acting out in the group.

Another problem is the diversity of judicial settings. Peters and Wexler (2005) also note that the therapeutic alliance will vary according to the judicial setting. Developing a therapeutic relationship with a prison inmate who will be incarcerated for a longer period of time will take more time, deliberation and patience. With a jail inmate where the stay is shorter, the working relationship may be less interpersonal and more task oriented, e.g., completing a short-term treatment program. As Springer et al. (2003) note: "One size does not fit all when it comes to treating the complex needs of substance-abusing offenders. In other words, 'start where the client is' " (p. 43).

The most challenging part of developing a therapeutic relationship with judicial clients is that correctional treatment is both client-centered and society centered. As discussed in some detail in *Chapter 1,* the provider/counselor represents both the judicial system and the client, and works at integrating the therapeutic and correctional system in the delivery of treatment.

An important focus in enhancing motivation and interest for change in judicial clients is that of developing "a more enlightened view of their self-interest and recognize that it is in their own best interest to anticipate the long-term consequences of their actions...." (Freeman et al., 1990, p. 229). This model is designed to help judicial clients to control impulsivity long enough to perceive the consequences of drinking and committing a crime as not as rewarding as the long-term consequences of prosocial behavior. In essence, motivation is enhanced by helping clients take a long-term view of their self-interest. This can only be done when the provider takes a collaborative approach to treatment (a key component of CBT) and a trust-based working relationship has been developed. These two objectives of treatment - building a collaborative relationship and helping the client take a long-term view of self-interest - are primary focuses in the treatment of substance abusing judicial clients.

Therapeutic alliance with the group

Most of our discussion of the therapeutic alliance has been in relationship to the client and provider. Since *SSC,* and probably most correctional treatment programs, are administered in a group modality, it is important to apply the principles we have discussed to the group as a whole. It is also important to recognize that the group, in and of itself, is a social unit that has its own resistance, set of values, goals and objectives, stages of change, relationship with the provider, and need for change. In this sense, the group becomes "the client" and all of the skills used to develop the therapeutic alliance should be applied to the group as well as the individual. We will discuss this approach and the "treatment of the group" in more detail in *Chapter 7.*

The Client as Person

Therapeutic alliance and motivation to change is in the hands of both the provider and the client. We looked at the characteristics of providers that contribute to the establishment of the therapeutic relationship and therapeutic alliance. However, *Figure 2.1* also shows that the client as a person is a critical variable that coalesces with the therapeutic relationship to effect change.

Given that the therapeutic alliance is a powerful tool to effect change, what contributions do clients make towards this alliance? *Figure 2.1* provides categories of client characteristics and circumstances that influence the therapeutic alliance. At a more specific level, Roth and Fonagy (2005) summarize findings from their review of the research on client characteristics that contribute to a poor therapeutic alliance and treatment outcome (see p. 465 for this review): At the intrapersonal level, a lack of hope, lack of psychological mindfulness, and a poor or negative view of others; history of difficulty in maintaining and sustaining good relationships with others and family; and an inability to establish secure attachments to others. Their summary also indicates that clients with higher expectations of improvement tend to predict the level of alliance and treatment outcome.

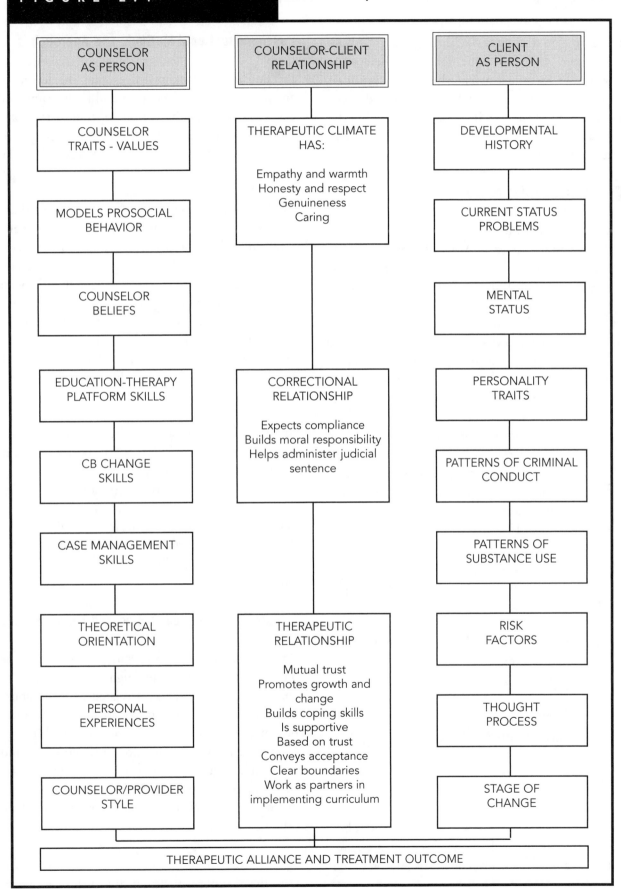

COUNSELOR AS PERSON

COUNSELOR TRAITS - VALUES

MODELS PROSOCIAL BEHAVIOR

COUNSELOR BELIEFS

EDUCATION-THERAPY PLATFORM SKILLS

CB CHANGE SKILLS

CASE MANAGEMENT SKILLS

THEORETICAL ORIENTATION

PERSONAL EXPERIENCES

COUNSELOR/PROVIDER STYLE

COUNSELOR-CLIENT RELATIONSHIP

THERAPEUTIC CLIMATE HAS:

Empathy and warmth
Honesty and respect
Genuineness
Caring

CORRECTIONAL RELATIONSHIP

Expects compliance
Builds moral responsibility
Helps administer judicial sentence

THERAPEUTIC RELATIONSHIP

Mutual trust
Promotes growth and change
Builds coping skills
Is supportive
Based on trust
Conveys acceptance
Clear boundaries
Work as partners in implementing curriculum

CLIENT AS PERSON

DEVELOPMENTAL HISTORY

CURRENT STATUS PROBLEMS

MENTAL STATUS

PERSONALITY TRAITS

PATTERNS OF CRIMINAL CONDUCT

PATTERNS OF SUBSTANCE USE

RISK FACTORS

THOUGHT PROCESS

STAGE OF CHANGE

THERAPEUTIC ALLIANCE AND TREATMENT OUTCOME

PROVIDER SKILLS IN INTEGRATING EDUCATION AND THERAPY

The third core strategy of *SSC* introduced in *Chapter 1* is integration of the educational and therapeutic process. We identified psychoeducation as being an important component of CB treatment and treatment of judicial clients. This strategy falls within the domain of the provider's skill necessary for effective treatment delivery.

The Adult Learning Model

The correctional treatment provider is both educator and therapist or - to use DeMuro's concept - assumes the role of a therapeutic educator (DeMuro, 1997). He points out the difference between pedagogy, or the art and science of helping children learn, and andragogy, which is the process of adult learning and education (Knowles, 1980, 1984, 1990). In pedagogy, the learner is viewed as underdeveloped and dependent upon the teacher. In andragogy, it is assumed that learners are diverse and have reached certain levels of physical, intellectual and emotional maturity allowing for greater collaboration between educator and learner in the process of learning. The adult learner "enters a learning situation with his or her own complete set of values, beliefs, attitudes, needs, life experiences, self-concept, and perceptions of life" (DeMuro, 1997, p. 59).

Knowles (1980) sees the adult educator as a teacher, facilitator, mentor and role model who has five main functions:

- to **help** individuals identify (diagnose) their needs for learning;

- to **plan** their learning experiences;

- to **motivate** the learner;

- to provide a **method** and **resources** for learning; and

- to **evaluate** the learning process.

The goal is for *SSC* providers to integrate these adult educator functions with those of the therapist, resulting in a role that helps individuals interpret their life experiences in order to change their behaviors (Demuro, 1997, p. 65).

Psychoeducational Methods and Approaches

Psychoeducation acknowledges that the learner is an adult with vast experiences and background and cognitive sets that have been operating for some time. However, effective integration must include more than the application of the adult educator functions.

Psychoeducation involves using a variety of methods in presenting, teaching, and explaining concepts and skills, and in helping clients to integrate these into the change process. To effect change, it must use methods that are interactive and experiential and clients must have a sense of personal identification with the material being presented and learned. These methods include in-session exercises, interactive journaling, role playing, cognitive and behavioral rehearsal, and interactive discussion of the concepts and ideas being presented.

Methods should be varied and use multi-media approaches such as flip-charts, chalk boards, drawing diagrams and presenting graphic presentations (see J. Beck, 2005, p. 258 for illustration of the use of diagrams in helping clients understand the process of change). Psychoeducational methods also include the use of video feedback, computer-assisted learning, actiongrams, reading assignments and homework.

Integrating Psychoeducation and Therapy

Psychoeducation is an important component of the *SSC* program. Clients are taught basic schemas for change, important concepts related to AOD abuse and CC, problem solving, negotiation skills, interpersonal skills, and how to restructure thinking. Clients are then helped to apply this knowledge and these skills to their own personal-emotional situation with the goal of enhancing prosocial and positive outcomes in the clients' relationship to themselves, others and the community.

The education approach of *SSC* is based on a learner-centered rather than an information-centered model (Hart, 1991) with the goal of giving personal meaning to learned content. *SSC* sessions create a learning environment whereby clients interact with the curriculum content so as to disclose personal information for the purpose of self-assessment and to identify personal problems. The curriculum encourages clients to make changes with the goal of preventing relapse and recidivism.

Throughout the *SSC* program, information and knowledge that are provided are always followed by interactive group activity and exercises designed to help clients apply the concepts and knowledge to their own personal situation. The goal is to help achieve the first step to change - facilitating self-disclosure. In the interactive process, clients identify and share how the concepts fit them. This helps to achieve an important second step towards change - self-awareness.

Clients then learn to use the knowledge and the specific skills to make changes and discover that these changes can lead to positive outcomes and more adaptive living. These changes get reinforced and strengthened by persons in their lives and by the treatment process (the provider and the group). Review of the concepts and skills and continual practice continue to result in positive outcomes, and change is further reinforced.

This model translates into an important mantra of *SSC:*

▶ self-disclosure leads to self-awareness (which includes mindfulness and acceptance);

▶ self-awareness leads to change;

▶ change results in positive outcomes that further strengthen change.

Thus, integrating education with the principles of therapy, *SSC* moves the client beyond the level of self-awareness to a level of cognitive, affective and behavioral change. Therapy helps clients deal with the realms of thoughts, feelings, attitudes and behavior at a more intense and deeper level. The client is more involved in the affective elements of change and there is greater focus on helping the client have more intense personal identification with the therapeutic themes and content. To use Patterson's (1966) concept, therapy (in contrast to education) is clearly more "conative" in nature - that is, it directs mental processes (thought and feeling) and behavior towards action and change. Therapy moves the client through the challenge (precontemplative-contemplative-preparation) stage of change to a commitment (action) and ownership (maintenance) level of change. These stages of change are discussed in more detail in *Chapter 3.*

THE CORRECTIONAL-THERAPEUTIC PARTNERSHIP

Most judicial clients are different from other AOD abuse clients in that they are usually required to attend treatment. In this sense they are coerced clients. This is the basis of the **eighth core strategy** of *SSC*: that the therapeutic and correctional roles and functions must be integrated for effective treatment of the SA judicial client. As discussed in *Chapter 1,* this means that the SA judicial counselor is part and parcel of the administration of the client's judicial sentence. *SSC* and the *SSC* provder are often part of that sentence.

The provider must be both a therapeutic and a correctional specialist, that is, a correctional practitioner (Milkman & Wanberg, 2007). Thus, it is important to understand the elements of an effective correctional counseling relationship and the correctional partnership. This relationship certainly includes the elements of the counselor-client relationship discussed above. The provider utilizes the skills and traits of warmth, genuineness, respect and empathy in developing and maintaining that relationship.

However, there are some unique elements of the correctional-therapeutic relationship that serve to enhance effectiveness in working with SA judicial clients. We review some of these elements that have been identified in the literature and some emerging out of the clinical experience of the authors and then define the correctional-intervention partnership.

Elements of Effective Correctional Counseling

Andrews and Bonta (2003) identify the following elements as essential for effective correctional counseling (pp. 311-319).

- **Establish high-quality relationship with clients.** Productive interactions between correctional counselors and clients are predicated upon staff enthusiasm and openness to the free expression of attitudes, feelings and experiences. Mutual respect and caring facilitate the meaningful disapproval of procriminal expressions. Within the limits of mutually agreed upon boundaries, counseling is offered in an atmosphere of genuineness, empathy and caring.

- **Model and demonstrate anticriminal expressions.** Judicial clients look for antisocial characteristics and behaviors and features in others in order to justify their own antisocial and criminal thinking and behavior. The effective correctional counselor must be consistent and unerring in demonstrating prosocial and high moral values.

- **Approve (reinforce) the client's anticriminal and prosocial expressions.** This is a vigilant process. Capturing opportunities to reinforce client changes and efforts to change may make significant differences in the overall change process. A continual reinforcement of abstinence from drug use and abuse and sustaining a crime-free life and reinforcing thinking and behaviors that prevent relapse and recidivism are absolutely essential in bringing about change in judicial clients. Acknowledging that it is difficult to stay free of crime and drug use, and that clients face daily temptations to return to these behaviors is part of this reinforcement repertoire.

- **Disapprove (punish) the client's procriminal and antisocial expressions.** Often, this must go beyond disapproval to actually engaging in the sanctioning process by reporting violations of probation and court sentencing conditions. This sanctioning should take place within the therapeutic process. Ultimately, the provider is obligated to be sure that the judicial system is informed of client infractions. It is not enough to disapprove of procriminal expressions such as spending time with old criminal associates. Effective correctional work will provide and demonstrate alternatives to antisocial and procriminal behaviors, e.g., help the client find social groups that are committed to change and recovery and prosocial behavior. Client advoca-

cy should be part of the correctional counselor's ongoing agenda.

Anticriminal Versus Procriminal Expressions

Many judicial clients do not see themselves as criminals or offenders per se. And many do not see themselves as antisocial or having serious characterological problems. One obvious goal of the self-disclosure and self-awareness phases of *SSC* treatment is for judicial clients to get an accurate picture of the degree to which they have engaged in criminal conduct. Many *SSC* exercises are geared towards achieving this objective. This involves understanding the difference between procriminal and anticriminal thinking and behavior.

However, making these distinctions is only half the picture. It is important for clients to understand the difference between criminal thinking and behavior and prosocial thinking and behavior. Clients may come to clearly see themselves as having committed crimes and may come to understand what criminal conduct is. But having a full understanding of and engaging in prosocial behaviors is another step.

Although providers will not see themselves as antisocial or procriminal, it is not difficult at times to give that impression to their clients. This is often very subtle. For example, providers can easily find themselves as having and expressing negative attitudes towards the "system", towards the law, police and the courts. Acceptance on the part of providers of rule violations or disregarding the law will communicate procriminal beliefs and attitudes. For example, knowing that a client is driving with a suspended license, or has done some minor shoplifting, or who has used an illegal drug on one or two occasions and has not therapeutically confronted those behaviors is modeling procriminal attitudes and behaviors. It is easy for providers to side with clients around "unfair" rules of probation, of the prison setting, or of a sentence issued by the courts.

Providers express anticriminal attitudes when emphasizing the painful consequences of the impact of criminal conduct on the community and victims; rejecting rationalizations for criminal conduct; and highlighting the hazards of associating with criminal associates. Correcting errors in thinking that judicial clients often have, such as "everyone uses drugs," "everyone breaks the law," "everyone speeds" will model anticriminal attitudes.

Reinforcing whenever possible prosocial attitudes and behaviors models prosociality. An example would be: reinforcing clients when they engage in alternative ways of acting in situations that are high risk for recidivism (spending time with criminal associates). Attending sessions and completing homework assignments are seen as prosocial expressions.

Therapeutic effects are significantly enhanced when group members begin to reinforce anticriminal and prosocial thinking and behaviors in each other. This is a strong indication that the group as a whole is developing an environment of prosociality.

Reinforcing Positive Thoughts and Behaviors

Rewarding positive thoughts and behavior requires the availability of a wide variety of reinforcers in the repertoire of *SSC* counselors. Minimal visual cues such as eye contact or approving smiles may sometimes be effective while other anticriminal expressions may call forth explicit comments reflecting agreement and support. The continuation of a positive and therapeutic counseling relationship serves as the most powerful reinforcer of prosocial attitudes and conduct.

Andrews and Bonta (1994, 1998, 2003) offer specific suggestions regarding high level reinforcement of offenders by their counselors or providers.

▶ Strong, emphatic and immediate statements of approval, support and agreement with regard to expressions of prosocial attitudes and conduct of clients, e.g., nonverbal expression, eye contact, smiles, shared experiences.

▶ Elaboration of the reason why agreement, approval and reinforcement are being offered, i.e., identifying specific attitudes and behaviors being approved of.

▶ Expressions of support should be sufficiently intense and have affective components.

▶ The provider's statement should at least match the client's statement in emotional intensity (i.e., be empathic) and his or her elaboration of the reason for support may involve some self-disclosure (i.e., openness).

Sanctioning Within the Therapeutic Context

Sanctioning and punishment around administering the judicial client's sentence should occur within a therapeutic context. Andrews and Bonta (1994, 1998, 2003) indicate that effective sanctioning and punishment occur within the context of a caring, genuine and empathic relationship. Providers should not let the fear of client retribution or termination prevent appropriate confrontation of antisocial and procriminal attitudes or conduct.

Expressed disapproval is more effective in an atmosphere of trust and mutual caring. Yet, supportive statements should outnumber disapproving ones, e.g., a ratio of 4-1 (Andrews & Bonta, 2003). The expression of disapproval should stand in contrast to the levels of interest, concern and warmth previously offered. The levels of disapproval should be immediately reduced and approval introduced when the client expresses morally responsible and prosocial attitudes and behavior.

Provider and Client Partnership

A strong alliance does not necessarily guarantee a working partnership, although the alliance is a foundation for an effective partnership. It is helpful to view the provider-client relationship as similar to a business partnership. That relationship is defined by the degree of investment the partners have in achieving the goals of the business. There is a mutual investment of their own sets of skills and talents in helping the business, an external entity, to prosper and thrive. Although profit may be the primary objective, and is the basis for the existence of the business, outcome is also measured by the satisfaction and meaning the partners derive from their involvement in the business entity.

In the case of the judicial treatment partnership, the counselor has a set of skills and knowledge to achieve

FIGURE 2.2 Collaborative Correctional-Intervention Partnership

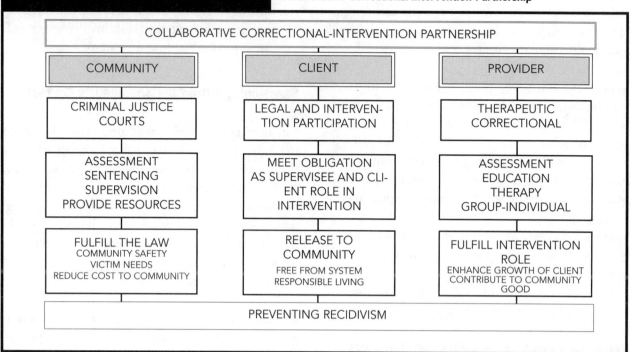

the goals of the therapeutic business. The client also brings to the partnership, skills and the potential to learn new skills as well as first hand knowledge of his/her problems and traits. The primary goal of the judicial treatment business is to achieve the bottom line profit that benefits the client, provider and community: prosocial outcomes and preventing relapse and recidivism.

The partners plan, problem solve, apply techniques and skills, and review work done so as to advance the external business entity and profit. Achieving prosociality and the prevention of relapse and recidivism are the overriding goals of the partnership. However, mutual satisfaction and meaningful involvement in the business is also important, and are predictors of the bottom line business profit - prosociality.

Interactive Partners with the Correctional System

The correctional-treatment system involves a three-way partnership: the community, the client and the provider. The success of the correction-intervention system in preventing relapse and recidivism depends on the development of a collaborative relationship among these three partners. Initially, clients do not

see themselves as being part of this three-way partnership. If intervention is successful, clients - mainly in the **Commitment** and **Ownership** phases of intervention - will begin to see themselves as part of the partnership.

Figure 2.2 describes this collaborative partnership and the parts that each plays in fulfilling the terms of the partnership. The payoff for the community is fulfillment of the law, safety, victim satisfaction and reduced cost to the community.

For clients, the payoff is: fulfilling their obligation to the community; increasing positive thoughts and feelings about self; having a sense of pride in being morally responsible in the community; freedom from further correctional involvement; and a sense of satisfaction in contributing to the good of the community and responsible living.

The payoff to the provider is: fulfilling the therapeutic and correctional role and obligation; enhancing client growth; contributing to the safety and good of the community; generating models for the prevention of recidivism; and fulfilling an important societal role of promoting community responsibility and safety.

PROFILE OF THE EFFECTIVE JUDICIAL PROVIDER

There are three broad dimensions that define the primary characteristics of the effective judicial counselor: 1) the counselor's personal characteristics and traits; 2) professional or technical development; and 3) philosophical perspectives (see Wanberg, 1990). *Figure 2.3* provides an outline of these three dimensions.

We consistently use the term provider to refer to a counselor or therapist delivering treatment services to judicial clients. At the broad level of correctional service delivery, these individuals represent correctional practitioners (Milkman & Wanberg, 2007) who deliver a variety of correctional treatment services to judicial clients. We will continue using provider (counselor or therapist) throughout this *Guide,* keeping in mind that they fulfill the role of correctional practitioners.

The Personal Dimension

The personal dimension is defined by the core counselor traits of warmth, genuineness, empathy and respect. Although some providers are able to express these more easily than others, as discussed above, each of these characteristics is observable, measurable, and thus trainable. Other personal characteristics that impact on effective criminal conduct intervention counseling are the counselor's values, beliefs, personal experiences, social role orientation and unresolved personal conflicts.

Biases and negative attitudes with respect to orientation towards social and cultural roles, representative groups within the society, and orientation towards job productivity can all influence the *SSC* provider's response to the client and the correctional system. As discussed above, biased attitudes can have a profound influence on the provider's therapeutic stance.

Each counselor has a set of unique personal experiences, personal values, attitudes and beliefs which can impact on treatment. Counselors with unresolved personal issues may find these issues getting in the way of being client-oriented and objective.

Effective counselors have full awareness of their own values, beliefs, attitudes, personal experiences and biases and will understand how these personal characteristics can contribute to or hinder effective treatment delivery to judicial clients. Self-disclosure is the primary skill through which these personal values, beliefs and experiences can be effectively utilized in treatment (Wanberg, 1990).

Self-disclosure is the sharing of personal, emotional and experiential feelings and experiences that are unique to the counselor. It can enhance the opening up process and increase treatment communication between the counselor and client or among clients. It can help the client feel more at ease knowing that the counselor has had very real and human feelings and experiences. There is evidence that self-disclosure is working when: 1) clients continue to share at a deeper and more personal level; 2) clients begin to utilize some of the personal approaches that the counselor has used in his or her own problem-solving and conflict resolutions; and 3) clients express greater acceptance of their own inner feelings and problems.

Self-disclosure can present major barriers in treatment (Wanberg, 1990). It can slow down or even stop the opening up and sharing process. If the counselor indicates having been through such and such an experience, the client may internally reflect that "there is no reason to go on; the counselor already knows what I've been through." Self-disclosure may cause the client to lose confidence in the counselor. As a consequence of self-disclosure, the client may move away from self-focus and focus more on the counselor's issues. Finally, self-disclosure may cause the counselor to lose concentration and attention on the content and affect flow of the client.

In summary, self-disclosure becomes effective when, following its use, clients think they are better understood and more deeply supported and then continue to share personal material at a deeper level. It should be used with caution. It is a complex factor in the treatment process. It does not necessarily enhance, and may inhibit, the client seeing the counselor as empathic, trustworthy or competent. It could reinforce antisocial behavior. It should never be used by the counselor for personal-emotional gain, but only when it clearly fits into the plan of enhancing the therapeutic alliance and providing clients with additional tools and information that will prevent relapse and recidivism.

The Professional Dimension

The second dimension that defines the effective judicial counselor and *SSC* provider is the area of professional training and development. This involves the development of the psychoeducation and therapy skills necessary to deliver a manual-guided and group-based intervention program as well as skills of assessment and of client management. These skills form an important component of the conceptual framework of the treatment platform discussed in *Chapter 1*.

In *Chapter 7* and *Section III*, specific skills are outlined that providers need in order to effectively deliver each *SSC* treatment phase. Most of these skills are learned by counselors in professional training, and are used continually in their work with clients.

A standard for the application of the professional dimension is found in the practice of surgery in medicine. During a surgical procedure, a physician's knowledge, skills and ethical behaviors are continually used. At any given moment in the surgical process, the surgeon knows what skills are needed for successful surgery. The surgeon knows the process for each surgical procedure. The skills, tools and instruments are precisely labeled and identified, and the surgeon knows under what conditions the application of the skills and the use of the instruments are needed. You would not only expect, but require that of a surgeon operating on you. Imagine being operated on, and you wake up and hear the surgeon say: "Gee, that's an interesting instrument. Don't know what it is, but I'll try it." Needless to say, you would be in shock.

Let us apply the same standard to counseling and psychosocial treatment and in the delivery of *SSC*. We should have an awareness of the process and goals of *SSC* and the necessary knowledge and skills for effective delivery. We should be able to label our therapy skills and tools, and then we should know when in the intervention and change process we ap-

ply those skills and tools. We should also have a fairly decent idea of the outcome of the application of the process and skills. We would expect no less of our surgeon; our clients should expect no less of us.

In psychosocial treatment, we may not always have definitive knowledge of the process and the skills, as in medicine. Yet we should be grounded in a process that works and in which we have confidence, and which allows us to label and effectively use skills to implement therapeutic and correctional change. A model for the process, skills and strategies for the treatment of judicial clients and the delivery of *SSC* was provided in *Chapter 1, Figure 1.1*. This model provides a guideline for the adaptation and use of psychosocial and correctional treatment.

One important component of the professional dimension is being culturally competent in capitalizing on the strengths of diversity. This is discussed in a separate section below. Another important component of the professional dimension is the ethical and professional standards of judicial counselors. This area is covered in more detail in the *Resource Guide* (Wanberg & Milkman, 2008). Some of the key ethical considerations are: confidentiality; complete avoidance of dual relationships (e.g., business, romantic); giving or receiving favors including money, objects, gratuities; bartering; and abusing the power that providers may have in relationship to the client (see Masters, 2004, pp. 19-24). Providers will hold to the ethical and professional standards defined by their respective profession, e.g., addictions counselor, psychologist, probation office, etc.

Philosophical Perspectives

Finally, the philosophical dimension defines the theoretical orientation and knowledge structure used in the delivery of services to judicial clients. It is important that providers have some theory of human personality, a theoretical view of education and teaching (e.g., learner-centered model), and of counseling and treatment (e.g., cognitive-behavioral, client centered), a theory of drug abuse and alcoholism, and some perspective on the nature, etiology and development of criminal conduct. Teaching and imparting knowledge is the primary skill through which counselors directly bring to bear their knowl-

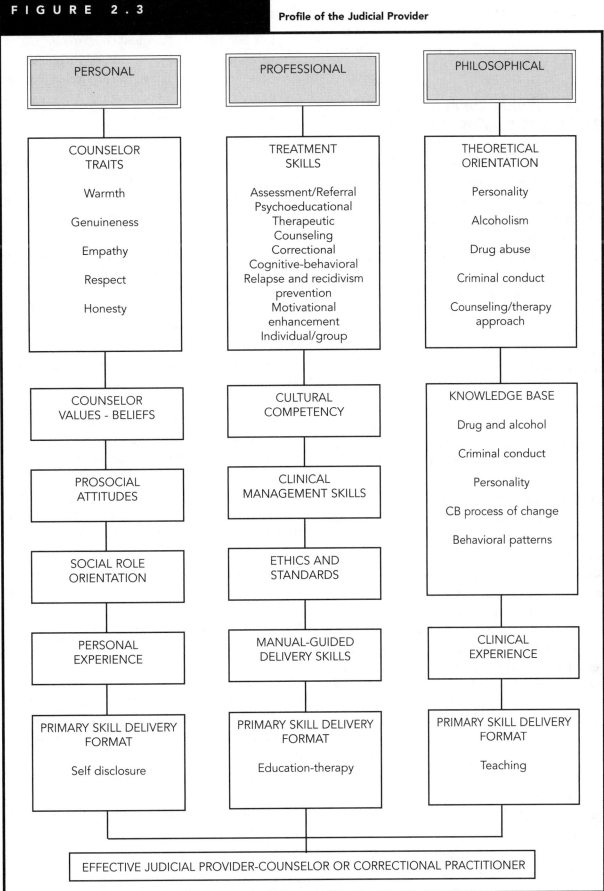

FIGURE 2.3 Profile of the Judicial Provider

PERSONAL

COUNSELOR TRAITS

Warmth

Genuineness

Empathy

Respect

Honesty

COUNSELOR VALUES - BELIEFS

PROSOCIAL ATTITUDES

SOCIAL ROLE ORIENTATION

PERSONAL EXPERIENCE

PRIMARY SKILL DELIVERY FORMAT

Self disclosure

PROFESSIONAL

TREATMENT SKILLS

Assessment/Referral
Psychoeducational
Therapeutic
Counseling
Correctional
Cognitive-behavioral
Relapse and recidivism prevention
Motivational enhancement
Individual/group

CULTURAL COMPETENCY

CLINICAL MANAGEMENT SKILLS

ETHICS AND STANDARDS

MANUAL-GUIDED DELIVERY SKILLS

PRIMARY SKILL DELIVERY FORMAT

Education-therapy

PHILOSOPHICAL

THEORETICAL ORIENTATION

Personality

Alcoholism

Drug abuse

Criminal conduct

Counseling/therapy approach

KNOWLEDGE BASE

Drug and alcohol

Criminal conduct

Personality

CB process of change

Behavioral patterns

CLINICAL EXPERIENCE

PRIMARY SKILL DELIVERY FORMAT

Teaching

EFFECTIVE JUDICIAL PROVIDER-COUNSELOR OR CORRECTIONAL PRACTITIONER edge and theoretical orientation on the therapeutic process. *Section I* of this *Guide* provides grounding in a theoretical and philosophical perspective in the treatment of SA judicial clients and in the delivery of *SSC*.

PROVIDER CULTURAL COMPETENCE: CAPITALIZING ON THE STRENGTHS OF DIVERSITY

Counselor cultural competency falls within the professional dimension of the judicial counselor profile. The *Resource Guide* (Wanberg & Milkman, 2008) devotes a chapter to cultural competence, cultural issues and sensitivity, and specific needs and concerns defined by cultural diversity. Here, we point to some of the more important considerations regarding the ability of counselors to be competent in capitalizing on the strengths of diversity among judicial clients.

First, treatment should be culturally responsive and sensitive and address the cultural values, competencies and strengths of judicial clients. It utilizes these strengths and competencies to promote growth and change. The goal is for providers to have the skills and competence to recognize and capitalize on the strengths of diversity in the judicial population.

Judicial clients are very diverse as to ethnic and demographic differences, age, gender, and different populations with specific needs. There is strength in age, in gender, in ethnic heritage, and even in being classified in a judicial group with specific needs. For example, recognizing that a judicial client has a co-occurring disorder will move the judicial system to provide specialized services that can enhance change and prevent recidivism. There is strength in recognizing that a client has an AOD problem since in doing so, such clients will receive treatments that are known to increase the probability of positive outcomes for those clients.

Second, it is important that providers establish a clear awareness of their own orientation towards other cultures, level of cultural competence and specific biases and prejudices. This can range from the position of being:

▶ exclusionary, negativistic and prejudicial attitudes;

▶ to the middle ground of being sensitive to the cultural issues that need to be addressed;

▶ to a higher level of cultural competency that involves openness to cross-cultural interactions, a commitment to valuing diversity, seeing strength in diversity and even celebrating diversity (Cross et al., 1989; Guajardo-Lucero, 2000).

Third, providers should be able to effectively evaluate the system within which they work with respect to its cultural competency. Does the system value diversity, acknowledge the dynamics of interacting cultures, and build in methods and programs that recognize, capitalize on and enhance the positive expression of diversity (Cross et al., 1989)?

Fourth, a set of effective communication skills should be used relative to cultural diversity. This involves recognizing the verbal and language skill level of the group. When using important terms that the group has not integrated into its vocabulary, time should be taken to explain the meaning and purpose of those terms. For example, many, if not most, judicial clients will not understand the term self-efficacy or self-mastery. Since this is an important concept in CB treatment, time needs to be taken to be sure the group understands its meaning. Making a deliberate effort to understand accent and dialect and valuing the individual's primary language are important.

Staying with normative language and not engaging in jargon is important. The goal is to integrate the client into normative language and normative culture with respect to prosocial attitudes and behaviors. Thus, "dig the jive, but don't talk it."

Be sensitive to communication styles that might be offensive. For example, direct eye contact for some people in some cultures is offensive. It is important not to use profanity. It may not bother most, but the few it does is not worth the risk of alienation. After all, an important goal of treatment is to rise above conditions and conditioning (e.g., to extinguish conditioned responses such as profanity, drug taking, and violence) that are part of many offenders' lifestyles.

Finally, providers need to have the skills to work

with the cultural biases and prejudices that surface among judicial clients. Providers will find strong biases and even intense feelings of enmity among judicial groups, and many of these are ethnic and racially focused. The manifestation and even eruption of these intense prejudices can be damaging to group cohesion and provide major barriers to the treatment process.

Here are some guidelines in mitigating and managing these issues when arising in group:

▶ Foster positive interactions among group members and when these biases surface, remind the group that the principal guideline for all therapeutic activity is respect for self and others.

▶ Facilitate therapeutic processing around prejudice and negative stereotyping using the basic therapy skills of encouragers to share and offer reflective feedback.

▶ Give members an opportunity to share their thoughts and feelings within the framework and boundaries of civil discourse.

▶ Keep confrontation at the therapeutic reflective-acceptance level when possible while at the same time not reinforcing strong biases, prejudices and enmity.

▶ Allow only civil language and set clear limits on and prohibit prejudicial expressions and behaviors, use of racial slurs, demeaning and disparaging language.

▶ Set limits on the time spent on such issues. Do not try to resolve the biases and prejudicial attitudes of group members, and acknowledge that these attitudes and differences will exist, and that individuals have the right to hold these views, but not the right to act them out in harmful ways.

▶ Keep the group on task - on the goals and objectives of *SSC* in general and the specific objectives spelled out in each session.

▶ It may be necessary to ask group members who want to keep the group focused on these issues and whose attitudes and behaviors are disruptive to the group treatment process to leave the group.

▶ The goal is always to work towards and foster a cohesive and prosocial group environment.

CHAPTER REVIEW

This chapter focused on the therapeutic relationship and the specific characteristics of the effective SA judicial counselor, and more specifically, delivery of the *SSC* curriculum. One of the most robust findings in the treatment literature is the impact of the client-counselor relationship in producing positive treatment outcomes. The therapeutic relationship is a common factor that cuts across different treatment approaches and contributes to treatment efficacy. The provider-client relationship is determined by the specific counselor characteristics of warmth, genuineness, respect, and most important, empathy. It is also determined by the characteristics and motivation of the client.

The therapeutic relationship is forged through the counselor's therapeutic stance, developing a therapeutic alliance with the client, and using skills to enhance client motivation for a positive response to treatment. Empathy, a learned skill, is the key player in the process of developing the therapeutic relationship. It is also a key player in the development and fostering of prosocial attitudes and behaviors.

Motivational enhancement and the therapeutic alliance interact in such a manner that motivational enhancement helps to build the therapeutic alliance and, in turn, the therapeutic alliance provides the basis upon which client motivation is fostered and nourished. Resistance and ambivalence are the resting points from which change emanates, and need to be resolved for change to take place. The therapeutic alliance and the skills of reflective acceptance are the vehicles to move clients past that resting point.

Other provider characteristics and skills that contribute to the effective treatment of judicial clients are forming a therapeutic alliance with the group, knowing how to integrate psychoeducation with the therapeutic process, and practicing the principles that facilitate effective correctional counseling. Modeling anticriminal and prosocial attitudes and behaviors are ongoing responsibilities of the judicial provider.

CHAPTER 3: Treatment Phases: Facilitating Learning, Growth and Change

CHAPTER OUTLINE

OVERVIEW

TRADITIONAL THEORIES OF LEARNING

A DYNAMIC MODEL FOR LEARNING AND GROWTH

Lewin's Model of Growth and the Orthogenetic
  Principle
Application to the Therapy Process

THE STAGES OF CHANGE AND THE *SSC* TREATMENT
STRUCTURE

Transtheoretical Model
Integrating Learning, Growth and Change into the
  SSC Treatment Structure

> *Phase I: Challenge to Change - The Global,*
>   *Undifferentiated Response*
> *Phase II: Commitment to Change - The*
>   *Differentiation Response*
> *Phase III: Ownership of Change - The*
>   *Integration Response*

FUNDAMENTAL ISSUES REGARDING LEARNING AND
CHANGE

The Orthogenetic Learning and Growth Model
Stages of Change

> *Change is multidimensional*
> *Change is differential*
> *Change is not always congruent with a treatment*
>   *phase*
> *Stages of change are cyclical*

CHAPTER REVIEW

CHAPTER OBJECTIVES

▶ Describe a dynamic model for learning and growth and apply the model to the process of therapy and treatment.

▶ Describe the transtheoretical model of the stages of change.

▶ Present the structure and phases of treatment of *SSC* and show how these phases of treatment are structured around the models of learning, growth and change.

▶ Describe some fundamental issues around the process and dynamics of change.

OVERVIEW

The purpose of *Chapter 3* is to define a conceptual framework for the process of learning, growth, self-improvement and change in treatment. This is the **fourth core strategy** and one of the foundational models of *SSC*.

The chapter starts with providing an understanding of how psychosocial learning and growth take place. It then shows how this theory of learning is integrated into a stage of change framework. We then show how these two models - psychosocial learning and growth and stages of change - provide the treatment structure for *SSC*. Finally, some fundamental issues regarding the dynamics of learning, growth and change are discussed.

The reader is reminded of the distinction we make between self-improvement and change and is asked to review this discussion on page 8 in the Introduction to this *Guide*. Throughout this chapter, and the entire text of this *Guide*, we use the word change to include self-improvement for the convenience of not having to repeatedly use both terms.

TRADITIONAL THEORIES OF LEARNING

Learning and behavioral reinforcement are commonly explained through two stimulus-response (S-R) theories and the concept of observational learning. These three approaches are briefly discussed.

Classical conditioning (e.g., Pavlov's dogs) occurs when a response (salivation-unconditioned) that an organism automatically makes to a stimulus (food-unconditioned) is transferred to another stimulus (bell-conditioned) that is new and neutral, resulting in an association occurring between the two stimuli. After a number of matching trials, the response (salivation) now occurs when the new or conditioned stimulus is presented without the presentation of the food.

Classical conditioning is often used to explain various kinds of maladaptive behaviors such as phobias, posttraumatic stress responses, panic responses, and withdrawal symptoms that occur in response to neural stimuli that have become associated with powerful effects of drugs (syringe or other paraphernalia, drug-taking associates, other stimuli in the environment). An acute anxiety attack (panic) may be triggered by a set of circumstances that may seem neutral, but is associated with prior trauma-causing stimuli, such as observing a traumatic event that was the origin of the panic response.

Operant conditioning is also used to explain how behaviors are reinforced. In this theory, the response occurs prior to the stimulus. The stimulus may be pain, a positive experience, or the turning off of a negative experience. When a behavior results in a reward or positive outcome, or results in eliminating a negative circumstance, that behavior gets reinforced (strengthened).

In *Session 5,* we utilize the operant conditioning model when explaining how certain behaviors, such as alcohol use or criminal conduct, get strengthened and reinforced. Taking a drug brings on a positive experience or turns off negative events or stimuli which strengthens the use of the drug.

Modeling and observational learning, an important component of social learning theory, is another way to explain how behavior is learned and reinforced. Bandura (1969) described how people learn behavior by imitating those whom they encounter. Behaviors such as drug abuse, domestic violence, emotional loss of control, and criminal conduct are all subject to Bandura's principles of observational learning. When we observe models, we not only learn how to behave, but we also develop expectations of reward or punishment depending on the behavioral consequences that we have observed (Bandura, 1989). Through modeling, behaviors get strengthened and reinforced - and learning occurs.

Although the S-R theories have value in providing understanding of how learning takes place, they do not integrate the social and internal motivating factors related to learning, nor do they give a dynamic view of learning and growth, particularly as it takes place in psychotherapy and treatment. Modeling and observational learning as described by social learning theory does provide us with a more complete explanation of the complexities of human behavior and learning.

A DYNAMIC MODEL FOR LEARNING AND GROWTH

As explained in *Chapter 1*, a significant goal of treatment is to enhance the learning, growth and change of clients. Although all of the above theories provide us with an understanding of how learning takes place and how behavior is reinforced, they do not provide us with an understanding of the process and dynamics of learning and growth. What is needed is a more comprehensive and dynamic view of these processes, certainly, one that fits into the context of social learning theory, and one that we could use to structure the treatment process and provide a framework for change.

Lewin's Model of Growth and the Orthogenetic Principle

Kurt Lewin's steps of learning and growth (Ham, 1957; Lewin, 1935, 1936, 1951) and Werner's *Orthogenetic Principle* (1957) provide a more dynamic and comprehensive explanation of the process and structure of how learning and growth occur. These learning and growth models also provide an explanation of the phases that people go through when making psychosocial changes.

Kurt Lewin conceptualized the process of learning and growth as involving three response phases: 1) undifferentiated or global; 2) differentiation; and 3) integration. The **first** phase involves a **global or undifferentiated response** to a set of stimuli or a situation. This response can be observed in all living organisms. It occurs in a rapid, undifferentiated multiplication of cells in the first stages of a new organism; it can be observed in an infant child whose whole body responds to a stimulus.

The global response is experienced when encountering a new and unfamiliar environment. For example, when getting off an airplane and entering a particular terminal for the first time, there is a global and even somewhat confused response until one finds the signs pointing to the main terminal or baggage claim. Or clients who attend their first treatment group will experience a global, undifferentiated response. All faces are unfamiliar; clients are unsure what to expect. And, if there is some degree of distrust and doubt about attending treatment, the confusion and global experience are intensified.

The **second** response phase of growth occurs when the individual units of the organism begin to **differentiate** among each other. This is the "sorting out" phase of learning and growth. Different sizes and shapes of cells begin to emerge; now the infant can reach out with his arms without the rest of the body moving. This sorting out or differentiation starts when the signs point to the main terminal and the baggage claim area is located. Confusion, at least for a short period of time, is alleviated.

Clients find common ground as they share personal experiences. They introduce themselves and faces now have names. There is no indication that they will be accused of wrong-doing, anxiety lowers, and there occurs a settling-in process. Lewin describes this as the differentiated phase of learning and growth.

The **third** response phase of growth occurs when the various cells in the new organism begin to show purpose and **functional integration.** Now the elongated cells of the plant carry water and minerals to the flat leaf cells responsible for photosynthesis. The embryonic cells now form a cardiovascular system and serve to bring blood to all parts of the fetus. The infant's reach now is for food, which she successfully places in her mouth.

The main terminal is found and the baggage claim area located. The client is introduced to the group, the group leader introduces him/herself, and a workbook and schedule are provided. There has occurred a level of learning and growth.

Werner, in his *Orthogenetic Principle,* conceptualizes growth and development taking place in a very similar manner. "Wherever development occurs it proceeds from a state of relative globality and lack of differentiation to a state of increased differentiation, articulation, and hierarchic integration" (Werner, 1957, p. 126).

The constructivists use the *Orthogenetic Principle* to illustrate how the cognitive system develops and sustains itself (Delia, O'Keefe & O'Keefe, 1982). The differentiation phase provides the basis for the development of mental constructs, the most basic units of cognitive organization. The most general units of cognitive organization are called "interpretive schemes" (Delia et al., 1982), similar to Kelly's (1955) causal schemes constructs and Heider's balance schemes (1958). The "interpretive scheme" is simply a concept or classification method that people use to make sense of the world. The new client has constructed an interpretive scheme to make sense of the first group session. The sorting out and differentiation of locations in the airport terminal helps to find the baggage claim area.

The "interpretive scheme" becomes one of the main units of focus in cognitive therapy (J. Beck, 1995). The focus is also on the emotional and behavior units that interact with the mental or cognitive units or interpretive schemes used to make sense of the world (Delia et al, 1982). These cognitive constructs are continually developing and become the basis through which individuals make their adjustment to the world. Their development is in accord with the process of learning, growth and change described above by Lewin and Werner.

Thus, we can use the Lewin model and the *Orthogenetic Principle* in understanding how individuals develop and change the specific units of cognitive responding and behavior. Or, we can use this principle in understanding how people respond in general to learning, education and treatment processes. From hereon we will refer to this model of learning and growth as the *Orthogenetic Principle*.

Application to the Therapy Process

Utilizing the concept of the process of learning, growth and development provided by the *Orthogenetic Principle,* Wanberg (1983, 1990) and Wanberg and Milkman (1998) developed a dynamic cyclical or spiral model to explain the process of therapeutic learning and growth and a counseling skill structure to facilitate this growth and change. This is illustrated in *Figure 3.1.*

This model explains how growth and change occur over the course of treatment; or how they occur within one treatment session. It is not a linear model that occurs in a stepwise fashion. Rather, it describes growth and change as spiral in nature, and the model is applied to each individual growth experience. It is dynamic in that each stage of learning provides the energy to move the organism to the next level of growth. For example, when the organism achieves an integrative stage of learning, it provides the energy to move on to a new level of learning that begins with a new global or undifferentiated response to external or internal stimuli.

Just as the infant child integrates the grasp into a movement that successfully puts food into the mouth, there is a global response to that experience such as wanting more food; or to be more efficient about putting food in her mouth. The fingers are used to grasp a cracker or a spoon is differentiated from the hand, and used to get food in the mouth.

When seeing the baggage claim area, again there is the global response to multiple baggage carousels. A monitor is found or the sign indicating which flights are served by each carousel. The client now begins to engage in a session exercise and there is a global and even confused response as to the meaning of the exercise. Yet, each prior integration experience services and energizes the movement into the next global experience.

Within the framework of correctional treatment, we see this process taking place for clients. **First,** there is the global, undifferentiated phases of unpacking. Judicial clients respond in a global or undifferentiated way to all of the events they encounter in the judicial system, e.g., arrest, jail, conviction. The response might be undifferentiated anger, shame, guilt, withdrawal, or thoughts of blaming others or helplessness. When starting treatment, clients may have a global response of being confused, overwhelmed, resistant or defensive.

Second, to each of these events or experiences, there is the sorting out phase. Following the arrest event, the client goes beyond the global response, understands the charges, gets detoxed, calls a lawyer, makes decisions about contacting a family member or friend, and begins to sort out various responses that can be made. As clients experience treatment, they hear specific information about AOD use, about CC, receive feedback about their own story, and begin to label and identify thoughts, feelings and behaviors.

Third, there is the acting on the story and integrating the events. With respect to the arrest event, the client hires an attorney, the responses of family members are accepted and life is pulled back together with certain decision responses. The client enters treatment, a new event that again takes him/her through the three phases. Now, as a consequence of getting feedback, understanding and learning cognitive and relationship coping skills, these skills are applied, recidivism and further CC are prevented, certain levels of freedom are restored, and irresponsible thinking and errors in logic are corrected or replaced so as to lead to more positive outcomes.

Thus, the phasic-spiral of the learning and change process occurs with both micro and macro life events. These phases of unpacking (clients receive information or tell their story), sorting out (clients hear their story) and integrating (clients act on their story) may: 1) occur when encountering a new skill or concept in therapy; 2) occur several times in the course of one session; 3) occur over several sessions around one theme, skill, concept, problem or topic; or 4) be descriptive of the clients' total treatment experience, e.g., over the entire *SSC* treatment program.

FIGURE 3.1   The Cyclical Process and Change in Treatment

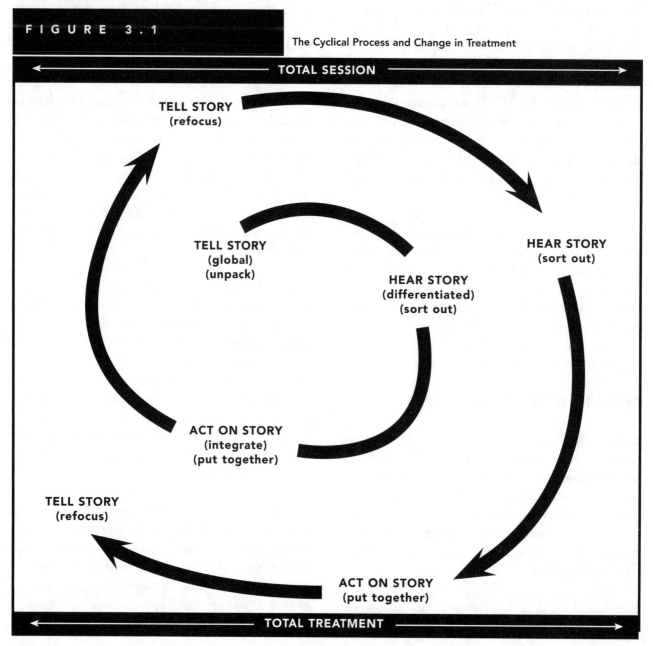

The spiral concept illustrates that clients never return to the same place, but each cycle is dynamic in that it moves them further away from the baseline conditions that brought them into treatment. Thus, clients may relapse, but if therapeutic intervention and change is effective, the relapse does not take the client back to the pre-treatment level of morbidity. Likewise, clients may find themselves being confronted with high-risk exposures that led to recidivism in the past, however, by applying the concepts and skills learned in treatment, full recidivism (returning to CC) is prevented.

THE STAGES OF CHANGE AND THE *SSC* TREATMENT STRUCTURE

Research has indicated that people go through various stages when making change. Prochaska and associates (Connors, Donovan & DiClemente, 2001; Prochaska & DiClemente, 1992; Prochaska, DiClemente & Norcross, 1992) identify six stages of change in their transtheoretical model of how people change addictive lifestyles. We first look at these six stages, and then present a three-stage model that integrates the transtheoretical model.

Transtheoretical Model

In accordance with the transtheoretical approach an array of theoretical models, e.g., motivational enhancement, cognitive-behavioral, psychopharmacologic, are involved in bringing about change. The deployment of specific therapeutic interventions is matched with the client's level of openness to disclose and change, specific patterns of resiliency and risk, and commitment to modify and change specific life problems. This deployment and use of different interventions are integrated into the client's stage of change.

At the **precontemplative stage,** clients are resistive, do not process information about their problems, give little or no thought or energy to self-evaluation or serious change in their behavior, and resist other people's suggestion of change. The problem behavior is often evident to others, but not to the individual with the problem. Resistance to acknowledging or even registering clarity about the problem is increased when others point out the problem to the

person who is perceived to have it. There is defensiveness around developing cognitive awareness of the impact of their behaviors on others. Or cognitive distortions can occur around events that happen to them. Many judicial clients see being arrested as the problem, and not the behavior that led to the arrest.

Clients in the **contemplative stage** give some thought to change, may even have made attempts to change in the past, but are ambivalent about change, and take little action to change since they are not sure if the problem is serious enough to warrant action. Even though they may be more open and responsive to consciousness-raising and educational procedures, and may even seek to assess and try to understand their problems, they still hold on to old patterns that lead to those problems. The ambivalence is increased when they compare the difficulties they have from their problems with the effort and difficulty of making change. There is some increase in self-reflection and self-evaluation and even an increase in awareness of the problem and how it affects others. Some discomfort may arise from this awareness. There is still defensiveness around being confronted by others about the problem. If the ambivalence about change is resolved, this stage becomes a turning point for clients.

As clients move into the **determination or preparation stage** they continue to increase the use of cognitive, affective and valuative processes of change. They begin to take steps towards using specific techniques to reduce or even discontinue their use of substances, to manage their life-problems with methods other than using substances, and avoid engaging in CC. Although there is a lack of commitment to any goals or course of action around change, there may be some efforts to change, although it may involve looking for an "easy cure." As this stage evolves, there is evidence of a movement towards and even engaging in the change process, there is preparation to make a commitment to change, and even making a decision to change. Yet, some ambivalence still tends to operate to prevent taking firm action.

In the **action stage,** a sense of self-direction and self-liberation begins to develop. There is greater internalization of self-determination and self-regulation and more openness to using reinforcement tools and techniques to change behavior. There is an increased reliance on support and understanding from significant others and helping relationships. Clients not only verbalize a commitment to specific goals and a course of action, they take action by using skills and strategies to change thoughts and behaviors for better outcomes. The judicial client takes specific actions such as discontinuing associating with criminal associates, changing thinking that can lead to recidivism, or committing to not using drugs. There is an observed commitment to treatment and using the tools and skills learned in treatment. The development of alternative responses to substance use and to CC is an important part of this stage.

The **maintenance stage** involves the prevention of relapse and recidivism through the development and reinforcement of alternative responses. Strategies and skills that have been learned are put in action to reinforce established changes and stimulus control (e.g., urge to drink when with friends, spend time with criminal associates). More advanced and extensive life-management skills are learned in this stage. There is a commitment to therapy and receiving support from significant others and a continued practice of established skills to manage high-risk exposures for relapse and recidivism. Clients report less frequent lures into substance use or criminal conduct, although those that do occur may be more intense. Self takes on a greater value. Change supporters are an important part of this process, and there is an increase in self-mastery of high-risk exposures (high-risk thinking, feelings, and situations).

Prochaska and DiClemente (1992) have postulated **relapse** as a sixth stage where the individual engages in behaviors and thinking that indicate a process of relapse or relapses into the full pattern of use; or engaging in thinking and behaviors that portend involvement in CC. The potential for relapse and recidivism is increased when clients "let down their guard" and lose sight of the power of high-risk exposures that can lead to R&R. In the stage of change model, relapse is recognized as normal in the recovery process, i.e., "each slip brings you closer to recovery." Rather than inviting clients to relapse, the aforementioned phrase may simply prevent patients and staff from demoralization when unsteadiness or backsliding occurs.

The relapse stage in the transtheoretical model is not applicable to what we call full recidivism (to be discussed in *Chapter 5*). With respect to CC, full recidivism is not recognized as a "normal" process of change. However, engaging in high-risk thinking and situations that can lead to CC are part of this process and can be addressed within the transtheoretical model of the relapse stage of change.

Integrating Learning, Growth and Change Into the *SSC* Treatment Structure

Our clinical experience suggested that a simpler model was needed to help judicial clients with co-occurring substance abuse understand the stages of change and more easily apply these stages to their personal experiences. Thus, based on the transtheoretical model, we reduce the stages to three (Milkman & Wanberg, 2005; Wanberg & Milkman, 1998; Wanberg, Milkman & Timken, 2005): **Challenge to Change, Commitment to Change,** and **Ownership of Change.**

This three-stage approach integrates many of the concepts of the transtheoretical model. They provide **the framework or structure for the three phases of the *SSC* treatment program.** The purpose of treatment is to facilitate clients through these stages of change and through the three treatment phases of *SSC*.

Before looking at the three phases of *SSC* treatment, it is important to understand how we apply the Lewin model and the *Orthogenetic Principle* of learning and growth to the *SSC* phases of treatment. As discussed above, this model of growth is cyclical. And this cyclical process occurs at both the micro and macro levels of learning and change.

At the micro level, when clients encounter a new concept or skill in *SSC*, they go through the global, differentiation, and integration processes. For example, when the *SSC CB Map* is introduced in *Session 1 (see Chapter 4)*, clients experience a global and undifferentiated response. It looks confusing; it may even look incomprehensible to many clients. However, as they learn to apply the *SSC CB Map* to a specific situation, they begin to sort out each of the components of the *Map*. In applying it to a specific situation in their lives, they differentiate and sort out: 1) specific thought responses to that situation; 2) they identify some of the emotional outcomes; and 3) they connect these thoughts and emotions to specific actions. Then, through repetitive exposure to the *CB Map Exercise* in each session, they begin to use (integrate) the *CB Map* to restructure thoughts and core beliefs so as to have more positive emotional and behavioral outcomes. The skill of using the CB model for change becomes integrated (functional) in their everyday lives and results in more self-control over outcomes.

At the broader and more macro level, we also apply this model of learning and growth to the *SSC* phases of treatment. *Phase I* represents an overall global response to change, with resistance, confusion, and doubt that they can make changes. It also represents the beginning of the sorting out or differentiation phase where clients identify major problem areas and begin to see solutions through the concepts and skills learned in *SSC*.

Phase II continues that differentiation phase, but also begins the phase of the integration - taking action to effect change - of the *SSC* concepts and skills in their lives. *Phase III* represents a fuller integration of the skills and concepts with the client taking ownership of these changes, and change is strengthened through multiple resources of reinforcement.

Although the Lewin and Orthogenetic models suggest that there is a natural process of learning involving the global, differentiation, and integration phases of development and growth, both dynamic internal and external influences are important in facilitating individuals through these phases of learning and development. For example, the integration of the infant child's self-feeding is facilitated by the parent (external influence) putting a spoon in the child's hand, guiding the hand towards the mouth, and provides social reinforcements of verbal praise. Treatment represents a complex of these external influences including providing specific skills and tools, giving social reinforcement when clients experience success in the use of these skills, and modeling skill-use and prosocial attitudes and behaviors.

Phase I: Challenge to Change - The Global, Undifferentiated Response

Built into the global and undifferentiated phase of learning and growth is the potential for a **Challenge to Change.** It is a challenge for the infant to begin to move from gross motor movements to refined and more differentiated responses. It is a challenge for judicial clients to move beyond the global response of blame and anger when arrested to a more rational and functional response to their dilemma.

The **Challenge to Change,** *Phase I* of *SSC,* represents the transtheoretical pre-contemplative, contemplative and movement towards the preparation stages of change. It also represents the macro level of global learning and growth. Providers use specific skills that facilitate self-disclosure or "unpacking" - to get clients to tell their story and then facilitate the clients' awareness of their story - what is going on with them.

Judicial clients differ with respect to the degree of global, undifferentiated states they are in when entering treatment. Thus, information given to clients and facilitation of their self-disclosure should be at their level of cognitive organization. It should adhere to the principle of responsivity (Andrews & Bonta, 2003).

In this stage of change, and this broad phase of learning, some clients are defensive and resist self-disclosing and sharing. Individuals in a highly defensive state or who are experiencing considerable anxiety or stress are often unable to get thoughts and feelings into organized mental and verbal components. Although this is often interpreted as resistance to change or ambivalence about changing, it is best viewed as a phase in the learning and growth process and an essential step that people go through when learning and making changes. Other clients may do just the opposite and openly share and there may even be a spurting forth of material that, at the most severe level of dysfunction, may be disconnected and uncontrolled.

Phase I challenges clients to listen to information about AOD use and CC that is relevant to their situation, and then challenges them to disclose their own history in these areas. It integrates psychoeducation and therapy and, as discussed above, provides clients with basic information around how change occurs, skills that can be used to effect change, AOD use and abuse, and CC, and then helps clients relate these concepts to their own situation. This sets the stage for self-disclosure that in turn sets the stage for greater self-awareness of the need to change. An important part of self-awareness is acceptance - accepting that one has a problem and accepting that change is needed.

In *Phase I*, clients begin to become involved in a supportive and **self-discovery feedback** loop process. Although direct therapeutic feedback is essentially reserved for *Phase II, Phase I* involves a process of self-discovery feedback that results from the completion of session worksheets and exercises and feedback from group members. Provider feedback is restricted to a **reflective-acceptance** level. This is more of an informal, yet systematic, feedback approach that helps clients "sort out," identify, and label thoughts and core attitudes, beliefs, and overt behaviors in the areas of CC and AOD abuse. This process prepares clients to make a commitment to take action to change, the goal of *SSC Phase II.*

The skill structure for facilitating clients through the **Challenge to Change** stage and through *Phase I* includes responding attentiveness (both verbal and nonverbal), encouragers to share (open statements and open questions), and reflective acceptance. The latter skill uses a variety of reflection and acceptance statements that openly accept client sharing without judgment and without confrontation. Resistance is not confronted, but is accepted as part of the challenge stage of change.

Facilitation methods and techniques used in *Phase I* and subsequent phases of *SSC* treatment include interactive teaching, interactive worksheets and journaling, modeling, role playing, multimedia methods, skills rehearsal and group processing. Utilization of these skills helps clients to self-disclose and share concerns and problems, lower defenses, and experience a release of cognitive and affective material. This provides the basis for the next phase of growth, differentiation of feelings, thoughts and behaviors. It is a necessary step in cognitive-behavioral change.

Although provider confrontation in *Phase I* is at the reflective-acceptance level, when the behaviors of clients become disruptive to the group, or are perceived to be of potential harm towards others and the community, direct correctional confrontation, which may include sanctioning, must be used. When possible, the provider will engage the group in helping to resolve these kind of problems. However, ultimate responsibility lies with the provider. If providers carefully spell out the ground rules of the group, discussed in *Chapter 7*, this type of confrontation is seldom needed.

The **Challenge** phase begins with the screening and assessment process, which challenges clients to self-disclose through formal, psychometric methods and through structured interviews. Self assessment occurs in each session as clients explore and share their past AOD abuse and CC history and their current thoughts, beliefs, attitudes and emotions in areas other than AOD use and criminal conduct.

In this treatment phase, comprehensive assessment is completed. This assessment facilitates a structured self-disclosure and sets the stage for enhancing the clients' awareness of their life-situation problems, their AOD use patterns, and of their cognitive schemes and behavioral patterns associated with CC and AOD use.

Structured self-disclosure is further facilitated through the completion of the *Master Profile (MP)*, which directly challenges clients to look at their life-adjustment problems. The *Master Assessment Plan (MAP)* is completed, which challenges clients to look at the areas of change they need to address in order to prevent relapse and recidivism.

The first step, then, in the **Challenge to Change** stage is self-disclosure which leads clients to being self-aware and accepting of the seriousness of their AOD problems and CC. Self-disclosure is enhanced through the use of the therapeutic relationship, motivational enhancement, client-centered counseling skills, and a structured self-assessment through the completion of psychometric instruments and completing the MP and MAP. The overall goal and objectives of *Phase I* are provided in *Table 3.1.*

GOAL OF PHASE I: CHALLENGE TO CHANGE

Through a positive therapeutic environment, facilitate the development of client trust in and rapport with the purpose of *SSC*, the *SSC* provider and *SSC* group so as to motivate clients to begin engaging in the learning and change process.

OBJECTIVES OF PHASE I

▶ Develop a clear understanding of the meaning, purpose, guidelines and rules of *SSC*.

▶ Learn the stages of change, and clients evaluate themselves as to the stages that they are in.

▶ Facilitate self-disclosure and "unpacking" and have clients share critical information about self including their CC and AOD history.

▶ Clients learn the rules and a cognitive-behavioral model (*SSC CB Map*) for change and apply this model to making changes in their lives.

▶ Develop a core knowledge base in the area of AOD use and abuse and have clients evaluate their level of AOD problems, abuse and dependence.

▶ Understand criminal and antisocial thinking and behavior, and have clients evaluate themselves on the extent to which they fit the antisocial pattern.

▶ Learn and practice the basic communication skills of active listening and active sharing.

▶ Understand the pathways to R&R and the pathways to R&R prevention and have clients define their R&R prevention goals.

▶ Clients develop a plan for change by completing the *Master Profile (MP)* and *Master Assessment Plan (MAP)*.

▶ Through feedback from session exercises, worksheets, and group members, clients begin to identify and become aware and accepting of their thoughts, core beliefs, overt behaviors, and problems related to AOD abuse and criminal conduct.

▶ Clients evaluate their level of knowledge and skills learned in each session and their progress and change during *Phase I*.

▶ Motivate and prepare clients to make a commitment to change.

Phase II: Commitment to Change - The Differentiation Response

The second stage of change in the Wanberg and Milkman model (1998) is commitment. *Phase II* of *SSC* is designed to facilitate the **commitment** process. This phase essentially represents the transtheoretical action stage of change, however, some clients may still be in the preparation phase, at least in the early part of *Phase II*.

If *Phase I* was successful in helping clients understand the key concepts around substance abuse and CC, and was successful in getting clients to "unpack" their own problems in these areas, and sort out and differentiate these problem areas, clients can begin to respond to *Phase II* or commitment. They continue to have global, differentiated, and integrated responses around each new concept and skill that is learned and presented in *Phase II*. However, the goal of *Phase II* is to get clients to **commit to taking action to change.**

Although the feedback process was started in *Phase I* through the self-discovery process, a formal and provider-directed feedback loop is systematically used in this phase. This is the key process through which the clients hear their story and their dilemmas. Through the feedback loop, clients "hear and see" more clearly - become more aware of - old problems and discover new problems, dysfunctions and pathological responses to the world. Clients continue to receive self-discovery feedback from session exercises, worksheets, interactive journaling and the group.

However, feedback now is now more formal and is provider-directed. The provider also facilitates the group in giving feedback to its members. The defensive system begins to open up and allows increased self-awareness and self-understanding, critical to the growth and change process.

As mentioned, with each new skill or new concept introduced, the client goes through the phases of learning and growth. Yet, at the macro level of growth, *Phase II* represents the differentiation phase where clients sort out and differentiate the specific areas that need change, and differentiate and learn specific skills and concepts to implement that change. Clients also begin taking action to integrate these skills and concepts so as to manage high-risk exposures for relapse and recidivism and to enhance self-control and prosocial and responsible behavior towards others and the community.

The awareness and acceptance of needed growth and change continues during this phase, as throughout all of *SSC*. But *Phase II* involves more than awareness and acceptance of problems. It involves a commitment to taking action to manage and correct those problems. Although this commitment often begins in *Phase I,* it is the main focus of *Phase II.* In this phase, both therapeutic and correctional confrontation approaches, discussed below, are used.

The *MP* and the *MAP* completed in *Phase I* provide guidelines for change in *Phase II.* The client engages in specific coping and responsibility skills training experiences (e.g., intrapersonal, interpersonal and community responsibility skill development) to bring about shifts in cognitive schemes and actual behaviors associated with CC and AOD abuse.

Phase II is devoted to testing out and practicing cognitive and behavioral changes. The principles and methods of preventing relapse and recidivism are continually practiced throughout this phase.

The provider skill structure for *Phase II* includes the categories of feedback skills (reflection, paraphrasing, summarization, change clarification) and confrontation skills (therapeutic and correctional). Through change clarification and confrontation, clients begin to hear their own story, sort out the feelings, thoughts and behaviors involved in dysfunctional and pathological responding and begin to develop a clear perspective of specific areas in which growth and change are needed in order to prevent R&R. When change is made, it is acknowledged and reinforced.

Therapeutic and correctional confrontational skills are used in this phase. As discussed in *Chapter 2, SSC* is designed to blend these two approaches in the treatment of the judicial client.

Therapeutic confrontation is client centered, and clients are confronted with the discrepancies between behaviors, feelings and thoughts (i.e., "you say you don't want to drink, but you keep spending time in the bars with your friends!"). Correctional confrontation directly confronts clients with the potential consequences of their antisocial and criminal thinking and engaging in high-risk exposures that can lead to recidivism.

Assessment in this phase of treatment involves two components. The first is utilizing the assessment results of *Phase I,* including the *MP* and *MAP,* to provide clinical data for the feedback process of helping clients sort out their own patterns of criminal behavior, AOD use, feelings, thoughts and emotions. The second component of assessment in this phase and in *Phase III* is to monitor and give feedback to clients as to their progress and change, using the *Progress and Change Evaluation (PACE) Monitor.* The various instruments and methods used to implement *PACE* are presented in *Chapter 6.*

The objectives of *Phase II (Table 3.2),* are to help clients learn skills to develop cognitive self-control, positive interpersonal relationships and responsible behavior in the community.

GOAL OF PHASE II: COMMITMENT TO CHANGE

Through continued facilitation of a positive therapeutic environment, clients strengthen their commitment to take definite action to use the *SSC* concepts and skills to change cognitive structures and behaviors so as to prevent relapse and recidivism.

OBJECTIVES OF PHASE II

▶ Through a formal and systematic feedback confrontation process, clients sort out, label and identify (awareness and acceptance) the intrapersonal, relationship, and antisocial attitudes and behaviors that need to be changed in order to prevent relapse and recidivism.

▶ Increase skills in using the *CB Map* for change, and focus on the positive outcome pathway by using the STEP Method: **S**ituation, **T**hinking change, **E**motions, and **P**ositive action and outcome.

▶ Identify and learn cognitive restructuring skills that facilitate management and control over intrapersonal issues and problems that contribute to R&R, such as, negative thinking and attitudes, errors in thinking, stress, anger, guilt and depression, with the goal of enhancing positive emotional and behavioral outcomes.

▶ Identify and learn concepts and skills that facilitate positive and meaningful interpersonal relationships that help prevent R&R: self-directed and other-directed communication; problem solving; assertiveness; regulating and managing anger; and developing meaningful family and intimate relationships.

▶ Through *Social Responsibility Therapy* (SRT), identify and learn concepts and skills that promote social and community responsibility (prosocial) behaviors. SRT involves strengthening character and prosocial attitudes and behaviors; understanding and learning the skills of empathy; understanding and preventing aggression, abuse and violence; learning skills of conflict resolution; strengthening values and morals; making a constructive contribution to the community.

▶ Evaluate level of knowledge and skills learned in each session and progress and change during *Phase II*.

▶ Prepare clients for **Ownership of Change.**

Phase III: Ownership of Change - The Integration Response

Phase III of *SSC* is the integration and **Ownership** stage of intervention. It focuses on integrating and reinforcing (strengthening) the concepts and skills learned in *Phases I* and *II* with the goal of maintaining the lifestyle changes that clients have made. It represents both the action and maintenance stages of change in the transtheoretical model.

In this phase, clients put together the meaning of the intervention experience and demonstrate consistency in changes they have made. Although the change goals may still be those of some external system - the court, family, marriage, the motor vehicle authority, criminal justice system - what is important is that there is consistent demonstration of change and clients internalize change and claim it to be theirs.

Evidence of these changes comes from worksheets and group processing and discussions. These may include reports of staying AOD free, not engaging in criminal behavior, improved communication with significant others, and increased ability to handle stress and manage high-risk episodes that can lead to recidivism or relapse. The difference between the commitment and ownership phases of intervention is that clients in the ownership phase talk about "owning" these changes and the desire for these changes independent of expectations from external systems. Clients also talk about longer range goals that are compatible with responsible and prosocial living.

At the macro level of the Lewin and *Orthogenetic* models, the **Ownership** phase of intervention is the integrative phase of growth and learning. Clients integrate what they have learned in such a manner that there is consistent involvement in self-control and positive outcomes. There is also a demonstration of self-efficacy or self-mastery in the management of thoughts and situations that are high risk for recidivism and relapse. And, there is evidence of broad lifestyle changes.

However, as in *Phases I* and *II*, with each new skill or new concept introduced, the client goes through the phases of learning and growth. For example, many clients respond in a global and undifferentiated manner to the presentation in *Session 47* of the basic concepts of healthy play - that it involves moving freely within boundaries, that it is not harmful to self or others, and that it is prosocial and demonstrates moral responsibility. To many judicial clients, "healthy play" involved partying and getting high. Clients begin to move beyond the global, and see different forms of healthy play (differentiation) and then discover positive outcomes from engaging in healthy play (integration).

In this ownership phase, intervention builds on the client's increased self-awareness and the coping and change skills the client has learned and practiced in *SSC*. The provider helps clients tie together various feelings, thoughts and behaviors that have emerged in the overall treatment experience and reinforces and strengthens improvement and change in specific areas. R&R prevention training is continued in this phase. Clients are taught to utilize community resources and self-help groups in maintaining change, model prosocial and AOD-free living, and some begin to mentor others who are going through the same treatment experiences. Most important, clients begin to feel the strength of the maintenance of the changes they have made.

The counselor skill categories used to help clients achieve ownership include those used in the commitment phase of treatment, but most important, there is a systematic use of change reinforcement skills. Therapeutic and correctional confrontation are used on occasion, but are less important and less necessary for clients who are taking ownership and showing maintenance of change. Even in this phase, improvements and changes that can be made are clarified, since the change process is ongoing. Providers are constantly vigilant in observing for and reinforcing even small improvements and changes in the client's life.

Important in this phase of intervention is the concept of attribution. The ideal model for change is one that facilitates change from within the individual. The most effective changes occur when clients attribute change to themselves, or when the changes are attributed to an inner motivation by the client (Kanfer, 1970, 1975, 1986). This self-attribution or internalization of change is most apt to occur when feedback reinforcement skills are utilized in such a manner that clients feel that self-improvement and change are due to their own efforts. This is an **evoking** feedback reinforcement process: "You feel good about how you handled that situation." "You are proud of the self-control you showed in not going to that party with those old buddies." However, **invoking** feedback reinforcement is also important in strengthening improvement and change: "I'm really proud of the way you handled that problem." Evoking seeks to draw or elicit the reinforcement from within the person and gives the ownership to the client. Invoking lays the reinforcement on the person from an outside source.

In the ownership stage, clients experience the strength of cognitive, affective and behavioral change. Yet, ownership begins in *Phase I* of *SSC* intervention and continues throughout the *SSC* program. Evidence indicating ownership is found in completing homework assignments, putting the *SSC* skills to work each day, taking the initiative to become involved in self-help groups, and in modeling and mentoring others who are going through the same change process. The goal and objectives of *Phase III* are provided in *Table 3.3*.

TABLE 3.3

Goal and Objectives of Phase III: Ownership of Change

GOAL OF PHASE III: OWNERSHIP OF CHANGE

Through continued facilitation of a positive therapeutic environment, clients take ownership of the changes they have made and demonstrate maintenance of these changes over time.

OBJECTIVES OF PHASE III

▶ Learn critical reasoning and independent thinking so as to prevent being pressured by antisocial peers to engage in criminal conduct.

▶ The formal and systematic feedback confrontation process is continued with the objective of continuing self-disclosure and increasing self-awareness, particularly around changes the client has made.

▶ Clients continue to use the STEP component of the *CB Map:* **S**ituation, **T**hinking change, **E**motions, and **P**ositive action/outcomes to bring about positive changes in their lives.

▶ Further develop, strengthen and maintain cognitive restructuring skills and skills that lead to prosocial and positive relationships with others and the community.

▶ Strengthen and enhance clients' R&R prevention plan with a balanced and healthy lifestyle in the areas of work, play and healthy relaxation.

▶ Internalize and take ownership of values and morals which provide guides for prosocial living.

▶ As a result of taking ownership of change, clients learn to receive and give support and they provide role modeling for other clients who are engaged in the process of change.

▶ Develop a sense of confidence about not engaging in CC and have clients develop ownership of their recidivism prevention goals.

▶ Evaluate level of knowledge and skills learned in each session and evaluate progress and change during *Phase III* and in the overall *SSC* program.

▶ Prepare clients for program completion, reentry and reintegration.

FUNDAMENTAL ISSUES REGARDING LEARNING AND CHANGE

There are a number of basic issues regarding the understanding of learning and growth, and the stages of change. Some of these have been discussed above, but will be reiterated.

The Orthogenetic Learning and Growth Model

The *Orthogenetic Principle* provides a model for understanding how growth and learning take place at various levels of human responding. As noted, it can be applied to one specific episode of learning, e.g.,

finding the airport baggage claim; to what happens in a series of experiences; or within one treatment session; or it explains the overall process of clients' involvement in the three phases of *SSC.* The three phases of growth help provide a basic structure for *SSC.*

The phases of learning and growth - global, differentiation, integration - are a natural process that can be nurtured. They are facilitated by individuals who have an investment in the learning and growth of another person, e.g., parents, teachers, therapists. They are facilitated through reflective listening feedback, and change reinforcement skills.

The *Orthogenetic Principle* of learning and growth is cyclical. Every phase of integration opens the door for another global and undifferentiated response to a new experience, situation or challenge. However, the new global response or experience always begins at a higher level than the last integrative response.

This model sees learning and growth as dynamic. Each phase provides energy and force for the next learning response. Yet, the dynamic is both internal and external.

External influences — teacher, environment, therapist, group — provide energy and force to help the individual reach a new level of learning and growth. Yet, there are internal physiological (physical growth, relief from drug withdrawal) and psychological (motivation) processes that move learning and growth along.

Finally, the *Orthogenetic Principle* provides a structure that is compatible with the stages of change, and both provide a structure around which to organize specific therapeutic experiences that facilitate both growth and change.

Stages of Change

There are a number of issues that are important when understanding and applying the stages of change to treatment.

Change is multidimensional

First, the change process and efforts to influence self-improvement and change in treatment are multidimensional. Change may be occurring across several problem behavior dimensions at one time. Connors et al. (2001) and Prochaska and DiClemente (1992) stress that stages of change will apply to specific target behavior such as alcohol use, criminal conduct, smoking and that "commitment to change one behavior, such as alcohol use, may say nothing about commitment to change another, such as cigarette smoking" (Connors et al., 2001, p. 6).

When several targets become the focus of change, as is the case of criminal conduct and substance abuse treatment, therapeutic efforts need to focus on both.

Changes in one area will not necessarily produce changes in another area. However, the response generalization principle of psychology would suggest that change in one area could generalize to another area or problem.

Change is differential

Second, change is differential. An individual may be in one stage of change with respect to one target and another stage with respect to another target. Our experience is that judicial clients tend to move through the challenge to change stage at a quicker pace in the area of criminal conduct than in the area of substance abuse. There seems to be greater resistance and defensiveness in giving up old patterns of substance use than patterns that lead to CC.

This differential change process means that the evaluation of a client's stage of change must be done across all of the target behaviors. This may be true for specific targets within a more general target of change. For example, judicial clients may be more open to changing their criminal thinking, but may be less open to cutting off their relationships with old criminal associates.

Change is not always congruent with a treatment phase

A client's stage of change is not necessarily congruent with the *SSC* treatment phase that the individual may be in. Not all clients are at an equal pace with respect to change. The pace of *SSC* often stays somewhat ahead of the stage of change that some clients are in.

Each *SSC* treatment phase is designed to address certain stages of change. The goal of *Phase I* is to challenge clients to change their AOD abuse and CC patterns, and the 20 sessions of *Phase I* are designed to do that. However, an individual may complete the 20 sessions of *Phase I* and in some important domains (e.g., marijuana use) still be in the challenge phase - still contemplating change, or still making some preparation to change.

Yet, we move such clients along with the expectation that they will make a commitment and take action to change. And, if treatment is working, most clients' stage of change will be congruent with the treatment phase.

This pace incongruence occurs mainly in the group treatment modality. We cannot expect all clients in the group to be at the same stage in a particular phase of treatment, just as we cannot expect clients to be in the same stage for different problem behaviors.

Pace incongruence is further compounded by the use of open groups. New members entering the group will clearly be at different stages of change than group veterans. Again, the expectation is that, as clients progress through all of the sessions in a particular treatment phase, they will begin to match the expected stage of change level that the treatment phase addresses.

There are several ways to address this lack of congruence or pace differential. First, clients are therapeutically prepared for the possibility that they will be at different stages of change when they enter treatment than other group members.

Second, in orientation, the stage or change model can be explained, providing clients with an understanding of the process they will be experiencing. They should be told that their stage of change may be different for different problem areas, e.g. different for substance abuse vs. CC.

Third, by having different groups for each of the treatment phases (to be discussed in *Chapter 7*), providers can use the skills that are appropriate for each of the treatment phases. Skills used for the challenge stage of change or *Phase I* group will be different from those used in the commitment *Phase II* group, etc.

Fourth, providers need to attend to the individual needs of each client based on his/her stage of change. Because the *SSC* phases are flexible, and because the provider can be flexible, clients who are in the challenge stage for specific treatment targets can be in *Phase II,* which is designed for commitment, yet not be threatened because, overall, their understandings and skills for relapse and recidivism prevention have met the criteria for acceptance into *Phase II* of treat-

ment. The methods and approaches of *Phase II* still meet the needs of clients in early stages of change in some important areas of their life.

Finally, a cohesive group will tend to "understand" where individual members are with respect to identified treatment targets and actually relate to them based on their stage of change. This is why it is important for providers to build a cohesive and prosocial group that is supportive of its group members. This is one of the core *SSC* strategies and is discussed in more detail in *Chapter 7*.

Stages of change are cyclical

As discussed above, the *Orthogenetic Principle* describes the process of learning and growth as cyclical. The three phases of growth are replicated across the various encounters with new treatment stimuli.

Just as with the *Orthogenetic Principle* of growth and learning, the stages of change are also cyclical. Connors et al. (2001) note that even though the transtheoretical model describes change in a linear manner, "in practice people commonly cycle back from an advanced stage to an earlier one. This may happen a number of times before the person makes it to the maintenance stage for good" (p. 8). The cyclical nature of change described by Prochaska, DiClemente and Norcross (1992) shows that even though a person may cycle back to a former stage of change, "in most cases, the person does not go all the way back to the precontemplation stage" (Connors et al., 2001, p. 9).

We see the same cyclical concept applying to the three stages of change in *SSC*. Clients in the commitment stage of change are often faced with going back to substance use or criminal conduct, particularly when encountering high-risk exposures. They may slip back to seeing old criminal associates at a bar, cruising the old neighborhoods where they bought drugs. However, if they apply the skills they have learned to **manage** high-risk exposures, they are able to reestablish the commitment process, and move on in that stage of change.

What is important, however, is that even though clients in *Phase II* of *SSC* find themselves again in a challenge to change position relative to specific treatment targets, they continue in *Phase II*. This is the strength of programs like *SSC*.

The group and provider continue to keep the client on track and moving towards ownership and maintenance of change. In this sense, treatment, the treatment group, and the overall influence of the *SSC* process become the stabilizing components in their lives.

CHAPTER REVIEW

This chapter began with a presentation of a dynamic model for understanding how learning and growth take place. This model, based on the work of Kurt Lewin and Werner's *Orthogenetic Principle,* sees learning as involving three response phases: a global or undifferentiated response; a differentiated or sorting out response; and an integration of responses into a functional interaction with the environment. Various examples were given to illustrate how this process takes place. It was then used as a model to explain the process of growth and learning in the therapy and treatment experience.

The next task of this chapter was to provide a conceptual framework for the stages that people go through when making changes in their lives. The traditional transtheoretical model was described that provides six stages of change. Then, a simpler model was provided, based on the transtheoretical stages, but boiled down to three stages: **Challenge to Change; Commitment to Change; and Ownership of Change.**

The chapter then focused on how the phases of learning and growth and the three-stage model of change are integrated into a three-phase treatment structure for the *SSC* curriculum. Each of these phases was then discussed with its respective goals and objectives.

Finally, some fundamental issues regarding the models of learning, growth and change were discussed. It was stressed that the phases of learning and growth are cyclical and dynamic: learning and growth continually cycle back through the three phases but not back to an original position of growth; and that each

phase provides the energy and force to move to the next growth and learning step. The same cyclical process also occurs in stages that people go through in making changes.

Change is also described as being multidimensional and differential. The pace of change at the individual level differs across persons and differs for each target area that is the focus of change.

Most important with respect to the treatment process, clients will be at different stages of change within a particular *SSC* treatment phase. The stage of change for some clients, in some important life domains, may not keep pace or may not be parallel with their movement through the *SSC* treatment phases.

Providers can minimize the impact of this differential pace by explaining to new clients the concept of stages of change, informing new clients that, with respect to certain patterns of thinking, feeling, and action, they may be at a different stage of change from other group members. Providers attend to individual needs based on differences in the change pace, and build a strong and cohesive group that provides support for all members regardless of where they are with respect to the change process.

CHAPTER OUTLINE

OVERVIEW

BRIEF SUMMARY OF HISTORICAL ROOTS OF CB TREATMENT

Behavioral Therapy
Cognitive Therapy
Merging of Cognitive and Behavioral
    Approaches - CBT

EFFECTIVENESS OF CBT

CB ASSUMPTIONS UNDERLYING AOD ABUSE AND CC AND THEIR TREATMENT

COGNITIVE STRUCTURES THAT ARE THE FOCUS OF TREATMENT

Level I: Proximal Structures
Level II: Mediating Structures
Level III: Core Beliefs and Assumptions

COGNITIVE PROCESSES THAT ARE THE FOCUS OF CB TREATMENT

Automatic Thinking
Decision Making
Cognitive Distorting
Automatic Assuming
Being Mindful and Aware
Accepting
Interaction of Thoughts, Emotions and Behaviors

COGNITIVE-BEHAVIORAL METHODS USED IN *SSC*

Cognitive Restructuring or Intrapersonal Skill
    Building
Social or Relationship Skills Training (SRST)
Social Responsibility Therapy (SRT)

SELF-EFFICACY: A FOCAL ISSUE IN CB TREATMENT
THE CONTEXT OF CHANGE

THE EMOTIONAL COMPONENT OF CBT

THE *SSC* CB MODEL FOR CHANGE: THE COGNITIVE-BEHAVIORAL MAP

CHAPTER REVIEW

CHAPTER OBJECTIVES

▌ Provide an overview, historical perspective, and key components of CBT that help lay the foundation for the development of a CBT model for the *SSC* program and curriculum.

▌ Identify and describe the core cognitive structures that are the focus of CBT.

▌ Identify and describe core processes or actions of CBT, the vehicles and dynamics through which cognitive structures are expressed, and that define the action focus of CBT in the *SSC* program.

▌ Show that change occurs within the context of a biopsychosocial process.

▌ Show that self-efficacy is a key focus in effective CB treatment.

▌ Integrate the concepts and skills of CBT into a model that provides a map - the *SSC CB Map* - for guiding judicial clients through the process of cognitive and behavioral change with the goal of preventing relapse and recidivism.

OVERVIEW

Cognitive-behavioral (CB) therapy is the primary foundational model for *Criminal Conduct and Substance Abuse Treatment: Strategies for Self-Improvement and Change (SSC)*. In the *Resource Guide* (Wanberg & Milkman, 2008), we summarize the historical roots, the underlying principles and key focuses of CB approaches. The purpose of this chapter is to describe a specific model for the use of CB in working with judicial clients, and more specifically, the CB model upon which *SSC* is based.

We first give a brief historical background to the development of CB approaches. We then look at the CB assumptions that explain criminal conduct (CC) and its relationship to AOD abuse and problems. The core cognitive structures that are the focus of CB change in judicial clients, and which are the focus of *SSC,* are then discussed. This discussion is followed by describing some underlying processes through which the cognitive structures are expressed and manifested. These processes provide an important basis of *SSC* treatment. The three primary focuses of CB treatment of substance abusing judicial clients are then presented. The contextual understanding of how CB change occurs is then described. Finally, a specific CB model designed for use with *SSC* clients is outlined.

BRIEF SUMMARY OF HISTORICAL ROOTS OF CB TREATMENT

Cognitive-behavioral therapy (CBT) emerged from two paths: cognitive theory and therapy; and behavioral theory and therapy. We briefly look at these two paths and their merging into CB approaches to treatment.

Behavioral Therapy

The development of behavioral therapies in the late 1950s and 1960s provided the foundation of the behavior component of cognitive-behavioral therapy. The roots of this development go back to the early work of Pavlov, Skinner, Watson, and others in the first half of the 20th century. The early focus was on changing behaviors through the management of anxiety, and applying contingency reinforcements to desirable behaviors and behavioral change.

Contemporary behavior therapy places the focus on current determinants of behavior with an emphasis on changing overt behavior guided by specific treatment objectives (Kazdin, 1978). It involves environmental change and social interaction using approaches that enhance self-control (Franks & Wilson, 1973-1975) and a focus on client responsibility and the therapeutic relationship (Franks & Barbrack, 1983). The common intervention approaches used in behavioral therapy are coping and social skills training, contingency management, modeling, anxiety reduction and relaxation methods, self-management methods and behavioral rehearsal (Glass & Arnkoff, 1992).

Cognitive Therapy

Cognitive therapy is premised on the idea that our view of the world shapes the reality that we experience. The cognitive approach was a reaction to the narrow view of early behavioral psychology which did not attend to, and even rejected, the importance of the effect of the inside-the-mind happenings on behavioral outcomes.

Thus, independent movements of cognitive therapy began mainly with the work of Albert Ellis and Aaron Beck, both of whom introduced cognitive restructuring therapies beginning in the 1950s and 1960s. Beck is often seen as the founder and developer of cognitive therapy in his work with depression in the early 1960s (Leahy, 1996).

The underlying principle of contemporary cognitive therapy is that disturbances in behaviors, emotions and thought can be modified or changed by altering the cognitive processes (Hollen & Beck, 1986). In simplistic terms, "cognitive therapy is based on the simple idea that your thoughts and attitudes -- and not external events -- create your moods" (Burns, 1989, p. xiii). Thus, emotions are experienced as a result of the way in which events are interpreted or appraised (Beck, 1976). "It is the meaning of the event that triggers emotions rather than the events themselves" (Salkovskis, 1996, p. 48).

Cognitive psychology assumes an interplay between thought, emotion and action. As Freeman and colleagues (1990) note, "the cognitive model is not simply that 'thoughts cause feelings and actions'" (p. 6). Emotions and moods can change cognitive processes. Actions can have an influence on how one sees a particular situation.

The common intervention thread across the spectrum of cognitive therapy is cognitive restructuring. The more specific approaches are: 1) restructuring cognitive distortions found in negative thinking, maladaptive assumptions, and automatic thoughts; 2) self-instructional training; 3) problem solving; 4) mental coping skills; 5) relaxation therapy; 6) modeling strategies; and 7) specific cognitive techniques such as thought stopping, thought replacement, thought conditioning, thought countering, etc.

Merging of Cognitive and Behavioral Approaches - CBT

Although behavioral therapies and cognitive restructuring approaches seemed to develop in parallel paths, over time, the two approaches merged into what we now call cognitive-behavioral therapy. Bandura's work on behavioral modification, social learning theory, and how internal mental processes regulate and modify behavior provided an important bridge in the merging of behavioral and cognitive approaches (1969, 1977a).

Following the work of Ellis and Beck, the different approaches to cognitive therapy and cognitive restructuring were blended with the elements of behavioral therapy. Early examples of this blending include coping skills training and self-instructional training (Meichenbaum, 1975, 1977). Other blending approaches include problem solving, assertiveness and other social skills training, and managing relationship stress.

Contemporary CBT, then, is an integration of the key components of behavioral and cognitive therapy. It is common to see cognitive restructuring as the cognitive part of CBT and social skills training as the behavioral component of CBT.

Our take from the literature is that the key combin-

ing element of cognitive and behavioral approaches is found in the principle of **self-reinforcement.** It represents one of the most important principles of social learning theory (Bandura, 1977a, 1997). This concept simply states that cognitive and behavioral changes reinforce each other. When changes in thinking lead to positive behavior outcomes, the outcomes strengthen both the behavior and the cognitive structures that lead to those outcomes. In turn, the changes in thinking reinforced by the changes in behavior further strengthen those behavioral changes. It is not just the reinforcement of the behavior that strengthens the behavior; it is the reinforcement of the thought structures leading to the behavior that strengthens the behavior.

This self-reinforcing feedback process is a key principle which becomes the basis for helping clients understand the process and maintenance of change and is the basis for the cognitive-behavioral approach to change in this work - *Criminal Conduct and Substance Abuse Treatment - Strategies for Self-Improvement and Change.*

The underlying principle of *SSC* is that both cognitive and behavioral approaches bring combined strengths to the implementation of effective treatment of substance abusing judicial clients.

EFFECTIVENESS OF CBT

There is a large body of literature supporting the efficacy and effectiveness of CB treatment in general, and the specific approaches that fall within the domain of CBT. More specifically, there is also strong research support for the efficacy of CB and its related approaches to the treatment of antisocial behavior, criminal conduct and its co-occurrence with substance abuse. A more comprehensive review of this literature is provided in the *Resource Guide* (Wanberg & Milkman, 2008) and in *Cognitive-Behavioral Treatment: A Review and Discussion for Corrections Professionals* (Milkman & Wanberg, 2007). We briefly summarize the most salient of these findings.

As to the treatment of CC and its co-occurrence with AOD abuse, the general conclusion, in terms of meta-analyses and individual studies, is that there is strong evidence to support the efficacy of correctional treatment as to the reduction of relapse and recidivism. Andrews and Bonta (2003) have concluded over the years that the efficacy of correctional treatments is enhanced by the use of cognitive-behavioral therapy approaches. They identify a number of principles that contributed to effective correctional treatment. Among these is "using generally powerful influence and behavioral change strategies (general responsivity principle: use behavioral/social learning/cognitive-behavioral strategies..." p. 95).

The extensive meta-analysis work of Lipsey and associates provides cogent support for the use of CBT with judicial clients. In their most recent meta-analysis summary (Landenberger & Lipsey, 2005), they state that their findings confirm other recent meta-analyses of the positive effects of CBT on reducing recidivism among offenders (Lipsey, Chapman & Landenberger, 2001; Lipsey & Landenberger, 2006; Pearson et al., 2002; Wilson, Bouffard & MacKenzie, 2005).

Landenberger and Lipsey (2005) conclude that, when controlling for client characteristics and implementation differences, "no significant differences were found in the effectiveness of the different types or 'brand names' of CBT" (p. 471). However, they further state that, given the specific elements that characterize effective CBT programs, "...any representative CBT program that is well implemented might have results in practice that approach the very positive effects on recidivism produced by the most effective programs documented in the available research studies" (p. 471). Finally, they state: "...the consistency and magnitude of the effects found in the research to date leave little doubt that CBT is capable of producing significant reductions in the recidivism of even high risk offenders under favorable conditions" (p. 472).

CB ASSUMPTIONS UNDERLYING AOD ABUSE AND CC AND THEIR TREATMENT

The CB assumptions underlying AOD misuse and CC is that cognitive structures and processes operate within the person in such a manner so as to prevent self-control over the use of substances and irresponsible behavior in the community. AOD abuse and CC are consequences of the individual's cognitive

organization (or disorganization) and cognitive processes through which these structures are behaviorally expressed.

The CB approach to treatment is to first modify and change the proximal or short-term structures which we call thought habits or automatic thoughts, e.g., outcome expectancies, that lead to the loss of control over AOD use and irresponsible behavior in the community; and second, work on changing the distal or long-term structures, e.g., beliefs and attitudes. This change process involves:

- Identifying the thought habits or automatic thoughts that lead to substance abuse and criminal behavior;

- Changing thought habits or proximal structures to those that lead to self-control and adaptive prosocial outcomes;

- Helping clients to be mindful of and identify the more distal and ingrained structures of attitudes and beliefs that reinforce the thought habits or proximal structures that led to substance use problems and CC;

- Challenging old beliefs and transforming them into or replacing them with a belief system that generates and strengthens the thought habits or proximal structures that lead to self-control and prosocial outcomes; and

- Having clients practice these changes so that both the behaviors and cognitive changes are reinforced (strengthened).

COGNITIVE STRUCTURES THAT ARE THE FOCUS OF TREATMENT

The CB model developed for the *SSC* treatment approach is built upon three levels of cognitive structures. This model utilizes a combination of the work of Seligman et al. (2001) and J. Beck (1995) and builds on the work of A. Beck (1976) and Bandura (1977a).

Level I: Proximal structures

In the *SSC* treatment model, these are referred to as thought habits or automatic thoughts. Seligman et al. (2001) refer to these as short-term, more surface cognitive processes. We refer to them as structures. We take these structures and draw upon Bandura's work (1977a) to expand them to five essential proximal structures.

▶ **Outcome expectancies** are the individual's judgment about whether the performance of a particular behavior will lead to a certain outcome. It is the knowledge of what to do and what will result from that action. If the behavior and the outcome expectancy thoughts are fulfilled, both the thoughts and behavior are reinforced. Example: "If I take a drink, I'll relax." If this in fact occurs, the thoughts and behaviors are likely to increase in both intensity and frequency.

▶ **Efficacy expectations** refer to the individual's assessment of his or her ability to successfully execute a particular behavior. This is the belief that one can carry out a certain course of action to get a certain outcome. If there is the belief that one can perform a particular behavior, then most likely one will engage in that behavior. If the behavior is performed successfully, this reinforces the efficacy expectation. Example: "If I hold my cool, I won't get into an argument with my boss - and I can hold my cool."

▶ **Appraisals** are proximal structures that evaluate the value and meaning of what we are experiencing and our responses to those experiences. These can become distorted resulting in thinking errors. Examples: "When he yelled at me in front of my kids, it was big-time disrespect." I feel better because she respects my opinion." "I must be a failure because I can't hold a job."

▶ **Attributions** are explanations of why things happen or the explanations of outcomes. They might be internalized, "I'm responsible for the accident," or externalized, "The reason I got arrested is the cops were after me."

▶ **Decisions** are structures that lead to the behaviors that can result in good or bad outcomes. They are important components of Marlatt's (1985a) relapse prevention model, and represent the individual's conscious choices to take certain actions. This component provides the basis of the underlying philosophy of freedom of choice

in change, self-determination, self-control and self-improvment.

Level II: Mediating structures

J. Beck (1995) refers to these as intermediate beliefs. We will refer to these as mediating structures. They mediate between the underlying core beliefs and the thought habits or automatic thoughts. They line us up with our inside world or the outside world. Some important intermediary structures noted in the literature are attitudes, values and rules. We focus on these in the *SSC* curriculum.

▶ **Attitudes** orient us for or against an idea, a situation or person outside of ourselves: "That person is a jerk." "It's a cruel world." "He's a great guy." Attitudes also provide an orientation for or against ourselves: "I'm a real dummy." "I'm a good skier." Attitudes are usually emotionally based and we place a good or bad valence or charge on them.

▶ **Values** define the position we take in relationship to ourselves and the outside world. These are guiding principles in our lives. We attach ourselves to our values, and this attachment can position us as being for or against others or the outside world. If we value family, then we will align ourselves with family. If we value work, money, power or status, then we will engage in activities that achieve goals related to those values.

▶ **Rules** define how we relate to ourselves and the outside world. They determine our behavior. Rules define how we live up to our values. If we have an internal rule that "I will not steal" (a value), that rule will determine how we associate ourselves with people and with systems. The person who has a strict rule of "never cheating," will point out to the waiter that the dessert was left off of the bill. Rules are important in mediating core beliefs into thought habits or proximal structures. For example, a core belief that "I am an honest person" will translate into a rule of "I will never cheat someone," leading to the automatic thought "I need to tell the waiter" the dessert was left off of the bill.

Level III: Core beliefs and assumptions.

Although some put assumptions as the intermediary structure (J. Beck, 1995), assumptions and core beliefs are used synonymously in the *SSC* model. Core beliefs are concepts that are used to judge or evaluate ourselves, situations, people, the world. Beliefs bond or connect us to ourselves and to the outside world. We see these as the "truth," "the fact" or a "conviction." Core beliefs are usually 100 percent and deeply ingrained. There are two kinds of core beliefs or assumptions that become the focus in CB treatment.

▶ Beliefs about self bond us to our sense of self. They include the core belief of self-efficacy, self-importance and self-value. Self-efficacy is an important focus in treating substance abuse and antisocial behavior. Examples of these beliefs about self are: "I'm a good person," "I feel I can handle life's problems," "I've made a contribution," "I can't handle life," and "I'm worthless."

▶ Beliefs about the world bond us to the outside world. They involve a basic assumption about how we see and perceive the world. Some core beliefs are "the sacredness of life," "right to make choices," "people are created equal," "all persons should live in a government that is for the people, by the people, of the people." These beliefs are mediated by attitudes, rules and values and surface into automatic thoughts or thought habits. A belief that "the world is a hostile place" may support an attitude of entitlement that surfaces as a thought habit of "I'm going to take what's coming to me."

Figure 4.1 provides a schemata for these three levels of cognitive structures. Certainly, there are other cognitive structures that could be added to these levels. For example, a core belief that one should "treat fellow humans with respect," may be mediated by the rule of being "courteous," and an automatic thought of "I'm sorry" when making a mistake or offending someone. In *Figure 4.1,* the base of the pyramid is represented by the core beliefs about self and the world, which are mediated by the intermediary structures to surface in thought habits and automatic thoughts.

FIGURE 4.1

Model of Cognitive Structures and Processes

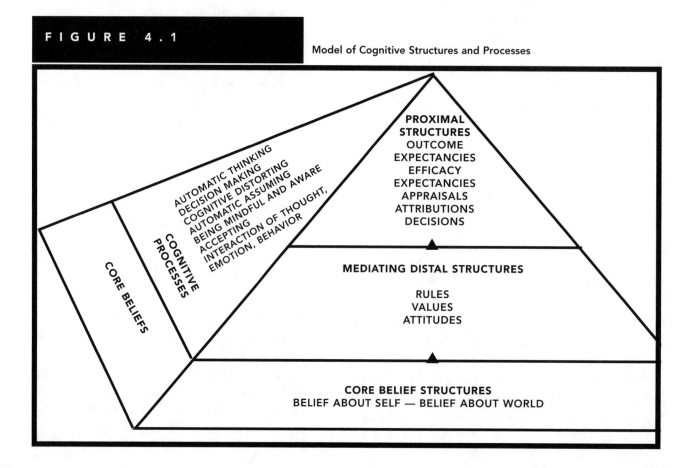

COGNITIVE PROCESSES THAT ARE THE FOCUS OF TREATMENT

There are important **cognitive processes** that operate in such a manner as to allow the expression and manifestation of the **cognitive structures** described above. These processes or actions (they are stated as verbs) provide the dynamics (energy) for the expression of cognitive structures. These processes help direct the *SSC* treatment - they are treatment actions. We look at seven cognitive processes that underlie the expression of the core cognitive structures that are noted in the three-dimensional pyramid of *Figure 4.1*.

Automatic Thinking

Automatic thinking is a process that allows a series of thought habits (proximal structures), already inside our head, to emerge and lead to certain outcomes. This is a response to the events that we experience. Automatic thinking allows the surfacing of the various thought structures described above. It usually involves a series of different kinds of thought structures that result in a certain outcome. "I've had a hard day" (appraisal). "If I had a drink, I'd relax" (expectation). "I have about an hour before I have to get home, so I'll stop by and see John" (decision). "He'll understand" (appraisal).

The goal of treatment is to: help clients learn to interrupt and/or change the process of automatic thinking that leads to bad emotional and action outcomes; and to create a process where new thoughts can be developed that lead to better outcomes. This involves using cognitive skills that lead to increased self-control.

The goal is to make thinking non-automatic, at least until there is assurance that the automatic thinking will lead to positive outcomes. For example, a client may automatically engage in a series of thought habits that leads to meeting and spending time with criminal associates. The situation of being with a criminal associate may subsequently lead to engaging in another series of criminal thinking or thought habits. However, recognizing that this high-risk thought pattern and subsequent high-risk situation will lead to further high-risk thinking around criminal conduct, the goal is to change the thinking process where the individual will not "automatically" gravitate towards this high-risk situation. Thoughts are replaced or new thoughts formed. The high-risk situation is avoided. However, to be effective, it must involve more than avoidance; it must involve thinking about positive alternatives to spending time with criminal associates. Soon, this avoiding and replacement process becomes automatic. It then becomes self-reinforcing because it leads to positive outcomes.

An important method in interrupting automatic thinking is thought mapping and belief searching. This is part of learning cognitive self-control, and is a focus of *Module 8,* and particularly, *Sessions 21* and *22.*

Decision Making

Decision making is another cognitive process that allows the surfacing of decision thoughts that lead to certain outcomes. With respect to the above example, at some point, the individual engages in a series of automatic decision-making thoughts. Making a left turn to go to Joe's Bar and meeting some old criminal associates, instead of a right turn to go home, is a decision. Going into the bar where "my old buddies hang out" and making the decision to go with them in their plans to break into a liquor store is decision making. Decision-making processes are based on many proximal thought structures described above. Again, treatment is directed at interrupting the decision-making process. It starts with learning skills to enhance conscious awareness of where the person is with respect to specific thoughts and specific situations. It involves learning to clearly identify those high-risk exposures (high-risk thinking, situations) that lead to the automatic thoughts.

Cognitive Distorting

This is a process where our reaction to the outside world leads to thought habits that are errors in judgment about what we are experiencing. Cognitive distorting is based on cognitive structures that are appraisals of self or the outside world. These appraisals can become thought habits or automatic thoughts that emerge out of core beliefs.

These distortions are often "all or nothing" kinds of thoughts. "She **always** puts me down." "My boss **never** gives me credit." "I can **never** handle things." These are appraisals that, for the most part, constitute errors in thinking.

The process for changing errors in thinking first involves using skills to recognize thinking errors. This requires being critical of one's cognitive and behavioral responses: "Am I correct?" "Is he always that way?" It then involves using internal cognitive processing, such as self-talk, to verbally challenge the error. Then, one actually changes the thinking error internally through self-talk. "She **does** support me at times." "I **did** handle that job well this morning." "My boss **did** give me a raise."

What is important is the dynamic, or the force, behind these errors in thinking. Cognitive distorting becomes a process that has power and strength. It is a primary process for justifying criminal behavior. Several *SSC* sessions focus on thinking errors and cognitive distorting. Thought mapping and belief searching are important methods in changing automatic cognitive distorting.

Automatic Assuming

Another cognitive process related to the above structures is **automatic assuming.** This is the operational process through which attitudes, values and core beliefs get expressed without conscious awareness or thoughtfulness. It is a deeper process than automatic thinking, which allows the surfacing of automatic thought structures. Automatic assuming results in thinking and acting based on our core beliefs and allows core beliefs or assumptions to surface. In a sense, these core beliefs are "always stirring around, ready for action" but usually without conscious awareness. When we encounter a specific situation, and find ourselves reacting in a strong manner, we are automatically assuming. Automatic assuming does not let the outside realities or facts determine our response. It is a process that moves from the inside out. It is judging and evaluating.

For example, if we have a strong belief that today's

teenagers are lazy and up to no good, and drive by a park where there is a large group of teens milling around, that core belief will most likely result in a strong judgmental statement - "Why aren't they in school?" and maybe even result in calling the police. Further investigation may reveal that it is a high school picnic.

Automatic assuming is a dynamic process that drives criminal conduct and underlies the expression of cognitive structures, e.g., **expectations,** "I won't get caught" that can result in criminal conduct; **appraisal,** "I deserve more than what I have" that is supported by the **attribution,** "I did that because they had it coming." Yet, the process of assuming is so automatic that the cognitive structures are not noticed or recognized. The process of assuming functions like an automatic transmission in a car.

The goal of treatment is to have clients get a conscious grasp on "automatic shifting" to help them learn "manual shifting." It involves consciously putting one's hands on the process of shifting beliefs (and thoughts) to effect self-control and guide the change process. It involves many skills, including stopping and observing where one is at any moment in time, being mindful and aware, e.g., "I'm in a high crime neighborhood." It involves looking at the assuming process and its related cognitive structures, e.g., core beliefs, that emerge in this process, within a therapeutic environment using role playing, interactive journaling, worksheets, etc. It is developing cognitive structures that prepare for high-risk situations in which core beliefs and automatic thoughts tend to take over. It is putting to work the skill of mindfulness and being vigilant in situations and environments that are high-risk for criminal conduct.

Being Mindful and Aware

In *SSC,* we see self-awareness as a critical step in the change process. Acceptance commitment therapy (ACT: Hayes, Follette & Linehan, 2004) and dialectical behavioral therapy (DBT: Linehan, 1993a, 1993b; Robins, Schmidt, & Linehan, 2004) have enhanced our thinking about and the value of mindfulness and awareness in treatment. These models are discussed in more detail in the *Resource Guide* (Wanberg & Milkman, 2008). Mindfulness generally includes awareness and attention, focusing on the present, sensitivity to surrounding stimuli, awareness of the connections between self and the outside world, and a lack of desire or urge to escape the current situation (Fruzzetti & Iverson, 2004).

It is a practice that has to do with being aware of and taking part in everyday living. "It is a way of living awake, with one's eyes wide open" (Robins et al., p. 37). It is rooted in the thoughtful approaches common to Eastern and Western spiritual disciplines and "allows" experiences rather than suppressing or avoiding them (p. 37). It is a conscious process of observing, describing, and taking part in the reality of the moment, putting aside judgment, conclusions, and opinions. It is looking at thoughts as thoughts rather than looking from thoughts or looking at the world through thoughts (Robins et al., 2004).

Linehan sees mindfulness as involving "what to do" (1993a) and "how to do" skills (1993b: Fruzzetti & Iverson, 2004, primary source). The "what to do" skills in being mindful are:

◗ observing, noticing, awareness of the present;

◗ verbally describing what has been observed or experienced; and

◗ taking part fully in the behavior and letting go without a lot of self-conscious activity.

The "how to do" skills involve:

◗ not being judgmental or evaluative, or focusing on the "good" or "bad" of the thoughts or experience;

◗ focusing on the present, here and now, and on one thing at a time; and

◗ engaging in actions that are congruent with one's life goals, purpose or values.

In *SSC,* mindfulness and awareness are important parts of the treatment process. They are enhanced through group exercises and worksheets. These are structured efforts to enhance awareness of the past within the context of the present; or just awareness of present thoughts and emotions.

Accepting

Achieving a goal or making change may involve accepting one's condition or situation without the immediate intention of making change. Acceptance can be defined as "behavioral tolerance" which is not actively working on change, but accepting the current situation to get a certain outcome.

One may accept being in a boring required college class because it leads to getting the necessary credit for graduation. One has the choice to make some changes within that context such as engaging in some positive interactive discussion in class. Accepting being treated rudely and then moving on requires the cognitive processing of accepting the rude treatment, but making no effort to change the thinking about being treated rudely - only engaging in thinking that is accepting and moving on. It also involves looking at broader goals than just getting an apology.

Robins et al. (2004) talk about radical acceptance - "focusing on the current moment, seeing reality as it is without 'delusions,' and accepting reality without judgment" (p. 39). In DBT, "clients are taught and encouraged to use skills for accepting life completely and radically, as well as for changing it" (p. 39). The latter, "changing it," is crucial to the treatment of criminal conduct. The focus on accepting one's past criminal conduct, one's current judicial sentence, or even one's current criminal thinking is part of the awareness component of change. However, the treatment of criminal conduct must unequivocally go beyond mindfulness and awareness and involve change. Just as with suicide. Being aware of and accepting one's suicidal thinking (and options) is only part of the picture. It is essential to engage in cognitive restructuring to get prosocial outcomes (as in the case of criminal conduct) and continued living (as in the case of suicidal thinking).

Fruzzetti and Iverson (2004) identify several components or defining features of acceptance:

◗ The person is fully aware of what is being accepted;

◗ Regardless of whether the experience is pleasant

or unpleasant, wanted or not wanted, the focus is not on mobilizing resources to change the situation or experience (the judicial sentence);

▶ The person has some understanding of how the experience is related to stimuli that preceded it.

They see acceptance at two levels: pure acceptance with no efforts to change; and acceptance in balance with change. As discussed above, the treatment of criminal conduct must involve both of these levels.

Interaction of Thoughts, Emotions and Behaviors

Another cognitive process is the **interaction that occurs between thoughts, emotions and behaviors.** Thoughts can lead to emotions and behaviors. Emotions can lead to behaviors and thoughts; and behaviors can lead to thoughts and emotions. In *SSC,* we take the position that the starting point for change is with our thoughts.

However, often we experience the emotion as coming first. We feel anger, but may not be aware of the thoughts that lead to the anger. Thus, we may have to label the emotion first and then work back to the thought habit: "I'm really angry - but what are the thoughts that make me angry?" Many judicial clients will say: "I just go mad. Didn't have any thoughts." Or, "I just hit him. Didn't have any thoughts." The goal of CB treatment is to interrupt the automatic thinking and assuming long enough to identify and manage those thoughts that lead to bad emotional and behavioral outcomes. However, the change process often involves identifying the emotions first and then asking "What am I thinking?"

COGNITIVE-BEHAVIORAL METHODS USED IN SSC

As noted above, there are two traditional focuses in CB learning and change: **cognitive restructuring** and **social skills training.** The third method is **social responsibility therapy (SRT)** and its focus on social-community responsibility skills training. These three approaches are the focus of *Phase II* of *SSC.* It is important to remember that the primary purpose of the use of these three approaches in *SSC*

is to prevent relapse and recidivism.

Cognitive Restructuring or Intrapersonal Skill Building

There are two primary goals for using cognitive restructuring in the treatment of criminal conduct and co-occurring substance abuse. The first is to change the proximal structures (thoughts) and distal or deeper structures (beliefs) that lead directly to substance abuse and criminal conduct - relapse and recidivism. For example, changing criminal thinking; changing thoughts that lead to substance use.

The second purpose for using cognitive restructuring is to help clients manage negative emotional states that can lead to relapse and recidivism. There is a significant link between negative cognitive-emotional states and relapse (Marlatt & Witkiewitz, 2005). AOD relapse is also associated with positive emotional states (Marlatt & Witkiewitz, 2005). Hodgins and colleagues (1995) show that both positive and negative emotional states can predict relapse. However the former was more associated with lapses whereas the latter was more associated with heavy drinking. In fact, Borland (1990) shows that lapses linked to positive moods were more likely to lead to a positive outcome such as abstinence.

Negative emotional states also increase the risk of recidivism. For example, increased levels of depression and anxiety among offenders tend to increase the probability that clients will drop out of treatment and reoffend (Moos, Finney, & Moos, 2000; Hiller, Knight, & Simpson, 1999).

Most substance abusing judicial clients will experience negative emotional states. Andrews and Bonta (2003) conclude from their literature search that most offenders have some kind of mental health diagnosis across the broad gamut of disorders. However, they conclude that the more major and serious mental health disorders such as schizophrenia, other psychotic disorders or major depression are relatively rare in the judicial population.

Findings regarding the prevalence of serious mental health disorders among criminal justice populations vary according to setting and methods of collecting data. For incarcerated offenders, the figure varies from seven to 16 percent (Ditton, 1999; Guy, Platt, Zwerling, & Bullock, 1985; Steadman, Fabisiak, Dvoskin, & Holohean, 1989; Teplin, 1990).

With respect to mental health disorders co-occurring with substance abuse in jail and prison populations, the estimates vary from three to 16 percent (Abramson, 1972; Pepper & Massaro, 1992; Steadman, Cocozza, & Melick, 1987; Teplin, 1990) with one report of 26 percent (Cote & Hogins, 1990). Peters and Hills (1996) provide a more conservative range of three to 11 percent.

We can view emotional or psychological disturbances among judicial clients as being either primary or secondary to substance abuse and criminal conduct (Mueser, Bennett & Kushner, 1995; Wanberg & Milkman, 1998). A primary psychological disturbance or disorder exists relatively independent from, yet interacts with, substance abuse and criminal conduct. For example, depression, anxiety or psychotic symptoms are underlying and primary.

The purpose of cognitive restructuring is to establish mental self-control. The skills of cognitive restructuring have been shown to be highly effective in achieving their goal of changing both proximal (thought habits) and distal (beliefs) structures that can result in positive and adaptive emotional and behavioral outcomes.

The eight sessions in *Module 8* address these areas with the assumption that most judicial clients have had psychological and emotional issues that interact with their substance abuse and criminal conduct; and that self-control over emotional problems reduces the risk of relapse and recidivism. Yet, the provider needs to be observant relative to which judicial clients have primary mental health issues and problems that need to be addressed beyond the scope of *SSC.*

The sessions in *Module 8* provide clients with specific cognitive restructuring skills to manage: negative thinking and beliefs; stress; errors in thinking; and the emotions of anger, guilt and depression. The methods and approaches used in *Module 8* are evidenced-based and there is a robust body of literature that supports the efficacy of this component

of CBT (see *Resource Guide,* Wanberg & Milkman, 2008). Some of the specific methods that are used in the *SSC* curriculum to help clients learn to change both the proximal and distal maladaptive cognitive structures that are used in are:

- self-talk;
- thought stopping;
- thought replacement;
- changing negative thinking;
- changing thinking errors;
- relaxation skills;
- managing and changing thoughts and core beliefs that lead to anger, depression, guilt, stress.

The introduction to *Module 8* and to each of the eight sessions, as presented in *Section III* of this *Guide,* provide substantive information around addressing the intrapersonal problems and issues of offenders.

Social and Relationship Skills Training (SRST)

Cognitive restructuring and mental self-control skills are essential for building positive relationships with others and the community. Yet, there are specific skills that can be used to develop and strengthen these relationships. They are usually referred to as coping and social skills training. *SSC* puts these into the category of social and relationship (interpersonal) skills training (SRST).

SRST emerged out of social learning theory (Bandura, 1977a) and has solid empirical evidence from outcome research that supports its efficacy in improving and increasing effectiveness of relationships, reducing psychological symptoms and increasing adherence to treatment involvement (e.g., Monti et al., 1989, 1995; Segrin, 2003). The various skills training components of SRST are widely applied to a variety of psychosocial problems (Segrin, 2003, p. 384). Its substantive approach began with assertiveness training (Alberti & Emmons, 1995; Lange & Jakubowski, 1976).

Libet and Lewinsohn (1973) define social skills as behaviors directed at producing or increasing positive reinforcement and reducing the possibility of punishing responses from the social environment. The result is an increased ability to engage in appropriate and effective interactions and communication with others, more meaningful living and "more satisfying, effective, and enjoyable interactions with other people" (Segrin, 2003, p. 385).

Appropriate social and interpersonal actions respect the rights of others, are prosocial, and stay within social and relational norms. Effective SRST will allow individuals to achieve their relationship goals (Segrin, 2003). However, the converse is true: it allows those interacting with others to achieve their goals. Effective interpersonal relationships are win-win.

Effective SRST approaches will involve several components and methods.

▶ **Assessment** or evaluating the specific social skills deficits of clients (Segrin, 2003).

▶ **Clarifying** the rationale for and description of the use of a particular skill which involves direct instruction or coaching (Segrin, 2003).

▶ **Modeling** or demonstrating both effective and ineffective responses to sample situations (Monti et al., 1995; Segrin, 2003).

▶ **Role playing** and practicing SRST skills using either standard vignettes or real situations in their lives followed by feedback on the effectiveness of skill usage.

▶ **Behavioral rehearsal** and continued practice over the course of several sessions. Providers will continually reach back to previously learned skills (including those in the mental self-control category) and have clients practice them in the current session or as homework.

▶ **Structured homework** and application to real-life situations.

▶ **Follow-up** and reassessment of skill application and proficiency.

The seven sessions in *SSC Module 9* focus on several specific areas that are designed to increase positive interpersonal and social relationships. These areas include:

▶ Refusal training;

▶ Communication skills which include conversation building and giving and receiving positive reinforcement;

▶ Assertiveness training;

▶ Interpersonal problem solving;

▶ Managing anger and other emotions in relationships;

▶ Building and maintaining close and intimate relationships.

The introduction to *Module 9* of this *Guide* discusses in more detail the concepts, issues and approaches to SRST, and each session provides guidelines in the delivery of SRST.

Social Responsibility Therapy (SRT)

SRT, referred to as either *Social Responsibility Therapy* or social responsibility training, is a sociocentric approach to enhance social and moral responsibility towards others and the community (Wanberg & Milkman, 1998; Wanberg, Milkman & Timken, 2005). SRT is seen as an expansion of and based on the core principles of CBT. We consider SRT to be a new wave of CB therapy in the treatment of substance abusing judicial offenders. We discuss SRT in more detail in the *Resource Guide*.

SRT is sociocentric, is directed at restructuring relationships with the community and addresses moral and social responsibility. Developing skills for social and moral responsibility and prosocial behavior in the community is an essential component of correctional treatment. This was an important part of our first edition of this work (Wanberg & Milkman, 1998), in our work on the education and treatment of impaired driving offenders (Wanberg, Milkman & Timken, 2005) and in our work *Criminal Conduct and Substance Abuse Treatment for Adolescents* (Milkman & Wanberg, 2005). SRT helps clients live not only according to their own values (egocentric focus), but also according to the values and laws of community and society - to live prosocially.

As stressed in several places in this *Guide,* traditional

CB treatment focuses on cognitive restructuring and interpersonal and social skills building. These are egocentric-oriented therapies. Both social skills training and cognitive restructuring focus on meeting the therapeutic needs of the individual and bringing about positive emotional and behavioral outcomes that are adaptive for the individual. They are crucial in the change process and provide the foundation for SRT. However, even though the spinoff from using these methods may be that others benefit from the individual's change and that the person becomes more prosocial, they alone are not sufficient in the treatment of substance abusing judicial clients.

In several places in this *Guide,* we define moral and community responsibility. Because of its importance in the treatment of offenders, we repeat the definition. Moral and community responsibility represent a set of ethical and principled thoughts, attitudes and behaviors that: respects the rights of others; adheres to laws of society; demonstrates positive regard for and caring about the welfare and safety of others; and contributes to the good of the community. It is engaging in responsible thinking and actions towards others and society.

One of the key components of SRT is empathy skills building. In *Chapter 2,* we discussed empathy in some depth, particularly empathy as a skill and as the basis of prosocial behavior. It is the specific focus of *Session 37* of *Module 10.* SRT is the primary focus of *Module 10.* Following are some specific focuses of SRT:

- Character building;
- Moral development and reasoning;
- Values clarification and development;
- Building prosocial attitudes and behaviors;
- Empathy skills building;
- Conflict resolution;
- Preventing aggression and preventing violence;
- Critical reasoning;
- Role modeling and mentoring;
- Changing criminal thinking and thinking errors;

- Engaging social and community reinforcement resources; and
- Integrating judicial sanctioning with the SRT focus.

SELF-EFFICACY: A FOCAL ISSUE IN CB TREATMENT

Self-efficacy (SE) is an important focus in CBT (e.g., Bandura, 1977b, 1995; Beck et al., 2004; Freeman, et al., 1990; Goldfried, 1995; Maisto, Carey & Bradizza, 1999; Rokke & Rehm, 2001; Wilson & O'Leary, 1980). Bandura (1977b) sees SE as the unifying construct of the social-cognitive framework of therapy and is a cognitive construct that relates to and strengthens self-control (Bandura, 1978). For a psychosocial intervention to be effective, it must alter a person's expectation of self-efficacy (Bandura, 1977b).

Wilson and O'Leary (1980) conclude that "efficacy expectations play a major part in the initiation, generalization, and maintenance of coping behavior" (p. 269) and are key concepts in behavioral change. Goldfried (1995) sees the facilitation of SE and the perceived sense of self-mastery and competence as a key focus in treatment. Marlatt (1985b) sees SE as a critical link in relapse prevention and an important determinant of self-control over substance abuse problems (Marlatt, Baer & Quigley, 1995).

Self-efficacy is defined as "a perception or judgement of one's capability to execute a particular course of action required to deal effectively with an impending situation" (Abrams & Niaura, 1987, p. 134). It is "perceived control," a belief that one is able to execute successfully the behavior required to produce a particular outcome, and "refers to the strength of our convictions about our personal effectiveness" (Sarason & Sarason, 1989, p. 76). Efficacy expectations have a major effect on whether a person initiates a coping behavior and how much effort will be put towards implementing that behavior (Bandura, 1982). SE is reinforced if the person copes successfully over time (Dimeff & Marlatt, 1995).

Bandura sees SE as perceived performance competency in specific situations and differs from the constructs of self-esteem and self-concept, the latter of which refers more to global constructs of self-image (Bandura 1977b, 1981, 1982). Marlatt also concludes (1985c) that SE is not a global, cross-situational construct or trait like self-esteem or locus of control, but a state-condition that refers to expectations or judgments about coping with specific situations. Helping clients increase their sense of self-efficacy is of particular importance during the action stage of change. Increasing perceived SE involves focusing on successful outcomes, strengthening positive decisions, and helping clients take ownership of their own change.

There is empirical evidence to indicate SE has a strong relationship to treatment outcome. This research is presented in the *Resource Guide* (Wanberg & Milkman, 2008). Perceived situational SE significantly affects: self-appraisals of adequacy in handling specific situations (Marlatt, 1985d, p. 130); performance accomplishments (Bandura, 1982); alcohol use outcomes (Maisto et al., 1999; Witkiewitz & Marlatt, 2007a); abstinence outcomes (Moore et al., 1996); alcohol consumption (Young et al., 1991); future alcohol use by adolescents (Hays & Ellickson, 1990); longer term abstinence (Miller et al., 1989); and levels of average daily consumption of alcohol (Solomon & Annis, 1990).

There is some debate as to whether SE is a short-term expectancy construct or a long-term, underlying belief structure. Although it is common to see SE as situation-specific (e.g., Bandura, 1977b, 1982; Marlatt, 1985b), it is also identified in some studies as a global or generic construct. Rokke and Rehm (2001) see SE as central to adequate functioning and to a sense of self-competency. Although they do not see it as a "single, overarching trait" (p. 177), they do see it as representing a system of beliefs. Each of these beliefs is specific to a particular area of functioning and refer to a set of cognitive skills. These skills are founded on the basis of experience and are situational and behavior specific.

Gleaning from our review of the literature, it appears that SE can be seen as both a short-term expectancy thought structure that leads to certain behaviors and outcomes (as in Seligman, Walker & Rosenhan, 2001, and Bandura, 1977b) and a generic belief

about self. We see it as part of the belief structure about the self and as an efficacy expectation as a thought habit or short-term structure that leads to specific emotional and behavioral outcomes. These outcomes will strengthen or weaken the efficacy expectancy thought habits and strengthen or weaken the underlying belief construct of self-efficacy.

THE CONTEXT OF CHANGE

The CB model as designed for *SSC* addresses the process of change and preventing relapse and recidivism within the context of the interaction of the individual's environmental situation and personality (including genetic predispositions, biochemical processes, and prior social learning experiences). It is a biopsychosocial process. It utilizes a variety of strategies to manage high-risk exposures that increase the probability of engaging in problematic AOD use (relapse) and criminal conduct (recidivism).

These high-risk exposures can be biological such as a strong physical urge to get high. High-risk exposures can be an increase of neurochemicals, resulting from drug withdrawal, that produces a state of agitation and stress and an urge to use a drug. They can be emotional such as in the arousal of anger. They can be cognitive, such as the manifestation of a core belief into thoughts that "I've been cheated" that subsequently lead to criminal thinking. They can be overtly behavioral such as committing a criminal act. They can be social-situational such as spending more time with former criminal associates. We look more closely at these high-risk exposures in *Chapter 5*.

The strategies for self-improvement and change include the management and change of environmental conditions and the engaging of social and community reinforcement resources. The approach is holistic in that it uses all concepts, methods, and approaches that increase clients' understanding of their past and present condition and provides them with the essential skills for self-control, management of high-risk exposures, and the development of prosocial attitudes and behaviors.

THE EMOTIONAL COMPONENT OF CBT

Most CB models assume that our thinking can lead

to certain emotions that result in certain behavioral outcomes. And most CB theorists see emotions and feelings as the consequence or outcome that precedes the behavior. The basic *SSC* model is that thinking leads to emotions, and these emotions are representations of self-control or lack of self-control. Thus, the automatic thought, "He's cheating me," leads to feelings of "I'm damn mad about that." The next logical consequence is a behavioral response. The CB model identifies a number of core emotions that result from thought habits coming out of intermediary cognitive structures and core beliefs. These are usually anger, guilt, depression or sadness.

THE *SSC* CB MODEL FOR CHANGE: THE *SSC* COGNITIVE-BEHAVIORAL MAP

The *SSC* cognitive-behavioral map (*SSC CB Map*), presented in *Figure 4.2,* is the core model used in *SSC* to help clients learn how cognitive structures lead to emotional and behavioral outcomes. The *SSC CB Map* provides clients with a tool for understanding and evaluating mental, emotional and behavioral responses to specific situations. It also provides them with a schemata and tool for changing cognitive structures (thoughts, attitudes, beliefs) that can lead to positive and adaptive outcomes. It is a powerful method that helps clients learn skills to manage and control emotional and behavioral outcomes in their lives.

The application of the *SSC CB Map* to changing AOD patterns and criminal conduct is based on five important assumptions. The **first assumption** is that patterns of AOD misuse and criminal conduct are determined by the individual's cognitive structures and processes that lead to emotions and feelings and result in overt AOD misuse and criminal behavior. *SSC* treatment is directed at restructuring the thinking and underlying beliefs resulting in a change in emotions and subsequently bringing about change in behavior.

The **second assumption** is that external events or inside memories and feelings can lead to automatic thoughts (thought habits) that are based on core beliefs about self and about the world. A primary focus is to help the client recognize those automatic thoughts or thought habits and the errors and dis-

tortions in thinking associated with those thoughts, and to change the core beliefs and intermediary attitudes, values, and rules that underlie the automatic thoughts and thinking distortions. The key guiding principle of *SSC* is that we can have control over our thoughts and feelings - we can change and choose our thoughts and our beliefs. Cognitive restructuring, interpersonal skills training and social responsibility therapy (SRT) are the vehicles through which change is achieved.

The **third assumption** is that automatic thoughts, which are based on core beliefs and attitudes, can lead to both positive and negative emotional outcomes, e.g., anger, resentment, guilt, depression, joy, happiness, contentment, and positive or negative behavioral outcomes. One objective of *SSC* is to help clients identify those emotions and their underlying cognitive structures. Sometimes it is necessary to first focus on the emotion and then work back to the underlying thought or thoughts leading to the emotion.

The **fourth assumption** is that cognitive structures team up with emotional outcomes to produce behavioral choices. The CBT model holds that individuals consciously choose their behavioral responses (e.g., criminal conduct) to external events and to their internal thoughts and feelings. Social and community responsibility skills training provides key interventions in helping judicial clients learn to choose adaptive behaviors that manage outside events and internal feelings and that lead to prosocial outcomes.

Finally, the **fifth assumption** is that the coping behaviors or actions we choose and the outcomes of those actions reinforce internal thoughts, underlying beliefs and the mediating assumptions that lead to those behaviors. When the outcomes are positive (increase pleasure, decrease negative events), the behaviors leading to the outcomes are reinforced. When the outcomes are negative, they should decrease the probability of the behavior leading to the outcome. This does not always happen, and behaviors that result in bad outcomes often repeat themselves. This is because both positive (adaptive) and negative (maladaptive) outcomes can strengthen the cognitive structures that lead to these outcomes. Unless these structures (thought habits and underlying beliefs) are changed, the behaviors resulting from these structures will continue to occur. Thus, there are two reinforcement pathways to the *SSC* CB model: behaviors are reinforced because they lead to desirable outcomes; the cognitive structures that lead to behavioral outcomes are reinforced.

Figure 4.2 provides the basic CB model for the process of learning and change used in *SSC* and explains the two pathways for behavioral reinforcement. Using *Figure 4.2*, we summarize the above five assumptions that explain how the *SSC CB Map* model works. Automatic thoughts (based on underlying beliefs, attitudes, values) are responses to specific internal or external situations. These responses lead to emotions and behaviors that are adaptive (they lead to positive outcomes) or maladaptive (they lead to negative outcomes). If the behavior results in a positive outcome, then that behavior gets reinforced, as

indicated by the return arrow from positive outcome back to adaptive positive action (upper right corner of *Figure 4.2*). Note that there is no comparable return arrow in the lower right of *Figure 4.2*, from negative outcomes back to negative maladaptive behavior or action. However, there are return arrows leading back to automatic thoughts from both positive outcomes and negative outcomes. This implies that the automatic thoughts and underlying beliefs can get reinforced, whether the outcome is positive or whether the outcome is negative.

In *Phase I,* the *SSC CB Map* is used in each session to help clients understand their responses to external and internal events and the CB process resulting from those events. Clients use the *SSC CB Map* to analyze their responses to internal and external situations in their daily experiences. The *Map* is applied to both good and bad outcomes. At times, the provider will

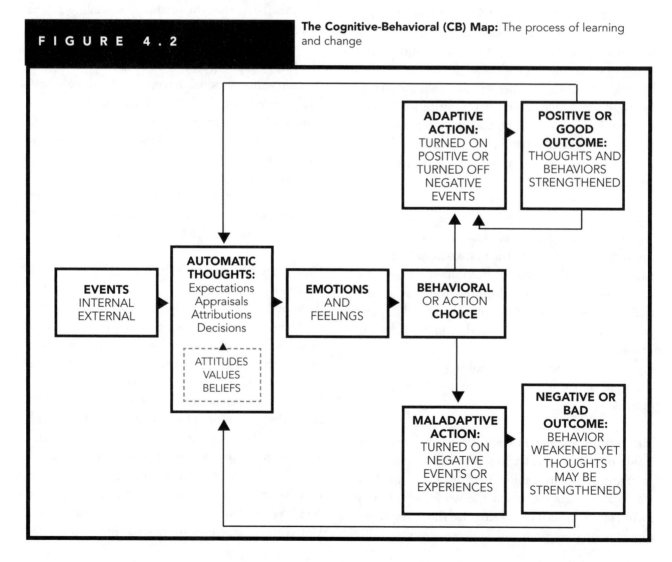

FIGURE 4.2

The Cognitive-Behavioral (CB) Map: The process of learning and change take the client back through the *Map* in order to get a positive outcome. In *Phase II*, the focus is on using the *CB Map* to generate positive outcomes. This is the *STEP* model - **S**ituation - **T**hinking change - **E**motional response - **P**ositive outcome.

STEP is a component of the *SSC CB Map* that facilitates an immediate thought pattern that generates positive outcomes. However, the *CB Map* is the core *SSC* model for understanding the change process and the ongoing basic tool for helping clients change cognitive structures that lead to negative and maladaptive outcomes.

We use this report by Kevin, a 26-year-old *SSC* client who had completed *Modules 8 and 9* to explain how the *CB Map Exercise* is utilized and to identify the cognitive-emotional-behavior components of the *CB Map*.

I got a call from an old friend - I won't call him a friend now - who I used to get high with, did some dealing with and we did some break-ins to get dough for our drugs (**Situation**). He wanted to get together - you know, go over the old stuff we did. He'd served four and had been out about a month. I said - "OK" (**decision**) and thought, can't do no harm (**appraisal**). Anyway, thought it'd help get me out of feeling like shit, you know, depressed because my boss has been screwing me over (**attribution-appraisal**). And that old thought came back - "I've been screwed over so many GD times - life is not worth shit" (**core belief**). But I got kind of excited (**emotions**) - the thought of talking about old times and even getting high - hadn't gotten high since being out on parole - what's it been 6 months. He led me to believe that he was doing drugs and also making some hits on some houses on the east side. Now I know that's a big high-risk deal - I saw that (**appraisal**). But I told him I'd meet him after work (**decision**). So I was on my way the next day - was getting close to the hangout to have a couple beers. Now, I've been clean since hitting the streets. Then bam! It hit me. I got all sweaty. I'm thinking, "I'm setting myself up" (**appraisal - moving from automatic transmission to manual shifting**). And I thought back on what I've learned here. And I said, "No way man! Too much to lose" (**appraisal - thought change and enhanced self-efficacy in handling high-risk situation and thinking**). So I pulled my car over and got on my cell. Hell, everybody has one. I told him "Listen man, I'd like to see you, but I can't (**decision**). I'm not strong enough. But tell you what. I'm going to a meeting at Vine. Meet me there if you want (**assertiveness skill**)." I hung up and just sat

there - so relieved (**appraisal - positive outcome**) even shaking. I got on it again and told my woman what had happened - that I'm going to a meeting - but be home at six. I could tell she was relieved - she said she was proud of me (**external reinforcement**). But it works. I even felt proud of myself (**internal self-reinforcement**).

CHAPTER REVIEW

Contemporary CBT is an integration of the key components of behavioral and cognitive therapy with cognitive restructuring representing the cognitive part and social skills training the behavioral component. The combining element of CBT is found in the principle of **self-reinforcement.**

Literature support for the efficacy of CBT with substance abusing offenders was summarized. The CB assumptions underlying criminal conduct and substance abuse were discussed and the specific cognitive structures and the processes that energize the expression of these structures were summarized. These structures and processes are a primary focus in *SSC* for bringing about self-improvement and change. These structures are often manifested through automatic thinking. One goal of treatment is to help clients learn to move to "manual shifting" and get conscious control of these automatic thoughts.

The three CB methods used in *SSC* were discussed: 1) cognitive restructuring; 2) social and relationship skills training (SRST); and 3) social responsibility therapy (SRT). SRT is a sociocentric therapy and is a shift from the traditional CBT treatment paradigm. It is an essential component in the treatment of substance abusing judicial clients with a focus on character building, moral development, and building prosocial attitudes and behaviors.

The *CB Map* is used throughout *SSC* to help clients learn how cognitive structures lead to emotional and behavioral outcomes and to use this map as a tool for changing thoughts, attitudes and beliefs that result in positive and adaptive outcomes. The *SSC CB Map* provides clients with a powerful method to manage and control behavioral outcomes in their lives.

CHAPTER 5: Relapse and Recidivism Prevention

CHAPTER OUTLINE

OVERVIEW

RELAPSE PREVENTION: A MAJOR PARADIGM SHIFT

ADDRESSING RECIDIVISM PREVENTION

OVERVIEW OF MARLATT'S RELAPSE PREVENTION MODEL

THE RELAPSE AND RECIDIVISM MODEL USED IN *SSC*

**Defining Relapse and Recidivism
Adaptation of the Marlatt Model**

*High-risk exposures and R&R
Weak versus strong coping skills
Self-efficacy or self-mastery
Expected outcomes
Rule violation effect (RVE)
Perceived self-control and attribution*

**Pathways to Relapse and Recidivism
Pathways to R&R Prevention
Developing a Relapse Prevention Plan
Strengthening R&R Prevention: A Balanced and
  Healthy Lifestyle
SSC as an Integrated Effort to Prevent R&R**

CHAPTER REVIEW

CHAPTER OBJECTIVES

▶ Introduce the reader to the major paradigm shift that brought relapse prevention to the forefront of substance abuse treatment.

▶ Provide a brief summary of the Marlatt relapse prevention model.

▶ Show how the Marlatt model is adapted and used to develop a relapse and recidivism (R&R) model that can be utilized in the treatment of the SA (substance abusing) judicial client.

▶ Discuss the specific R&R approach used in *SSC* and show how this model provides the map for describing the pathways to R&R and the pathways to preventing R&R.

▶ Provide an understanding of how R&R prevention is strengthened through changing living patterns that can lead to a balanced and healthy lifestyle.

▶ Describe how *SSC* as a whole is an integrated effort in preventing R&R.

OVERVIEW

Criminal conduct and substance abuse treatment is about preventing relapse and recidivism (R&R). As discussed in *Chapter 1,* this is the **sixth core strategy** of *SSC* and one of its five foundational models.

In the *Resource Guide* (Wanberg & Milkman, 2008), we more thoroughly address relapse and recidivism in the treatment of the SA judicial client. We describe the evolution and development of relapse prevention (RP) and also different models and approaches to both relapse and recidivism prevention.

The purpose of this chapter is to describe the relapse and recidivism (R&R) model and strategies specifically used in *SSC.* These strategies are based on an adaptation of the Marlatt RP model (1985a: Marlatt & Witkiewitz, 2005). We first look at the major paradigm shift in addressing relapse in the treatment of substance abusing clients that occurred around the mid-1980s. We then provide a brief summary of how recidivism has been addressed in the correctional literature. Marlatt's RP model is then briefly summarized. We then describe the R&R model used in *SSC* and start with showing how the Marlatt model was adapted to apply to both relapse and recidivism in the treatment of SA judicial clients. *SSC* approaches the treatment of R&R prevention in two steps. First, clients are presented with the pathways to R&R which are discussed in this chapter. It is important that clients clearly understand these pathways and the process of R&R. Second, clients are shown the pathways and process to preventing R&R along with a skills map for R&R prevention. These pathways and skills map are also presented in this chapter.

Although this chapter provides a presentation of R&R and the R&R prevention model used in *SSC,* some of the most important information in this chapter is again summarized in the *Introduction to Module 6, Understanding and Preventing Relapse and Recidivism* of this *Guide,* and in *Sessions 15, 16, 43* and *44* of the *Workbook.* This repetition is intentional considering the extreme importance of the role of R&R prevention in the overall treatment approach of *SSC.*

RELAPSE PREVENTION: A MAJOR PARADIGM SHIFT

Prior to the 1980s, alcohol and drug treatment programs did not address relapse. In fact, the first author's experience working in alcohol treatment programs in the 1960s and 1970s found that the topic was often avoided. This was based, in part, on what Washton and Zweben (2006) identify as the "clinician's fears that even raising the topic of relapse with patients might communicate an expectation of failure and promote a self-fulfilling prophesy of failure by giving patients 'permission' to use alcohol and other drugs again" (p. 207).

Whether or not it was addressed in treatment, the fact was that relapse did happen. Early studies by Marlatt and associates and others in the field in the 1980s indicate that one-year post-treatment relapse rates ranged from 50% to 80% (see Milkman & Wanberg, 2007; Wanberg & Milkman, 1998; Wanberg & Milkman, 2008).

Recognizing these attitudes and findings, Marlatt and Gordon (1985) addressed the relapse problem head on and published their seminal - and classic - work: *Relapse Prevention: Maintenance Strategies in the Treatment of Addictive Behaviors.* This work resulted in a major paradigm shift in the treatment of addictive disorders. Since then, relapse prevention has become an integral part of the treatment of addictive disorders. Virtually every text addressing addictions treatment includes a substantive focus on relapse prevention.

ADDRESSING RECIDIVISM PREVENTION

The issue of recidivism and operational treatment models designed to prevent recidivism is not as clearly addressed in works that address the treatment of offenders with the co-occurrence of substance abuse. Perusal of the indexes or tables of contents of texts in the area of correctional treatment, and more specifically, treatment of SA judicial clients, will reveal substantive treatment of relapse prevention, but not a clear and distinct approach to recidivism prevention - although recidivism as a general topic is certainly addressed. It is of note that Andrews and Bonta, who provide probably the most thorough review of the correctional treatment literature, did not reference any major work that provided a discrete and substantive presentation of recidivism prevention per se.

Taxman (2004), in her chapter on *Reducing Recidivism,* did provide 12 principles for effective systems of care that are designed to reduce recidivism and increase treatment retention within the judicial system. They are briefly summarized.

1. Make recidivism reduction the goal.

2. Treatment and criminal justice system features must be policy driven.

3. Treatment and criminal justice professionals must function as a team. This is compatible with the *SSC* strategy of integrating the therapeutic and the correctional.

4. Use drug testing to manage offender behavior.

5. Target offenders whose treatment will have broad impact.

6. Use treatment matching practices.

7. Create a treatment process and extend length of time in treatment.

8. Use behavioral contracts.

9. Use special agents to supervise offenders in treatment.

10. Sanction non-compliant behavior.

11. Reward positive behavior.

12. Focus on quality, not quantity.

Even though these principles do not represent a specific treatment model for recidivism prevention, they provide important guidelines for the judicial system in addressing recidivism.

Most often, recidivism prevention is addressed within the framework of relapse prevention. All too often, it is assumed that when treating substance abusing judicial clients, if one prevents relapse, then recidivism is taken care of. This is simply not the case. It is argued in a number of places in this work that relapse and recidivism are separate but related phenomena. Each must be addressed in its own right.

If we boil down the essence of the treatment of offenders with the co-occurrence of substance abuse, it has to do with relapse and recidivism prevention. We contend that these are the two primary treatment goals of the treatment of individuals with a history of substance abuse and criminal conduct. Efforts to address other areas of concern, such as anxiety, depression, relationship problems, etc., are done with these two primary treatment goals in mind.

In our first edition to this work, we provided a clear and distinct model for addressing recidivism prevention, based on a modification of the Marlatt relapse prevention model. Since that edition, we have modified and enhanced this model and applied it to the education and treatment of impaired driving offenders (Wanberg, Milkman & Timken, 2005) and adolescents (Milkman & Wanberg, 2005). We briefly review the Marlatt RP model and then present the specific R&R model used in *SSC.*

OVERVIEW OF MARLATT'S RELAPSE PREVENTION MODEL

Relapse prevention (RP) is a CBT self-management program "that combines behavioral skills training with cognitive intervention techniques to assist individuals in maintaining desired behavioral changes" (Marlatt & Barrett, 1994, p. 285). Clients are taught new coping responses (e.g., alternatives to addictive behavior); they learn to modify maladaptive beliefs and expectancies concerning their behavior; and they learn to change personal habits and lifestyles. The Marlatt RP model has been used as an adjunct to treatment programs and also as a stand-alone program for the cessation and maintenance phases of addiction treatment (Dimeff & Marlatt, 1995). A stand-alone Marlatt RP program is summarized in Dimeff and Marlatt.

In the Marlatt model, relapse is defined "as any violation of a self-imposed rule regarding a particular behavior" (Dimeff & Marlatt, 1995, p. 180). The model stresses that relapse must be reframed from the traditional "all-or nothing" view to the idea that it is a transitional process in which slips or lapses may or may not result in a full return to the level of the pretreatment substance use pattern. A single occurrence is different from a full-blown relapse (Dimeff & Marlatt, 1995). The model defines prolapse as another outcome of a lapse - getting "back on track" in the direction of a positive change (Marlatt, 1985a; Marlatt & Witkiewitz, 2005).

The Marlatt model is presented in *Figure 5.1*. The specific elements of the model are briefly discussed, and then presented in more detail as they are applied to the relapse and recidivism (R&R) model used in SSC. We first look at the left side of *Figure 5.1*. The initial step to relapse occurs when the individual's self-control is confronted with **high-risk (HR) situations.** HR situations can be external or internal cues that can set off the relapse process.

An **ineffective coping response** to a HR situation makes the person more vulnerable to relapse. A lack of effective coping responses may lead to a **decrease in self-efficacy** - a sense of not being able to successfully manage a given situation. The potential for relapse is increased when the lack of effective coping skills and decreased self-efficacy is combined with the individual's perception of **positive outcome expectancies** from drinking or using other drugs.

Thus, the dynamic interaction of multiple factors (e.g., HR situation, ineffective coping skills, etc.) can lead to an **initial lapse** - taking a few drinks after being abstinent for several weeks or months. An important part of the Marlatt RP model is to help clients deal with a lapse so that it does not lead to a full-blown relapse.

Interacting with these various factors is the **rule violation effect** (RVE). RVE is used to explain how lapses can lead to full relapse and to help the client manage lapses or slips (Curry & Marlatt, 1987; Dimeff & Marlatt, 1995; Marlatt, 1985a). RVE is the result of violating the individual's rule to change target behaviors. When RVE refers specifically to abstinence, then it is appropriate to use the expression abstinence violation effect (AVE), a term used earlier and also in Marlatt's most recent treatment of RP (Marlatt & Witkiewitz, 2005).

The right side of *Figure 5.1* shows the prevention process. The first step in Marlatt's RP model is to help the client identify HR situations. The second step is to help the client build coping and problem solving skills to deal with HR situations without returning to the use of substances. Utilization of effective coping responses to replace ineffective coping responses results in an increase in self-control and self-efficacy. Self-efficacy is strengthened over time. As this occurs, and as the individual experiences success in coping with high-risk situations through using effective coping skills, the probability of relapse decreases.

Finally, the Marlatt Relapse Prevention (RP) model focuses on helping the client deal with life-style imbalances that occur between the individual's perceived external demands or "shoulds" and perceived desires or "wants." Strong imbalances in the direction of "shoulds" may lead to strong feelings of being deprived and a desire to indulge (even to the point of a craving or urge). The goal is to help the client build a balanced life-style which ultimately helps to manage HR situations that can lead to relapse. The Marlatt RP model has developed global intervention procedures aimed at helping the client to build a balanced life-style. This includes developing coping skills to effectively manage factors that are precursors to high-risk situations and relapse (Dimeff & Marlatt, 1995).

The Marlatt model identifies intrapersonal and interpersonal determinants of lapse and relapse which, when redefined, are also determinants of decreased probability of relapse (Marlatt & Witkiewitz, 2005). The intrapersonal determinants include:

▶ Self-efficacy or the degree to which individuals perceive their ability to perform certain behaviors in specific situations - **or** lack of self-efficacy reduces the capacity to handle a specific HR situation and increases the probability of relapse;

▶ Outcome expectancies or the positive effects that are perceived to be derived from AOD use or other behaviors associated with substance use - **or** expectations of the positive outcomes of preventing relapse;

▶ Lack of motivation to engage in change - **or** motivation for positive behavioral change;

- Lack of cognitive and behavioral coping skills to manage HR situations - **or** CB coping skills that manage those situations that are high-risk for relapse;

- Negative or positive emotional states which are strong predictors of relapse - **or** restructuring thoughts leading to positive emotional states that prevent relapse;

- Cravings and urges with some individuals can lead to relapse - **or** managing these cravings and urges to prevent relapse. A thorough discussion of cravings and urges is found in *Session 17* of *Section III* of this *Guide* and *Session 17* is devoted to helping clients manage urges and cravings.

The interpersonal determinants relate mainly to the lack of social support as a predictor of relapse or the positive social support that is highly predictive of long-term abstinence (see references in Marlatt & Witkiewitz, 2005, p. 20).

Building on the model described in *Figure 5.1,* Marlatt and Witkiewitz (2005; Witkiwitz & Marlatt, 2007b) have provided a more dynamic reconceptualization of the relapse process. This conceptualizes the determinants of relapse as multidimensional and that there is a dynamic interaction among the several conditions that lead up to a relapse. The composite of an individual's responses leading up to a relapse is seen as a self-organizing system that comprises: distal factors (family history of drug abuse or antisocial behavior, co-morbidities, history of lack of social support); and proximal factors such as cravings, motivation, decision making, and CB coping skills. Although these factors may be going on at the same time, small changes in one can precipitate relapse.

Marlatt and Witkiewitz (2005) point out that this dynamic and multidimensional approach is congruent with catastrophe theory (Thom, 1975), which is based on a nonlinear model, and explains large and sudden changes resulting from slight yet continuous alterations in situational, behavioral or environmental variables. Hufford et al. (2003) applied this model to predicting post-treatment relapses. They found it to be a better predictor of relapse, predicting, for example, 58% of inpatient relapses versus a linear

model predicting 19% of inpatient relapses.

The dynamic-multidimensional model is also congruent with seeing relapse as an erosion process. A number of factors can contribute to the eroding away or deterioration of the topsoil. Each of these factors, by itself, will have little impact on soil erosion and deterioration. Yet, a moderate rain storm that typically may not cause serious erosion and deterioration, but that is preceded by an unusually dry period, failure to maintain proper levels of organic matter in the soil, and failure to adequately rotate crops, can result in more serious soil deterioration. The same holds true with relapse. A client, after being exposed to a series of HR situations and getting lax in applying coping skills to these situations, may relapse after having a rather minor conflict with an intimate partner.

Seeing relapse as based on the dynamic interaction among several conditions is similar to Andrews and Bonta's (2003) dynamic and static risk factors of predicting recidivism. They would see the distal factors as static, and the proximal (readily available) factors as dynamic.

THE RELAPSE AND RECIDIVISM MODEL USED IN *SSC*

SSC uses an adaptation of the Marlatt model to develop a model for relapse and recidivism (R&R) prevention. Justification for this adaptation is based on two important facts that are found in the literature addressing substance abuse and criminal conduct. **First,** there is a robust relationship between substance abuse and criminal conduct (see Wanberg & Milkman, 2008). Drug-involved offenders comprise the majority of incarcerates. The number of offenders reporting use of illicit drugs during their lifetime varies from 70% to 90%. From 50% to 70% report regular use of alcohol. From 50% to 70% have a lifetime diagnosis of substance abuse or dependence. And, studies reporting the percent on drugs or alcohol at the time of the committing offense varies from 50% to 80%.

Second, our review of the relapse and recidivism literature (Wanberg & Milkman, 1998; Wanberg, Milkman & Timken, 2005) showed striking similar-

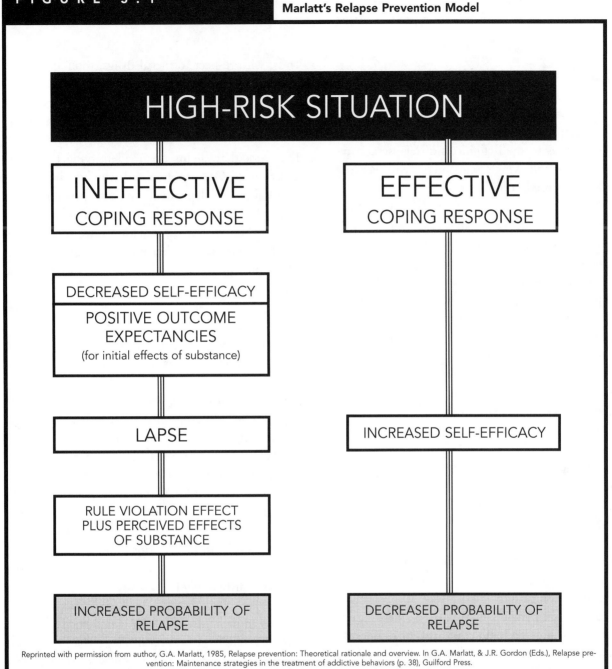

FIGURE 5.1   **Marlatt's Relapse Prevention Model**

HIGH-RISK SITUATION

INEFFECTIVE
COPING RESPONSE

EFFECTIVE
COPING RESPONSE

DECREASED SELF-EFFICACY

POSITIVE OUTCOME
EXPECTANCIES
(for initial effects of substance)

LAPSE

INCREASED SELF-EFFICACY

RULE VIOLATION EFFECT
PLUS PERCEIVED EFFECTS
OF SUBSTANCE

INCREASED PROBABILITY OF
RELAPSE

DECREASED PROBABILITY OF
RELAPSE

Reprinted with permission from author, G.A. Marlatt, 1985, Relapse prevention: Theoretical rationale and overview. In G.A. Marlatt, & J.R. Gordon (Eds.), Relapse prevention: Maintenance strategies in the treatment of addictive behaviors (p. 38), Guilford Press.

ities between relapse and recidivism with respect to the process, the outcome rates (about 65% to 70%), and the high-risk thinking and situations that can be triggers for both relapse and recidivism.

The work of Andrews and Bonta makes it clear that punishment and sanctioning do not prevent recidivism, and that clinically relevant treatment services have the best promise for reducing recidivism (1994, 2003). Any viable approach for substance abusing judicial clients must include both relapse and recidivism prevention using a structured and evidence-based model. We concluded that the most clinically relevant model would be an adaptation of the Marlatt model to address both relapse and recidivism in judicial clients (Wanberg & Milkman, 1998).

In this second edition of *SSC*, the adaptation of the Marlatt RP model is further refined and is shown in *Figures 5.2, 5.3* and *5.4*. These same figures are provided in *Sessions 15* and *16* of the *Participant's Workbook.* Before looking at the specific R&R model used in *SSC,* we will define terms related to relapse and recidivism.

Defining Relapse and Recidivism

It is important to have a working definition of terms around relapse and recidivism. Sources in the literature vary as to the definitions of relapse and recidivism. The following discussion presents working definitions as used in *SSC.*

We define the **process of relapse** as engaging in HR (high-risk) exposures (to be discussed below) that put the individual at risk of returning to AOD use or a pattern of AOD use that can lead to prior levels of abuse. Engaging in a pattern of thinking about having a few drinks puts the person into the process of relapse. A **lapse** is any use of alcohol that can lead to a problem use pattern after the individual has committed to a non-harmful pattern of alcohol use; or for the goal of total abstinence, any use of alcohol or illegal drugs. For illegal drugs, a lapse is the use of any illegal drug.

A **full relapse** is engaging in or returning to a pattern of alcohol use or the use of other drugs that causes problems, is harmful and upsetting to the individual and to others. Although there is some debate around when to define relapse, the *SSC* position is that the concept of relapse applies to situations where the individual has made the decision to stop use or stop the problem use pattern. In our view, relapse would not apply to the person who is into a clear pattern of problem use, **has made no conscious or deliberate decision to change or stop that use,** but who may stop for a short time and then again take up the pattern of use.

Although clients are asked to determine their own relapse prevention (RP) goal, it is made clear that *SSC* identifies two acceptable goals of relapse prevention.

▶ Total abstinence from AOD use - or living an AOD-free life which *SSC* recommends for all clients.

▶ Living an alcohol-problem free life; and abstaining from the use of all illegal drugs and from the misuse of prescription drugs.

Thus, with respect to illegal drugs, total abstinence is the only goal acceptable in the *SSC* program. As well, use of illegal drugs involves the possession of illegal drugs, which is engaging in illegal behavior.

The work that clients do in identifying the severity of their AOD problem and whether they fit the AOD abuse or dependence pattern provides them with information to make the decision of which RP goal to choose. For those with a history of alcohol problems, particularly dependence or abuse, a strong case is presented that total abstinence should be the goal.

Definitions around recidivism are somewhat different from those concerning relapse. We define the **process of recidivism** as engaging in high-risk exposures that can lead to recidivism. For example, a person is into recidivism when thinking about committing a crime, spending time with criminal associates, or engaging in patterns of thinking and behaving that have preceded criminal conduct in the past. We define **full recidivism** as reoffending or committing a criminal act. With CC, we apply the rule of zero tolerance. We do not need to apply zero tolerance criteria to alcohol use, or for that matter, in most cases, relapse into illegal drugs. Thus, an individual may return to the use of illegal drugs, and that does not necessarily imply CC recidivism.

Relapse into the use of illegal drugs involves a grey area. Certainly, possession of illegal drugs is breaking the law. And, relapse into illegal drugs will require informing the judicial system of this behavior. The provider can have treatment tolerance towards relapse into the use of illegal drugs without instituting sanctioning as long as this relapse:

▶ does not constitute a major reoffending act, such as selling illegal drugs;

▶ is addressed within the context of and involvement with the judicial system and the judicial system agrees not to sanction the relapse; and

▶ constitutes a brief regression within a larger pattern of treatment progress and the judicial client shows a positive effort to reengage the treatment process, reestablish the use of R&R prevention skills, and again commit to the goal of total abstinence from the use of illegal drugs.

Outside of this grey area of relapsing into the use of illegal drugs, the zero tolerance criterion to criminal conduct is applied. Thus, correctional treatment works with the process of recidivism, giving clients cognitive and behavioral skills to manage high-risk exposures to recidivism. The provider works with the judicial client therapeutically and correctionally.

This is not to say that judicial clients who reoffend are "written off." When possible, they are provided continued treatment services. In the *SSC* model, clients' lapse and relapse patterns are accepted and worked with through educational and treatment processes. With criminal behavior, full recidivism is sanctioned.

Adaptation of the Marlatt Model

There are a number of elements of the Marlatt model that we have enhanced so as fit the substance abusing (SA) judicial client, and to best explain recidivism and recidivism prevention. As well, it is important to note that the *SSC* R&R model is congruent with the *SSC* CB Model for change presented in *Figure 4.2,* page 78 of this *Guide.* The *SSC* R&R approach is also discussed in *Modules 6* and *11* in *Section III* of this *Guide,* and also in the *SSC Resource Guide* (Wanberg & Milkman, 2008). *Figures 5.2* through *5.4* provide a graphic description of the process and prevention of R&R used in the *SSC* curriculum.

Figure 5.2, an adaptation of the Marlatt model presented in *Figure 5.1,* shows the process of relapse and recidivism. Again, although it is presented in a linear fashion, the process does not necessarily follow in the step-wise fashion illustrated. Also, for some clients, one of the steps may have greater weight than others in either precipitating or preventing relapse or recidivism.

The Marlatt model has been adapted and enhanced

in several ways. First, we use the term HR exposures to take into account cognitive, emotional, and behavioral factors that can increase the risk of both relapse and recidivism. Second, we have included criminal conduct (recidivism) along with AOD use and abuse (relapse) in the various components of the model. Third, we have enhanced the elements on the right side of the figure. We discuss each of the components presented in *Figure 5.2.*

High-risk exposures and R&R

R&R is a dynamic and multiple-factor process encompassing gradual processes of erosion that involve HR exposures: HR thinking (I'll get drunk); HR situations (drinking soft drinks with friends at the bar); HR feelings (intense anger); and HR distal cognitions such as attitudes and beliefs (I won't get caught). Relapse can start with the HR thought "I deserve to get high, just one more time." Or, recidivism can begin with the thought "The only way I can pay my rent is to sell some drugs." Thus, R&R refers to lapsing back to thoughts, feelings, and actions that lead to AOD use or committing a crime. R&R does not necessarily mean that the person has engaged in committing a crime or using a substance.

HR exposures threaten the sense of self-control (self-efficacy) thereby increasing the risk for R&R. These exposures can be internal or external. An example of an external HR exposure would be making the decision to spend time with an old criminal associate who is still into doing crimes. An internal HR exposure would be memories of being physically abused by a parent that justifies thinking "I have more coming, I deserve more."

Weak versus strong coping skills

A major focus of *SSC* is to help clients learn and strengthen skills to manage HR exposures and to develop a healthy relationship with self, others and the community. Weak coping skills enhance the probability of R&R; strong coping skills decrease the probability of R&R. Strong coping skills include cognitive, interpersonal, and community responsibility skills.

Module 8 focuses on building intrapersonal or cognitive restructuring skills to change thinking, attitudes and core beliefs that can lead to relapse or recidivism. *Module 9* focuses on building relationship or interpersonal skills that lead to positive and prosocial relationship outcomes. Social and relationship skills training (SRST) represents the basic treatment approach for this focus. *Module 10* focuses on the goal of building social responsibility skills that enhance victim empathy, moral responsibility and prosocial behavior in the community. Social responsibility therapy (SRT) is the therapeutic approach used to achieve this goal.

Self-efficacy or self-mastery

As discussed in *Chapter 4,* self-efficacy was described from two different perspectives.

▶ Efficacy expectation is a short-term cognitive structure (i.e., state) that determines or influences the individual's perception of how well specific situations can be handled or whether a person can initiate a specific coping skill in specific situations.

▶ A belief structure (i.e., trait) about the self that is central to adequate functioning and to a sense of self-confidence.

Self-efficacy as 1) an expectation in self-performance in specific situations and 2) as an underlying belief about the self is focal to CBT and to the treatment of substance abuse. Specific to R&R, self-efficacy or self-mastery is the clients' judgement about how well they are coping with the HR exposures and whether they have succeeded or failed when exposed to similar past HR exposures. If clients have learned skills to manage high-risk exposures, they will develop stronger coping responses, an increased sense of self-mastery, and a decrease in the probability of relapse or recidivism. Failure to use skills to cope with HR exposures will result in a decrease in a sense of self-efficacy.

Expected outcomes

An expected desired effect from AOD use such as feeling good, or committing a crime to feel powerful or in control will further increase the risk of R&R.

These positive outcomes are powerful reinforcers of these behaviors. The expected positive effects of AOD use or CC will have greater impact when the individual lacks the skills to handle HR exposures and subsequently experiences a decrease in efficacy expectations in handling specific HR exposures. Expected positive outcomes of AOD use and CC will tend to override the sense of self-efficacy clients may have, and set the stage for an initial AOD lapse or engaging in patterns of thinking and behaving that lead to CC.

However, expected positive outcomes of the deliberate and conscious use of learned skills to manage HR exposures can be just as powerful in preventing lapses into AOD use or behaviors and thinking that lead to CC. Positive outcomes serve to reinforce the use of these skills. The result is an increase in self-control and self-efficacy, a sense of self-empowerment and control, and a strengthening of a positive belief about self.

In both of these cases, "expected effects" may be quite different from "real effects." Although clients may expect a positive outcome of AOD use or CC, the actual outcome is often negative. The treatment process can capitalize on this negative outcome and help the client to reengage in the necessary skills to prevent full relapse. Or, clients may "catch" themselves in the process of recidivism and reengage in the use of skills to manage criminal thinking or behaviors that would set themselves up for engaging in CC.

Likewise, the expected outcome of using strong coping skills may be different from the "real effects." Clients discover that the skills do not always work with some HR exposures, and find themselves engaging in thinking and behaviors that make them vulnerable to engaging in CC. Providers who see clients in this position need to increase their therapeutic and even correctional support, and maximize the opportunity to reinforce positive outcomes from the use of coping skills so as to prevent full recidivism.

Rule violation effect (RVE)

Clients become vulnerable to the RVE when they have established a self-perception of being "clean" or "going straight." Then, when they violate the rule of "never using drugs," or to "never to see old criminal buddies again" they experience the RVE. Their sense or view of self is violated. They experience inner conflict. One way to solve this conflict is to return to their old view of themselves - acceptance of using drugs, or engaging in criminal thinking and even behavior. The strength of this rule violation will depend on: 1) how much conflict and guilt they experience in violating their rule; 2) how much they attribute their relapse or engaging in the process of recidivism to their own personal weaknesses; and 3) how much they blame others for their RVE.

When RVE is combined with a perceived positive outcome from engaging in AOD use or CC and a perceived decrease in self-efficacy, the probability for R&R increases. However, when clients continue to hold on to the view that they will not relapse into a problem of AOD use or recidivate back into criminal conduct, and when their use of coping skills brings positive outcomes, the probability of R&R decreases.

Perceived self-control and attribution

When clients find themselves engaging in relapse or recidivism behavior and believe that these behaviors are due to personal "weakness," they experience a sense of loss of self-control and decreased self-efficacy. This attribution strengthens the impact of the RVE and increases the probability of continuing in the process of relapse and recidivism. This attribution becomes a more powerful influence in R&R, and in loss of self-control, when clients experience a high degree of guilt and conflict around the RVE.

As noted above, another factor that can strengthen the impact of RVE is when clients blame others for their lapses or for engaging in thinking and behaviors that can lead to CC. Externalizing blame will mitigate the use of coping skills and provide justification and rationalization for the R&R process in which they find themselves. This kind of attribution represents a regression into cognitive processes that were foundational to the development of CC.

However, when clients engage in skills that handle HR exposures and credit themselves with stopping

at the point of initial relapse or stopping at initial recidivism (deciding not to go visit an old criminal associate) then the probability of R&R is reduced. This self-attribution involves accepting responsibility for their engaging in the process of R&R. The consequence is an increase in self-control and self-efficacy.

Pathways to Relapse and Recidivism

Figure 5.2 is an important map that is used in helping *SSC* clients understand the process of R&R prevention. However, *Figure 5.3* provides a graphic representation of examples of specific high-risk exposures that can lead to relapse or recidivism. Note that the arrows that lead back and forth between the high-risk exposures to relapse and recidivism indicate that the pathways of relapse and recidivism are linked. For example, HR thinking around relapse can cross over to HR thinking around criminal conduct. Or, relapse behaviors, such as drinking at a bar, could lead to meeting criminal associates to plan a crime.

Yet, the pathways should be viewed as separate processes that can occur independent of each other. For example, a judicial client may engage in criminal thinking that can lead to committing another crime independent of any HR related to relapse. Thus, the two pathways can interact or they can operate separately. When the two do interact, they may strengthen the probability of both relapse and recidivism.

The pathways to R&R are not linear (even though *Figure 5.3* might indicate so). A client might experience high-risk thought independent of a high-risk situation. Also, any one of the high-risk exposures alone could lead to relapse or recidivism. Furthermore, using the multidimensional and dynamic model of Marlatt and Witkiewitz (2005), although one risk exposure could precipitate a relapse, it is usually a combination of factors that ultimately leads to a full relapse or full recidivism.

Pathways to R&R Prevention

Figure 5.4 provides the cognitive-behavioral skills map for preventing R&R. This figure shows the pathways to R&R. The left column reiterates the high-risk exposures and pathways leading to R&R.

FIGURE 5.2

The Process of Relapse and Recidivism Prevention: How it works

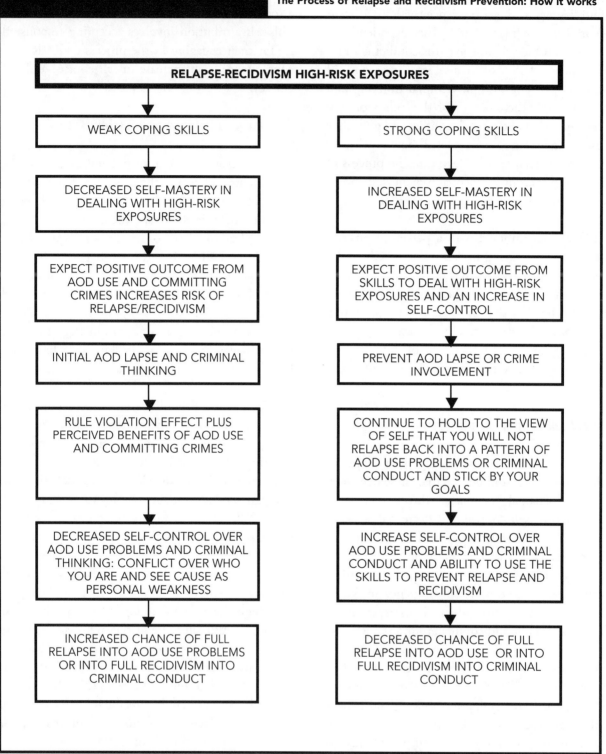

RELAPSE-RECIDIVISM HIGH-RISK EXPOSURES

WEAK COPING SKILLS	STRONG COPING SKILLS
DECREASED SELF-MASTERY IN DEALING WITH HIGH-RISK EXPOSURES	INCREASED SELF-MASTERY IN DEALING WITH HIGH-RISK EXPOSURES
EXPECT POSITIVE OUTCOME FROM AOD USE AND COMMITTING CRIMES INCREASES RISK OF RELAPSE/RECIDIVISM	EXPECT POSITIVE OUTCOME FROM SKILLS TO DEAL WITH HIGH-RISK EXPOSURES AND AN INCREASE IN SELF-CONTROL
INITIAL AOD LAPSE AND CRIMINAL THINKING	PREVENT AOD LAPSE OR CRIME INVOLVEMENT
RULE VIOLATION EFFECT PLUS PERCEIVED BENEFITS OF AOD USE AND COMMITTING CRIMES	CONTINUE TO HOLD TO THE VIEW OF SELF THAT YOU WILL NOT RELAPSE BACK INTO A PATTERN OF AOD USE PROBLEMS OR CRIMINAL CONDUCT AND STICK BY YOUR GOALS
DECREASED SELF-CONTROL OVER AOD USE PROBLEMS AND CRIMINAL THINKING: CONFLICT OVER WHO YOU ARE AND SEE CAUSE AS PERSONAL WEAKNESS	INCREASE SELF-CONTROL OVER AOD USE PROBLEMS AND CRIMINAL CONDUCT AND ABILITY TO USE THE SKILLS TO PREVENT RELAPSE AND RECIDIVISM
INCREASED CHANCE OF FULL RELAPSE INTO AOD USE PROBLEMS OR INTO FULL RECIDIVISM INTO CRIMINAL CONDUCT	DECREASED CHANCE OF FULL RELAPSE INTO AOD USE OR INTO FULL RECIDIVISM INTO CRIMINAL CONDUCT

Adapted with permission from author, G.A. Marlatt, 1985, Relapse Prevention: Theoretical rationale and overview (p. 38). In G.A. Marlatt, and J.R. Gordon (Eds.), *Relapse Prevention: Maintenance Strategies in the Treatment of Addictive Behaviors* (p. 38), Guilford Press.

FIGURE 5.3

Cognitive-Behavioral Pathways for Relapse and Recidivism

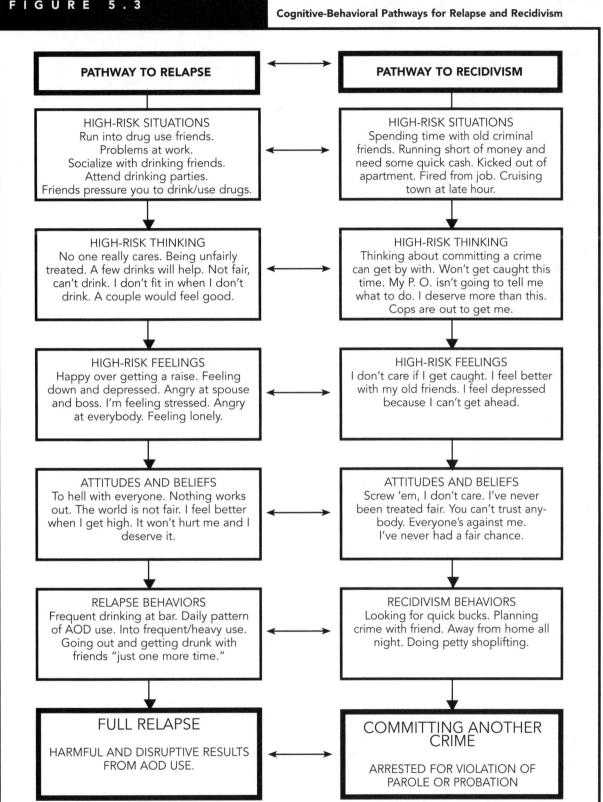

Adapted with permission from author, G.A. Marlatt, 1985, Relapse Prevention: Theoretical rationale and overview (p. 38). In G.A. Marlatt, and J.R. Gordon (Eds.), *Relapse Prevention: Maintenance Strategies in theTreatment of Addictive Behaviors* (p. 38), Guilford Press.

FIGURE 5.4

Pathways for Relapse and Recidivism Prevention

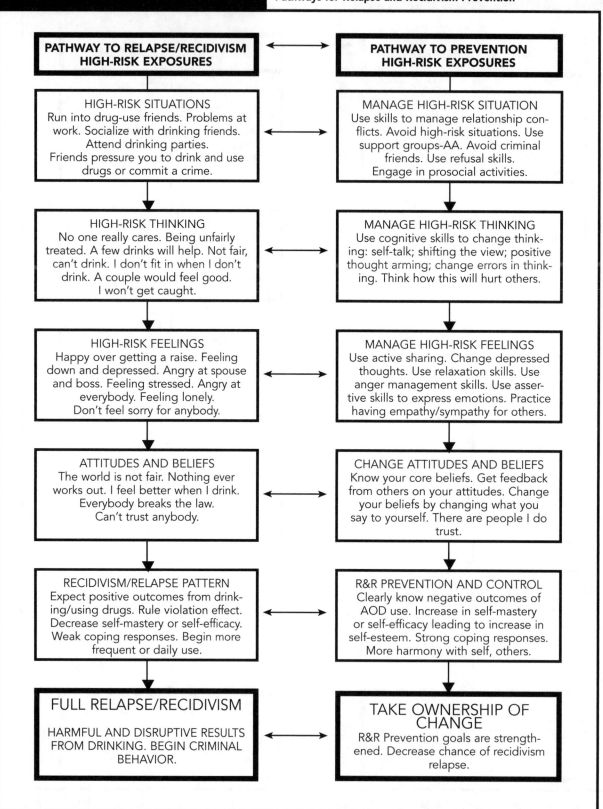

PATHWAY TO RELAPSE/RECIDIVISM HIGH-RISK EXPOSURES

PATHWAY TO PREVENTION HIGH-RISK EXPOSURES

HIGH-RISK SITUATIONS
Run into drug-use friends. Problems at work. Socialize with drinking friends. Attend drinking parties. Friends pressure you to drink and use drugs or commit a crime.

MANAGE HIGH-RISK SITUATION
Use skills to manage relationship conflicts. Avoid high-risk situations. Use support groups-AA. Avoid criminal friends. Use refusal skills. Engage in prosocial activities.

HIGH-RISK THINKING
No one really cares. Being unfairly treated. A few drinks will help. Not fair, can't drink. I don't fit in when I don't drink. A couple would feel good. I won't get caught.

MANAGE HIGH-RISK THINKING
Use cognitive skills to change thinking: self-talk; shifting the view; positive thought arming; change errors in thinking. Think how this will hurt others.

HIGH-RISK FEELINGS
Happy over getting a raise. Feeling down and depressed. Angry at spouse and boss. Feeling stressed. Angry at everybody. Feeling lonely. Don't feel sorry for anybody.

MANAGE HIGH-RISK FEELINGS
Use active sharing. Change depressed thoughts. Use relaxation skills. Use anger management skills. Use assertive skills to express emotions. Practice having empathy/sympathy for others.

ATTITUDES AND BELIEFS
The world is not fair. Nothing ever works out. I feel better when I drink. Everybody breaks the law. Can't trust anybody.

CHANGE ATTITUDES AND BELIEFS
Know your core beliefs. Get feedback from others on your attitudes. Change your beliefs by changing what you say to yourself. There are people I do trust.

RECIDIVISM/RELAPSE PATTERN
Expect positive outcomes from drinking/using drugs. Rule violation effect. Decrease self-mastery or self-efficacy. Weak coping responses. Begin more frequent or daily use.

R&R PREVENTION AND CONTROL
Clearly know negative outcomes of AOD use. Increase in self-mastery or self-efficacy leading to increase in self-esteem. Strong coping responses. More harmony with self, others.

FULL RELAPSE/RECIDIVISM
HARMFUL AND DISRUPTIVE RESULTS FROM DRINKING. BEGIN CRIMINAL BEHAVIOR.

TAKE OWNERSHIP OF CHANGE
R&R Prevention goals are strengthened. Decrease chance of recidivism relapse.

Adapted with permission from author, G.A. Marlatt, 1985, Relapse Prevention: Theoretical rationale and overview (p. 38). In G.A. Marlatt, and J.R. Gordon (Eds.), *Relapse prevention: Maintenance Strategies in the Treatment of Addictive Behaviors* (p. 38), Guilford Press.

The right column provides examples of adaptive and management responses to manage the various high-risk exposures.

Note that weak coping responses, decrease in self-efficacy, the expected positive outcomes from AOD use and CC, the rule violation effect, blaming others for initial lapses and engaging in thinking and actions that can lead to recidivism all contribute to a decrease in self-control and increase the probability of R&R.

Figure 5.4 suggests that both relapse and recidivism occur together as one process. Again, they should be viewed as separate processes that can occur independent of each other.

For example, a client may be in the ownership (maintenance) stage of change with respect to CC, yet still be in the commitment (action) stage of change with respect to AOD use and abuse. Clients may be in a stable pattern and maintaining abstinence from AOD use for a year, yet find themselves confronted with HR exposures with respect to criminal conduct. Thus, the skills the client uses to manage the HR exposure must be specific to preventing recidivism, and may have little to do with the management of relapse.

Developing a Relapse Prevention Plan

Figures 5.3 and *5.4* are used to help clients develop a R&R prevention plan. In *Session 15*, clients complete worksheets based on *Figure 5.3* that help them identify their unique HR exposures and triggers for R&R and their own pathways to R&R.

In *Session 16*, clients complete worksheets based on *Figure 5.4* in which they first identify the HR thinking, action and situation patterns that can lead to R&R and then, using the skills that they have learned, replace these with thoughts, actions and situations that prevent R&R.

The *Master Assessment Plan (MAP)* is also used as a R&R prevention plan in that it identifies problem areas that are targets for change. When these life-situation problems are managed or resolved, the client's R&R prevention efforts are strengthened.

Strengthening R&R Prevention: A Balanced and Healthy Lifestyle

An important component of the *SSC* R&R prevention approach is for clients to develop strategies for lifestyle changes and for developing a **balanced lifestyle.** Having clients learn specific skills to manage HR exposures is not sufficient in preventing R&R. Recognizing this, Marlatt (1985a) generated several global strategies that help clients to develop a broader set of skills and concepts for preventing relapse. These strategies help clients intervene in their overall lifestyle so as to increase their ability (self-efficacy) in handling stress and difficult life situations. *SSC Module 11* is dedicated to this component of R&R prevention and provides clients with guidelines in developing a more balanced lifestyle.

However, *SSC* goes beyond this lifestyle balance strategy and provides clients with strategies for developing and maintaining a **healthy lifestyle.** *Module 12* focuses on providing clients with the concepts and skills for implementing healthy choices and lifestyle approaches in the areas of work, job, recreation and play, relaxation, healthy eating, personal care, physical activity and using community resources to support achievement of the client's R&R prevention goals.

SSC as an Integrated Effort to Prevent R&R

As mentioned several times in this *Guide,* the primary goals of *SSC* are: relapse and recidivism prevention; and helping clients to live a responsible and meaningful life. Even though *Modules 6* and *11* are specifically dedicated to the topic of R&R prevention, *SSC* as a whole is a recidivism and relapse prevention program.

In this respect, all of the concepts and skills taught and utilized in *SSC* are dedicated to R&R prevention. For example, *SSC* clients are provided relevant information regarding alcohol and other drugs and the psychobiological and social impact of AOD use and abuse. Clients see how they fit the AOD information provided to them. They then complete a variety of worksheets to determine how they fit the various AOD use and abuse patterns and what category of AOD problems they fit, i.e., problem user, abuse or dependence. This information is then used to help clients understand the different categories and definitions of relapse and then have them determine their own relapse risk and their own relapse prevention goal based on the results of their self-assessment.

A similar approach is used to heighten awareness of antisocial behavior, criminal conduct and the CC cycle. Clients relate this information to their own CC history and how they fit the CC cycle. They evaluate themselves across measures of antisocial attitudes and behaviors and determine their own risk for recidivism and identify their own recidivism prevention plan.

Research has shown that there are four broad triggers for relapse and recidivism: 1) intrapersonal stress and emotions; 2) relationship stress and conflict; 3) peer pressure to engage in AOD use and criminal conduct; and 4) change in self-image. Many *SSC* sessions are directed at helping clients manage HR exposures that emerge from these four R&R triggers.

Finally, clients set their own relapse and recidivism goals, and these goals are continually reevaluated, and the skills of achieving these goals are continually learned and practiced as clients proceed through the program. In the orientation sessions, clients are asked to state their initial R&R goals. These goals may not be congruent with providers' expectations or even the expectations of the judicial system or society in general.

For example, some clients may indicate that their goal is to use drugs, but to not have drug use interfere with their lives. They might indicate that the primary goal is to stay out of jail, or to not get rearrested, which could imply not getting caught committing another crime. Or, some clients may write goals that they think the judicial provider or counselor wants to hear while at the same time having in mind goals different from those stated.

Providers need to use reflective acceptance skills when responding to these early goal expressions and statements, keeping in mind that these reflect early stages of change, e.g., challenge, contemplative. As clients begin to respond to *SSC* in a productive and positive way, their goals will change; they will become more adaptive and more compatible with the R&R goals of the judicial system and society.

CHAPTER REVIEW

During the 1980s there occurred a major paradigm shift in the treatment of individuals with alcohol and other drug problems. Faced with the reality of the prevalence of relapse among those completing treatment for substance abuse, and prompted by the work of Alan Marlatt and associates, treatment programs gave relapse prevention (RP) a major role in substance abuse treatment.

A similar trend has also occurred in the treatment of the SA judicial client. The reality of recidivism - at rates similar but even somewhat higher than relapse - among judicial clients was apparent in studies emerging in the 1970s and 1980s. It was clear that specific programs to address recidivism in correctional treatment were needed.

However, with SA judicial clients, recidivism tended to be dealt with by addressing relapse prevention. It was believed, at least with SA judicial clients, the problem or recidivism would be resolved by preventing relapse. Thus, early on, correctional treatment programs gave relapse prevention a prominent role. Yet, it was apparent that specific and independent efforts were needed in addressing separately relapse and recidivism among offenders.

Guided by the two primary goals of the treatment of SA judicial clients - preventing relapse and recidivism - in our 1998 edition of this work, we adapted Alan Marlatt's (1985a) relapse prevention model to address both relapse and recidivism in correctional treatment. This adaptation was enhanced in our work on the education and treatment of impaired drivers (Wanberg, Milkman & Timken, 2005), and is again further enhanced in this work.

The first part of this chapter gives a brief description of the Marlatt RP model and describes the key components of that model. The rest of the chapter focuses on the adaptation of this model in generating a specific approach for *SSC* that describes relapse and recidivism as linked but also as independent processes. A starting point for discussion of the *SSC* R&R approach was to define both relapse and recidivism and the specific goals related to R&R prevention.

Relapse is seen as a process that may involve lapses and that can evolve into a state or condition that emulates substance abusing pathological conditions found in the history of SA judicial clients. *SSC* identifies two potential relapse goals regarding alcohol use: total abstinence; and not returning to a pattern of alcohol use that results in harm to the client, to others and the community.

SSC takes the position that the only acceptable relapse prevention goal for illegal drugs is abstinence. However, given that relapse into the use of illegal drugs is a reality among judicial clients, providers can develop a position of treatment tolerance and intermediate sanctions in working with clients who relapse into the use of illegal drugs.

Thus, *SSC* distinguishes between the process of relapse and full relapse. Clients are into the process of relapse when they engage in high-risk exposures that can lead to full relapse. This may not involve an actual lapse (use of a drug). The process of relapse can lead to two outcomes: **full relapse** which is the violation of the client's relapse prevention goal of either total abstinence from alcohol and other drugs or not returning to a pattern of alcohol use problems; and **prolapse,** getting "back on track" by using skills to manage the high-risk exposures preventing full relapse.

The process of **recidivism** is engaging in thinking and behaving that lead to full recidivism - committing another criminal act. *SSC* assumes a zero tolerance approach towards full recidivism - engaging in any criminal conduct - which requires a sanctioning response. The only acceptable recidivism goal is to abstain from involvement in criminal conduct. However, providers accept that judicial clients will engage in criminal thinking and in actions that are precursors to criminal conduct. These pre-criminal conduct conditions become the fodder for correctional treatment and for preventing recidivism. The concept of prolapse can be applied to recidivism. Clients who engage in high-risk thinking or actions can get "back on track" by managing the high risk

exposures and prevent recidivism.

Even though *SSC* takes a "zero tolerance" approach to full recidivism, this does not mean that the "door is shut" with respect to the opportunity of judicial clients to receive continued treatment services. Clients who reoffend and are sentenced should be re-evaluated for need of further treatment services. That evaluation will address motivation, the client's stage of change, and specific treatment needs before determining what services might be offered.

The grey area is in the use of illegal drugs, the possession of which constitutes an illegal act. Providers can have treatment tolerance towards this involvement as long as it does not involve and offense beyond possesion, that it is addressed in cooperation with the context of the judicial system, and that clients show a positive effort to work towards the goal of total abstinence from the use of illegal drugs.

The rest of the chapter defines the R&R model used in *SSC*. The key elements of this model are: HR exposures, developing cognitive and behavioral coping skills, understanding the power of expected positive outcomes, initial lapse into R&R, the rule violation effect, and decrease or increase in self-control. Self-efficacy, or the perceived ability to handling specific situations that can lead to R&R, is the conceptual glue that holds together the *SSC* R&R approach. The pathways to R&R are defined and described and the approach used in *SSC* to help clients identify their specific HR exposures and pathways to R&R is described.

A R&R map is provided that describes the pathways to prevention and skills that can be used to handle HR exposure. The outcome of this R&R prevention approach is increased self-control and self-efficacy, and achieving the goal of helping clients take ownership of change. The importance of developing a plan to guide clients in the process of R&R prevention and the strengthening of R&R through developing a balanced and healthy lifestyle are discussed.

Finally, the concept that *SSC* represents an integrated approach to R&R prevention is discussed. Taken as a whole, *SSC* is a recidivism and relapse prevention program.

SECTION II

OPERATIONAL GUIDELINES

Section I defined the conceptual framework and treatment platform of *Criminal Conduct and Substance Abuse Treatment: Strategies for Self-Improvement and Change (SSC) - Pathways to Responsible Living.* The purpose of *Section II* of this *Guide* is to delineate the operational guidelines for the delivery of *SSC. Chapter 6* outlines an assessment program for evaluating the treatment needs, the progress and change of *SSC* clients. The assessment program is based on a convergent validation model which identifies self-report and other-report as essential sources of information for identifying the client's problems and strengths and to discern progress and change. The *Progress and Change Evaluation (PACE) Monitor* provides a formal operational framework for this assessment program. However, the chapter stresses that the assessment of change goes beyond the formal *PACE* program and is an ongoing process that takes place in each *SSC* session. It also stresses that treatment efficacy and outcome are not just measured at some point following treatment, but all measurements of change at any point in the assessment process are an indication of treatment efficacy and outcome.

Chapter 7 presents general guidelines and procedures for *SSC* delivery. It discusses intake and admission guidelines, presents different delivery options, identifies basic provider skills necessary to deliver each phase of *SSC,* and outlines program agreements and ground rules for client participation. It also identifies specific skills that enhance interactive learning and client participation. Principles of effective group management and leadership are discussed. The efficacy of *SSC* depends on the degree of the client's involvement in self-evaluation. Likewise, provider effectiveness in *SSC* delivery will depend on a continual process of provider self-evaluation. *Chapter 7* provides mechanisms for providers to evaluate the effectiveness of their delivery of the *SSC* program.

*There can be a paralysis of self-analysis
unless the analysis moves the person to action.*
-AUTHOR UNKNOWN

CHAPTER OUTLINE

OVERVIEW

THE CONVERGENT VALIDATION MODEL OF
ASSESSMENT

Components of the Assessment Process
Objectives of Assessment
Sources of Information and Report Subjectivity
Valuing Client Self-Disclosure
The Convergent Validation Model

SCREENING FOR *SSC*: DISCERNING CRIMINAL
CONDUCT AND AOD PROBLEMS

Level of Antisocial Behavior and Criminal Conduct
Level of Substance Use Problems

 Minimum symptom criteria
 The Impaired-Control Cycle
 Self-selection
 Self-report - standardized psychometric instruments

PROGRESS AND CHANGE EVALUATION (PACE)

Differential Screening and Intake
Comprehensive Multiple-Factor Assessment

 Multiple-factor assessment
 Assessment of cognitive-behavioral processing
 *Assessment of motivation and readiness for
   treatment*
 Assessment of strengths

Assessment of Treatment Progress and Change
Assessment of Outcome

 Assessment of readiness for program continuation
 Program closure assessment
 Post-discharge assessment

PACE CASE EXAMPLE PRESENTATION

Admission to *SSC*
Comprehensive Assessment
Progress and Change Documentation

 Program Attending Record
 Client Program Response: CPR-C and CPR-P
 Status Assessment Questionnaire (SAQ)
 Retesting on the ASUS-R and AdSAP

Status at Discharge From *SSC* and Follow-up

CLIENT SELF-ASSESSMENT DURING *SSC*

Cognitive-Behavioral Map
Autobiography
Master Skills List (MSL)
Master Profile (MP) and Master Assessment Plan
  (MAP)
Weekly Thinking and Action Patterns (TAP)
  Charting
Thinking and Re-thinking Reports
SSC Change Scales

SUMMARY OF *PACE* AND THE AUTOMATED *PACE*
MANAGER

CHAPTER REVIEW

CHAPTER OBJECTIVES

▶ Provide an overview of the structure and process
of assessment and the multiple-factor and convergent validation model to estimate the client's
multiple problems and conditions.

▶ Provide guidelines for determining the level of
AOD use problems and criminal conduct.

▶ Describe the *SSC* assessment program and the
PACE Monitor that defines the process and
structure of assessment.

▶ Present a case example to illustrate *PACE*.

▶ Discuss the client self-assessment components.

OVERVIEW

Multidimensional assessment using the convergent validation approach is the second core strategy of *SSC*. It is also one of the five foundational models upon which this program was established. The purpose of this chapter is to provide a specific operational assessment model used for evaluating the treatment needs, progress and change, and the treatment outcome of substance abusing judicial clients entering *SSC*.

This chapter begins with a brief presentation of the convergent validation model used in substance abuse and criminal conduct assessment (Wanberg, 1997, 2000, 2004; Wanberg et al., 2005). That model is described in more detail in the *Resource Guide's* chapter on *Perspectives on Assessment* (Wanberg & Milkman, 2008). A comprehensive assessment program that can be used specifically with *SSC* clients is then presented. This program is identified as the *Progress and Change Evaluation (PACE) Monitor*.

PACE includes three components: 1) evaluation of the treatment needs at admission and in the early part of treatment; 2) evaluation of the progress and change clients make during treatment; and 3) evaluation of immediate and longer-term treatment outcomes. The instruments used in each of these components will be described.

An important part of the overall comprehensive assessment process is the client's own self-assessment summary. Before completing this summary, clients are given feedback on the results of the *PACE Monitor* assessment. Then, using this information, clients complete the *Master Profile (MP)*, which is *Program Guide 2* in the *Workbook*, and the *Master Assessment Plan (MAP)*, *Program Guide 3* of the *Workbook*. The *MP* helps clients identify critical areas that need to be addressed in treatment. The *MAP* is the client's map or plan for change. The initial or preliminary *MP* and *MAP* are completed within the first month of the program and then continually updated. *Session 20* of *SSC* focuses specifically on the *MP* and *MAP* and provides opportunity for clients to share their findings and their progress and change with the group. The *MP* and *MAP* are discussed at the end of this chapter.

It is recognized that some agencies will have their own screening and up-front assessment instruments, particularly those used to evaluate client treatment needs. Although it is recommended that the provider use those in *PACE* for *SSC* clients, providers can use the ones they have established for use in their agencies in place of those in the *PACE Monitor*.

SSC is an assessment-driven program. The formal assessment is structured through the *PACE* instruments. However, in each session, *SSC* clients complete worksheets and exercises that continually evaluate their current status with respect to the change targets of *SSC*. Many of these worksheets are psychometric in nature - that is, they provide quantitative measurement of specific problem areas and provide clients with a normative group with which to compare their results. For example, in *Session 6*, clients complete self-reports that measure how they fit the AOD use patterns of Social, Solo and Benefits.

THE CONVERGENT VALIDATION MODEL OF ASSESSMENT

It is general practice of most judicial agencies to use some form of screening to evaluate clients in order to determine appropriate intervention placement and the need for further assessment. It is also common practice for treatment agencies to do a comprehensive assessment in order to determine the more specific needs of the client and to develop an individualized treatment plan (ITP).

Much of the information gathered in these assessment efforts relies on self-report of the client. It is commonly believed by many correctional workers and evaluators that these self-reports are not reliable and are often not to be trusted. Given that most would agree that both screening and comprehensive assessment are essential in the process of developing an effective treatment placement and plan for judicial clients, how do we approach assessment so as to resolve the dilemma between this importance and the problem of report validity (veridicality)? Although this dilemma is discussed in detail in the *Resource Guide*, it is briefly summarized here since it is critical to understanding the *PACE Monitor* used in the evaluation of the *SSC* client's treatment needs and change.

Components of the Assessment Process

Assessment is a continual process that begins with screening and continues through the assessment of treatment outcome. This process has four major components.

- **Screening:** This can be formal or informal. It can start with simple screening to determine whether a certain problem exists, e.g., substance abuse. It can then proceed to a differential screening process, i.e., clients are screened for specific problem areas (such as mental health and criminal conduct). An important purpose of screening, particularly differential screening, is to determine service referral needs.

- **Comprehensive or in-depth assessment** looks at distinct and multiple conditions that need to be addressed in substance abusing judicial clients. It provides a comprehensive understanding of the client in order to formulate a treatment plan and determine specific treatment needs and services.

- **Treatment progress and change assessment** looks at clients' response to *SSC*, beginning with the initial assessment and continuing through the last contact made with clients. Although this component of assessment focuses more specifically on clients' response to the treatment process, it is a focus at every level of client involvement.

- **Outcome assessment:** This includes immediate assessment that is done when the client finishes the formal treatment program. It also includes short-term outcome at three to six months post-discharge, and long-term outcome evaluation, or assessment at points one year or more post-discharge.

Objectives of Assessment

The overall goal of assessment for all of the components and levels of evaluation is to collect sufficient information in order to make intelligent decisions around the general and specific service needs of the judicial client. There are a number of specific common objectives that guide the process of assessment within each of the assessment components.

- **To provide clients opportunity to disclose information about themselves or to tell their story.** It begins with screening and continues throughout treatment and follow-up. It is essential in that it defines how clients see themselves and provides a baseline of the client's willingness to self-disclose at the various points of assessment.

- **To gather information from other individuals associated with the client or other sources of information.** These include: persons who have direct contact with the client, such as family members, probation supervisor; legal records; records of prior treatment; and the evaluator's own view of the client.

- **To discern the level of openness or defensiveness of the client at the time of assessment.** This is important at screening, comprehensive assessment and throughout treatment. As the client's willingness to disclose increases, defensiveness decreases, and the motivation to engage in change is enhanced.

- **Estimate the "true" condition of the client.** We never know the client's "true" condition. We only estimate this condition. Our estimate at screening will not be as veridical as our estimate at the comprehensive level of assessment or at later points in treatment. This estimate is ongoing and converging.

- **To make a referral and placement that match the presenting problems with appropriate services.** At screening, the decision might be to refer the client to a specific program such as *SSC,* or to more generic outpatient AOD treatment. This matching is ongoing, and even after a client is in treatment for several months, continued assessment may reveal a new problem or condition that needs a new or different service.

- **To evaluate progress and outcomes during treatment.** Clients who do not show adequate change and progress will be re-evaluated for different or enhanced service needs. Some judicial clients continue to be resistant and defensive. This finding may require changing the treatment plan.

All of these objectives are viewed within the context of the partnership between the provider and client. The client is continually involved as a partner in determining the level of problems and service needs to address these problems.

Sources of Information and Report Subjectivity

There are two types of data that are used in every component of the assessment process. They are: other-report and self-report.

Other Report (OR) Data are collateral to the self-report and are sorted into two categories.

1. Includes reports from individual third parties who have some familiarity with the client such as probation or parole officers, family members, treatment specialists, and other individuals who have had substantive contact with the client.

2. Includes official documentation such as laboratory reports or legal records.

These data are always subjective, and in fact, are double-subjective. Information given to the evaluator by the client or collaterals is subjective. The evaluator's interpretation of the information is subjective making the evaluator's final impressions or ratings double-subjective.

Self-Report (SR) Data include interview (narrative) and psychometric test data and are also subjective. Interview SR provides a basis for understanding the client, particularly when recorded in a verbatim fashion. However, the interviewer's assessment statement around these data are considered to be OR information. SR data become most meaningful and more objective when they are based on the principles of psychological measurement. This approach reduces the subjectivity of SR data and makes them more reliable and veridical (valid). The subjectivity of SR can also be reduced when trust and rapport are developed with that client.

Valuing Client Self-Disclosure

SR is viewed from two perspectives: the content of the data used in estimating the client's "true" condi-

tions; and the changes in the self-disclosure of these conditions as they are reported over time. The content of the data gathered at any particular point in time is relevant only as it is viewed within the process of change.

The results of any one point of testing should never be taken as a fixed and final description of the client. Any point in testing only provides us with an estimate of the client's condition and gives us guidelines for treatment needs at that point in time. From this perspective, the process of assessment is just as important as the content of assessment.

As noted earlier, judicial evaluators and providers tend to distrust the "so-called" validity of client SR. There is a tendency to conclude that clients are "lying" or "into denial" when they think that clients are not reporting their "true" condition. However, when we see assessment as a process, we view all SR data as a valid representation of where the client is at a particular point in time. If we believe the client is not accurately reporting his or her "real condition," we should view this within the framework of self-defensiveness, rather than denial.

SR data are viewed as a baseline measure of the client's willingness to disclose his or her problems or conditions at any point of assessment. It tells us the degree of openness around this self-disclosure. The degree of validity or veridicality of how well SR data estimate the "true condition" of the client is directly related to the level of defensiveness. Thus, when looking at SR data, we must first look at this level of defensiveness.

SR is also essential in the assessment process in that it tells us where to begin treatment. This is where the change process and intervention begin - with the client's self-perception, or the willingness to disclose information around that self-perception.

If SR in the initial assessment is not veridical with what is going on in the client's life, say, based on OR data, and if treatment is working, later SRs will reflect a change in this self-disclosure. The first indication of treatment efficacy is found in the client's increase of self-disclosure and openness in treatment. Retesting should reveal any change occurring in this self-disclosure.

Within this model of assessment, every client SR is seen as a valid representation of the client's willingness to disclose perceptions about the conditions being evaluated at a particular point of assessment. If we have evidence that the self-report is not veridical with collateral information, and the client is highly defensive around self-disclosure, then the report is valid in the sense that we have an estimate of the discrepancy between what the client says is going on and what the other-reports indicate. We may then conclude that our estimate of defensiveness and discrepancy is valid. This discrepancy then becomes the basis for where we start treatment.

From this perspective, a self-report is never invalid - as some tests indicate to be the case. Report invalidity must always be interpreted as indicating the discrepancy between sources of data, level of defensiveness and willingness on the part of the client to not only self-disclose, but to engage in intervention and treatment services. This approach prevents us from getting caught up in the question of whether the client is "lying," "under-reporting," "denying," or "falsifying."

The Convergent Validation Model

The convergent validation model (Wanberg & Horn, 1987; Wanberg, 1992, 1998, 2000; Wanberg et al., 2005) utilizes self-report and other-report as valid representations of where the client is at the time of assessment. It is based on Campbell and Fiske's classic multitrait-multimethod matrix approach (1959). They found that using several methods of assessment and several sources of data was more effective than using one method or one source of data when predicting outcome in research studies.

The convergent validation model uses all sources of information to converge on the most valid "estimate" of the client's condition in key areas of assessment. We can hypothesize about this condition. Our data then can test that hypothesis.

SCREENING FOR *SSC:* DISCERNING CRIMINAL CONDUCT AND AOD PROBLEMS

Some form of screening is important in order to determine appropriateness for *SSC,* which addresses co-occurring substance abuse and criminal conduct. Yet the questions around screening for *SSC* have to do with what degree of CC and substance abuse clients should have for them to be appropriate for this program.

With respect to level of criminal conduct, Andrews and Bonta (2003) argue that correctional treatment should target those who are high-risk for recidivism. This would mean that higher-risk judicial clients would be selected into treatment. Yet, those at low and medium risk also have treatment needs that can be effectively addressed by *SSC.* Thus, screening for *SSC* includes some determination of level of risk.

The other screening issue is what level of substance abuse problems clients should indicate that would make them appropriate for *SSC.* Finally, there are other areas that should be considered when discerning appropriateness for *SSC* such as motivation for services, level of defensiveness, psychological problems, etc. We first look at the two main areas of screening at a more general level and some other considerations regarding appropriateness for *SSC.* Then, when discussing the elements of the *PACE Monitor,* we look at more specific guidelines for admission into *SSC.*

Level of Antisocial Behavior and Criminal Conduct

First, it is recommended that screening for *SSC* include some determination of past level of antisocial behavior and criminal conduct and level of risk for recidivism. Most judicial jurisdictions have criteria to determine the level of recidivism risk, usually based on both interview or instrumentation. The *Level of Service Inventory - Revised* (LSI-R: Andrews & Bonta, 1995) is a commonly used instrument to determine level of risk and recommended levels of supervision.

Most often, risk determination procedures usually categorize offenders into a low-, medium- or high-risk category. First, if there is available space in the treatment program, all judicial clients should have a chance to be included in *SSC,* regardless of their risk level. However, if there is a limit as to the number of clients that an agency can include in *SSC* treatment, then, following Andrews and Bonta's (2003) suggestion, it is recommended that those falling in the medium and high-risk categories have first priority.

For example, for agencies using the LSI-R, those with LSI-R total scores of 21 or higher would have first priority for inclusion into *SSC*. Those with LSI-R scores of 14 through 20 would be given second priority. And those in the score range of zero through 13 are given third priority.

SR instruments can also be used as guidelines for determining the level of antisocial behavior and involvement in criminal conduct and the potential for recidivism. There are two scales in the *Adult Substance Use Survey - Revised* (ASUS-R: Wanberg, 2004), to be discussed below, that can be used for determining the

level of past involvement in antisocial thinking and behavior and involvement in criminal conduct: SOCIAL NON-CONFORMING and LEGAL NON-CONFORMING. It is recommended that judicial clients with scores around the 50th percentile rank on SOCIAL NON-CONFORMING and LEGAL NON-CONFORMING Scales be given priority for admission into *SSC*. The case study profile of the ASUS-R in *Figure 6.1,* page 115, is a client who was admitted into *SSC*. This client has scores above the 50th percentile on both SOCIAL NON-CONFORMING and LEGAL NON-CONFORMING. As well, the client's total LSI-R score placed him in high-risk status.

Part of the assessment of criminal conduct should involve an evaluation of antisocial attitudes and be-

---

TABLE 6.1

Characteristics of the Antisocial Personality Pattern

▶ Repeatedly performing acts that do not conform to social norms with respect to obeying the law and that are grounds for being arrested;

▶ Impulsivity and failure to plan ahead;

▶ Patterns of deceit, lying, conning others for personal gain or pleasure;

▶ Inability to handle anger in adaptive ways;

▶ Low frustration tolerance;

▶ Ineffective problem solving in relationships;

▶ Irresponsibility in finances, relationships, and societal obligations;

▶ Reckless disregard for the safety of others and of self;

▶ Inability or unwillingness to delay gratification;

▶ Aggressive and even assaultive behavior;

▶ Denial of personal responsibility and blaming others;

▶ Associating with friends who are antisocial and who engage in illegal conduct and devious behavior;

▶ Manipulating and exploiting relationships;

▶ Lack of empathy for others;

▶ Lack of remorse and guilt;

▶ Aggrandizement of self and inflated view of self.

havior. As we discussed in previous chapters in this *Guide,* criminal conduct is antisocial behavior; and the treatment of CC must involve changing antisocial attitudes and behaviors and facilitating the development of prosocial responses towards others and the community.

As discussed in the *Resource Guide,* we prefer to use the concept of antisocial personality pattern (APP) which includes, but is not limited to, criteria in the DSM-IV that define the antisocial personality disorder (APD). APD is represented by a pattern of behavior involving "disregard for, and violation of, the rights of others." "By definition, a personality disorder is an enduring pattern of thinking, feeling, and behaving that is relatively stable over time" (American Psychiatric Association, 1994, p. 632).

When evaluating for antisocial attitudes and behaviors, the features of an antisocial personality pattern (APP), more commonly called character pathology, should be considered. These are outlined in *Table 6.1* (e.g., DSM-IV: American Psychiatric Association, 1994; Sarason & Sarason, 1989, 1995, 2005). There are varying patterns within the antisocial domain. Not all of the antisocial features described in *Table 6.1* are found in all individuals who fit the APP. For example, not all people with APP, or with APD, have engaged in criminal behavior.

Level of Substance Use Problems

This is a second major area for screening. Although there are many ways to discern whether a person has a substance abuse problem, and the extent of that problem, we provide four basic procedures to help providers address this assessment issue.

Minimum symptom criteria

The minimum symptom criteria approach involves defining AOD problems in terms of a set of diagnostic criteria and requiring that a certain number of these criteria be met for inclusion into the category of AOD problems, abuse or dependence. The evaluator rates the client across specified inclusion or diagnostic criteria. Minimum symptom criteria are considered to be OR (rater data). The most commonly used minimum symptom criteria are the

Diagnostic and Statistical Manual of Mental Disorders IV - DSM-IV (American Psychiatric Association, 1994) and the text revised version of this work (2000). Those who fall into either the Substance Abuse or Substance Dependence classifications should be given priority with respect to admission into *SSC*. *Table 6.2* provides the criteria for Substance Abuse and *Table 6.3* provides the DSM-IV criteria for Substance Dependence.

The impaired-control cycle

The concept of impaired control and the impaired-control cycle (ICC) can be useful in identifying the presence and extent of an AOD problem (Wanberg, 1974, 1990; Wanberg & Horn, 1987; Wanberg & Milkman, 1998). Impaired control occurs when notable negative consequences result from drug use (loss of job, physical problems, relationship and marital problems, etc.).

The cycle begins when drugs are used to solve problems that result from their use and continues when the individual continues to use drugs to solve the problems that come from drug use. In this approach, a person who develops significant negative consequences from alcohol use would be considered to have had an alcohol problem. An individual who uses alcohol to manage problems coming from alcohol use would be identified as a problem drinker. The clinical judgment of whether a person fits the impaired control cycle is considered to be other-report data.

Self-selection

Self-selection is another approach for concluding that the individual has an AOD problem and thus would be a candidate for *SSC*. Those who openly self-select into an AOD problem category will also be up-front with respect to their AOD use involvement and problems.

Self-selection is enhanced when the individual experiences some emotional concern about the disruptive quality of drug use. For treatment to be effective, substance abusing judicial clients must move towards some degree of self-selection and acceptance of treatment.

TABLE 6.2

DSM-IV Criteria for Substance Abuse

A. A maladaptive pattern of substance use leading to clinically significant impairment or distress, as manifested by one (or more) of the following, occurring within a 12 month period:

▶ recurrent substance use resulting in a failure to fulfill major role obligations at work, school, or home (e.g., repeated absences or poor work performance related to substance use; substance-related absences, suspensions, or expulsions from school; neglect of children or household)

▶ recurrent substance use in situations in which it is physically hazardous (e.g., driving an automobile or operating a machine when impaired by substance use)

▶ recurrent substance use despite legal problems (e.g., arrests for substance-related disorderly conduct)

▶ continued substance use despite having persistent or recurrent social or interpersonal problems caused or exacerbated by the effects of the substance (e.g., arguments with spouse about consequences of intoxication, physical fights)

B. The symptoms have never met the criteria for Substance Dependence for this class of substance

From American Psychiatric Association (1994), Diagnostic and Statistical Manual of Mental Disorders (4th ed.) with permission.

Self-report - standardized psychometric instruments

A variety of self-report screening devises are used with judicial clients to discern the presence of substance abuse and inclusion into SA treatment. The *Perspectives on Assessment* chapter in the *Resource Guide* provides a summary of some of these instruments and resources to find these instruments. These instruments are usually identified as being simple screening instruments or differential screening instruments. Simple screening instruments should not be used for discerning appropriateness for *SSC*.

Differential screening instruments go beyond the single task of AOD problem screening and measure other conditions relevant to offender intervention service needs and, more specifically, admission into *SSC*. This is a multidimensional approach to screening. For example, within the domain of AOD assessment, differential screening will measure the extent to which individuals are involved in various kinds of drugs and the extent of negative consequences or symptoms resulting from this involvement. Other

domains include mental health, treatment motivation and level of defensiveness. These are the most important areas of evaluation at the screening level. The standardized psychometric differential screening instrument that we recommend to discern appropriateness for *SSC* is the *Adult Substance Use Survey - Revised* (ASUS-R: Wanberg, 2004). The ASUS-R may be used by providers for screening clients into *SSC*. The ASUS-R is a differential screening instrument that provides measures across multiple factors including: AOD involvement and disruption; mood and mental health assessment; benefits of AOD use; social and legal non-conformity; defensiveness; motivation for services; and strengths. The ASUS-R can be used to evaluate a number of critical areas of SA judicial clients, can be helpful in making treatment referrals and recommendations, and can guide both judicial supervision and counselors (providers) in developing an effective treatment plan.

A number of scales can also be used to measure change in treatment. These are dynamic scales and include: AOD SIX MONTH, AOD BENEFITS, LEGAL NON-CONFORMING SIX MONTH,

A maladaptive pattern of substance use, leading to clinically significant impairment or distress, as manifested by three (or more) of the following, occurring at any time in the same 12-month period.

1. tolerance, as defined by either of the following:

   ▶ a need for markedly increased amounts of the substance to achieve intoxication or desired effect

   ▶ markedly diminished effect with continued use of the same amount of the substance

2. withdrawal, as manifested by either of the following:

   ▶ the characteristic withdrawal syndrome for the substance

   ▶ the same (or a closely related) substance is taken to relieve or avoid withdrawal symptoms

3. the substance is often taken in larger amounts or over a longer period than was intended

4. there is a persistent desire or unsuccessful efforts to cut down or control substance use

5. a great deal of time is spent in activities necessary to obtain the substance, or use the substance

6. important social, occupational, or recreational activities are given up or reduced because of substance use

7. the substance use is continued despite knowledge of having a persistent or recurrent physical or psychological problem that is likely to have been caused or exacerbated by the substance

Specify if:

With Physiological Dependence: evidence of tolerance or withdrawal (either item 1 or 2 is present)

Without Physiological Dependence: no evidence of tolerance or withdrawal (neither item 1 or 2 is present)

American Psychiatric Association (1994), Diagnostic and Statistical Manual of Mental Disorders (4th ed.) with permission.

MOOD ADJUSTMENT, DEFENSIVE, MOTIVATION TO CHANGE, and STRENGTHS. Also, a change scale based on the dynamic variables in the SOCIAL NON-CONFORMING and LEGAL NON-CONFORMING scales can also be used as a reassessment measure. *Figure 6.1,* page 115, provides a case illustration of the ASUS-R for a judicial client screened into *SSC.*

PROGRESS AND CHANGE EVALUATION *(PACE)*

Following the outline provided above with respect to the process and components of assessment, *PACE* is

built around five components or tasks that provide the structure for evaluating the *SSC* client at various stages of *SSC* involvement. These are:

▶ Differential screening and intake;

▶ Differential and comprehensive assessment;

▶ Progress and change during treatment;

▶ Treatment closure;

▶ Follow-up assessment.

PACE utilizes specific instruments for this assessment process. As acknowledged above, many agencies have their own instruments for assessment. In cases where the agency is unable to introduce new instruments for evaluating *SSC* clients, providers will need to match the areas of assessment of those instruments with the screening and comprehensive assessment areas of *PACE.*

Table 6.4 provides a summary and description of the *PACE* instruments. The rater instruments are based on data taken from the counselor's observation and interaction with clients through formal interviews (e.g., intake), clients involvement in all group activities (e.g., group processing, worksheets, role play), and individual sessions with clients.

As noted in *Table 6.4,* retesting of the intake ASUS-R and the comprehensive AdSAP and AdSAQ are recommended but do not impact on the *PACE* process. These retests will provide enhanced information on the progress that clients are making in *SSC.*

The following sections discuss the instrumentation and concepts that go into achieving the objectives of the specific components or tasks of *PACE.* This chapter will only summarize the *PACE* instruments and procedures. The specific instruments and their scoring and interpretive procedures are included in the *Progress and Change Evaluation (PACE) Monitor Handbook,* which is a supplement to this *Provider's Guide.* An Automated *PACE (A-PACE)* is also available on CD, discussed at the end of this chapter.

Differential Screening and Intake

There are three tasks that are addressed in this component of *PACE:* 1) determine which judicial clients are appropriate for *SSC*; 2) clients complete an intake form as required by treatment agency standards; and 3) completing the *Self Evaluation Questionnaire* (SEQ) which provides a baseline measure of the dynamic variables that represent targets of change in *SSC.* When discussing the use of the various instruments in this process, the abbreviations provided in *Table 6.4* will be used.

With respect to appropriateness for *SSC* based on level of AOD use problems, placement guidelines have been established based on weighted scores on

five ASUS-R scales: INVOLVEMENT, DISRUPTION, AOD BENEFITS, SOCIAL NON-CONFORMING, and LEGAL NON-CONFORMING. The weighted guidelines are provided in the *PACE Handbook* along with the ASUS-R, the ASUS-R profile and scoring instructions.

The screening process should include an interview with the client. This interview should explore the AOD use history and other clinical areas that help determine whether clients have a substance use problem. The DSM-IV criteria should be used in this process, but should not be used as the sole criteria for making this determination. Individuals who fall into the category of substance abuse or substance dependence will certainly be appropriate for *SSC.* However, there will be some, and possibly many, clients who will not meet these criteria and yet are appropriate for *SSC.* These are clients who do show evidence of a history of substance use problems but also fall into the medium and high risk of criminal conduct and recidivism.

The *Adult Self-Assessment Questionnaire* (AdSAQ: Wanberg & Milkman, 1993, 2004) provides a measure of the client's motivation and readiness for treatment services. Again, guidelines for using this instrument for determining treatment readiness are provided in the *PACE Handbook.*

Note: The instruments provided in the *PACE Handbook* may only be used by providers with clients in *SSC.* Providers and agencies who wish to use these instruments for their clients who are not in *SSC,* or who want to use them for general purposes for screening and assessment, will need to purchase an annual contract for their use (see footnote 1 at end of chapter).

If the client is accepted for admission into the *SSC* program, then the evaluator can proceed to complete the PDQ and the SEQ. Most agencies have their own intake form to record individual data and demographics on their clients and obtain the essential data for the client's record. *PACE* includes a *Personal Data Questionnaire* (PDQ), provided in the *PACE Handbook* (and in *Appendix A),* that provides the essential data elements for this task.

Tasks and Instruments Used in PACE

PACE TASKS	INSTRUMENTS
Differential screening and intake	▶ ASUS-R: Differential screening ▶ Personal Data Questionnaire (PDQ): Descriptive information ▶ Adult Self-Assessment Questionnaire (AdSAQ): Completed by client and measures motivation and readiness for treatment ▶ Self Evaluation Questionnaire - (SEQ): Completed by client at intake and describes the cognitive-behavioral status of clients
Differential and comprehensive assessment	▶ Adult Self-Assessment Profile (AdSAP): Measures basic psychosocial problem areas and risk factors ▶ Rating Adult Problems Scale (RAPS): Evaluator's rating of client's psychosocial problem areas ▶ Cognitive Assessment Guide (CAG)
Progress and change during treatment	▶ Program Attending Record (PAR): Measures client's program involvement ▶ Client Program Response - Client (CPR-C): Measures client's response to treatment and CB changes every 4th session ▶ Client Program Response - Provider (CPR-P): Same as CPR-C and completed by provider every 4th session ▶ Self Evaluation Questionnaire - (SEQ): Completed by client every three months and/or at the end of each *SSC* Phase of treatment ▶ AdSAP/RAPS Retest (optional): Completed by client after being in program six months and are used to compare client's intake responses with six months post-admission responses ▶ AdSAQ Retest (optional): Completed by client after being in program six months and used to compare client's intake motivation and readiness for treatment with six months post-admission ▶ ASUS-R Retest (optional): Completed by client after being in program six months and used to compare client's intake responses with six months post-admission responses
Treatment closure: immediate treatment outcome	▶ Phase I Review Guide (PI-RG) ▶ Program Closure Inventory - Client (PCI-C): By client when completing or terminating program ▶ Program Closure Inventory - Provider (PCI-P): By provider when client completes or ends program ▶ Self Evaluation Questionnaire - (SEQ)
Treatment follow-up	▶ Follow-up Assessment Questionnaire (FAQ) - six months: Includes retest of SEQ and components of the ASUS-R and AdSAP (because of limited resources, it is recommended a random sample of clients be followed) ▶ Follow-up Assessment Questionnaire (FAQ) - one year or more

One of the objectives of *PACE* is to measure the client's progress and change throughout all of the *SSC* phases of treatment relative to the targets of change. These change targets are dynamic factors that can be influenced by the treatment process. The *Self Evaluation Questionnaire* (SEQ) provides this capability and provides a baseline measure with respect to:

▶ Mental self-control, relationship, and community responsibility skills at the time of admission;

▶ Concern about and ability to handle an AOD and criminal conduct problem.

▶ Criminal conduct and AOD involvement in the three months prior to last arrest and in the three months prior to admission to *SSC;*

▶ Response to prior treatment experiences;

▶ Adjustments in the areas of family, mental health, employment, antisocial behavior and AOD use in the three months prior to last arrest (for judicial clients who are incarcerated, this would be the three months in the community prior to their last arrest);

▶ Understanding of and satisfaction with *SSC* and ratings of providers perfomance.

Clients are retested every three months on the SEQ.

Comprehensive Multiple-Factor Assessment

There are a number of issues related to comprehensive assessment. This topic is discussed in more detail in the *Perspectives on Assessment* chapter of the *Resource Guide.*

Multiple-factor assessment

There is strong support in the literature for a multiple-factor, comprehensive assessment of clients entering AOD treatment (Caddy, 1978; Connors, Donovan & DiClemente, 2001; Hart & Stueland, 1979; Hyman, 1976; Miller, Westerberg & Waldron, 1995; Pattison & Kaufman, 1982; Pattison, Sobell & Sobell, 1977; Wanberg & Horn, 1983; Wanberg & Horn, 1987; Wanberg & Milkman, 1998). This kind of assessment should be done for clients entering *SSC.* This includes the assessment of

the following major life-concerns and life-functioning domains.

▶ Concerns about problems during the years of development;

▶ Family, marital and relationship problems;

▶ Mental health and psychological concerns;

▶ Employment and vocational adjustment;

▶ Involvement in antisocial behavior and history of criminal conduct;

▶ AOD use and abuse problems and patterns;

▶ Motivation and readiness for change and treatment and perceptual defensiveness;

▶ Medical/physical health;

▶ Client strengths and assets;

▶ Clients perception of treatment and service needs.

These major domains represent multiple risk factors that contribute to the development and maintenance of AOD problems and criminal conduct. A number of life-adjustment problems, i.e., marital, job, mood adjustment, legal, can interact with and reinforce a pattern of alcohol use and abuse.

There are a number of instruments that provide measurement across these various factors, including AOD use and abuse. These instrument options are presented in the chapter on *Perspectives on Assessment* in the *Resource Guide.* For clients in *SSC,* we recommend the use of the *Adult Clinical Assessment Profile* - ACAP (Wanberg, 1998, 2006), which includes the *Adult Self-Assessment Profile* and the *Rating Adult Problems Scale* (AdSAP-RAPS: Wanberg, 1998, 2006). These two instruments and scoring instructions are provided in the *PACE Handbook* along with brief instructions for scoring.

The *Resource Guide* also provides a conceptual framework for describing multidimensional drug use patterns and conditions. As well, it provides a conceptual framework for comprehensive and in-depth assessment of judicial clients. This framework includes all of the problem conditions and risk factors that should be addressed in treatment.

Assessment of cognitive-behavioral processing

The rationale behind cognitive therapy is that emotions and actions are determined by the individual's cognitive structures and processes. The task of assessment is to understand the way the individual organizes that world through various cognitive structures which were discussed in *Chapter 4.*

CB assessment involves identifying the client's cognitive structures that determine specific responses to various life situations and that lead to pathological or disruptive emotional or behavioral outcomes. The assessment starts with identifying the pathological or disruptive emotional and behavioral responses and work back to those cognitive responses that lead to those emotions and behaviors. The treatment goal is then to replace or learn new cognitive responses that lead to healthier and more positive emotional and behavioral outcomes. The selection of new cognitive responses is based on those most relevant to target emotions or behaviors. The *Cognitive Assessment Guide* (CAG) in the *PACE Handbook* provides a structure for completing the CB assessment.

CB assessment is a formal part of the comprehensive assessment component and also an integral part of each treatment session. The following cognitive-behavioral assessment model is congruent with the basic cognitive-behavioral approach to change that is used in the client's workbook, and more specifically, with the *SSC CB Map.*

▶ First, identify the general and specific disturbed and pathological emotional and behavioral targets for change, e.g., depression, criminal conduct, addictive behavior, and the degree of pathology or disturbance related to those targets, using both interview and instrument data.

▶ Identify the specific relevant internal and external events or situations that are part of emotional and behavioral outcomes, e.g., relationship with criminal associates, stressful relationship, etc.

▶ Identify the individual's cognitive structures (thoughts, attitudes and beliefs) that are responses to these situations and that lead to maladaptive emotional and behavioral outcomes.

▶ Identify the cognitive processes through which the cognitive structures are expressed, e.g., cognitive distorting.

▶ Identify cognitive skills (thought restructuring, relaxation exercises) that can help replace, change or manage maladaptive cognitive structures and processes with those that are predicted to produce healthy and more adaptive emotional and behavioral outcomes.

▶ Identify the social and community responsibility skills congruent with the improved or changed cognitive responses that can lead to positive outcomes, e.g., prosocial behaviors.

▶ Evaluate the effectiveness of the new cognitive responses and the new interpersonal and community responsibility skills to determine their efficacy in producing positive outcomes.

Assessment of motivation and readiness for treatment

The work on stages of change has demonstrated that an essential task in assessment is determining the client's readiness and motivation for treatment. The area of treatment motivation and readiness is not only assessed in the intake interview but is ongoing during intervention and treatment. For *SSC,* the following are the most salient elements for assessing treatment readiness and motivation:

▶ degree of problem awareness;

▶ acknowledgement of the need for help;

▶ acknowledgement of the perception that others also see a need for change and help;

▶ willingness to be involved in treatment;

▶ established thoughts about making changes in particular areas;

▶ whether changes have actually been made.

The *SSC* instrument for this kind of assessment is the *Adult Self Assessment Questionnaire* (AdSAQ: Wanberg & Milkman, 1993; 2004) It provides six specific and two broad measures of readiness and change.

Assessment of strengths

Those concerned about resiliency and strength assessment might conclude that the above multiple-factors do not consider the client's strengths. Inherent in the above-identified problem factors are strengths. Persons who score low on job and economic problems indicate strengths in these areas. So is the case across all of the assessment factors. However, the direct measurement of strengths is also important. Thus, assessment needs to include a factor that measures the client's strength, from both a self-report and an other-report perspective. The ASUS-R and the AdSAP/RAPS provide both a self-report and an other-report client strengths measure.

Assessment of Treatment Progress and Change

This area of assessment is most often addressed in treatment progress notes. However, these notes do not give a quantitative description of the progress and changes clients make in treatment.

PACE is comprised of several instruments that allow for the discernment of progress and change. The results of these changes are graphed so that they can be compared across multiple testings. These instruments are summarized in *Table 6.4*.

The PAR (*Program Attending Record*) records the client's attending behavior. We use the word "attending" to indicate the degree to which the client is giving attention to the program. This includes number of sessions completed, number of worksheets completed, number of sessions in which the client verbally participated, and the number of units in 30-minute segments completed. The Automated *PACE Monitor* will allow a graphic printout of the attending data for each client at any point in *SSC*. As well, the *A-PACE Monitor* has capabilities of providing attending information by group, by agency, and by individual provider (counselor). This provides a valuable management information process for the agency at large as well as for the client.

The *Client Program Response - Client* (CPR-C) and the *Client Program Response - Provider* (CPR-P) are completed by the client and provider every 4th session. Providers may choose to use a different

schedule, such as every month or every 5th session. Whichever the case, the CPR-C and CPR-P can be scored and plotted on a graph. This will show the client's progress and change across session segments.

The SEQ is re-administered every three months. Some of the items in the SEQ are based on retrospective responding around adjustment factors over the "past three months." This lends the retesting to be compared with previous testing, and the scale score results to have comparability over sequential three-month testing periods.

The scores generated for the CPR-C, CPR-P and SEQ scales are the percent of the total possible score on a particular scale. This allows for a current measure to be compared with previous measures on the same scale. For example, if the total score on the scale Problem Involvement in CC and AOD Use is nine, and the client's score is three, then the percent of the total score would be 33. This is similar to how the subscales on the LSI-R are scored and represented. For example, if a client has eight checks on the LSI-R Criminal History Scale, the score would be .80 (80%), since there are 10 items on that scale. Since the progress and change questions on *PACE* have multiple responses, the total score on any one item may be three or four. Thus, the total score is more than the number of items on the scale.

The provider can also choose to re-administer the ASUS-R, the AdSAP/RAPS and the AdSAQ after the client has been in the program for six months. This retesting lends itself to comparing the six-month scales on the ASUS-R and AdSAP, as well as the measures that are more dynamic (e.g., MOOD ADJUSTMENT, STRENGTHS, etc.) with the testing done at intake and comprehensive assessment.

These testings and retestings not only indicate progress and change, but also areas that still need to be addressed in treatment. They can be helpful in updating the individual treatment plan of clients, but also help clients update their *MAP.*

Assessment of Outcome at Treatment Closure and Follow-up

In essence, all of the components of the assessment

process address treatment outcome. For example, the increase in the client's willingness to self-disclose from the time of initial screening to comprehensive assessment represents change and is a measure of treatment outcome. The decrease in cognitive pre-occupation with criminal involvement or AOD use as measured by the CPR-C represents change and treatment outcome. These observed changes (clinically or psychometrically) during treatment are good predictors of post-treatment outcome.

However, a comprehensive program of assessment should include evaluating the client's status at discharge and at some period post-discharge.

Assessment of readiness for program continuation

At the end of *Phase I,* clients are evaluated for readiness and motivation to continue into *Phase II.* An individual session is held with clients during the two weeks prior to the completion of *Phase I.* The *PACE* results are reviewed with the client. The key areas of work clients did in that phase are also reviewed, using the *Phase I Review Guide* (PI-RG). The PI-RG is part of the *PACE Monitor.* An individual interview is also held with clients at the end of *Phase II* to evaluate their motivation and readiness to continue *SSC.* However, the assessment at the end of *Phase II* is informal. The methods, procedures and guidelines for these phase reviews and closure assessments are discussed in detail in *Chapter 7.*

Program closure assessment

The *Program Closure Inventory - Client* (PCI-C) and the *Program Closure Inventory - Provider* (PCI-P) are completed by the client and provider (counselor) respectively at the time the client completes or leaves the program. Providers compare their results with clients. The SEQ is again completed at program closure unless the closure process for the client is within two weeks of having completed the last SEQ.

In the case of clients who discontinue *SSC* without notice, providers will not be able to administer the self-report closure instruments. However, in the case where clients decide not to continue *SSC,* and there is notice that they will be discontinuing, providers should make every effort to have them complete these instruments.

For clients who discontinue without notice, providers will want to complete the PCI-P. This will provide some measure of the client's progress and change from the perspective of the provider.

Post-discharge assessment

As noted above, how a client does in treatment is a good predictor of post-discharge outcome (Horn, Wanberg & Foster, 1990). However, some sense of how clients are doing at some point following returning to the community or following discharge from treatment is important and provides for a well-rounded program of evaluating client outcome and treatment program efficacy. The *Follow-up Assessment Questionnaire* (FAQ) provides the instrument structure for this objective. It combines many of the scales in the SEQ, ASUS-R, and AdSAP. Although ideally, all clients should be followed at some point following discharge, this is not a practical objective. Thus, it is recommended that a random sample of clients is identified for both short- and long-term follow-up. The sample should include at least 10% of any particular treatment cohort.

PACE CASE EXAMPLE PRESENTATION

One way to gain further understanding of *PACE* is to present a case study. This client completed the intake instruments and was seen as appropriate for *SSC.* Instrumentation results will be presented for this client for the ASUS-R, AdSAP/RAPS, and the AdSAQ. The rest of the *PACE* measures are completed based on expected or hypothetical outcomes. Only example scales of the PAR, CPR-C, CPR-P and SEQ will be presented to illustrate *PACE.*

Admission to SSC

This client was referred for evaluation by community corrections. He was placed in a community corrections facility in lieu of being sent to a minimum security prison setting. It is routine for this particular jurisdiction to process the client through a diagnostic workup and administer the LSI-R and a simple AOD problem screening instrument to determine whether AOD differential screening is needed. This client was screened into the process of being administered the ASUS-R. Results of the ASUS-R are found in *Figure 6.1* along with descriptive information from an instrument comparable to the PDQ and the total LSI-R score.

This 31-year-old, never married, Anglo male has had five prior judicial adult convictions, was not arrested prior to age 16, has had prior incarcerations, has had suspensions while on probation and has a record of assaultive behavior. However, his recent conviction was not for assault. He was placed in community corrections and was employed at the time of being evaluated. He has a fairly good employment history and has a skilled trade. Although claiming to be never married, he has had disruptive marital-type relationships. He reports having past criminal friends or associates and very few if any prosocial or anticriminal associates. Interview results indicated a rather poor attitude towards his sentencing and changing criminal conduct.

Results from the LSI-R and ASUS-R indicated significant history and current AOD problems with alcohol abuse diagnosis and possible dependence. His psychophysical problems related to AOD use are low. The primary area of AOD abuse is loss of behavioral control when using drugs. He has a history of extensive involvement in marijuana, alcohol and amphetamines.

ASUS-R results also indicate marginal motivation for treatment, and he sees himself as having minimal mental health or mood adjustment problems. However, the LSI-R indicated a history of psychiatric treatment. Thus, there is resistance and defensiveness towards admitting to problems in the area of mental health. There is also some defensiveness around admitting to criminal conduct and antisocial attitudes and behaviors, and his case record indicates more than what is reflected in the ASUS-R. However, on both the SOCIAL NON-CONFORMING and LEGAL NON-CONFORMING ASUS-R scales, he scores higher than 50% of the offenders in the normative sample. His score on DEFENSIVE is not extremely high, but in the range to indicate he is holding back some; yet, overall, relatively self-disclosing, particularly in the AOD problems area. He rates himself relatively low with respect to strengths

in psychosocial adjustment and in being able to prevent involvement in AOD abuse and criminal conduct.

The total LSI-R score of 39 and the sum of the weighted scores from the ASUS-R INVOLVEMENT, DISRUPTION, BENEFITS, SOCIAL NON-CONFORMING and LEGAL NON-CONFORMING scales placed this individual at the high range of the regular outpatient treatment category. However, his profile could justify placement in enhanced treatment services, e.g., intensive outpatient versus regular outpatient. The evaluator rated this individual as having AOD involvement and disruption (ASUS-R RATER Scale) at a higher level than the client rated himself and actually placed him in enhanced AOD treatment services. His high risk for criminal conduct and recidivism and his AOD problem level made him eligible for *SSC*. However, his low scores on motivation posed some concern around this placement.

Comprehensive Assessment

Although the LSI-R and the ASUS-R provide substantive information on clients at the time they are screened for AOD services, comprehensive assessment broadens this assessment and adds to the depth of understanding clients. The comprehensive assessment is usually done a few days or even weeks after the screening assessment, and clients will have made some adjustment in self-understanding and thus self-disclosure.

Figure 6.2 provides the summary profile of the *Adult Clinical Assessment Profile* (ACAP) which includes the profile from the AdSAP and RAPS. *Figure 6.3* provides a summary of the AdSAQ, which is a measure of readiness for change and motivation for treatment. The AdSAP supports the results from the ASUS-R indicating significant AOD problems, sustained AOD use, moderate benefits from use, and some prior help to address AOD problems. There is a history of significant relationship and interpersonal problems, most likely due to his history of violence which mainly was confined to close relationships. He scores high on childhood problems, and, congruent with the ASUS-R results, moderate on legal problems, and low on motivation to change and self-perceived strengths. The AdSAP indicates that, in addition to a history of legal problems, these problems and his criminal conduct have been recent (last six months). He continues to see himself as having minimal mental health concerns or problems, in spite of some past treatment in this area.

The AdSAP also confirms the findings at screening that he has been able to sustain stable employment and has a skilled trade to rely upon. Also, across both the ASUS-R and AdSAP, his overall global psychosocial disruption is in the moderate range when compared to other adult offenders being processed through assessment.

The results from RAPS (evaluator's perception of client) validates the client's self-disclosures and self-perceptions. However, the evaluator sees him as having more problems in the mood adjustment and mental health areas than the client's self-disclosure.

The results from the AdSAQ, *Figure 6.3*, indicates that this client has contemplated change, yet does not see a strong need for change in the emotional or interpersonal relationship area, even though he discloses having problems in the latter. He also minimizes his need to change in the area of community responsibility which includes complying with the law and also being gainfully employed. The latter is one of his strengths. He does perceive others as seeing him needing to change, does not strongly acknowledge the need for help, sees himself as having made some change, has low to moderate overall readiness for change and help, and indicates he has taken little action to change. Overall, he would fall in the contemplative to early preparation stage of change.

The comprehensive assessment supports entering *SSC*. The treatment targets are clearly criminal conduct and substance abuse. However, other areas that need to be addressed are: unresolved problems of childhood, disruptions in his interpersonal, and most likely, close and intimate relationships, and overall motivational enhancement to help this client have a positive response to treatment. He seems to have low self-efficacy as to confidence to handle his life problems, however, the one area of strength to be capitalized on is that of job productivity and employment. The comprehensive assessment also

shows that specialized services in anger management and violence prevention are clearly needed, and should be parallel with or follow at least the completion of *SSC Phase I*.

Progress and Change Documentation

Although this client had not yet started *SSC*, we proceed to rate this case on the various *PACE* measures to illustrate how change and progress are measured as a client proceeds through *SSC*. Only a sample of the change and progress scales of *PACE* will be illustrated for this client at the end of *Phase I*. *Phase I* includes 20 sessions, 50 worksheets, and, considering each session to be two hours, 40 hours of therapy.

Figures 6.4 through *6.6* provide a summary of the *PACE Monitor* at the end of *Phase I* or 20 sessions delivered over a period of five months or one session a week. The CPR-C and CPR-P would have been completed every four sessions, or five times. The SEQ would have been completed once after the client finished three months and then once more at the completion of *Phase I*. The provider would have re-administered the ASUS-R one time and the AdSAQ one time. We will not illustrate the re-administration of these two instruments.

Although the illustration is for the entire *Phase I* period, the provider can generate a client's *PACE* profile for shorter time intervals. It should be done at least twice during *Phase I* for each client. The value of the automated *PACE* is that the client's *PACE* profile is automatically calculated and can be visited at any time by the provider.

Program Attending Record

The *Program Attending Record* (PAR) can be used as a management information system. As noted above, it is referred to as "attending" since it measures a number of variables that indicate the degree to which the client gives attention to and is involved in the program. It measures the percent of sessions attended relative to those held during the time the client was enrolled in *SSC*. For example, if 10 sessions were held and the client attended eight of 10 sessions, he would have an 80% attendance score. It also provides an estimated percent of worksheets the client completed, the hours of *SSC* attended, and the number of sessions in which the client verbally participated and the degree of that verbal participation.

Figure 6.4 illustrates that this client attended 90% of the *Phase I* sessions, completed 88% of the worksheets and verbally participated in 94% of the sessions. This will be the extent of measures that are generated by the hand scoring procedure.

The automated *PACE* enhances the amount of information that indicates program attention. For example, it can show the verbal participation for any particular session, for the total group, or for the total of *Phase I*. The percent of client attendance can be generated for different providers and different groups. Furthermore, this program will allow for the gross session fee charges and gross receipts by session, by client, by program, by month, etc. It allows for providers to enter various kinds of data in addition to summarizing the basic attending variables.

Client Program Response: CPR-C and CPR-P

The CPR is completed every four sessions and done by the client and the provider. There are three subscales and one general scale. The general scale measures the overall response to the program, including program participation and cooperation, awareness of AOD and CC problems, changes in criminal and AOD thinking, degree of willingness to change, and a measure of overall progress made over the past four sessions. The general scale is a sum of all of the individual scales and provides an overall measure of the client's participation, response, and change efforts.

For the case being illustrated, only the Global Response measure is charted. *Figure 6.5* provides the CPR for the client's self-ratings (CPR-C) and *Figure 6.6* the CPR completed by the provider (CPR-P). The illustration is rather typical in that the first ratings by the client represent the honeymoon stage of treatment where response to the program and change are usually rated high. For the second four sessions, the ratings tend to drop; then for the subsequent sessions, the ratings tend to increase and surpass the first segment's ratings. Also typical is that the ratings by the provider or counselor are usually lower than those by the client. Yet, the same honeymoon, slump, and then acceleration trend is usually observed even with the provider ratings. The case being illustrated shows that at the end of *Phase I*, the client's self-ratings are quite good as are the provider's ratings of the client.

Again, the automated *PACE* provides enhanced capabilities of charting progress in treatment. The ratings can be summarized by group, by provider, and even compared to other programs.

Self Evaluation Questionnaire (SEQ)

The SEQ is administered at admission and then every three months. This allows for two administrations during *Phase I* if sessions are held once a week. If *Phase I* is delivered twice a week over a period of about three months, the SEQ is administered at the end of this treatment phase.

Figure 6.7 illustrates a comparison of the measures at admission into *SSC* with those taken after three months of *SSC* for six scales of the SEQ. Scale 1 measures the degree of self-perceived involvement in AOD problems and criminal conduct in the three months prior to the client's last arrest and then for the first three months in *SSC*. The results suggest that the client had some involvement in these behaviors during the first three months of *SSC*.

Scale 2 measures the client's perceived benefits from prior programs and efforts to prevent AOD use and CC. The results would suggest that the client perceives the three months in *SSC* to be of greater benefit than prior program involvements.

Scale 3 measures perceived progress and improvement in the attempt to prevent AOD involvement and CC. Scale 4 provides a global measure of the extent to which the client perceived himself to be involved in the five major risk or problem areas: family and relationships; psychological, employment and jobs, AOD abuse and criminal conduct.

Scale 5 provides a measure of the degree to which the client was involved in thinking about criminal conduct and substance use. The comparison of testing at admission is made with that done after three months in *SSC*.

F I G U R E 6 . 1

Adult Substance Use Survey - Revised (ASUS-R) Profile Summary

AGE 31	MALE	EDUCATION 11 YEARS	ANGLO-WHITE AM	NEVER MARRIED	NO PRIOR AOD TREATMENT	EMPLOYED FULL TIME

PRIMARY DRUGS AND AGE LAST USE: ALCOHOL (31), MARIJUANA (30), AMPHETAMINES (31)	TOTAL LSI-R: 39	COMMUNITY CORR.

ASUS-R BASIC PROFILE

	SCALE	Low	Low-medium	High-medium	High
SCALE NAME	SCORE	1 : 2 : 3	4 : 5	6 : 7	8 : 9 : 10
1. AOD INVOLVEMENT1	17				18:19 24 40
2. AOD DISRUPTION1	22			24 28:29 32 37:38	42 49:50 58 80
3. AOD LAST 6 MONTHS	1	2:3 4 5:6 7 8:9	10 12:13 15 17:18	21 25:26 30 37:38	51 99
4. AOD USE BENEFITS	9			10:10 13 14:15	17 19:20 24 30
5. SOCIAL NON-CON	11		12 13 : 14 : 15	16: 17 18 :19	21 36
6. LEGAL NON-CON	15		15 16 : 17 18 : 19	20 :21 22 23:24	26 42
7. LEGAL 6 MONTHS	4		5 : 6 : 7	8 : 9 10 :11	14 33
8. MOOD ADJUSTMENT	3	: 5 6: 7 : 8	:9 10 : 11	12:13 14 15:16 17	19:20 22 27
9. GLOBAL AOD-PSYSOC	51			55:56 61 65:66 73 79:80	87 97:98 177
10. DEFENSIVE	10			11: 12	13:14 15 21
11. MOTIVATION	6	7 8: 9 10 11: 12	13 :14 15 16: 17	: 18 19 : 20	: 21
12. STRENGTHS	8	9 10 11:12 13 :14 15	: 16 17: 18	:19 20 : 21	22:23 24 25: 26 27
13. ASUS-R RATER	16				: 18
14. +AOD INVOLVEMENT2	16		:17 18 19:20 22 23:24	25 26:27 30 32:33	36 40
15. +AOD DISRUPTION2	22	26:27 30 34:35 38 41:42	45 47:48 50 53:54	57 59:60 63 65:66	69 80

ADULT JUDICIAL NORMS 　 1　10　20　30　40　50　60　70　80　90　99
PERCENTILE　　+INPATIENT/IOP NORMS

ASUS-R SUPPLEMENTAL PROFILE

	SCALE RAW	Low	Low-medium	High-medium	High
SCALE NAME	SCORE	1 : 2 : 3	4 : 5	DECILE RANK 6 : 7	8 : 9 : 10
16. BEHAVIORAL DISRUPT	11		12 :13 14 15: 16	17: 18 19 :20	21 24
17. PSYCHOPHYS DISRUPT	7	8 11:12 14 15:16 18 19:20	21 23:24 25 26:27 28	30:31 32 33:34	36 40
18. SOCIAL ROLE	4	: 5 6 7: 8 : 9	10 11 : 12 13: 14	:15 : 16

INPATIENT/IOP NORMS　　1　10　20　30　40　50　60　70　80　90　99
PERCENTILE

ASUS-R EVALUATOR SUMMARY

16. AOD Use Involvement?	Minimal　Low　Moderate　High	No Services Suggested	
17. AOD Use Disruption?	Minimal　Low　Moderate　High　9	Alcohol/Drug Education	
		AOD Ed.+ Evaluation for WOP	
18. AOD service readiness?	Minimal　Low　Moderate　High　　4　5　6　7　8　9	Evaluation for Enhanced Tx: IOP or Residential	

Reprinted with permission of author, K. W. Wanberg, Copyright (c) 2004

Adult Clinical Assessment Profile (ACAP) Summary
ADULT SELF-ASSESSMENT PROFILE (ADSAP)

SCALE NAME	RAW SCORE	DECILES Low 1 ¦ 2 ¦ 3	Low-medium 4 ¦ 5	High-medium 6 ¦ 7	High 8 ¦ 9 ¦ 10
1. CHILDHOOD	17				18 20 36
2. FAMILY-MARITAL	7				8 9 10¦11 13 21
3. INTERPERSONAL	5				6 7 8¦9 10 21
4. MENTAL HEALTH	3	¦ 4	¦ 5 6 ¦ 7 8	¦ 9 10 11¦12 14 16¦17 21 42
5. PRODUCTIVITY	4		5 ¦ 6 ¦ 7	8 ¦ 9 10 11¦12 14 21
6. LEGAL-NON-CON	13	14 ¦ 15 16¦ 17 18	¦19 20 21¦22 25 45
7. AOD INVOLVEMENT	17				19¦20 25 40
8. AOD SUSTAINED	11				12 15
9. AOD BENEFITS	10			11¦12 13 15¦16 18 20¦21 25 33
10. AOD DISRUPTION	16				¦17 19 22¦23 27 36
11. PRIOR AOD HELP	1	¦ 2 ¦ 3	¦ 4 5 ¦ 6 7 8¦ 9 11 16
12. AOD GLOBAL	35	37¦38 41 44¦45 52 58¦59 68 99
13. PHYSICAL HEALTH	3	¦ 4	¦5 6 7¦ 8 10 18
14. MOTIVATION	1	¦ 2 ¦ 3 ¦ 4 ¦ 5	¦ 6 7 8¦9 11 21
15. HELP NEEDS	3	¦ 4 5 ¦ 6 7¦ 8 10 24
16. STRENGTHS	11	¦12 13 14¦ 15 16¦ 17 18 ¦ 16 20¦ 21 22¦ 23 24¦25 26 27¦28 30 33
17. FAM-INTER. 6 MO	5	¦ 6 7¦ 8 9 10¦11 13 14¦15 19 42
18. MEN. HEALTH 6 MO	3	4 ¦ 5 ¦6 7 8¦ 9 11 12¦13 17 42
19. PRODUCTIVI. 6 MO	2	¦3 4¦ 5 ¦ 6 7¦ 8 9 10¦11 14 21
20. LEGAL-NON-C 6 MO	3	¦4 ¦5 6 ¦ 7 ¦ 8 9 10¦11 14 45
21 AOD INVOLVE 6 MO	0	¦ ¦ ¦ ¦ 1 ¦ 2 ¦ 3 4¦5 6 7¦8 10 36
22. AOD GLOBAL 6 MO	2	¦ 3 ¦ 4 5 ¦ 6 7 8¦ 9 12 14¦15 19 25¦26 36 99
PERCENTILE SCORES		1 10 20 30 40	50 60	70 80	90 99

RATING ADULT PROBLEMS SCALE (RAPS)

SCALE NAME	SCORE	DECILES Low 1 ¦ 2 ¦ 3	Low-medium 4 ¦ 5	High-medium 6 ¦ 7	High 8 ¦ 9 ¦ 10
1. CHILDHOOD	19				20¦21 23 28
2. FAMILY-INTERPER	11			¦12 13 14¦ 15 16 ¦17 18 24
3. MENTAL HEALTH	7	¦ 8 ¦ 9 ¦ 10 11¦ 12 13 ¦14 15 16¦17 19 32
4. WORK-JOB	5	¦6 7 ¦ 8 ¦9 10 ¦11 12 ¦13 15 16¦17 18 24
5. LEGAL	12	¦ 13 14 ¦ 15 16 ¦17 18 19¦20 22 32
6. AOD GLOBAL	18	19¦ 20 21¦ 22 23¦24 27 32
7. HEALTH	2	3 ¦ 4 ¦ 5 6 7¦ 8 9 ¦10 13 20
8. STRENGTHS	21	22 23¦ 14 15 ¦26 27 28¦ 29 30¦ 31 32 ¦33 34 35¦36 39 44
PERCENTILE SCORES		1 10 20 30 40	50 60	70 80	90 99

Reprinted with permission of author K.W. Wanberg, copyright © 2006

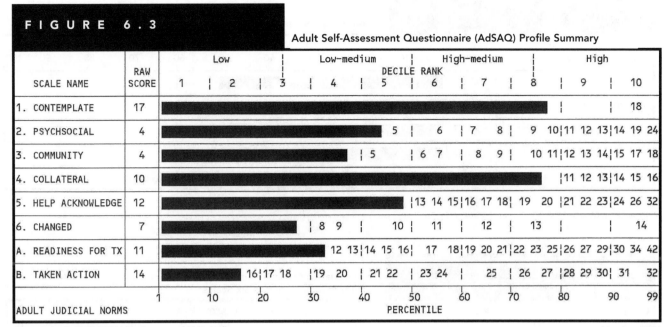

FIGURE 6.3

Adult Self-Assessment Questionnaire (AdSAQ) Profile Summary

SCALE NAME	RAW SCORE	Low			Low-medium		High-medium			High		
		DECILE RANK										
		1	2	3	4	5	6	7	8	9	10	
1. CONTEMPLATE	17										18	
2. PSYCHSOCIAL	4					5	6	7	8	9 10 11 12 13 14	19 24	
3. COMMUNITY	4					5	6 7	8 9		10 11 12 13 14 15	17 18	
4. COLLATERAL	10									11 12 13 14 15 16		
5. HELP ACKNOWLEDGE	12						13 14 15 16 17 18	19	20 21 22 23 24	26 32		
6. CHANGED	7				8 9	10	11	12	13		14	
A. READINESS FOR TX	11				12 13 14 15 16	17	18 19 20 21 22 23 25 26 27 29 30 34 42					
B. TAKEN ACTION	14		16 17 18	19 20	21 22	23 24	25	26 27 28 29 30 31	32			

	1	10	20	30	40	50	60	70	80	90	99	

ADULT JUDICIAL NORMS   PERCENTILE

Copyright © 2003 K.W. Wanberg and H.B. Milkman   Version 0504

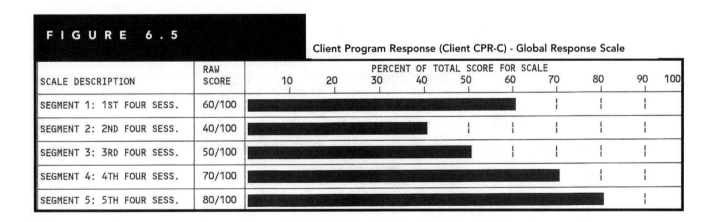

FIGURE 6.4

Program Attending Record - PAR for Client at End of Phase I

SCALE DESCRIPTION	RAW SCORE	PERCENT OF TOTAL SCORE FOR SCALE
		10 20 30 40 50 60 70 80 90 100
PHASE I ATTENDANCE	18/20	
PERCENT WORKSHEETS DONE	44/50	
PERCENT OF SESSIONS ACTIVE	17/18	

FIGURE 6.5

Client Program Response (Client CPR-C) - Global Response Scale

SCALE DESCRIPTION	RAW SCORE	PERCENT OF TOTAL SCORE FOR SCALE
		10 20 30 40 50 60 70 80 90 100
SEGMENT 1: 1ST FOUR SESS.	60/100	
SEGMENT 2: 2ND FOUR SESS.	40/100	
SEGMENT 3: 3RD FOUR SESS.	50/100	
SEGMENT 4: 4TH FOUR SESS.	70/100	
SEGMENT 5: 5TH FOUR SESS.	80/100	

FIGURE 6.6

Client Program Response - Provider (CPR-P) Global Response Scale

SCALE DESCRIPTION	RAW SCORE	PERCENT OF TOTAL SCORE FOR SCALE
		10 20 30 40 50 60 70 80 90 100
SEGMENT 1: 1ST FOUR SESS.	50/100	
SEGMENT 2: 2ND FOUR SESS.	30/100	
SEGMENT 3: 3RD FOUR SESS.	60/100	
SEGMENT 4: 4TH FOUR SESS.	60/100	
SEGMENT 5: 5TH FOUR SESS.	70/100	

FIGURE 6.7

Self Evaluation Questionnaire (SEQ): Admission Results Compared with *SSC* Three Months Across Six Scales

SCALE 1: INVOLVEMENT IN AOD USE AND CRIMINAL CONDUCT	RAW SCORE	PERCENT OF TOTAL SCORE FOR SCALE
		10 20 30 40 50 60 70 80 90 100
THREE MONTHS BEFORE ARREST	9/12	
SSC THREE MONTHS	2/12	

SCALE 2: PERCEIVED BENEFITS FROM TREATMENT	RAW SCORE	PERCENT OF TOTAL SCORE FOR SCALE
		10 20 30 40 50 60 70 80 90 100
THREE MONTHS PRIOR TO ADMIT	6/20	
SSC THREE MONTHS	14/20	

SCALE 3: PROGRESS IN PREV- VENTING AOD PROBLEMS AND CC	RAW SCORE	PERCENT OF TOTAL SCORE FOR SCALE
		10 20 30 40 50 60 70 80 90 100
THREE MONTHS PRIOR TO ADMIT	6/20	
SSC THREE MONTHS	14/20	

SCALE 4: GLOBAL MEASURE OF LIFE-ADJUSTMENT PROBLEMS	RAW SCORE	PERCENT OF TOTAL SCORE FOR SCALE
		10 20 30 40 50 60 70 80 90 100
THREE MONTHS PRIOR TO ADMIT	80/100	
SSC THREE MONTHS	35/100	

SCALE 5: AOD AND CC THINK- ING AND BEHAVIOR	RAW SCORE	PERCENT OF TOTAL SCORE FOR SCALE
		10 20 30 40 50 60 70 80 90 100
THREE MONTHS PRIOR TO ADMIT	36/40	
SSC THREE MONTHS	16/40	

SCALE 6: COGNITIVE-SOCIAL RESPONSIBILITY SKILLS	RAW SCORE	PERCENT OF TOTAL SCORE FOR SCALE
		10 20 30 40 50 60 70 80 90 100
THREE MONTHS PRIOR TO ADMIT	10/100	
SSC THREE MONTHS	60/100	

Scale 6 is a measure of the client's perception of competency in using 25 skills that are the focus of *SSC*. At admission, the client is asked to reflect on the ability to use these skills; and then after three months of *SSC*.

Retesting on the ASUS-R and AdSAP

For this particular client, it is recommended that he be retested on the ASUS-R and AdSAP mainly due to his having positive scores on the six-month measures on these two instruments. It would be important to determine whether the six months in *SSC* had an impact on reducing his adjustment problems that he indicated in the six months prior to admission. This will provide more substantive information regarding updating the client's treatment plan.

Status at Discharge from *SSC* and Follow-up

At discharge from *SSC*, both the client and provider complete the *Program Closure Inventory*. The PCI includes most of the scales of the SEQ and the CPR. These scales do not have a time-sequence comparison as does, for example, the SEQ. However, the scales will be scored on the same basis as the SEQ - percent of total score for each scale giving an idea of how the client perceives his overall response to *SSC*. The scale scores of the provider can be compared to the scores of the client, since the same items are used in both the client's and provider's versions of the PCI. The PCI is included in the *PACE Handbook*.

The FAQ (*Follow-up Assessment Questionnaire*) includes many of the same scales as does the SEQ and PCI. However, it also includes measures of the length of time the client was AOD free post-discharge and the length of time the client was also AOD problem-free. Measures of cognitive involvement in criminal and antisocial thinking and actual antisocial and criminal behaviors are included. The FAQ is included in the *PACE Handbook*.

CLIENT SELF-ASSESSMENT DURING *SSC*

SSC is self-assessment driven. Clients are constantly involved in self-disclosure and self-evaluation. This self-evaluation is accomplished mainly through the

tools of change, presented to clients in *Session 2* of *SSC* orientation. We summarize these tools.

Cognitive-Behavioral Map

The *CB Map* was discussed in *Chapter 4*. Although the *CB Map* is one of the primary tools for change in *SSC*, it also provides a structure for CB assessment and for determining specific targets for cognitive and behavioral change.

Autobiography

Although the autobiography is not a measurement instrument, it provides a qualitative assessment of the critical areas of the judicial client's life that may become targets for change. After clients complete the autobiography, they should be asked to underline those areas that can become foci for treatment and targets for change.

Master Skills List (MSL)

The MSL, *Program Guide 1* (page 291 of the *Workbook*), provides clients with a structure for ongoing assessment of their skill development and mastery. At the end of most sessions, clients are asked to update their MSL, which includes checking new skills learned and reevaluating their level of mastery of skills already learned.

Master Profile (MP) and Master Assessment Plan (MAP)

The *MP* is *Program Guide 2* and the *MAP* is *Program Guide 3*. They are listed on pages 292 through 299 of the *Workbook*. During the first month of *SSC*, clients should receive feedback from the results of the intake and admission differential screening (ASUS-R and AdSAQ) and the multiple-factor comprehensive assessment (AdSAP and RAPS). This feedback should be given in an individual session.

Clients use this feedback, plus the work they did on *Worksheet 4*, pages 19 and 20 of the *Workbook*, to complete the *MP* and *MAP*. They complete the initial *MP* and *MAP* in the first month of *SSC*. The provider completes the *MP* on the client, and in an individual session, reviews the client's and provider's profile and the client's *MAP*. *Table 6.5* shows the initial *MAP* for the case illustration.

Weekly Thinking and Action Patterns (TAP) Charting

TAP Charting or Program Guide 4, is a tool that helps clients monitor their thinking around AOD use, their actual use, and their thinking about criminal conduct. *TAP* is of particular importance in terms of seeing changes and progress around being open and self-disclosing over time. Clients will initially be defensive in using *TAP,* and will not trust how the information will be used. As trust and rapport are developed, and as clients begin to take ownership of their own change, they will be more self-disclosing on their *TAP* charting. Although clients are asked if they did use alcohol or other drugs, they are **not** asked if they were involved in actual criminal behavior - but only in thinking about criminal conduct. *TAP* also asks clients if they were in a place where they could have used alcohol or other drugs. Such disclosure in a prison setting could put clients at risk of harm from other inmates. How to manage this situation is dealt with in more detail in *Section III, Session 2,* page 157.

Thinking and Re-thinking Reports

Thinking and re-thinking reports are part of the ongoing CB assessment process. These reports provide a continual practice of identifying high-risk situations and thought structures that lead to relapse and recidivism; and practice using skills to manage those situations. Thinking and re-thinking reports provide both providers and clients with tools to monitor skill development and change in the process of self-disclosure and self-awareness.

SSC Change Scales

At the end of each session, clients are asked to rate themselves on the level of the knowledge and skills they learned and practiced in the session. One method of monitoring progress and change is for clients to periodically go back to previous sessions and rerate themselves on the *SSC Change Scales.* As clients

continue to use and practice the concepts and skills learned in prior sessions, they will indicate higher ratings on these scales. This is also a good review of the concepts and skills learned in *SSC.*

SUMMARY OF *PACE* AND THE AUTOMATED *PACE* MONITOR

The *PACE Monitor* is comprehensive program of client assessment. It is comprised of instruments and methods that evaluate critical life-situations and adjustment problems across a variety of domains which include substance abuse, mental health, criminal conduct, job productivity, relationship and family problems, and physical health concerns. It also measures client responsivity in the areas of motivation and defensiveness. It provides for the measurement of progress and change over the course of treatment and post-treatment outcome. *PACE* provides the mechanism and tools for both client and program evaluation.

The *Pace Handbook* is the user's guide for the *PACE Monitor.* It includes all of the instruments, a brief description of each instrument and its scales, instructions for scoring, and profiles that provide graphic results of the scale scores. It is highly recommended that the provider or counselor have access to the full user's guides for the ASUS-R, AdSAP/RAPS and the AdSAQ. These guides provide information on instrument administration, scoring, and a full description of each scale and scale reliability and construct validity. Information regarding the access of these guides is found in footnote 1 below.

The *Automated PACE Monitor* (A-PACE) is available on a compact disc. The disc includes a PDF file for each instrument that can be used to print copies. The instruments are completed by the client and provider and then entered into the computer. The *A-PACE* scores each instrument, plots the profile, and shows profile comparisons over time. It can chart changes on individual clients and also provide aggregate-change information across group, provider and agency. It can be used as a management information system for individual clients (e.g., client demographics, attendance, fee charges and payments) and for aggregate-level reports for the group, provider and agency. Information regarding the access

Master Assessment Plan (MAP)

I. ALCOHOL AND OTHER DRUG USE PROBLEM AREAS

PROBLEM AREA AND DESCRIPTION	CHANGES NEEDED IN THOUGHT AND ACTION	RESOURCES TO BE USED TO MAKE CHANGES
Have continual thoughts and desire to get high with friends (marijuana)	Replace with thoughts of going out with non-using friends; manage urges and cravings	Learn and practice skills in *Session 17* on coping with urges and cravings; use assertiveness skills; Master Skills 6 and 20

II. CRIMINAL CONDUCT PROBLEMS

PROBLEM AREA AND DESCRIPTION	CHANGES NEEDED IN THOUGHT AND ACTION	RESOURCES TO BE USED TO MAKE CHANGES
Getting angry and violent in relationships when feeling not in control	Learn to manage anger in relationships; change angry thoughts to get better outcomes	Learn the skills to manage anger as in *Session 27* and prevent violence, *Session 39*; Master Skills 12 and 25

III. THINKING, FEELING, TRIGGERS AND ATTITUDE PATTERNS THAT LEAD TO CRIMINAL CONDUCT AND SUBSTANCE ABUSE

PROBLEM AREA AND DESCRIPTION	CHANGES NEEDED IN THOUGHT AND ACTION	RESOURCES TO BE USED TO MAKE CHANGES
Get depressed because live alone and have hopeless thoughts about ever having a trusting relationship with a woman	Change depressed thoughts; identify underlying beliefs that lead to hopeless thoughts about having trusting relationship	Cognitive restructuring; develop social skills to help meet people and get involved in social groups; Master Skills 1, 13-18, 26

IV. CURRENT LIFE SITUATION PROBLEMS

PROBLEM AREA AND DESCRIPTION	CHANGES NEEDED IN THOUGHT AND ACTION	RESOURCES TO BE USED TO MAKE CHANGES
Conflicts and power struggles with female partner over money issues that lead to anger and thoughts "she doesn't care," that further leads to thoughts of emotional and physical control over her	Change need to be in control and dominate partner; improve on communication skills and how to resolve conflicts around money issues; identify underlying beliefs that lead to "she doesn't care"	Thought restructuring around controlling partner; develop interpersonal and prosocial skills to get better relationship outcomes; interpersonal skills training; couples counseling; conflict resolution skills; Master Skills 1, 19, 20, 21, 30, 31

of the *A-PACE* is found in footnote 2 below.

Agencies will have their limitations as to resources that can be devoted to the use of *PACE* for client assessment and program evaluation. Because of this, the provider or agency may elect to use only portions of the *PACE Monitor*.

CHAPTER REVIEW

This chapter provides a specific operational assessment program for evaluating the treatment needs, progress and change, and the treatment outcome of substance abusing offenders who are admitted to *SSC*. An effective approach to assessment of clients at the beginning of treatment and throughout the treatment process is the convergent validation model. This approach uses two sources of data to estimate the valid condition of the client: self-report and other-report. This model also treats self-report as a valid representation of the client's willingness to self-disclose, and represents a baseline measure of where the client is at each point in the assessment process. Other-report data are used to determine the level of defensiveness of the client and, combined with self-report, provide the most effective way to determine the problem conditions of the client. Effective assessment also evaluates all of the conditions relevant to the client's psychosocial problems and adjustment. This multiple-factor, comprehensive approach provides the basis upon which a valid treatment plan for clients can be developed.

An important component of assessment is screening clients for appropriateness for the *SSC* program. Clients with higher risk for criminal conduct and higher levels of antisocial attitudes and behaviors along with higher levels of disruption related to AOD use are seen as most appropriate for *SSC*. However, clients with low CC risks and low to medium AOD problems should also be considered as candidates for *SSC*. Instruments are described that can be used to discern these problem areas and their level of expression were described.

A specific program of client assessment and evaluation for *SSC* based on the *PACE Monitor* was described. *PACE* is comprised of five basic assessment components: 1) intake and admission; 2) compre-

hensive assessment; 3) evaluation of the progress and change during treatment; 4) treatment closure and 5) follow-up assessment.

The specific instruments used in each component of *PACE* were briefly described. A case example was presented that included the client's intake information, differential screening profiles, and comprehensive assessment profiles. The progress and change instruments of *PACE* were illustrated through the presentation of profiles estimating the client's response to treatment.

The formal program of client assessment through *PACE* represents only part of the effort to evaluate client progress and change. The specific change tools used in *SSC* also provide a picture of the client's effort to change during *SSC*. This self-evaluation of progress and change is a continual process and takes place within each session and is formalized through the client's completion of the *Master Profile (MP)* and the *Master Assessment Plan (MAP)*. The *MP* and *MAP* represent the client's self-analysis and plan for change and are continually updated during *SSC*.

Overall, *SSC* is assessment-driven through both a formal and structured program of assessment defined by the *PACE Monitor* and through a continual process of self-evaluation that occurs in each session and is accomplished through the use of specific *SSC* change tools. These tools include the *CB Map Exercise*, the *Autobiography*, the *Master Skills List*, the *MP* and *MAP*, the weekly *TAP Charting, Thinking and Re-thinking Reports*, and the *SSC Change Scales* completed at the end of each session. This assessment program can be summarized through the *SSC* mantra: Self-disclosure leads to self-awareness, self-awareness leads to change.

1. User's Guides for the ASUS-R, AdSAQ and AdSAP/RAPS may be ordered from the Center for Addictions Research and Evaluation, P. O. Box 1975, Arvada, CO 80001-1975. Additional information regarding these instruments may be found at: www.aodassess.com

2. A compact disc with the *PACE Monitor,* which includes the instruments and automated scoring may be ordered from: Diversion Services Inc., 4435 O Street, Suite 96, Lincoln, NE 68515 or by visiting www.aodassess.com/PACEMONITOR

CHAPTER OUTLINE

OVERVIEW

INTAKE AND ADMISSION PROCEDURES AND GUIDELINES

Referral Information and Data
Screening and Intake
Admission Interview and ITP

PROGRAM AGREEMENTS AND GROUND RULES
EXPECTATIONS OF PROVIDERS
STRUCTURE AND STRATEGIES OF DELIVERY

The Structure of *SSC:* The Treatment Phases
SSC Orientation and Format
Participant's Workbook
Program Delivery Strategies

> *Group format*
> *Delivery options*
> *Minimum-maximum time delivery guidelines*
> *Creativity within fidelity to the SSC program*
> *Delivery settings and service resources*
> *No-entry points for open group format*

PHASE AND PROGRAM CLOSURE GUIDELINES

Phase I Review and Closure
Phases II and *III* Closure
Recognition of Program Completion

REMOVAL OF CLIENT FROM PROGRAM
MANUAL-GUIDED DELIVERY PRINCIPLES

Integration of Psychoeducation and Therapy
Sessions Are Lesson Based
Sessions Are Skill Development Based
Personalizing Curriculum Content and Themes
Multi-Media and Multi-Sensory Formats
Keep Focused on Concepts and Skills
Delivery Setting and Seating Arrangements

> *Setting*
> *Seating arrangement and work space*

PROVIDER KNOWLEDGE AND SKILLS NECESSARY IN *SSC* DELIVERY

Differential Screening and Comprehensive Assessment
Referral Knowledge and Skills
Basic Knowledge Areas
Core Counseling Skills
Motivational Enhancement Skills
Implementing Change: The *CB Map Exercise*
Utilizing *SSC* Tools for Change
Maximizing Participation and Skill Development
Delivering Social Responsibility Therapy - SRT

PRINCIPLES OF GROUP LEADERSHIP: BUILDING A COHESIVE, PROSOCIAL GROUP

Methods of Group Treatment
Depersonalizing Leadership Authority
Center the Authority Within the Group
Center the Authority With Group Members
Keep the Focus on Curriculum Themes and Concepts
Keep the Focus on CB Change
Provider-Group Collaborative Relationship
Maximize Individual Involvement

THE PROVIDER'S MANY HATS
REENTRY AND REINTEGRATION
PROVIDER SKILL EVALUATION AND SUPERVISION
PROVIDER QUALIFICATIONS
EVALUATING SESSION DELIVERY EFFICACY
CHAPTER REVIEW

CHAPTER OBJECTIVES

▶ Define intake and admission procedures and program agreements.

▶ Outline the strategies and methods of program delivery.

▶ Define provider knowledge, skills qualifications required for program delivery.

OVERVIEW

The purpose of this chapter is to present basic guidelines and procedures for the delivery of *Strategies for Self-Improvement and Change (SSC) - Pathways to Responsible Living*. The structure and process of *SSC* will be briefly reviewed. General guidelines for the admission and intake of clients into *SSC* are outlined including samples of intake and admission forms. Program agreements and expectations of clients along with the role expectations of providers are presented. Various options and delivery strategies are discussed along with the provider skills that are necessary for effective *SSC* delivery. Guidelines regarding effective group facilitation and management are also provided. Finally, methods for the evaluation of session delivery are presented.

INTAKE AND ADMISSION PROCEDURES AND GUIDELINES

There are a number of intake and admission procedures that should be followed when admitting clients to *SSC*. Most agencies have these procedures well defined in their policy and procedures manual. We summarize what we see as the essential components and tasks of this procedure and provide sample forms for each of these components in *Appendix A*.

Referral Information and Data

Many judicial clients referred to *SSC* are evaluated for level of criminal risk and AOD problems by the referring judicial agency. Probation departments usually complete a pre-sentencing report and offenders processed for community corrections or incarceration placement usually undergo a diagnostic workup that includes a sentencing and placement report. Referral packages should be sent to receiving treatment agencies that include summary profiles and reports generated from these assessments.

It is also helpful to standardize the referral data and to get some impression from the referring staff member of the nature and extent of the client's problems. The *Referral Evaluation Summary (RES)* provides this basic information. Treatment agencies can distribute these to judicial agencies referring clients to *SSC*.

The *RES* is included in *Appendix A*.

Screening and Intake

At least one hour should be devoted to the screening and intake process. Procedures for screening were discussed in *Chapter 6*. Many judicial agencies do their own screening using instruments such as the *Level of Supervision Inventory-R* (LSI-R) and the *Adult Substance Use Survey-R* (ASUS-R). These screening results should be included in the referral package. If not, then the treatment agency should do a criminal conduct (CC) risk assessment and administer an AOD screening instrument to determine appropriateness for *SSC*.

Once the client has been accepted for *SSC*, then appropriate intake forms are completed. Forms that should be included are listed below and samples are provided in either *Appendix A*..

- *Personal Data Questionnaire* (PDQ: *Appendix A* and *PACE Handbook*).

- *Consent for Program Involvement (Appendix A):* A description of the program and client's agreement to participate.

- *Consent for Release of Confidential Information (Appendix A):* Reviews confidentiality issues and discusses reports clients want sent to components of the judicial system, e.g., court, probation, etc. Have client read and sign these consents.

- *Client's Rights Statement (Appendix A):* Includes:

  - treatment fees and cost;

  - the length and nature of the treatment program;

  - confidentiality laws and requirements;

  - a disclosure that states that sexual contact between client and counselor is not a part of any recognized therapy, that such contact or intimacy between client and counselor is illegal and should be reported to the state grievance board.

- *Notice of Federal Requirements Regarding Con-*

fidentiality of Alcohol and Drug Abuse Patient Records (Appendix A) which apply to staff and participants in the program;

▶ *Full Disclosure Statement (Appendix A):* Required by many states. Must include information about the counselor, including education, training and certifications. The counselor also provides clients with a card indicating name, certification, degree, address and phone number.

In summary, the following are the specific tasks for screening and intake:

▶ Complete the ASUS-R (see *PACE Monitor Handbook*);

▶ Complete the AdSAQ (see *PACE Monitor Handbook*);

▶ Complete intake forms as described above;

▶ Schedule client for orientation to *SSC.*

Admission Interview and Individual Treatment Plan (ITP)

A formal interview is conducted and a comprehensive self-report instrument administered (e.g., *Adult Clinical Assessment Profile - ACAP* (Includes the AdSAP and RAPS). This procedure is discussed in *Chapter 6*. Information from these tasks are used to develop an initial ITP. The client's *MAP* can be used as the ITP.

PROGRAM AGREEMENTS AND GROUND RULES: EXPECTATIONS OF CLIENTS

The orientation session presents the program agreements and guidelines provided in *Session 1* of the *Workbook*. Here are the minimal expectations of clients as to their participation in *SSC.*

▶ **Attendance, promptness and make up missed sessions:** On-time and consistent attendance is required. Missed sessions are made up either when the missed session occurs again in the program cycle or in an individual or group make-up session. Clients are expected to give notification if they anticipate being late or absent.

▶ **Active positive participation:** Participation in exercises, role-playing demonstrations, completion of all worksheets and timely completion of homework assignments is expected. A positive attitude towards the provider and peers is expected.

▶ **Confidentiality:** Clients are expected to not discuss group conversations with outsiders. Providers explain that confidentiality is maintained to the extent that behavior of clients does not reflect imminent danger to themselves or others, the requirement to report suspected child abuse, or a past unreported crime that is required by law to be reported. Providers do not commit to keeping secrets about anything the sponsoring agency or supervisory personnel need to know. Thinking reports and self-disclosing statements should not become a part of the client's official correctional record. Clients should expect and agree through signed consent that summary progress reports will be submitted to supervising agencies, including the court.

Providers make explicit that information about specific crimes or planned crimes might be shared with appropriate authorities where such reporting is required by law. However, *SSC* should not require nor ask for such information. While we expect open communication about thoughts and beliefs, detailed information that constitutes legal evidence is not required.

▶ **Complete all worksheets and homework:** These are measures of program motivation and are attending variables measured by *PACE*. Group members can assist clients who have reading problems and difficulty in completing some assignments.

▶ **Abstinence from substance use during treatment:** Two long-term relapse prevention goals are seen as acceptable for clients: total abstinence from alcohol or other drugs; and preventing involvement in alcohol use patterns that lead to problem or disruptive outcomes. Clients are expected to abstain from the use of all illegal drugs or illegal use of legal drugs. They are expected to abstain from all drugs (including alcohol) while in treatment. Clients whose terms of probation do not require alcohol abstinence may resist this expectation, at least initially. Lapses need to be dealt with therapeutically as well as from a correctional perspective. Correctional confrontation is necessary in the case of the use of illegal drugs. Such breaches are reported to judicial supervisors. Reporting should be done within a therapeutic framework. Every effort should be made to have clients be responsible for disclosing "lapses" to judicial supervisors.

▶ **Clients do not attend during lapses or when they have drugs in their system.** These conditions prevent appropriate program participation and are disruptive to group members' efforts to maintain abstinence. Drug testing is required if there is a question of participants' being drug-free. Clients with positive tests are not allowed in group. If there is a threat to the safety of others because of intoxication, then appropriate measures are taken to protect the community (e.g., police called, client taken to detox, etc.). Clients with a positive drug test are staffed to determine disposition, e.g., temporary suspension from *SSC,* referral to detox, or program dismissal. These decisions are made on a case-by-case basis. Again: releases are obtained at admission to allow reporting of these events to appropriate personnel.

▶ **Cravings and urges:** Encourage clients to discuss these at the beginning of each session for a short period (less than 10 minutes). Reinforce the effort to self-disclose these problems. Help clients identify the high-risk exposures that precede these urges and cravings.

EXPECTATIONS OF PROVIDERS AND GROUP LEADERS

Expectations and ground rules also apply to providers. The most basic guideline is that providers maintain a high level of ethical and professional standards in all contacts with clients. This includes maintaining appropriate dress and appearance and model normative and prosocial behavior. Providers are thoroughly prepared and ready to present each session. The presentation guides for each session in *Section III* of this *Guide* should be studied.

STRUCTURE AND STRATEGIES OF PROGRAM DELIVERY

The structure and process of the delivery of SSC is built around its three overarching goals: Prevent relapse; prevent recidivism; and live a meaningful and responsible life. In accomplishing these goals, different strategies and options can be used in program delivery.

The Structure of *SSC:* The Treatment Phases

Chapter 3 provides a detailed description of the structure and phases of *SSC* and the goals and objectives of the three phases of treatment. We only summarize how these three phases are structured.

▶ *Phase I:* **Challenge to Change** is comprised of 20 two-hour sessions and two individual sessions: one to review the client's *MP* and *MAP;* and one at the end of *Phase I* to review the progress and change of clients and discuss their decision to proceed into *Phase II.*

▶ *Phase II:* **Commitment to Change** is comprised of 22 two-hour sessions. One individual session is held to review progress and change and discuss continuing into *Phase III.*

▶ *Phase III:* **Ownership of Change** is comprised of eight two-hour sessions and an individual session at closure to review progress and change and the client's continuing care plan.

SSC Orientation and Format

Module I, comprised of two sessions, is program orientation. These are delivered before clients proceed in *SSC.* Agencies using open groups will present orientation in either a group or in individual sessions. Agencies that have two or three admissions or more per month can conduct a monthly orientation group. Agencies admitting only one or two a month may need to do orientation in individual sessions.

Orientation to *Phase II* can be done at the same time that clients receive the *Phase I* individual closure session. The same procedure can be used for *Phase II* closure and *Phase III* orientation.

Participant's Workbook

Each client receives a *Workbook* at orientation. It is the client's handbook or user's guide for *SSC* and enhances a sense of program ownership. It is evidence of program motivation and prosocial commitment and is used to evaluate progress and change during treatment.

Some agencies try to cut expenses by using the same *Workbooks* over and over and then copying the worksheets. This is **not** an acceptable delivery strategy as it compromises the effectiveness of the program by diminishing client ownership of the change process. Also, the *Workbook* is under copyright and its materials cannot be copied unless specified in this *Guide*. An example is *Worksheet 6,* page 36. Providers may want clients to practice this CB exercise around different topics. Thus, it is permissible for this worksheet to be copied for repetitive practice.

During and after participation in *SSC,* probation and parole personnel may use the *Workbook* as a tool to enhance individual supervision sessions by referring to specific lessons when discussing situations, thoughts, feelings, and actions related to successful compliance with community based judicial supervision. In this case, the client's completed *SSC Workbook* is used as a parole or probation worker's desk reference.

Program Delivery Strategies

Within the structure of the *Participant's Workbook* and the *Provider's Guide* there are different strategies and options that providers can use in program delivery.

Group format

SSC is delivered in a group format. Individual sessions are used at certain points to review and reinforce changes in clients. Some agencies elect to present *SSC* to incarcerated judicial clients who are in isolation, using an individual session format. This is labor-intense and requires considerable individual-provider effort. It will require one-to-one contact with inmates and considerable self-instruction on the part of the judicial client. This method should be used only if there is no option for group involvement.

Delivery options

Closed group format: The same group begins together and proceeds through *Phase III.* Although effective, it is not practical unless an agency has five or six *SSC* groups going at any one time. It would take a closed group receiving sessions two times a week, 25 weeks to complete the program. If an agency had five groups, then a new group would be started every five weeks, requiring clients to wait as long as five weeks to start a group. This wait period increases entry attrition. This may be feasible in an incarcerated or residential setting if staff resources are available. Closed groups are not as efficient since, over the course of one delivery cycle, fewer clients end up being served because of client dropout.

Open group format for all phases: This requires three separate groups operating at the same time, one for each phase. This is more efficient since dropouts are replaced by new admissions. This is the most practical option for most agencies.

Closed group for *Phase I,* open for *Phases II and III.* At two sessions a week, *Phase I* can be delivered in 10 weeks. To cut the maximum admission wait time to five weeks, an agency would need to have two *Phase I* groups going at any one time; plus a group for *Phase II* and one for *Phase III.*

***Phase I* as stand-alone in residential settings and *Phases II* and *III* delivered in outpatient setting.** This format is used by residential settings where treatment is limited to four or five weeks. *Phase I* can be delivered five times a week and completed in four weeks. Clients are then referred to outpatient for subsequent phases. In this option, continuity of treatment is maintained because clients take their *Workbooks* into the agency where they continue the program. *Phase I* introduces clients to the necessary and essential strategies, content, and skill development of *SSC.* However, this phase has a limited focus on social responsibility therapy (SRT). Effective delivery of *SSC* will include *Phase II.*

Minimum-maximum time delivery guidelines

The structure of the judicial sentence will limit the time that some clients can spend in *SSC*. Their sentence or judicial supervision time may expire while they are in the middle of a treatment phase. Providers should schedule closure sessions for those unable to complete a particular phase to provide a sense of completion. This problem can be mostly avoided by working closely with the judicial system to clarify the time frames necessary to complete *SSC*.

Clients who have less than two or three months of judicial time are not candidates for the total *SSC* program. For example, as noted, *Phase I* offered five times a week in a residential care setting requires four weeks to complete. If the subsequent two phases are delivered in outpatient settings twice a week, the remaining 30 sessions would take 16 weeks, requiring five months for full program delivery. *Phase I* alone, delivered twice a week, would require almost three months. Thus, the minimum program time frame, even using an accelerated delivery schedule, should be four months. The literature is quite clear that SA judicial clients should have a minimum of six to nine months of treatment involvement regardless of the specific program used.

Creativity within fidelity to the SSC program

Providers are expected to have fidelity to the *SSC* module and session content, concepts and interactive exercises provided in the *Workbook* and *Guide*. However, most *SSC* providers are experienced therapists and counselors who have information, concepts, skills, and exercises that they have used with their clients. When these are used in *SSC*, they should fit into the overall objectives, theme and purpose of a particular session. Creativity, within the framework of these objectives, is certainly encouraged.

Delivery settings and service resources

SSC can be delivered in any judicial setting. It can be nested (or embedded) within a broader-scoped program, such as a therapeutic community. Or it can be a stand-alone program offered in an outpatient setting. Whether embedded or stand-alone, other treatment services should be available to cli-

ents within the delivery agency or through service referral. These services should include:

- the broad spectrum of treatment modalities including individual, family and marital treatment, unstructured process groups, and family support groups;

- availability to self-help programs such as Alcoholics Anonymous or Narcotics Anonymous;

- mental health treatment services;

- medication management including psychotropic and abstinence medications such as antabuse, naltrexone;

- vocational/educational development and job placement services;

- aftercare groups and continuing care services.

No-entry points for open group format

For open groups, clients do not enter a session where the prior session was a perquisite. Following are the session no-entry points:

- *Phase I: Sessions 4, 6, 8, 10, 12, 14, 16, 19 and 20;*

- *Phase II: Sessions 23, 26, 28, 30 and 39;*

- *Phase III: Session 44.*

PHASE AND PROGRAM CLOSURE GUIDELINES

Closure sessions are addressed in two ways. First, there is closure within the group for clients in their final session of each phase of treatment. In that session, they reflect on the progress and changes they have made, share the most important parts of their autobiography, and receive feedback from group members as to their progress and change. About five to 10 minutes are allowed for each client completing a particular phase. When several clients are up for closure at one time, the closure exercises can be spread out over several sessions.

Second, closure at the end of each phase is addressed through an individual session. These are discussed in the following sections.

Phase I Review and Closure

This is one of the most important individual sessions in *SSC*. Provider and client work together as partners to discern the client's readiness and motivation for continuing in *SSC*. Even for clients where completion of *SSC* is a required part of judicial supervision, their readiness and motivation for continuing *SSC* should be evaluated and discussed.

The *Phase I* closure session is described on page 152 of the *Workbook* and guidelines for its delivery are provided in *Section III* of this *Guide*. Conducted within two or three weeks of completion, this session reviews the client's improvement, progress and change and overall response to *SSC* as measured by *PACE* and as observed by the provider. Here are guidelines to determine a client's response to *Phase I* and readiness and motivation for *Phase II*.

▶ Overall positive engagement demonstrated by attending to group discussions and engaging in session exercises and worksheet activities. Positive engagement should not be measured only by level of involvement in verbal discussions. Some clients may be very attentive and engaging in treatment but reticent around verbal involvement due to lack of self-confidence, introverted personality features or limited verbal skills.

▶ Completion of 80% of the 50 *Phase I* worksheets. Sincerity and intent in worksheet completion should be the guideline, and not verbal or writing skills.

▶ The *Client Program Response - Client* (CPR-C) ratings, the *Client Program Response - Provider* CPR-P) ratings, and the *Self Evaluation Questionnaire* (SEQ) responses in *PACE* are at levels to indicate steady improvement and progress.

▶ A review of the key areas of work clients did in *Phase I,* using the *Phase I Review Guide* (PI-RG), *Table 7.1* below. It follows the outline provided for clients on page 156 of the *Workbook* and is provided in the *PACE Handbook*. It is copied and given to clients to complete as homework a week before the *Phase I* review and closure interview. Clients rate themselves as satisfactory or unsatisfactory as to completing and achieving the areas of work listed in the PI-RG. During

this interview, the provider and client go over the PI-RG together and mutually come to a final rating. Four or five unsatisfactory ratings would indicate a need for additional tutoring before the client proceeds into *Phase II*. For the unsatisfactory ratings, it is recommended that the client do some additional work in those areas to bring them to a satisfactory rating level. The *PI-RG* is part of *PACE,* and listed as a *PACE* task in *Table 6.4*.

This review and closure session should be an enabling rather then a restrictive experience; and done in a partnership with the client. Every effort is made to motivate and prepare clients for *Phase II*. If the *PACE* results indicate little or no progress, the PI-RG is generally unsatisfactory, the client is still unmotivated, and shows an inability to understand or use the *SSC* concepts and skills to implement change, then a treatment plan is developed to mobilize resources to bring the client to a satisfactory level of progress and accomplishment.

These resources include repeating certain sessions or being assigned to individual or group tutoring that is designed to bring clients to an acceptable level of performance and progress. Providers continually evaluate clients relative to progress and change, and identify those who need this tutoring. It is best not to wait until a client has almost completed *Phase I* to assign him or her to this group. In rare cases, providers may facilitate transfer to alternative treatment or behavioral management services if a client us unable to fulfill the expectation of *SSC Phase I*.

If the client and provider decide the client will continue in *SSC,* then orientation to *Phase II* is provided. This is done in the individual *Phase I* review session or in a *Phase II* orientation group. The *Preparation Session* for *Phase II* is found on page 154 of the *Workbook* and guidelines for its delivery are in *Section III*.

Phases II and *III* Closure

An individual session is held at the end of *Phase II* to evaluate the motivation of clients to continue into *Phase III,* review the results from the *PACE Monitor,* and orient them to that phase. At this point, the main criterion that is applied for continuation will be an observed desire and motivation to continue in the program.

A final interview is conducted within two weeks of completing *SSC* and clients discuss the improvements and changes that they have made and the *Program Closure Inventory* (PCI) is completed.

Recognition of Program Completion

A certificate of completion is awarded to clients at the end of the first two phases and at the completion of the entire *SSC* program. Providers hold a special graduation ceremony for these clients. Family members and friends are invited and agency staff who have had contact with these clients will also want to attend to support their achievement.

Completing all 50 sessions is a very significant accomplishment that should be celebrated. This recognition is an integral part of the change reinforcement process.

REMOVAL OF CLIENT FROM PROGRAM

Each agency will have its own policy for the removal of a client from group or for program termination. Therapeutic skills and approaches should always be the basis for dealing with adverse and disruptive client behavior both at the group and individual level. Even when taking a correctional role when dealing with fractious and infractious behaviors, that role should be implemented within the framework of

TABLE 7.1	Phase I Review Guide (PI-RG): Each Area Rated as Satisfactory (S) or Unsatisfactory (U) as to Completion and Achievement.

PHASE ONE AREAS TO BE REVIEWED AND EVALUATED WITH CLIENT	RATING
1. What are the three goals and objectives of *SSC: Figure 1*, pg. 11	
2. Compare your *SSC* goals you wrote at the beginning of your program with those you now have for *SSC*: pg. 17	
3. How does the *CB Map* show us what causes our emotions and actions: *Figure 2*, pg. 14	
4. What were your specific patterns of AOD use before the last time you entered the criminal justice system: pg. 63	
5. What was your AOD use and problems profile before you last entered the judicial system: *Profile 2*, pg. 80	
6. What AOD problem group or classification did you fit prior to your entering the judicial system: *Worksheet 22*, pg. 82.	
7. Explain your relapse and recidivism prevention goals: pgs. 126 and 127	
8. Explain your own pathways and skills to preventing relapse and recidivism: *Figure 20*, pg. 130	
9. Name four mental and behavior change skills you use to prevent relapse and recidivism: pg. 146	
10. With your counselor, re-rate yourself on the *SSC Scales* at the end of each session.	
11. Update your *MP* by re-rating yourself on each of the scales. Use a different mark or different colored pen: pgs. 292-294.	
12. Name four strengths that you developed in *SSC* and that you take into *Phase II*	
13. Briefly go over your *MAP* and make sure it is updated as to problems worked on and worked out: pgs. 295-299	
14. Review your *MSL* and the skills learned in *Phase I* and see if all are rated fair to very good: pg. 292	

therapeutic skills and communication.

MANUAL-GUIDED DELIVERY PRINCIPLES FOR SSC

In *Chapter 1,* 10 core strategies were identified upon which *SSC* is built. From these strategies, several manual-guided treatment principles can be identified that guide the provider's delivery of this program. These are also discussed at certain delivery points in the session delivery guides in *Section III.*

Integration of Psychoeducation and Therapy

This strategy was presented in *Chapter 1* and its general issues discussed in *Chapter 2.* Effective psychoeducation methods and approaches are learner-centered based on interactive teaching (Weimer, 2002). This involves actively engaging clients in the concepts being taught with the goal of clients assuming ownership of learning, self-improvement, and change. Hart (1991) identifies the features of a learner-centered approach.

▶ The goal is to improve and change performance, not to just get information across.

▶ The learner is a source of expertise as well as the provider.

▶ Learners are actively involved and express their thoughts, views, beliefs versus being in a passive, "soaking up" role.

▶ Feedback from learners is for the purpose of determining whether ideas and concepts are being applied rather than whether the learner just retains and understands information.

▶ Risk-taking and exploration are reinforced versus control through reward and punishment.

▶ Learning is experiential.

Sessions Are Lesson Based

Although we learn from experience, experience is not a good teacher because experience gives us the test before the lesson. Effective teaching and learning will give the lesson first, and then the test. Judicial clients have failed many life-tests because of not hav-

ing learned important lessons of living. The primary goal of *SSC* is to give clients important lessons so as to prevent relapse and recidivism. Thus, *SSC* has a strong lesson-based component. It is structured around specific therapy themes that are the basis of interactive participation.

Sessions Are Skill Development Based

SSC skill development is built around three broad therapeutic themes: 1) developing cognitive skills for self-control; 2) developing skills to enhance positive relationship outcomes; and 3) developing skills to enhance responsible behaviors and actions in the community (SRT). All of these skills are specifically directed at preventing relapse and recidivism and developing strategies for responsible living and change.

Personalizing Curriculum Content and Themes

Every effort should be made to maximize the interaction of clients with the curriculum material and to help them personalize and identify with its content and themes. When using a didactic format, providers facilitate client sharing of personal experiences that illustrate the concepts and ideas being presented. Worksheets and thinking reports maximize the interaction of clients with the material and the application of the material to their own experiences.

The use of reflective-interactive and reflective-acceptance approaches help enhance personal identification with the material. For example, to a comment, "all my friends steal," the reflective-interactive response might be "How is that an error in thinking? Are all your friends thieves? What about some friends in this group who don't steal?"

Multi-Media and Multi-Sensory Formats

Using various media formats enhances interactive participation with the curriculum material. These include posters, overhead transparencies, Power Point presentations, charts and worksheets. A wall poster illustrating the basic cognitive-behavioral change schemata (*Figure 2,* page 14 in the *Workbook*) and a laminated billfold-sized card of this schemata are effective reminders and reinforcement tools. Effective media formats are multisensory - seeing, listening, talking and kinesthetic approaches.

Keep Sessions Moving and Focused on Concepts and Skills

Therapeutic processing in manual-guided formats is more structured than traditional process therapy groups. A process treatment group may spend an entire session around a particular client's problems. In a manual-guided format, this is avoided. If the needs of some clients go beyond the manual-guided session, structured individual sessions and unstructured process therapy groups should be available to clients. However, some therapeutic processing is important. Although best deferred to the session closure time, at times, individual therapeutic issues must be addressed during the group session.

Manual-guided approaches keep the focus on session content, topics and skills. When therapeutic processing is used to address individual client issues, it should be done within the context of these concepts and skills. Again, sessions outside of the *SSC* format may be needed for resolution.

Providers continually balance client and group therapeutic issues with fulfilling the objectives of each session. Treatment is most effective when following the "teaching to fish" metaphor. Solving individual problems in group is "giving clients a fish in order to feed them for a day." Having clients learn the skills of resolving and working through their individual problems is "teaching them to fish which feeds them for a lifetime."

Delivery Environment and Seating

Setting

SSC is delivered in a location that has minimum extraneous or outside activities or noises that distract members from giving complete attention and focus on the session. Each session, the group meets in the same location dedicated to the delivery of *SSC*. Other programs and groups may use the same room, yet, the location should be "home" to *SSC* clients. This helps clients become comfortable with the surroundings and enhances the therapeutic environment. The room should have wall space on which to place posters and media that display key concepts of *SSC* such as the *CB Map* or the *STEP* method.

In secure judicial settings where higher risk clients are involved in treatment, even though the treatment room should be set aside from distracting activities, security and safety are critical issues. Thus, providers need to have access to security staff in case a behavioral management problem arises with a client or the group. Although sometimes distracting, this accessibility is essential to treatment delivered in these kinds of settings.

Seating arrangement and work space

In manual-guided treatment delivery, it is essential that clients have tables on which to write in their workbooks and do interactive journaling. Seating must be arranged so that clients can see each other in order to maximize group interaction. Manual-guided treatment is counselor-directed and client-oriented. The provider is the group leader, and is in charge.

What is important when considering seating arrangements and other styles of program delivery is for providers to establish themselves as knowledgeable and capable therapists and group leaders while at the same time avoiding being authoritarian or exhibiting power and dominance over the group. The basic principles of reflective acceptance, maximizing client participation, enhancing interaction around the content and among group members, and modeling reflective listening, assertiveness and prosocial responding are the important principles that guide the delivery of manual-guided treatment.

Providers differ as to how they want the tables arranged. Some prefer to have the table in a square where clients can sit in a semblance of a circle, and the provider is located in the square along with other group members. Other providers prefer to arrange the tables in a rectangle with the provider at one end and clients seated on the other three sides. This allows the provider to have a more definitive or authoritative role in the group. If this rectangle arrangement is used, it is recommended that the provider sit at the table when presenting the program.

Some providers like a U-shaped arrangement and keep the space in front of the group open so they can stand, or even walk around, during the treatment session. This tends to put the leader in a more commanding role in the group, and "above" group members. Judicial clients may see this style as paternalistic, patronizing, and even demeaning. With judicial clients this approach is discouraged.

Placing the provider in the position of authority in the group tends to enhance and increase individual client and group authority transference issues and problems with the provider. Most, if not all, judicial clients have a history of strong reactions to and transference problems with those in authority. This transference is often unconscious, and the problems that judicial clients had with authority figures in their past, particularly in early and middle childhood, get unconsciously transferred to persons in authority in present life, e.g., counselor, therapist, *SSC* provider. However, many offenders are very aware and conscious of their anger at those in authority even though most do not understand the etiology of that anger.

It is of note that in reviewing numerous works on the treatment of substance abusing judicial clients, the transference issue, particularly with respect to authority, is seldom dealt with. Masters (2004) did address this issue and its importance in working with substance abusing judicial clients.

What is important is that judicial clients develop a working relationship with their provider/counselor, who is an authority with respect to being the group leader, having knowledge about the treatment process and curriculum, and who is "in charge" of and responsible for the management of the group. Given this *a priori* definitive role, it is important that providers avoid making worse the problems with authority most judicial clients have. The problem is made worse when providers act in a dominating and authoritarian manner. There is some risk of this occurring, at least initially, when providers stand at the head of the group arranged in a U-shaped arrangement, or even sit alone at the head table of a rectangle arrangement. Thus, providers need to weight out these issues when making decisions around how to position themselves in relationship to the group setting and seating arrangement. The ultimate goal is that clients take charge of their treatment and become authorities in and of themselves in the process of self-improvement and change. The provider is a director and a catalyst in this process of change.

PROVIDER KNOWLEDGE AND SKILLS NECESSARY IN *SSC* DELIVERY

In addition to the principles that guide the delivery of *SSC,* effective manual-guided delivery also depends on specific knowledge and the use of specific skills. These are discussed at various places in this *Guide* and are summarized.

Differential Screening and Comprehensive Assessment

Chapter 6 provides a comprehensive approach to differential screening and comprehensive assessment. Assessment is ongoing and starts with the first client contact and continues through final contact. Providers need the basic knowledge and skills in assessment interviewing, interpreting the results of assessment instruments, evaluating and determining treatment needs, writing a summary report, and generating an individual treatment plan (ITP).

Referral Knowledge and Skills

Providers are skilled in making referrals for specific treatment and aftercare needs. Differential screening and comprehensive assessment identify needs of clients that go beyond the goals and objectives of *SSC*. Providers need to have knowledge of available resources for these special needs, particularly for settings where *SSC* is a stand-alone program without direct access to these resources. A list of the minimum resources that should be available to clients is described above in the section on *Delivery Settings and Service Resources.*

Basic Knowledge Areas

Providers should have a basic knowledge of how substances affect the mind and body, basic concepts of the patterns of substance use, the cycles of addiction, and the categories that define substance use problems, e.g., substance abuse, substance dependence, and relapse prevention. Providers will have a core knowledge of criminal thinking and conduct, the CC cycle and the pathways to recidivism. It is also expected that providers have a basic understanding of the principles of cognitive-behavioral learning and change or an understanding of how both thoughts and behaviors are changed and reinforced.

Core Counseling Skills

There are a number of core counseling skills essential for effective *SSC* delivery. These are:

- Invitational skills of attending, open statements and open questions to facilitate self-disclosure and getting clients to **share their story**;

- Feedback clarification and confrontation skills such as reflection of thoughts and feelings, paraphrasing, summarization, therapeutic and correctional confrontation to get clients to **hear their story** so as to increase self-awareness; and

- Change clarification and change reinforcement skills to get clients to **act on their story** and take action to change their thoughts, emotions and behaviors so as to enhance the probability of positive outcomes.

Motivational Enhancement Skills

Skills and principles of motivational interviewing and enhancement are based on the core counseling skills described above. The initial stages of motivational enhancement involve being non-confrontational around resistance, avoiding argumentation, maximizing individual sharing, expressing empathy, rolling with the resistance and using reinforcement feedback skills around changes in attitudes and behavior.

Implementing Change: The *CB Map Exercise*

Although all of the above approaches are used to bring about CB changes, there are two specific techniques that *SSC* providers use to implement changes

in thinking and action.

First, there is the use of the *CB Map* (page 14 in the *Workbook*) and the *CB Map Exercise* to identify and label specific thought structures and core beliefs that lead to various outcomes, regardless of whether those outcomes are positive (adaptive) or negative (maladaptive). The goal is to help clients learn how the CB process works and learn to be conscious of cognitive structures that result in certain outcomes; and to make the process non-automatic. Initially, the specific outcome is not as important as learning this process. The *CB Map Exercise* uses past events, recent or current situations which may or may not deal with CC or AOD use. Every session begins with this exercise. Once clients learn the process, then providers help them use the exercise to change thoughts and beliefs. Many session worksheets and thinking reports support the use of the *CB Map* in learning and implementing CB change. The exercise also helps clients build a database on the re-occurring thought structures and core beliefs that can lead to relapse and recidivism.

Second, the *CB STEP* method is used to facilitate immediate thought structures that lead to positive outcomes. Although this technique is specifically introduced at the beginning of *Phase II,* it is an integral part of the *CB Map Exercise* and the goal of the re-thinking report. The *CB STEP* cuts directly to developing cognitive structures that result in positive outcomes. The goal is for clients to automatically use *STEP* to implement cognitive and behavioral change. However, *STEP* does not replace the *CB Map Exercise* which is the core model for change used throughout *SSC.*

Utilizing *SSC* Tools for Change

Providers are skilled in utilizing the 10 specific tools for change which include the four *SSC* program guides. In review, they are: 1) *CB Map*; 2) autobiography; 3) *Master Skills List (Program Guide 1)*; 4) *Master Profile (Program Guide 2)*; 5) *Master Assessment Plan (Program Guide 3)*; 6) the *Weekly Thinking and Action Patterns* (TAP) *Charting (Program Guide 4)*; 7) the thinking report; 8) the re-thinking report; 9), the *SSC Change Scales,* completed at the end of each session; and 10) the *CB STEP* method, introduced in *Phase II.* These tools are also discussed at various places in the next section of this *Guide.*

Maximizing Participation and Skill Development

There are specific skills that maximize interactive participation around the session themes and concepts. These skills have a dual purpose. They are used by providers to maximize interaction and participation. They are learned by clients to help implement learning and change and develop prosocial attitudes and behavior. These are structured and counselor-directed techniques. The provider orchestrates the process and initially role-models the specific technique.

▶ **Role playing:** A client role-plays a specific event that involves a person or persons in the client's life. The client selects another group member to play the role of that person. Usually, the event involves some problem or unresolved issue.

▶ **Role Reversal:** This is switching roles during role play. A client who chooses another group member to play the role of a person in his/her life around a specific event reverses roles and plays the role of the person identified. For example, a client who chooses another group member to play the role of his/her intimate partner, is asked to take the role of the intimate partner and the group member plays the role of the client. Role reversal helps the person playing the role of the person in the client's life understand the kind of responses that person will make and thus more realistically play that role. Most important, role reversal puts the client in the role of the person in his/her life and helps him/her understand how that person thinks and feels, an important step in learning the skill of empathy.

▶ **Doubling:** Another person reflects what a certain client is saying during a role-play. For example, during a role playing episode where a client is talking to a person playing the role of his intimate partner, another group member will stand by the client in the role-play and reflect out loud what the client might be thinking. When the client says: "you don't listen to me," the double might say, "and you don't really understand me." The objective is to help the client playing

the role listen to what he/she is saying and learn the skill of recognizing covert thoughts of others. The double tries to "get inside" the thinking and emotions of the person in the role-play. The double makes the same physical motions and actions as the role-play client and reflects verbally what the client is saying. The provider demonstrates the skill first, and from time to time, will "slip" into the role of a double when clients are engaging in role-play. Doubling is an important tool in teaching empathy. Providers can have clients practice doubling by using a mirror-technique involving one group member standing opposite another and mimicking or mirroring the physical actions of the other person.

▶ **Round robin:** Involves each group member briefly sharing thoughts or feelings proceeding around the group one member at a time. For example, each member shares one idea learned during the session. The sharing should be crisp and brief.

▶ **Wagon wheel:** Used in practicing interactive skills such as active listening and active sharing. For example, one client shares a brief experience and the person directly across from that person makes a reflective statement to that sharing. The next group member to the left does the same, and the group member opposite that member reflects the experience, etc.

▶ **Skill practice and rehearsal:** Once a skill is presented, it is recalled for practice in subsequent sessions. Rehearsal of skills is usually not prompted in subsequent session delivery guides. Providers will make a list of these skills and recall them for practice at appropriate points in a session. For example, once clients learn the skill of active listening, they practice this skill in subsequent sessions when presenting a new skill and concept, such as "starting a difficult conversation" as in *Session 30.* Although clients tend to complain about the redundancy of skill practice and rehearsal, the goal is for the skills of change to become automatic in and part of the daily life and routine of clients.

▶ **Giving and receiving feedback:** Involves one group member giving feedback to other group members. The ground rule is that the group member receiving the feedback responds in a positive manner without minimizing the feedback or without getting defensive. This technique helps clients learn interpersonal self-control.

▶ **Reflective-interactive skills:** Involves reflecting back the responses that group members make to information, ideas and skills presented to the group. For example, when presenting the concept of the Mental-Behavior Impaired-Control Cycle (MB-ICC) in *Session 7,* group members are asked to share how they identified with the concept. The provider then reflects back what group members say.

▶ **Reflective-acceptance skills:** Providers reflect back in an accepting way defensive or resistive statements made by clients. For example, when presenting the *SSC* assumption that CC is angry conduct, a client may respond by saying "I wasn't mad when I committed that crime." A reflective-acceptance response would be: "That idea just doesn't fit you."

▶ **Facilitating elaboration and personal identification:** Involves getting clients to elaborate on specific concepts and skills presented and then personally identify with those concepts. This is done through invitational and reflective counseling skills. For example, when presenting the MB-ICC concept, providers maximize client sharing around and personally identifying with the concept.

▶ **Sharing the content presentation:** This involves several approaches: Clients read portions of the *Workbook* text; share the most important idea they learned when reading the session material; read to the group an idea that helped; or describe a key concept, such as the MB-ICC. It is important to know the reading level of the group and to not put any client who does not feel comfortable reading or who cannot read in an embarrassing position.

▶ **Adjunct exercises:** These are occasionally presented in the session delivery guidelines in *Section III* for the purpose of enhancing the efficacy of various sessions. Providers will need to judge whether there is time to use these exercises.

▶ **Actiongrams:** Group members take the role of certain concepts and ideas. An actiongram can be used when presenting the *CB Map Exercise.* A client presents a specific event that led to a negative outcome, and identifies the thoughts, feelings, behaviors and the negative outcome. Group members play the role of each of these elements, e.g., the event, the thoughts, etc. With the assistance of the provider, clients are asked to orchestrate a change in each of these elements in order to get a positive outcome. Other group members are brought in to play the role of the new thoughts, emotions, behaviors, and outcomes.

▶ **Updating and review:** Involves bringing forward to a current session prior concepts and skills learned. This skill and concept updating should be done within the context of a new skill or concept being presented and learned.

▶ **Skills for effective group delivery:** Discussed in a separate section below.

Delivering *Social Responsibility Therapy - SRT*

SRT is the **seventh core strategy** of *SSC* and is discussed in a number of places in this *Guide*. It focuses on character building, social and moral responsibility, developing prosocial attitudes and behaviors, managing anger and preventing violence, settling conflicts, and understanding and practicing empathy.

Although SRT is more defined by its focus, it is premised on the use of basic counseling and motivational enhancement skills, and on the provider's modeling of prosocial attitudes and behaviors. It is also based on correctional confrontation - confronting clients with the expectations of society and integrating the use of sanctioning and punishment with therapeutic approaches.

The two most important focuses of SRT are: 1) empathy development; and 2) building prosocial attitudes and behaviors. Earlier discussions in this *Guide* showed a strong link between prosociality and empathy. Positive group participation and interaction provide the basis for building a prosocial group and the learning matrix for developing prosocial attitudes and behaviors.

Several of the techniques identified above that enhance interaction and participation also help build prosociality and empathy skills. These include role reversal and doubling.

One of the most important elements in developing client prosociality is the client-counselor relationship. Through modeling and the processes of healthy identification and mimicry, clients take on the positive characteristics of their providers, e.g., caring for others, honesty and genuineness, making positive contributions to family, friends, and society at large.

PRINCIPLES OF GROUP LEADERSHIP: BUILDING A COHESIVE PROSOCIAL GROUP

Group management and leadership are seen as part of the provider skills necessary for effective *SSC* delivery and for building a cohesive, prosocial group, the **ninth core strategy** of *SSC*. Guidelines and principles for effective group facilitation, management and leadership are presented. These are particularly relevant with respect to the delivery of manual-guided treatment.

Methods of Group Treatment

Glassman (1983) identified three major approaches to group treatment. The first is treatment **in** the group. This focuses on individuals in the group and is actually doing individual counseling within a group setting. The vehicle for change is the personal experiences of individual group members.

The second approach is to facilitate interaction among individuals in the group. This is called treatment **with** the group. The leader facilitates and uses interpersonal interactions to help individual clients to disclose themselves, work on their problems, and learn effective relationship skills. The vehicle for change is the interaction the client experiences in the group.

The third approach involves seeing the group as an individual. Glassman (1983) calls this treatment **of**

the group. In this approach, the treatment of the client occurs through the treatment of the group. The group "is the client," and becomes the vehicle for change and growth in the individual. It is based on the idea that a healthy group produces healthy members. The skills that the counselor uses to facilitate the expression and change in individual counseling is used with the group. The counselor invites the group to share, disclose and tell its story. The counselor reflects the group's feelings, thoughts, actions, gets the group to change and then reinforces that change. The development of group cohesion and trust becomes a primary focus. The group becomes a powerful initiator and reinforcer of the changes in its members. The group leader will look after the group to nurture it, to help it grow, to protect it, and to facilitate its growth.

With judicial clients, an important goal of the "treatment of the group" approach is to **build a healthy prosocial group.** Offender groups have high potential to be antisocial and procriminal by virtue of the fact that its members have histories of antisocial and criminal thinking and conduct. The counselor works at changing the group's thinking and core beliefs from antisocial and criminal to anticriminal and prosocial. Just as the session worksheets and exercises are designed to build moral and social responsibility in the client, they also are designed to do the same with the treatment group. The skills of social responsibility therapy (SRT) are applied to the group as well as individual clients.

Depersonalizing Leadership Authority

Judicial client groups tend to see the authority for controlling and sanctioning behavior as centered in the group leader or counselor. An effective approach is to allow the structure, rules and guidelines of the program to manage the group and the individual behaviors of group members. This centers the authority on the program rules and guidelines.

Bush and Bilodeau (1993) identify this as depersonalizing the use of leader authority while maintaining control of the process and upholding the rules. The group leader makes it clear that the process will proceed as it has been defined, not because of leader power, but because this is a change process that works, i.e., "it's nothing personal." Managing disruptive behavior is part of the group leadership role. The leader communicates, within the context of therapeutic skills, that: 1) the behavior disrupts the task at hand; 2) the client has the choice whether or not to participate; and 3) there are consequences related to not fully participating in the group. With regard to rules, leaders will communicate that the intent is not to force clients to comply, **but rather help them to succeed.**

Center the Authority Within the Group

Every effort should be made to center the authority for group management within the group itself. This is congruent with the "leadership of the group" model described above. The group leader facilitates group responsibility in developing positive behavioral responses in the group. This is not always possible, and the center of authority may, at times, fall back on the group leader. In most cases, control and management of individual behavior in groups can be done through the group itself. This will not work if the group leader is unwilling to relinquish the power and control, or gets caught up in a power struggle with the group.

Center the Authority With Group Members

Another method for effective group management is to place the authority and responsibility with the individual offender on questions of appropriate behavior. Group leaders need to draw out participants' own recognition of their patterns of thinking and behaving, rather than imposing their own views. The goal is to empower the judicial client by enhancing self-control through skill development. Part of the therapeutic and correctional confrontation strategy of *SSC* is stressing that the locus of control is always internal and the decision to change or not to change is always within the power of the client.

Keep the Focus on Curriculum Themes and Concepts

Group process and interaction are not the primary focus of manual-guided programs. A focus on process is important; however, providers can get caught up with process and interaction at the expense of

not focusing on helping the client interact with the curriculum content and theme. Strong process-oriented providers will have to shift their therapeutic paradigm in order to effectively deliver manual-guided programs. Clients, however, do need time to process both the experiences with the group and the content.

Keep the Focus on CB Change

Each group session should focus on underlying cognitive-behavioral patterns. The group is continually reminded that the purpose is preventing relapse and recidivism and to focus on the CB processes of change that achieve this purpose. Participants should have a clear understanding of how the session content, exercises and worksheets assist in the process of self-directed change. Each session should leave clients with an improved skill and ability to think (cognitive) and act (behavioral) to specific high-risk episodes that results in increased self-control and prosocial outcomes.

Provider-Group Collaborative Relationship

Group management is always directed at achieving cooperation between the group and the provider. The initial posture of "us or them" must eventually be worked through to achieve this collaborative relationship (Bush & Bilodeau, 1993). Patterns of hostility and social conflict need to be replaced with patterns of prosocial cooperation between the group and provider. When angry and hostile attitudes block channels of communication, these attitudes may be exposed as disruptive and challenged according to the established guideline for program participation. Members' resentment of the leader's authority may indicate a need to allow clients more freedom to express their views.

Maximize Individual Involvement

Effective group leadership is directed at maximizing participation of group members, using the skills outlined above. At the same time, the leader needs to be aware that individuals differ with respect to group comfort, feeling at ease in a group and ability to be open and to share. As group cohesion and trust build, even the most "threat sensitive" group member will begin to feel a greater degree of comfort in sharing with the group.

Providers use skills to attend to all group members while at the same time attending to the group itself. This will involve helping each member to be actively involved in the discussions. Although the group leader may work with a single group member on a given exercise, all participants should be actively contemplating the exercise. Leaders may "check in" with the group to be sure that everyone is following what is going on.

Finally, using the "treatment of the group" approach, the group leader helps the group learn to facilitate participation of its members. This involves reinforcing the behavior of group members that gets other members to participate and share. The group is a powerful element in getting members to interact and engage.

THE PROVIDER'S MANY HATS

The *SSC* provider wears "many hats" when working with judicial clients. These "many hats" have been discussed in previous chapters of this *Guide*. The provider wears the **personal** "hat" in expressing empathy, warmth, genuineness and respect. There is the **therapeutic** "hat" where the provider utilizes all the skills of effective counseling. The **philosophical** "hat" gets expressed through the teaching of a theoretical view of alcoholism, drug abuse, CC or a particular approach to counseling. The provider will need to wear the **correctional** "hat" when holding the client responsible for violating the terms of probation or the law.

Clients should have a clear understanding that providers are advocates for both the client and the court. This is made very clear at the start of the client-provider relationship. Again: signed releases for reporting to the judicial system are obtained at the first contact with the client. The provider is always in the process of effectively integrating these various roles when working with judicial clients.

REENTRY AND REINTEGRATION

The **tenth *SSC* core strategy** is to facilitate re-entry

and re-integration into the community. As discussed in *Chapter 1*, reentry and reintegration are often seen as only applicable to incarcerated judicial clients returning to the community. They are just as applicable to probation clients. Probationers also experience separation and isolation from the community, though not to the extent as those incarcerated. As well, reentry services are often seen as limited to judicial supervision, e.g., parole. Judicial supervision is not adequate for effective reentry.

The process of reentry and reintegration is effective when clients are linked to services that meet their treatment and rehabilitation needs. The process includes servicing needs identified in the various judicial programs in which offenders were involved, such as mental health treatment, vocational assessment, housing and health care. Ideally, reentry services should begin once offenders enter the judicial system when reintegration needs and services are first identified.

An important component of reentry and reintegration is continuing care and the continuing care plan (CCP). Continuing care involves connectedness with prosocial resources in the community. The CCP is part of the client's ITP and is developed in partnership with the judicial client. When *SSC* is nested in a broad-based treatment program, the *SSC* provider will work with other staff and services to develop and implement the CCP. When *SSC* is offered as a stand-alone program, the provider will have more responsibility, and need more skills and resources to implement the CCP.

Although *Phase III* sessions address reintegration, providers need specific skills and knowledge to help clients develop a CCP and make successful reentry. Some of these are summarized.

▶ Knowledge and understanding that the community reinforcement model for judicial clients involves maintaining continuity of connectedness with prosocial groups and resources in reentry.

▶ Knowledge of general community support resources such as self-help groups.

▶ Knowledge of resources that can meet specific rehabilitation and treatment needs, e.g., mental health, medical, and AOD.

▶ Skills in connecting and reconnecting judicial clients with primary support units in the community such as family and prosocial friends.

▶ The skill of connecting judicial clients with specific prosocial resources, e.g., self-help groups, religious organizations, volunteer groups.

PROVIDER SKILL EVALUATION AND SUPERVISION

Professional development of *SSC* providers involves learning new skills and sharpening existing skills that influence self-improvement and change in clients. There are several methods through which this professional development occurs.

Continued Self-Evaluation of Knowledge and Skills

This chapter has outlined many of the skills that are essential in the delivery of treatment programs such as *SSC*. *Table 7.2* is an evaluation worksheet that helps providers assess their current level of knowledge and skills, and provides guidelines for continuing education, clinical supervision and professional development.

Receiving Clinical Supervision

It is recommended that providers receive a minimum of one hour a month of supervision around *SSC* delivery and addressing clinical problems that arise in treatment. It is helpful if the supervisor can observe the provider's delivery of the program either through video or attending a group. It is important that supervisors have an understanding of and even experience in the delivery of manual-guide CB programs. Providers who complete a three day formal training program on *SSC* are better qualified to provide supervision and to do *SSC* training within their agency (see Footnote 1, pg. 142).

Giving Clinical Supervision and Training

After providers have delivered one full round (50 sessions) of *SSC*, professional growth is enhanced in providing supervision to others delivering *SSC*.

PROVIDER QUALIFICATIONS

Providers should have from one to two years of experience providing AOD treatment and counseling services. Some experience in working with judicial clients is desirable. Providers should also have undergraduate or graduate work in psychology and counseling and have completed basic AOD counseling training; or have completed a master's degree in the field of human services, e.g., counseling, psychology, correctional treatment, etc.

EVALUATING SESSION DELIVERY EFFICACY

Effective providers are self-reflective around their own performance and are also open to receiving feedback from clients around this performance. To measure delivery efficacy, providers and clients rate the provider's delivery performance and the client's response to the performance. These ratings are part of the measures of client program responsivity (understanding or discernment) that are in the Self Evaluation Questionnaire (SEQ) and the Client Program Response ratings (CPR-C). These instruments are found in the *PACE Handbook*.

Over the course of *SSC*, the provider will notice trends around delivery. For example, clients will provide lower ratings of providers in their early evaluations; but as rapport and trust are established, delivery effectiveness, satisfaction and program responsivity will increase. It is expected that delivery efficacy ratings, on the average, will show a slump in the rating segments that include sessions that are more difficult to understand and present.

CHAPTER REVIEW

This chapter provides a comprehensive presentation of the methods, strategies and skills that are used for effective *SSC* delivery. The old adage that the first step is the most important and getting started is the most difficult applies to intake and admission into *SSC*. This process begins with the first client contact and continues into orientation. This chapter presents guidelines and tasks for conducting an effective intake and admission process. The tasks involve get-

TABLE 7.2   Provider's Master Knowledge and Skills List

	KNOWLEDGE AND SKILLS	Poor	Fair	Good	V. Good
BASIC KNOWLEDGE	1. Differential screening				
	2. Differential assessment				
	3. Referral knowledge/skills				
	4. Substance use patterns				
	5. Substance abuse cycles				
	6. Knowledge of criminal thinking				
	7. Understand criminal conduct				
	8. Understand CC cycle				
	9. Basic principles of CBT				
BASIC SKILLS	10. How thoughts/behaviors change				
	11. Basic counseling skills				
	12. Motivational enhancement skills				
	13. Implementing CB change				
	14. Using the CB Map Exercise				
	15. Specific SSC tools of change				
	16. CB STEP Exercise				
	17. Directing role playing				
	18. Directing role reversal				
	19. Directing doubling				
	20. Using round robin technique				
	22. Using wagon wheel technique				
	23. Skill practice and rehearsal				
	24. Reflective-interactive skill				
	25. Reflective-acceptance skills				
	26. Conducting an actiongram				
	27. Interactive teaching				
	28. Updating				
	29. Delivering SRT				
	30. Conducting manual-guided group				
	31. Group facilitation skills				
	32. Facilitate reintegration				

ting relevant referral information about the client, determining appropriateness for *SSC,* completing forms that protect the rights of clients, provider and sponsoring agency, and developing an initial individual treatment plan.

This chapter also provides guidelines for identifying and establishing clear program agreements and ground rules for *SSC* clients. Just as with clients, there are expectations of providers delivering the program. These are summarized.

Many of the strategies, principles, and skills used in *SSC* delivery are generic to the delivery of treatment services to individuals with a history of substance abuse and/or criminal conduct. However, most of the strategies, principles and skills presented in this chapter are germane to the delivery of *SSC* as a manual-guided treatment program.

Although providers are asked to adhere to the concepts, content, objectives and skills in the *SSC* curriculum, there is considerable latitude with respect to delivery structure and strategies. Provider's are asked to study the various delivery structures and options outlined in this chapter, and then to select the one that best fits their staffing patterns and delivery capabilities. A delivery task that all providers are asked to complete is conducting an individual session with clients at the end of *Phase I* to evaluate their progress and change and to determine their motivation and readiness to continue into *Phase II.*

Counselors and providers with limited experience in manual-guided treatment will find this chapter helpful in shifting from the process-oriented group treatment paradigm to a curriculum-based, manual-guided format and structure. This chapter provides basic manual-guided delivery principles specific to *SSC.* Inherent in these principles is the objective of helping clients identify their own personal situation and problems with the curriculum content and themes.

This chapter also presents the specific areas of knowledge and therapy skills that are necessary in the delivery of *SSC.* Relevant knowledge areas are around AOD use and abuse, criminal conduct, and basic principles of CBT. The skill areas include assess-

ment, core counseling skills, enhancing motivation, utilizing the basic *SSC* skills for change which includes the *CB Map Exercise,* enhancing client participation in skill development, and the delivery of social responsibility therapy (SRT).

One of the most difficult aspects of delivering treatment to judicial clients is the multiple roles providers and counselors must assume. The most difficult is balancing the role between delivering therapeutic and correctional services. As discussed often in this *Guide,* providers are correctional practitioners who are advocates of both the client and community. Building trust and rapport with clients while at the same time working with the correctional system in helping to administer the judicial sentence is often a balancing act. As is stressed often, much of the difficulty is resolved when this dual role is made clear to clients at the time they enter treatment.

SSC counselors provide an important role in implementing successful reentry and reintegration of judicial clients into the community. Although *Phase III* sessions address skills and lifestyle changes that support these efforts, this chapter outlines the important objectives and tasks in this area. Research shows that effective continuing care programs significantly reduce the probability of relapse and recidivism (see *Resource Guide,* Wanberg & Milkman, 2008).

Throughout this *Guide,* we have emphasized that this program is assessment-based with a strong focus on client self-evaluation. Just as important is provider professional development and self-evaluation. This chapter discusses the vehicles of supervision and formal training in enhancing professional development. Methods and procedures are also outlined to assist providers in the evaluation and assessment of their own skills and of the effectiveness of their delivery of *SSC.*

1. Information regarding the three-day formal training for *SSC* may be made at: CIS, P. O. Box 16745, Golden, CO, 80402 (303.830.8500); or CARE, P. O. Box 1975, Arvada, CO, 80001-1975 (303.421.1261).

SECTION III

THE TREATMENT CURRICULUM
Strategies for Self-Improvement and Change
Pathways to Responsible Living

The purpose of *Section III* of this *Provider's Guide* is to describe the methods and approaches for the delivery of *Criminal Conduct and Substance Abuse Treatment: Strategies for Self-Improvement and Change - Pathways to Responsible Living (SSC)*. In this *Guide,* for each of the three phases of *SSC* and for each of the 12 modules, an overview is provided and specific goals and objectives are defined. Service delivery guidelines for each of the specific sessions are outlined in some detail. These guidelines include session overview and rationale, summary of session content and presentation sequence, summary of key concepts, and guidelines for therapeutic processing and session closure.

Our overarching theme of *SSC* is *Pathways to Responsible Living.* As discussed in *Section I,* this represents the sociocentric or *Social Responsibility Therapy* (SRT) component of criminal conduct treatment. The goal of responsible living is to help the judicial client have a prosocial and harmonious relationship with the community and society. Yet, this sociocentric goal also results in an egocentric treatment outcome in that it brings meaning, fulfillment and positive outcomes in the lives of judicial clients. We use the "pathways" metaphor to symbolize that there are specific directions that lead to responsible living. The program provides maps and guidelines for these pathways. The *SSC* provider is encouraged to use this metaphor and to help the judicial client stay on these pathways to ensure positive outcomes for the client and for the community.

"What a man thinks of himself, that is
what determines his fate."
-HENRY DAVID THOREAU

INTRODUCTION TO SECTION III

OVERVIEW

Sections I and II of this *Guide* give research and theoretical perspectives and foundational models for understanding, assessing and treating persons with a history of substance abuse and criminal conduct. The material in these sections came from our review of the literature and from our other works (Milkman & Wanberg, 2005; Wanberg & Milkman, 1998; Wanberg, Milkman & Timken, 2005). From these sources we identified ten strategies and principles for effective treatment of the substance abusing judicial client. These strategies and principles of treatment are presented in detail in *Section I* of this *Guide*. They are summarized since they are the foundation of the *SSC* curriculum.

1. Developing therapeutic relationship through motivational enhancement and therapeutic alliance.

2. Multidimensional and differential assessment.

3. Integrating the educational (knowledge) and therapeutic within a manual-guided format.

4. Facilitating learning and growth and the stages of change.

5. Utilizing cognitive-behavioral therapy principles and methods.

6. Relapse and recidivism prevention.

7. Focus on moral responsibility to the community and concern for the welfare and safety of others - *Social Responsibilty Therapy* (SRT).

8. Integrating the therapeutic and correctional.

9. A cohesive group which elicits positive "within group" identity and prosocial attitudes.

10. Reentry and reintegration into the community.

Sections I and II also describe the important components of the platform upon which this program is built. A conceptual framework for the treatment of the judicial client is provided. We identify key characteristics of the *SSC* provider and the relationship between the provider and the client. An assessment protocol is described that provides guidelines for referral into *SSC* and for developing a generic and unique treatment plan for clients. Specific operational guidelines are outlined that give the provider the methods and procedures to effectively deliver the *SSC* treatment curriculum.

Section III of this *Guide* presents delivery guidelines for the 50 treatment sessions. We took what we learned from our literature and curricula reviews, input from treatment providers working with substance abusing judicial clients, the authors' previous works (Wanberg & Milkman, 1998; Wanberg, Milkman & Timken, 2005) and from our combined 80 years of clinical experience and treatment program development for AOD abusing clients, and constructed an intervention protocol with a specific course of treatment. This course of treatment includes standard and innovative approaches to the treatment of substance abuse and criminal conduct.

In the first edition of *SSC,* much of the session content was included in the *Provider's Guide* and only a summary of the session material was given in the *Participant's Workbook.* In this second edition, all of the content and material necessary for the delivery of each session are included in the *Participant's Workbook* and the *Guide* will include only a summary of the session content. Occasionally, **adjunct exercises** and material are provided for certain sessions in the *Guide* that are not in the *Workbook.* Before the delivery of each session, the provider should carefully study the session rationale, support material, and presentation guidelines provided in this *Guide* and the material in the *Workbook.*

Providers are expected to demonstrate fidelity to the *SSC* session content, concepts and interactive exercises. However, providers are encouraged to be flexible and creative in the delivery of *SSC.* They may occasionally want to use additional exercises and material they have utilized in their treatment experience. When doing this, it is important that these additions support and strengthen the concepts, content and themes of each *SSC* session.

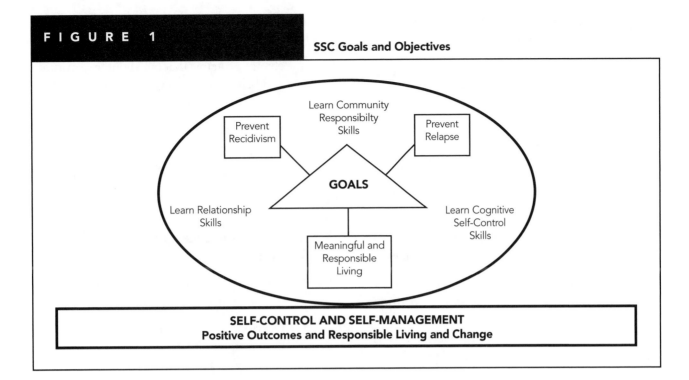

GOALS AND OBJECTIVES OF *SSC*

There are three broad goals of *SSC*. These goals are the threads that are woven through the tapestry of self-improvement, change, and responsible living.

▶ Prevent recidivism into criminal thinking and conduct.

▶ Prevent relapse into substance use and abuse.

▶ Clients live a meaningful and responsible life.

SSC has three primary objectives.

▶ Learn, practice and apply cognitive self-control and change skills to everyday living.

▶ Learn, practice and apply relationship skills that lead to prosocial and positive outcomes.

▶ Learn, practice and apply community responsibility skills that lead to prosocial behavior, a positive relationship with others and the community, and that promote respect for the rights, welfare and good of others and the community.

Achievement of these goals and objectives provides the foundation for helping the substance abusing judicial client make successful reentry and reintegra-tion into normative, meaningful and responsible living. *Figure 1* provides a graphic representation of the goals and objectives of *SSC*.

KEY TOPICS OF THE TREATMENT CURRICULUM

The treatment curriculum is built around key topics or themes that support the goals and objectives of *SSC*. These topics define the tasks of the provider-client partnership that work towards helping clients learn the strategies and skills for self-improvement, change and responsible living. These topics define the expectations of client involvement in *SSC*. The following is a summary of these topics.

▶ **Developing a treatment alliance**

   ◆ Building trust and rapport.

   ◆ Developing a motivation and readiness for treatment.

▶ **Self-Assessment and evaluation**

   ◆ Be open to self-disclosure and sharing per-sonal problems and experiences.

   ◆ Enhance self-awareness through self assess-ment and self-disclosure and through receiv-ing feedback from others.

- Engage in a continuing process of self-assessment by rating oneself on current levels of skill acquisition and learning.

- Be willing to explore and disclose social-emotional issues and relate these issues to past substance abuse and past criminal thinking and behaviors.

▶ **Developing a knowledge base for change**

- Learn the cognitive-behavioral approach to change.

- Understand the process, steps and stages that people go through when making changes.

- Develop an understanding of AOD use patterns, problem outcomes and the pathways and cycles of addiction and help clients see the value of a "zero risk" goal around AOD use - commit to living an AOD-free life.

- Understand how criminal thinking leads to criminal conduct and understand the cycle of criminal thinking and conduct.

- Have an understanding of the principles of relapse and recidivism (R&R) prevention and understand the high-risk exposures and pathways to R&R and to R&R prevention.

- Understand the communication pathways for self-awareness and other-awareness.

▶ **Applying the knowledge base and skills to prevent relapse and recidivism**

- Apply the knowledge of AOD diagnostic descriptions and problem outcomes to the client's own patterns of use.

- Learn and apply skills to change AOD use patterns to get positive and problem-free outcomes.

- Learn and apply skills to change criminal thinking that leads to criminal conduct.

- Learn and apply skills to manage the high-risk exposures that lead to R&R.

- Develop a R&R prevention plan.

- Strengthen the skills of preventing R&R through developing a healthy life style.

▶ **Applying the knowledge base and skills for**

mental self-control

- Help clients apply to everyday living the CB change principle that our thoughts, attitudes and beliefs, not the events outside ourselves, lead to our feelings and behaviors.

- Develop and strengthen the basic skills for changing thought, attitudes and beliefs.

- Develop and strengthen skills to cope with and manage intrapersonal problems of stress, anger, guilt, depression.

▶ **Applying the knowledge base and skills for effective interpersonal relations**

- Apply to daily living the communication skills of active sharing and active listening.

- Develop, strengthen and maintain the skills for engaging in positive, meaningful and empathy-based interpersonal relationships.

▶ **Applying the knowledge and skills for a positive and harmonious relationship with the community and society**

- Develop and strengthen the basic skills for engaging in positive, meaningful and empathy-based relationships with society.

- Develop and strengthen the basic skills for prosocial behavior, community responsibility and moral reasoning though *Social Responsibilty Therapy* (SRT).

HOW *SECTION III* OF THIS *PROVIDER'S GUIDE* IS ORGANIZED

The curriculum is comprised of three phases: *Challenge to Change, Commitment to Change* and *Ownership of Change.* Each is divided into specific modules that address various themes of *SSC.*

Phase I, Challenge to Change: Building Knowledge and Skills for Responsible Living, has seven modules and 20 therapy sessions. *Phase II, Commitment to Change: Strengthening Skills for Self-Improvement, Change and Responsible Living,* has three modules and 22 therapy sessions. *Phase III, Taking Ownership of Change: Lifestyle Balance and Healthy Living,* has two modules and eight therapy sessions.

The *SSC Workbook* provides the substance of the treatment protocol and a full description of the goals and objectives, content and exercises for each session. Except for some key figures and illustrations, the tables, figures, and worksheets are included only in the *Workbook*. The presentation guidelines of the sessions in this *Guide* are divided into four parts.

▶ Rationale and overview including documentation of sources used in session development.

▶ A summary of session content and presentation sequence, process and guidelines. Additional content and exercises are included for some sessions to enhance presentation effectiveness.

▶ Key session concepts.

▶ Session closure and guidelines for therapeutic processing.

PARTICIPANT'S WORKBOOK

Each session is divided into three parts.

▶ Introduction and objectives.

▶ Session content and focus.

▶ Summary of session activities, homework, and guidelines for therapeutic processing.

The *Session Content and Focus* part of each session has specific structured experiences followed by interactive processing through the use of skill modeling, worksheets, role playing, discussion exercises and structured group sharing. These are the key session delivery methods. *Thinking Reports and Re-thinking Reports* are included in many sessions. Tables and figures are used in order to illustrate the relevant content of various sessions. The *Workbook* also includes homework assignments in the form of verbal and written exercises and worksheets.

The *Workbook* is written to address the client in the second person. This helps to personalize the session content and also allows the provider to present directly from the curriculum content in the *Workbook*. Sometimes the content is presented in a factual manner without personalizing it in the second person.

The entire *Workbook* is given to the client at the intake session. This enhances the client's sense of program ownership. Have clients put their name in the *Workbook*. Encourage the client to read the session before coming to group. Since the *Workbook* includes all the necessary material to deliver *SSC*, clients may be overwhelmed by the amount of content in **some sessions.** Be flexible. Don't expect them to learn all of the material. But help them understand and learn the key ideas and concepts.

The provider introduces the client to the purpose and structure of the *Workbook* during the intake and initial interview. The *Workbook* should be presented as representing the client's handbook for successful completion of the program. Providers facilitate the formation of a respectful attitude for the *Workbook* which can represent a record of individual efforts towards self-improvement and change. This written record can serve as evidence of prosocial commitment that may be used by judicial supervisors to evaluate progress in treatment and supervision.

PROGRAM AGREEMENTS AND GROUND RULES: EXPECTATIONS OF CLIENTS

Session 1 spells out what is expected of clients. These expectations are also discussed in *Chapter 7*. We summarize the program agreements and ground rules.

▶ Be on time, attend each session and make up any missed sessions.

▶ Take an active part with a positive attitude in all sessions.

▶ Keep names and all information clients learn about other people in trust and confidence.

▶ Complete all classroom worksheets and homework.

▶ Clients agree to not use alcohol or any mind-altering drugs while in the program.

▶ Clients are expected not to come to group during any lapses into AOD use and are willing to discuss lapses with the group and/or provider.

▶ Clients agree to take part in AOD testing required by their sentence or treatment agency.

▶ Clients will not take part in any illegal activity including driving with a revoked license.

Judicial clients who fail to meet these expectations may be asked to repeat *Phase I* or to take leave from the program until they are ready to fully experience all aspects of the program.

SERVICE DELIVERY OPTIONS AND APPROACHES

The options for delivering *SSC* are presented in *Chapter 7.* In all options, clients receive *Module I* in either an orientation group or in individual sessions. The delivery options are reviewed.

▶ **Closed group option:** The same group begins *Phase I* and proceeds through *Phase III.* The number of sessions offered each week will be determined by the provider.

▶ **Open group:** Provider has an open group for each phase. The number of sessions offered each week in each of these phases will be determined by the provider. Guidelines with respect to session schedule and frequency are given in *Chapter 7.* It is recommended that new clients start SSC at the beginning of a new module. However, here are the sessions in which clients **should not begin** *SSC.*

  ◆ Phase I: No entry at 4, 6, 8, 10, 12, 14, 16, 19 and 20.

  ◆ Phase II: No entry at 23, 26, 28, 30, and 39.

  ◆ Phase III: No entry at 44.

▶ **Closed group for** *Phase I* **and open groups for** *Phases II and III.* Clients who complete *Phase I* enter open *Phase II* group. Those completing *Phase II* enter an open *Phase III* group.

▶ *Phase I* **as a stand-alone program and** *Phase II and III* **provided in another outpatient or aftercare setting.** Some programs are set up to be delivered in a four-week period or limited to 20 to 25 sessions. For example, a 28-day inpatient treatment program could provide *Phase I* five times a week and then refer clients to outpatient or aftercare for *Phases II and III. Phase*

I now includes all of the essential and necessary strategies, content, and themes that make up *SSC,* and *Phases II* and *III* build on this foundation. When this option is used, clients would take their workbook into the receiving agency where they continue in the *SSC* program.

INTAKE AND IN-DEPTH ASSESSMENT

The intake and in-depth assessment is completed prior to or during the first orientation session. Feedback of the results of the assessment should be given to the client after the first orientation session. Clients will use these results to complete their list of problems to work on while in *SSC, Worksheet 4,* page 19, in the *Workbook.* A recommended protocol for the in-depth assessment is described in *Chapter 6.*

CLIENT PROGRESS AND CHANGE EVALUATION

The client *Progress and Change Evaluation (PACE) Monitor* should be explained to the client in the first orientation session. *PACE* has been described in *Chapter 6,* and involves completion of instruments by the provider and the client which measure the client's progress and change in the program. These instruments are completed during the initial screening, in-depth assessment, while the client is progressing through the program, and at program completion, e.g., the *SSC Program Closure Inventory (PCI).* The specific *PACE* instruments and schedule for their administration are outlined in *Chapter 6.* The complete *PACE* program and its instruments are provided in the *PACE Handbook.*

ORIENTATION SESSION

Module I provides the content and structure for orientation to *SSC.* These two sessions can be conducted in individual sessions or in scheduled orientation groups. The orientation session should follow the intake and assessment process. During orientation, inform clients that the nature of growth and change involves reflecting back, practicing and updating skills and concepts that were covered during earlier sessions. This referring back and forth throughout the *Workbook* is essential to the successful completion of *SSC.*

PHASE I
challenge to change

Building Knowledge and Skills
for Responsible Living

We make changes when we are challenged. This is the first stage of change and the first phase of *SSC: Challenge to Change*. We are challenged to change when our thinking and behaviors have led to bad outcomes, such as losing an important relationship or our freedom.

An important concept to convey to the substance abusing judicial client is that change takes place in steps - sometimes ever-so-small - and that change is not easy. But also important is to help clients understand that these steps are like a spiral. We may slip back to earlier stages of change, but never back to where we started. The spiral of change is different for different areas of change. Clients might be in one stage of change with respect to criminal thinking and another stage in changing destructive and harmful patterns of AOD use.

Phase I involves seven modules and 20 two-hour treatment sessions. The time for completion depends on the number of *Phase I* sessions that are offered each week.

It is recommended that a minimum of two hours is used for the presentation of each *Phase I* session. Providers will find that for some sessions, it is desireable to spend more than two hours of delivery time. This is particularly true for sessions in *Module 3*.

Note: As discussed in the *Introduction* to *Section III*, effective delivery of *SSC* requires having clients reflect back, practice, and update the concepts and skills that were introduced and learned in earlier sessions. This will involve going back and forth in a number of places in the *Workbook* to accomplish this goal. In almost every session, clients will update the program guides at the back of the *Workbook*. It is suggested that participants put "sticky markers" on the critical reference pages in the *Workbook*. For *Phase I*, these include pages 14 *(Figure 2, CB Map)*, 35, 87, and 99 *(Johari Window)* and the program guides: pages 291, 292, 295, and 300. Some are referred back to only once, and marking those is not necessary.

"Our life is what our thoughts make it."
-MARCUS AURELIUS

Phase I, **Challenge to Change,** sets the stage for self-improvement and change. Since the first step in change is self-disclosure, there is a strong emphasis on getting clients to self-disclose and share through interactive experiences - group exercises, open sharing and worksheets. The second step to change is self-awareness which comes through the feedback clients receive in the process of self-disclosure. Clients increase their self-awareness by understanding the process of change and setting their own targets for change. **A key mantra for *Phase I* is: self-disclosure leads to self-awareness and self-awareness leads to change.**

Phase I is designed to inspire and motivate clients to change. But inspiration and motivation are not enough to make change happen. *Phase I* helps clients to learn the rules, tools and targets for change. Yet change must have a focus and a goal. For *SSC,* that focus and goal are responsible and prosocial living and conduct.

The therapeutic alliance provides the basis upon which the provider achieves the goals of *Phase I* and is the foundation of the *SSC* program. It involves developing and maintaining a working partnership and trusting relationship with the client and the treatment group. Building a therapeutic alliance is an ongoing task. It gets challenged when the provider must assume the role of correctional specialist and, in partnership with the judicial system, help administer the judicial sentence.

The elements and principles of motivational enhancement and interviewing are important applications in *Module 1* as in all of *Phase I.* The focal counselor skills to be used during *Phase I* are: responding attentiveness; encouragers to share; and feedback clarification and reflective confrontation.

PROVIDER GOALS AND OBJECTIVES FOR *PHASE I*

▶ Develop a therapeutic, trust-based relationship with clients and the group.

▶ Help clients understand the purpose and goals of *SSC* and how it works.

▶ Help clients resolve the ambivalence around commitment to treatment and change.

▶ Help clients understand the stages of change and apply these stages to their own change process.

▶ Have clients assess and evaluate their progress and change in knowledge and skill development using the *SSC Change Scales* at the end of each session and the *PACE Monitor.*

▶ Provide opportunity for self-disclosure and self-awareness which lay the groundwork for change.

▶ Maximize clients' understanding and utilization of the basic rules, tools and skills of the cognitive-behavioral (CB) approach to change.

▶ Maximize clients' understanding of AOD use and abuse and apply this understanding to clients' own history and pattern of AOD use.

▶ Maximize clients' understanding of antisocial and criminal thinking and behavior and apply this understanding to their own history and pattern of criminal conduct.

▶ Maximize clients' understanding of the pathways to relapse and recidivism (R&R) and the pathways to R&R prevention and help them learn skills to prevent R&R.

▶ Help clients develop and commit to a plan for change.

▶ Finally, help clients inculcate the pathways metaphor and see that self-improvement, change and responsible living are journeys that continue throughout *SSC* and their lifetime.

MODULE I

Orientation: How This Program Works - the Rules, Tools and Targets for Change

OVERVIEW OF *MODULE 1*

The attitude and response of clients in this module set the tone for their involvement in *SSC*. Hard work may be required in dealing with the ambivalence, resistance and even anger of some clients at being in the program. Although individual attention may be needed for highly resistive clients, these issues are best resolved through group process and support. Clients whose attitudes and behaviors are disruptive to the flow of the group may have to be asked to discontinue the group.

The attitude and response of clients depend on the development of a readiness and motivation to change. *Module 1* focuses on developing a working relationship with clients and helping clients understand the process of self-improvement and change. As noted, building and maintaining client trust and rapport are ongoing tasks in every module and phase of treatment. *Module 1* also provides the basic understanding of what *SSC* is about, its objectives and goals and the tools and rules for change. The *SSC* cognitive-behavioral map or model for change is presented, and the *CB Map Exercise* is used at the beginning of each *SSC* session.

GOALS OF THIS MODULE

▶ Building a therapeutic alliance and a working relationship.

▶ Helping clients learn who *SSC* is for and what it is about.

▶ Helping clients learn to use the *CB Map* for change and understand that it is used in every *SSC* session.

▶ Learning the rules, tools and targets of change.

INTRODUCING THE *PARTICIPANT'S WORKBOOK*

Thoroughly review the introduction of the *Workbook* in a positive and motivating manner. Some providers may want to review the *Workbook* in its entirety during the first session of this module. The *Workbook* should be presented as representing the client's handbook for successful completion of the program.

If you are using a closed group approach, then *Module 1* will be presented in the *SSC* group you will be working with over the next 20 sessions. If you are using an open-group model, with new clients introduced as the program progresses, then *Module 1* will be presented in either an individual session or in an orientation group conducted on a periodic basis.

RATIONALE AND OVERVIEW

Developing a working relationship involves a complicated blend of building a therapeutic alliance within the context of the system's expectations of the judicial client. It involves the blend of applying both the therapeutic and correctional approach in judicial treatment. It involves being a partner with both the judicial client and the judicial system. Often, this is walking a "thin line." AOD counselors and treatment programs can become agents of substance control or "watch dogs." This readily compromises the therapeutic effort. While there are overall common goals that the therapeutic and judicial system share, the two systems are not one and the same. The goals and objectives of both must be made clear to the judicial client.

In *Chapter 2,* we addressed the importance of developing the treatment relationship using motivational enhancement and therapeutic alliance skills. The provider is asked to review this chapter.

The treatment literature makes it clear that positive treatment outcomes are dependent on the therapeutic alliance and trust and rapport that are the matrix of the alliance. This alliance is developed using the skills of motivational enhancement, rolling with the resistance, using reflective rather than direct confrontation, accepting self-disclosure without judgmental responses, using "accurate empathy" (Miller et al., 1994) and utilizing "ethical, decent and humane" approaches (Andrews & Bonta, 2003).

Correctional confrontation approaches, initially, need to be minimized. Research has shown that confrontation of denial regarding criminal or substance abuse motives and attitudes may well increase resistance and have an adverse effect on treatment outcomes (e.g., Miller, Benefield & Tonigan, 1993).

The work of Andrews and Bonta (2003) shows that what is important to the provider-client relationship "is an open, flexible, and enthusiastic style wherein people feel free to express their opinions, feeling, and experiences. Also needed are mutual liking, respect, and caring" (p. 314). Springer, McNeece, and Arnold make it clear: "Regardless of practitioners' theoretical orientation in working with offenders, we advocate that they operate from a stance of nonpossessive warmth and empathic understanding" (2003, p. 42).

Although the traditional treatment literature sees therapeutic alliance as an essential and necessary component of outcome, the correctional treatment literature has not strongly or explicitly addressed the therapeutic alliance and partnership with the judicial client. In these works, no specific chapter or section was found that was devoted to the provider-client treatment relationship. There is, however, a strong emphasis on developing offender readiness and motivation (e.g., Dansereau et al., 2004; Dees, Dansereau & Simpson, 2004; Kennedy & Serin, 1999). Certainly, part of this emphasis is the therapeutic alliance and relationship.

Clients beginning *SSC* may be anxious and even confused as to what is to happen in the program. The first sessions are therefore geared toward establishing group comfort while at the same time presenting the purpose and approach of *SSC,* its goals and objectives and the tools and rules for change.

The staff presenting the program should be introduced including counseling and educational background. The provider then gives a preview of the two orientation sessions.

Some clients may enter the program having recently become detoxified from alcohol or other drugs. They may have attention and concentration problems, and may still be experiencing emotional and physical discomfort.

Encourage these clients to give their best effort and assure them that they will have ample time to grasp the material presented in *Module I*. For these clients, an individual orientation booster session may be helpful at the onset of *SSC*.

SUMMARY OF CONTENT, PRESENTATION SEQUENCE AND GUIDELINES

Providers are asked to present the session objectives at the beginning of each session. The following sequence is used for this orientation session.

▶ Start with presenting the Introduction, page 1, which includes the welcome, program phases, stages of change, goals and introduction material of *Phase I*. Then introduce *Module 1*.

▶ Present the objectives of *Session 1*, **Who the Program Is For and How the Program Is Set Up.**

▶ Present the three **Goals of SSC,** and have clients write down their recidivism prevention goal and their relapse prevention and community commitment goal.

  ◆ Carefully go over the recidivism and relapse prevention goals from which they can choose.

  ◆ Take time to discuss the two relapse prevention goals they can choose from. Present the *SSC* expectation of abstinence from all illegal drugs. Facilitate an open discussion of this expectation and accept arguments and disputes of this goal in a non-judgmental way.

  ◆ Discuss the difference between the goal of living alcohol-free and the goal of living an alcohol problem-free life. Discuss the *SSC* position of "zero-risk" or alcohol-abstinence, particularly for those who have had significant and serious past problems around AOD use.

▶ When presenting the **Objectives and Benefits of This Program** and *Figure 1,* emphasize that meaningful and responsible living is a primary goal of *SSC*.

▶ Carefully present **What Is Expected of Clients and the Program Agreements.** Some of these may spark some resistance and even anger. Again, deal with the resistance from a therapeutic perspective. *Worksheet 1* gives clients opportunity to define their own goals. How are the client's goals different from the *SSC* goals?

▶ Present **What Is the Approach of** *SSC* and the *Cognitive-Behavioral (CB) Map, Figure 2* below and *Figure 2,* page 14 in the *Workbook.* Introduce the *CB Map Exercise* and then take one or two group members through that exercise. To prepare for this section, the provider should review *Chapter 4, CB Approach as the Platform for Change* and the guidelines for presenting the *CB Map Exercise* in *Chapter 7,* page 134. Then present the next two sections on **What the CB Map Tells Us About AOD Use and CC.**

▶ Discuss **Trust and Rapport** in the program, and have clients introduce themselves and share the areas discussed in this section. Take time to go over the trust and rapport section. Help clients understand the concept of rapport - harmony with themselves and others. After doing *Worksheet 2,* have clients feel free to openly discuss their concerns about trust in *SSC*.

▶ Again, openly discuss the expectations of clients not only **Being Alcohol and Drug Free** during *SSC,* but the expectation is that clients abstain from the use of all illegal drugs.

▶ Use *Worksheet 3,* the CSAS, as a baseline self-rating of clients perceptions of their own AOD problems and criminal conduct history. Explain the *Progress and Change Evaluation (PACE)* to be done during *SSC*. This is outlined in *Chapter 6* and presented in the *PACE Handbook Monitor*.

▶ *Worksheet 4* can be done in group or as homework. It is the basis for developing their *Master Profile (MP)* and their *Master Assessment Plan (MAP)* that are introduced in *Session 2*.

SUMMARY OF KEY CONCEPTS

▶ Three stages of change that occur in steps and over time.

▶ Overall goals of *SSC* and for *Phase I.*

▶ Concepts of relapse and recidivism.

▶ The CB approach to change and the *CB Map Exercise.*

▶ How substance abuse and criminal conduct are connected.

▶ Trust and rapport.

▶ Self-assessment of AOD use and history of CC and the *PACE Index.*

SESSION CLOSURE AND GUIDELINES FOR THERAPEUTIC PROCESSING

Allow at least a brief time for closure. Important areas to focus on are the program agreements, trust in *SSC*, and having clients share their R&R goals.

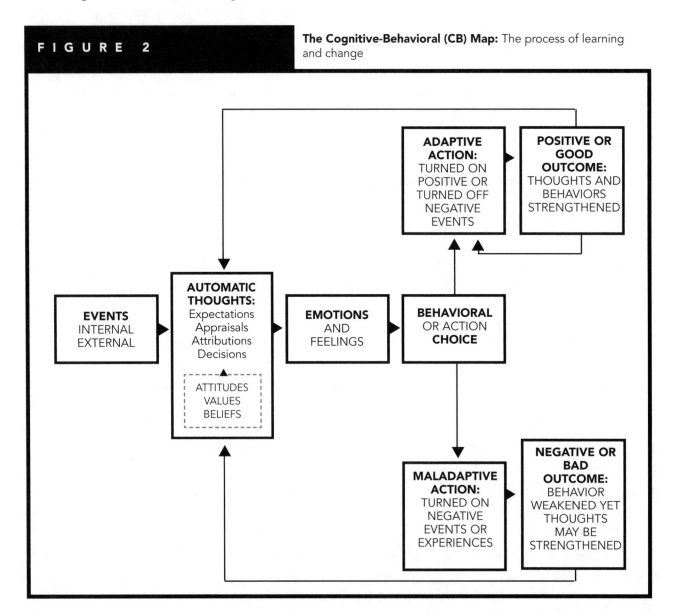

F I G U R E   2   **The Cognitive-Behavioral (CB) Map:** The process of learning and change

RATIONALE AND OVERVIEW

An assumption of *SSC* is that change is more apt to occur through a partnership among the provider, judicial client, and the group. In that partnership, the client has the opportunity for self-disclosure and to receive feedback, both of which are part of the self-assessment process.

Review of Provider Skills and Approaches

Providers are always challenged to improve their skills and approaches for effective delivery of *SSC*. In *Section II, Chapter 7*, we looked at the approaches and skills that providers need in delivering *SSC*. Following is a review of these skills.

▶ Assessment and referral.

▶ Using psychoeducational methods and interactive teaching.

▶ Skills to enhance client participation, which include: actiongrams; skill learning and rehearsal; role playing; role reversal skills; doubling; different methods of structured sharing such as the round-robin approach; and group sharing.

▶ Using basic counseling skills to: build trust, rapport and motivation; maximize client self-disclosure and self-awareness; and maximize and strengthen change.

▶ Presenting the basic concepts of AOD abuse and criminal conduct and their cycles.

▶ Delivery of the cognitive-behavior approach to learning and change.

▶ Integrating the correctional and therapeutic approaches.

▶ Group facilitation skills.

We also summarize the most salient guidelines and skills that more specifically enhance effectiveness in working with judicial clients.

▶ A non-confrontational approach in the early stages of treatment.

▶ Avoid argumentation.

▶ Express empathy.

▶ Roll with the resistance.

▶ Reinforce positive involvement and sharing.

Overview and Rationale for Session 2

Session 2, the second orientation session, continues to build trust and rapport and enhance motivation and treatment involvement. If the provider is using the closed group option, there should be a special emphasis on building group cohesion and strengthening client commitment to the *SSC* group. If an open group approach is being used, then more focus is given to developing a working relationship with clients in the two orientation sessions and preparing clients for involvement in an ongoing open group they will enter in their next session.

At this point, the in-depth assessment should be completed, which will include an interview with the client and a completion of self-report psychometric instruments, as outlined in *Chapter 6*. *SSC* is an ongoing process of self-assessment through self-disclosure and receiving feedback. Self-disclosure opens the door for feedback which enhances self-awareness and lays the groundwork for change. This session helps clients to learn and use the rules, tools and targets of self-assessment and change. These rules, tools and targets are the maps and guidelines to monitor change and keep clients on the pathway to responsible living.

SUMMARY OF CONTENT, PRESENTATION SEQUENCE AND GUIDELINES

Presentation of this session involves a thorough coverage of its content using an interactive teaching approach. Yet, clients should be given the opportunity to share their thoughts and ideas around session content. The following presentation process and sequence is recommended.

- Begin with the *CB Map Exercise*, which would also involve a review of the CB model, *Figure 2* above or *Figure 2*, page 14 in the *Workbook*. Then present the section objectives.

- Review the objectives and benefits of *SSC*, page 11 in the *Workbook*.

- Briefly review the expectations and program agreements and guidelines, page 12 in the *Workbook*.

- Review the three core skill strategies of *SSC* that are designed to prevent relapse and recidivism and keep individuals on the pathways to responsible and meaningful living, page 11.

  - Mental restructuring or thought-changing skills.

  - Social and relationship skills.

  - Community responsibility skills.

- Present the six **Rules That Guide Change.**

- Present the nine **Tools and Targets for Change**.

  1. The *CB Map Exercise,* used to start each *Phase I* session.

  2. *Autobiography:* Review the elements of the autobiography. Clients who have difficulty writing may have someone help them, or even do it with drawings and pictures. Ask clients to include their future biography. A good time line for completion is within four to six weeks of starting *SSC*. Have clients share elements of their autobiography from time-to-time in group. Develop a schedule as to when clients are to complete their autobiographies.

  3. *Master Skills List (MSL), Program Guide 1,* in the back of the *Workbook*. Go over the skills, and indicate that when a skill is introduced, clients will initially rate themselves, and then update the skills list.

  4. *Master Profile (MP), Program Guide 2, Workbook,* page 292. Have clients practice rating themselves on one area, e.g., Level of Involvement in Drug Use. Have clients complete the *MP* during their first month in *SSC* or before completing eight sessions. Once the *MP* is completed, the provider rates each client either on the client's own MP or on a copy of one and then give it to client for comparison.

  5. *Master Assessment Plan (MAP), Program Guide 3* in the back of the *Workbook* defines the clients' targets for change. They are asked to complete the *MAP* in the first month of *SSC* or before completing eight *SSC* sessions. The *MAP* is the client's ITP (individual treatment plan or plan for change). With permission, providers may want to use the client's initial *MAP* as a starting point for the provider's ITP. Have clients practice using the *MAP* by entering one problem in any problem area of their choice. *Worksheet 4,* the comprehensive assessment and the MP are the primary resources for developing their *MAP*. Review *Workbook 4,* page 19, to see if clients need to add problems to the list.

6. *Weekly Thinking and Action Patterns (TAP) Charting* is *Program Guide 4* in the back of the *Workbook*. Initially, clients will be defensive in using this tool and will not trust how the information will be used. They will be guarded against admitting to AOD use or having thoughts about committing crimes. As trust and rapport are developed and as clients begin to take ownership around their own change and discover that self-disclosure and self-assessment are important in preventing relapse and recidivism, their self-report on *TAP* will be more candid.

   CAVEAT: Clients in a prison setting may choose not to respond to the *TAP* question of whether they were where they could have used alcohol or other drugs because they may see such disclosure as putting them at risk of harm from other inmates. This specific part of *TAP* should be discussed with clients and that, as with all exercises and worksheets, they should disclose within their own comfort zone. All information disclosed by clients must be kept confidential, as required by the Federal confidential guidelines, except for where the client is of imminent danger to self or others or in the case of suspected child abuse. The *TAP* question is an important part of helping clients managing high-risk exposures, and part of the R&R process. It should be dealt with therapeutically, and not at a correctional (sanctioning) level.

7. *Thinking Report:* Daley and Marlatt (1992) identify the use of inventories as an important relapse prevention strategy. These inventories have the goal of getting clients to monitor their lives so as to identify high-risk factors that would contribute to a relapse. The *Thinking Report* is such an inventory.

8. *Re-thinking Report* changes the thoughts, beliefs and actions to produce positive outcomes. It is a map for change and a plan as to how to handle similar future events. We change the thoughts and then hypothesize what underlying beliefs would have to change in order to produce those thoughts. Then, we hypothesize actions that could result from those changes and which lead to good outcomes.

9. *SSC Change Scales:* At the end of each session, clients are asked to rate their level of knowledge and skill use for the specific concepts and skills they learned and practiced in the session. They start in this session, rating themselves on their understanding of *SSC* and the degree to which they see themselves taking part in the program. The *SSC Change Scales* and *PACE* are the basic tools to monitor change.

SUMMARY OF KEY CONCEPTS PRESENTED

▶ *CB Map Exercise.*

▶ Core goals of *SSC.*

▶ Expectations and program agreements and guidelines.

▶ Three core skill strategies of *SSC.*

▶ The six rules that guide change.

▶ The nine tools and targets for change.

▶ The *PACE Monitor.*

SESSION CLOSURE AND GUIDELINES FOR THERAPEUTIC PROCESSING

Most of this session will be spent presenting the session content. If this orientation session is done in a group, a **round-robin exercise** could be used where clients share their level of trust and comfort in *SSC,* and how they see themselves with respect to making changes in their lives. Again, when using this technique, have clients share in a crisp quick manner, using around 10 to 20 seconds of time per client.

MODULE 2

Cognitive-Behavioral Approach to Change and Responsible Living

OVERVIEW OF MODULE 2

Learning and using the skills of changing thoughts, feelings and actions are premised on having knowledge of how we change and what we change. This module provides the basic understanding as to how thinking and behavior are learned and changed.

A key to this module and to success in making change is the cognitive-behavioral (CB) model for learning and change (*Figure 2* in this *Guide* and *Figure 2* in the *Workbook*). Clients were introduced to this model in *Session 1* and the rules for change in *Session 2*. This module devotes two sessions to understanding and applying this key to change and learning five rules of thinking that lead to action outcomes.

The distinction between *Session 3* and *4* is somewhat subtle with respect to the *CB Map* and model for change. In *Session 3,* we focus only on how this model applies to thinking and how our thoughts get reinforced and strengthened. *Session 4* describes how thinking **and** behavior are learned and strengthened. At the end of this module, we want clients to have the skill to use the *CB Map* to change thoughts so as to have positive outcomes - outcomes that prevent relapse and that result in prosocial and responsible behavior in the community.

The concepts and skills in this module are basic to a lot of the material covered in subsequent *SSC* sessions. Some clients in the open group option will enter *SSC* after this module has been presented. Since each *SSC* session starts with a *CB Map Exercise,* these clients will be quite skilled in using the model in changing thinking, attitudes and beliefs. It is suggested that the provider, from time-to-time review and update the group on the material in this module.

GOALS OF THIS MODULE

A general purpose of *Module 2* is to help clients apply the concepts of CB learning and change to making changes in their lives. Here are the more specific provider goals.

▶ Help clients understand how thinking and emotions fit into self-improvement and change.

▶ Help clients understand how behavior and actions are learned and changed.

▶ Facilitate the application and practice of the CB model to help make changes in their lives.

RATIONALE AND OVERVIEW

Research findings support the efficacy of cognitive-behavioral (CB) approaches in developing self-control and change and in intervening in AOD misuse (e.g., Marlatt & Witkiewitz, 2005) and criminal conduct (e.g., Andrews & Bonta, 2003; Landenberger & Lipsey, 2005; Wanberg & Milkman, 1998; Milkman & Wanberg, 2005, 2007). The CB approach is the underlying strategy of the *SSC* curriculum. It is important that clients have an understanding of the cognitive and behavioral processes that lead to both maladaptive and adaptive thinking and acting and to enhancing self-control and change. Meichenbaum (1977, 1985, 1993b), who has made major contributions to cognitive therapy, emphasized the importance of providing the client with an early, clear and distinct framework for therapy. He suggests that clients should be taught the basic concepts of CB therapy and how change takes place and this instruction should precede any specific treatment intervention.

An important component of change is enhancing clients' belief that they have the skills and confidence to develop self-control over thoughts, feelings and behaviors that cause problems and lead to bad outcomes. The content and material of this session are based on the sources referenced in *Chapter 4* and on the previous work done by the authors (Milkman & Wanberg, 2005, 2007; Wanberg & Milkman, 1998; Wanberg, Milkman & Timken, 2005).

The main purpose of this session is to apply the principles of cognitive-behavior therapy to prevent criminal conduct recidivism and AOD relapse and getting positive outcomes. There are two pathways through which self-control and positive change are strengthened:

▶ through reinforcing thoughts that lead to positive outcomes and behavior; and

▶ by reinforcing the behaviors that produce positive outcomes or events.

This session focuses on the first of these two pathways.

Traditional behavioral therapy focuses mainly on the idea that when behavior leads to favorable outcomes, that behavior is reinforced; and when behavior leads to unfavorable outcomes or to neither good nor bad outcomes, that behavior is weakened or will extinguish. The cognitive model adds a new link to the reinforcement path: that favorable and unfavorable outcomes often strengthen the thoughts that lead to the behaviors that produce them. This provides one explanation as to why behaviors from negative outcomes often do not become weakened or extinguished. No matter how unfavorable the outcomes, if that outcome reinforces the thoughts that produce it, then those behaviors producing those outcomes are likely to occur again.

SUMMARY OF CONTENT, PRESENTATION SEQUENCE AND GUIDELINES

The first part of this session explores how our thoughts, attitudes and beliefs lead to substance abuse or to antisocial and criminal conduct. Five rules of thinking are presented to help the client see how this happens. Explain to clients that the first three rules of thinking that lead to actions are the same as change rules one, two and four presented in *Session 2*.

The material in this session needs to be presented in a deliberate and slow-paced fashion. The concepts and ideas should be given in small segments and clients are asked to discuss these concepts as they are presented. The following provides the presentation sequence of this session.

▶ Start with the session objectives and then do the *CB Map Exercise* and sharing the *TAP Charting*.

▶ Present the **Five Rules of Thinking That Lead to Actions or Behaviors.**

Thinking Rule 1: Thoughts control emotions and behaviors. This rule is at the heart of the CB model for change. Clients learn the concepts of automatic thoughts, attitudes and beliefs and apply them to their past criminal conduct and AOD use and abuse and to getting positive outcomes. Help clients understand that automatic thoughts, attitudes and beliefs are cognitive or mental habits. Draw the analogy between these cognitive habits and behavioral habits. We also want clients to understand that these thought habits lead to positive as well as negative outcomes.

Thinking Rule 2: We fight or resist changing our thinking. Clients often defend against or resist change. They may externalize and blame the system, others and even those close to them for their current predicament. Change is not necessary if their problems and circumstances are the fault of others. "It's the outside world that needs to change." Do not argue with this position, but roll with the resistance (Miller & Rollnick, 2002). Reflect their perceptions and position. This helps judicial clients hear themselves think and hear the errors in their thinking and to take ownership of those thoughts. Part of this rule is that each person sees the world differently. No view is right or wrong. Yet, clients who resist change think their views and ideas are right. **However, make it clear that society does form common views of what is right and what is wrong.** These become rules and laws of society. Review the concepts of the belief clutch.

Thinking Rule 3: We choose our thoughts. Many judicial clients find it difficult to accept that they consciously decide or choose to commit crimes. When presented with this idea, many judicial clients will say: "It just happened. I didn't choose to break the law."

Thinking Rule 4: Our thoughts can become distorted and illogical. Focusing on thinking errors is an important part of the treatment of criminal conduct. Take time to do *Worksheet 5,* page 35. Thinking errors become the focus of other sessions, which will refer back to this session, particularly *Worksheet 5.*

Thinking Rule 5: Good and bad outcomes strengthen thoughts. This helps clients understand why they repeat behavior that results in negative outcomes and punishment.

▶ Present the section on **Mapping the Pathway to Change our Thinking.** Carefully go over *Figure 3,* page 32, in the *Workbook* (*Figure 3* below) and the four automatic thought structures. These four structures - expectations, appraisals, attributions and decisions - determine many of our emotional and action outcomes. They can lead to criminal conduct and AOD abuse behaviors. Go over the example of "the boss wants to see you," page 32, which shows how these structures can lead to certain outcomes. Have clients look over how these thought structures determine John's emotional and behavioral outcomes (page 32). These examples can also be used to explain concepts and skills that are presented in other *SSC* sessions.

▶ Have clients note the difference between *Figure 3,* page 32 and *Figure 5,* page 41, in the *Workbook (Figures 2* and *3* in this *Guide). Figure 3* (page 32 in *Workbook* and below) only focuses on how thoughts are reinforced - there are arrows going back from the positive and negative outcome blocks to automatic thoughts. This illustrates that both positive and negative outcomes can strengthen thoughts that lead to those outcomes. Explain that this session is the cognitive part of the cognitive-behavior model. The behavior part is discussed in *Session 4.*

▶ Present **How Thoughts, Emotions and Actions Interact,** using *Figure 4* in the *Workbook.*

▶ Present the **Steps to How Thoughts Lead to Actions.** Have one or two clients use personal examples to illustrate this.

▶ Go over the **Steps to Change Thoughts.** Again, have one or two clients share an experience that illustrates how thoughts can be changed.

▶ **Exercise:** Do *Worksheet 6,* page 36, in group. Have clients use the event of their last arrest. Walk clients through the automatic thinking and thought habits, feelings, underlying attitudes and beliefs, the behavioral choice and the outcome of that arrest. Then have clients replay the process by changing thinking to get a positive emotional and behavioral outcome from the event that preceded their last arrest. Take time to do *Worksheet 6.* It is probably one of the most important exercises in *SSC.*

▶ Have clients update their *Master Skills List* (MSL), particularly Skill 1, using the *Cognitive Behavioral Map* and Skill 8, Changing Thinking Errors.

▶ Have clients update their *MAP* and remind them to do their *TAP* charting

▶ Have clients use the *SSC Change Scale* to rate their understanding of how thoughts lead to behavior.

▶ Have clients take one of the steps to changing thoughts, e.g., identify attitude, and practice it all week.

SUMMARY OF KEY CONCEPTS

▶ Five rules of thinking that lead to action outcomes.
▶ How to map the pathway to changing thinking.

▶ Steps to how thoughts lead to actions.
▶ Steps to changing thoughts.

SESSION CLOSURE AND GUIDELINES FOR THERAPEUTIC PROCESSING

Have clients share what thoughts and behaviors will be most difficult for them to change. Give some time for unstructured processing.

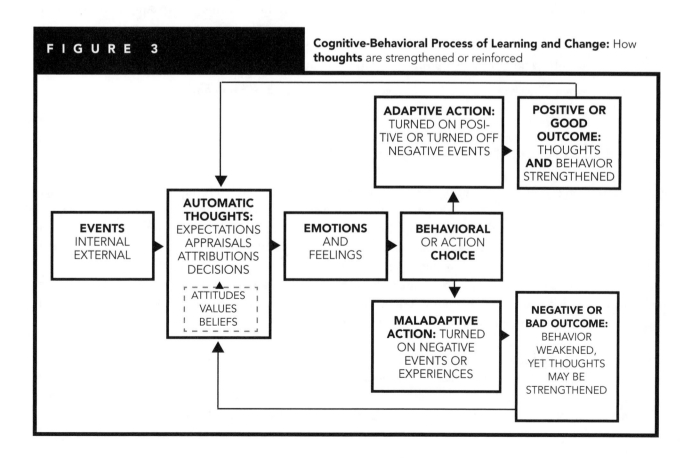

FIGURE 3

Cognitive-Behavioral Process of Learning and Change: How **thoughts** are strengthened or reinforced

SESSION 4: How Behavior Is Learned and Changed

RATIONALE AND OVERVIEW

For the open group structure, there is no new client entry for this session. It must be preceded by *Session 3.* Cognitive learning and change are only part of the overall picture of how people learn and change behavior. The other piece of the puzzle involves understanding how behavior is learned and reinforced or strengthened. This piece must be in place in order for clients to fully see how the cognitive-behavioral learning process applies to their own AOD use and criminal conduct.

The purpose of this session is to give substance abusing judicial clients a firm understanding of how their substance use and abuse and their criminal behavior get strengthened and reinforced. The three rules that determine how behavior is learned and reinforced (or weakened) are discussed, along with how they are related to AOD abuse and criminal conduct.

Attention is given to helping clients understand why Rule III doesn't always work - that a behavior that is punished or that leads to bad outcomes often continues to persist and repeat itself. The final goal of this session is to show how the two methods of reinforcing thinking and reinforcing behavior are integrated into the overall cognitive-behavioral model of developing self-control and change.

SUMMARY OF CONTENT, PRESENTATION SEQUENCE AND GUIDELINES

Whereas *Session 3* focuses on **thought habits** (automatic thoughts), this session focuses on **action or behavior habits** or automatic behaviors. Action habits are developed and reinforced through **two simple rules** of operant conditioning:

▶ **First,** when a behavior produces a positive or good outcome it gets reinforced;

▶ **Second,** when a behavior turns off a negative event or prevents a bad outcome, that behavior is strengthened (negative reinforcement model).

Both of these pathways to reinforcement are powerful in developing behaviors that are resistant to change.

Important Concept: When presenting the behavioral reinforcement model, it is important that clients understand that some behaviors that are maladaptive and lead to negative outcomes can also be perceived as adaptive and leading to positive outcomes. For example, maladaptive drinking that leads to negative outcomes such as violence, impaired driving and criminal conduct, initially were (and may continue to be) perceived as adaptive and leading to positive outcomes (it reduces stress or turns on positive events). The fact that such maladaptive and negative-consequence behaviors continue to lead to good outcomes is one of the reasons why the bad results from those behaviors often do not weaken or extinguish the behavior. These subtle nuances are important in helping clients understand the power and complexities of the model.

The third rule is that behavior that is punished or leads to negative outcomes will extinguish or drop out of the behavioral repertoire. This rule often confuses people. If that rule works, then why do people repeat behaviors that lead to bad outcomes? Why do people commit another crime after being punished for a previous crime? The answers to these questions are presented in the *Workbook* and time should be taken to discuss this issue.

This session puts together how our thinking and acting lead to the process of learning. *Figure 5,* page 41 in the *Workbook*, provides this integration and a careful explanation of how thinking and behavior are reinforced.

The following presentation sequence is suggested.

▶ Start with session objectives and then do the *CB Map Exercise* and sharing the *TAP Charting*.

▶ Review **How Thoughts and Beliefs Get Strengthened**, the key ideas of *Session 3.* Use the example of Betty (page 37 in the *Workbook*) to illustrate how beliefs that lead to a positive outcome get strengthened and the example of John (page 32 of the *Workbook*) to illustrate how beliefs that lead to bad outcomes can get strengthened.

▶ Interactively present the three **Rules of How Behaviors or Actions Are Learned.** Have clients present examples to illustrate the rules.

▶ Discuss **Why Doesn't Rule 3 — Turning Off Negative Events — Always Work?** Again, this helps clients understand why behaviors that lead to bad outcomes get reinforced rather than weakened.

▶ Using *Figure 5* in the *Workbook,* page 41 (*Figure 2, Session 1* above, which introduced clients to the *CB Map*), discuss **How Thinking and Behaviors Are Learned and Strengthened** and behavior habits and how these are integrated in the cognitive-behavior model of learning self-control and change. Again, have clients see the difference between *Figure 3,* page 32, and *Figure 5,* page 41 in the *Workbook.*

▶ **Exercise: Practicing Cognitive-Behavioral Change.** Do *Worksheet 7,* having clients use a past event that led to a bad outcome, and then go back over the process and replace the thoughts, emotions and behaviors that will lead to a positive outcome. The provider may want to make copies of this worksheet and use it in subsequent sessions around other topics and issues.

▶ Using the *SSC Change Scales,* have clients rate their knowledge and skill in changing thoughts and behaviors. Have them update their *Master Skills List* (MSL). For clients in the first month of *SSC* or the first eight sessions, have them continue working on their *MP* and *MAP.*

SUMMARY OF KEY CONCEPTS

▶ Rules on how behaviors and actions are learned.

▶ Both positive **and** negative outcomes can strengthen the thoughts that lead to them and become thought habits.

▶ Behaviors that lead to positive outcomes or eliminate negative outcomes will get strengthened and lead to action habits.

▶ Some behaviors that lead to positive outcomes can become maladaptive and lead to negative outcomes.

▶ Behaviors that are punished or lead to negative outcomes are not necessarily extinguished unless the thoughts that lead to those behaviors are changed.

SESSION CLOSURE AND GUIDELINES FOR THERAPEUTIC PROCESSING

Have clients apply the CB change model to a situation where a friend offers another person illegal drugs. Have clients share how they see themselves doing in *SSC.* Give some time for unstructured processing.

MODULE 3

Alcohol and Other Drug (AOD) Use Patterns and Outcomes

OVERVIEW OF MODULE 3

Change is dependent on knowledge and understanding about the areas that we seek to change, e.g., substance abuse, criminal thinking and action. The **first step** to change is developing generic knowledge about these areas. The **second step** is to apply these understandings to the individual's specific and unique situation where change is needed using **interactive self-assessment** approaches. This involves having clients measure and evaluate their own specific status in relationship to the knowledge base and then self-disclose and receive feedback around their findings. The **third step** in the change process is to generate skills from the knowledge base and then have clients apply these skills in practical ways to their own situation to bring about cognitive, emotional and behavioral change.

The focus of *Module 3* is to achieve the first two steps of this process in the area of AOD use and abuse: 1) develop the knowledge base; 2) self-disclose and receive feedback; and then provide the basis for skill acquisition and application to prevent relapse and recidivism. This module takes important elements of AOD education and helps clients develop an understanding of their own AOD use and problem outcomes. This provides a basis for developing AOD relapse goals and a relapse prevention plan.

Because this module is based on the principles of psychoeducation, one of the *SSC* core strategies, the provider is asked to review the discussion of this strategy in *Chapter 1,* pp. 15-17 *and Chapter 2,* pp. 36-37. Also, the chapter *Substance Abuse and the Brain* in the *Resource Guide* (Wanberg & Milkman, 2008) provides additional information that can be used in presenting this module.

GOALS OF THIS MODULE

▶ Provide basic information on how the abuse of alcohol and other drugs present imminent and long-term danger to the brain, mind and body;

▶ Help clients see how the facts and knowledge about drugs fit them;

▶ Provide understanding of AOD use and abuse patterns and have clients see how these patterns fit them;

▶ Define the AOD impaired control cycles or the pathways to addiction and have clients see how they fit these cycles.

▶ Define the problem outcome patterns of AOD use and help each client define or detect his or her own AOD problem outcome pattern.

This module could easily be expanded to six AOD change-education sessions.

RATIONALE AND OVERVIEW

SSC challenges clients to change behaviors and patterns in AOD use and abuse and consider the "zero-risk" relapse prevention plan of living AOD-free. A part of this challenge, and the purpose of this session, is to provide basic knowledge about alcohol and other drugs. This material is presented in a factual and non-theoretical manner. Information for this session as well as *Session 7* comes from a variety of sources, including: Acosta, Haller & Schnoll, 2005; Boehm, Valenzuela & Harris, 2005; Dilts & Dilts, 2005; Dupont & Dupont, 2005; Johnson & Ait-Daoud, 2005; Kosten, George & Kleber, 2005; Lin & Anthenelli, 2005; Lowinson et al., 2005; McDowell, 2005; Nace, 2005; Ray & Ksir, 1996; Ray, Ksir & Hart, 2006; Wesson et al., 2005; Wanberg, 1990; Wanberg & Milkman, 1998; Wanberg, Milkman & Timken, 2005; Welch, 2005; Grinspoon, Bakalar & Russo, 2005; and the material presented in the chapter, *Substance Abuse and the Brain,* of the *Resource Guide* (Wanberg & Milkman, 2008).

SUMMARY OF CONTENT, PRESENTATION SEQUENCE AND GUIDELINES

Generally, there are two kinds of drug direct effects: the system is suppressed or sedated; or the system is stimulated or enhanced. Some drugs are biphasic - they can first stimulate the system and then suppress it. In our previous works (Wanberg & Milkman, 1998; Wanberg, Milkman & Timken, 2005) we put drugs into the two categories based on the intoxicating or direct effects: those that suppress or sedate the system; and those that stimulate or enhance the system. We also indicated that some of these drugs can do both, such as cannabis or nicotine. We also showed that drugs have a withdrawal or indirect effect. We then indicated that, generally, the withdrawal effect of a drug is the opposite of the direct effect.

In this *SSC* edition, we define five drug categories (*Table 1*, page 46 of the *Workbook*) and then show the direct and indirect effects of drugs in these categories. We indicate which of these drugs are system suppressors or system enhancers or both. We want clients to have an understanding of the five kinds of drugs and which drugs they have used. However, we also want clients to understand the concept of direct and indirect effects, since this concept is basic to understanding the mental-physical impaired control or addiction cycle described in *Session 7.* This cycle shows that use of a particular drug for its direct effect (e.g., to relieve anxiety) can result in a need to use the drug to relieve symptoms resulting from its indirect effect (anxiety). Often overlooked in the literature is that the indirect or withdrawal effects of a drug can be just as disruptive and dangerous as its direct effects.

This session also discusses drug toxicity, tolerance, drug interactions, and drug withdrawal (indirect effects). Special focus is devoted to alcohol since this drug is commonly abused by judicial clients and often associated with criminal conduct. Understanding BAC and its level effects is an important focus.

Marijuana is also a focus (*Table 4,* page 55), since it is widely used by judicial clients. General health risks related to drug use are discussed including AIDS and FAS. Another focus is the relationship of specific drug groups to criminal conduct, *Table 5,* page 57, in the *Workbook.*

The following presentation sequence is recommended for this session.

▶ Start with the *CB Map Exercise* and sharing the *TAP Charting.* Then have clients apply one of the thinking rules in *Session 3* to an event they experienced this past week. Present session objectives.

▶ Discuss the question posed at the first part of the session: What is an alcohol or drug problem?

▶ Present the section on **Basic Facts and Knowledge about Drugs**. Here are some enhancements to the information in the *Workbook* around topics in this part of *Session 7.*

- **Definition of Drug:** A drug is defined as any substance, natural or artificial, that by its chemical or physical nature, changes physical, psychological or chemical functioning of a living organism (Ray & Ksir, 2002). For our purpose in this program, we are referring to drugs that have a direct or indirect effect on the person in such a way that it changes or alters the persons's states of consciousness, emotions and moods, thinking and actions (Wanberg, 1990; Wanberg & Milkman, 1998). Even though the word drug comes from the French word "drogue," or dry substance, **drug** in this work refers to any chemical that changes or alters the person's states of consciousness.

- **Drugs work** because they change the nervous system's flow of electricity and the release of natural nerve chemicals called neurochemicals or neurotransmitters. These neurotransmitters are stored in the nerve endings and are released into spaces between the neuron called synapses. *Chapter 4* presents a thorough discussion of how drugs influence mood and behavior largely through their effect on the levels of dopamine in the pleasure centers of the brain (Blum, et al., 1996).

- **Drugs change the way that our neurochemical system works.** They may slow down (drugs that suppress the system) or speed up (drugs that enhance the system) the action of the nerves by increasing or decreasing the release of nerve chemicals in the nerve endings. They can also directly affect the nerves. For example, alcohol not only affects the release of the nerve chemicals in the nerve endings, but also can change the lining of the nerves to cause a "leakage of electricity" so as to slow down their action.

- Most of the **five types of drugs** in *Table 1,* page 46 of the *Workbook,* have one of two types of effects on the nervous system. Drugs that slow down the nervous system or **system suppressors** are referred to as downers or sedatives such as alcohol, barbiturates, tranquilizers. This group of drugs also includes drugs that slow down or block sensitivity to internal stimuli, such as pain, and includes opioids and synthetic pain killers. We label drugs that speed up the nervous system as **enhancers** or stimulants. Some excite or speed up our mental world, e.g., hallucinogens (acid). Others excite or speed up the physical part of the body as well as the mental part, e.g., amphetamines.

- **Drugs have a direct and an indirect effect on people:** The **direct** effect is when drugs are in the system and change the flow of electricity and nerve chemicals in the nerves and nerve ending. The **indirect** effect occurs when the drug leaves the body and the body reacts to its absence. This is the abstinence reaction discussed more in *Session 7.* Example: the direct effect of alcohol is sedation, sleepiness; the indirect or withdrawal effect is stimulation, agitation, insomnia, shakiness of the hands.

- **AOD tolerance causes physical and mental dependence:** Prolonged use of certain drugs leads to the need to use more and more of the drug to get the same reaction; or the same amount of drug will give less of an effect. Tolerance occurs because the brain cells that have receptors or transporters gradually become less responsive to the stimulation by an external drug, e.g., alcohol (Kosten, George, & Kleber, 2005). For example, where two drinks may initially have brought on a "buzz" or a feeling of relaxation, after using alcohol for several years, it may take four or five drinks to get the same "buzz" or to feel the same amount of relaxation. A daily quart of vodka may be required to get the same effect as once did a half pint. As much as a ten- to twenty-fold increase with some narcotics may be needed to maintain the desired effect. This is one basis of drug dependence (Portenoy, Payne & Passik, 2005; Repetto & Gold, 2005).

▶ Discuss the issues **About Alcohol.** Some topics will require more focus and attention. In addition to the information presented in *Chapter 4,* of the *Resource Guide,* the provider is referred to Ray, Ksir and Hart

(2006) and Nace (2005) for more detailed information around the drug alcohol.

- ◆ Take time to go over the meaning of BAC, its different level effects, and BAC *Tables 2* and *3* in the *Workbook.* Use *Figure 6* to show how the amount of alcohol affects certain parts of the brain.

- ◆ Metabolism of alcohol is an important topic, particularly when helping clients understand that the mind has no control over the breakdown of alcohol. Time is the key factor, as can be seen in the BAC *Tables 2* and *3*. We summarize additional information not given in the *Workbook.*

When the body breaks down alcohol, it goes through the following chain:

Alcohol → **acetaldehyde** → **acetic acid** → **water** + **CO2**
↓ ↓
hydrogen **hydrogen**

Hydrogen, which is given off when alcohol is broken down, becomes a source of energy for the liver. The liver uses hydrogen in lieu of using fat as its source of energy. This causes fatty tissue to build up in the liver and is one of the basis for liver disease, discussed in the *Workbook* on page 49. The breakdown of alcohol depends on gender and body fat. A person with a lot of body fat will break down alcohol at a slower rate. That person may actually end up with a higher BAC. As discussed in the *Workbook, Table 2* shows that if a heavier person drinks the same as a lighter person, the heavier person may have a lower BAC. But, the heavier person with more body fat may end up with a higher BAC level since body fat slows down the metabolism of alcohol. The person with high body fat may also have a greater risk of alcohol damaging or harming the body.

Because women have a higher percentage of body fat, they are at more risk in developing health problems from drinking. Body fat may be only one of the contributing factors to putting women at higher risk of health problems due to drinking. For example, when weight and body fat are controlled (that is, taking men and women with the same body fat and weight), women still have higher BAC for the same amount of alcohol over time. Thus, the difference between gender may be due to differences in hormones and levels of certain enzymes in the digestive tract. Women also metabolize alcohol slower and have higher levels of acetaldehyde than men.

❱ Present the health risk of alcohol use and loss of tolerance. Here is a summary of these effects.

- ◆ Alcohol can damage both the body and the brain. It can damage and destroy neurons in the *hippocampus and frontal cortex.* These areas of the brain are responsible for learning, memory and cognition.

- ◆ Alcohol can have serious health effects on the heart and cause liver disease and strokes. Alcohol affects men and women differently as discussed above.

❱ Many clients are concerned about the inheritability of alcoholism and drug dependence. There is a brief discussion of this in the *Workbook.* However, it is appropriate to give additional information and facilitate discussion in this area. The provider should review the material on biological perspectives in the *Resource Guide* (Wanberg & Milkman, 2008). Here are the most salient points regarding this area.

- ◆ There appears to be no specific genetic pathway or gene for alcohol abuse or dependence or the abuse of or dependence on other substances.

- ◆ There is a common genetic influence on the risk of developing alcoholism and substance abuse and clients are at higher risk for developing AOD abuse or dependence problems if biological family members, particularly parents, have AOD abuse and dependence.

- Research has shown (Blum et al., 1996; Gardner, 2005) that a high percent of persons with addictive problems have a reduction in the dopamine D2 receptors which activate the brain's pleasure centers. This deficiency can cause an individual's sense of well being to be replaced by feelings of anxiety, or a craving for the substance that can relieve anxiety. This depletion of the D2 receptors is related to the dopamine D2 receptor gene called the A1 allele. They found that a higher percent of persons with alcohol and cocaine addiction had this A1 allele variation.

- Research has also shown that enzyme differences play into decreased availability of dopamine in the reward circuits of the brain. Dopamine is produced from phenylalanine which is present in foods such as meat. Phenylalanine is converted into dopamine by a series of reactions, each of which requires a special enzyme. Deficiencies in any of these enzymes will decrease the production of dopamine. Since enzymes are proteins that are formed through genetic templates, another genetic factor in the development of alcoholism and other drug problems may be tied to variations in enzyme levels.

- Biogenetic factors work together with psychological, social and environmental factors to increase the risk of developing AOD abuse and dependence patterns and problems. Psychological and social risk factors are very potent in the development of AOD abuse problems.

▶ Present **What About Marijuana** and **Other Health Risks From Alcohol and Other Drugs.** There is overwhelming evidence that chronic marijuana usage has serious negative effects on memory, learning and cognition. There is some dispute regarding how long these effects last. However, with animal studies showing destruction of cells in the hippocampus, there can be little doubt that long-term marijuana smoking impacts the ability to remember and especially to learn new information. One of the most deleterious effects of marijuana smoking is permanent damage to the lungs including respiratory illness, obstructed breathing, lung cancer, frequent pneumonia, bronchitis and possible emphysema.

▶ Present **Drug Use Increases Risk of Criminal Conduct** and the relationship of drugs to CC.

▶ **Exercises:** *Worksheets 8* through *12* should be done in class and completed at the points noted in the *Workbook*. These worksheets help clients apply the material to their own drug use and criminal conduct. One approach is to have clients work in pairs when doing the worksheets. These exercises will show to what degree clients are willing to openly self-disclose. Give the more defensive clients special support. Remember, our approach is to use reflective or therapeutic confrontation in dealing with defensiveness.

▶ Clients update their *MSL,* particularly Skills 4 and 5, their *MAP* and continue working on their autobiography and use the *SSC Change Scale* to rate their understanding of how drugs have affected their lives.

SUMMARY OF KEY CONCEPTS

▶ Facts and knowledge about alcohol and other drugs.

▶ How drug use increases risk of criminal conduct.

SESSION CLOSURE AND GUIDELINES FOR THERAPEUTIC PROCESSING

Have clients discuss their drug use and abuse patterns and the impact of drugs on their lives. Have clients share their drug of choice. Present the question: Can they live life without using drugs?

RATIONALE AND OVERVIEW

New clients do not start *SSC* with this session since *Session 5* is its prerequisite. This session is based on the assumption that from 60 to 80 percent of persons in the judicial system have an established pattern of alcohol or other drug use that was an integral part of their legal problems. This session focuses on helping clients learn the different kinds of AOD use patterns and then to identify their own AOD use pattern or patterns.

Defensive clients initially will have a hard time with this task and may even resist the idea that they have a unique AOD use pattern, let alone see that this pattern may have been the basis of their criminal conduct. Such clients will score high on the self-report defensive scales.

Material for this session is based on some 40 years of research by Wanberg and associates on alcohol and other drug use patterns of individuals identified as having AOD use problems (Horn & Wanberg, 1969, 1973; Horn, Wanberg & Foster, 1990; Wanberg, 1992, 1997, 1998, 2004; Wanberg & Horn, 1970, 1983, 1987, 1991, 2008; Wanberg, Horn & Foster, 1977).

Once clients identify their own AOD use styles and patterns, they may see how those patterns are linked to their past criminal conduct. If this link is established, then the door is open to help the client make the necessary changes to prevent further CC.

SUMMARY OF CONTENT, PRESENTATION SEQUENCE AND GUIDELINES

This session presents three kinds of AOD use patterns:

▶ Quantity-Frequency-Prediction (QFP) pattern for both alcohol and other drugs;

▶ Social use (solo or gregarious or both) patterns; and

▶ Benefits derived from use.

Several exercises and worksheets in the *Workbook* help clients put a label on their unique use styles. Clients identify their Quantity, Frequency and Prediction (QFP) pattern for alcohol and for other drugs (checklists on pages 60 and 61). They look at whether they are a **social or solo user** (*Worksheets 13* and *14*, pages 65 and 66). Clients then measure themselves on a use benefits scale (*Worksheet 15*, page 67). *Profile 1* (page 67) provides a graphic representation of the client's patterns and styles of use.

A client might be described as a moderate, frequent, daily consistent drinker who drinks at bars with friends and to relax. Clients often resist doing these exercises. The purpose of this drinking style description is to give clients some idea of their risk for recidivism.

Worksheet 16 provides an estimate of how closely the clients' AOD use is related to their criminal conduct. A high score would indicate a close relationship and a higher risk for recidivism if clients do not change their AOD use patterns. The following is the presentation sequence for this session.

▶ Start with the *CB Map Exercise* and sharing the *TAP Charting*. Then have clients apply one of the thinking rules in *Session 3* to an event they experienced this past week. Go over session objectives.

- Discuss again: What is an alcohol or drug problem? Are the responses different now from what they were in *Session 5?*

- Have clients review *Worksheet 8,* page 58, about different drugs they have used.

- Facilitate group interaction around how clients see their different patterns of use: periodic, sustained, solo, gregarious, etc.

- Present the sections on **QFP, Social Patterns (Gregarious - Social Versus Solo) and Benefits of AOD Use.**

  - ◆ Have clients use these variables to describe their AOD use pattern.

  - ◆ **Exercise:** Complete *Worksheets 13, 14* and *15,* and *Profile 1* to help clients identify their AOD use patterns. Structure some discussion around their findings. Clients will need guidance in scoring these worksheets and plotting *Profile 1.* Explain the meaning of the percentile score. For example, a client with a 60th percentile score scores higher than 60 percent of a sample of persons with AOD problems.

- Present **Summary of Different Patterns of AOD Use.**

- Present **Alcohol Use and Criminal Conduct. Exercise:** Have clients look at the relationship between their AOD use and CC and complete *Worksheet 16,* which shows the extent to which these two areas are related. **Exercise:** Have clients identify the specific AOD use pattern that was part of their CC. Are they defensive about this? How serious did clients take this exercise? Was it accurately presented by clients?

- Present **Changing our AOD Use Patterns.** Work on helping clients see how their thought habits, attitudes and beliefs are part of and lead to their AOD use. **Exercise:** Complete *Worksheet 17,* how thoughts, attitudes and beliefs are part of AOD use.

- Have clients update their *MSL,* their *MAP* and continue working on their autobiography. Clients who have been in the program for more than a month (or for eight sessions) will have completed their initial *MAP.* They are asked to update or add to it.

- Clients who have been in the program from four to six weeks should be close to completing their autobiography.

- Have clients use the *SSC Change Scale* to rate their understanding of their own AOD use pattern.

SUMMARY OF KEY CONCEPTS

- Quantity-Frequency-Prediction pattern.

- Benefits pattern.

- AOD use profile.

- Changing thoughts that lead to specific AOD use patterns.

SESSION CLOSURE AND GUIDELINES FOR THERAPEUTIC PROCESSING

Have clients talk about how hard it will be for them to change their AOD use patterns. Discuss their commitment to living an AOD-free life. How do they see AOD use connected to their history of CC?

RATIONALE AND OVERVIEW

In *Chapter 5* of the *Resource Guide,* we presented a summary of discussions in the literature around the best terms that describe AOD use problem outcomes and that these outcomes can include negative consequences in the psychological, social, economic, legal and physical areas. We also noted that there are disagreements around whether addiction or dependence is the best term to use when referring to the psychophysical problems related to AOD use (Ling, Wesson & Smith, 2005).

The *American Society of Addiction Medicine* (ASAM, 2001) uses the term addiction to define a primary, chronic, neurobiological disease whose development is influenced by genetic, psychosocial and environmental factors and which is characterized by: impaired control over drug use; and/or compulsive use; and/or continued use despite harm; and/or craving. The *American Psychiatric Association* (2000) prefers the term dependence to indicate a variety of psychosocial and physical negative outcomes and symptoms.

We take the position that both addiction and dependence are appropriate terms to describe two impaired control cycles that are pathways to psychophysical problems related to AOD use. In this session, which is a prerequisite to *Session 8,* we describe these two problem outcome and addiction cycles: the *Mental-Behavior Impaired Control Cycle* (MB-ICC) and the *Mental-Physical Impaired Control Cycle* (MP-ICC). Most judicial clients will identify with some aspects of these cycles, and some will see themselves as closely fitting them. The two ICC models are also used in *Session 8* as a basis for defining different types of AOD problem outcomes. The main purpose of this session is to help clients see how their past AOD use fits the two impaired control cycles. Although the two addiction pathways are clearly described in the *Workbook,* we will review some of the key concepts of and provide literature support for these two models.

Mental-Behavioral Impaired Control Cycle (MB-ICC) Pathway

The MB-ICC provides an understanding of how thinking and behavior get reinforced around alcohol or other drug use. It is built on the concepts of cognitive-behavioral learning and change as illustrated in the *CB Map* and on the learning rules of how behaviors are strengthened and reinforced. These learning rules are important in understanding the MB-ICC model: if a behavior turns on a positive event, that behavior gets strengthened; if a behavior turns off a negative event, that behavior gets strengthened. *Figure 7,* page 69 of the *Workbook* provides a summary of these two rules. *Figure 8,* page 71 in the *Workbook* gives a full description of the MB-ICC.

There are a number of theories that have been used to explain the ICC model including Social Learning Theory (Bandura, 1969, 1977a; Abrams & Niaura, 1987; Collins, Blane & Leonard, 1999), Expectancy Theory (Collins, Blane & Leonard, 1999; Goldman, Brown & Christiansen, 1987; Goldman, Del Boca, & Darkes, 1999; Hull & Bond, 1986; Webb, Baer, Francis, & Caid, 1993), Opponent Process Theory (Shipley, 1987), Tension Reduction Theory (Cappell & Greeley, 1987), the Self-Awareness Model (Hull, 1987), and the Stress Reduction Dampening Theory (Sher, 1987). Expectancy and coping (stress and tension reduction) are the two key concepts of the ICC model. It can also be seen as an operant conditioning model.

Therapeutic gains can come from learning the MB-ICC model and understanding that specific expectations (thought structures) of short-term benefits (direct effects as described in the *Workbook, Table 1,* p. 46) are thought habits that need to be changed in order to break the cycle of dependency on drugs to get positive outcomes.

Mental-Physical Impaired Control Cycle (MP-ICC) Pathway

The MP-ICC model provides a psychophysical explanation of addiction or drug dependence and is based on physical and chemical changes in the nervous system. The identification and description of this pathway to addiction is based on the work of Stanley Gitlow (1966, 1970, 1982, 1988) and Stuart Gitlow (2001). It has been illustrated by Glenn and Hockman (1977), Glenn and Warner (1975), and Glenn, Warner, and Hockman (1977), has been further discussed by Peyser (1988) and Grilly (1989) and has been illustrated in detail by Wanberg (1990), Wanberg and Milkman (1998) and Wanberg, Milkman and Timken (2005). It has support in Fromme and D'Amico's descriptions of the neurobiological bases of the psychological effects of alcohol (1999), Kosten, George and Kleber's (2005) description of the neurobiology of substance dependence and in the chapter on *Substance Abuse and the Brain* in the *Resource Guide* (Wanberg & Milkman, 2008)

The material on the direct and indirect (withdrawal) effects of drugs presented in *Session 5* provides a basis for understanding the MP-ICC. The MP-ICC is described in the *Workbook* and is illustrated by *Figures 9* through *12,* pages 72 through 74. The following discussion provides some of the more technical nuances of this model.

The mental-physical pathway to addiction is based on the withdrawal effects of drugs and the neurochemical imbalances resulting from the use of drugs. These withdrawal effects and neurochemical imbalances are mitigated or relieved by the use of the substance causing withdrawal. This pathway to addiction can be explained, to some extent, by the theory of classical conditioning (see Collins, Blane & Leonard's discussion of classical conditioning and addiction, 1999). However, the essence of this theory of addiction is the imbalance of the neurochemical system resulting in a "rebound" from the use of a drug.

When a suppressor or sedative type drug such as alcohol begins to wear off, the system can experience a "rebound" or nerve-excitement effect (Fromme & D'Amico, 1999). This neurological stress or tension is explained by an increase of natural stimulant drugs in the system that get stored up and suppressed due to the effects of the sedative, e.g., alcohol. This is the withdrawal reaction from the use of a sedative drug.

This rebound effect is what Gitlow (1966, 1970, 1982, 1988) and Peyser (1988) call the asynchronous relationship between the short-term large-amplitude sedative effect of alcohol and its long-term agitating (withdrawal) effect. Every alcohol dose has to work against the "rebound" effect of the drug. This is similar to what Ray and Ksir (1996, 2002) describe as the continuation of the body's response to compensate for the sedation of the body resulting from using a sedative or suppressor (alcohol) drug.

One of the players involved in reinforcing alcohol use and the rebound of alcohol withdrawal appears to be the endogenous or internal opioids (endorphins) in the nervous system. Research supports the theory that alcohol use enhances or increases the presence of the natural, internal opioids in the system (Boehm, Valenzuela & Harris, 2005). The pleasure effects resulting from the increase of natural opioids during alcohol use may be an important component in alcohol reinforcement and dependence. The use of naltrexone, which blocks the action of natural opioid receptors, has been effective in reducing alcohol cravings. When alcohol leaves the system, there appears to be a decrease in the natural endogenous opioids (Boehm, Valenzuela, & Harris, 2005). Thus, the symptoms of withdrawal, e.g., agitation, irritability, anxiety, tremors, etc., may be due, in part, to the system withdrawing from the enhanced presence of the natural opioids as well as other neurochemical imbalances related to alcohol leaving the system (Chang & Kosten, 2005).

Acamprosate is another pharmaceutical used in the management of alcohol withdrawal or rebound. Acamprosate works by stimulating the production of the brain chemical GABA. GABA helps to reduce the rebound effects of irritability, agitation and dysphoria that often occurs in early recovery and are thought to be partially due to depletion of GABA (McGregor & Gallate, 2004; Boeijinga et al., 2004).

Kosten, George and Kleber (2005) use opioids to describe this phenomenon. One direct effect of opioids is to suppress the production of noradrenaline (NA), which stimulates wakefulness, breathing, alertness, etc. This suppression results in drowsiness, slowed respiration and other effects of opioid intoxication. When opioids are not present or after prolonged intoxication, they leave the body, and "...the neurons release excessive amounts of NA, triggering jitters, anxiety, muscle cramps, and diarrhea" (p. 9). This is the rebound or withdrawal effect of the drug.

The work of Fromme and D'Amico (1999) supports this theory. They contend that acute alcohol withdrawal from chronic alcohol intake is associated with increased norepinephrine (noradrenaline or NA) activity, which contributes to sympathetic arousal (i.e., increased blood pressure, heart rate) as well as the delirious features of withdrawal (i.e., hallucinations, delirium tremens). At the behavioral level, NA increases arousal and alertness. Whereas low doses of alcohol increases NA release, high doses of alcohol decrease NA release which, contributes to the sedative-hypnotic effect of alcohol.

Stanley Gitlow contends that the rebound or withdrawal effect may continue for several weeks or even months following a longer period of alcohol use. The stimulation and agitation effects become less intense and less noticeable. However, the very presence of this agitation creates an ongoing level of stress. When this low level of stress is added to normal daily tension, stressful events are more difficult to handle. This may be a factor that contributes to relapse. Thus, one may be more vulnerable to relapsing during the several weeks or months following quitting drinking.

A person who has developed a pattern of daily, steady drinking may need to use the drug every one or two hours during non-sleep periods in order to avoid the agitation of withdrawal and relieve the rebound effect. This describes the case of the "strung out" user. Thus, the rebound effect reduces the strength of each dose of alcohol. This process explains one reason why people become addicted to a drug.

For many people, this process is one explantion as to how they get into the addiction cycle or the impaired control cycle where the drug is needed to manage the withdrawal effects of the drug. Peyser (1988) calls this the "autonomous self-perpetuating" factor of addiction. The body demands more of the drug to maintain the body balance (homeostasis) - the very drug that set off the state of nervous system imbalance. It is related to what the drug does to the nerve chemistry at the nerve endings themselves.

A steady use of the drug may be for only the purpose of relieving the discomfort of the rebound or withdrawal phase of use. If the drug is discontinued after a period of use, minor symptoms such as inability to sleep, shakes or being irritable may occur within 24 hours. For the person who has been drinking sustained and heavy for several days to several weeks, more serious symptoms will begin to occur within 72 hours (Chang & Kosten, 2005; Ciraulo & Ciraulo, 1988; Hodding, Jann & Ackerman, 1980), e.g., convulsions, hallucinations.

Note: There are many mechanisms through which chronic or excessive alcohol abuse results in symptoms of withdrawal as well as short and long-term impairment of mental and physical functioning. One is the effect of alcohol on glutamate and GABA receptors as well as the rush associated with alcohol. When alcohol enters the brain, it attaches itself to glutamate receptors in many parts of the brain and distorts the structure of the receptor. Damage to glutamate receptors in the hippocampus can result in the impairment of memory.

The effects of the rebound or withdrawal from a drug are the opposite of the direct or intoxicating effects of the drug (Grilly, 1989, p. 94). Thus, this psychophysical model can be applied to other drugs such as stimulants. The direct effects of a stimulant (amphetamines, cocaine) would be physical and mental excitability, stimulation or agitation. When the blood level of the stimulant drug drops, the rebound or withdrawal process begins resulting in depression, tiredness, and a "crashing" effect. Some of these symptoms could also include a decrease in vital signs (blood pressure, heart rate). Again, the most effective short-term way to relieve or "cure" these reactions is to re-engage in the use of the drug.

Cocaine and Amphetamine Addiction and the Neurochemical Process

Because stimulants, particularly cocaine and methamphetamines, are drugs used by many judicial clients, *SSC* clients will benefit from an explanation of how MP-ICC can be used to explain addiction and dependence on these drugs.

Some of the direct effects of stimulant drugs are: increased system activity (increase in blood pressure, heart beat, diaphoreses); euphoria; pleasurable stimulation; loquacity; and hyperactive behavior. Individuals use stimulants to not only achieve these effects, but also to decrease or alleviate the opposite of these effects - depression, discouragement and hopelessness. Often, the direct effects of these drugs are negative stimulation such as agitation, irritability and anger. Taken in high amounts, the direct effects can produce dangerous levels of stimulation such as convulsions and cardiac arrhythmias (Acosta, Haller & Schnoll, 2005).

As the presence of cocaine or other stimulants in the system declines, an opposite effect of euphoria, pleasure and stimulation occurs - depression, neurological slowing, and loss of pleasure. This effect (both physically and psychologically) can be "treated" by using more of the stimulant. During this period, there can occur intense cravings for the drug.

There is extensive evidence in the literature on the relationship between cocaine and other stimulants and brain chemistry that explains both the direct and indirect effects of these drugs (Acosta et al., 2005; Blum et al., 1996; Gold & Jacobs, 2005; Milkman & Sunderwirth, 1987, 1998; Ray & Ksir, 1996, 2002; Repetto & Gold, 2005; Roehrich, Dackis & Gold, 1987; Volkow et al., 1993). The *Resource Guide* (Wanberg & Milkman, 2008) also provides a good summary of the direct and indirect effects of cocaine and other stimulants.

With respect to cocaine, the principal place where this drug takes effect is the dopamine D2 receptor. Neuronal excitement can induce the flow of dopamine, a neurotransmitter that activates the brain pleasure centers. Under normal conditions of dopamine flow, the excess is recycled into the dopamine-releasing nerve cells and deactivated. When cocaine is used, the excess dopamine is prevented from being recycled and excessive pleasure or euphoria results. More dopamine stimulates other neurons to produce still more dopamine, leading to increased euphoria or pleasure. In essence, cocaine prevents the dopamine-releasing neurons from performing the normal reuptake process. Although dopamine is the key player in cocaine reward, some studies suggest that "...discrete subpopulations of dopamine, serotonin, glutamate, and gama-aminobutric acid (GABA)-releasing neurons are responsible for cocaine reward" (Acosta et al., 2005, p. 189).

After prolonged use, cocaine leaves the system, there is a depletion of the D2 receptors, and an opposite effect of pleasure and euphoria is felt. Chronic administration of cocaine results in a decrease of D2 receptors, resulting in a craving for cocaine to achieve effects of pleasure and euphoria.

SESSION CONTENT AND PRESENTATION SEQUENCE AND GUIDELINES

Use psychoeducational and interactive-teaching format when presenting the two ICC models. The material in this session is rather extensive, and providers may want to use an additional session to cover the content and allow interaction and discussion around the content. An important component in presenting this session is to have clients identify and then share how and where they see themselves fitting in the two ICC cycles.

◗ Start with the *CB Map Exercise* and the *TAP Charting*. Present the session objectives.

◗ Present the **Mental-Behavioral Impaired Control Cycle, MB-ICC.** Start with reviewing the two ways that behaviors are reinforced, illustrated in *Figure 7*. Then go through the MB-ICC model, using *Figure 8*. Have a large chart on the wall illustrating *Figure 8* or a flip chart to go through each of the elements of *Figure 8*. Have clients identify how they fit the cycle. Most clients will have at least gone as far as block D of this cycle. Through group discussion, have clients identify how far they have gone in this cycle.

◗ Present the **Mental-Physical Impaired Control Cycle, MP-ICC.**

◆ Review the direct and indirect (withdrawal) effects of drugs, the basis of this model.

◆ Explain that the time frames in *Figures 10* through *13* are estimates and only illustrate the "rebound" effects. Illustrate how the MP-ICC model applies to stimulant drugs.

◆ Anecdotal material from Stanley Gitlow's research of monkeys in the 1970s can be used to illustrate the rebound phenomenon. He found that monkeys reached a seizure threshold much sooner when withdrawing from alcohol than when in an alcohol-free state. This supported his theory that when withdrawing from sedative-hypnotic drugs, i.e., alcohol, the body moves towards higher levels of stimulation, or, moves towards a seizure. A certain percent of persons who withdraw from an extended period of alcohol use do have seizures, unless the withdrawal or abstinence syndrome is treated. One relief for the withdrawal is to use more of the drug.

◗ Have clients update their *Master Skills List (MSL)*, and their *Master Assessment Plan (MAP)* and continue working on their autobiography.

◗ Some clients may have finished their autobiography. In these cases, the provider may want to review the client's autobiography in individual sessions.

SUMMARY OF KEY CONCEPTS

◗ Mental-Behavioral Impaired Control Cycle.

◗ Mental-Physical Impaired Control Cycle.

SESSION CLOSURE AND GUIDELINES FOR THERAPEUTIC PROCESSING

Have clients discuss how they fit the two impaired control cycles. Discuss whether their understanding of these cycles and how they fit them impacts on their thinking as to whether the relapse prevention goal of "zero-risk" or total abstinence is a good choice.

Note: The majority of judicial clients will have a distinct drug preference or drug of choice (Milkman & Frosch, 1974; Milkman & Sunderwirth, 1987, 1993, 1998). Treatment providers are encouraged to photocopy and make available relevant sections of the chapter, *Substance Abuse and the Brain*, in the *Resource Guide* (Wanberg & Milkman, 2008) for clients who have an inclination to delve deeper into the brain mechanisms, and mental and physical risk factors associated with the specific drugs or drug categories that have been salient in their personal impaired control cycles. That chapter provides in-depth information about alcohol, methamphetamine, cocaine, marijuana, opiates, Ecstasy, inhalants, hallucinogens, prescription drugs and tobacco.

RATIONALE AND OVERVIEW

Session 7 is a prerequisite to *Session 8*. **Thus, new clients do not enter at this session.** A basic assumption for this session is that all *SSC* clients will have a history of some problem outcomes from AOD use. The two ICC pathways to addiction models provide the basis for developing the four AOD outcome classifications. These four categories are:

▶ **Drinking-drug use problem;**

▶ **AOD problem user** without abuse or dependence;

▶ **The problem user with AOD abuse;** and

▶ **The AOD problem user with AOD dependence.**

The main purpose of this session is to help clients understand these four problem outcome patterns and have them classify their own problem outcomes with respect to the above four outcome categories.

Most if not every substance abusing judicial client can identify with some component of the AOD impaired control cycles presented in *Session 7*. Those cycles, and the outcome categories presented in this session, are based on social learning theory and cognitive-behavior approaches to self-control and change and a biosocial-psychological basis for addiction.

These cycles and categories provide clients with considerable flexibility in identifying their own problem outcome patterns and reduce defensiveness in looking at the reality of their drug use problems. The ICC models also provide a basis for presenting and describing AOD abuse and dependence a la the DSM-IV-TR (American Psychiatric Association, 2000).

However, many judicial clients will be defensive around seeing themselves as fitting any AOD problem outcome category, let alone the more traditional addiction or disease model. Defensive thinking and so-called "denial" are common responses of judicial clients when they are confronted with the realities of their own AOD abuse and criminal conduct history. Depending on the level of defensiveness of the provider's treatment group, it may be helpful to address and facilitate discussion around the area of defensiveness and so-called "denial."

SSC takes the position that we use the concept of denial in a positive light - that it represents a step towards change rather than a resistance to change. Defensiveness (denial) is a way of saying "I don't want to be that way." What we are being defensive about, or "denying," gives a clue of how we "don't want to be" and what we might need to change if we "don't want to be that way." When we "deny" we are setting up a **contrast in self-perceptions** as to how we see ourselves. "I do not have a drug use problem. I am not a criminal." This implies that the person also has the opposite perception of "having a drug use problem" or being a "criminal." The powerful need to defend the self results in, "But, I see myself the opposite way," or "opposite" from having a drug problem. "I don't have one." This sets the stage for change. The view of "not having a drug problem" is a perception that we want to actualize - for the client to not have a drug problem.

Thus, the client's "denial" is in the direction in which we want the client to move or what we want the client to be. That is, to not have a drug problem. In this sense, "denial" is the first step to change. The goal is to get the client to see the contrasting view of the self, or the view "**I do have** a drug problem," or what it means to have a drug problem. Once the client can "tolerate" that view, "maybe I do have a drug problem, and here are some reasons why," the defensiveness is lowered, and the client moves in the direction of changing thoughts and actions so as to be what he/she was initially defensive about - not having a drug problem or not being a criminal.

SSC sees the first step in resolving defensiveness or "denial" is giving clients information about AOD use and abuse patterns and problems. This sets up the second step of resolving defensiveness, to provide clients with the opportunity to see whether and how they might fit these patterns. This is achieved through self-disclosure and receiving feedback. This approach is effective in helping very defensive clients accept and gain insight into their AOD problems or criminal conduct.

Many clients are forthcoming with their view "I have a problem." They have worked through the defensiveness. The door is open to make the kind of changes to achieve, now in a realistic way, the initial defensive perception of the self that "I do not have a problem because I've done something about it."

Providers should review the sections in *Chapter 2, Therapeutic Relationship and Enhancing Client Motivation,* to cultivate a clear understanding of how their counseling skills may be honed to reduce client defensiveness around their AOD abuse patterns, with the likely result of improved treatment outcomes.

SESSION CONTENT, PRESENTATION SEQUENCE AND GUIDELINES

This session is very heavy in self-evaluation around substance use and abuse. The worksheets can be demanding, and providers will need to take time to walk clients through their completion. The provider may want to use two two-hour group sessions for this session.

The following presentation sequence is suggested.

▶ Present the objectives of the session.

▶ **Start with** the *CB Map Exercise.* Share the *TAP Charting* and then do some sharing around *Worksheet 18,* page 75, *The Thinking Report,* on an event that led to a desire to drink.

▶ Review the AOD use patterns in *Session 6* and the impaired control cycles presented in *Session 7.*

▶ Present **Problem Outcomes and Symptoms for Different Drugs. <u>Exercise:</u>** Have group members go to *Table 1*, page 46, and put a circle around the drugs they have used and check what direct and indirect symptoms they have experienced from the use of those drugs. This sets the stage for determining the category of AOD problem outcome they might fit.

▶ Present **Four Types or Classes of AOD Problem Outcomes.**

   ◆ *Worksheet 19* measures the degree of AOD use disruption and negative consequences. This is the DISRUPTION scale in the ASUS-R (Wanberg, 2004). Have clients put their raw score from *Worksheet 19* on the AOD PROBLEM row of *Profile 2* and then find their percentile score and explain that this shows how they rank in a large group of judicial clients.

   ◆ **Type 3** and **Type 4** problem outcomes are based on the criteria of Substance Abuse and Substance Dependence (American Psychiatric Association, 2000). *Worksheet 20* is based on the criteria for Substance Abuse and *Worksheet 21* is based on the criteria for Substance Dependence.

   ◆ **Several points around these worksheets should be clarified with clients. First,** *Worksheets 20 and 21* are based on the criteria for the disruptive outcome patterns of *Substance Abuse* and *Substance*

Dependence, and are not the exact criteria per se. **Second,** clients are not diagnosing themselves, but only getting an indication of how they might fit these two disruptive outcome patterns. **Third,** only a qualified professional can make a diagnosis of *Substance Abuse* or *Substance Dependence.*

▶ Present the section on **Putting It Together.**

   ◆ Have clients bring their scores from *Profile 1,* page 67, on the SOCIAL, SOLO, and BENEFITS scale and put their scores on *Profile 2,* page 80. This gives a more complete picture of their AOD use social style (gregarious or solo or both), their use benefits pattern and their AOD disruption or problem outcome pattern. Help clients find their percentile score and explain that this compares them with large group of judicial clients. Have them share if this is the way they see themselves.

   ◆ **Exercise:** *Worksheet 22* gives a summary of their AOD problem outcome classification. Discuss the results in group. Clients who check row 4 in *Worksheet 22* should also check rows 1 through 3. Again, clients are not diagnosing themselves, but only seeing how they fit these outcome patterns.

▶ What is most important about this session is for clients to have a clear understanding of the problem outcomes they have experienced around AOD use. The purpose of having them identify what problem outcome category they fit is to have them understand the degree of severity of these outcomes.

▶ Based on what clients learned in this session, have them update their *MSL* (particularly Skills 4 and 5), their *MAP* and continue working on their autobiography. Clients in the program for more than a month (or for eight sessions) will have completed their *MAP.* They are asked to update or add to it.

▶ Have clients use the *SSC Change Scales* to rate their understanding of the two ICCs, their own AOD use pattern in which problem outcome category they fit.

SUMMARY OF KEY CONCEPTS

▶ AOD use problem.

▶ Problem user.

▶ Problem user - Substance Abuse.

▶ Problem user - Substance Dependence.

SESSION CLOSURE AND GUIDELINES FOR THERAPEUTIC PROCESSING

Have clients share whether they have a different view of their AOD use and abuse patterns as a result of this session. Discuss how they now see their relapse prevention goal. Did any clients decided to adopt the goal of abstinence because of the self-assessment work done in this session?

If time permits, have clients share how the sessions in *Module 3* help improve their understanding of how AOD abuse and dependence problems develop. How does this improved understanding of specific patterns of abuse and cycles of impairment help develop strategies for relapse and recidivism prevention?

MODULE 4

Understanding and Changing Criminal Thinking and Behavior

In the *Preface* to this *Guide,* we discussed the necessity of including a sociocentric approach to the treatment of the judicial client. This focus of cognitive-behavioral treatment is on learning skills to enhance responsible attitudes and behaviors towards others and the community. This module is an introduction to this focus of criminal conduct (CC) treatment. *Module 10* in *Phase II* provides the in-depth component of this treatment focus.

This module provides the important elements of CC education and the basis for developing CC prevention goals and a recidivism prevention plan. Knowledge and understanding about criminal conduct, antisocial behavior, and prosocial and responsible living provide judicial clients with the basis for preventing recidivism. They can apply these understandings to their specific and unique criminal conduct history. Such application is made effective through **interactive self-assessment** approaches. This involves having clients measure and evaluate their own specific status in relationship to the knowledge base and then self-disclose and receive feedback around their findings. These understandings then build the foundation for developing and applying skills to change criminal thinking and conduct. Here are the provider goals of *Module 4.*

▶ Help clients understand prosocial, antisocial and criminal thinking and conduct.

▶ Have clients do a personal evaluation of their antisocial attitudes and behaviors.

▶ Help clients understand their risk of future CC involvement.

▶ Facilitate client understanding on how thinking errors can lead to CC recidivism.

▶ Help clients understand and apply to their unique situation the criminal thinking and conduct correction cycle.

▶ Help clients see the relationship between AOD abuse and CC.

▶ Help clients evaluate their prosocial strengths.

▶ Provide clients with an opportunity for **interactive self-disclosure** around their criminal conduct history.

▶ Provide the basis for skill acquisition and application to prevent recidivism.

Important note: This module encourages clients to increase their level of self-disclosure around criminal thoughts and actions. It should be stressed that the intent is to improve the capacity to think and act prosocially, and not to gather information that would incriminate them or further entrench them in the criminal justice system. Clients should be reminded that there is no need to reveal facts about specific crimes other than those that are on their legal and official record.

RATIONALE AND OVERVIEW

Andrews and Bonta (2003) see "criminal behavior as antisocial acts that place the actor at risk of becoming a focus of the attention of criminal and juvenile justice professionals" (p. 38). Based on this definition, an underlying assumption of *SSC* is that **criminal conduct represents a pattern of antisocial behavior.** The overall goal of this session is to help judicial clients understand the differences between antisocial and prosocial attitudes and behaviors. There is a strong emphasis on self-assessment in the area of antisocial attitudes and behaviors.

We often "walk softly" in being straightforward with judicial clients around our assessment of their psychological and behavioral problems. Just as we want our physicians who care for our physical health to be open and direct about our medical condition, we should expect that our clients also want to know what we assess as being "wrong with them" from a psychological and behavioral standpoint. Certainly, discretion is needed with respect to how we share our assessment of clients. We need to do so within a therapeutic and supportive framework. Yet, clients need to know what they need to change - from a correctional as well as a therapeutic perspective. We want judicial clients to clearly understand the nature and extent of their antisocial and criminal thinking and conduct.

Antisocial behavior and attitudes involve a pattern of disregarding and violating the rights of others, doing harm to others and going against the standards, morals, rules and laws of society. We are making the distinction between antisocial behaviors and attitudes and the antisocial personality disorder (APD) in the DSM- IV-TR (American Psychiatric Association, 2000), which is defined by a "pervasive pattern of disregard for and violation of the rights of others occurring since age 15 years." To fit the APD diagnosis, one has to meet three or more of the following criteria:

- failure to conform to social norms with respect to lawful behaviors by repeatedly performing acts that are grounds for arrest;

- repeated deceitfulness, lying, conning others for personal profit or gain;

- impulsivity or failure to plan ahead;

- irritability and aggressiveness, as indicated by repeated physical fights or assaults;

- reckless disregard for safety of self or others;

- consistent irresponsibility, as shown by repeated failure to sustain consistent work behavior or honor financial obligations;

- lack of remorse, indicated by being indifferent to or rationalizing having hurt, mistreated, or stolen from another.

One can engage in antisocial behavior and attitudes and not fit the APD as defined by these criteria. Yet, criminal conduct is antisocial. Most, if not all, judicial clients will fit one or more of the above DSM-IV-TR APD criteria.

Our intent in this session is to help clients look at their behaviors and attitudes that go against the norms, laws and expectations of society and that violate the rights of others **and** to see how these behaviors and attitudes play into their criminal conduct. This session also focuses on prosocial values - values that emphasize positive relationships with others, with our community and with society.

We also want *SSC* clients to understand what it means to be prosocial and morally responsible. Moral responsibility represents **a set of ethical and principled thoughts, attitudes and behaviors directed at respecting the rights of others, being accountable to laws and rules of our community and society, having positive regard for and caring about the welfare and safety of others, and contributing to the ongoing good of our community.** In essence, it means responding in a responsible way to others and to our community.

SUMMARY OF CONTENT, PRESENTATION SEQUENCE AND GUIDELINES

This session utilizes **interactive self-disclosure** and discussion around the key topics. Following are the guidelines and presentation sequence for this session, including resources for session content.

▶ Start the session with the *CB Map Exercise* and sharing the *TAP Charting*. Then have clients share their views on the meaning of crime and criminal behavior. Review the session objectives.

▶ The **Guidelines for Responsible Living** discuss what prosocial values and moral responsibility involve. Construct a wall chart to outline the elements of prosocial values and moral responsibility to the community.

▶ Present the meaning and definition of **Antisocial Attitudes and Behaviors**. Clients discuss their views of whether their criminal conduct is antisocial. Andrews and Bonta (2003) define criminal behavior as antisocial. **Exercise:** *Worksheet 23* is a self-report measurement of antisocial attitudes and behaviors. Clients share their scores and their rating with respect to whether they need to make changes so as to become more prosocial. The higher the score, the higher their risk of future involvement in antisocial behaviors unless they change their thinking and action patterns. Although *Worksheet 23* includes all of the elements of the DSM-IV-TR criteria for determining APD, specific APD criteria (described in *Chapter 6*) should be presented on a flip or wall chart. **Exercise:** Clients make a prosocial statement out of questions in *Worksheet 23*.

▶ Present **What Is Criminal Conduct?** This section is based on Andrews and Bonta's (2003, p. 38) four definitions of criminal behavior: legal, moral, social, and psychological. **Exercise:** Have clients check which definitions fit their past criminal conduct.

▶ Present **What Leads to Criminal Thinking and Conduct (CC)**. Discuss the past (static) and present (dynamic) risk factors. Most of the risk items in *Worksheet 24* represent the "Big Four" factors identified by Andrews and Bonta (2003): *antisocial attitudes, antisocial associates, a history of antisocial behavior, and antisocial personality pattern.* **Exercise:** Clients rate themselves on these risks using *Worksheet 24*.

♦ Help clients see that they cannot change the static or past risk factors and events (first part of *Worksheet 24*) but they can **reinterpret** these past events to get better emotional and action outcomes. They can understand how these events have influenced and changed their lives and work through the feelings resulting from these life situations. They can learn to accept them as realities and not try to justify them through irrational and distorted thinking.

♦ The present or dynamic risk factors (second part of *Worksheet 24*) are the best predictors of involvement in criminal conduct and are targets for change in treatment. Andrews and Bonta (2003) see these as criminogenic needs "that when changed, are associated with changes in the probability of recidivism" (p. 261). In essence, these are treatment needs that guide judicial clients in making cognitive and behavioral corrections. **Exercise:** Using *Worksheet 24,* have clients write down a thought or action that reduces each of the dynamic risk factors or criminogenic needs. *Table 1* below provides some examples of thinking and action changes for each of the dynamic or present risk factors (criminogenic needs) in *Worksheet 24*. Judicial clients often find it hard to write a thought or action that reduces the risks in *Worksheet 24* or meets the criminogenic treatment need.

◗ Based on what clients learn in this session, have them update their *MSL* (particularly *Skills 25, 26* and *27*), their *MAP* and continue working on their autobiography. Clients who have been in the program for more than a month (or for eight sessions) will have completed their *MAP*. They are asked to update it.

SUMMARY OF KEY CONCEPTS

◗ Prosocial values and moral responsibility.

◗ Antisocial attitudes and actions.

◗ Definitions of criminal conduct.

◗ Past risk factors.

◗ Present or dynamic risk factors.

◗ Criminogenic needs and targets for change.

SESSION CLOSURE AND GUIDELINES FOR THERAPEUTIC PROCESSING

Judicial clients often resist the idea that their actions have been antisocial, let alone having a history of criminal conduct. Help clients define their own antisocial thoughts, attitudes and behaviors. Facilitate candid sharing around past and dynamic risk factors. Do structured sharing around criminogenic needs.

TABLE 1	Examples of Cognitive-Behavioral Responses that Reduce Risk Factors and Criminogenic Needs
RISK FACTOR/CRIMINOGENIC NEED:TARGETS FOR CHANGE	**COGNITIVE-BEHAVIORAL SELF-CORRECTION RESPONSES/CRIMINOGENIC TREATMENT NEED**
1. Antisocial/criminal peers	Develop associations with prosocial peers
2. Have criminal role models	Develop relationships with prosocial role models
3. Criminal thinking/attitudes	Develop anticriminal thoughts
4. Time with criminal peers	Join a group that helps people
5. Lack family closeness	Develop positive ties or family-like relationships
6. Get rewards through crime	Get rewards living a prosocial, crime-free life
7. Spend time in high-crime neighborhoods/communities	Move to lower-risk neighborhood or community
8. Poor relationship skills	Develop interpersonal skills through social skills training
9. Lack emotional support	Become emotionally available to people close to you
10. Rebel against authority	Understand what it means to be in an authority role
11. Poor problem-solving skills	Learn and apply the steps and skills of problem solving
12. Need to manipulate others	Experience the relief of letting go and not controlling others
13. Lack moral reasoning	Develop prosocial and other-reflective moral codes
14. Angry and hostile attitude	Learn self-regulation of angry and hostile feelings
15. Act on spur of the moment	Learn to think before acting
16. Impaired AOD use	Choose an AOD-free lifestyle

RATIONALE AND OVERVIEW

New clients do not enter *SSC* **at this session.** An assumption of *SSC* is that criminal thinking and conduct are learned. These behaviors are responses to the individual's internal and external world. Criminal conduct (CC) is used to turn on positive events and to cope with life problems and situations and the stress resulting from these problems and situations. CC is reinforced when it becomes an effective tool in dealing with the problems and stresses of living. The *Criminal Thinking and Conduct (CTC)* cycle begins when an individual engages in CC to cope with the problems that come from CC.

An important dynamic in the perpetuation of the *CTC* cycle is cognitive distortion or thinking errors. Some work on thinking errors was done in *Session 3*. The current session makes a more specific connection between these errors and criminal conduct. Another dynamic in the perpetuation and strengthening of the *CTC* is substance use and abuse. This session helps the client increase understanding of how CC and AOD abuse are related. Although, an assumption of *SSC* is that judicial clients have core antisocial attitudes and beliefs that lead to criminal conduct, most judicial clients also have prosocial values, attitudes and strengths that can be capitalized on in treatment. In this session clients evaluate their prosocial values and strengths and see how these strengths can control and override their antisocial attitudes and values.

SUMMARY OF CONTENT, PRESENTATION SEQUENCE AND GUIDELINES

▶ Start this session with the *CB Map Exercise*, sharing the weekly *TAP Charting* and session objectives. Then inform the group that work done in previous sessions will be reviewed and integrated with the current session.

▶ Present **Thinking Errors That Can Lead to Criminal Conduct.** Have clients review *Worksheet 5*, page 35. Clients who have not had *Session 3* can complete *Worksheet 5*. **Exercise:** Have clients do *Worksheet 25*, page 92. Spend time practicing replacing these errors with prosocial thoughts and beliefs. In *Session 3*, clients evaluate their thinking errors and assess how these errors are part of their CC and AOD use. Thinking errors are cognitive distortions that are often automatic to the point that we continue to engage in the errors of thinking even though our experiences and the facts do not support the thinking error. Yochelson and Samenow (1976, 1977) see thinking errors as the mental process required by the offender to live his/her lifestyle; and that they are habitual and obvious in day-to-day transactions of the offender. Correcting or eliminating criminal thinking errors is an essential part of the treatment of the judicial client. Whereas *Worksheet 5*, page 35, introduces clients to thinking errors in general, *Worksheet 25* identifies the thinking errors and social relationships that have potential to lead to CC and antisocial behaviors. These were compiled from a variety of sources (Beck, 1976; Burns, 1980, 1989, 1999; Leahy, 2003; Marlatt, 1985c; Yochelson & Samenow, 1976, 1977; Wanberg & Milkman, 1998; Wanberg, Milkman & Timken, 2005).

▶ Present the **Criminal Conduct and Thinking (CTC)** cycle, *Figure 14*, page 90. Have clients see the similarity between the *CTC* and the MB-ICC (page 71 in the *Workbook*). Help clients see how the negative results from CC (punishment) can contribute to the weakening of this cycle; but they can also strengthen *CTC* because they reinforce the automatic thoughts, attitudes and beliefs of the individual. Just as with AOD use and abuse, CC occurs in a cyclical manner and the cycle gets reinforced. *Figure 14* provides a description of this cycle. Criminal justice clients will differ as to the precipitating events and the unique cognitive responses (different thoughts, attitudes and beliefs) to these events. As well, criminal justice clients differ as to the kind of criminal conduct they choose to engage in and the kind of victim targeted. Even though individuals will differ as to particular thinking and behavioral responses, this cycle applies to most individuals who engage in criminal conduct. The following are the important parts of this cycle.

- ◆ **External and internal events** that trigger criminal thinking and conduct.

- ◆ CC involves conscious **mental choices** as to the type of criminal conduct the offender chooses to engage in and the victims that are the target of this conduct.

- ◆ A pattern of **criminal thinking** involving errors in thinking and thinking about criminal conduct which are supported by core criminal beliefs.

- ◆ Powerful **emotional outcomes** and sentiments resulting from criminal thinking.

- ◆ **Criminal behavior and actions** resulting from criminal thinking and emotions.

- ◆ **Criminal outcomes and consequences** resulting from criminal actions. These outcomes cycle back to strengthen criminal thinking and reinforce the *CTC*.

Correction and change can occur at any point in this cycle.

- ◆ **Change external and internal events,** which may involve changing living environments.

- ◆ **Change criminal thinking choices to prosocial thinking and choices.**

- ◆ **Enhance positive emotions that lead to prosocial outcomes.**

- ◆ **Change specific criminal actions to prosocial behaviors.**

Exercise: Clients complete *Worksheet 26* to show their own *CTC* and how to correct the cycle.

▶ Present **Relationship Between AOD Use and Criminal Conduct** and show how the two interact, feed into and reinforce each other.

▶ Present **Evaluating Prosocial Values and Strengths. Exercise:** *Worksheet 27* provides clients an opportunity to identify prosocial values and strengths. Judicial clients are often surprised at the degree to which they do have these strengths. **Adjunct Exercise:** Clients practice cognitive change skills that allow prosocial thinking to override and rule out antisocial and criminal thinking.

▶ Have clients update their *MSL* (with particular attention given to *Skills 25, 26* and *27*), their *MAP* and continue working on their autobiography.

▶ Have clients use the *SSC Change Scales* on page 91 to rate their understanding and skills learned in this session.

SUMMARY OF KEY CONCEPTS

▶ Thinking errors and how these are related to CC.

▶ The criminal thinking and conduct cycle.

▶ CC and AOD abuse are interactive and reinforce each other.

SESSION CLOSURE AND GUIDELINES FOR THERAPEUTIC PROCESSING

Focus question: How do each of the participants see AOD use leading to their criminal conduct? How do participants see how their CC leads to AOD use?

MODULE 5

Sharing and Listening: Communication Pathways to Self-Awareness and Other-Awareness

OVERVIEW OF MODULE 5

A mantra of *SSC* is that self-disclosure leads to self-awareness and self-awareness leads to change. The pathway to self-awareness is active sharing or **self-oriented communication.** The communication skills required for active sharing are: self-disclosure and receiving feedback. The pathway to other-awareness is active listening or **other-oriented communication.** The active listening skills are: inviting others to share; and giving feedback. Active listening increases our understanding of others and self.

An important task of this module is for clients to learn and practice these two skills. They represent the foundation of engaging in meaningful, positive, effective and responsible social and interpersonal relationships. They are pathways to effective communication **and** to effective involvement in treatment. These skills are the focus of *Sessions 11* and *12* and the basis of much of the work that is done in *SSC.*

Another focus of this module is to give clients an opportunity to more deeply explore their personal-emotional experiences, particularly as these are related to their history of substance use problems and criminal conduct. The challenge for clients in this module is engaging in honest and open sharing and taking the risk of receiving feedback as to how others see them.

GOALS OF THIS MODULE

▶ Learn and practice the skills of active sharing and active listening.

▶ Encourage clients to take a deeper look at their personal-emotional experiences as these are related to substance abuse and criminal conduct.

Important note: This module facilitates an open and honest look at thoughts and emotions related to the client's history of substance abuse and criminal conduct. Stress that the intent of this self-disclosure is to increase self-awareness and to help clients to better understand their thoughts and emotions so as to make changes in their lives. Encourage clients to share their deeper thoughts and emotions about their substance abuse and criminal conduct within the boundaries of their own comfort zone and at their own pace. Clients need to feel supported and affirmed by the group and the provider in this process. It is helpful to focus on thoughts and emotions related to life experiences rather than the details of these specific experiences. Some clients may open up areas that they have not explored or talked about. Efforts should be made to help clients resolve cognitive and emotional issues that arise in group. However, some clients may need individual sessions to work through the therapeutic material that arises in group.

RATIONALE AND OVERVIEW

Because *Sessions 11* and *12* provide a basis for many *SSC* sessions, a more extensive overview of and rationale for their content and concepts will be presented. This session is a prerequisite to *Session 12*.

Interpersonal cognition is an area of investigation that provides important understandings of how individuals form and sustain relationships and become a part of interpersonal interaction. Interpersonal cognition is about what people think about their relationships, their mental representation of others, what they think others think about them, their thoughts about acceptance and rejection, and the mental schemas they use to understand and form relationships (Baldwin, 2005). The work in this area has provided "models of the mechanisms whereby people think about their interpersonal experiences and the effects of this thinking on their subsequent interactions and sense of self" (p. xi).

Interpersonal communication is a manifestation of interpersonal cognition. It forms the basis of a positive and prosocial relationship with the community. Interpersonal communication has been identified as having three functions (Dance, 1982; Littlejohn, 1999):

▶ **The linking function:** it provides a link between the person and others, including the community.

▶ **The mentation function:** We think, therefore we communicate (Dance & Larson, 1976). We can reflect on the past and the future. This function allows us to imagine locations and activities other than the present (Littlejohn, 1999). We do not have to be tied to ourselves. This is the process of **decentering**. It formulates the basis of empathy (Littlejohn, 1999), an essential cognition for prosocial attitudes and actions.

▶ **The regulatory function:** Through interpersonal communication, one's behavior is regulated by others, one regulates one's own behavior, and one regulates the behavior of others (Littlejohn, 1999). Thus, interpersonal communication provides the structure for self-regulation. It directs us in doing what is proper, listening to others, fulfilling a role that is consistent with what is expected of us, in lieu of what our own impulses and desires say. It is an important component in determining prosocial attitudes and behavior.

Effective and healthy communication skills, then, link us with others in a prosocial way, allow us to step outside of ourselves in order for us to understand and have empathy for others, and provide a basis for self-regulation.

Communication skills training is a key component of the interpersonal restructuring focus of cognitive-behavior treatment (Wanberg & Milkman, 1998). It is widely used in CB treatment and treatment manuals (Oliver & Margolin, 2003).

Most interpersonal communication theories describe people as engaging in two kinds of interactions (Littlejohn, 1999):

▶ a presentation of themselves to others; and

▶ an attempt to understand others.

We have defined these as the communication pathways of active sharing and active listening (Wanberg & Milkman, 1998). *Sessions 11* and *12* provide a basic understanding and practice of the skills needed to engage in active sharing and active listening. These have been referred to as speaker and listener skills (Oliver & Margolin, 2003). Thus, we see these as more than just skills. They are roles that people assume. The goal of these two sessions is to help clients learn the skills of active sharing and active listening, **and** to inculcate the role of being an active sharer and an active listener.

These two sessions also focus on nonverbal communication since it is an important part of interpersonal communication. There is a large corpus of literature pointing out the importance of nonverbal cues and signals in interpersonal communication (e.g., Burgoon, 1985; Ekman, 1973; Ekman & Friesen, 1969, 1975; Knapp, 1978; Knapp & Daly, 2002; Knapp & Hall, 1997; Littlejohn, 1999).

Developing Communication Skills

Many substance abusing judicial clients have never developed effective communication skills. Because of this, they are often unable to communicate their positive or negative thoughts and emotions and to have a positive connection with others. This inability increases the probability of acting out negative (e.g., anger, resentment) thoughts and feelings resulting in criminal conduct.

Many clients share feelings and thoughts only when AOD-intoxicated. This helps overcome the fear or anxiety they experience when relating to others. Thus, talking about the self and sharing feelings and thoughts will have to be learned under a new condition - that of being free of alcohol and other drugs. As well, many judicial clients are unable to **allow others** to openly and effectively express their thoughts and feelings. They lack the communication skills to step outside of themselves and put themselves in the place of others, which makes it difficult for them to have empathy towards others. This is part of the focus of *Session 12,* and of *Session 37* in *Phase II.*

Sharing thoughts and feelings and listening to feedback are learned skills and their benefits are considerable. These skills increase reciprocal understanding, overcome barriers to communication, and strengthen relationships. Self-disclosure is a way to build trust, to let others know they are not alone in their thoughts and emotions. Listening lets the other person know we are interested and helps us learn about others, the world, and about ourselves (Wanberg & Milkman, 1998).

Emotions and Self-Disclosure

One of the most important parts of self-disclosure is sharing feelings and emotions. *Chapter 4* discusses the importance of managing emotions in cognitive-behavioral change. *Module 8* deals specifically with using cognitive skills to manage emotions. The goal of self-control is to let our thoughts be in control of our emotions. We control our emotions when we are able to identify the thoughts that lead to those emotions. Yet, it is important that we share our emotions and feelings. "If I am to tell you who I am, I must tell you how I feel." This session is about learning the skills to share our thoughts **and** our emotions.

Barriers to Self-Disclosure

Self-disclosure is difficult for most people, let alone judicial clients. Much of their lives they were told to not express their feelings, to not talk about themselves, or if they did express their feelings and thoughts, they often experienced disapproval and even punishment. They were often told: not to get angry; to be happy when they were sad; to not be too happy or something bad will happen; or that showing affection and positive feelings was a sign of weakness.

For many clients, this led to a holding-in and storing-up process. Thus, when they did show negative feelings, they came out by "blowing up" or throwing a tantrum or pouting. Or, if there was not the open permission to feel good and express positive emotions, these would be stored and then released in a more intense and inappropriate manner, such as through getting drunk or high, committing a crime for excitement, or sexual acting out.

Thus, many judicial clients had no real outlet, with parents or other adults, to talk about and express negative or positive thoughts and feelings; or when they were expressed, they were often not received and accepted by parents and adults. As well, few judicial clients had role models for showing both positive and negative emotions.

Judicial clients often engaged in faulty or distorted automatic thinking that make it difficult for them to see clearly, let alone share, their own problem cognitions and behaviors. This also caused them to feel misunderstood. Errors in thinking are barriers to sharing thoughts, emotions, and experiences with others.

Not only did many judicial clients lack opportunity to express their feelings and thoughts during their developing years, they most likely did not learn or were not taught the important skills and tools to express themselves in healthy ways. They were often taught to blame others, since that is the way most adults solve their frustrations and problems. Or, they learned that you solved problems between people by someone being right and someone being wrong. As most adults mature, they try to move away from the "child" ways of expressing thoughts and feelings. Yet they tend to hold on to unhealthy ways of showing thoughts and emotions.

Another barrier to self-disclosure is that, even though clients learn and are able to effectively use the skills of self-disclosure, persons to whom they might self-disclose may not be skilled in active listening. Such persons may be unable to deal with personal sharing and not have the reflective listening skills to allow clients to think and feel that they are being heard. Their self-disclosure may fall on "deaf ears," or is a threat to other persons, and may not be received in an open and accepting manner. This is a risk that occurs with all persons who enter self-improvement and change programs - that they are often "way ahead" of others around them in terms of using good communication skills.

Receiving feedback from others is also difficult for the judicial client. For one reason, much of the feedback they have received in the past was a **reaction** to rather than an **interacting** with their disclosure. Feedback often came in a blaming manner, and not in a way that other persons communicated that this was their view or perception. Feedback is given as if "this is the way you are." When people tell us that this is their opinion of us, but that they may be wrong, it is much easier to accept that feedback.

Preparing the Judicial Client for Self-Disclosure in Treatment

The above discussion would suggest that when judicial clients enter treatment, they have a long history of guarding against sharing and listening to what other people have to say about them. They have been through an adversarial system that has judged them as breaking the law and as being wrong. Treatment expects just the opposite - to be open and share. Many are not prepared for this. When we encourage judicial clients to self-disclose, to talk about themselves, to be open for nonjudgmental feedback and to explore their past and present feelings, thoughts and actions, we need to be prepared for initial guarded and distrustful responses.

It is helpful to inform clients that when they agree to enter a treatment program, they essentially agree to self-disclose and receive feedback. This is an unwritten though stated contract. But they also need to know that, although the feedback will be given in a non-blaming manner, it will be around their substance use problems and their criminal conduct. Thus, they may initially see the feedback as being judgmental. Hopefully, over time, they will see that the feedback is designed to help them increase self-awareness and lead to change. Even then, judicial clients are prone to be defensive around receiving feedback.

SUMMARY OF CONTENT, PRESENTATION SEQUENCE AND GUIDELINES

Remind clients that the skills in *Sessions 11* and *12* are among the most important to be learned in *SSC*. Following is the recommended presentation sequence and guidelines for this session.

▶ Start with the *CB Map Exercise* and sharing the *TAP Charting.* Summarize objectives and key concepts.

▶ Present **What Keeps Us From Self-Disclosure?** The *Workbook* provides a summary of the barriers to self-disclosure described in more detail in the Rationale section above.

▶ Present the **Two Kinds of Communication: Nonverbal and Verbal** and do the two exercises in this section.

◆ When presenting **Nonverbal Communication**, discuss the problem of not saying the same thing with words that we say without words. To "read" nonverbal cues and signals, we must observe carefully and not jump to conclusions. We often misinterpret the nonverbal signals of others when they do not accurately communicate their thoughts and feelings. Sometimes people say one thing and mean another. A person may get red-faced and furious yet insists he is not angry. Ask the group for examples of people saying one thing, but their body language indicating something else. By being more observant and careful when watching and communicating with others, we can improve our ability to communicate accurately and to solve problems with other people.

Research in nonverbal communication has shown that there are core or universal emotions that are expressed across cultures. These studies initially came out of the work of Ekman and associates (Ekman & Friesen, 1969, 1975) but are supported by other studies (Knapp, 1978; Knapp & Hall, 1997; Knapp & Daley, 2002). These studies support the notion that there are universal associations between specific facial muscular patterns and discrete emotions (Knapp, 1978; Knapp & Hall, 1997). These emotions are: happiness, fear, sadness, surprise, anger, and disgust or contempt (Ekman, 1973). What is important for clients to understand is that these emotions are communicated through both verbal and nonverbal channels and that good communication occurs when there is a congruency between the verbal and nonverbal expression of these emotions.

Exercise: Clients practice showing the emotions of anger, fear, shame, joy, love, surprise and sadness through nonverbal channels. It is helpful in this exercise to have clients express these emotions, and then identify the thoughts they had when showing these emotions.

Adjunct Exercise: After presenting each of the following situations, have group members vote their opinion. Then go back and briefly discuss each situation. After the discussion, give the information following the three scenes below (exercise adapted from Ross, Fabiano & Ross, 1986):

1) When a judge asked a young man whether he stole the money, the man holds his head down and claims to be innocent. In your opinion, is he innocent or guilty?

2) After a funeral, you see a woman dressed in black speaking quietly and seriously to another woman. Is she expressing her sorrow or discussing business?

3) You are interviewed for a job. The human resource director did not smile throughout the interview. When he finishes, he smiles briefly. Does the smile mean you can do the job, or he is being polite?

Additional information about the three scenes:

1) The man is from a country in which it is considered rude to look a judge in the eye.

2) The woman in black is holding a calculator.

3) You learned that the human resources director did not show any feelings at all when he interviewed some of your friends. You are the only one he has smiled at.

These examples illustrate how we tend to interpret what is going on around us even if we can't hear what people are saying. No matter how we try, we cannot NOT communicate.

Adjunct Exercise: If time permits, break group into dyads and have one person share something emotional that happened to him or her in the recent past. Have the listener look for the nonverbal expressions and body language that also help tell that story, e.g., voice tone, body posture, and eye expressions, and then give feedback on the nonverbal expressions.

Adjunct Exercise: If time permits, show a brief video without the audio in which individuals are expressing emotions. Show only one or two scenes at a time. Then, have clients try to identify the emotions being expressed. This exercise also helps clients learn empathy skills.

- ◆ Present **Verbal Communication** - "talking with words." Verbal communication is not as natural of a skill as most believe. One problem in verbal communication is that we are inclined to believe that our way of thinking or viewing the world is the "only way" and "the right way." This thinking error sets us in conflict and invites problems and hassles with those around us. It is common for judicial clients to engage in this thinking error.

  Judicial clients resolve this problem by thinking and believing that it is good to have different opinions and different likes and dislikes. Help them see that almost everyone is different from us and has different opinions and that's OK! This thinking is an important part of learning the skill of empathy, which we focus on in *Session 37, Module 10,* of learning to understand and take the other person's point of view. Thinking, "wouldn't it be boring if each of us thought the same way, dressed the same way, liked the same things and never had a different opinion?" helps us to accept that others are different.

  Another problem in verbal communication is that we are inclined to believe that everyone else is thinking what we are thinking, therefore, there is no need to check that we are being understood.

  Failure to distinguish the difference between opinion and fact also creates problems in verbal communication. We may not agree on our opinions, but there is common ground in understanding the facts - what is camera-checkable. It is difficult to solve problems if we don't stick to the facts, or if we believe our opinion is "fact." **Adjunct Exercise:** Give the group a statement and have them decided if it is a statement of fact or an opinion. Example: Fact - the sun set at 5:00 p.m. Opinion: It was a beautiful sunset. Then have each member give a statement of opinion and a statement of fact.

  Our language often makes verbal communication difficult. For example, one word can have different meanings. The meaning of different words is shaped by our experiences. Do the exercise: where the group shares the meaning of a word that can have different meanings.

▶ Present the **Two Pathways to Communication:** self-oriented (active sharing) and other-oriented (active listening) communication. Explain that active listening is the topic for *Session 12.*

▶ Present the **Active Sharing or Self-Oriented Communication** pathway and the two active sharing skills: **self-disclosure** and **receiving feedback.** Help clients see that this is more than learning skills. The goal is to learn the role of being an active sharer.

- ◆ Present **First Active Sharing Skill: Self-Disclosure.** There is overwhelming evidence of the efficacy of self-disclosure in producing reciprocity in communication. Based on the classic work of Jourard (Jourard, 1959; Jourard & Friedman, 1970; Jourard & Resnick, 1970) and many others (e.g., Cappella,

1985; Knapp & Miller, 1985; Knapp & Daly, 2002) self-disclosure not only facilitates self-disclosure in the others, but partners tend to match the level of self-disclosure.

Discuss the important concept that our communication is improved when we talk about ourselves in relation to the other person and not talk about the other person. This involves using "I" messages and avoiding "you" messages. Go over the "tips" on how to make active sharing have positive outcomes. Discuss the difficulty of being open to feedback and how being defensive can stop that feedback.

◆ Present **Second Active Sharing Skill: Receiving Feedback.** Help clients see how defensiveness blocks receiving feedback. Go over *Figure 15* in the *Workbook* which is a picture of active sharing or self-oriented communication.

▶ Present and discuss the **Active Sharing Window.** The Johari window (Luft, 1969) provides a descriptive understanding of the two communication pathways and illustrates what happens in treatment.

▶ Do the **Exercises** in the section on **Practicing Active Sharing.** They can be done in the total group rather than breaking into groups of three if time is short. This is often a more efficient and time-saving approach. It takes time to divide the group and then reassemble. Structure the time carefully and stick to a good timetable when doing exercises.

▶ Have clients update their *MSL* with particular focus on *Skills 12* and *13.* Clients also update their *MAP.* Remind them to do their *TAP Charting* and continue working on their autobiography. Go over the "I" message homework.

▶ Have clients complete the *SSC Change Scales* on their knowledge of and skills in using active sharing.

SUMMARY OF KEY CONCEPTS

▶ Nonverbal and verbal communication.

▶ Active sharing or self-oriented communication.

▶ Active listening or other-oriented communication.

SESSION CLOSURE AND GUIDELINES FOR THERAPEUTIC PROCESSING

If time permits, for a closing **exercise,** focus on the "Hidden Area" part of the Johari window, and have each individual share something about themselves that they think others don't know. Have clients share only what they feel comfortable sharing. Then, have those in the group raise their hands if they did know this about the other person. This same exercise can be done with the "Blind Area" of the window. Make this exercise crisp and move fast.

Have group members communicate a perception they have of another group member. After group members receive the communication, have them state whether this was a new awareness or something they already knew about themselves.

RATIONALE AND OVERVIEW

The rationale and overview section of *Session 11* provides a good foundation for why we have clients learn and practice the skills of active listening and active sharing. **New clients do not enter *SSC* at this session.**

One of the characteristics of being human is the capacity to understand others. This involves putting ourselves in the place of others. This is the basis of empathy and the foundation of prosocial attitudes and actions. The skills of active listening help us actualize this human capacity to understand others. **Active sharing** through the skills of self-disclosure and receiving feedback **increases self-awareness. Active listening increases our awareness and understanding of others.** It is other-oriented communication.

There are two broad skills that make active listening possible: invitation to share; and giving feedback or reflective responding. These are basic skills that we use with clients in counseling and therapy. Thus, we are asking clients to learn the skills that we use in everyday clinical work.

It has been the experience of the authors that counselors in training have a difficult time learning basic counseling skills. As well, we often have observed that many clients who have been in therapy for several years and exposed to these skills through interaction with their therapist still have difficulty putting into practice these skills in everyday living. Thus, the skills of active listening and the role of being an active listener will take time for clients to learn. This session introduces clients to this communication pathway which enhances awareness of others. Throughout *SSC,* providers are encouraged to continually have clients practice and apply these skills in group and in their daily lives.

SUMMARY OF CONTENT, PRESENTATION SEQUENCE AND GUIDELINES

Introduce the session by again reminding clients that the skills learned in *Sessions 11* and *12* are among the most important to be learned in *SSC.* Explain that these are foundational skills to be used by clients in their interactions with providers and group members throughout their involvement in *SSC.* Following is the recommended presentation sequence and guidelines for this session.

▶ Start out with the *CB Map Exercise* and sharing the *TAP Charting.* Summarize the key concepts in the session and session objectives.

▶ **Have clients share** the *Session 11* homework on active sharing, *Worksheet 29.*

▶ Present **Reviewing Your Work on Active Sharing.** Review the concepts and ideas of nonverbal and verbal communication and active sharing. **Adjunct Exercise:** Practice self-disclosure by having clients share a humorous or funny experience they had over the past week. After each client shares, have a client across the circle reflect back what the client shared. **Make this exercise brief.** This prepares clients for learning the skill of reflective feedback. **Exercise:** Do *Worksheet 30* and have a few members share their work.

▶ Present **What Is Active Listening or Other-Oriented Communication?** Role model both the invitation and reflective feedback skills. Demonstrate the difference between closed and open questions and statements. Give clients some basic introduction statements to reflective listening, e.g., "I hear you...," "I see you...," etc. Since this is an introduction to these skills, we want to keep the concepts and presentation as simple as possible. Start with the most basic skills.

- ◆ **Invitational skills:** "How are you...?" "Tell me...," "Give me your thoughts...," etc.

- ◆ **Feedback skills:** Start with the most simple skill of parroting - repeating back verbatim what the other person said. Then, raise the bar some by having clients reflect back, in their own words, what the other person is saying. As the group catches on, raise the bar even more and have clients reflect the other person's feelings, thoughts and actions.

In *Session 29* of *Module 9,* we enhance and strengthen these interpersonal communication skills by broadening the base of open invitation and reflective listening approaches.

▶ Present **How to Make Active Listening Work.** Discuss how thinking filters create closed listening channels. In order to have an open listening channel, we have to bypass our thinking filters. Again, we focus on nonverbal communication by practicing the skill of **"listening" to body language** or body talk.

    Adjunct Exercise: From time to time during the session, after a person speaks or shares, have group members state what kind of body language they observed in the speaker. Discuss the meaning of clear and accurate feedback. Review the tips for effective active listening.

▶ Present **Practicing Active Listening. Exercise:** Practice both active sharing and the active listening skills. The goal is to learn the simple communication process of accurate sending and receiving of messages (Oliver & Margolin, 2003). **Exercise:** Closely monitor the role-playing exercises where a client tells another person playing the role of his/her spouse a problem he or she is having with that spouse. This could open up marital conflict issues that need to be resolved.

▶ Have clients update their *MSL,* focusing on *Skills 12, 13* and *14,* and their *MAP.* Remind them to do their *TAP Charting* and continue working on their autobiography.

▶ Go over the homework.

- ◆ Practice active listening during the week and have clients look for the results.

- ◆ **Exercise:** Go over *Worksheet 31.*

▶ Have clients complete the *SSC Change Scales* on their knowledge of and skills in using active listening.

SUMMARY OF KEY CONCEPTS

▶ Active sharing or self-oriented communication.

▶ Active listening or other-oriented communication.

▶ Thinking filters, open and closed channels.

▶ "Listening" to body language.

▶ Accurate feedback.

SESSION CLOSURE AND GUIDELINES FOR THERAPEUTIC PROCESSING

When starting the therapeutic processing, encourage clients to use the skills of active sharing and listening during the session as well as in subsequent therapeutic processing. A focus topic for the closure group is sharing how clients get defensive with people close to them.

RATIONALE AND OVERVIEW

As clients move closer to the **Commitment to Change** phase of treatment, it will be important that they have a firm grip on the nature of their past problems with AOD use and criminal behavior. As they progress through the **Challenge to Change** phase of *SSC,* they will move to a deeper level of sharing thoughts, feelings and past experiences. This session is designed to help clients have a greater awareness of the negative outcomes of their AOD use and the effect of that use on others. Clients reevaluate themselves across self-report instruments to see if they have changed as to being more self-disclosing and less defensive. This session also facilitates a deeper sharing of past and present emotions. *Sessions 13* and *14* are presented in sequence.

The *Johari Window* (Luft, 1969), page 99 in the *Workbook,* provides a model for the self-disclosure process of this session and *Session 14.* It is focusing on the HIDDEN AREA of the window with clients using the active sharing communication skills.

Important note: This session may be difficult for some clients since it encourages them to increase the depth of their self-disclosure. Advise clients to stay within the boundaries of their own comfort level. Take a client-centered, supportive, positive regard, and empathic approach. Some clients may get in touch with thoughts and feelings and past experiences they need to explore in individual counseling.

SUMMARY OF CONTENT, PRESENTATION SEQUENCE AND GUIDELINES

Introduce this session by reviewing the stages of change, and that looking deeper into their AOD use history and emotional experiences is part of the **Challenge to Change.** As part of this introduction, review the two pathways to communication, **active sharing and active listening**, since these are the skills needed for involvement in this session. Clients will need tutoring and instruction to complete the exercises and worksheets. Here are the suggested presentation process and guidelines for this session.

❱ Start out with the *CB Map Exercise* and sharing the *TAP Charting.* Summarize the key concepts and objectives of the session.

❱ **Have clients share** the *Session 12* homework on **active listening,** *Worksheet 31,* page 105.

❱ Present **A Deeper Sharing of Your AOD Use History.** This section will take careful deliberation.

◆ **Exercise:** Clients complete *Worksheet 32,* page 109, of the *CSAS* and put their score in the 2nd column of the table on page 107. Explain that there are no right or wrong answers and to respond to the questions as to how the see themselves now. **Then have clients take their score from the CSAS they did in orientation, *Worksheet 3,* page 18, and put that score in the "1st score" column in the table on page 107.** Take a few minutes for them to compare scores. Have them share whether their scores went up or down. The scores of most clients will increase because of greater willingness to self-disclose. Those with very high scores on the first *CSAS* will probably have slightly lower scores on the second testing.

◆ **Exercise: Clients retake the survey in *Worksheet 19,* page 79 in the *Workbook, Negative Outcomes of AOD Use.*** Instruct them to use a different mark for the second testing. Have them put their first and second scores on the table on page 107. For those clients who have not completed *Session 8,* have them complete *Worksheet 19* and put their score in the first column of the table. They will retake the test when they do *Session 8.* Have them discuss their findings. Did their scores increase or decrease?

- ◆ **Exercise:** Clients retake the differential screening instrument they took when entering *SSC*. If they took the *Adult Substance Use Survey-Revised* (ASUS-R) have them compare their first scores with their second scores across all scales. Then, have them put the score on the ASUS-R GLOBAL Scale of the first and second testing in the table on page 107. If they took another survey, they can put the first and second scores on the line "Other Survey." Take time to discuss how their scores differ on these two testings. Were clients more self-disclosing on the second testing? Were the results more reflective of their "true" condition around AOD use and abuse?

- ◆ **Exercise:** *Worksheet 33* provides opportunity for clients to look at the results of their AOD abuse in greater depth. Encourage clients to be as self-disclosing as possible on this worksheet. Have clients share their thoughts and feelings around their disclosures. The goal is to prevent relapse by heightening their awareness of the negative outcomes of their AOD use and abuse.

- ◆ **Exercise:** *Worksheet 34* may be difficult for some clients. This raises the bar around self-disclosure of negative outcomes around their AOD use. Encourage clients to stay within their self-disclosure comfort zone. Observe for clients who may be distressed when recalling those who were negatively affected by their AOD use. Remind clients that they cannot change these past negative consequences, **but they can change their thinking around these consequences so as to have better emotional outcomes.**

- ❱ Present **Sharing Deeper Feelings.** Again, encourage clients to stay within their comfort zone. **Exercise:** When doing the exercise in this section, ask clients to write down only the feelings they had about a particular emotional event, and not the event itself. When doing group sharing, they can share the specific event if they want, but sharing the emotions is the important goal. Again, remind them that they can't change the event, but they can change how they think about it to get better emotional outcomes. Also, some clients may choose to write down their emotions about a positive event. This effort should be supported. **Monitor the group for persons who may be distressed by this exercise and evaluate whether they could benefit from individual sessions around the event or related experiences.**

- ❱ Have clients update their *MSL* and their *MAP*. Remind them to do their *TAP Charting*. This would be an appropriate session for some clients to share parts of their autobiography.

- ❱ Have clients complete the *SSC Change Scales* on their ability to be open around their past AOD use problems and their deeper feelings.

SUMMARY OF KEY CONCEPTS

- ❱ More honest look at AOD problems and how these problems affected others.

- ❱ Deeper sharing of past emotional experiences.

SESSION CLOSURE AND GUIDELINES FOR THERAPEUTIC PROCESSING

The provider should keep the structured interactive portion of this session moving at a comfortable pace so that there is time for therapeutic processing. Have clients interact around their thoughts and emotions about what they shared in the exercises and worksheets.

SESSION 14: A Deeper Sharing of Your Criminal Conduct History

RATIONALE AND OVERVIEW

Introduction to Session

As clients move closer to the **commitment to change** phase of treatment, it will be important that they have a good understanding of the nature of their past criminal conduct (CC) and offenses. This will be a difficult session for some clients. Even though judicial clients can access their official judicial records and history, and are aware of their past criminal offenses and convictions, most have not carefully processed that history. Few offenders have looked at the real cost of their CC. With many offenders, there is a strong defense system which prevents a full awareness, let alone the emotional processing, of this history.

This session involves a rather extensive exploration of the judicial clients' involvement in criminal conduct and the impact of that involvement on their lives. It could easily be expanded into two structured group sessions. **It is also recommended that the provider meet in a 20- to 30-minute individual session with clients to explain the purpose of the session, assist them in doing and discussing their self-report on** *Worksheet 35,* **and discuss their official record.** If the group is small, e.g., five or fewer clients, this individual attention can be done in group. **New clients do not enter at this session.**

Guidelines and Caveats Around Disclosure of Criminal Conduct

Whereas *Module 4* focused on the process and cycles of criminal thinking and conduct, the focus of this session is on specific CC and what that conduct has cost the judicial client in money and time. The purpose of having clients list their arrests and disposition, and to peruse their official criminal record, is to help them confront directly the extent of their CC involvement. This provides a platform for changing criminal thinking, preventing recidivism, and engaging in prosocial thinking, attitudes and actions.

Clients are reminded that there is no need to reveal specific crimes other than those for which they were arrested and/or prosecuted. **The purpose of this session is not to further incriminate clients, nor to discover the details of crimes for which they have not been arrested or prosecuted. The purpose is to improve cognitive, emotional and behavioral outcomes, again, with the goal of preventing recidivism.**

Criminal Conduct and Substance Abuse Patterns and Types

In *Chapter 3* of the *Resource Guide,* we discussed several offender patterns and types. Based on the work clients did in *Session 9* and in this session, have them discuss how they might fit two patterns or types of criminal conduct discussed in that chapter: Life-course sustained (LCS) and Time-limited (TL).

This session will give clients some understanding of how they might fit three different patterns and types around the interaction of substance abuse and criminal conduct: AOD abuse primary and criminal conduct secondary to AOD abuse; CC is primary and AOD abuse secondary; CC and AOD abuse are secondary to other psychosocial circumstances. Determining the kinds of patterns clients fit will provide guidelines for treatment and judicial supervision. Clients with primary AOD and secondary CC will need to have consistent UA monitoring. Clients who have features of the *life-course sustained* (LCS) CC pattern will need extended and more intensive judicial supervision. The *Participant's Workbook* does not present the LCS or TL patterns.

SUMMARY OF CONTENT, PRESENTATION SEQUENCE AND GUIDELINES

Introduce this session by reminding clients that studying their CC history is part of the **Challenge to Change.** Discuss the caveats presented in the session overview and rationale. Reflect understanding that it may be distressful looking at one's criminal history. Here are the guidelines for presenting this session.

▶ Start out with the *CB Map Exercise* and sharing the *TAP Charting.* Summarize the session's key concepts and objectives. Have clients briefly reflect on the work they did in *Session 13.*

▶ Present **Deeper Sharing of Your Criminal Conduct.**

◆ **Exercise:** Have clients compare their first and second responses to items 3 and 5 on the CASA.

◆ **Exercise:** Take time to do the *Criminal Conduct History Log, Worksheet 35.* Explain that, for this exercise, they only complete the first five columns.

◆ **Exercise:** Often, the official record does not reveal the full extent of a client's criminal history. When available, have clients compare their official record with their work on *Worksheet 35,* which may be more revealing than their official record.

◆ Moffitt (1993) defines two adolescent offender patterns or types: *Life-course persistent (LCP)* and *adolescent-limited.* Based on the Moffitt model and data from the *Adult Substance Use Survey* (ASUS: Wanberg, 1998, 2004), we postulated two adult patterns of CC: *Life-course sustained (LCS)* and *time-limited (TL).* We see *LCS* as similar to Moffitt's *LCP,* however, this pattern may not necessarily be evidenced in adolescence, but does evolve during the early adult years. It is defined by consistent and sustained involvement in adult CC and antisocial behavior that are integral parts of the offender's lifestyle. *LCS* offenders continue their antisocial attitudes and behaviors even during periods where they are not involved in criminal behavior. There is a commitment to a criminal lifestyle and evidence of a long history of antisocial and CC starting in adolescence and continues into adulthood. Most *LCS* types will have significant to severe antisocial and other personality disorders and will have high scores on antisocial and antilegal measures. They are quite open around their CC history. Judicial clients with high scores on both past and present risk factors on *Worksheet 24,* page 87, and whose *Criminal Conduct History Log* in *Worksheet 35* shows a long legal record, with consistent arrests across time (outside of periods of incarceration), may fit the *LCS*-type. *LCS*-type judicial clients will need to have greater cognitive-behavioral focus in preventing criminal and antisocial thinking and behaviors and will need to closely monitor and avoid their involvement in high risk exposures that lead to recidivism.

The *TL*-type is defined by a specific period or periods of criminal involvement or even limited to one or two episodes. The antisocial and criminal attitudes and behaviors are not persistent and they may go into remission temporarily or permanently. There are defined periods of prosocial adjustment and responsible living. CC may be more situational, dependent on environmental factors, and **may not** be based on pathogenic personality traits. Moffitt (1993) defines the adolescent-limited pattern in a similar way, but she sees this pattern as not typically going beyond adolescence. It is not uncommon to see the *TL*-type with minimal criminal conduct in adolescence. Yet, it often starts in adolescence. Persons with low to moderate scores on both past and present risk factors on *Worksheet 24* and who indicate on their *Criminal Conduct History Log* in *Worksheet 35* they have a spotty, periodic, and time-limited patterns of arrests may be more apt to fit this pattern.

The provider should not take a deterministic attitude around the *LCS*-type and communicate that *LCS*-types are not treatable and doomed to recidivism. Nor would it be wise to communicate that those fitting the *TL* type can let down their defenses to high-risk exposures for recidivism.

Adjunct Exercise: Describe the two offender types and then have clients evaluate their work on *Worksheet 24,* page 87, and *Worksheet 35,* in this session, to see if they can discern whether they fit either type or neither type. Open the group up to discussion around what it means to fit a certain type.

- ◆ **Adjunct Exercise:** Have clients share their thoughts and feelings about reviewing their criminal history. Set limits on this initial discussion, since clients can easily see that if time is taken on this discussion, there will be little time to complete other exercises.

▶ Present **How Are Your AOD Use and Criminal Conduct Related?** Have clients look at their recordings in column 6, *Related to AOD Use,* of *Worksheet 35.*

Adjunct Exercise: Use the following typology model, and have clients evaluate and discuss which pattern or patterns they fit.

- ◆ CC is primary and AOD abuse is secondary. In this case, the trajectory of CC operates independently, but is supported by AOD use and abuse.

- ◆ AOD abuse is primary and CC is secondary. There is an established pattern of AOD abuse and CC emerges out of that pattern or supports the continuation of the AOD abuse pattern.

- ◆ CC and AOD abuse are secondary to psychosocial factors such as posttraumatic stress syndrome.

▶ Present **What Has Your Criminal Conduct History Cost You?** **Exercise:** Complete *Worksheet 36.* Clients may want to do this as homework. If this is done, then discuss their findings in the next session.

▶ Have clients update their *MSL* (particularly *Skill 25*), and their *MAP.* Remind them to do their *TAP Charting.* This would be an appropriate session for some clients to share parts of their autobiography.

▶ **Exercise:** Clients will need help with the *Thinking and Re-thinking Report* around an event where the use of alcohol or other drugs led to committing a crime. This can be part of the closure group, or part of the structured session. Providers can use *Thinking Reports* and *Re-thinking Reports* in any session where there is time and it is done in relationship to the session topic or focus. These reports can be used as homework exercises. This would be a good time to review the basic elements of a *Thinking and Re-thinking Report:* EVENT, THOUGHTS, BELIEFS, FEELINGS, OUTCOMES.

▶ Have clients complete the *SSC Change Scales* on their ability to be open around their criminal history.

SUMMARY OF KEY CONCEPTS

▶ Deeper sharing of criminal conduct and *CC History Log.*

▶ AOD abuse and CC primary or secondary.

▶ How AOD abuse and criminal conduct are related.

▶ Cost of CC in terms of time and money.

SESSION CLOSURE AND GUIDELINES FOR THERAPEUTIC PROCESSING

Because of the extensive nature of this session, there may be limited time for therapeutic processing. Using an individual meeting to explain the session and assist in completing *Worksheet 35* will provide more group time.

MODULE 6

Understanding and Preventing Relapse and Recidivism

OVERVIEW OF MODULE 6

Preventing relapse and recidivism (R&R) are the two primary goals of *SSC*. One step in achieving these goals is challenging clients to look at their own AOD use and misuse patterns and their patterns of criminal conduct. Much of the work in other *SSC* sessions is built around this challenge. Another step in R&R prevention, and a major task of this module, is for clients to understand the risk exposures and conditions that lead to R&R. Still another step is learning coping skills to avoid or manage those risk exposures.

An important component of skill building to prevent R&R is to manage urges and cravings that lead to substance use and criminal conduct. An important part of managing drug and crime-seeking behavior is learning refusal skills.

Another task of this module is to have clients define what relapse and recidivism mean to them, and define their pathways to R&R. Self-confrontation, self-awareness, and coping skills are powerful influences in preventing relapse and recidivism and are most likely more powerful than sanctions imposed on them by the courts.

R&R prevention approaches are based on the theory that AOD use and abuse and criminal conduct are learned behaviors. Social learning theory (SLT) provides an explanation for this learning process (Bandura, 1977a, 1997). SLT holds that through a variety of factors and influences, individuals have learned thoughts, underlying attitudes and beliefs, and emotions that determine and explain problem behaviors, e.g., substance abuse and criminal conduct. These factors include *operant* and *classical conditioning*, sociocultural influences, peer and adult role modeling, and biogenetic predispositions. A basic premise of SLT is that cognitive mediating factors (e.g., thoughts and beliefs) are critical in determining and reinforcing problem behaviors. Two of these cognitive factors central to Bandura's SLT reinforcement model and important to the explanation of AOD abuse and criminal conduct are: outcome expectancies; and efficacy outcomes. Cognitive-behavioral therapy is based on SLT and is the core treatment approach to relapse and recidivism prevention.

PROVIDER GOALS OF THIS MODULE

▶ Facilitate client understanding of the pathways to R&R and the pathways to R&R prevention.

▶ Facilitate the learning and practice of skills to prevent R&R.

▶ Facilitate the learning and practice of skills to manage cravings and urges.

THE RELAPSE AND RECIDIVISM PREVENTION APPROACH IN *SSC*

Relapse prevention was designed specifically to address the intervention and treatment of addictive behaviors. *SSC* takes the approach that engaging in criminal conduct is a habitual and addictive process and that the principles and concepts applied to the understanding of relapse can be applicable to criminal behavior and conduct. The provider is asked to review the material in *Chapter 5* that explores in more detail the theories and approaches to R&R. This introduction to *Module 6* reviews how the Marlatt relapse prevention (RP) model was adapted to the R&R prevention approach used with judicial clients, and more specifically, describes the essential components of the R&R prevention approaches used in *SSC*.

The R&R approach presented in this module should be seen as a specialized derivative of the basic *CB Map* used throughout the *Participant's Workbook*. It is important for clients to understand the relationship between the *SSC* CB model for learning and change and how the embodied principles in that model are specifically designed for relapse and recidivism prevention.

THE MARLATT MODEL

Marlatt and Gordon's (1985) classic work on relapse prevention (RP) caused a major paradigm shift in the treatment of persons with alcohol and other substance use problems. Prior to the 1980s, treatment programs would not realistically address the issue of relapse. In many treatment programs, it was a "taboo" subject. If you talk about it, "it might happen." The reality was that it did happen.

Research in the late 1960s and 1970s clearly indicated from 60 to 80 percent of AOD treatment clients went back to do some drinking or other drug use within one year of coming out of treatment programs (see Wanberg & Milkman, 1998, and *Chapter 5* of *Section 1* for a summary of relapse findings). Many who went back to some drinking experienced full relapse - returning to the same or similar pre-treatment problem outcome pattern.

Marlatt concluded from these "sobering" findings that relapse was a reality that needed to be addressed within a formal treatment model. His early work and investigations in the 1970s and early 1980s (e.g., Marlatt, 1978, 1979, 1982; Marlatt & George, 1984) set the stage for his and Gordon's seminal work that produced the shift in treatment to address relapse and build RP approaches using social learning and cognitive-behavioral theory. Today, with variations, most RP programs are modeled after the Marlatt approach. This RP approach, which is presented in some detail in *Chapter 5*, is the basis for developing the R&R models for *SSC*.

APPLICATION OF RP TO RECIDIVISM

The same concerns regarding relapse and substance abuse also surfaced with offenders in the criminal justice system. Recidivism rates were similar to the relapse rates. About 65 to 70 percent of the offenders in the criminal justice system re-offended.

The seminal work of Andrews and Bonta (1994) makes it very clear that, whatever the roles of punishment and sanctioning are in the society, they do not prevent recidivism, and in some studies, resulted in an increase of recidivism rates. They concluded that clinically relevant interventions involving treatment services have the best promise for reducing recidivism rather than interventions based only on criminal sanctions (Andrews & Bonta, 1994, 2003).

A search of the relapse and recidivism literature (Wanberg & Milkman, 1998) showed striking similarities between relapse and recidivism - the process, the outcome rates, the triggers related to high-risk thinking and situations. Thus, using the Marlatt (1985a) model, Wanberg and Milkman (1998) developed a model for recidivism based on the essential concepts of relapse and relapse prevention. This model has also been developed for impaired driving offenders (Wanberg, Milkman & Timken, 2005).

Any viable intervention and treatment protocol for judicial clients must address both recidivism and relapse prevention with a structured, evidenced-based model. The *SSC* R&R approach is built on the Marlatt model and on the adaptations of this model by Wanberg and Milkman (1998) in the first edition of this work. *Figures 5.2, 5.3 and 5.4* in *Chapter 5* (also included in *Sessions 15* and *16*) are adaptations of the Marlatt (Doualhy, Stowell, aprk and Daley, 2007; Marlatt, 1985a; Marlatt & Witkiewitz, 2005) model (*Figure 5.1* in *Chapter 5*).

GOALS OF R&R TREATMENT

Marlatt and Witkiewitz (2005) state that the major goal of relapse prevention (RP) is to directly address the problem of relapse and to generate techniques for preventing or managing its occurrence (p. 1). In the Marlatt model, RP works at identifying high-risk situations that make the individual vulnerable to relapse, and uses cognitive-behavioral coping strategies to prevent relapse in similar situations. There are two objectives of RP (p. 1):

▶ To prevent an initial lapse and maintain an abstinence or harm reduction treatment goal;

▶ To manage a lapse in such a manner so as to prevent further relapse.

The ultimate purpose is to help clients learn skills to prevent complete relapse, regardless of the situation or possible risk factors (Marlatt, 1985a; Marlatt & Witkiewitz, 2005).

SSC has taken these goals of RP and applied them to understanding and preventing relapse **and** recidivism in the judicial client. Again, operating under the assumption that criminal conduct is a learned, and in many cases, an addictive behavior, the principles of RP as presented by Marlatt and his associates down through the years are applicable to preventing recidivism.

BASIC ELEMENTS IN R&R TREATMENT

Whereas the approaches to RP will differ depending on the kind of addiction being treated, there are several common elements to the RP approach (e.g., Donovan, 2005). These commonalities form the basis of our approach to the first and and current edition of *SSC,* and more specifically to R&R prevention.

▶ Educate or help clients learn about the process of relapse and recidivism. As Donovan (2005) notes, despite having firsthand knowledge of relapse, most clients do not understand the many factors that enter into relapse. This makes them think that relapse "just happens," giving them little sense of having cognitive and behavioral control over the event. This also applies to recidivism. Most judicial clients do not understand the many factors that enter into recidivism.

▶ Help clients identify high-risk exposures, or in the Marlatt model, high-risk situations. These exposures are the "caution signs" on the pathway to R&R. An important part of this approach is to have clients identify the high-risk exposures specific to their own situation that portend R&R, or what Donovan (2005) calls the personal "warning signs."

▶ Help clients learn and practice skills to manage these high-risk exposures. These skills must be practical, portable and transferable - they can be used in managing different kinds of high-risk exposures.

EMPIRICALLY SUPPORTED APPROACHES

There has been a significant debate over the preference of evidence-based or empirically supported treatments (EST) over other approaches (see Norcross, Beutler & Levant, 2006, for a comprehensive treatment of this debate). However, there has been an increase focus on using the EST approaches in the treatment of mental health disorders (Norcross et al., 2006) and addictions (McCrady, 2000).

The cognitive-behavioral intrapersonal and interpersonal skills development approaches used in *SSC*, and more specifically, used in the *SSC* R&R prevention approach in this module, are based on ESTs (e.g., problem-solving skills, coping skills training, cognitive restructuring, refusal skills, etc.) Relapse prevention approaches, and more specifically, coping skills training, have shown to be efficacious with many addictive disorders (see Donovan, 2005, p. 7 for summary of cites supporting RP efficacy).

DEFINITIONS OF RELAPSE AND RECIDIVISM USED IN THIS MODULE

The problem of defining relapse has been discussed in *Chapter 5*. It is complex and has multiple meanings, as Miller's paper connotes: *What is Relapse? Fifty Ways to Leave the Wagon* (1996). The term relapse is most appropriately used when an individual has made an effort or commitment to change a problem behavior and then "slips" back into that behavior. It has been common practice to differentiate between a lapse and a relapse (Marlatt, 1985a, 1985b; Marlatt & Witkiewitz, 2005; Witiewitz & Marlatt, 2007a). A lapse is an "instance of a previously cessated behavior" (Marlatt & Witkiewitz, 2005, p. 2) whereas a relapse follows that instance and is a "return to the previous problematic behavior pattern" (p. 2). Marlatt also refers to a prolapse or "getting back on track" in the direction of positive change (p. 2).

In this work, we utilize the Marlatt definitions, but clearly distinguish **being into the process of R&R** from **actual R&R occurrence.** This differentiation allows for the integration of the recidivism prevention model with the **zero-tolerance** approach for criminal conduct. Being **into the process of R&R** involves engaging in cognitions and behaviors that lead to full R&R. With AOD treatment, we can tolerate, accept and work with full relapse.

However, with criminal conduct, we can only work with the cognitive and behavioral events and processes that **lead to** full recidivism - returning to committing a crime. We have **zero tolerance** for full recidivism. If we know the individual has returned to criminal conduct, the judicial process takes over, and this essentially ends our treatment effort, or at least the current treatment episode. Certainly, we can work with some clients who are rearrested, but those opportunities occur at some point down the road. For clients who relapse into AOD problem behavior, we not only tolerate that relapse, but can work with and capitalize on the relapse in the current treatment episode.

Using these modifications, we see three components to the definition of relapse.

▶ We first define the **process of relapse** as involving cognitive events that lead to thinking about AOD use or engaging in high-risk exposures that put the client at risk of a lapse or lead to full relapse.

▶ We define **lapse** as any use of alcohol or other drugs that can lead to problem use after being committed to a pattern of non-harmful use; or for the goal of total abstinence, any use of alcohol or illegal drugs.

▶ **Full relapse** is returning to a pattern of drinking or other drug use that causes problems and is harmful and upsetting to the client or others.

With relapse, we distinguish between alcohol and illegal drugs. With alcohol, we see two options: clients choose the relapse prevention goal (upon completion of treatment and judicial supervision requirements) of not returning to a pattern of alcohol use that causes further use problems; **or** total abstinence. **With illegal drugs or the illegal use of legal drugs, we state that the only acceptable goal is total abstinence.** The extensive self-assessment that clients do around AOD use problems in *Module 3* provides a basis upon which they can make a decision regarding their alcohol relapse prevention goal. *SSC* strongly recommends total alcohol abstinence for clients who have a significant history of alcohol use disruption.

With respect to recidivism, we use these definitions.

▶ A person is **into the process of recidivism** when taking part in high-risk exposures that can lead to CC.

▶ **Full recidivism is committing another crime.**

The "zero tolerance" model for recidivism — being crime-free — is the only option. Thus, the viable recidivism prevention goal is preventing involvement in high-risk exposures (situations, thoughts, feelings) that lead to criminal conduct. We make it clear that the options regarding a relapse goal are a personal choice of the judicial client. But the "zero tolerance" goal of recidivism is both the client's choice and society's choice.

We present these definitions of R&R and then ask clients to write down their definitions. We then have clients define their R&R prevention goal options.

RELAPSE AND RECIDIVISM: A PROCESS OF EROSION

An important concept in the RP model is that relapse is a gradual process that occurs over time. This gradual process includes what Marlatt originally called *apparently irrelevant decisions* (1985a), and later called *seemingly irrelevant decisions (SIDS).*

The erosion starts with high-risk exposures. Most clients think that the initial lapse into AOD use or criminal thinking is "sudden" or "on the spur of the moment." However, when relapse or recidivism clients are interviewed, invariably, the R&R episodes are preceded with gradual involvement in high-risk exposures.

RELAPSE AND RECIDIVISM: SIMILAR BUT DIFFERENT

Relapse and recidivism processes are similar and have similar features. Both have common high-risk exposures, and prevention for both involves managing these exposures. Both involve an erosion process and occur gradually. The process of each is advanced and reinforced by positive outcome expectancies (from AOD use and criminal conduct). Each has greater probability of occurring with persons who have low self-efficacy relative to specific high-risk exposures. Both end up in negative outcomes for the individual and the community. Both respond to similar treatment approaches. For example, the literature suggests that cognitive-behavioral approaches are effective for both relapse (Marlatt & Witkiewitz, 2005) and recidivism (Andrews & Bonta, 2003).

Even though similar, there are distinct differences. A person can relapse without engaging in CC recidivism. A person can go back to CC without relapsing. An alcohol relapse does not usually violate criminal statutes and usually does not have judicial ramifications. Other drug relapses often do not lead to sanctioning. Recidivism always has judicial ramifications and always leads to sanctioning. Providers take a **zero-tolerance approach** to full recidivism but there can be tolerance to full relapse.

HIGH-RISK EXPOSURES AND TRIGGERS

We have extrapolated the Marlatt high-risk situation model to a more inclusive concept: high-risk exposures. Although Marlatt views high-risk situations to include internal and external events or circumstances that increase the probability of relapse, we wanted to use terms that more explicitly defined these events. This gives clients more specific handles in spotting these events.

Here are the high-risk exposures used in the *SSC* R&R.

- High-risk thinking or thought habits (automatic thoughts). These include changes in how one thinks about self or changes in self-image.

- High-risk situations.

- High-risk feelings and emotions.

- High-risk attitudes and beliefs.

- High-risk behaviors.

These high-risk exposures or triggers are the cognitive-behavioral expressions of the determinants of relapse as outlined by Marlatt (1985a; Marlatt & Witkiewitz, 2005) and discussed in *Chapter 5*.

PREVENTING RELAPSE AND RECIDIVISM

In preparation for working on R&R prevention skills and plans, clients engage in a number of assessment exercises. They identify and evaluate their own specific high-risk exposures and their specific triggers for R&R. They define their own pathway to R&R, and then look at their past R&R history by doing an R&R log.

Clients define their own relapse and recidivism prevention goals within the framework of the *SSC* options. Some clients may choose not to stay within these option guidelines, e.g., some clients may decide to return to AOD use and "let the cards fall as they may."

The adapted Marlatt model (Marlatt, 1985a; Marlatt & Witkiewitz, 2005) is used to help the judicial client understand the process of preventing R&R. Skills in preventing R&R are then identified within this framework. Clients then develop a R&R prevention plan and identify the specific skills to make this plan work.

Each day that clients prevent relapse and recidivism, they become stronger. The patterns of living AOD and crime-free are reinforced. Yet, it is important that clients understand that R&R prevention is based on the use of self-control and relationship skills. Whether or not clients use these skills depends on whether they are in the commitment stage of change. These R&R prevention patterns become strengthened when clients take ownership of their change.

RATIONALE AND OVERVIEW

A basic approach of *SSC* is to provide clients with knowledge and information about the life-adjustment areas relevant to changing their patterns of substance abuse and criminal conduct. *Module 3* focuses on providing clients with basic information around drugs and drug use patterns and then challenges clients to apply these concepts and understandings to their specific situations.

Module 4 provides clients with information around CC and the CCT (criminal conduct and thinking) cycle and then challenges clients to apply information to their unique situations. *Module 5* provides clients with tools for: sharing their histories; listening to others; and being open to and giving constructive feedback – promoting the development of realistic plans to prevent relapse and recidivism.

Module 6 provides clients with a basic understanding of and information around what leads to relapse and recidivism (R&R) and the pathways and skills to preventing R&R. Clients are challenged to apply this understanding to their unique situations.

In preparation for this session, the provider should review the introduction to this module as well as *Chapter 5* of this *Guide.* This will provide a good understanding of the key issues related to R&R. This session focuses on the process and pathways to recidivism. **It is a prerequisite to *Session 16.***

SUMMARY OF CONTENT, PRESENTATION SEQUENCE AND GUIDELINES

Although clients are asked to define their own relapse and recidivism prevention goals in *Session 16,* in this session, they are challenged to look at two possible goals around relapse. As well, definitions of relapse and its process are presented. Clients are then asked to present what relapse means to them.

Providers may find that some clients define relapse quite differently from how it is defined in the *Workbook.* Some discussion can be held around these differences, giving clients the freedom to express their views. Although this discussion may not lead all clients to agree with the definitions in the *Workbook,* the goal is to help clients see the value of the *Workbook's* definitions and how these can lead to positive outcomes in their lives.

▶ Start with presenting the objectives of the session and then facilitate the *CB Map Exercise* and sharing the *TAP Charting.*

▶ Present **Relapse and Recidivism - A Process of Erosion.** Use the metaphor of soil erosion - the gradual wearing away of an individual's ability to handle high-risk exposures - or an erosion of self-mastery (the Marlatt model uses the term self-efficacy). Discuss *Figure 17* (Daley & Marlatt, 1992, 2005). Have someone read the example of the erosion process on page 117. Discuss the concept of self-efficacy or self-mastery, a term we use that may have more meaning to clients.

Self-mastery is seen as both: 1) a global or generic trait or construct that serves to operate as a core belief in handling life situations; and 2) an efficacy outcome expectation, based on a set of skills, to handle specific life situations. We are using the latter meaning when referring to self-mastery in this session and *Session 16* in managing specific situations that can lead to R&R. The provider will want to review the discussion of self-efficacy in *Chapter 4,* pg. 75.

- Present **Understanding Relapse.** *SSC's* position is that clients abstain from all illegal drug use or from the illegal use of legal drugs. *SSC* identifies two viable choices: total abstinence from alcohol and illegal drugs; or living alcohol problem-free and abstinence from all illegal drugs. This is a harm-avoidance approach to alcohol use and not abstinence.

- When presenting the definitions of relapse, make it clear that the **process of being into relapse** is both cognitive and behavioral, and this process does not necessarily involve actual use of alcohol or other drugs, e.g., thinking about getting high is in the process of relapse. It could involve a lapse. There are two possible outcomes of engaging in the process of relapse which may include a lapse: 1) full relapse or returning to a pattern of drinking or other drug use that causes problems, is harmful and upsetting to the individual and to others; and 2) "getting back on track" by using skills to manage the relapse process and prevent full relapse.

  - Have clients write down what relapse means to them.

  - **Adjunct exercise:** Discuss what relapse means to clients.

  - **Exercises:** Present high-risk exposures for relapse and have clients complete the left column of *Worksheet 37,* listing their high-risk exposures. These provide warning signs for relapse. In response to these exposures, cognitive-behavioral shifts occur that lead to R&R.

- Present **Understanding Recidivism** and the **process of being into recidivism** versus **full recidivism** (actually engaging in criminal conduct). **Exercise:** go over the high-risk exposures for recidivism and then have clients list their own high-risk exposures in the right column of *Worksheet 37.* These are clues or warning signs for recidivism. Discuss the question: Does using illegal drugs put a person into full recidivism?

- Present **Triggers for Relapse and Recidivism** which are specific examples of high-risk exposures. They differ for each person. An important task of treatment is for clients to identify their unique triggers. By understanding their high-risk exposures, they can figure out what triggers involvement in AOD abuse or in criminal conduct. They can test out ways other than AOD use or CC to respond to high-risk exposures. Even though each client has unique triggers or high risk exposures, research has identified four major categories of triggers that help clients understand their specific vulnerabilities (Emrick & Aarons, 1990; Marlatt, 1985a; Marlatt & Witkiewitz, 2005).

1) **Interpersonal conflict:** Frustration and anger from interactions with another person.

2) **Social or peer pressure:** Being offered a drug; pressured into committing a crime by a close friend.

3) **Unpleasant emotions** such as stress, depression, intense anger. Using substances or involvement in a criminal event may serve to cope with being depressed, anxious, bored or lonely.

4) **A change in self-image:** This involves change from seeing self as an abstainer to again being a user; change from the image of living a straight, crime-free life to one who does criminal acts. Taking a drink or using a drug after a period of abstinence may lead to continued drug use because of a change in self-view - the client now sees him/herself not as an abstainer, but as a user. A change in social roles, e.g., divorced, unemployed, being victimized may serve as triggers for relapse.

Exercise: On *Worksheet 38,* clients identify personal instances for each of the four triggers for both relapse and recidivism, and the thoughts, emotions and actions (positive or negative) related to those instances. If their examples led to negative outcomes, have clients practice restructuring their thoughts so that they have positive outcomes. This takes advantage of the "change moment" to facilitate clients' construction of alternative, positive strategies for thinking and acting. The *CB Map* and *Thought Report* formats are useful tools to highlight the client's ability to achieve mastery over thoughts, feelings and actions. Clients are reminded that the model for this change is the *CB Map, Figure 2,* page 14, of the *Workbook.*

Adjunct exercise: Have one or two group members role-play an ineffective coping response or negative outcome for one of the triggers in *Worksheet 38*. Follow this with a role play of an effective coping response to the same instance.

▶ Present **Your Risk of Relapse or Recidivism - Review.** Have clients re-evaluate their R&R risk by reviewing the work they did in *Sessions 8, Worksheets 19* through *21,* pages 79 to 81, and *Session 9, Worksheets 23* and *24.*

▶ Present **Pathways to Relapse and Recidivism.** Carefully go over *Figure 18,* one of the most important in *SSC.* **Exercise:** Using *Worksheet 39,* have clients map their potential R&R pathway.

▶ Present the **Relapse and Recidivism Log. Exercise:** Clients will need some guidance doing *Worksheet 40* (adapted after Gorski, 1993; Wanberg & Milkman, 1998). The log represents a portion of the clients R&R history. R&R prevention starts with understanding one's R&R history and how AOD and legal problems are related.

▶ Based on what clients learned this session, have them update their *MSL* and *MAP.* Use an individual session for clients who have finished their autobiography to review their work.

▶ Have clients use the *SSC Change Scales* to rate their understanding of their process of relapse and recidivism.

SUMMARY OF KEY CONCEPTS

▶ R&R is a process of erosion.

▶ Definition of relapse.

▶ Definition of recidivism.

▶ High-risk exposures for relapse.

▶ High-risk exposures for recidivism.

▶ Triggers for R&R.

▶ R&R pathways.

▶ R&R Log.

SESSION CLOSURE AND GUIDELINES FOR THERAPEUTIC PROCESSING

Have clients visualize the contrast between continuing a life of AOD use and abuse and CC, and living a life free of AOD problems and CC. How are their relationships, health, family life, financial life, and psychological well-being affected and changed by living AOD and crime free? Have them imagine and visualize the benefits. Will people hold them in higher regard? Will they feel better about themselves? Will they be relieved in not having legal burdens? Have them visualize other positive outcomes related to this change.

RATIONALE AND OVERVIEW

New clients do not begin *SSC* with this session since *Session 15* is its prerequisite. The concepts of R&R apply to individuals who have made decisions to change cognitive-behavioral and other life patterns so as to prevent a return to AOD use or abuse and criminal conduct. Individuals committed to continuing AOD abuse patterns and criminal conduct do not relapse or recidivate. They just continue involvement in these patterns at the same cognitive and behavioral levels. In essence, one cannot relapse or recidivate unless deciding to establish a R&R goal.

Many judicial clients have not made these decisions when they start treatment. They may say, "I'm going straight," or, "I'm never getting high again," which are important steps to change, but do not represent concrete R&R prevention goals. The purpose of this session is concretize these goals. These goals evolve. This is why we ask clients to generate their goals in the orientation session, and then do it again in this session, after having considerable exposure to the meaning of R&R and learning the *SSC* concepts and skills for change. We want to see how their R&R prevention goals evolve.

Remind clients that R&R is a process that occurs long before lapsing into use or committing a criminal act. Part of this process is involvement in exposures and triggers - the warning signs and clues to R&R. R&R are shifts away from adaptive cognitive-behavioral responses to these exposures. They are shifts away from the thoughts, attitudes and beliefs that have been adopted and learned to prevent recidivism.

A person is **into the process of relapse** when shifting the thinking: "I'm strong and I can handle this by being calm and in control" to thinking, "A couple of drinks will help me handle this situation." Or, the cognitive shift from "I'll put off buying new boots so I can make the rent" to thinking, "If I sell a few drugs, I can make next month's rent and buy those boots." Or, the thought, "I'm getting a lot of rewards and comfort going straight," is shifted to "I used to have money in my pocket when I was doing those 'jobs'; and anyway, I'm bored." These shifts result in decreased confidence in coping abilities coupled with anticipated pleasure or relief following transgression of previously valued standards of conduct. These **risky shifts** in cognitive–behavioral processes trigger relapse and recidivism.

At the front end of treatment, most judicial clients do not see these **risky shifts** or warning signs but see their past substance abuse and CC episodes as "just happening." They learn there are almost always cognitive events that precede AOD relapse and involvement in CC. Clients learn to identify these shifts as links in a relapse (and recidivism) chain of events (Marlatt, 1985a).

Many offenders who experience full relapse or return to criminal conduct report that warning signs appeared weeks, months or longer before using drugs or committing a crime. When clients review their experiences in detail, they learn the connection between their cognitive-behavioral events and relapse (Daley & Marlatt, 1992). Understanding this process better prepares clients to handle the challenges of high-risk exposures and see that R&R do not occur in a vacuum, but within a context of biological, psychological, and social events. This is the goal of *Session 15*.

This session builds on the awareness of the steps to R&R and provides a model and skill development approach for preventing R&R. Based on their own R&R goals and their unique high-risk exposures, clients develop a relapse and recidivism prevention plan.

SUMMARY OF CONTENT, PRESENTATION SEQUENCE AND GUIDELINES

As clients define their R&R prevention goals, remind them that their recidivism prevention goal is not just their choice, but the choice and expectations of society - to live a crime-free life. Their relapse prevention goal **is** mainly their choice, unless that goal is a violation of their judicial requirements or legal status.

▶ Present the objectives of the session and then facilitate the *CB Map Exercise* and *TAP Charting* sharing.

▶ Present **Setting Your R&R Prevention Goals.** Clients compare those goals with the ones they defined for themselves in *Session 1,* page 9.

▶ Present the section on **Relapse and Recidivism (R&R) Prevention.** *Figure 19,* page 129, is an adaptation of the Marlatt Model. The left side of the map provides the process of R&R. The right side provides the process of prevention. Go over each step, using the following material to enhance the discussion.

  ◆ **High-risk exposures:** Both internal and external events that threaten self-control.

  ◆ **Weak or strong coping skills:** These are cognitive and behavioral. A strong cognitive skill is changing negative thinking to positive thoughts. A strong behavioral skill is reflective listening.

  ◆ **Decrease or increase of self-efficacy or self-mastery:** This is based on ineffective or effective use of coping skills. It is self-competence in dealing with high-risk exposures. It is self-judgement (appraisals) of clients on how well they cope with different situations.

  ◆ **Expected outcome:** What the person expects the outcome to be, such as expecting a drug to have a desired effect, e.g. "makes you feel good". The expected effects may be different from real effects. When the prospect of AOD use is hooked in with a positive (albeit short-term) outcome of AOD use, the probability of relapse increases. Or, correspondingly, when offenders think that the crime they are about to commit will make them feel more powerful, they are at high risk for recidivism.

  ◆ **Initial lapse into recidivism or preventing lapse or criminal thinking:** Again, it is helpful to distinguish between the process of recidivism and full recidivism.

  ◆ **Rule Violation Effect (RVE):** This is a shifting of self-perception, from being one way, e.g., "being clean and sober" to being "a drunk." The self-perception has to do with internal rules. "This is how I am." When that rule is violated, or thinking and behavior go against it, inner conflict or cognitive dissonance is experienced. Returning to an old view of self resolves the conflict. The strength of the effect of RVE depends on: 1) degree of cognitive dissonance - how much conflict and guilt are felt due to R&R; and 2) personal attribution—how much perceived personal weaknesses are attributed to the cause of R&R. With criminal conduct, RVE occurs when the person is into the process of recidivism, e.g., thinking about committing a crime. Our clinical experience indicates that greater degrees of cognitive dissonance and self-attribution of personal weakness result in more extreme episodes of relapse or recidivism.

  ◆ **Decrease or increase of self-control:** This emerges out of the RVE. A belief that an initial relapse is due to personal weaknesses can advance the process of R&R. This can lead to a belief in a loss of self-control or that the process is beyond one's control. However, an increase of self-control comes through using cognitive-behavioral skills to stop at the point of initial relapse (stop or change thinking and actions that lead to use) or stop at initial recidivism (change obsessive CC thinking). In either case, self-attribution (of personal weakness or competence) strengthens a decrease or increase of self-control.

  ◆ **Increase/decrease of chances for full R&R:** This outcome is directly related to level of self-mastery, strength of positive outcome expectations, RVE and perception of self-control.

We return to the example of soil erosion. The farmer has learned to prevent high-risk exposures to erosion. He uses skills to prevent the eroding away of the top soil. Fertilizers are added to refresh and build up the soil. The same is true with our lives. We build and use good mental and action skills to change our errors in thinking and to manage high-risk exposures. We refresh ourselves with healthy friends and positive activities. And we are always aware of the R&R warnings.

Adjunct Exercise: Go back to the example on page 117 of the *Workbook*. First have the group identify the high-risk exposures for this judicial client. Then, have the group identify how each of the steps on the left column of *Figure 19*, page 129, applies to this client. Then, go back through the story and have the group point out how each of the steps in the right column applies to the client.

▶ Present the **Skills in Preventing Relapse and Recidivism.** Using *Figure 20*, page 130, clients take another look at the pathways to R&R and learn to make cognitive-behavioral shifts from that pathway to taking ownership of change and preventing R&R. That shift is made through the use of skills to manage each of the high-risk exposures. Refusal skills are important in this process and are covered in *Session 17*.

   ◆ **Adjunct Exercise:** Have clients go back to *Worksheet 36*, page 114. In the right margin, have clients write down the money and time they **will save each year** by being crime-free and AOD free.

   ◆ **Exercise:** Clients write down, in the right margin of *Figure 20*, their own unique skills to handle the high-risk exposures.

   ◆ **Adjunct exercise:** Use the following example of a high-risk situation. **Larry runs into an old girlfriend with whom he used to do a lot of drugs. He just got out of prison for possession - his third conviction. He is committed to abstinence. His old girlfriend is also committed to not using. They start reminiscing. He suggests they get high, one more time for old-times sake.** Using *Figure 19*, page 129, as a guide, group members are asked to go through the two pathways for Larry and his old girlfriend: one that leads to R&R; and the other leading to prevention. Have clients think of outcomes based on ineffective and effective coping skills.

▶ Present **Your Relapse and Recidivism Prevention Plans,** using *Worksheets 41* and *42*, pages 131 and 132. Clients may want to use a separate notebook to have more room for recording. Have them be skill-specific. Have them continue this as homework. These plan's can serve as the client's R&R prevention guide as they continue in the program.

▶ Have clients update their *MSL*, particularly *Skills 23* and *25*, and their *MAP* and use the *SSC Change Scales* to rate their self-control over relapse and recidivism.

SUMMARY OF KEY CONCEPTS

▶ R&R prevention goals.

▶ R&R prevention skills.

▶ Pathways to prevention.

▶ R&R prevention plan.

SESSION CLOSURE AND GUIDELINES FOR THERAPEUTIC PROCESSING

For discussion focus, have clients look at the example of John's R&R process at the bottom of page 32 of the *Workbook*. First, have the group identify John's high-risk exposures. Then, do role playing around this example, with someone being John and other group members helping John develop an R&R prevention plan.

RATIONALE AND OVERVIEW

Many judicial clients will not experience cravings. However, clients who do not have cravings or urges for alcohol or other drugs may have desires or strong impulses to continue to engage in a drug use lifestyle, such as stopping off at the bar after work or getting together with a friend and getting high. These desires can place clients at high risk for recidivism. We briefly summarize the most salient issues around cravings and urges.

Our discussion here and the work in this session refers to cravings and urges that occur after the individual has made a decision to stop the use of drugs, or after a period of abstinence from AOD use. We are not referring to urges and cravings that occur during withdrawal which provides a strong negative reinforcement effect - using a drug to reduce or eliminate painful or negative withdrawal effects.

The literature provides a number of important findings regarding urges and cravings. **First,** there is a strong corpus of literature that supports these phenomena in drinkers and other drug users (e.g., Fisher & Harrison, 2000). **Second,** there is also support for a neural, neurochemical and cortical basis for addictions and the phenomena of cravings and urges (Borg, Czarnecka, Knande, Mossberg & Sedvall, 1983; Fromme and D'Amico, 1999; Masters, 2004; Volkow & Fowler, 2000).

Third, both conditioned reinforcement models (Li, 2000) and cognitive processing models (Tiffany, 1990) provide cognitive-behavioral understanding of cravings and urges and their prevention. **Finally,** one common finding is the lack of a strong association between **subjective reports** of cravings and relapse (e.g., Drummond et al., 2000). However, even though subjective reports may not predict relapse, Sayette et al. (2000) suggest that other factors congruent with a cognitive social learning model (cognitive processing, conditioned reinforcement, outcome expectancies) may be predictive of relapse.

Congruent with the cognitive social learning approach, Marlatt (1985a; Larimer, Palmer, & Marlatt, 1999; Marlatt & Witkiewitz, 2005) defines a **craving** as the degree of **subjective desire** for the positive effects of substance use and an **urge** as the **behavioral intention** to engage in use to satisfy the craving. Thus, a craving is the desire for the drug - drug-wanting. An urge is moving towards fulfilling that desire - drug-seeking.

One issue relevant to this session is that individuals who seek alcohol or other drugs, e.g., have cravings and urges, do so in the absence of drug reinforcement. That is, even though the individual no longer gains benefits from use, e.g., reduce tension, manage stress, relax, etc., the person still seeks drugs. This explains why some individuals will score high on the obsessive-compulsive drinking and disruption scales on the *Alcohol Use Inventory* (Horn & Wanberg, 1990), yet low on the psychosocial benefits scale: their urges and cravings are powerful even though no direct psychological or social reward is forthcoming.

Another issue related to the goals of this session is shifting from automatic processing that leads to drug use to the non-automatic processing as an attempt to discontinue use. Tiffany (1990) argues that automatic processing is often the basis of drug use behavior. Automatic processing (or automatic thinking) leads to the automatic behavior. Under this condition there is a low cognitive demand for drugs, and cravings and urges may not be experienced because the process of automatic thinking and action occurs quickly and effortlessly. If the automatic process is interrupted, such as when individuals make the conscious effort to halt the process and stop using drugs, the non-automatic process takes over and the person may experience cravings. The client gets in touch with the automatic thoughts leading to drug use. Cravings occur when the automatic thinking process is short-circuited.

This concept has important implications for treatment. Treatment in general and cognitive therapy in particular might, at least initially, increase cravings and urges (drug-seeking behavior) because treatment interrupts the automatic process which has allowed the person to go right to drug-using behavior without experiencing the drive for or urge to drink. Through enhancing the individual's cognitive awareness of and efforts to stop the thoughts that lead to use, the automatic thinking process now is replaced by the non-automatic process. This is why continual practice and application of thought restructuring (the non-automatic process) is essential so as to give the individual cognitive control over the drug-seeking behavior.

There are cognitive-behavioral approaches that can be used to manage drug-wanting and drug-seeking behavior and "cravings may be reduced or eliminated by focusing on the client's subjective biases and outcome expectancies for a desired substance" (Marlatt & Witkiewitz, 2005, p. 19). This is the objective of this session.

We can apply the concepts of drug cravings and urges to criminal conduct. Crime-wanting and crime-seeking are powerful determinants in moving offenders towards recidivism. The neurochemical and neural processes as a basis of cravings and urges seem relevant to CC. Masters (2004) suggests there may be a neural basis for criminal behavior. Impulsive behavior, the need for immediate gratification, seeking excitement, and arousal have neurobiological components. Since these are important aspects of most criminal behavior, they provide support for the CC-neural link. More important is the relevancy of the cognitive-behavioral component of cravings and urges for CC. As with substance use, CB approaches can be used to prevent crime-wanting and crime-seeking behavior.

Relative to both relapse and recidivism, cravings can be triggered by exposure to environmental cues (Daley & Marlatt, 2005; McKay, 1999; NIDA, 1993; O'Brien et al., 1998; Staiger, Greeley, & Wallace, 1999). Two rather opposite approaches have been used to manage these cues: **cue avoidance** and **cue extinction.** The former helps clients avoid overwhelming exposures to cues that can trigger relapse. The latter sets up cognitive and imagery conditions where the client is confronted by cues that can trigger relapse, and then taught skills to handle those cues.

As to the cue avoidance approach, *SSC* helps clients work at developing supportive environments and avoid overwhelming cues for relapse, particularly in the early stages of treatment when clients are learning skills to manage high-risk exposures. *SSC* recommends and works at helping clients restructure life-styles so as to avoid environments that are high-risk exposures for recidivism, e.g., high crime environments.

As to cue extinction *SSC* does not use formal and structured methods where several sessions are designed to use cognitive and imagery exposure to cues and triggers (e.g., NIDA, 1993). However, several of the cue extinction methods are integrated into the *SSC* curriculum. Clients do worksheets that identify high-risk situations and triggers that can lead to R&R. And, specific skills are taught and practiced to confront and manage high-risk exposures and triggers that can lead to cravings and urges. These steps are learned in this session.

The purpose of this session is to enhance self-mastery in preventing R&R by learning skills to:

▶ manage urges and cravings;

▶ resist social pressure to use or become involve in CC through refusal skills; and

▶ learn the skill of thought solutions in managing high-risk exposures.

SUMMARY OF CONTENT, PRESENTATION SEQUENCE AND GUIDELINES

Although new clients can enter at this session, it is recommended that it be presented as a sequence to *Sessions 15* and *16*. The following are guidelines for presenting this session.

▶ Present the objectives of the session and then facilitate the *CB Map Exercise* and *TAP Charting* sharing.

▶ **Adjunct Exercise:** Review the key concepts of *Sessions 15* and *16*, particularly *Figures 19* and *20* of the *Workbook*. Have a few clients share high-risk exposures they experienced this week and the R&R prevention skills they used.

▶ Present **Urges and Cravings** and their definitions. Go over the scenario of Harry, and ask clients to identify his high-risk exposures and his cravings and urges.

◆ Discuss the **triggers for cravings and urges for substances** (Kadden et al., 1992; Monti et al., 1989, 1995; Wanberg & Milkman, 1998; Wanberg, Milkman & Timken, 2005). **Adjunct Exercise:** Have clients share their own triggers for AOD use.

◆ Present the **triggers for cravings and urges for criminal involvement.** This may spark some discussion. Many judicial clients will resist the idea that they crave CC. Again, roll with the resistance and facilitate open and non-judgmental discussion in this area.

◆ Present the **steps and skills in coping with cravings and urges** (Kadden et al., 1992; Lloyd, 2003; Monti et al., 1989, 1995; Wanberg & Milkman, 1998). **"Toughing it out"** or **"urge surfing"** (Lloyd, 2003) is an effective component of CB treatment packages and is widely used with AOD dependent clients (Copeland et al., 2001). Although it has a quality of being an avoidance approach, it is an important component of the acceptance strategy of *Dialectical Behavioral Therapy* (Linehan, 1994; Hayes, Follette & Linehan, 2004). It does not fight the urge to make it go away; rather, it teaches clients how to experience the urge, to see its error or irrationality, look at the bad and negative consequences of following through with the urge, and the positive benefits of passing through the urge.

Exercise: *Worksheet 43*, page 137, lists clients' joys and pleasures and determines whether relapsing or going back to CC would cause them to lose those joys. This is an important exercise of *SSC* and a basic step in coping with and passing through cravings and urges.

◆ Have clients **practice managing cravings and urges.**

Exercise: Have clients take turns choosing an episode of craving and applying the management skills.

Exercise: *Worksheet 44*, page 137, sets a plan for dealing with cravings or urges to use or commit a crime. This plan can be used to manage future cravings and urges.

▶ Present **Refusal Skills and Steps to Handle Pressure to Use Drugs or Do a Crime.** There are internal and external high-risk exposures that are triggers for relapse (Daley & Marlatt, 2005). One of the most important is peer pressure and influence to use drugs or to get involved in CC. Learning to "just say no" to these pressures is usually not sufficient in the early stages of change. Difficult situations will arise, even if the client has been successful in avoiding old companions and the peer pressure they exert. When the bar becomes a "second home," or the neighborhood where past criminal associates hang out is comfortable and familiar, it makes resistance to this pressure more difficult. Peers are often unaware of a client's commitment to change. Some peers are acting out their anger when being forceful in getting clients to go back to the old ways. Some are just thoughtless. Different situations will present different difficulties. We draw on many resources in constructing a simple method to learn and put to practice refusal skills (Hester, 1995; Kadden et al., 1992; Monti et al., 1989, 1995; Smith & Meyers, 1995; Wanberg & Milkman, 1998; Wanberg, Milkman & Timken, 2005).

- Go over the specific refusal skills and steps.

- **Exercise:** Select a few group members to role-play refusal skills. Take the role-play scenarios from actual experiences of clients.

The refusal skills approach will depend on whether the relapse prevention goal is total abstinence or a harm-avoidance goal. Discuss this difference with clients.

It is important to be sensitive to cultural differences when teaching refusal skills. Eye contact, body language and degree of assertiveness may vary across cultural groups.

▶ Present **Thought Solutions in Preventing Relapse and Recidivism. Exercise:** Using *Worksheet 45,* page 138, clients practice thought solutions to each example. The thought solution model can be used throughout *SSC* in teaching coping skills.

▶ Present **Your Highway to Responsible Living or Collapse.** *Session 15* and *16* present pathways to R&R and R&R prevention. The R&R prevention plans developed in *Session 16* are maps for responsible living. *Figure 21,* page 136, adapted after Parks and Marlatt (1999), provides a summary highway map for those pathways and the R&R prevention plan. **Adjunct Exercise:** Have clients adapt *Figure 21* to describe their unique situation.

▶ Clients update their *MSL* and rate themselves on *Skill 6, Managing Urges and Cravings.*

▶ Have clients review and update their *MAP.*

▶ Clients use the *SSC Change Scale*s to rate their skills in handling cravings and urges and their level of refusal skills.

SUMMARY OF KEY CONCEPTS

▶ Urges and cravings.

▶ Triggers to R&R.

▶ Refusal skills and thought solutions.

▶ Highway map to responsible living.

SESSION CLOSURE AND GUIDELINES FOR THERAPEUTIC PROCESSING

Begin the closure group with an unstructured processing. Determine whether there are clients who may need individual sessions to resolve issues that cannot be dealt with in group, either because of time limitations or they are not appropriate for group.

MODULE 7

Steps, Stages and Skills for Self-Improvement and Change

This module raises the bar for the challenge to change. Clients who have been in *SSC* for several weeks are still struggling with whether they want to change. Most have decided: yes! For those clients, it is a matter of continuing to learn the specific skills and targets of change. For clients where this is the second module in *SSC,* there will be greater ambivalence and skepticism regarding whether they want to change. All of *Phase I* is a preparation for the commitment to change. This module is designed to clarify how the sequential process of change is made possible through self-disclosure, openness to feedback and taking responsibility for control over thoughts, feelings and actions.

THE PROCESS OF CHANGE

As often noted in this *Guide,* a key mantra of *SSC* is that change starts with self-disclosure, self-disclosure leads to self-awareness which leads to change. The effectiveness of this model for change has a long history of empirical support beginning with the work of Carl Rogers (Rogers, 1942, 1951).

Self-disclosure involves exploring and disclosing personal experiences and problems in the areas of desired change. The client becomes open to experience (Zimring & Raskin, 1992). Self-disclosure is facilitated through:

▶ Differential screening and in-depth assessment instruments; and

▶ Group discussions, worksheets, role playing and experientially based, interactive exercises. Providing generic information to clients around their core life-adjustment problem areas also enhances self-disclosures.

Self-disclosure is the pathway to self-awareness. Self-awareness is facilitated by giving clients feedback and more specific information around their own unique problems and life difficulties. The source information for this feedback comes through self-report assessments, session interactive discussions, worksheets and exercises.

Finally, although self-awareness leads to change, change is based on more than self-awareness. It involves understanding how change takes place, understanding roadblocks to change, learning and practicing specific change skills, and constructing a plan with specific targets for change.

This process builds self-efficacy (Bandura, 1977b), the self-expectation of successfully performing behaviors that lead to certain outcomes. "Self-efficacy is the final common pathway through which different treatments are considered to produce change" (Kazdin, 1983, p. 279).

CHANGE IS NATURAL

It is a common and popular belief that most substance addicted persons and offenders cannot change. Portrayal of the "alcoholic" and drug addicted persons in movies and theatrical productions, for example, usually leaves the viewers with the inevitability of the "alcoholic" relapsing. Portrayal of offenders usually depicts one outcome: going back to a life of crime.

Yet, change is built into life. Life is dynamic and ever changing. Plato saw reality as unchanged and based on fixed forms behind what we observe (Collingwood, 1949; Tarnas, 1991). This cosmology or worldview persisted up to the Copernican revolution and the development of Newtonian physics.

The thinking of Locke, Hume and Kant shook us out of this static view and brought us to the view that our understanding of the world and reality grows and changes as we observe, study and gather data (Tarnas, 1991). Kuhn (1970) concluded that scientific paradigms are in constant shift with the gradual accumulation of conflicting data resulting in a paradigm crisis and a new creative synthesis (Tarnus, 1991).

In the view of the constructivist, we are constantly recreating, changing and organizing our experiences and realities through our cognitive interpretations (Delia, O'Keefe & O'Keefe, 1982). **If change is built into the nature of reality, then substance abusing offenders can change.**

STAGES OF CHANGE

There is empirical evidence to support the theory that "behavior change involves a process that occurs in increments and that involves specific and varied tasks" (DiClemente & Velasquez, 2002, p. 201). This evidence was used to construct what DiClemente and Prochaska (1985, 1998; Prochaska & DiClemente, 1992) call the transtheoretical model of change. Within this model, research has isolated specific stages of change across various problem behaviors, and has demonstrated the efficacy of the model to provide a structure for change (DiClemente & Velasquez, 2002).

Chapter 3 of this *Guide* provides a description of the DiClemente and Prochaska stages and an adaptation of this model by the authors to generate a three stage model that is used in the process and structure of *SSC*. These three stages are described in *Chapter 2* and for *SSC* clients in this session of the *Workbook.* They are:

▶ Challenge to change;

▶ Commitment to change; and

▶ Ownership of change.

ENHANCING MOTIVATION TO CHANGE

As discussed above, change is natural, and this is our greatest hope. Yet, change that results in positive outcomes for the individual and the community often requires a formal and structured treatment effort. In *Chapter 2*, we discuss motivation enhancement approaches to increase client engagement in the process of growth and change, utilizing the approaches of client-centered treatment and motivational interviewing (Miller & Rollnick, 2002). The most salient elements of motivational enhancement are briefly summarized.

▶ **Therapeutic stance:** This is based on the core elements of client-centered therapy: warmth, empathy, genuineness and positive regard (Rogers, 1951, 1957).

- **The therapeutic alliance.** This builds on the therapeutic stance and involves a collaborative relationship, affective bonding, rapport building, and a mutual understanding and sharing of the intervention goals between the client and treatment provider.

- **Reflective confrontation in managing resistance and ambivalence.** This involves: encouraging clients to share thoughts and feelings of resistance and defensiveness; and using reflective-acceptance skills to help clients hear their resistance and ambivalence. The key principles in this motivational enhancement task are: avoid argumentation (Miller & Rollnick, 1991); and develop discrepancy and roll with the resistance (Miller & Rollnick, 2002).

- **Enhancing interest in change.** This is enhancing the internal desire to change. Lasting change occurs when clients attribute change to themselves (Kanfer, 1970, 1975, 1986). In the end, the client makes the changes. Yet, key principles that help in enhancing self-attribution are: support self-efficacy; express empathy; and emphasize personal responsibility for change (Miller & Rollnick, 2002).

CONSTRUCTING THE CHANGE ENVIRONMENT

The **challenge to change** is done within the context of a therapeutic alliance and a collaborative relationship that is trust based. It is client-centered in that the ultimate decision for change rests with the judicial client.

We cannot force clients to change. We can only construct a change environment that is non-threatening but challenging. The FRAMES model (Miller, 2006a, p. 146), discussed in *Chapter 2*, provides guidelines in constructing that environment.

- **FEEDBACK** of personal risk or impairment.
- **RESPONSIBILITY** for change.
- **ADVICE** to change.
- **MENU** of alternative change options.
- **EMPATHY** through counseling skills.
- Facilitation of client **SELF-EFFICACY** or optimism.

In a similar way, Freeman and colleagues (1990) emphasize that criminal conduct must also be recognized as counter productive; that, in the long run, prosocial behavior is in the offender's best interest.

PROVIDER GOALS FOR THIS MODULE

- Give clients an understanding of the steps and stages of change and their current stage of change in specific areas.
- Facilitate understanding of the barriers to change.
- Facilitate learning and practicing cognitive change skills.
- Facilitate the identification of the targets for change and develop a plan for change.
- Assist clients in identifying their strengths that support change.

RATIONALE AND OVERVIEW

In the *Introduction* to the *Workbook,* a three-stage model was presented to explain how people change and showed that the three phases of *SSC* are built around these stages. One purpose of this session is to review these stages of change within the context of the *SSC CB model* for change illustrated in the *SSC CB Map* (*Figure 2* above, *Figure 2,* page 14 in the *Workbook*).

The three stages of change - **Challenge, Commitment and Ownership** - incorporate all of the stages in DiClemente and Prochaska's transtheoretical model of change (DiClemente & Prochaska, 1985, 1998; Prochaska & DiClemente, 1992; DiClemente & Velasquez, 2002).

This session continues to challenge clients to change by having them evaluate the stage they are in relative to changes in the areas of substance abuse and criminal thinking and conduct. Clients also identify the barriers and roadblocks that they put in the way of change.

SUMMARY OF CONTENT, PRESENTATION SEQUENCE AND GUIDELINES

As clients progress through *Phase I,* they will become more committed to changing the thought habits that lead to their self-defeating CC and AOD behavior. Most judicial clients are initially resistant to and/or ambivalent about change. Clients who take this session earlier on in *SSC* will have a higher level of resistance and ambivalence.

Clients who have been in the program for a longer period of time are positive role models for the more resistant clients. Here are this session's presentation guidelines.

▶ Start with presenting the objectives and key concepts of the session. Then, facilitate the *CB Map Exercise* and sharing the *TAP Charting.*

▶ Present **Review the Key to Change - the CB Map** including the four thought structures (i.e., expectations, attributions, appraisals, decisions) and the concepts of attitudes, values, and beliefs. Have clients give examples of these and practice labeling their thought structures and their underlying attitudes, values and beliefs.

Exercise: When doing the outcome-change exercise in this section, it is helpful to use *Worksheet 7,* page 42, as the model, putting it on a wall display and making copies to distribute. Remind clients that they choose what behaviors and actions they take part in.

▶ Present **Stages of Change: Where Are You Now?** Review the stages of change using the material in the *Workbook Introduction* (pages 2-4) and in this session.

Where do clients see themselves as to their stage of change? Some remain resistive to change and avoid self-evaluation. Many clients have met the challenge to change and are open to receiving feedback about their own AOD use and their CC. Some have probably not taken any firm action to change. They may be just beginning to consider the existence of problems and some awareness that they have the potential that they can overcome them. Others are fully committed and have clearly made changes that have persisted.

Exercise: Using *Worksheets 46* and *47,* clients rate themselves on each of the key elements that identify each stage of change for substance abuse and CC. The provider then rates each client on these worksheets.

Explain that clients may be in different stages for different areas of change. They may have higher ratings for CC than for substance abuse. Clients who are eager to change will often overrate themselves. How realistic are their change ratings? How do the clients' ratings compare with the provider's ratings?

▶ Present **Barriers or Roadblocks to Change.** Resistance to and ambivalence about change is experienced by most people, regardless of the nature of their problems or degree of disturbance. Part of resolving this resistance is understanding the barriers to change. One barrier is that change is just too uncomfortable or too much of a burden. "Getting tired of pleasing people" can be another barrier. Or, "it's not worth the effort." Most often, resistance to change involves **thinking barriers,** some of which are provided in the *Workbook* for clients to check if they fit them (adapted from King et al., 1994; Wanberg & Milkman, 1998). The use of these barriers is reinforced particularly for the person who does not want to change.

Adjunct Exercise: Have clients take one thinking barrier or roadblock in the *Workbook* and give examples of how they use it to block change. Have them give alternative ways of thinking that do not block change. Have the group look for patterns of thinking that are barriers to change. For example, **excuse thinking** is one pattern. "Can't exercise today, not enough time." "Can't tomorrow, have to work late," etc.

Discuss **making the effort.** Clients must perceive some reward in change. Changing one thought or behavior that keeps a client out of trouble makes life better. There is reward in that. They then look for another thought or behavior to change to make it better. The reward may be feeling the power of self-control. They are now "practicing change" and, with practice, they overcome one of the greatest roadblocks to change: **not making the effort** (Bush & Bilodeau, 1993, pp. 3-64). Challenge clients to be honest if they are not really trying to change. Recognizing the **long-term negative consequences** of AOD abuse and CC is essential to embracing the challenge to change.

▶ Have clients update their *MSL* based on the skills learned or practiced in this session, which include changing thinking errors.

▶ Clients also update their *MAP.* Remind them to do their *TAP Charting.*

▶ Have clients complete the *SSC Change Scale* on the degree to which they are resisting change.

SUMMARY OF KEY CONCEPTS

▶ The *CB Map*

▶ Stages of change.

▶ Barriers or roadblocks to change.

SESSION CLOSURE AND GUIDELINES FOR THERAPEUTIC PROCESSING

Have clients discuss what they think and feel about the comparisons between their own ratings and the ratings of the provider. Have clients share what stages of change they see themselves in for both substance abuse and criminal conduct. Have the group give each client feedback if they agree with the client's self-assessment.

RATIONALE AND OVERVIEW

The basic premise of CB treatment is that our thoughts, attitudes and beliefs lead to emotional and behavioral outcomes. Positive outcomes come through self-control. Our thought processes and structures determine self-control. As discussed in *Chapter 8,* the foundation for the cognitive model was laid by Kelly's (1955) definition of personal constructs and the building blocks provided by the work of Beck (1963, 1964, 1976, 1996) and Ellis (1962, 1975; Ellis & Harper, 1961).

An important part of change and self-control is learning to connect specific thoughts with these outcomes. As Leahy puts it, "before you can challenge and change thoughts, you have to understand how thoughts affect your feelings" 2003, p. 9). Once we understand these thoughts and connections, and how they take place, then we can change our thinking to get different outcomes.

One objective of this session is to have clients learn the skill of connecting thoughts, emotions and behaviors. Resources for the methods in this session to guide clients in connecting thoughts with feelings and actions came from several sources, including Leahy's (2003) technique of explaining how thoughts create feelings, Ellis's (2003) work on cognitive restructuring, and the authors' previous work (Wanberg & Milkman, 1998).

Changing thoughts is not enough to get consistent and productive outcomes. We need to change the beliefs and attitudes that underlie our thoughts. This is much more difficult since these beliefs are often so deep we are unaware of them. They are often hidden - the blind or unconscious part of the *Johari Window.* They operate automatically. These core beliefs underlie thought, emotional, and behavioral patterns.

Focusing on core beliefs is also referred to as schema-focused therapy (Beck, 1996; Leahy, 2003). Again, this approach is based on the foundational work of Kelly (1955) and the seminal work of Beck and Ellis. Beck sees core beliefs as consisting "of the most sensitive component of the self-concept (e.g., vulnerable, helpless, inept, loveless, worthless) and the primitive view of others (rejecting, hostile, demeaning)" (1996, p. 14). There are core beliefs that underlie an individual's pattern of substance abuse ("I have a right to drink, I've had a rough life") and criminal thinking ("The world has screwed me over and I'll take what I can get").

Another objective of this session is learning to connect core beliefs with automatic thoughts and then to generate a list of master core beliefs that lead to AOD problems. The first task and step in learning change is identifying thoughts that lead to certain emotions and behaviors. We will never know all of the thoughts that lead to feelings and actions, but we can learn the skill of identifying them. Once we have become proficient in identifying the thought antecedents to our emotional and behavioral outcomes, we can begin to identify the core beliefs that underlie these thoughts. In *Session 21,* clients do more in-depth work and practice identifying these core beliefs using the thought mapping and belief searching model.

The real power of change comes when we master mental or cognitive change skills. Another objective of this session is to have clients begin to learn a core set of mental change skills. The efficacy of these skills has considerable empirical support. This session introduces clients to some of the most salient self-control and cognitive change skills. A number of resources were used to develop the list of self-control and cognitive change skills in the *Workbook* (e.g., Bush & Bilodeau, 1993; Kaplan & Laygo, 2003; Leahy, 1996, 2003; McMullin, 1986, 2000; Monti et al., 1989; Monti et al., 1995; Wanberg & Milkman, 1998).

SUMMARY OF CONTENT, PRESENTATION SEQUENCE AND GUIDELINES

This is one of the most important sessions in *SSC* with respect to identifying and changing thoughts, attitudes and beliefs. Clients do further work on these skills in *Session 21*. In subsequent sessions, the provider will want to refer back to these skills, and from time to time reinforce their use in exercises in subsequent sessions. These skills are also basic to the cognitive self-control and change work done in *Module 8*. Here is the presentation sequence for this session.

▶ Start with presenting the objectives and key concepts of the session. Then, facilitate the *CB Map Exercise* and sharing the *TAP Charting*.

▶ Present the section on **Specific Thoughts That Produce Emotions and Behaviors. Exercises:** The role-play exercise around the example of John and *Worksheet 48,* page 148, give clients practice in learning how to connect specific thoughts, feelings and behaviors. Clients fill in the missing thoughts, feelings or behaviors in *Worksheet 48.*

▶ Present **Seeing How Specific Beliefs Produce Specific Automatic Thoughts.** This is the schema-focused therapy approach (Beck, 1996; J. Beck, 1995; Leahy, 2003; Young, 1994; Young & Flanagan, 1998). **Exercise:** Using *Worksheet 49,* page 149, clients practice identifying thoughts that can emanate from core beliefs often associated with persistent problem behaviors, e.g., AOD addiction or CC. Notice that items 3 and 6 are beliefs that can lead to thoughts that change these problem behaviors.

▶ Present **Your Core Beliefs and Life Themes.** Another schema-change approach is to identify core beliefs related to problem behavior. **Exercise:** *Worksheet 50* provides a start for this task. The provider will want to refer back to this *Worksheet* in subsequent sessions and have clients add to it.

Adjunct Exercise: Using a cognitive-behavioral testing approach (Dobson & Hamilton, 2003), have clients put these beliefs to test in two ways. **First,** clients validate core beliefs by giving examples of beliefs that lead to specific criminal acts. **Second,** clients restructure the core beliefs so that they will lead to positive thoughts that generate positive emotional and behavioral outcomes. This validates that belief change. For example: a core belief might be: "I can't live without drugs." A validation of this belief is that the person views self as a life-time user. A restructuring of this belief might be: "But I can live without drugs." A validation of this belief change is to see the specific periods that he/she has gone without drugs. Have clients practice testing the restructuring of the beliefs they listed in *Worksheet 50.*

▶ Present **Mental-Cognitive Skills for Self-Control and Good Outcomes.** These cognitive restructuring and self-control skills are referred to as "self-talk" methods (e.g., Kendall & Bemis, 1983; Meichenbaum, 1977) and have been an integral part of the cognitive restructuring approach. This is instructing the self to think or act in a certain way or to change a target thought or behavior. Self-talk is "thinking inside yourself," or "what you say to yourself." It is deliberate thinking. A formal use of self-talk is called self-instructional training (Meichenbaum, 1977). The *Workbook* provides only a select list of these skills. McMullin (1986, 2000) provides a comprehensive list of cognitive restructuring techniques that is an invaluable resource for the provider. Have clients practice each of these self-talk methods in group and apply them to their core beliefs in *Worksheet 50*. *Session 21* refocuses on these skills. These skills will be discussed along with their reference resources. Help clients feel the power of these change and self-control skills.

Thought stopping or thought braking (e.g., J. Beck, 1995; Burns, 1980, 1989, 1999; Bush & Bilodeau, 1993; Donohue & Cavenagh,, 2003; Wanberg & Milkman, 1998) is a mainstay in cognitive restructuring. Have clients add to the list of thought stopping skills in the *Workbook*.

Countering or arguing against the thought (e.g., McMullin, 1986, 2000) makes the thought weaker. It works best when one argues against an error in thinking or an irrational thought every time it occurs.

Shifting the view (perceptual shifting). McMullin (2000) provides discussion of this method. It works to change our mental sets or how we see things inside and outside ourselves. Getting caught up in destructive (to ourselves and others) beliefs and thoughts often leads to problem behaviors. Shifting our view allows us to see the other side of the belief or thought. Studies by Hobson and McCarley (1977) indicate that not only does our brain take in and store information and tries to understand the information it takes in, but it also changes how we see that information. The brain transforms the information and turns it into ideas, beliefs, and story themes. A good example of how the brain can change what it brings in is in *Figure 22,* page 146, of the *Workbook,* Boring's (1930) famous "old woman-young woman" visual shift picture. Holding on to the belief **"I'm taking what I can get - no one's done a damn thing for me"** can lead to problem behavior. Changing this belief requires shifting the view to **"There have been people who have done good to me."**

Thinking "their position." (Bush & Bilodeau, 1993; Wanberg & Milkman, 1998). This is one cognitive component of empathy and prosocial behavior. This involves thinking "how would I feel if I were in their place." This increases respect for others. Judicial clients have difficulty consistently using this skill.

Thinking "taking responsibility." This is another component of empathy and prosocial attitudes and behaviors. *Responsibility* is the basis of taking ownership of our actions.

Planting positive thoughts. It's the negative thoughts that often lead to bad outcomes that need to be replaced with positive thoughts. For this to work, it has to be done every time. However, some negative thoughts can be helpful if they are used to problem solve. But not if they are dwelled on. Positive thinking must be realistic thinking in order to be effective. *Sessions 22* and *23* focus on negative thinking.

Exaggerate or overstate the thought (paradoxical intent). This technique was developed by Victor Frankl (1959, 1980) when he was in the German concentration camps. Overstating the thought or paradoxical thinking forces us to look at the error in thinking or the irrational belief. It is like "typing the error" to realize you make the error and then you correct it.

Conditioning. Making our thoughts weaker or stronger (McMullin, 1986, 2000). This is rewarding or punishing your thoughts. This is difficult for judicial clients who resist change. They may not want to see the negative consequences of their drug use or CC, since this is a challenge to give them up. As well, judicial clients tend to see themselves as the victim of others, but not victims of themselves.

Logical (sensible) study. Going to court with your thoughts (McMullin, 1986, 2000) requires turning thoughts back into self and internalizing, a difficult task for judicial clients. It requires accepting that one's thinking is irrational or distorted. This task is particularly difficult for the impulsive person since it requires thought deliberation.

Relaxation skills. Managing stress is the focus of *Sessions 25* and *26.* Relaxation skills enhance self-control, and help shift from automatic to non-automatic thinking. It gives "breathing space." Spend time teaching clients these skills. It is recommended that the provider have training in the use of these relaxation skills. Clients are advised that they will receive additional relaxation skills instruction in *Phase II, Session 26.* In this session, they learn the following four relaxation skills.

- **Progressive muscle relaxation** (see Benson, 1975; Bernstein & Carlson, 1993; Ferguson, 2003; Jacobson, 1938; Norris & Fahrion, 1993);

- **Calm scene relaxation.**

- **Passive body focus or what we call autogenic training** (Benson, 1975; Linden, 1993); and

- **Deep breathing** (Benson, 1975; Fried, 1993; Hazlett-Stevens & Craske, 2003): This can be done at any time in most situations. Every time you come to a stop sign, take a deep breath.

Some clients may find certain relaxation techniques more helpful than others. Encourage clients to select one(s) that works best for them. For clients who have experienced trauma in association with letting down their guard, relaxation exercises may elicit memories that trigger anxiety and fear. Providers should be sensitive to these issues and encourage clients to find their own levels of comfort with relaxation exercises.

Adjunct Exercise: Have volunteers role-play the following examples and then have another person use one of the interventions described above. For the **scene** examples, have two people role-play with one giving the intervention response. Then, let several group members give responses. For the **thought** examples, have one person think out loud and another person do his/her "self-talk" out loud using one of the interventions. We call this **doubling.** Discuss which intervention works best for the various scenes or thoughts.

Scene: Your boss has just caught you arriving late to work. He tells you this is the last time he will tolerate tardiness. What do you do? Intervention example: RESPONSIBILITY What are you doing to contribute to the situation?

Scene: You **are** the boss and you have just caught an employee arriving late to work. What do you do? Intervention example: What if I were in THEIR POSITION?

Scene: You are approached by a dealer who offers to sell you drugs. How do you respond? Intervention example: COUNTER OR ARGUE AGAINST THE THOUGHT.

Scene: You and your mother-in-law have never gotten along. She is at your house for dinner and finds something wrong with everything. Intervention example: PLANT A POSITIVE THOUGHT.

Thought: "Taking a few drinks is about the only way a person can really let down and relax." Have the **double** use an intervention or method to change the thought.

Thought: "Every boss is usually going to end up screwing you over and taking advantage of you."

Thought: "I'm worried about whether I'm going to get fired."

Thought: "I feel depressed about my job. It's getting me down."

Adjunct Exercise: Clients practice the relaxation skills.

▶ Have clients update their *MSL, Program Guide 1,* based on the skills learned and practiced in this session: mental self-control skills, relaxation skills, changing negative thoughts. Clients also update their *MAP, Program Guide 3.* Remind them to do their *TAP Charting.*

▶ Have clients complete the *SSC Change Scales* on the degree to which they are resisting change.

SUMMARY OF KEY CONCEPTS

▶ Connecting thoughts, feelings and behaviors.

▶ Hooking core beliefs to thoughts.

▶ Core beliefs.

▶ Mental-cognitive skills for self-control and change.

SESSION CLOSURE AND GUIDELINES FOR THERAPEUTIC PROCESSING

Have clients discuss their core beliefs and how these beliefs are related to their substance abuse and criminal conduct.

RATIONALE AND OVERVIEW

A theme throughout *SSC* is that self-disclosure leads to self-awareness and self-awareness provides a vision for change. An important part of the self-disclosure and self-awareness process is an in-depth assessment of life adjustment issues and problems. The purpose of the in-depth assessment is to identify and select target areas for change. Clients define these change targets through the use of all of the *Progress and Change Evaluation (PACE) Monitor* instruments completed at intake, admission, and during *SSC*. This includes the following resources.

▶ The *Adult Substance Use Survey - R* (ASUS-R) profile or other differential screening instruments.

▶ Profiles from the *Adult Self-Assessment Profile* (AdSAP) and the *Rating Adult Problems Scale* (RAPS) or other in-depth differential assessment instruments administered during the initial stages of treatment.

▶ *Adult Self-Assessment Questionnaire* (AdSAQ) *Profile,* or other measures of motivation and treatment readiness.

▶ *Worksheet 4, List of Problems to Work On, Workbook* pages 19-20.

▶ Self-assessment worksheets pertaining to AOD patterns and CC, and psychosocial problems.

▶ Results from the Client Progress Rating (by client and provider).

▶ The *Master Profile (MP), Program Guide 2,* page 292 in the *Workbook.*

Clients use all of the above resources to complete the *MP.* The *MP* identifies the specific life-problem areas in which change is needed. The *MP* is completed within the first month in *SSC.*

Once the target areas for change are determined, the next step is to develop the *MAP, Program Guide 3,* page 295 in the *Workbook.* This is the client's **plan for change.** The *MAP* lists: the specific problem areas; the thoughts, beliefs and actions that need to be changed related to these problem areas; the specific methods to be used for change; and the outcome or results.

Clients begin their initial work on the *MP* and *MAP* during intake and orientation. They are enhanced and updated in each session based on emerging self-awareness and changing needs. Clients are expected to complete a preliminary *MP* and *MAP* by the end of the first month or 8th session of *SSC.* The *MP* and *MAP* guide the work clients do in *SSC* and are the basis for the development of an *(ITP) Individualized Treatment Plan* by the provider. The *MAP* should project the treatment needs for clients for *Phases II* and *III.*

The *MAP* provides evidence of clients' adherence to the goals and objectives of *SSC.* It can provide a system of accountability for judicial oversight of treatment progress. Satisfactory completion of *Phase I* sessions and successful completion and sharing the results of the *MAP* in the treatment planning process qualifies the client for *Phase I* graduation and entry into *Phase II.* Before starting this session, most clients will have completed their *MP* and *MAP.* **As well, the provider will have conducted an individual session with each client to review all of the *PACE* results and to complete, to date, their work on these two program guides.**

The **purpose of this session** is for clients to review their *MP* and *MAP* and to have them share their most salient findings in group, including targets and areas of change and their plan for change. **New clients do not start *SSC* with this session.** Since *Sessions 18* and *19* are presented in sequence, all clients will have had at least two sessions before entering *Session 20.* It will be necessary to meet with some clients within two weeks of starting the program to review their *MP* and *MAP.*

SUMMARY OF CONTENT, PRESENTATION SEQUENCE AND GUIDELINES

The preparation for this session begins at *Orientation*. It includes an individual session with the provider.

▶ Start with presenting the objectives and key concepts of the session. Then, facilitate the *CB Map Exercise* and sharing the *TAP Charting*.

▶ Present **The *Johari Window* as a Guide for Self-Assessment.** Most clients will have been introduced to this window in *Session 11,* page 99. Show clients how this fits in with the self-assessment process of sharing and receiving feedback.

▶ Present **Your Targets and Steps for Change.** First go through the steps which represent the four columns in the *MAP.* Some targets may be specific thoughts, such as planning a crime. Others may be a general area such as improving relationship with spouse. **Adjunct Exercise:** Ask for volunteers to provide an example of a target thought or behavior from their *MAP* they want to change and then go through the four steps.

   ◆ **Pick the target** - a specific problem from their *MAP.* For **thought change** targets, have clients identify the attitudes and beliefs behind the thought target.

   ◆ **Set a goal.** Use the "think for a change" metaphor. What do clients want their new thoughts and behaviors to be (goals)? Are the goals realistic? Clear and concrete? Goals require a gradual change and time to make change. What high-risk exposures prevent achieving these goals?

   ◆ **Choose a method** or skills to change the targets. This is the **intervention.** *Session 18* focused on specific methods to change target thoughts. The power of the CB method is that clients can begin NOW to make changes in their target thoughts.

   ◆ **Have clients evaluate their efforts and outcome.** Are they working?

▶ Present **Your Master Profile,** *Program Guide 2,* page 295 in the *Workbook.* Clients have completed the *MP.* Now, have them go back and rate themselves again. **Exercise:** Have them share their ratings with the group at their level of comfort. Did their ratings change? How did their ratings differ from those done on them by the provider (other-report data)?

▶ Present **Your Plan for Change - The Master Assessment Profile (MAP).** Clients update their *MAP* in group. When doing the exercise of having clients share the most important parts of their *MAP,* explain that they share at their level of comfort.

▶ Have clients update their *MSL, Program Guide 1.* Remind them to do their *TAP Charting.*

▶ Have clients complete the *SSC Change Scale.*

SUMMARY OF KEY CONCEPTS

▶ *Johari Window.*   ▶ Targets and steps for change.

▶ *Master Profile (MP)* and *Master Assessment Plan (MAP).*

SESSION CLOSURE AND GUIDELINES FOR THERAPEUTIC PROCESSING

Since considerable therapeutic processing and sharing occur during the session, take a few minutes at the end to have clients share an area that they are working on that needs more attention. Have then share whether they need individual work on these areas.

Clients who have finished the 20-session *Phase I* program should be praised and reinforced for their performance and given a certificate of completion. For most judicial clients, this is a major accomplishment. Few judicial clients complete a program of self-improvement and change as represented by the *SSC* program.

For clients in the closed group setting, the *Phase I Closure Session* will be done in the total group. For an open *SSC* setup, time should be set aside for clients in their last *Phase I* group to bring their *Phase I* journey to a close. They will be asked to do the closing reflections and sharing exercise as outlined in the *Workbook* on page 152. This exercise involves:

▶ Sharing their perception of the change and progress they have made, including the most important parts of their autobiography.

▶ Receiving feedback from group members as to their perception of the client's progress and change.

A *Phase I* review and closure individual session is held with clients to evaluate their progress and change and received feedback from the *PACE* (*Process and Change Evaluation*) instruments they completed during the program. In that session, clients will be asked to make a decision as to whether they plan to continue *SSC* into *Phase II*. The *Phase I Review Guide* (PI-RG) is used during this closure session. **Providers should carefully review the guidelines** for this session found on pg. 129 of this *Guide*.

The following *PACE Monitor* instruments will be completed by the client and the provider as part of the client's *Phase I* progress and change evaluation.

▶ Client Program Response - Client (CPR-C)

▶ Client Program Response - Provider (CPR-P)

▶ Self-Evaluation Questionnaire - (SEQ)

The provider will also score the CPR-C and CPR-P and chart the change process for each client. Clients

then receive feedback as to the change profile and feedback as to how the client did in the overall *SSC* program.

Clients will then rate themselves on the *SSC Change Scales* (pg. 152 in the *Workbook*) as to their stage of change regarding AOD use patterns and their stage of change for CC thinking and conduct.

Many judicial clients referred to *SSC* will be required by the judicial system to proceed into *Phase II*. However, it is best if the provider approaches this juncture with the idea that clients do have some choice as to whether to proceed into *Phase II*.

An honest discussion should transpire regarding what the client wants to do. However, judicial requirements may rule against this "client choice" approach. Clients who simply do not want to continue into *Phase II* should be given alternative options and choices.

The *Phase I* experience will impact on most judicial clients with respect to self-improvement and change. The degree of impact will certainly depend on the extent to which clients utilize the skills and concepts of *SSC* and commit themselves to change. Continuing into and completing *Phase II* will increase the probability of actualizing more lasting change.

Making the completion of *Phase I* a positive experience for clients fits in with the overall spirit of *SSC*: That clients have the capacity and have been given the skills and concepts to make permanent and positive changes in their lives and to engage in:

▶ Living an AOD-free life

▶ Living a crime-free life

▶ Responsible living

PHASE II
commitment to change

Strengthening Skills for Self-Improvement, Change and Responsible Living

Change starts with a **challenge.** Ongoing change requires a **commitment.** *Phase II* represents a commitment to change and is action-oriented treatment. It is based on two important processes:

▶ Enhancing commitment to change through more intensive feedback using both therapeutic and correctional confrontation;

▶ Enhancing cognitive self-control skills and prosocial attitudes and actions towards others and the community.

The feedback process confronts clients with their story and dilemma, their problems and dysfunctions and their antisocial and pathological responses to the world. It is the foundation for getting clients to take action on that story. Through the feedback loop, the defensive system opens up and allows greater reception for self-understanding. Clients receive feedback around their change, or lack of change, and their motivation and willingness to change. Both therapeutic and correctional confrontation are important components of the feedback process.

The second process upon which *Phase II* is built is enhancing cognitive self-control and relationship skill-building. The test for commitment is whether clients resolve the ambivalence to change and take action to learn and put into practice, on a daily basis, the skills that enhance self-control and responsible living. Time in each session is devoted to getting feedback from and giving feedback to clients on how they are doing with this test. *Phase II* is structured around strengthening skills in three focal areas:

▶ Cognitive or mental self-control and change;

▶ Social and interpersonal relationships;

▶ Prosocial and community responsibility.

These skills bring about shifts in the client's cognitive sets and behaviors in order to prevent relapse and recidivism. Thinking and behavioral changes are practiced and reinforced.

"It is caring about others and living in harmony with our community that makes us human."

-AUTHOR UNKNOWN

SUMMARY OF *PHASE I*

Phase I, the **Challenge to Change,** took clients through the stages of contemplation and preparation for change (DiClemente & Prochaska, 1985, 1998; Prochaska & DiClemente, 1992) and prepared clients for a **commitment to change.** *Phase I* is about building a core knowledge of the critical areas of change and learning the rules, tools and targets for change. There is a strong emphasis on self-disclosure and increasing self-awareness of the client's own unique problems. Thoughts and feelings are identified and explored in greater depth. Clients learn the *CB Map* and specific skills to changing thinking, attitudes and beliefs. Roadblocks to change are clarified. Communication skills are learned to improve relationship outcomes. Clients learn the pathways to relapse and recidivism and to R&R prevention. A plan for change - the *MAP* - is developed that identifies targets and methods to implement change. Clients view their progress through the *PACE Monitor.*

Providers in *Phase I* develop a working relationship with clients within the framework of a non-judgmental, empathy-based and caring environment so as to maximize self-disclosure and self-discovery. Providers utilize the principles of motivational enhancement. Confrontation is reflective and non-judgmental. There is maximum use of the skills of:

▶ responding attentiveness,

▶ encouragers to share, and

▶ feedback clarification.

Prochaska (1999) stresses that judicial clients who are in a contemplative or preparation stage of change and placed in an action (commitment to change) type treatment are at greater risk for intervention and treatment failure. Even though some *SSC Phase I* clients are in the commitment to change stage, it is oriented towards a contemplative-preparation (challenge) treatment approach.

PROVIDER SKILLS AND TREATMENT STRATEGIES FOR *PHASE II*

▶ **Assessment: The *PACE Monitor* and the *MP* and *MAP*** developed in *Phase I* provide a basis for the feedback process to help clients sort out their own patterns of criminal behavior, AOD use, and psychosocial problems that need change. This assessment is ongoing and continues throughout *Phase II.*

▶ **Invitation to share,** a core provider skill in *Phase I,* is continually used in *Phase II.*

▶ **Reflective feedback skills** which include reflection and clarification of thoughts and feelings, paraphrasing, summarization, and change clarification are utilized in *Phase I* but are important skills in *Phase II.* Through these skills, clients sort out the feelings, thoughts and behaviors involved in dysfunctional and pathological responding and help clients develop a clear perspective of needed growth and change (assisted by the *MAP*).

▶ **Confrontation feedback skills** which include both *therapeutic and correctional confrontation.* These skills not only confront clients with antisocial and drug abuse problems, but also confront clients with the changes that need to be made. The *MAP* is an important component of the change confrontation process.

▶ **Change reinforcement skills:** When changes occur, the provider utilizes reinforcement skills to strengthen changes in thinking and behavior.

▶ **Facilitation of the learning and practice** of mental self-control, relationship and community responsibility skills.

- **Group facilitation skills:** *Phase II* represents an increase in the use of group interaction and processing to achieve program objectives. The utilization of these skills, as outlined in *Chapter 7,* will help the provider achieve this purpose.

- **Action therapy approaches:** This involves role playing, doubling, actiongrams, action dramas, and role reversals. These skills are discussed in *Chapter 7.*

- **Teaching and facilitation of the *CB STEP*** method, which focuses on the positive outcome component of the *CB Map.*

PROVIDER GOALS AND OBJECTIVES FOR *PHASE II*

- Facilitate a higher level of commitment to changing criminal thinking and conduct and AOD abuse patterns.

- Help clients learn and practice the skills of mental self-control, relationship building and moral responsibility.

- Help clients see how AOD abuse and CC interact and reinforce each other and feed into further involvement in both criminal thinking, conduct and AOD abuse.

- Help clients make substantial changes in cognitive sets and in behaviors to prevent R&R and strengthen prosocial actions and AOD abstinence or AOD harm avoidance.

- Help clients function in a cooperative yet self-directed manner, assisting others to complete the tasks of *Phase II.*

FOCUS ON POSITIVE ACTIONS AND OUTCOMES - THE *STEP* APPROACH

Phase I focused on helping judicial clients identify and change thoughts and behaviors that lead to negative outcomes - substance abuse and criminal conduct. The *SSC CB Map* provided the bases for understanding the process and pathways of how various cognitive responses (thoughts, attitudes and beliefs) to external and internal events lead to emotional and behavioral outcomes. Almost every session in *Phase I* started with the *CB Map Exercise* to see how specific situations or events resulted in these outcomes, regardless of whether they were negative or positive. In some of the exercises, clients were asked to change thinking so as to get positive outcomes.

Phase II will continue to use the *CB Map Exercises* to center on having clients identify the thoughts and emotions that come from high-risk exposures which potentially lead to substance abuse (relapse) or criminal conduct (recidivism). However, *Phase II* will also use the *SSC STEP* method that focuses on the positive change process of the *CB Map.* That process is spelled out in *Figure 4* below, and in *Figure 23,* page 155 in the *Workbook.*

In the 1950s, Gordon Allport, one of the founders of modern personality theory, in his book *Becoming,* pointed out that individuals in treatment make progress towards health in proportion to the lessening of their resentment, hostility, and hatred (negative outcomes), and in proportion to the increase of feeling accepted and wanted by treatment providers, family members, and their life affiliations (1955, pp. 32-33). He then went on to say: "We have paid more attention to the pathology of becoming than to its normal course, focusing upon disease rather than health, upon bad citizenship rather than good, and upon prejudice rather than tolerance and charity" (p. 33).

Implied in Allport's thinking is that the treatment process needs to attend not just to problem behavior, but to adaptive and positive behaviors and outcomes for the individual (egocentric focus) and the individual's relationship to others and society (sociocentric focus). Certainly, *Phases II and III* will continue focusing on problem thinking and behavior that lead to disruptive outcomes for the client and society. But, the *STEP Method* is a primary *Phase II* and *III* platform which facilitates a thought pattern that generates positive outcomes such as prosocial behavior and drug-free living.

PREPARATION SESSION FOR *PHASE II*

For the closed group structure, the *Preparation Session* for *Phase II* can be done in the ongoing *SSC* group. For open group structures, this session can be done in a small group of clients who have completed *Phase I*, or on an individual basis.

Remind clients that change takes place in steps and that these steps are like a spiral. We may slip back to earlier stages of change, but never back to where we started. Also, review the three overarching goals of *SSC*: 1) preventing relapse; 2) preventing recidivism; and 3) living a comfortable and meaningful life without the use of drugs and criminal involvement.

The outline and content for *Phase II* orientation are found in the *Workbook*, pages 154 through 156, *Preparation Session for Phase II*. Take time to present the *STEP Method*, which focuses on the **thinking change** process that will lead to positive outcomes. Whereas every session in *Phase I* started with the *CB Map Exercise*, in *Phase II* some sessions start with the full *CB Map Exercise* and others start with *STEP*. The *Preparation Session* for *Phase II* will take up to one hour. *Phase II* involves three modules and 22 two-hour treatment sessions. Completion time depends on the number of *Phase II* sessions are offered each week.

Note: There are a number of critical reference pages that are referred back to several times in *Phases II* and *III* which clients should mark for easy referral. These are pages: 14 *(CB Map)*; 35 (errors checklist); 71 (MB-ICC); 99 *(Johari Window)*; 92 (antisocial thinking errors); 131 and 132 (R&R prevention plan); 143 and 144 (Rating on Stages of Change); 160 *(Table 6)*; 180 (Table 7); 184 (anger management skills); and the program guides, pages 291, 292, 295, and 300. Those referred back to only once do not need to be marked.

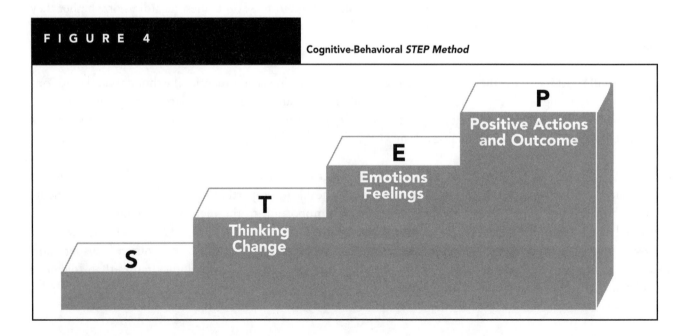

FIGURE 4

Cognitive-Behavioral *STEP Method*

P Positive Actions and Outcome

E Emotions Feelings

T Thinking Change

S

MODULE 8

Mental Self-Control: Managing Thoughts and Emotions

OVERVIEW

An important objective that guides our work with judicial clients is facilitating the development of self-control that leads to positive outcomes for the client, others and the community. *Phase I* introduced clients to a number of cognitive control and change skills and gave them practice experience in applying them to everyday living. *Phase II,* and more specifically, *Module 8,* moves clients into the action and commitment stage of change with respect to utilizing mental self-control skills.

GOALS OF *MODULE 8*

The general goal of *Module 8* is for clients to further develop and put into action cognitive skills that facilitate change and self-control over thoughts, feelings and behaviors. The provider's objectives are to help clients learn the concepts and skills to:

▶ Manage and change negative thoughts, attitudes and beliefs;

▶ Change and correct errors in thinking;

▶ Manage anxiety and stress;

▶ Manage and regulate anger;

▶ Manage and change cognitions that lead to guilt and depression; and

▶ Increase positive emotional outcomes.

PRESENTATION LOGISTICS

The ideal delivery strategy for this module is to present the eight sessions in sequence, starting with *Session 21.* For agencies using the open group format, this is not practical. For example, if *Phase II* sessions are presented on a once-a-week basis, some clients would have to wait as long as seven weeks to start *Module 8.* Thus, *Module 8* is designed so that there are only two no-entry points: *Sessions 23* and *26. Sessions 22* and *23* are presented in sequence; as are *Sessions 25* and *26.*

OPTIMAL COGNITIVE-EMOTIONAL STIMULATION

This module focuses on the intrapersonal self-control of thoughts and emotions related to negative thinking, thinking errors, stress, anger, guilt and depression. The literature has identified these internal states as being major triggers for AOD relapse. When these are at high to very high levels of arousal or stimulation, they are considered to be high-risk exposures that can lead to relapse and recidivism.

Yet, there are optimal levels of these cognitive and affective states that can contribute to good performance and positive outcomes. To illustrate this concept, we refer to the well-known Yerkes-Dodson Law (1908), which points out that we are better able to cope with the cognitive-affective stimulation of negative thinking, stress, anger, guilt and agitation when they are at low to moderate levels. At these levels, these arousals can contribute to good performance and positive outcomes.

For example, low to moderate stress can contribute to good performance; but high to very high levels of stress, or very low or no stress at all, can lead to poor performance or bad outcomes. Low to moderate levels of cognitive and affective guilt can contribute to prosocial and responsible behavior; but little or no cognitive or affective guilt can lead to antisocial behavior. High or very high levels of guilt can constrict normal interactions and lead to unsatisfactory relationships with others.

Figure 5 illustrates the application of the Yerkes-Dodson Law to the various thoughts and emotions that are the focus of this module. We will refer back to this Law when focusing on these internal cognitive and affective states. We use a scale of zero to 10 to illustrate different levels of cognitive and emotional arousal, with zero to 3 being none or very low (inadequate), and around eight to 10 being high to very high (excessive).

Several cautions should be heeded when using the Yerkes-Dodson Law. First, the optimal level of arousal will vary from person to person. For some, an anxiety arousal of six may result in excessive stimulation and bad outcomes. For others, an anxiety arousal of six is required for good performance. Second, optimal arousal depends on the tasks. Difficult tasks may require an anxiety arousal of seven or eight. Third, optimal arousal depends on the specific type of emotions. An anger arousal of six or seven may result in bad outcomes, where a stress arousal of six or seven may be optimal for good performance. We do not use the arousal model to evaluate optimal levels of depression. Depression can be triggered by high levels of stress and anxiety, as seen from the perspective of the opponent process model (Shipley, 1987). Yet, some depression can be a way of managing anxiety and stress.

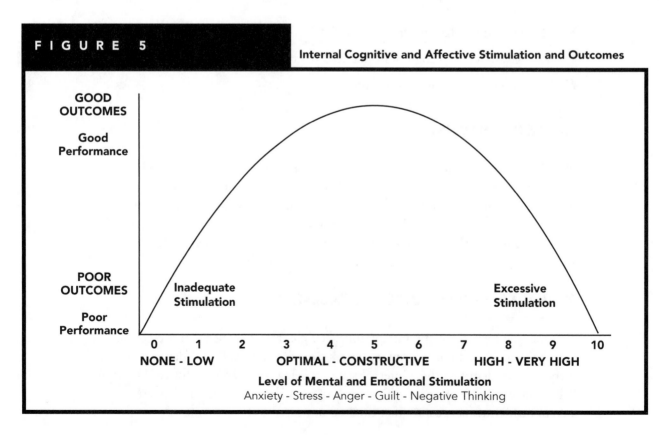

FIGURE 5 — Internal Cognitive and Affective Stimulation and Outcomes

RATIONALE AND OVERVIEW

This session focuses on practicing cognitive change skills and learning thought mapping and belief exploring. Long-term positive outcomes are based on changing core beliefs.

SUMMARY OF CONTENT, PRESENTATION SEQUENCE AND GUIDELINES

Present the session by following the topics in sequence in the *Workbook* and using the following guidelines.

▶ Start with a *STEP Method Exercise* and share the *TAP Charting*.

▶ Reviewing **How Thoughts and Beliefs are Hooked Together** will involve reviewing work done on *Worksheets 49* and *50,* page 149 in the *Workbook.*

▶ **Thought Mapping and Belief Exploring** maps the thought chain that leads down to or up from core beliefs. Go over *Figure 24* and then illustrate *Worksheet 51* on a flipchart or chalkboard, having a client volunteer an example. Then, have clients do *Worksheet 51,* using a core belief they identified in *Worksheet 50,* page 149. Resources used for the development of this method were Leahy's (2003) technique of Vertical Descent and McMullin's work on finding beliefs and belief grouping (2000).

▶ The **Mental Skills for Self-Control and Good Outcomes** presents the skills learned in *Session 19* and summarized in *Table 6.*

◆ Note that the skill of acceptance, based on the work of Hayes (2004), is new. The concepts of acceptance and mindfulness in cognitive-behavioral change and therapy are presented in *Chapter 4.*

◆ McMullin (2000) conceptualizes the practice of cognitive change skills in four ways: visual, auditory, role-playing, diary research, and environmental practice. *Figure 25,* page 159 of the *Workbook,* provides a graphic representation of these practice modalities, with daily living representing the environmental component. For example, thought stopping can be practiced by: visualizing a STOP sign; hearing by shouting STOP or thinking a thought out loud and a group member says STOP; writing down STOP; or acting it out by role playing.

◆ When doing the exercises in this section, have clients apply these four methods - **see, hear, act** and **write.** Review the *STEP* method with clients before doing the last exercise in this section - role-playing events that lead to thoughts about using drugs or doing a crime.

▶ Have clients update their *MSL* and their *MAP* and do their *TAP Charting.* Have clients complete the *SSC Change Scale* on their ability to use mental control skills.

SUMMARY OF KEY CONCEPTS

▶ Thought mapping and belief exploring.

▶ Mental cognitive restructuring and change skills.

SESSION CLOSURE AND GUIDELINES FOR THERAPEUTIC PROCESSING

Some clients may be overwhelmed with the challenge of this session. Give them room to share their negative thinking and practice using skills to change that thinking to positive thoughts.

RATIONALE AND OVERVIEW

Negative Thinking and Cognitive-Behavioral Therapy

Negative appraisals and thinking, and negative schemas and beliefs have been important focuses in the CB treatment of depression, anger, anxiety and other disruptive psychological problems, such as posttraumatic stress disturbances (e.g., Burns, 1999; Clark & Ehlers, 2004; Leahy, 2003; Scher, Segal, & Ingram, 2004). Many errors in thinking are based on negative schemas. Negative thoughts are often automatic thoughts. Criticisms of self and others are a part of the negative thinking schemas.

An important component of Beck's theory of depression (see Scher, Segal & Ingram, 2004) is the activation of cognitive structures or schemas that view the self, others and the world in a rigid and unrealistically negative manner (Beck, 1963, 1972, 1987). Beck defines the negative cognitive triad as comprised of negative views of self, the world and the future (Beck, 1976; Weissenburger & Rush, 1996).

Burns (1999) makes an even stronger case for negative thinking as the basis of depression and painful emotions: "Every bad feeling you have is the result of your distorted negative thinking. Intense negative thinking always accompanies a depressive episode; or any painful emotion for that matter" (p. 28).

Discerning Realistic Negative Thinking

The difficulty with addressing negative thinking is that of discerning to what extent the negative thoughts are realistic or true, constructive or functional? Moorey (1996) asks the question: "What about negative thoughts that are a realistic interpretation of the situation in which people find themselves?" (p. 463). To ignore or change negative thoughts before determining if they are real or functional could decrease self-confidence and self-efficacy.

"The sky is really black. We're going to get a tornado." Although this is a negative view at the moment, it does alert us to be prepared for a potentially grave danger. Some negative thinking can lead to good outcomes and good performance. This relates to the Yerkes-Dodson Law (1908) on optimal arousal.

An important step in changing negative thinking is to test the negative thought as to whether it is true or false, realistic or irrational. Let's test the statement "She always blames me." This statement cannot be proven to be true. In fact, "there are times when I screw up and she doesn't blame me." Thus, we can prove it to be false. Thus, it is irrational. All-or-nothing statements (Leahy, 2003) ignore information or evidence. We shut the door to changing them. Yet, we spend a lot of time focusing on all-or-nothing statements that cannot be proven true and are irrational.

Thus, determining whether a negative thought is irrational is important in deciding whether or not to change the thought. The word rational is derived from ratio, meaning perspective or proportion (Leahy, 2003). Thus, a rational view involves having a realistic perspective of negative thoughts.

Importance of Negative Thinking in AOD and CC Treatment

Negative thinking becomes a problem and a target for change when it creates an extreme view of self or the world and consequently leads to emotional and behavioral outcomes that are harmful to self or others. It also becomes a problem for treatment focus when it leads to relapse and recidivism.

Marlatt and Gordon's (1980) early studies of relapse showed that negative emotional states were the strongest predictors of relapse in a sample of male alcoholics (Marlatt & Witkiewitz, 2005). Many other studies have provided evidence for a strong link between negative emotions and relapse to substance use and an underlying motive for using substances (see Marlatt & Witkiewitz, 2005, p. 16, for a comprehensive list of references supporting this finding).

Kadden and Cooney (2005) see negative thoughts as automatic thoughts that are high-risk for drinking. They see the identification, management and change of negative thinking as an important component of cognitive skills therapy.

Criminal thinking is negative thinking. It creates negative outcomes and goes against the positive and prosocial purpose of individuals and society. The view that "the world has screwed me over therefore I am justified in hurting others" has high potential to lead to behavior that goes against the good of others and "screws over" other people. "Hurt or be hurt" is a core belief of many offenders that can lead to recidivism.

Goals of This Session

Negative thinking can become a way of life to which people may cling. Negative thinking will lead to negative emotions that are generally accompanied by tension from which we want to escape. The escape may take the form of drinking, spending time with criminal associates or committing a crime. Negative thinking can set the conditions for CC. The results of this behavior will subsequently lead to negative feelings about oneself including reduced self-respect, anger and depression.

With depressed clients, our goal is to focus more on the negative self-view part of the Beck triad (1972, 1996). However, with judicial clients, in addition to a negative self image, it is the **negative view of the world and the future** that will be strong contributors to engaging in criminal conduct.

The goal of this session is to help clients understand negative thinking, how negative thinking can lead to relapse and recidivism, and have clients identify their own dysfunctional negative thoughts. *Session 23* focuses on the management or changing of negative thinking. *Sessions 22* and *23* are presented in sequence.

SUMMARY OF CONTENT, PRESENTATION SEQUENCE AND GUIDELINES

When introducing this session, make the point that not all negative thinking is bad, unrealistic or irrational. As discussed above, some negative thinking is realistic and functional. Thus, an adjunct exercise that is added to this session is having clients develop the skill to identify realistic negative thinking, or realistic parts to negative thinking and beliefs.

Present the session by following the topics in sequence in the *Workbook* using these guidelines.

▶ Start with a *STEP Method Exercise* and use an event (situation) that could lead to negative thinking. Clients share the *TAP Charting*. Review the session objectives.

▶ When presenting **How Negative Thoughts and Beliefs Lead to Problem Outcomes,** use these guidlines.

- Present the issue that some negative thoughts are realistic and functional and can lead to good outcomes, using material discussed above. Use the Yerkes-Dodson Law (1908) to illustrate how some (optimal) negative thought arousal can lead to good outcomes or performance. **The Yerkes-Dodson Law is not covered in the *Workbook*. This is a good time to present this concept to clients with some discussion.**

  - <u>**Adjunct Exercise:**</u> Have clients identify negative thoughts that are not realistic or that are irrational. Usually these are all-or-nothing statements. "He always puts me down." Then have clients identify some of their negative thoughts that are realistic and functional and that have led to good outcomes. Use the tornado example above.

▶ The main purpose of the section **Recognizing Negative Thoughts and Beliefs** is to help clients be mindful of their negative thinking. Mindfulness involves self-disclosure, helps people to be flexible and can lead to acceptance and to change. It is a process of looking **from thoughts** and not just **at thoughts** (Hayes, 2004, p. 20). An important exercise in this section is linking negative thinking to thinking errors.

▶ The purpose of the section on **How Negative Thinking Can Lead to R&R** is to link negative thinking to R&R.

  <u>**Adjunct Exercise:**</u> Discuss how realistic negative thinking can prevent R&R. "When I go out with those guys, I usually get into trouble." This is preventive negative thinking.

▶ The **Negative Thought Mapping in Search of Negative Beliefs** will need some introduction for clients who have not had *Session 21*. Providers may want to make an enlarged copy of *Worksheet 52* to put on the wall in the therapy room for reference in other sessions.

▶ Have clients update their *MSL* and their *MAP* and do their *TAP Charting*.

▶ Have clients complete the *SSC Change Scale* on their ability to see and identify their own negative thoughts.

SUMMARY OF KEY CONCEPTS

▶ Negative thinking.

▶ Linking negative thinking to R&R.

▶ Linking negative thoughts to negative beliefs.

▶ Mindfulness and acceptance.

SESSION CLOSURE AND GUIDELINES FOR THERAPEUTIC PROCESSING

Have clients share the degree to which negative thoughts and beliefs have contributed to their problems. Also, have them discuss whether negative thinking may have led to positive outcomes or reduced negative outcomes.

RATIONALE AND OVERVIEW

Session 22 is a prerequisite to this session and new clients do not enter *SSC* at *Session 23*. *Session 22* provided guidelines and practice in recognizing and being mindful of and putting labels on negative thinking and beliefs. In that session, we looked at how mindfulness is related to acceptance and that a key goal of acceptance therapy "...is to support clients in feeling and thinking what they directly feel and think already ... and to help clients move in a valued direction, with all their history and automatic reactions" (Hayes, 2004, p. 17). A concrete approach in mindfulness and acceptance is to use the skills of negative thought mapping and negative belief searching, presented in *Session 22*.

Realistic Negative and Positive Thinking

Norman Vincent Peale wrote a famous book in 1952 called *The Power of Positive Thinking*. Although written from a religious perspective, and at the time, looked upon by psychologists and behavioral theorists with considerable skepticism, it set forth many concepts basic to cognitive therapy and the use of changing thinking to get positive outcomes. One could say that his work represents one of the first consistent presentations of the use of cognitive processes to bring about change. He notes that his book "..is written with the sole objective of helping the reader achieve a happy, satisfying, and worthwhile life" (1952, p. viii). Quite significant is that he quotes the famous statement by William James, who he sees as "one of the very few wisest men America has produced" (p. 201):

> "The greatest discovery of my generation is that human beings can alter their lives by altering their attitudes of mind."

Peale makes it clear that positive thinking must be realistic, and states "I certainly do not ignore or minimize the hardships and tragedies of the world, but neither do I allow them to dominate" (p. viii).

In the guidelines to *Session 22,* it was stressed that it is important for clients:

▶ To understand that **realistic negative thoughts** and beliefs can be functional and lead to good outcomes;

▶ To differentiate realistic negative thoughts and beliefs from those that are destructive and lead to harmful outcomes for the individual and society; and

▶ To see that **realistic positive thinking** is what is powerful, not just positive thinking. Leahy (2003) makes the point that "Cognitive therapy is not a process of bolstering defenses or proselytizing about 'the power of positive thinking.' Rather, it demonstrates the power of realistic thinking - that is, to the extent that we can know reality" (p. 2).

Goals of *Session 23*

The main goal of this session is to give clients skills and practice in managing, stopping or changing negative thoughts and replacing them with positive ones. The primary skills will be those of cognitive restructuring. These skills will be used in managing and dealing with many different thoughts and emotions. It will only be with repetition and practice that these techniques are learned. It will take participants time to notice a change, reflected in a more positive outlook on life.

SUMMARY OF CONTENT, PRESENTATION SEQUENCE AND GUIDELINES

Present the session by following the topics in sequence in the *Workbook*. Here are the session presentation guidelines.

▶ Start with the *CB Map Exercise,* having one client provide an example of a recent event.

▶ Have a few clients briefly share their *TAP Charting.* Here are some important issues to keep in mind when asking clients to share their *TAP.*

◆ Sharing should be within each client's comfort zone.

◆ Have them reflect back on the *TAP Charting* they did in *Phase I* to see the difference in their openness and willingness to self-disclose. Even though clients did the *TAP Charting* throughout *Phase I,* they will continue to be guarded in disclosing their thoughts about AOD use or actual use, or thoughts about engaging in criminal conduct. They will see such disclosures as making them vulnerable to punishment and sanctioning.

◆ The *TAP Charting* can put providers in the position of assuming a correctional role when such charting reveals activities that violate the client's legal requirements, e.g., AOD use violating the terms of parole or probation. Again, at the time clients enter correctional treatment, and during the process of treatment, providers need to make it clear that they wear both the therapeutic and correctional hat - they are an advocate for both the client and the community. Discussing this issue with the group from time to time will help clarify both client and provider responsibilities.

◆ As discussed earlier in this *Guide,* clients in a prison setting may choose not to respond to (or be unwilling to share in group) the *TAP* question of whether they were where they could have used alcohol or other drugs because they will see such disclosure as putting them at risk of harm from other inmates. Again, stress that they should disclose within their own comfort zone. Even though such disclosure must be kept confidential, as required by the Federal confidential guidelines, other clients in the group may discuss such disclosure with other inmates in the system. This could result in putting the disclosing client at risk of harm in the prison community. The *TAP* question is an important part of helping clients managing high-risk exposures, and part of the process of preventing R&R. Thus, it should be dealt with if there is assurance that disclosing clients will not be put at risk of harm. Also, it should be dealt with therapeutically, and not at a correctional (sanctioning) level.

▶ Review the negative thought mapping and negative belief searching approach presented and practiced in *Session 22.* **Adjunct Exercise:** Provide clients with a copy of *Worksheet 52,* page 164, and have them practice negative thought mapping and belief searching.

▶ Present **There Is Power in Realistic Positive Thinking.** Discuss the difference between unrealistic and realistic positive thinking. Again, use the Yerkes-Dodson Law to show there is optimal realistic positive thinking. Realistic positive thinking seldom leads to poor performance. Unrealistic or pollyanna positive thinking can lead to poor performance and outcomes. This is also a good time to review the concept of self-efficacy or self-mastery. It is the self-perceived ability to handle high-risk exposures that can lead to relapse or recidivism. The provider will want to review this concept as it is presented in *Chapter 4,* pg. 75.

▶ Present **The *STEP* Method in Changing Negative Thinking.** First, review this method. Then, apply *STEP* to changing negative thoughts and beliefs with examples provided by one or two clients.

▶ Present **Positive Thought Arming,** having clients complete *Worksheet 54.* These are standby positive thoughts that clients will want to refer back to when experiencing negative thinking. **Exercise:** When doing the exercise in this section, the provider may have clients identify a past negative outcome related to an episode of substance abuse or a criminal act. This exercise furthers the use of *STEP* in getting positive outcomes. Have clients reflect on these questions as they present the event leading to a negative outcome:

- ◆ What is the difference between the negative thinking that led to the negative outcome and the **thinking change** that can lead to a positive outcome?

- ◆ What is the difference between the emotions that led to the negative outcome, and the emotions resulting from the **thinking change**?

▶ **Adjunct Exercise:** Have clients work on identifying **realistic negative thoughts** and beliefs that can be functional, and avoid bad outcomes or lead to good outcomes. Often, these are thoughts about the consequences of AOD abuse, the consequences of committing a crime, loss of someone close, fear of an accident, getting well during a prolonged illness, etc. Use the following steps:

- ◆ **First,** have clients think of circumstances where it is appropriate to have negative thoughts, e.g., not having enough money at the end of the month to pay the bills.

- ◆ **Second,** have clients practice mindfulness and acceptance of the negative thoughts - just experiencing them, e.g., "I'll lose my car."

- ◆ **Third,** sort out the irrational negative thoughts from those that are realistic and can help solve the problem. Irrational negative thought: "I'll never get ahead. I'll lose everything." Realistic negative thought: "I'm going to live within my means, even though I won't be able to buy a better car for some time." Have clients pick one or two thoughts that are useful, helpful and can solve a problem, even though they are negative.

- ◆ Use *STEP* to identify some positive thoughts and outcomes that can come from realistic negative thinking. Does the positive thinking about the negative thoughts produce better emotional outcomes and potentially better action outcomes?

▶ Clients update their *MSL,* particularly *Skill 7, Changing Negative Thinking.*

▶ Have clients evaluate their *MAP* and do their *TAP Charting* for the week.

▶ Clients complete the *SSC Change Scale* on their ability to change negative thoughts and beliefs.

SUMMARY OF KEY CONCEPTS

▶ The *STEP Method* to get positive outcomes from negative thinking.

▶ Power in realistic positive thinking.

▶ Realistic negative thinking.

▶ Positive thought arming.

SESSION CLOSURE AND GUIDELINES FOR THERAPEUTIC PROCESSING

Use the closure session to have clients evaluate where they are at this time in the program. Some clients may feel discouraged about their progress. Have the group help them change these negative thoughts to positive thinking that will give better outcomes.

Some clients may be overly positive and optimistic. These clients may be apt to ignore the high-risk exposures of their everyday living. Have clients again review these high-risk exposures.

RATIONALE AND OVERVIEW

Thinking errors or cognitive distortions are thought habits that are powerful determinants of behavior and are a critical focus in the treatment of substance abuse, antisocial thinking, and criminal conduct. They are automatic to the point that we accept them, even without facts to support them (Bush & Bilodeau, 1993). They are "self statements that operate as permission-givers for engaging in offensive behaviors, and that function to bring the client from trigger or cue to a high-risk situation" (Brunswig, Sbraga & Harris, 2003, p. 324).

Thinking errors are based on core beliefs that have long-standing sociocultural and familial roots and are supported by strong social cognitions. This tends to give thinking errors a "factual" basis or "legitimate" roots. For example, offenders who grew up in an antisocial family adopt core antisocial beliefs such as "we deserve more," "the world's screwing us over," or "it's OK to steal, just don't get caught."

Antisocial role models become a powerful reinforcer of cognitive distortions. Mashek et al. (2004) found that connectedness to the criminal community was associated with endorsement of criminogenic beliefs (see Aron et al., 2005). Thus, offenders often do not see cognitive distortions that lead to criminal conduct as distorted thinking. As Yochelson and Samenow (1976, 1977) state, they are required and justified by the offender to live his or her kind of life and are basic to the day-to-day transactions of the offender.

Brunswig, Sbraga and Harris (2003) see the identification and challenging of thinking errors and cognitive distortions as a special focus in relapse prevention (pp. 324-325). Their treatment of thinking errors in relationship to relapse, using some of the key concepts of Marlatt (1985b), is also applicable to the treatment of antisocial and criminal thinking. They describe three cognitive distortions that are part of the Marlatt relapse prevention model and dealt with in the R&R sessions in this program.

▶ **Seemingly Irrelevant Decisions (SIDs).** Thinking error: "I'll just stop by and see my 'old buddy' and have a couple. No harm to that" (the "old buddy" is still into criminal thinking and conduct).

▶ **Problem of Immediate Gratification (PIG).** This is acting to get immediate rewards and detaching from the negative consequences that can result from that act. An offender, seeing a pair of leather gloves in the store impulsively puts them in his pocket because "I need those for work."

▶ **Rule Violation Effect (RVE).** RVE involves viewing a lapse as being so bad that "I might just as well get drunk." Brunswig et al., (2003) note that this thinking error "...recognizes a small failure, focuses on it as evidence that behavior control is not possible, and indulges in immediate positive reinforcement that comes with enacting the problem behavior" (p. 325). "I stole those gloves; just as well steal some beer."

Thinking errors increase the risk of relapse and recidivism. They support and perpetuate the *Mental-Behavioral Impaired Control Cycle (MB-ICC)* and the *Criminal Thinking and Conduct (CTC) Cycle*. A good example of the validation of the automatic and habitual nature of thinking errors is impaired driving. The average offender drives 800 to 1,000 times before being arrested. The thinking errors behind impaired driving, e.g., "I haven't had that much," are powerfully reinforced by the fact of not getting caught.

Cognitive distortions are an important focus in *Phase I*. In *Session 3*, clients rated themselves across a list of common thinking errors and then evaluated whether these thinking errors were a part of their AOD abuse or criminal conduct (*Worksheet 5*, page 35 in the *Workbook*). In *Session 10*, clients looked at specific cognitive distortions that support criminal conduct. They practiced replacing those thinking errors with thoughts that can lead to prosocial outcomes (*Worksheet 25,* page 92). The purpose of this session is to do further work on identifying the common cognitive distortions and to help clients identify the errors they use that can lead to AOD abuse and CC. The *CB STEP Method* is used as a tool in changing thinking errors. One of the most powerful thinking errors - entitlement - is explored.

SUMMARY OF CONTENT, PRESENTATION SEQUENCE AND GUIDELINES

The following are some presentation guidelines for this session.

▶ Begin by reviewing the *MSL* and *MAP* and inviting group members to share their *TAP Charting.*

▶ Review the MB-ICC (*Figure 8,* page 71) and the CTC correction cycle (*Figure 14,* page 90).

▶ Present **Review Your Work on Thinking Errors.** When clients re-rate themselves on *Worksheet 5,* page 35, have them do it based on the time they were involved in CC. Then, have them check those errors that they have changed. Using *Worksheet 25,* page 92, clients add or enhance prosocial thinking and attitudes that counter antisocial thinking errors.

▶ When the **Common Thinking Errors** section is presented, have clients share all of the thinking errors they can at this point, and put them on a chalkboard or flipchart.

▶ When presenting **Correcting Thinking Errors Using the *CB STEP Method,*** use the cognitive change skills in *Table 6,* page 160, to illustrate the **Thinking Change** component of *STEP.*

▶ The section, **Practice Changing Thinking Errors** uses the mental change skills in *Table 6, Workbook* page 160, to change the thinking errors in *Worksheet 5,* page 25 and *Worksheet 25,* page 92. Example: for the thinking error **Just Deserts,** "They had it coming," use the mental change skill, **Their Position,** to correct the error. The thinking change might be, "They're not doing anybody any wrong, and it'd hurt them to get ripped off."

▶ **The Entitlement Trap** is a thinking error that is a powerful determinant of AOD abuse and CC. Offenders often see themselves as victims, being treated badly, short-changed, and "deserving more." Many judicial clients have been mistreated or abused as children, adolescents and young adults. However, the fact of their negative circumstances does not justify harming others (i.e., The Entitlement Trap). Take time to do the exercise on discussing and role-playing the offender story in this section. Have clients use *Worksheets 5,* page 35, and *25,* page 92, to identify the kind of thinking errors used by the offender.

▶ Clients update their *Master Skills List (MSL),* particularly *Skill 7, Changing Negative Thinking.*

▶ Using the *SSC Change Scale,* have clients rate their ability to change thinking errors.

SUMMARY OF KEY CONCEPTS

▶ Thinking errors.
▶ *CB STEP Method* in changing thinking errors.

SESSION CLOSURE AND GUIDELINES FOR THERAPEUTIC PROCESSING

Have clients share the thinking errors that are most apt to lead them to relapse and recidivism. Close with having each client share how they see themselves adjusting at this time in their lives.

RATIONALE AND OVERVIEW

As discussed in the introduction to *Module 8,* emotional or psychological disturbances found among judicial clients can be viewed as either primary or secondary. A primary psychological disturbance or disorder exists relatively independent from, yet interacts with, substance abuse and criminal conduct.

SSC assumes that most judicial clients will have experienced or are experiencing secondary psychological and emotional issues that increase their risk of relapse and recidivism. These are problems that are interactive with or are consequences of involvement in criminal conduct and substance abuse. Stress, anxious moods, guilt, self-blame, anger and depressed moods are common with persons recovering from a pattern of substance abuse and misuse or a history of criminal conduct. The focus of this session and *Session 26* is stress and anxiety. The following discussion and cited sources provide the resources for the development of this session.

Stress: A Double-Edged Sword

For the person who uses alcohol or other drugs, stress is a double-edged sword. First, stress is an important reason why people use alcohol or other drugs. The literature indicates that emotional distress and anxiety are important factors that lead to AOD use and abuse. The stress and emotional discomfort that people experience on a daily basis are often handled by AOD use. People use drugs to reduce stress, to "not feel bad." That is only one edge of the sword. The other edge is that stress can result from the negative consequences related to the use of alcohol or other drugs.

The same can be said of criminal conduct. Stress is an important reason why many offenders commit crimes. Anxiety related to lack of money, lack of a sense of security and importance, loneliness and isolation, etc., is often relieved through criminal behavior. Subsequently, a consequence of criminal conduct is anxiety and fear, albeit, being arrested and jailed.

Major Events and Triggers Producing Stress

There are three major life-events that produce stress (e.g., Bloom, 1985; D'Zurilla & Nezu, 2001).

- Major negative life events such as death of a loved one, divorce, loss of job, major illness.
- Daily negative life events such as not getting work done, daily demands of family life and marriage.
- Major positive events such as getting married, a new job, salary raise, having a baby.

One of the main triggers of AOD relapse identified in the literature is unpleasant emotions such as anxiety, sadness, depression or anger (Wanberg & Milkman, 1998). Feelings of guilt and depression should be considered high-risk emotions, for they may lead to relapse and a vicious cycle of repeated failures.

Biopsychological Tension

One source of tension that can lead to relapse is the rebound that occurs in the mental-physical impaired control cycle, described in *Session 7.* The chemical imbalance in the system created by the prolonged use of and withdrawal from drugs creates system tension or stress that can be relieved by further AOD use.

Cravings and urges, presented in *Session 17, Workbook* page 133, also create biopsychological tension. Cravings are described as drug-wanting or drug-desiring thoughts and feelings. Urges are defined as drug-seeking behaviors and are actions towards fulfilling the cravings. Cravings and urges are high-risk thoughts, feelings and behaviors. They increase once a commitment is made to AOD abstinence and to not being involved in criminal conduct. Cravings and urges are sources of stress. They create an imbalance or tension in the biopsychological system and thus can become triggers for relapse and recidivism.

Part of the tension or imbalance in the biopsychological system created by cravings and urges is the conditioned-response process (Li, 2000). When using alcohol or other drugs, or engaging in criminal conduct, the biopsychological system gets conditioned to external stimuli that become reinforcers of AOD use and CC. Thus, when an individual makes the decision to stop use or CC, and then is again exposed to these conditioned stimuli, it can create system imbalance and tension. This can set up a high-risk exposure for relapse and recidivism. Relapsing into use can relieve the tension and reestablish homeostasis or system balance. The same can be said for CC. Certainly, this conditioned response interacts with cognitive processing (Tiffany, 1990).

Neuropsychological research on relapse for alcohol dependence (Heinz, 2006) supports the conditioned response model, and cravings and urges as triggers for relapse. Heinz sees two parts to this process.

▶ **Conditioned desire.** A person who has consumed alcohol in a situation (conditioned stimulus) similar to one in which they presently find themselves may experience an almost irresistible feeling of need (craving) for the substance. This need creates system imbalance and tension relieved through drinking.

▶ **Conditioned withdrawal.** This is a powerful feeling of physical discomfort associated with inaccessibility of alcohol when previously available to cope with negative emotions. The inaccessibility can create imbalance and system tension. Relief comes through relapse. This fits in with the findings that cravings and urges, and system tension, increase when a commitment is made to abstain from use.

Although **conditioned desire** and **conditioned withdrawal** are triggered by different brain mechanisms, neuroscientists have shown how frequent and high-dose alcohol consumption changes circuitry in the brain, which produces biopsychological stress in the user's attempt to manage sobriety. This body of neuropsychological research supports the concept of a neural, neurochemical and cortical basis for addictions and the phenomena of cravings and urges (Borg et al., 1983; Fromme & D'Amico, 1999; Volkow & Fowler, 2000).

Defining Stress

Selye (1956, 1976), the famous stress researcher, defines stress as "the nonspecific response of the body to any demand made upon it" (1974, p. 27). He states that it is more than merely nervous tension. He categorizes over 1,000 physiological responses that happen in stress and adaptation (Selye, 1974).

Fried (1993) sees it as an orienting response in which activity, especially breathing, is inhibited. This is followed by an excitatory increased metabolic demand for oxygen. Fried states that the body cannot sustain this intermittent orientation and sympathetic arousal for very long without relief. He uses the example that we are like quarter horses. We can run fast, but not for long. He concludes that the nonspecific response identified by Selye is "not so nonspecific after all; it is increased tissue air hunger, and all that this entails" (p. 302).

Bloom's (1985) definition is generally accepted by most clinicians: *that stress occurs when the coping responses fail to deal with stressful life events that present a person with strong demands for personal, social or biological readjustment.* This is a transactional view of stress (e.g., Meichenbaum, 1993a; Lazarus & Folkman, 1984). This model proposes that stress occurs when the perceived demands of a situation or event go beyond the perceived ability or resources of the system to meet those demands, especially when the security or well-being of the individual is threatened or challenged (Meichenbaum, 1993a, p. 382) The important cognitive-behavioral components of stress are that the perceived demand is the **appraisal** of the situation and the perceived ability to handle the demand is the **coping ability** of the person. The appraisal and coping abilities are cognitive **and** behavioral. Thus, stress is characterized by the interaction or relationship between the environment and the person wherein the person perceives (appraises) the adaptive demands as taxing or going beyond internal or external available coping resources (Meichenbaum, 1993a, p. 382).

The Stress Syndromes

Where do depression, guilt and anger fit in with stress and anxiety? Emotional stress refers to the immediate emotional response of a person to a stressful event, as modified or transformed by appraisals and coping processes (Lazarus, 1999, p. 220). Beck (1993) becomes more specific with respect to these emotions and identifies guilt, fear, anger and depression as stress syndromes (p. 348). He sees these as cognitive schemas with their own content and structure and which lead to behavioral outcomes.

It is also important to see stress as not only negative e.g., depression, anger, but as also coming from and representing positive experiences such as hope, relief, exhilaration (D'Zurilla and Nezu, 2001, p. 220). Thus, we can add positive psychological responses to the list of stress triggers. Again, use the Yerkes-Dodson Law to illustrate that there is an optimal level of stress that can contribute to good performance and outcomes.

The Coping Model

Stress, then, is the system's response to situations that exceed coping abilities and become manifested in specific syndromes of depression, anger and guilt. This understanding of stress fits in with the *Mental-Behavioral Impaired Control Cycle (MB-ICC)* model described in *Session 7,* where AOD use is one way of coping with stress and the emotional syndromes associated with stress. Since this coping works, AOD use is reinforced.

There are a number of theories that have been used to explain AOD abuse and dependence as coping mechanisms to defend against stress. These include Social Learning Theory (Abrams & Niaura, 1987; Maisto, Carey & Bradizza, 1999); Expectancy Theory (Goldman, Del Boca & Darkes, 1999; Goldman, Brown & Christiansen, 1987); Opponent Process Theory (Shipley, 1987); Tension Reduction Theory (Cappell & Greeley, 1987; Leonard & Blane, 1999); Self-Awareness Model (Hull, 1987; Sayette, 1999); the Stress Reduction Dampening Theory (Greeley & Oei, 1999; Sher, 1987); Self-Medication Model (Khantzian,1977); and Drug of Choice Model (Milkman and Frosch, 1973; Frosch & Milkman, 1977).

The Biopsychosocial Model

The above discussion points out that the etiology, development and maintenance of stress is best explained though an interplay among biological, psychological and social-environmental factors (Kaplan & Laygo, 2003, p. 411). There are stress cycles within each of these domains.

▶ Stress produces a **biological cycle** (Kaplan & Laygo, 2003) where the body produces hormones (e.g., cortisol) that help fight stress, reduce tissue inflammation and resist illnesses. These body hormones such as cortisol can also weaken the immune defense system and make the person more susceptible to illnesses, as body stress continues. This susceptibility can lead to increased body stress.

▶ **Psychological cycle:** Stress can mobilize psychological strengths and coping mechanisms. With prolonged stress, these coping mechanisms can break down, leading to increased stress.

- Both positive and negative **social-environmental** factors are sources of stress. Yet, the social and interpersonal world can provide sources of support. However, negative psychosocial reactions to external stresses can erode these external support sources.

SUMMARY OF CONTENT, PRESENTATION SEQUENCE AND GUIDELINES

Present this session using the following presentation guidelines.

- Begin by reviewing the *MSL* and the *MAP* and inviting group members to share their *TAP Charting*. Then review the basic concept of the CB approach: that it is not the outside or inside events that make us stressed, but our automatic thoughts about these events that cause behavioral and emotional stress.

- Present **Understanding Stress.** Review the automatic thought structures that determine emotional and behavioral outcomes: **expectations, appraisals, attributions and decisions.** Use the *CB Map Exercise* to show how stress works. Have clients share different kinds of stress thoughts and then identify the thought structure they fit. Example: "I'm feeling uptight" (appraisal); "a drink would calm me" (expectation).

- Discuss **The Roots and Sources of Stress.** Have clients give examples of internal/external stressors. Some clients may need individual counseling around some of these stress events. Present **conditioned desire** and **conditioned withdrawal,** discussed above. These are not in the *Workbook.*

- **Stages and Effects of Stress on the Body** provides a biological perspective. Selye (1956, 1974, 1976) defines three biological stages of stress: alarm; revolt; and exhaustion. **Adjunct Exercise:** Have clients share one event where they experienced these three biological stages of stress.

- In presenting **Signs of Stress and Efforts to Cope,** explain the concept of **homeostasis.** The body and mind work hard to keep a balance through coping responses and behaviors. These coping responses are ways to manage stress, but they are also signs of stress. They can also be the sources of stress. For example, taking a few drinks may be a sign of stress, a mechanism to cope with stress, and a source of stress. A person has a couple of beers to relax after working hard all day. The "working hard" suggests stress.

- **How Problems Come From the Reaction to Stress** describes how the effort to cope actually leads to specific problems. As a result of the few beers, defenses are lowered, and there is less control of anger, and the result is a fight with one's spouse.

- The section **How Stress Triggers the R&R Cycle** uses the *MB-ICC* to show how stress can trigger R&R.

- **Looking at Our Stress** provides clients with a self-assessment of stress in their lives. Again, these assessments may trigger a need for more counseling support than can be given through the *SSC* group.

- Clients update their *Master Skills List (MSL),* particularly *Skill 9, Managing Stress and Anxiety.* Using the *SSC Change Scale,* have clients rate themselves on understanding their own stress.

SUMMARY OF KEY CONCEPTS

- Roots of stress.
- How stress triggers R&R.
- Effects of stress on body and signs of stress.
- Self-evaluation of stress.

SESSION CLOSURE AND GUIDELINES FOR THERAPEUTIC PROCESSING

Have clients share their areas of stress and whether they need further resources to manage stress in their lives.

New clients do not enter this session since it is sequential to *Session 25.* Understanding and managing stress and its emotional syndromes of guilt, anger and depression are crucial in developing and maintaining cognitive self-control. Stress plays an important role in emotional and mental health problems and in physical illnesses. In this session clients apply the self-control and self-management skills of cognitive-restructuring to cope with and manage stress, i.e., worry, anxiety, panic.

An important issue related to stress is the posttraumatic stress disorder (PTSD). This is discussed in the *Resource Guide* (Wanberg & Milkman, 2008) and in the *Women's Adjunct Guide* (Milkman & Wanberg, 2008) PTSD is found among female and male offenders with varying expressions and etiologies. Some if not many *SSC* clients will have histories of PTSD. Although the concepts and approaches in this current session will help clients manage PTSD in a general way, it is not designed to treat or address specific PTSD issues with clients. Certainly, these issues will arise in *SSC* groups and some judicial clients will spontaneously share such past or present traumatic events. Providers should give, and facilitate the group to provide, reflective support when this happens, and to bring appropriate cognitive and emotional closure to such disclosures. This would involve an affirmation and confirmation of the importance of what the client has shared, and that others in the group may have had similar experiences.

SSC **group sessions should not examine, and providers are cautioned to avoid opening "the window" into the details of specific situations and associated thoughts and feelings that may emanate from a traumatic life-event, e.g., the what, where, when, how, and why of such an event.** Addressing and treating the thoughts and emotions associated with past traumatic events are done in a specialized therapy setting by counselors and therapists with training and experience in this area. Providers should evaluate whether these clients need further specialized resources. Referral should be voluntary.

SUMMARY OF CONTENT, PRESENTATION SEQUENCE AND GUIDELINES

Present this session following the topic sequence in the *Workbook*. The following are presentation guidelines.

▶ Begin by reviewing the *MSL* and the *MAP* and inviting clients to share their *TAP Charting*.

▶ Review the session objectives. Then, have a client volunteer a recent event that led to a negative outcome, and then apply *STEP* to create a positive outcome.

▶ Present **The States of Stress.** Although stress and anxiety are often used synonymously, stress is viewed as a broad concept that is expressed through worry, anxiety and panic.

▶ When presenting **Identifying Your Stress Responses,** clients complete *Worksheet 58,* the *Stress Response Questionnaire.* There are no established norms for this worksheet, and the score values that refer to different levels of stress are only approximated. **Also, make sure that the following scoring procedure is used:** Never=0; Some=1; A lot=2; and All the Time=3. After doing *Worksheet 58,* some clients may decide they need further stress management services beyond this session. Have clients discuss their findings.

▶ **Steps in Managing Stress: Worry, Anxiety, Panic** should be presented in a studied manner. Discuss the rule: **Manage the stress reaction before managing the stress event.** The steps in the *Workbook* may not always be used in the order in which they are presented when dealing with stress. For example, **Step 3,** identifying thoughts, may be done first, or be part of **Step 1.** Because stress responses often occur automatically, it may be necessary to focus on that response first and then "back into the thoughts."

- **Step 1** focuses on the **internal stress response** - What's happening to me? Have clients look more specifically at the items they checked in *Worksheet 58.* This will give them a clue as to how they express stress. This step can involve identifying the thoughts related to the response.

- **Step 2** focuses on the level of stress. When writing a stressful event in their lives, clients **do not have to put the most stressful event,** although they tend to do that. **Adjunct Exercise:** Have clients think of other stress events and practice using the Stress Scale.

- **Step 3** focuses on the thoughts about the stress event and the stress response. Although this can be part of **Step 1, Step 3** involves "stopping and thinking" about the stress event and response and applying management skills. This is looking at the stress response before looking at the thoughts. Although both the thoughts and the stress response can occur at the same time, the *SSC* CB model holds that thoughts lead to the stress response. Yet, sometimes it is best to identify the stress response, and use the "back into the thoughts" approach. Review *Worksheets 56* and *57,* pages 175 and 176, which help clients identify and understand specific areas and events that trigger stressful thinking.

- **Step 4** focuses on using skills to manage stress. Go over *Table 6,* page 160, introduced in *Session 19,* page 147. The skill of grounding (Najavits, 2002) helps manage panic episodes and stress related to past traumas. **Adjunct Exercise:** Demonstrate the skills in *Table 6.* Providers should have experience and/or training in teaching these skills. Have clients practice using the Stress Scale and visually "implanting" this scale in their thinking so they can capture it at any time when experiencing stress. Events rated "high" in their thinking may need more management attention.

- **Step 5** evaluates how the client did in managing the stress event.

- When presenting **The Stress Ladder,** encourage clients to stay within their comfort zone. This could open up some unresolved issues for some clients. Clients should not be pressured to self-disclose in verbal discussion or in doing *Worksheet 59.* Clients may need assistance in ranking the stress areas and then rating these areas using the Stress Scale. Apply *STEP* to number FIVE to get a positive outcome.

- When presenting **Positive Faces of Worry and Stress,** review the Yerkes-Dodson Law (1908) around optimal cognitive-emotional arousal and stimulation (Introduction to *Module 8*), and that some stress can be functional and productive and contribute to good performance and positive outcomes. We often are too quick to consider all stress responses as negative.

- Clients update their *Master Skills List (MSL),* particularly *Skill 9, Managing Stress and Anxiety.*

- Have clients rate their ability to manage stress on the *SSC Change Scale.*

SUMMARY OF KEY CONCEPTS

- Worry, anxiety and panic as states of stress.
- Steps in managing stress.
- Stress ladder.

- *The Stress Response Questionnaire.*
- The Stress Scale.
- The positive faces of worry and anxiety.

SESSION CLOSURE AND GUIDELINES FOR THERAPEUTIC PROCESSING

Clients should process their self-disclosures in this session. Check with each client to ensure that anxiety or panic which may result from examining specific sources of stress are not likely to cause increased risk for R&R. Where there is concern, an individual counseling session and/or referral options are strongly recommended.

RATIONALE AND OVERVIEW

The emotion of anger is ubiquitous in Western and Eastern, ancient and contemporary writings (Chon, 2000). The early sages were poignant when speaking to the emotion:

> "When anger rises, think of the consequences" - Confucius.

> "Holding on to anger is like grasping a hot coal with the intent of throwing it at someone else; you are the one who gets burned" - Buddha.

As Chon notes, "...anger appears to be a fundamental and vital human emotion, the experience of which appears to be universal" (2000, p. 148: in Kassinove & Tafrate, 2002). Yet Novaco in 1978 wrote that anger is the most talked-about emotion but it has been the least studied. O'Neill (1999), some 20 years later, commented that "if it was studied, it was usually in conjunction with aggression or hostility rather than as an emotion in its own right" (p. 6). She then noted that this may be due to the fact that it has no formal clinical status of its own and does not have a formal diagnostic classification (e.g., in the DSM IV-TR, American Psychiatric Association 2000), even thought it is seen as a component of posttraumatic stress disorder, borderline personality disorder and other DSM disorders (O'Neill, 1999; Novaco, 1986).

Anger as a Disorder and Anger Management Treatment

The psychology and psychotherapy literature point out that anger can be a major contributor to or direct cause of disturbances in emotions, thoughts and behavior and thus should have prominence in research and treatment (e.g., Donohue & Cavenagh, 2003; Eckhardt & Deffenbacher, 1995; Kassinove & Tafrate, 2002; McKay, Rogers & McKay, 1989; Novaco, 1978, 1994; O'Neill, 1999; Wanberg & Milkman, 1998; Wexler, 2000). Kassinove and Tafrate note that, even though anger is widespread, both in terms of literary treatment and in the everyday lives of people, it becomes a disorder when it "...is excessive in frequency and duration, and is disproportionate to the event or person who triggered it" (2002, p. 1). For these people, anger leads to highly negative outcomes. They are appropriate for an anger management program.

Kassinove and Tafrate (2002) argue for officially recognizing anger "as a disorder of the emotions, along with anxiety and depression," noting that "each of these three human problems has self-report, biophysical, and behavioral components and, given what we already know, there is little reason to ignore anger" (p. 69). Eckhardt and Deffenbacher (1995) propose a five level diagnostic classification (see Kassinove & Tafrate, 2002, pp. 69-72, for a summary of these classifications).

▶ **Adjustment Disorder With Anger Mood** is an anger-based adjustment problem, triggered by psychosocial stressors, does not extend more than six months, and is defined by periods of agitation, irritability, and angry outbursts.

▶ **Situational Anger Disorder Without Aggression** is a strong reaction to a specific situation or a series of triggering events and that persists for six months or more. There is minimal aggressive (physical or motor) reactions. The anger may have an impact on work, education and social life.

▶ **Situational Anger Disorder With Aggression** involves enhanced anger and aggressive motor (physical) actions that are habitual and predictable anger responses to specific experiential situations or triggers.

▶ **General Anger Disorder Without Aggression** consists of generalized, extensive, pervasive, chronic, and perpetual angry responses to many different kinds and degrees of provocative situations and triggers, is disruptive to normal functioning at home, work, school, social settings, and does not usually involve physical aggression.

▶ **General Anger Disorder With Aggression** involves the above General Anger Disorder features but with frequency of aggressive motor and physical actions that are damaging to objects and people.

These classifications are presented to illustrate that there are different levels and areas of anger expressions. In *SSC,* these are seen within the context of intrapersonal disruptions (*Session 27*), managing anger in interpersonal relationships (*Session 34*), and aggression, abuse and violence in relationship to others and the community (*Sessions 38* and *39*). The above review indicates two basic areas of focus.

▶ That everyone has anger that can contribute to negative outcomes and that needs to be managed in appropriate ways.

▶ There are some whose anger becomes pathological and who have an anger disorder.

What Is Anger Management?

Kassinove and Tafrate (2002) see anger management as referring to the "reduction of disruptive, excessive anger arousal and expressions..." with the goal of teaching clients "to react to the stressors of life with minimal and infrequent anger and, when it is experienced, to express the anger appropriately" (pp. 1-2). It is the starting point with most clients, to manage or change thinking in order to prevent negative outcomes.

Using the *SSC STEP* (thinking change leads to positive outcomes), anger management also involves helping clients achieve positive outcomes resulting from their use of skills to manage anger. An important goal of this session is to help clients express anger in an appropriate and constructive manner - with the goal of getting a win-win with everyone involved. Constructive anger communicates responsibility and does not blame others. It builds communication. It leads to problem solving.

Catharsis or "Letting Go" Is Not the Answer

By "expressing" anger, we do not mean blowing up or "getting it off your chest" at the expense of others. The literature is relatively clear: that catharsis or "letting it go" or getting angry "just to feel better," is neither a short-term nor a long-term solution to the problems that are behind the anger. Just getting angry can actually feed anger. As Kassinove and Tafrate (2002) note, it has been a popular view and "conventional wisdom" that ventilating just to "feel good" leads to good emotional health. "Decades of scientific research, however, contradict this view" (p. 91).

Criminal Conduct Is Angry Behavior

SSC also takes the position that criminal conduct is angry behavior, and anger drives much of the behavior of the substance abusing offender. When a person's behavior potentially hurts another person, particularly when intentional, it is an angry act. Getting high or drunk often hurts others. This is an angry act. Criminal conduct involves a victim and hurts others. It is an angry act. On first or even second pass, many judicial clients will reject this statement. After working through their defensive posture and looking at how much harm their behavior has caused others and the society, most judicial clients will agree with this statement. Judicial clients who accept the concept that CC is an angry act are in the commitment stage of change.

The important issue, however, is not only that CC is an angry act, but that anger is a threat to self-control and is one of the major triggers to relapse and recidivism. Helping clients recognize and manage anger and hostility and prevent aggressive and violent behavior stands as one of the most important parts of the treatment of the substance abusing judicial client.

SSC is Not Anger Management Treatment: Guidelines for Referral

This *Workbook* devotes four sessions to looking at emotions and behaviors associated with anger. However, these sessions are not to be looked upon as an anger management program per se. They introduce clients to the topic of anger and anger management and provide concepts and skills in the management of angry thinking so as to avoid negative outcomes and lead to positive outcomes. Some, or even many judicial clients will need referral for specialized work in this area. The four *SSC* sessions will provide a good foundation for individuals who need such referral, or provide a booster and reinforcement of concepts and skills for those having had a formal anger management program.

O'Neill (1999) provides a list of suitability inclusion and exclusion criteria for referring clients into anger management programs. Here are some of her suitability inclusion criteria.

▶ Aggression to objects or others that is fed by anger.

▶ Being upset because anger caused a loss of freedom or loss of objects or relationships.

▶ Gets easily upset by external events or triggers.

▶ Impatience and impulsivity that lead to reacting to triggers with anger.

▶ Low self-esteem.

▶ Is motivated for help and wants treatment.

Here are some other inclusion criteria to consider.

▶ Person is impulsive and irrationally reacts to external frustrating events.

▶ There are repeated patterns of blow-ups.

▶ The person is aware that angry episodes are irrational.

▶ Inability to recall the reasons or events that preceded past anger, but only remembers getting angry.

▶ Anger results in negative and harmful outcomes.

O'Neill (1999) suggests that persons who display the following may not be candidates for more concentrated anger management treatment.

▶ Show deliberate and planned, instrumental, rather than angry aggression.

▶ Do not want to change the anger pattern and in fact perceive benefits from getting angry.

▶ Involved in current and consistent use of drugs.

▶ Signs of psychosis, memory problems or language functioning that does not allow for self-instruction.

SUMMARY OF CONTENT, PRESENTATION SEQUENCE AND GUIDELINES

Present this session following the topic sequence presentation in the *Workbook* using the following guidelines.

▶ Begin with reviewing the *MSL* and the *MAP* and inviting group members to share their *TAP Charting*.

▶ Start the section **Understanding Anger** with the acknowledgement that the concept of anger, like other emotions, cannot be defined with complete clarity and is often fuzzy (Russell & Fehr, 1994). Yet, there are clear concepts related to anger that most will agree on (Kassinove & Tafrate, 2002). It is learned, it varies as to intensity, duration, and frequency, and it involves different emotional, behavioral, and physical responses. It is defined as a learned cognitive state involving thinking distortions and errors (Beck, 1999) and is a felt emotional state (Kassinove & Tafrate, 2002). If anger is a learned state, it can be managed and changed. Here are some specific guidelines for presenting this section.

  ◆ Emphasize the CB model: Events do not cause anger; it is the thinking about those events.

  ◆ Anger is neither good nor bad: it is the actions and outcome of angry thoughts and emotions.

  ◆ Discuss the difference between constructive and destructive anger.

  ◆ When doing the *Anger Scale,* clients do not have to choose the situations that made them most angry. In cases where this is done, this may open areas of anger that clients have not looked at or resolved. **Be alert for these clients and be prepared to evaluate their need for further support and therapeutic resolution.** The goal is to help clients learn to use the *Anger Scale* so as to be alert to situations that require special self-control attention and to move from automatic angry thinking to conscious awareness of angry thoughts (moving from automatic to manual shifting).

  ◆ **Exercise:** Clients do a second rating using the *Anger Scale,* rating an event that happened in the "past couple of weeks." Have them compare the two ratings. These ratings can provide a baseline reference for future use of the *Anger Scale.*

▶ **Clues and Signs of Anger** helps clients learn to increase conscious awareness of their anger. Much of our anger is built on automatic processing. Thus, anger regulation is dependent on breaking this automatic responding (Kassinove & Tafrate, 2002, p. 113).

Adjunct Exercise: Help clients learn to apply the *Anger Scale* to each of the clues and signs in the *Workbook*. For example, have a client share a recent event where he/she experienced physical signs of anger, and rate that experience with the *Anger Scale*. One of the most important clues to being angry is angry self-talk. Have clients share their own angry self-talk. Because angry thoughts are so automatic, clients may have to use the "backing into" approach of identifying their angry responses first, and then working back to the angry thoughts and beliefs. The goal is getting to the point that automatic angry thinking is moved to mindful and controlled thinking.

▶ The section **High-Charged Events That Lead to Angry Thinking** is dealt with in greater depth in *Session 34,* which deals with anger in relationships. Most if not all anger ultimately relates back to one's social and interpersonal involvements. Anger related to misplacing one's car keys or other objects will ultimately relate back to the necessity of having that object to meet one's social and interpersonal obligations.

▶ The section **Self-Control Skills for Regulating Anger** integrates the cognitive, emotional, and behavioral components of anger into a two-phase skills process for regulating anger.

  ◆ The **first phase:** Being mindful and aware of angry feelings, thoughts and triggers. This involves **Skills 1 and 2.** Mindfulness and awareness are crucial to the management of anger. *Worksheet 60,* page 186, helps enhance awareness of anger triggers. Help clients understand the difference between expressing anger and getting angry. Distinguish between destructive and constructive anger.

- ♦ The **second phase** involves *Skills 3* through *6*. The goal is more than expressing anger in a constructive way. It is to resolve issues and problems and learn the skills in managing anger in multiple situations that lead to self-control and positive outcomes. This is a good place to relate constructive anger arousal to the Yerkes-Dodson (1908) Law. Optimal and constructive anger arousal can contribute to good outcomes and good performance.

  Adjunct Exercise: Have clients share either a personal or general situation where some anger arousal was constructive and contributed to a good outcome and good performance. Have them evaluate the appropriateness of that arousal.

- ▶ **Practice in Self-Control** is the key. Self-control and anger management are practiced through the use of role playing, using the *STEP Method* to bring an anger-arousing scene to a positive outcome, and applying the skills in *Table 6*, page 160, and *Table 7*, page 180, to change angry thinking.

  Adjunct Exercise: Working in dyads and using examples of anger that clients shared in group, have group members role-play these situations that demonstrate a constructive response and outcome.

  Adjunct Exercise: Have clients take another scene that brings up anger inside of them. This time, have them use self-talk to address the feelings of anger and to develop control over the anger. Use thought stopping to do this. Use the other tools clients have learned to manage anger.

- ▶ **Important:** In the exercises in this session, give clients room to operate within their own comfort zone, and make it clear that participation in the exercises is voluntary.

- ▶ Clients update their *MSL*, particularly *Skill 11, Anger Management Skills*.

- ▶ Have clients evaluate their *MAP* and do their *TAP Charting* for the week. Ask clients to see if their *MP* ratings are high on AOD use to cope with emotional discomfort and on loss of behavioral control due to AOD use. Should anger management be added to their *MAP* and their *Individual Treatment Plan?*

- ▶ Clients complete the *SSC Change Scale* on rating their ability to manage and regulate anger.

SUMMARY OF KEY CONCEPTS

- ▶ Criminal conduct and substance abuse are angry behaviors.

- ▶ "Getting it off your chest" does not solve the problem behind the anger, and by itself, is not necessarily good for your mental health.

- ▶ Constructive and destructive anger.

- ▶ The *Anger Scale*.

- ▶ Signs of anger and high-charged events for anger.

- ▶ Self-control skills for managing anger.

SESSION CLOSURE AND GUIDELINES FOR THERAPEUTIC PROCESSING

Use the closure session to have clients share their anger triggers. Close the group on a positive note. Be alert to clients who may have tapped into unresolved anger.

RATIONALE AND OVERVIEW

In the Rationale and Overview of *Session 25,* it was noted that emotional or psychological disturbances found among judicial clients can be viewed as either primary or secondary. A primary psychological disturbance or disorder exists relatively independent from, yet interacts with, substance abuse and criminal conduct.

Most studies of offender populations (e.g., Andrews & Bonta, 2003; Guy et al., 1985; Hodgins & Cote, 1990; Teplin & Swartz, 1989; Daniel et al., 1988; Cloninger & Guze, 1970) indicate that the prevalence of severe mental disorders, such as schizophrenia or other psychotic expressions, ranges from one to ten percent. These same studies indicate that the prevalence rates of primary depression or other affective disorders range from one to 17 percent. A report from the U.S. Department of Justice estimated that, in 1998, 16 percent of the inmates in the nation's prisons, 16 percent in local jails, and seven percent in federal prisons were mentally ill (Ditton, 1999). In the general population, about five percent is severely depressed, and about 15 percent will have at least one lifetime depressive episode (Seligman, Walker & Rosenhan, 2001). The upshot of these findings suggests that primary and severe emotional and psychological problems are found in around 15 to 16 percent or less in criminal justice populations; and around 15 percent or less would have a depressive disorder.

Yet, it is safe to assume that most judicial clients will have experienced or are experiencing secondary psychological and emotional issues that increase their risk of relapse and recidivism. These are problems that are interactive with or are consequences of involvement in criminal conduct and substance abuse. Guilt, self-blame, anger, depressive and anxious moods are common with persons recovering from substance abuse and misuse. As noted, Beck (1993) sees guilt, fear, anger and depression as stress syndromes (p. 348). He sees these as cognitive schemas with their own content and structure and which lead to behavioral outcomes.

Depression is one of the most widely studied mental health issues in the psychological and psychiatric literature. Beck (1963) began his work in cognitive therapy with depressed patients. He made depression a major focus in the application of cognitive therapy principles (e.g., 1972, 1996). He sees two processes that produce depression: the cognitive triad and errors in thinking. As discussed in *Session 22* of this *Guide,* the cognitive triad involves negative thoughts about: self; life experiences; and the future (Beck, 1976). Also noted, Burns (1999) makes an even stronger case for this theory and concludes that a depressive episode or any painful emotion always involves intense negative thinking (p. 28). The work done in *Sessions 22* and *23* on negative thinking is important in understanding and managing depression.

The literature is replete with studies, texts and manuals treating the subject of depression. No effort will be made to review this literature. Our goal in this session is to address the secondary nature of sadness, depression and guilt as these emotional states interact with substance abuse and criminal conduct. **This session does not purport to provide direction for the treatment of primary depression.** However, the provider should be aware of the signs and symptoms of depression. We summarize these primary symptoms or signs using a variety of resources (e.g., American Psychiatric Association, 2000; Burns, 1999; Gotlib & Hammen, 2002; Seligman, Walker, & Rosenhan, 2001). We organized the symptoms into four main components.

▶ **Affective:** Feeling sad, guilty, irritated, anxious, lack of joy, cry a lot, feel overwhelmed.

▶ **Cognitive:** Hopeless about future, thoughts of being a failure, disappointed in self, thoughts of suicide, unable to make decisions, negative thoughts about self, loss of interest, thoughts of inadequacy and incompetence, overly critical of self, negative self-image (look ugly), worthless thinking.

- **Behavioral:** withdrawing from others, sit around a lot (vegetate), no social involvement, difficult to get going (motivation deficit), gestures of self-harm or suicide attempts, hard time working, restlessness.

- **Somatic:** Loss of appetite, unusual weight losses or gains, unable to sleep, sleep too much, get fatigued and tired, morning fatigue, decrease of sexual drive.

There are several types of depression: including major depressive episode, major depressive disorder, dysthymic disorder and chronic depression (American Psychiatric Association, 2000; Seligman, Walker & Rosenahn, 2001).

The rationale for devoting a session to the management and control of guilt, sadness, and depression with judicial clients is that these unpleasant emotions are major triggers of AOD relapse (Wanberg & Milkman, 1998). Feelings of guilt and depression should be considered high-risk exposures, for they may lead to a cycle of repeated failures. One goal of this session is to enhance the awareness of emotions in general, and more specifically, the emotions of guilt and depression and to provide skills and tools in handling these emotions. Another goal is to help clients reinterpret (restructure their thinking) around situations that previously would bring on depression and guilt so as to have more positive emotional and behavioral outcomes.

SUMMARY OF CONTENT, PRESENTATION SEQUENCE AND GUIDELINES

Before presenting this session, the provider is asked to do an assessment reflection on group members to identify those who may be experiencing emotional problems, particularly depression. This session will help in discerning which clients may be appropriate for referral for treatment involving anxiety and depression.

Present this session following the topic sequence in the *Workbook,* using the following guidelines.

- Begin by reviewing the *MSL* and the *MAP* and inviting group members to share their *TAP Charting.*

- The section **Being Mindful: Putting a Name Tag on Our Emotions,** focuses on an approach that encourages clients to observe, describe, and participate in the reality of their own experience. "To be mindfully aware is to open oneself to the activity of exploration and inquiry, to complete the essential function of data collection and evaluation with as clear-eyed an approach as possible" (Robins, Schmidt, & Linehan, 2004, p. 38). Mindfulness leads to acceptance. As Robins et al. note in their discussion of Dialectical Behavior Therapy, "Radical acceptance is the fully open experience of what is, entering into reality just as it is, at this moment" (p. 39). The essence of this approach is that before change can take place, mindfulness and acceptance are essential. In this section, clients look at five basic skills of mindfulness and acceptance. The provider uses "acceptance-oriented" communication, involving non-judgmental responding with warmth and genuineness (Fruzzetti & Fruzzetti, 2003).

- **Understanding and Managing Guilt** deals with a topic that is grossly under-treated in the psychotherapy and treatment literature.

  - In a review of numerous books on psychotherapy and counseling, only one was found to give this important emotion substantive treatment. Burns (1999), in his chapter on *Ways of Defeating Guilt,* states: "No book on depression would be complete without a chapter on guilt" (p. 198). Seligman et al. (2001), in their abnormal psychology text barely mention that "sadness and guilt are the most obvious emotional symptoms in depressed people..." (p. 252).

  - The treatment of guilt and shame is usually done within the context of traditional, egocentric therapy: that it is defeating, debilitating, and only contributes to bad outcomes. With judicial clients, it must be dealt with from a sociocentric context: that appropriate guilt (both cognitive and affective) is an essential component for responsible living. Guilt is the emotional manifestation of the conscience or superego, and is important for balanced mental health. **Refer to the Yerkes-Dodson Law when discussing optimal guilt arousal.** Excessive and inappropriate guilt can be debilitating; having no guilt can lead to antisocial and criminal conduct. Optimal or constructive guilt is the emotional foundation of morality, character and prosocial living. Yet, excessive and inappropriate guilt can be major barriers to the effective management of depression, hostility, anger, and aggression and contribute to the anger-guilt cycle, dealt with in *Module 9*.

- Guide clients through the use of the *Guilt Scale*. When clients apply this scale to past episodes of guilt, have them discriminate between whether the guilt was **negative** (led to bad outcomes) or **functional** (led to good outcomes). **Adjunct Exercise:** Give examples of these kinds of guilt. For example, guilt leading to a bad outcome would be feeling guilty to the point that one withdraws and does not feel worthy of equal status in a relationship. Positive guilt would lead to behavior that rejects the request of a "friend" to help him sell drugs. Have clients give examples of these two kinds of guilt.

- Apply *STEP* to **thinking change** so that a positive outcome can result from an episode of guilt.

▶ Present **Understanding and Managing Depression** outlined in the *Workbook.* Here are some guidelines.

- When doing the exercise in **Being Mindful of Your Depression**, where clients write down a "depressed time in your life," make it clear that it does not have to be a time when they were the most depressed. Have them learn to use the *Depression Scale* in rating past times of depression. Have clients briefly share their ratings of depression "over the last two weeks."

- When presenting **Some Causes of Depression,** discuss *learned helplessness,* a cognitive model used to explain depression (Seligman & Beagley, 1975; Seligman & Maier, 1967; Seligman et al., 2001). Depression results from the **expectation** that there is nothing the individual can do to prevent bad outcomes (helplessness). When people are placed in inescapable situations, they learn to become passive and nonfunctional. Then, when placed in or experiencing events that are escapable or manageable, they continue to respond in a passive (depressed) way. They lack motivation to respond; they are unable to see that outcomes are based on their responding (Seligman et al., 2001, p. 270). The theory concludes that depression results from the expectation of no control and that something bad will happen with certainty. Depression is made worse when the individual internalizes the failure or helplessness (it's my fault), sees it as happening in all aspects of his/her life (global), and sees it as stable and permanent. Externalizing the helplessness (it's someone else's fault) may mitigate the manifestation of depression, yet fails to accept responsibility for bad feelings. The goal is to help clients develop a realistic perspective on the degree of self versus other contribution to a negative situation.

  Adjunct Exercise: Have clients apply the learned helplessness model to their involvement in the judicial system, e.g., being imprisoned. Does this lead to learned helplessness? Will this lead to a certain level of depression? If judicial clients externalize their plight (the police were out to get me), does this alleviate self-responsibility and put the blame on society? Yet, does this reduce depression? Help clients see that the solution to the dilemma of internalizing-externalizing is assuming responsibility to manage the depression related to these external events.

- In the section on **Measuring Your Depression,** clients complete the *Depression Questionnaire (DQ)*. There are no norms for this questionnaire, and the score ranges suggesting certain levels of depression are estimates based on the authors' clinical experience. These are only broad guidelines that clients can use to make some judgment around whether they might pursue further consultation. Providers clinically trained in evaluating depression may want to administer or make a clinical referral for the *Beck Depression Inventory* (BDI: Beck, 2006) or the *Burns Depression Checklist* (BDC: Burns, 1999).

- The section **Skills and Strategies in Managing and Coping With Depression** is a very brief summary of the techniques and skills to manage depression that is treated with great depth in numerous texts and documents. Again, it is important to remind clients that this session is not designed to treat depression, but to provide judicial clients with an understanding of and skills to manage the times when they feel depressed and discouraged. Clients who show signs of clinical depression, e.g., meets the criteria for one of the types of depression in the DSM-IV-TR (American Psychiatric Association, 2000), should be referred for evaluation for treatment.

▶ The **Positive Faces of Our Moods** again refers back to the Yerkes-Dodson Law (1908) around optimal cognitive-emotional arousal and stimulation: that there are optimal levels of guilt and stress that can be functional and productive and contribute to good performance and positive outcomes. As discussed earlier, the optimal levels of arousal will vary from person to person.

As well, we do not apply the Yerkes-Dodson Law to depression, since depression would represent the absence of arousal and stimulation. But, as noted, depression may be a response to high levels of stimulation, e.g., anger, anxiety.

▶ The section **Overcoming Negative Emotions by Increasing Positive Feelings** provides the foundation for helping judicial clients increase the probability of positive outcomes. Learning to prevent negative emotions such as depression, anxiety and anger, is only one part of the process. Responsible and meaningful living also comes from increasing the positive feelings and emotions in living, such as joy, love and pride.

▶ Clients update their *MSL*, particularly *Skills 10* and *21*.

▶ Have clients evaluate their *MAP* and do their *TAP Charting* for the week. Have clients look at the *MP* to see if ratings are high on AOD use to cope with emotional discomfort, problems with the law and if there are behavioral disruptions from use. See if managing depression needs to be added to their *MAP* and to the client's *Individual Treatment Plan*.

▶ Clients complete the *SSC Change Scale*s on rating their ability to manage guilt and depression.

SUMMARY OF KEY CONCEPTS

▶ Being mindful of our emotions.

▶ Balance between appropriate (constructive) guilt and excessive (inappropriate).

▶ The *Guilt Scale*.

▶ Being mindful of and managing depression.

▶ The *Depression Scale*.

▶ There is a positive side to our moods.

▶ Increasing positive emotions and feelings.

SESSION CLOSURE AND GUIDELINES FOR THERAPEUTIC PROCESSING

Have clients share how they see guilt, depression, sadness, and discouragement in their lives. Close the group on a positive note. Be alert to clients who may have tapped into unresolved issues that bring on depression.

MODULE 9

Social and Relationship Skills Building

OVERVIEW

As discussed earlier, *Phase II* moves clients into the commitment to change (action) stage. One component of commitment to change is the development of self-control skills to manage thoughts and emotions related to anger, depression, guilt, and negative thinking. These internal states can trigger R&R. Their management is critical to R&R prevention. This is the focus of *Module 8*.

Another category of triggers for R&R is interpersonal and relationship problems and stress. Although mental self-control skills provide the foundation for developing and building positive relationships with others and the community, there is a specific set of skills that can be used to develop and strengthen these relationships. These are often referred to as coping and social skills training. *SSC* puts these into the category of Social and Relationship (interpersonal) Skills Training (SRST).

BACKGROUND AND EFFICACY OF SOCIAL AND RELATIONSHIP SKILLS TRAINING

SRST evolved over the last two decades of the 20th century to become an essential component of CB therapy (Monti et al., 1995; Wanberg & Milkman, 1998; Wanberg et al., 2005). It is a widely applied and effective CB treatment for a range of psychosocial problems (Segrin, 2003, p. 384). It emerged out of social learning theory. One of the first approaches was assertiveness training, beginning in the 1970s (Alberti & Emmons, 1995; Lange & Jakubowski, 1976). SRST's efficacy has empirical support from outcome research in terms of increasing effective relationships, reducing psychologically disruptive symptoms, and increasing treatment involvement (e.g., Monti et al., 1995; Segrin, 2003).

DEFINING SOCIAL SKILLS AND SRST

Libet and Lewinsohn (1973) define social skills as behaviors directed at producing or increasing positive reinforcement and reducing the possibility of punishing responses from the social environment. The result is more meaningful living and "more satisfying, effective, and enjoyable interactions with other people" (Segrin, 2003, p. 385).

Social and interpersonal skills involve the ability to engage in appropriate and effective interactions and communication with other people (Segrin, 2003). Appropriate social and interpersonal actions respect the rights of others, are prosocial, and stay within social and relational norms. Effective SRST will allow the actor to achieve his or her relationship goals (Segrin, 2003). However, the converse is true: it allows those interacting with the actor to achieve their goals. Effective interpersonal relationships are win-win.

SPECIFIC AREAS OF FOCUS

There are a number of specific focuses of SRST (Wanberg & Milkman, 1998; Wanberg, Milkman & Timken, 2005). These provide the basis for the sessions in this module.

- ▶ Refusal training.

- ▶ Communication skills which include conversation building and giving and receiving praise.

- ▶ Assertiveness training.

- ▶ Interpersonal problem solving.

- ▶ Managing anger and other emotions in relationships.

- ▶ Building and maintaining close and intimate relationships.

- ▶ Conflict resolution.

SRST APPROACHES AND METHODS

The approaches and methods of SRST have been outlined in a number of literature sources, particularly in the areas of substance abuse (e.g., Kadden & Cooney, 2005; Marlatt, 1985b; Monti et al., 1989, 1995; Segrin, 2003; Wanberg & Milkman, 1998; Wanberg, Milkman & Timken, 2005). It was a foundational approach to Marlatt's seminal relapse prevention model (1985b). Drawing from these resources, we see the effective delivery of SRST to substance abusing judicial clients as involving several important steps, components and methods. These are briefly outlined. These components, although presented as steps, may not necessarily be followed in sequence when doing SRST. For example, sometimes role-playing may precede modeling.

- ▶ **Assessment:** Although *SSC* presents a generic approach to SRST in that all clients are exposed to its primary areas, providers should evaluate the social skills needs and deficits of clients (Segrin, 2003).

- ▶ **Present the rationale for and description of the use of a particular skill** (Monti et al., 1995) within the framework of high risk exposures (Kadden & Cooney, 2005; Wanberg, Milkman & Timken, 2005). This will involve direct instruction or coaching (Segrin, 2003). For substance abusing judicial clients, SRST is done within the context of those exposures that are high risk for R&R.

- ▶ **Modeling** is an important component of SRST. Bandura (1977a, 1997) sees modeling as a primary way that individuals develop new behaviors (1977a). It involves demonstrating an effective and ineffective response to a sample situation (Monti et al., 1995; Segrin, 2003). Modeling gives clients an example for their own behaviors. It is "making the unobservable observable" (Bandura, 1986, p. 66), and creates a condition of perceived self-efficacy. It shows the client that the behavior can be done and it can work (Segrin, 2003). Standard vignettes are used to illustrate the skill. The group discusses why the behavioral response was effective or not effective. Covert modeling (Kazdin, 1976, 1979) involves having the client imagine encountering a high risk situation and engaging in a successful coping response (Marlatt, 1985b).

- ▶ **Role playing:** Clients practice social and relationship skills in either standard vignettes or real situations in their lives. The provider and group give feedback on how effective the client was in using the skill. The role-play is done within a safe or controlled environment (Monti et al., 1995; Segrin, 2003). Positive and immediate feedback is given by the provider and group as to how the client did. Positive reinforcement increases the probability that the client will use these skills in situations outside of the treatment setting.

- ▶ **Behavioral rehearsal:** New skills are not likely to be learned in one session (Kadden & Cooney, 2005).

The skills need to be practiced in each subsequent session following their introduction. Continual practice is necessary for clients to develop a sense of mastery around different skills. An effective provider will continually reach back to previously learned skills (including those in the mental self-control category) and have clients practice them in the current session or as homework. Providers need to have these skills at the "tips of their fingers" and bring them to bear on current life experiences that clients discuss in the group closure sessions. For example, a client who discusses a situation involving conflict with a spouse can role-play the use of reflective listening to bring the conflict to a positive outcome.

▶ **Homework:** This is a standard method for all coping skills training, and particularly SRST. Most homework assignments will have clients apply the skills in everyday situations. Often, the most effective homework assignments are simple. It is important that these assignments be graduated in terms of difficulty. Before clients are asked to practice starting a conversation with an intimate partner around difficult and sensitive topics, homework should start with a more simple task of having clients just share simple daily happenings. Some clients may choose to intentionally place themselves in high-risk situations to test the relationship skills they have learned. However, this should only be on a voluntary basis, and for clients who want to prepare themselves for high-risk situations they anticipate they will have to face at some point in the future. This preemptive approach can be effective only when clients are sure that they have the skills to manage these situations. These eventual situations should be role-played first in group.

▶ **Follow-up:** Effective SRST will continually reassess client's social skills and evaluate the level of effectiveness of their use (Segrin, 2003). This reevaluation process is built into every *SSC* session and is the basis of *Program Guide 1,* the *Master Skills List, Participant's Workbook,* page 291. Most *Phase II* sessions begin with either the *CB Map Exercise* or the *STEP* exercise which provides the matrix for the application and practice of learned social and relationship skills.

RATIONALE AND GOALS OF *MODULE 9*

AOD abuse and criminal conduct (CC) are both the product and cause of relationship problems. One basis of the behavioral problems of judicial clients is the lack of effective relationship skills. Yet, the consequences of AOD abuse and CC are disrupted relationships. Effective SRST addresses relationship problems in order to: prevent AOD abuse and CC; and help repair disrupted relationships resulting from these behaviors. The specific provider objectives of this module are:

▶ Facilitate client development and strengthening of communication skills to increase positive relationship outcomes.

▶ Help clients learn and practice the skills of problem solving and being assertive.

▶ Facilitate client learning and practice of skills that regulate anger in relationships.

▶ Facilitate client skill development and maintenance of meaningful family and intimate relationships.

The concepts and skills that are learned and practiced in this module are also basic to developing responsible relationships in the community, the focus of *Module 10.*

PRESENTATION LOGISTICS

The ideal presentation strategy for this model is to present the seven sessions in sequence. Since this is not practical for agencies using the open group approach, *Sessions 29* and *30* are presented in sequence (no entry at *30*) and the remaining sessions can be presented as stand-alone.

RATIONALE AND OVERVIEW

"Communication is basic to human existence - indeed, to all life itself. In fundamental terms, all life around us demonstrates communication. To live is to communicate" (Patton & Giffin, 1981, p. 3). It takes place at the most basic cellular level of the nervous system and at the most complex level of human interaction. It is done knowingly and unknowingly. It is both an event and a process (Berlo, 1960). It is "the generation and attribution of meaning" (Patton & Giffin, 1981, p. 4). It involves, at the simplest level, a sender and receiver. Yet, it is complicated and circular in that it involves multiple circuits of feedback interaction (Berlo, 1960). It is a process that promotes change among humans (Patton & Giffin, 1981, p. 5). It takes place within the person (intrapersonal) and between persons (interpersonal). Its inevitability is best expressed by Watzlawick, Beavin, and Jackson's (1967) famous statement: "one cannot not communicate" (p. 48). Effective interpersonal communication requires and involves (Patton & Giffin, 1981):

▶ The direct presence of those involved;

▶ The assumption of the roles of sender and receiver;

▶ A separateness yet an interdependence of those involved;

▶ A mutual need to communicate;

▶ Defining the nature and meaning of relationships;

▶ The confirmation and validation of self;

▶ Different degrees of mutual understanding;

▶ A change in our views of self, others and the world; and

▶ Competencies in the use of communication skills.

Communication skills are the foundation for positive and healthy relationships. These skills provide the pathways for **self-awareness through active sharing** and **other-awareness through active listening.** These two skills provide one of the main components of the foundation of the *SSC* program and are presented in *Sessions 11* and *12*. These sessions also link together interpersonal cognition (what and how people think about their relationships) and interpersonal communication (the manifestation of these cognitions.

Communication Skills Training (CST) is considered to be an important component of cognitive-behavioral therapy (Oliver & Margolin, 2003). Based on social learning therapy, it established its prominence in behavioral-oriented marital therapy (e.g. Gottman et al., 1976; Jacobson & Margolin, 1979; Margolin, 1987; O'Farrell & Cowles, 1989). It has also become a mainstay in the cognitive-behavioral treatment of AOD abuse (e.g., Monti et al., 1989, 1995; O'Farrell & Cowles, 1989) and in the treatment of the substance abusing judicial client (Wanberg & Milkman, 1998; Wanberg, Milkman & Timken, 2005). Although CST is seen as a more specific focus within the broader domain of SRST, it provides the foundation for all of the specific areas of SRST, e.g., problem solving, assertiveness training, starting conversations, refusal skills, managing emotions in relationships, enhancing intimacy, etc. CST involves the specific learning and practice of the core communication skills of active sharing and active listening. There is considerable empirical support for the efficacy of CST and the broader areas encompassed within SRST (e.g., Chaney, 1989; Monti et al., 1995).

This session builds on the core communication concepts and skills provided in *Sessions 11* and *12*. Providers will refer to these skills in every other session that focuses on SRST.

SUMMARY OF CONTENT, PRESENTATION SEQUENCE AND GUIDELINES

The following are some presentation guidelines for this session.

▶ Begin this session by reviewing the *MSL* and the *MAP* and inviting group members to share their *TAP Charting*. Then, review the objectives of the session.

▶ Have clients briefly share their *Thinking Report* homework on an event that caused some depression, assigned in *Session 28*. Have the group do a *Re-thinking Report* on one client's *Thinking Report*.

▶ Before focusing on the two skills of active sharing and active listening, do a review of the following topics that are basic to participating in effective interpersonal communication.

  ◆ The *Johari Window* (page 99 in the *Workbook*) illustrates active sharing and active listening.

  ◆ Discuss the above points of effective interpersonal communication.

  ◆ Share the three functions of interpersonal communication outlined in the *Rationale and Overview* of *Session 11*: linking; thinking or decentering, the basis of empathy; and self-regulation.

  ◆ The barriers to self-disclosure, p. 96 of the *Workbook*.

  ◆ The two kinds of communication: nonverbal and verbal (*Session 11*, page 91 of the *Workbook*.

▶ Present the section **Skills of Active Sharing.** Make it clear that this is self-oriented communication and involves the two skills of self-disclosure and receiving feedback. The provider will want to review *Session 11* in the *Workbook* and in this *Guide*. Clear, correct and accurate sharing are the key concepts.

▶ Present **Active Listening.** This is a review of **How to Make Active Listening Work**, page 103 of the *Workbook*. Go back over the concepts of thinking filters, open and closed channels, and "listening" to body language. The skills of attending, inviting others to share and giving feedback are the main focus.

  ◆ Take time to do the four exercises in the *Workbook*. The first three exercises are done in the total group. Spend at least 20 minutes on the last exercise in groups of three.

  ◆ *Worksheet 64* arms clients with "ready to go" active sharing and active listening positive automatic thoughts. Start with having the group give examples and write them on a flipchart. Active sharing: "This is what I've been thinking." Open statement: "Tell me what happened." Reflection: "You sound upset." Then have clients put on *Worksheet 64* ones that will work for them.

▶ Clients update their *Master Skills List (MSL)*, particularly *Skills 12, 13* and *14*.

▶ Using the *SSC Change Scales*, have clients rate their skill levels of active sharing and active listening.

SUMMARY OF KEY CONCEPTS

▶ *Johari Window.*   ▶ Active sharing and active listening.

▶ Accurate and correct self-disclosure and accurate and correct feedback.

SESSION CLOSURE AND GUIDELINES FOR THERAPEUTIC PROCESSING

Since this session is very interactive with high levels of sharing and listening, only a brief closure and debriefing session may be needed.

RATIONALE AND OVERVIEW

This session builds on the foundation skills of **active listening** and **active sharing** and focuses on the skills of initiating **meaningful, prosocial** and **healthy** interpersonal interactions. These skills are the doorways to communicating with those we know, meeting new people, buying a car, getting a job, resolving conflicts, and starting and sustaining interactions around sensitive and difficult topics. Sometimes people find themselves lonely and isolated because they do not feel confident around developing meaningful interactions and relationships. Often, this is due to a reticence in initiating talk and interactions with others. For many people, this becomes one of the reasons for becoming involved in substance use. People who are highly anxious or who have negative feelings about themselves often feel they cannot function in a social situation without a drink or a fix.

An important component of relapse and recidivism prevention is ending relationships with old companions and associates who are still into AOD use and a criminal lifestyle. This means developing a new and different social network. This cannot be done without using basic communication skills which include starting and sustaining new **prosocial** interpersonal interactions and conversations. Initiating interpersonal interactions around sensitive and difficult topics are also important components of the process of preventing relapse and recidivism. Solving problems, resolving conflicts, getting thoughts and emotions out in the open, and mending relationships all involve skills in starting and keeping conversations going around difficult and sensitive topics. It is safe to assume that most judicial clients will find learning and using these skills a challenge.

It is important to emphasize that the focus is on meaningful, prosocial and healthy aspects of initiating conversation and approaching difficult topics. Judicial clients may find it easy to engage in jargon with criminal and/or barroom associates, which only reinforces substance use patterns and criminal conduct. Likewise, they can easily slip into an angry, reactive, and counterproductive interaction when dealing with sensitive, threatening, and difficult issues with co-workers, friends, family members, and intimate partners.

SUMMARY OF CONTENT, PRESENTATION SEQUENCE AND GUIDELINES

The first part of this session focuses on the basic skills of initiating prosocial interactions and conversations. We "raise the bar" considerably when we move to learning and practicing the skills of starting an interpersonal interaction around a difficult and sensitive topic. These should be reviewed in other sessions. Following are the guidelines for presenting this therapy session.

▶ Begin with a review of the *MSL* and *MAP* and *TAP Charting*. Then, present the session objectives.

▶ Review the foundational communication skills of **active listening** and **active sharing** and the topic of **nonverbal communication.** Effective communication around sensitive and difficult topics depends greatly on reading the other person's nonverbal messages.

▶ The offender's need for power is one basis of criminal conduct. Help clients see that: **THERE IS POWER IN PROSOCIAL COMMUNICATION. THEY CAN EXPERIENCE THIS POWER WHEN THEY PUT THE SKILLS OF ACTIVE SHARING AND ACTIVE LISTENING TO WORK.**

▶ Present **Guidelines and Skills for Starting a Conversation** (Monti et al., 1989, 1995; Wanberg & Milkman, 1998; Wanberg, Milkman & Timken, 2005). Emphasize that it is OK and unselfish to talk about yourself. Just as sharing your toys with friends was unselfish as a child, sharing your experiences as an adult is also unselfish. Remind the group that self-disclosing facilitates self-disclosure by others.

Adjunct Exercise: Have the group take turns role playing starting a conversation in these scenarios:

- Two strangers at a party;

- Two workers at a coffee break, one of whom just started working for the company;

- Two people who see each other for the first time since high school.

Discuss whether group members used the skills in the role-play that were introduced in this section of the *Workbook*.

Have group members practice: "I" messages and avoiding using "you" messages; receiving feedback from others; open-ended statements and questions; statements to reflect back what others are saying.

❱ Present and discuss the **Skills and Steps in Handling a Difficult Conversation.**

- When doing the exercises, encourage clients to stay within their comfort zone. Clients may become emotionally involved when role-playing a sensitive or difficult topic with a significant other. Use therapeutic skills when directing these role-plays and bring the role-play to a positive closure.

- After each role-play, have the group give feedback as to how well clients stuck to the skills.

- One important skill to be learned is talking about oneself and not the other person when approaching a sensitive topic. It involves the active sharing model of: "It's about me and not about you." "I want to share how I see myself, not how I see you." "I'm confronting you about me, not you about you."

- Use *role reversal and doubling* (see *Chapter 7*). These help clients learn the skill of empathy.

- Stress using "I" messages in these role-plays. This keeps the person on his or her agenda, and not on the agenda of the other person.

- **Adjunct Exercise:** Using the round robin and wagon wheel method, have each client briefly role-play one of the six skills in starting and keeping a conversation going around a difficult topic with someone in his/her life. Have the client identify who that person is before starting the role-play.

- Discuss which step is most difficult to achieve when starting a conversation around a difficult topic: the approach, setting the stage, sticking to the point, etc.

- After clients complete *Worksheet 65,* have them share their results with the group.

❱ Clients update their *Master Skills List (MSL),* focusing on *Skills 12* through *15.*

❱ Using the *SSC Change Scale,* have clients rate themselves on their skills in managing a difficult conversation.

SUMMARY OF KEY CONCEPTS

❱ Starting a conversation and interpersonal interaction.

❱ Starting and managing interactions around a sensitive and emotional topic.

❱ Initiating prosocial, meaningful and healthy interactions.

SESSION CLOSURE AND GUIDELINES FOR THERAPEUTIC PROCESSING

Have clients share relationship problems that might have come up during the session.

RATIONALE AND OVERVIEW

Building on the communication skills platform, clients learn and practice the interpersonal skills of giving and receiving positive reinforcement or praise. We strengthen the positive features of other people through giving and receiving compliments. Successful relationships depend on this feedback - and more specifically, an atmosphere of give and take where positive experiences are shared. The giving and receiving in relationships is quid pro quo - something for something. We get something when we give something. Frequently, people fail to share the positive thoughts they have about their friends and family assuming that other people know their thoughts and feelings. On the other hand, a person may have no problem telling other people how much they appreciate them, but may not be able to graciously accept compliments. Learning to give and accept praise and positive reinforcement in relationships is seen as an important component in the treatment of judicial clients with substance abuse problems (Monti et al., 1989, 1995; Ross et al., 1986; Wanberg & Milkman, 1998).

SUMMARY OF CONTENT, PRESENTATION SEQUENCE AND GUIDELINES

Present this session following the topic sequence in the *Workbook.* The following are presentation guidelines.

▶ Go over the session objectives, do the *CB Map Exercise,* update the *MSL* and the *MAP* and invite group members to share their *TAP Charting.* Review active sharing and active listening.

▶ Present the **Difference Between Praise (Compliments) and Thanks or Appreciation.**

▶ When presenting **The Skill of Giving Compliments and Praise,** show how this skill is the reflective or feedback part of active listening. *Worksheet 66, Practicing Giving Compliments,* can be done in group or as homework.

▶ **The Skills of Receiving Compliments** is the receiving feedback component of active sharing. *Worksheet 67* can be done in group or as homework. Discuss whether the group found it more difficult to give or receive praise and positive reinforcement.

▶ **Adjunct Exercise:** In groups of three, have two members of the group role-play giving and receiving positive reinforcement and praise to someone in their lives. The third person observes. Have the observer give feedback and practice complimenting them if they did well. Rotate roles. Have them share how it felt receiving and giving compliments. Was it difficult or easy? What were the consequences?

▶ Clients update their *Master Skills List (MSL),* particularly *Skills 16* and *17.*

▶ Using the *SSC Change Scales,* have clients rate their skill levels of giving and receiving compliments.

SUMMARY OF KEY CONCEPTS

▶ Active listening and active sharing.　　▶ Giving and receiving compliments.

SESSION CLOSURE AND GUIDELINES FOR THERAPEUTIC PROCESSING

Discuss why it is difficult to give and receive compliments and praise. How is this related to childhood experiences of receiving or not receiving praise from their parents? This processing may touch on sensitive childhood issues for some clients. Praise the group for its good work. Providers are role models for clients.

RATIONALE AND OVERVIEW

We could conclude that judicial clients are not good problem solvers. If they were, they would have solved the problem of placing themselves in situations that led to criminal conduct and the abuse of substances. One could argue that individuals who engage in criminal conduct while on drugs are too impaired to solve problems, let alone prevent involvement in criminal conduct. Yet, even for the individual under the influence of drugs, there was a period of time prior to AOD intoxication or impairment in which rational decision making and problem solving was possible. The fact is, the offender did not find a solution to the problem of being in a circumstance that led to criminal conduct.

Although some people are better problem solvers than others, everyone has used the skills of problem solving at one time or another. Everyone has at least the rudimentary knowledge and skills of problem solving, judicial clients included. Yet, the rationale for this session is that judicial clients have not learned or have not effectively and consistently used the skills of problem-solving, and that this has contributed to their involvement in AOD abuse and CC. Although there are many factors that contribute to the involvement in AOD abuse and CC, we want to be sure that it is not due to a lack of having or applying the skills of problem-solving.

A problem is a behavior, situation, or circumstance that presents uncertainty or causes difficulty. The difficulty might be not getting our way, not being sure what is expected of us, rebelling against custom or the law, conflict over how things should be done, a difference between our own goal and the goal of someone close to us, or trying to find someone or something. Usually, there is a goal attached to our problem. Problem-solving therapy is seen to have three focuses (Nezu, Nezu & Lombardo, 2003):

▶ Training in problem orientation;

▶ Training in the specific steps and skills of problem solving;

▶ Practicing these skills across real-life situations.

John Dewey (1910), the father of the problem-solving method, devised a six-stage protocol on how most people confront and solve problems. Since then, theorists have developed many refinements of that method. We have modified these steps, using a variety of sources (J. Beck, 2005; King et al., 1994; Monti et al., 1989; Myers & Myers, 1980; Nezu, Nezu & Lombardo, 2003; Perkinson, 2002; Smith & Meyers, 1995; Wanberg & Milkman, 1998; Wanberg et al., 2005). The efficacy of problem solving therapy and treatment has strong empirical support in the literature for a variety of psychosocial problems (D'Zurilla & Nezu, 1999, 2001; Nezu et al., 2003).

As with other skills clients learn in *SSC*, the goal of problem solving skills is to attain positive outcomes. Problem solving depends on the utilization of cognitive restructuring and interpersonal skills. Self-talk, for example, provides mental self-control in the midst of problem solving. Both active sharing and active listening are important components of the problem-solving process.

The purpose of this session is to provide clients with the skills of problem solving so as to prevent recidivism and relapse and to live a more fulfilling and responsible life. Although some clients will use the session to solve specific life problems they are currently facing, the goal is for clients to learn and apply the methods for everyday living. This follows the metaphor: give a person a fish, and he/she can eat for a day; teach the person to fish, and he/she can eat for a lifetime.

SUMMARY OF CONTENT, PRESENTATION SEQUENCE AND GUIDELINES

Present this session following the topic sequence in the *Workbook.* The following are presentation guidelines.

▶ Do the *CB Map Exercise,* update the *MSL* and *MAP* and share *TAP Charting.*

▶ Have clients share their work on *Worksheets 66* and *67,* giving and receiving compliments, which were done either in group or as homework.

▶ Present **Two Bad Ways of Problem Solving** (Nezu et al., 2003). Have all clients briefly share whether they used one of these methods in solving the last problem they had.

▶ Use interactive methods when presenting **What Is a Problem?** Basic to being a good problem solver is being able to identify problems or situations that are going to cause a problem (Ross, et al. 1986). Good problem solvers know when they have a problem. A major barrier to problem solving is failure to recognize having a problem. Substance abusing judicial clients often do not recognize that they have a problem. When confronted by others about the problem, they get defensive. Problem recognition begins in our thinking as does the solution. Spend time on discussing the example of Larry in the *Workbook.* **Adjunct Exercise:** Briefly have each client share a problem he or she has at the present time.

▶ Go over the five **Steps to Problem Solving.**

　◆ The critical step is based on the proverbial "a problem well-defined is a problem half solved" (Nezu et al., 2003). It involves the "who, what, when, where, how" of the problem. This is the problem orientation focus of problem solving (Nezu et al., 2003).

　◆ Stress that we begin solving problems at the cognitive level. Thus, many problems are solved mentally and never involve an interpersonal process.

　◆ Facilitate discussion of how problem solving can get short-circuited by the thoughts, feelings and actions involved in using drugs or committing crimes.

　◆ *Figure 27* in the *Workbook* provides these steps. The goal is not just to teach these steps, but for clients to apply them in their daily living. First, have the group apply the steps to the example of Larry. Then, using *Worksheet 68,* have clients apply the steps to a current problem each is facing.

▶ When presenting the **Rules to Keep in Mind,** stress that one of the major barriers to problem solving is the failure to think outside the box, to see only one choice and only one solution. Effective problem solving is solution focused and involves Fisher and Ury's (1981) three key steps: keep focused on the problem; understand the interest and needs of others involved; and work towards a win-win solution.

▶ Clients update their *MSL,* particularly *Skill 18,* and rate their level of problem-solving skills.

SUMMARY OF KEY CONCEPTS

▶ Bad ways to problem-solve.　　▶ What is a problem?

▶ Steps in problem-solving.　　▶ Think outside the box and be solution focused.

SESSION CLOSURE AND GUIDELINES FOR THERAPEUTIC PROCESSING

Give clients an opportunity to explore their current life-problems. If time is available, have one or two clients apply the problem solving steps to a life problem they currently have.

RATIONALE AND OVERVIEW

The sessions on *Giving and Receiving Praise and Positive Reinforcement* and *Skills in Problem Solving* are directed at building strategies for responsible living. This session takes a further step in that direction. Assertiveness skill building will help clients get their needs met within the framework of responsibility towards others. Individuals engaging in criminal conduct get their needs met at the expense of others - an aggressive style of relating to others and the community.

The purpose of this session is for clients to learn interpersonal skills that get their needs met within a win-win structure. Although developing assertiveness skills is included in *Module 9,* which focuses on learning skills that build positive relationships with others, it is also an important component of *Module 10 - Social Responsibility Therapy* (SRT).

Assertiveness training is a salient component of most AOD treatment programs. Numerous studies have documented the efficacy of assertiveness skills training (e.g., Monti et al., 1995). It is recognized as an important skill to form positive and productive relationships with others and to refuse involvement in behaviors that lead to bad outcomes.

The success of assertiveness training is premised on the effective use of active sharing and active listening skills and being tuned into nonverbal cues and behaviors. It is part of the entire set of social and interpersonal skills training. As well, it provides the foundation for problem solving, conflict resolution, giving and receiving positive reinforcement, and refusal skills competency.

The seminal work in this field was done by Alberti and Emmons, whose book *Your Perfect Right* (1995) has undergone over eight printings since its first appearance in 1971. It provides the key principles and foundation of virtually all cognitive-behavioral approaches to the delivery of assertiveness skills training (unfortunately, they are often not credited for this contribution). This book is an invaluable resource for more in-depth work in assertiveness training with clients. Their work, along with the work of Duckworth (2003), Monti et al. (1995), Wanberg and Milkman (1998), and Wanberg, Milkman and Timken (2005) were the resources for the development of this session.

This session contrasts three non-productive ways that people use to solve problems, deal with conflicts and get their needs met and which often lead to bad outcomes: 1) avoidance (flight); 2) aggression (fight); 3) being passive-aggressive (fake). These approaches most often result in outcomes where the needs of neither party are met, or the needs of one party are met at the expense of the other. The outcomes are either lose-lose or win-lose.

These non-productive methods are contrasted with the win-win assertive style basic to need fulfillment, problem solving, and responsible living. Duckworth (2003) cautions that the success of being assertive should not be evaluated only on the basis of tangible outcomes. Its success should also be seen in terms of the degree of self-control derived from being assertive and "the degree of personal control and personal respect that is achieved and maintained throughout the assertiveness exchange" (p. 16).

It is important to show clients how the cognitive restructuring model and the *SSC CB Map* are used in the learning and practice of assertiveness skills. The behavioral styles that we use to relate to others, whether they are aggressive or assertive, are manifestations of the cognitive responses to relationship events. What are the specific thoughts and underlying beliefs that lead to assertive behavior? Or to aggressive behavior? The goal is to help clients identify thoughts that lead to the counterproductive ways to get needs met and then help clients learn to restructure those into assertiveness thoughts and beliefs.

An important part of assertiveness training is modeling. In general, modeling is effective in addressing psychosocial problems in different kinds of clients and in different settings (Naugle & Maher, 2003). Modeling is discussed in *Chapter 7.*

SUMMARY OF CONTENT, PRESENTATION SEQUENCE AND GUIDELINES

Judicial clients may initially see assertiveness as being a weak approach to getting needs met. It goes against the aggressive approach that they are often accustomed to using; or it strikes at the heart of manipulation and conning. It is a style of relating that simply has not been in the repertoire of most, if not all, judicial clients.

▶ Start with presenting the objectives and key concepts of the session. Then, facilitate the *CB Map Exercise* and sharing the *TAP Charting.*

▶ Share the idea described above that the assertiveness style is vastly different from the relationship style of most individuals involved in criminal conduct and substance abuse.

▶ When presenting **Reviewing Refusal Skills,** *Workbook* page 134, explain that refusal skills work to prevent something negative from happening, i.e., relapse, whereas assertiveness works at bringing about something positive.

▶ **Relationship Style Choices That Lead to Poor Outcomes** focuses on the three styles that prevent problem solving, block prosocial interactions, and most often lead to negative outcomes.

- ◆ Have clients discuss how each style can lead to criminal conduct, and then have them rate themselves on the PASSIVE, AGGRESSIVE, and PASSIVE-AGGRESSIVE scales.

- ◆ Providers may want to model each of these styles, or have one or two clients volunteer modeling them. Clients can have fun doing these role-plays.

- ◆ The passive-aggressive style is often the most difficult for clients to role-play. Providers will want to model this relationship style before asking clients to role-play it. Some examples are: Employee is upset because of not getting an expected raise but does not confront his employer, but starts to come to work late; spouse or significant other is angry at mate, but doesn't say so and starts to vacuum in the room where he is watching a football game.

▶ When presenting **A Healthy Choice,** take time to define assertiveness and give the rationale for assertiveness skills (getting win-win outcomes and preventing R&R).

- ◆ Have clients rate themselves on the *ASSERTIVE Scale,* encouraging them to be as honest as possible.

- ◆ The 10 keys to being assertive are really an assertiveness test. Take time to facilitate discussion around each key. Have clients share personal examples of each key. Sometimes it is helpful to give an opposite example. **<u>Adjunct Exercise:</u>** After discussing each of the keys, have clients re-rate themselves on the *ASSERTIVE Scale,* page 211 of the *Workbook.*

▶ Two of the four **Specific Skills in Being Assertive** are familiar to clients. They are the core communication skills. Working towards a win-win and keeping the door open are new skills. They are styles of relating that, again, may be foreign to most judicial clients. Criminal conduct is not win-win, and it never leaves the door open to further discussion, except in court.

- Spend the rest of the session on **Practice What You Have Learned.**

    - Clients role-play the four styles of relating around the three examples. When using the assertive role, refer back to the 10 key ways of being assertive. Have clients identify how effective each of the different methods was in resolving the problem.

    - Go back over the case of Larry and have clients role-play the styles of relating around this case. Apply the *STEP Method* to Larry so that he can get a positive outcome. This is a good time to discuss the importance of clients applying *STEP* to their daily lives. *STEP* is about getting positive outcomes and helps clients achieve the *SSC* goal of meaningful and responsible living.

    - **Adjunct Exercise:** Have one or two clients choose a real situation to role-play. Keep the focus on the assertive style. Have the group give feedback and suggestions regarding how the assertive character could have achieved the desired outcome.

- Have clients review *Part III* of their *MP (Program Guide 2)*, page 293 in the *Workbook* to see how the various **Thoughts and Actions Scales** apply to the various styles of relating discussed in this session. Take each item and decide which style or styles it fits. For example, is **Blame Others for Problems** a passive style or passive-aggressive style? Then, have them restate the item so that it can be expressed in an assertive way. "I'm going to make it clear that I'm responsible for solving my problems." Based on this exercise, have clients update and add to their *MAP (Program Guide 3)*.

- Clients update their *Master Skills List (MSL)*, particularly *Skill 19, Assertive Skills*. Using the *SSC Change Scale*, have clients rate their ability to use assertiveness skills.

- Go over the homework assignment: *A Thinking Report* on a situation where clients could have been assertive but were not and then a *Re-Thinking Report* on how that situation could have been approached in an assertive way.

SUMMARY OF KEY CONCEPTS

- Styles that lead to bad outcome: flight, fight, fake.

- Fair - assertive, a healthy choice.

- Ten keys to being assertive.

SESSION CLOSURE AND GUIDELINES FOR THERAPEUTIC PROCESSING

Facilitate honest discussion around how realistic it is for judicial clients to be assertive in every situation. Can they apply this skill to their everyday living?

Have clients look at the core beliefs that underlie the three styles that lead to poor outcomes. What is the core belief of being passive, passive-aggressive, and aggressive? Often, sessions on assertiveness tend to confront people with their failures. Clients should be made to feel that whatever mistakes they have made in the past, they have the opportunity for change and growth.

RATIONALE AND OVERVIEW

The introduction to *Session 27* in this *Guide* provides a basic foundation for understanding anger and anger management. The provider is asked to review that material before presenting this session. As well, providers should review the core concepts in *Session 27,* page 183 in the *Workbook,* with the group. This review is of particular importance if there are clients who have not had *Module 8.*

The introduction to this session adds to the understanding and skill base of anger and anger management. These sessions are not intended to be a substitute for a specialized program in anger management which may be indicated for clients showing high levels of trait and state anger as described below.

Whereas *Session 27* focuses on understanding and managing anger at the more intrapersonal level, this session focuses on managing anger within relationships. It also describes a cycle of anger and guilt found in many relationships that, unless checked, can lead to relapse and recidivism.

The provider may want to spend two group periods on this session. *Sessions 38* and *39* look at understanding and managing the behavioral manifestations of anger that are harmful to others and the community: aggression, abuse and violence.

A number of resources were used for the development of *Sessions 27, 34* and *38*: (Carter & Minirth, 1993; Donohue & Cavenagh, 2003; Kassinove & Tafrate, 2002; Novaco, 1986, 1994; O'Neill, 1999; Wanberg & Milkman, 1998; Wanberg et al., 2005).

The *CB Map* for Managing Anger as an Episode or State-Condition

The *SSC* model for understanding and managing anger and an anger episode is based on the *CB Map:* **Events, activation of cognitive structures** (thoughts and beliefs), the **emotional** response, **behaviors** and **actions,** and **outcomes.** Most anger management approaches use similar models and utilize the anger episode in teaching anger management (e.g., Kassinove & Tafrate, 2002). When presenting this session, it is important for the provider to review the *CB Map* within the context of anger and anger management. Following is a summary of such a review.

▶ **Event:** First, events trigger anger. These events could be external or internal. They often occur within the context of interpersonal relationships. Research has shown that the most likely triggers are actions by others who are liked, loved or well known (Kassinove & Tafrate, 2002). Most, if not all, angry responses have some interpersonal connection or association.

▶ **Activation of thought and belief structures.** These usually involve the four cognitive structures of: **appraisals, expectations, attributions,** and **decisions. Appraisals** are evaluations of other people's actions as being negative, unfair, terrible, etc. Angry thoughts can also be **outcome** and **efficacy expectations.** When people fulfill our expectations, we will have positive feelings. When expectations are not met, then angry emotions can follow. Anger towards self can occur when one's efficacy expectation to handle a particular situation is not realized. Or, angry *attribution* thinking is blaming others or self for bad outcomes. The *decision* structure operates in the angry episode: "I'll give him a piece of my mind!" Most important in managing the cognitive activation of an anger episode is to understand and change the underlying beliefs that drive angry thoughts.

- **Emotional or feeling response:** Kassinove and Tafrate (2002) describe this as the "experiences" component of the anger episode (p. 39). As discussed earlier, individuals will often experience the emotions and feelings first. Unless there is a "backing into" the thoughts (and hopefully the beliefs) producing those emotions, the angry behavior is quite likely to result in a negative or bad outcome - and will likely repeat itself. Preventing the emotional response from dominating will depend on how well the individual is tuned into the clues and signs of anger. The *SSC* model holds that the emotions of anger are preceded by and hooked into angry thinking. The key is getting clients to be tuned into their angry thoughts and underlying angry beliefs.

- **Behavioral responses:** Anger can become manifest as constructive or destructive responses. Destructive responses include verbal abuse, passive aggression, hostility, overt aggression, violence. The outcome depends on how the cognitive responses to the anger event are managed or changed.

- **Outcome:** As the *SSC CB Map* shows, the outcome can be adaptive or maladaptive. Angry behaviors leading to bad outcomes get strengthened because they reinforced the thought structures and underlying beliefs that produced the angry behavior. Anger management must involve thought and belief restructuring.

Trait-Condition Anger

Anger is described as being both a state and a trait condition. The above discussion describes anger as a state condition. State anger is the temporary arousal of angry thoughts and emotions associated with an event that frustrates or thwarts one's needs and goals and results in some kind of anger episode. As discussed above, the *CB Map* is the *SSC* model for managing anger as a state-condition.

Trait condition anger is personality based, persists over time, is more tied into hostility, and has internal etiologies. Measurable evidence of these two anger conditions is found in Spielberger's *State Trait Anger Expression Inventory* (1988) and his *State-Trait Anger Expression Inventory 2* (STAXI-2: 1999). Those high on trait anger experience anger more often, often without provocation, in a variety of settings, are more temperamental and quick to arousal, and tend to be impulsive (Kassinove & Tafrate, 2002).

Whereas about half of average adults become angry one or more times a week, around 86 percent of individuals who are in the high trait category report angry experiences several times a week, and for half of these, angry episodes can last more than a day (Kassinove & Tafrate, 2002, p. 40). State-condition anger can lead to bad outcomes.

However, individuals who indicate **both high state and trait** condition anger are more likely to experience chronic anger that is disruptive to interpersonal and intrapersonal functioning. For clients suspected of fitting this group, referral for further assessment is important. Providers trained in anger assessment may want to use one or both of Spielberger's (1988, 1999) assessment instruments. Kassinove and Tafrate's (2002) chapter on anger assessment and diagnosis is an invaluable aid in this process.

Anger Is a Social Script That Is Learned

Evidence of trait-condition anger does not mean that anger is totally innate and only biologically determined. Anger does have animal underpinnings, is part of the animal flight-fight reaction, and these are carried over into the human condition. Yet, most authorities would explain anger from a social learning theory (SLT) perspective - that its cognitive structures and emotional expressions are developed and reinforced within a social matrix.

From the SLT perspective, anger is a socially learned script or role that we construct and learn to play, and that emerges out of our social and interpersonal interactions. We learn how and when to be angry. This social script takes on a "privately felt emotional state of varying intensity with associated verbal and motor behaviors, bodily responses, cognitive distortions and deficits, verbal labels, and interpersonal effects" (Kassinove & Tafrate, 2002, p. 20).

SUMMARY OF CONTENT, PRESENTATION SEQUENCE AND GUIDELINES

An assumption of *SSC* is that anger is a basic dynamic of criminal conduct (CC) and that CC is angry behavior. Even at this point in *SSC,* many judicial clients will reject this assumption.

This session should start with a summary of the key concepts and ideas in *Session 27* and indicate that *Sessions 38* and *39* focus on the harmful and dangerous manifestations of anger: aggression, abuse and violence. Clients in open groups may have had *Sessions 38* and *39* before *Sessions 27* and *33.* Again, discuss with group the importance of going back and forth in the *Workbook* to review and practice important skills and concepts learned in previous sessions. This linking and updating is important to successful delivery of *SSC.*

Clients should set their own pace in self-disclosure. Also observe for clients who need additional help in the area of anger management. Present this session following the content and topics in the *Workbook,* integrating the following guidelines.

▶ Review the *MSL* and the *MAP* and invite members to share their *TAP Charting.* Review the objectives of the session.

▶ Have clients share the *Thinking and Rethinking Report* homework on assertiveness.

▶ Present the introductory section in the *Workbook.* Have clients check the relationships to which this session applies.

▶ Present the definitions for **Hostility, Anger, Aggression, Abuse and Violence** in an interactive style, having clients share their views of hostility, anger, non-physical abuse, physical abuse and violence. These definitions are based on a variety of sources including: Eckhardt and Deffenbacher, 1995; Kassinove and Tafrate, 2002; Novaco, 1994; O'Neill, 1999; Wanberg and Milkman, 1998; Wanberg, Milkman and Timken, 2005. **Adjunct Exercise:** Have clients give examples and/or share their own personal experiences around these specific terms.

▶ Present **What Causes Anger in Relationships?** by first asking clients to share their thoughts around this question.

▶ Begin **Skills in Managing Relationship Anger** by reviewing and practicing the six **Self-Control Skills for Regulating Anger,** presented in *Session 27,* pages 184-185 of the *Workbook.* These are summarized as:

- ◆ Know the triggers;
- ◆ Be mindful and aware of your anger;
- ◆ Use cognitive self-control tools including thought stopping, relaxation training, self-talk, etc.;
- ◆ Communicate or express angry thoughts and feelings rather than act them out;
- ◆ Problem solve (most angry episodes are based on an unsolved problem);
- ◆ Reward yourself.

Present the seven skills specific to managing **relationship** anger. The main sources for these skills include: Eckhardt and Deffenbacher, 1995; Kassinove and Tafrate, 2002; Monti, et al., 1989; Novaco, 1978, 1986, 1994; O'Neill, 1999; Wanberg and Milkman, 1998; and Wexler, 2000. *Skills 4* and *5* are introduced in this session and are dealt with in more detail in *Session 39*. *Worksheet 69* may trigger anger in some clients. Encourage clients to work within their comfort zone, and observe for clients that may react emotionally to this and the other exercises in this session.

▶ **Managing Criticism** is an important part of anger management (e.g., Monti et al., 1995; Kassinove & Tafrate, 2002; O'Neill, 1999). Role model giving and receiving criticism before having clients role play a situation of not handling criticism well and that led to a bad outcome. Have clients apply *STEP* to get a positive action and outcome.

▶ **The Guilt-Anger (GA) Cycle.** Guilt and anger go together "like a horse and buggy." However, they switch back and forth in terms of which is in charge. At times, anger is in control; at other times, guilt is in control. Unhealthy and maladaptive guilt places a strong control over anger. Unhealthy and maladaptive anger overrides the controls of conscience and guilt. The *GA cycle* involves episodes of loss of control over both anger and guilt. Many judicial clients experience guilt when losing control over angry behavior and actions.

The exceptions are offenders who fit the psychopathic personality pattern (Hare, 1970, 1980, 1986, 2003) and who do not manifest guilt and conscience around their antisocial and criminal conduct. This accounts for between 10 and 20 percent of the offender population.

 ◆ Interactively present the GA cycle using the example of the intimate partner relationship and anger release during a drinking episode. Describe how anger builds up when it is not released in healthy and productive ways. It is then released in destructive and irrational ways during a drinking or drugging episode, when defenses are down, resulting in emotional and even physical harm to others. After sobering up, the user has strong thoughts and feelings of guilt. These thoughts and feelings suppress and prevent a healthy management of anger. Those affected now release their anger. After their angry episode, they experience guilt and fear that they may cause another drinking/drugging episode. They back off. Angry thoughts in the user builds, reaches a peak, triggers a drinking/drugging episode, anger is released resulting in another negative and destructive emotional and action outcome. *Figure 28* in the *Workbook* describes this cycle. **Exercise:** Have clients share how they fit the cycle and how this cycle is part of relapse.

 ◆ For some clients, the GA cycle is a hidden agenda for relapse, although some may not realize that the primary purpose of anger build-up is to justify the relapse.

 ◆ **Adjunct Exercise:** Have clients discuss how the GA cycle applies to criminal conduct and how the cycle is part of recidivism. For example, anger builds up during a period of going straight. Anger is released during a criminal act. This is followed by guilt and strong external legal suppressions, e.g., being incarcerated. During this suppressed period, anger builds, and when the opportunity arises, another criminal act is engaged - recidivism.

 ◆ The cycle is broken by using the self-control skills presented in *Session 27, Workbook* pages 184-185, and the skills in managing relationship anger presented in this session. Go over the additional strategies to break the cycle.

▶ **Adjunct Exercises:** Here are some additional exercises that can be used in advanced relationship anger management sessions. These exercises require therapeutic skills and having clients participate within their comfort zone. Always have clients debrief after using these skills. Have clients use these skills when they experience anger arousal.

- **Using self-control methods:** Have clients share out loud what they say to themselves when getting angry with someone. Then, have them use self-control skills (p. 146 in the *Workbook*) to change those thoughts, manage the angry emotions, prevent acting out, and have better outcomes.

- **Relaxation skills:** Relaxation training may be one of the most effective ways to deal with anger arousal and control (Deffenbacher & Stark, 1992; Deffenbacher et al., 1988, 1995, 1996). Have clients imagine a scene that arouses anger. Then lead them in breathing relaxation techniques. Have the group take several slow, deep breaths. Use these words: "Take a deep breath. Hold your breath. Hold it, hold it. Now, slowly blow out the air through your mouth. Clear your mind of your thoughts as you let go of the air. Now, tell yourself, 'I am relaxed, I feel calm, I feel relaxed.' If a thought interrupts, tell yourself, 'I am relaxed' and go back to do some deep breathing." Repeat this three times with the group. Then, have clients do it on their own. Providers trained in relaxation techniques may also have clients imagine a calm scene or lead them in autogenic and progressive muscle relaxation.

- Review the relaxation skills in Table 7, page 180 of the Workbook. Have clients discuss what skills might work better for them in managing anger.

▶ Have clients review their *MP* to see which scales they have high scores on that apply to anger management. Should they add anger to their *MAP* as a problem?

▶ Update their *MSL*, particularly *Skill 11,* anger management.

▶ Have clients use the *SSC Change Scale* to rate themselves on their skill in handling anger in relationships.

SUMMARY OF KEY CONCEPTS

▶ Hostility, anger, aggression, abuse, violence.

▶ Skills in managing relationship anger.

▶ Managing criticism.

▶ The guilt-anger cycle.

SESSION CLOSURE AND GUIDELINES FOR THERAPEUTIC PROCESSING

Have each client share whether he or she is currently struggling with unresolved anger around a specific person or situation. Identify clients who see themselves as struggling with anger control. These clients along with clients who have moderate to serious anger problems, should be referred for more intensive anger management.

RATIONALE AND OVERVIEW

A major trigger for relapse is conflict in close relationships and with family members. Criminal conduct (CC) is often a reaction to conflicts with parents, spouse, a significant other (SO) or other family members. **Yet, basic human needs are closeness and belonging.** When those needs are not met in primary relationships, people seek to meet those needs in other places, e.g., at the bar, with criminal associates.

Another trigger for R&R is loneliness. A study of 12,000 probation offenders (Wanberg, 2006) showed that 72.5% of the male offenders were single, divorced, separated or widowed, and only 27.5% married; and 75.9% of the female group were single, divorced, separated or widowed and only 24.1% married. In a study of a prison sample (Wanberg, 2006), 81.9% of the males were divorced, single, separated or widowed and only 18% married. In the female prison sample, 89% were divorced, separated, single, or widowed and only 11% married. These data show the degree of interpersonal isolation and loneliness found among offender populations.

The majority of judicial clients will not be in an intimate or close relationship. However, most of these clients want to be in a close or intimate relationship, or have been in the past, and the content and concepts of this session are just as applicable to them as to those in a marital or intimate partner relationship.

The role of healthy social support and closeness in maintaining physical and mental health is well documented. Following arrest, support from family members will lessen. Family members and intimate partners and girl/boyfriends are often frightened, hurt or angry. It takes time for those relationships to be repaired. The support of family and SOs is an invaluable resource in the rehabilitation and restoration process.

Another basic need is to be individual and separate, to be unique and different, to be ourselves. We seek activities to support our sense of self, our individuality and separateness. One basis of our conflicts with people with whom we share intimacy is the need to be separate and individual - to "do our own thing," to have freedom from the control of closeness. AOD use is one way to cope with and "break away" from a controlling and dominating relationship. CC provides a sense of power that defines individuality. It sets the individual apart from society and the mainstream. This meets the strong need for separateness.

These two needs, the need for intimacy and closeness **and** the need for separateness and individuality, are often in conflict. Maslow (1954) identifies these conflicts in his hierarchy of needs. He sees self-esteem and self-actualization as at higher levels of need than the need for relationships and closeness. Yet, the latter need is very powerful and can lead to problem behaviors. The need for friends, close associations and peer closeness can override our sense of what is right or wrong, moral or immoral. One of the most robust predictors of CC is criminal associates (Andrews & Bonta, 2003; Wanberg & Milkman, 1998).

AOD use problems and CC often result from the conflict between the need for closeness and intimacy and the need for separateness. AOD use with friends or engaging in criminal conduct are mechanisms for "getting away" from the control of family, parents, significant others or society at large. A healthy balance of separateness and closeness in relationships is one key to preventing relapse and recidivism.

This session helps clients address these relationship issues, see how they are related to AOD abuse and CC, and learn skills to build and support healthy families and intimate partner and social relationships. Clients also learn to value and preserve separateness and individuality in a prosocial and healthy way.

Family members and SOs often have a great deal of distrust of judicial clients because of the repeated patterns of AOD problems and CC. Thus, facilitation of interactions with family members and SOs and even skills training should initially be low-key, supportive, and avoid areas that are sensitive and conflictive (Monti, et al., 1989; Wanberg & Milkman, 1998). Working on basic communication skills is a good place to start. The general goal of this session is to encourage the beginning of honest and caring communication about concerns and problems with which judicial clients and their SOs are struggling.

Programs using *SSC* will have a number of resources available for clients and their families to address the treatment support needs of significant others, and to enhance prosocial support for and build positive connections between clients and family members during *SSC*, and upon re-entry into the community. These should include:

▶ An orientation session for family members of *SSC* clients, either on-site, through email, or other correspondence, to inform them of the program purpose, strategies, approaches, and structure;

▶ Family and couples support groups; and

▶ Marital and family counseling.

SUMMARY OF CONTENT, PRESENTATION SEQUENCE AND GUIDELINES

Welcome the guests and have each group member introduce themselves using only first names. When doing exercises, have those who do not have a SO present keep in mind some significant relationship to which they can apply the concepts and skills in this session.

▶ Start by summarizing the session objectives. Then, have clients review their *MP* and those scales pertinent to this session, which include:

◆ Benefits of AOD Use: Cope With Relationships;

◆ Negative Consequences From Use: Behavioral Disruption From Use and Social Irresponsibility;

◆ Thinking, Feelings and Attitude Patterns That Tend to Prevent Healthy Intimacy, e.g., Blame Others;

◆ Areas of Adult Problems Such as Marital-Family Problems, Social-Relationship Problems.

▶ Review and update the *MSL* and *MAP* and have volunteers share their *TAP Charting*.

▶ Have one client volunteer to do the *CB Map Exercise* around a recent relationship conflict. Then, apply the *STEP Method* to bring about a positive outcome. This will help the SOs attending to understand some of the tools clients use in *SSC*.

▶ Present **Conflict Between Need for Closeness and Need for Separateness,** using an interactive-teaching approach.

◆ Review and practice the skills of active sharing (self-oriented communication) and active listening (other-oriented communication) which are foundational to developing and keeping close and intimate relationships and in resolving the conflict between the need for closeness and separateness.

◆ **Adjunct Exercise:** Have clients and their guests share a closeness activity that they enjoy; then have clients share a separateness activity that they also value.

▶ **Defining Our Basic Needs** is based on Maslow's (1954) model of hierarchy of needs. The needs pertinent to this session are: closeness; self-esteem; and self-actualization - separateness. Society tends to place more value on the need for closeness, yet, individuals often lack the skills to fulfill this need.

- **Understanding Relationship** focuses on seeing a relationship "as a person" with specific needs, emotions and goals. Relationship is a powerful controlling factor in people's lives. A healthy relationship has limits and boundaries, just as healthy people set limits and boundaries on their thoughts and behaviors. The exercise in this section may help clients better understand this concept.

- **Stages of Change of a Relationship** focuses on learning to balance the needs of closeness and separateness, one key to a healthy relationship (Wanberg & Milkman, 1998). *Figure 29*, page 223 in the *Workbook*, shows the *Balanced Relationship Model*. Discuss the process of becoming enmeshed, establishing separateness and then integrating balance. Discuss how going to the bar and spending time with AOD-using friends may be an effort to establish separateness and individuality.

- The **Ten Tips for Keeping a Healthy Closeness** can be applied to intimate partner, family, and parent-child relationships. Have group members share how they can apply these tips in their relationships.

  Adjunct Exercises: Modeling and role playing exercises can be used with any of the Ten Tips.

- **Keeping the Balance** in a close and intimate relationship is achieved through good communication skills. Again, these concepts can be applied to family and parent-child relationships.

  - Caution clients that sharing the portrayal of their relationship with their SO on *Worksheet 70* could cause conflict or a strong emotional reaction if there is a large discrepancy between the portrayals. In such cases, and for unstable relationships, such sharing should be done in a structured marital counseling session. The same caution is in order for *Worksheet 71*. Have clients share their work with the group or their SO only if they feel comfortable doing so.

  - When practicing the active listening-active sharing skills, have couples or families work together. For those without a SO present, have someone role-play the SO, or have those persons be observers and give feedback to the couples for families working together.

  - **Adjunct Exercise:** Have clients review their results on *Scale 2*, Family Marital Adjustment, (questions 13 through 19) of the *Adult Self-Assessment Profile (AdSAP)*. Providers may copy that portion of the AdSAP so that clients can retake it in group. Have them compare the two testings.

- Have clients review their MP and update their *MAP*, particular problems related to SO relationships. Clients also update their *MSL*, particularly focusing on *Skills 11* through *21*.

SUMMARY OF KEY CONCEPTS

- Needs for closeness and separateness.
- Tips for healthy closeness.
- Relationship balance.

SESSION CLOSURE AND GUIDELINES FOR THERAPEUTIC PROCESSING

Have the group discuss the problems of keeping a balance between separateness and closeness. Facilitate client sharing around relationship problems.

MODULE 10

Skills for Social and Community Responsibility

OVERVIEW

Phase II moves clients into commitment to change and sets the stage for ownership of change. It is built around the three major focuses of *SSC*: the concepts and skills for cognitive self-control and change, *Module 8;* developing and maintaining positive social and interpersonal relationships, *Module 9*; and learning the concepts and skills of community responsibility, the focus of this module.

GOALS OF MODULE 10

SSC is about changing antisocial and criminal attitudes and behaviors. *Module 10* specifically focuses on the goal of helping clients develop and strengthen character and prosocial attitudes and behaviors through *Social Responsibility Therapy* (SRT). The specific provider objectives are to help clients learn the concepts and skills to:

▶ Strengthen character and prosocial attitudes and behavior;

▶ Understand empathy and learn skills of empathic reasoning;

▶ Understand and prevent aggression, abuse and violence;

▶ Resolve conflicts and gain win-win solutions;

▶ Strengthen values and morals for community responsibility;

▶ Make a constructive contribution to the community.

PRESENTATION LOGISTICS

For the closed group approach, *Sessions 36* through *42* are presented in sequence. For open groups, the only no-entry point for clients is *Session 39*, a sequel to *Session 38*. Providers may find a need to extend the time frame for some sessions beyond two hours.

SHIFTING TREATMENT PARADIGMS FOR ANTISOCIAL AND CRIMINAL CONDUCT

The *Preface* to this *Guide* discusses the need to include a strong emphasis on moral and community responsibility in judicial client treatment. Providers will recall that moral responsibility represents a set of ethical and principled thoughts, attitudes and behaviors directed at respecting the rights of others, being accountable to the laws and rules of our community and society, having positive regard for and caring about the welfare and safety of others, and contributing to the ongoing good of society.

Focusing on moral and community responsibility represents a shift in the treatment paradigm for judicial clients as discussed in the *Preface* and *Chapters 1* and *4* of this *Guide*. It is one of the core strategies of *SSC*. The most salient aspects of this discussion will be summarized.

Twentieth-century psychotherapy and treatment of psychosocial disorders were shaped by the worldview of modernity which made the individual supra-ordinate to any social role or obligation, focused on individualism, individual freedom and individual expression, idealized and codified the individual, and projected the individual outward (O'Hara, 1997). This resulted in psychotherapy and psychology being egocentric, putting the person at the center of its focus. Most therapies emerging out of this egocentric view of individuals - behavioral, humanistic, psychoanalytic, existential, cognitive-behavioral - were self-directed or self-focused. The focus was on relieving the pain and suffering of individuals, e.g., depression, anxiety, stress, disturbed thinking, substance abuse.

Within the framework of egocentric approaches, sociopathy, antisocial disorders, criminal conduct and character pathology were often viewed as not treatable. When traditional egocentric treatment was applied to these nosological groupings, the outcomes were poor. This merely reinforced the belief that antisocial patterns and criminal conduct would not respond to treatment.

Thus, a shift in the treatment paradigm was necessary in order to address antisocial and criminal patterns. There was a need to go beyond egocentric psychology to a sociocentric, holistic framework and move towards a connected consciousness and relational empathy (O'Hara, 1997). This means that we build on the gains and strengths of egocentric psychology and include a sociocentric approach, not only for the constituents of modern treatment and psychotherapy, viz, its clients, but also for civilization as a whole.

Within the sociocentric framework, treatment approaches for antisocial and criminal conduct developed several approaches. Generally, treatment of criminal conduct addresses the two dimensions of the antisocial personality pattern: 1) character which is based on learned schemas, formed out of the socialization process, and is defined by social and moral responsibility, cooperativeness, and concern about others; and 2) temperament, which is biosocial in origin, based more on innate and sociogenetic influences, and expressed through novelty-seeking, aggression and impulsivity (Cloninger, Svrakic & Prybeck, 1993; Costello, 1996; Sperry, 2006). Following are more specific approaches for addressing antisocial and criminal attitudes and conduct.

▶ Treatment is focused and structured with the provider taking an active role in implementing change.

▶ Use of supportive interventions that develop a therapeutic alliance and partnership with the client utilizing motivational enhancement approaches.

▶ Use of specific cognitive-behavioral approaches that develop prosocial attitudes and beliefs (schemas).

▶ Structured and measured external interventions, e.g., judicial supervision and sanctioning.

▶ A strong working partnership between the correctional and therapeutic systems.

▶ A strong focus on empathy identification, development and training.

IMPLEMENTING SOCIOCENTRIC APPROACHES IN *SSC*

The mental self-control component of *SSC (Module 8)* is essentially egocentric in nature. The skills of self-talk, thought-stopping, cognitive restructuring, changing negative thinking and managing internal emotional states are directed at enhancing ego strengths. However, these are essential in the treatment of the judicial client.

The Social and Relationship Skills Training (SRST) is a mixture of both egocentric and sociocentric approaches. Communication skills, problem solving, conflict resolution, and developing meaningful intimacy are directed at meeting the egocentric needs of clients, but also address the sociocentric goal of developing responsible relationships with others. This is the focus of *Module 9*.

Social Responsibility Therapy (SRT) is sociocentric, is directed at restructuring relationships with the community and addresses moral and social responsibility. It is the primary approach to changing antisocial thinking and behaviors. Such approaches involve replacing antisocial with prosocial thinking and behavior. It involves changing thinking errors that lead to criminal conduct. Empathy development is a key approach as are skills that contribute to the good of the community. Managing aggression and violence, prosocial approaches to conflict resolution, and facilitating cooperation between the judicial and therapeutic systems in judicial client management and treatment are sociocentric approaches. SRT is the focus of *Module 10*.

As noted, a common view of egocentric-oriented treatment literature is that antisocial patterns and characteristics are difficult, if not impossible, to treat. However, SRT can be effective in bringing about changes in antisocial patterns. As discussed in *Chapter 4*, Beck et al. (2004) see this as moving antisocial clients from concrete thinking operations and self-determination towards more abstract thinking, interpersonal consideration and moral functioning (p. 169). Beck sees moral functioning as ranging from concern for others based on what the individual has to gain or lose to a sense of responsibility towards others and a commitment to the guiding principles for the good of society (p. 179).

SRT offers promise to judicial clients committed to change and wanting better outcomes for themselves and their community. SRT strives to strengthen character and prosocial attitudes and behaviors. An important change skill is *STEP* which focuses on thinking change from antisocial to prosocial so as to bring about positive outcomes. In many ways, the essence of *SSC* is *Social Responsibility Therapy* (SRT).

CHARACTER BUILDING AND STRENGTHS

Module 10 focuses on building and strengthening character. Relevant to this focus are the six character strengths or moral virtues developed by Peterson and Seligman (2004). Each of these moral strengths is defined by specific characteristics. These will be briefly summarized along with their specific elements that are relevant to the treatment of judicial clients. These strengths provide the foundation for the SRT model used in *SSC*.

▶ **Wisdom and knowledge:** Open-mindedness, good judgment, critical thinking.

▶ **Courage:** Speaking up for what is right; integrity and honesty.

▶ **Humanity:** Love, kindness and social intelligence (awareness of the motives and feelings of others - empathy).

▶ **Justice:** Social responsibility, citizenship, treating others fairly.

▶ **Temperance:** Prudence (not taking undue risks; self-control and self-regulation).

▶ **Transcendence:** Being thankful and having gratitude; being mindful of the future; seeing a higher purpose beyond self; having a sense of meaning and purpose.

SESSION 36: Strengthening Character and Prosocial Attitudes and Behaviors

RATIONALE AND OVERVIEW

A strong argument made in this *Guide* is that providers be up-front and straightforward with judicial clients regarding the assessment of their psychosocial problems, particularly as they are related to the areas of sociopathy, antisocial and criminal conduct. This was an important part of *Module 4,* and is just as important in this session.

Module 4 focused on understanding and changing criminal thinking and behavior. *Session 9* provided strong focus on antisocial and criminal conduct. It gave guidelines for responsible living and defined antisocial and criminal attitudes and behavior. Clients measured their level of antisocial behavior and attitudes. *Session 10* linked thinking errors with criminal conduct (CC) and provided a graphic way of looking at the cyclical process of CC using the criminal thinking and conduct cycle. In that session, clients measured their level of prosocial values and strengths. In this session, the focus is on strengthening character, moral virtues, and prosocial values. As part of this focus, clients review the work they did in *Module 5.*

This session represents an important component of SRT: building moral character and prosocial values in order to help clients have a positive relationship with their community. One of the most important resources for clients in learning moral character and prosocial attitudes and behaviors is the role modeling done by the provider. This role modeling is much broader than demonstrating that the provider lives up to the specific elements of moral responsibility defined in the introduction to this module e.g., respects the rights of others, has positive regard for and caring about the welfare and safety of others, etc. Modeling character strengths has to do with the provider having fidelity and integrity around all of the concepts and skills that clients are learning in *SSC.*

For example, does the provider use the skills of active listening, giving and receiving praise, and problem solving in group? In essence, there is great burden on the provider to practice, not only in group, but in daily living, the concepts and skills that clients are expected to learn and integrate in their group experience and in their daily living.

Review the modalities through which clients practice self-control and mental change skills, *Figure 25,* page 159 in the *Workbook.* These modalities can also be used for practicing social-interpersonal and community responsibility skills.

▶ See or visualize the skill.

▶ Hear or listen to ourselves say the skill out loud.

▶ Act or role-play the skill.

▶ Write or journal the skill, as is done in the *SSC Worksheets.*

SUMMARY OF CONTENT, PRESENTATION SEQUENCE AND GUIDELINES

At the beginning of this session, stress that, throughout *SSC,* there has been an emphasis on building moral character and prosocial values through changing thinking to achieve positive outcomes for clients and for the community. This session builds on the work that clients did in *Module 4, Sessions 9* and *10.* Follow the presentation sequence of each section in the *Workbook.* Here are the guidelines for this session.

- Review the *MSL* and *MAP;* members *TAP Charting;* review the session objectives.

- Review of **Criminal Thinking and Conduct** involves going over the most important parts of *Sessions 9* and *10.* Have clients discuss changes in their scores on *Worksheet 24, Workbook* page 87. Also, have them discuss how they now see their criminal conduct cycle, *Worksheet 26, Workbook* page 93.

- The section **Understanding Antisocial, Moral Character, and Prosocial** defines these three important concepts and has clients re-rate themselves on the *Antisocial Behavior and Attitudes Scale, Worksheet 23, Workbook* page 86, and the *Prosocial Strengths Scale, Worksheet 27,* page 94 in the *Workbook.*

  - **Adjunct Exercise:** Present the six character strengths or moral virtues presented in this *Guide's* introduction to *Module 10.* Have clients discuss how they would rate themselves on these strengths, using the responses: "doesn't fit me," "fits me somewhat," "definitely fits me." It would be helpful to put these on a flip chart or poster board.

  - The exercise at the end of this section will help clients relate antisocial attitudes and behaviors to specific internal and external events. These events are high-risk exposures for recidivism. Apply *STEP* to only a few of the items in *Worksheet 23.*

- Here are some guidelines for presenting the **Ten Ways to Strengthening Moral Character and Prosocial Behavior,** which is one of the most important parts of the *SSC Workbook.*

  - Make a wall poster-board with the ten guidelines. Have clients give examples of each of these guidelines. For example, have clients discuss how they are a part of society and the benefits they get from society, e.g., they use public highways, transportation, and they are kept safe by law enforcement agencies. Clients review the antisocial thinking errors listed on page 92 of the *Workbook* and then use the *STEP Method* to change the errors to thoughts that can lead to prosocial outcomes.

  - Apply the 10 guidelines to the stories of John, page 32, and Larry, page 206, in the *Workbook.* Have one or two clients give personal examples on how they can apply the guidelines to their lives.

- Have clients review their *MP* to give them guidelines as to what areas they need to work on with respect to antisocial attitudes and behaviors. Have them review their *MAP* to see if they need to add new problems to work on related to character development and prosocial attitudes and behavior.

- Have clients update their *MSL,* particularly *Skills 26* and *27.* Have them use the *SSC Change Scale* to rate their ability to strengthen prosocial character.

SUMMARY OF KEY CONCEPTS

- Antisocial, moral character, prosocial.

- The six character strengths or moral virtues (not presented in the *Workbook*).

- Use *STEP* to get positive, prosocial outcomes.

- Ways to strengthen moral character.

SESSION CLOSURE AND GUIDELINES FOR THERAPEUTIC PROCESSING

Clients not fully into the commitment stage will be struggling with accepting that they have antisocial and criminal attitudes. Awareness and acceptance can be facilitated by having clients, again, share the nature and extent of their past criminal conduct and activities.

RATIONALE AND OVERVIEW

Defining and Understanding Empathy

Empathy is probably one of the most complex concepts in the fields of psychology and the behavioral sciences. "Empathy is frequently referred to as an elusive concept, difficult to define and even more difficult to measure" (Feshbach, 1997, p. 34). Since it is one of the most important concepts and skills that providers use in treatment and since empathy building and training are key components of SRT and of offender and antisocial treatment and change, its meaning will be explored in some depth. As discussed in *Chapter 2,* empathy is at the core of prosocial responding and responsible behavior towards others and the community.

Simply defined (Oxford English Dictionary), empathy is "the power of entering into the experience of or understanding objects or feelings outside oneself." Feshbach (1997, p. 36) proposed a three-component definition of empathy:

▶ cognitive ability to discriminate affective cues in others;

▶ taking the role or perspective of another person;

▶ experiencing the emotions of another person.

One way to understand the meaning of empathy is to distinguish it from sympathy. Sympathy is an emotional response that is aroused by a stimulus outside of ourselves. It is having a sense of or feeling the pain of others. The James-Lange theory of emotions (James, 1890) concludes that our subjective emotional experience (sympathy) is the awareness of our own bodily changes in the presence of outside emotionally arousing stimuli.

Cannon (1927) concludes that sympathy is more than purely autonomic (sympathetic nervous system) arousal. He sees emotional arousal as being more than just an awareness of our visceral responses or sympathetic nervous system's discharge since we are able to differentiate different kinds of emotions.

Schachter and Singer (1962) took a step further and emphasized the role of cognitive factors or processes in the emotional response. We attribute meaning to our emotional responses; or we interpret our emotional responses based on our prior experiences and what we experience going on around us. This cognitive interpretation of emotion lays some ground work for the understanding of empathy.

Sympathy is an emotional response that certainly involves a cognitive attribution process. Feeling sorry for someone must involve more than just a visceral response; it involves understanding. Gordon Allport (1937), however, states neither "... an 'instinct of sympathy' nor a theory of 'emotional contagion' will account for our understanding of others" (p. 529). He notes that Theodore Lipps was the first to discuss empathy in the psychological literature. Lipps saw empathy based on our capacity to imitate others. He saw knowledge as having three spheres: sensory perception; inner perception; and empathy (Lipps, 1907, as cited in Allport, 1937).

Empathy involves understanding another person and the ability to put oneself in the place of the other person. Allport (1937) states "...empathic knowledge achieves a unity through a welding of the objective and the subjective" (p. 533). Empathy is a deeper experience. It goes beyond the egocentric point of view. It assumes "... that the knowledge of others has complete priority over self-knowledge" (p. 533). Identification is emotional "and requires no specific mimicry." Empathy does not require identification, although it can be part of empathy. We can develop empathy for someone who has no emotional significance to us (Allport, 1937).

Carl Rogers (1980), who stamped empathic listening into the psychotherapy process, concluded that "a high degree of empathy in a relationship is possibly the most potent factor in bringing about change and learning" (p. 139). His formal definition focuses on "perceiving the internal frame of reference of another with accuracy and with the emotional components and meanings which pertain thereto as if one were the person, but without ever losing the 'as if' condition" (p. 140). It is "entering the private perceptual world of the other," it is "being sensitive," "it means sensing meanings," it means "temporarily living in the other person's life," it is a process of "desiring to know" (pp. 142-144).

Over the years, then, there has been theoretical debate as to whether the nature of the internal process of empathy is cognitive or emotional. Some (e.g., Allport, 1937, Rogers, 1980) see it as more cognitive. Others (Feshbach, 1997) see it as "a shared emotional response" between individuals, but "contingent on cognitive factors." However, the "general consensus is that empathy entails both affective and cognitive elements" (p. 36).

The Importance of Empathy Training in Judicial Client Treatment

Self-control is an important part of responsible living and change. Gottfredson and Hirschi (1990) suggest that low self-control is a single construct that accounts for a significant amount of variance in explaining antisocial behavior and criminal conduct. An important component of their low self-control construct is lack of empathy, self-centeredness, indifference and insensitivity to the suffering and plight of others, and not identifying with or putting oneself in the place of others.

Values and morals differ across all peoples and nations. Yet, there are laws across all nations that have one thing in common: the safety and welfare of people. This is basic to most communities and cultures. Basic to this concern for others is empathy.

The education and treatment protocols for judicial clients consider self-control as underlying the values of change, freedom, positive relationships with others and community, and concern about others. The latter two values have to do with empathy. Empathy is one of the most important parts of moral character, prosocial behavior and responsibility towards the community. Responsible living is considering the attitudes, feelings and views of others - or to become more understanding towards and caring of others.

Individuals with a history of substance abuse and criminal conduct have serious problems in identifying with the suffering of others, in placing themselves in the "shoes of another person," namely, their victims, and in being sensitive to and concerned about others and the community. Although some research would indicate that low empathy may not be a good predictor of recidivism (Andrews & Bonta, 2003), there is a strong agreement in the field that empathy training should be an important component of offender treatment (e.g., Agee, 1979, 1986; Feshbach, 1984; Ross, Fabiano & Ross, 1986; Wanberg & Milkman, 1998). A discussion of some of these research findings is presented in *Chapter 2* of this *Guide*.

Both sympathy and empathy are important in developing prosocial attitudes and self-control. Ross (Ross, Fabiano & Ross, 1986; Ross & Hilborn, 2005) considers empathy to be one of the most important values people can learn when moving from antisocial conduct to prosocial living and responsible attitudes towards the community. Ross and associates teach that offenders will have a greater chance to change thinking and beliefs when they learn to consider the attitudes, feelings, and views of others - or to become more understanding towards and caring of others.

Empathy as an Interpersonal Cognitive Construct

As discussed in *Session 11* of this *Guide,* **interpersonal cognition** is about what people think about their relationships, their mental representation of others, what they think others think about them, their thoughts about acceptance and rejection, and the mental schemas they use to understand and form relationships (Baldwin, 2005). The work in this area has provided "models of the mechanisms whereby people think about their interpersonal experiences and the effects of this thinking on their subsequent interactions and sense of self" (p. xi). An important component of interpersonal cognition is empathy.

Interpersonal Sensitivity - Decentering

Empathy is an interpersonal cognitive skill that allows the individual to be sensitive to others and the community. Interpersonal sensitivity, which is one operational definition of empathy, facilitates positive interactions with others. Research has shown that offenders have major deficits in the areas of interpersonal cognition that are needed to show social sensitivity and to deal effectively with social situations (Andrews & Bonta, 2003).

At the individual level, "egocentrism involves an inability to consider the perspective of others both cognitively and emotionally" (Andrews & Bonta, 2003, p. 201). Interpersonal sensitivity moves the individual beyond an egocentric to a sociocentric view of others and the world. This shift involves the process of decentering, discussed in *Session 11.* Decentering allows us to reflect on the past and the future, imagine locations other than place and activities of the present, and allows us to not be tied to ourselves (Littlejohn, 1999). Decentering begins in early childhood. It formulates the basis of empathy (Littlejohn), an essential cognition for prosocial attitudes and actions.

Empathy Training

Research findings indicate that individuals can move from an egocentric posture, and decenter towards a more sociocentric relationship towards others. For example, Chandler, Greenspan and Barenboim's (1973, 1974) classic studies showed that this decentering process can occur with delinquent juveniles after engaging in role-playing and journaling exercises. Feshbach's (1984) studies of the efficacy of her *Empathy Training Program* showed a decrease in aggressiveness and an increase in prosocial behavior in aggressive children.

A number of specific approaches are involved in empathy training. These are summarized.

- **Perspective taking:** This involves role-playing, and more specifically, role-taking of other individuals who are presented in either pictorial or vignette modalities. This facilitates getting into the world of others so as to increase interpersonal sensitivity.

- **Role reversal and doubling:** Empathy involves imitation, mimicry and putting yourself in the place of the other person. The techniques of role reversal and doubling (Bischof, 1964) are powerful methods for enhancing the understanding of the other person's position. It takes one beyond the self. In role reversal, the individual takes the role of the other person. In doubling, the double repeats back the words of the other person with the inferred meaning, emotional intonation and expression. It also involves kinetic mimicking of the other person. An example is when the observer of another person makes the actual bodily movement similar to that of the other person. Allport (1937) uses the example of observers of a high jumper actually lifting their legs as they watch a person clearing the high jump bar.

- **Communication skills:** Active sharing facilitates appropriate egocentric expressions and centering. Active listening facilitates the decentering process and enhances interpersonal sensitivity (empathy).

▶ **Moral dilemma exercise** (Arbuthnot & Gordon, 1986; Gibbs, 1995; Ross et al., 1986; Wanberg & Milkman, 1998): Although this approach focuses more on recognizing and resolving moral conflicts, it does get clients to think beyond their own egocentrism center, and consider the point of view of others. This is presented in *Session 41.*

Mutual and Community-Oriented Empathy

Most studies and approaches to empathy training are conducted within the relational context and within the interpersonal matrix. Treatment of the judicial client must include developing interpersonal sensitivity and empathy at the interpersonal level. However, effective judicial treatment also includes a focus on empathy for the community and for society as a whole. O'Hara (1997) moves beyond the relational context of empathy to a community and societal oriented model in the concept of mutual empathy. As she states:

> It is through mutual empathy that we develop a sense of ourselves in relationship, the security of knowing that we belong, the knowledge of who we belong to, and how we must participate if we are to be loved and recognized by our community. (p. 314).

Having judicial clients develop empathy for community and society is a difficult task. It is more abstract and less concrete than interpersonal empathy training. A strong group-oriented treatment program, where clients develop empathy for and understanding of their group, can represent the microcosm within which empathy towards the community can be learned. Therapeutic community treatment also provides this kind of microcosm for learning empathy towards the community and society as a whole.

Empathy and Sympathy: Both Are Needed

John Shlien (1997), as a student at the University of Chicago during the 1950s, had ongoing dialogues with Carl Rogers around the concept of empathy. Shlien concluded that empathy alone is not enough, either in treatment or in establishing a responsible relationship with others. "Although empathy is an important and perhaps essential factor in the service of understanding, it is not in itself the hoped-for consequence of understanding" (p. 67). He cautions that empathy may become "an easy substitute for the real motive, and the real work in therapy - sympathy and understanding" (p. 67).

Whereas empathy makes it possible to put yourself in the place of others, sympathy represents " 'a feeling for' - is a type of commitment" (p. 67). He sees sympathy as taking us to a higher state of moral development in that it represents a commitment to others. In fact, he concludes that "empathy alone, without sympathy, and even more, without understanding, may be harmful" (p. 67).

Empathy is such a powerful concept in therapy that it can overshadow the value and importance of sympathy. Shlien (1997) argued that the influence of empathy in treatment could "undermine and even obliterate the positive values of sympathy and understanding" (p. 67). He moves to a sociocentric (he does not use that term) perception around this concern, and sees the preservation of sympathy with empathy and understanding as going beyond the realm of treatment. "A whole society is currently affected, slowly losing the vocabulary and consciousness of compassion" (p. 67).

In *SSC,* we see understanding as an integral part of empathy. As well, we see that both empathy and sympathy are necessary for the development of a prosocial response to others and the community. Sympathy brings a stronger emotional commitment to being prosocial, caring, and responsible living. It provides the compassion component to moral responsibility and prosociality.

SUMMARY OF CONTENT, PRESENTATION SEQUENCE AND GUIDELINES

Introduce this session by sharing with clients that empathy is one of the most important parts of *SSC* with respect to preventing recidivism and developing a prosocial relationship with others and the community. Follow the presentation sequence in the *Workbook* utilizing the following guidelines.

▶ Start by briefly doing a *CB Map Exercise* with one volunteer in the group. Have that group member then apply *STEP* so that there is a thinking change and a positive outcome.

▶ Have clients share their *TAP Charting,* and then go over the session objectives.

▶ When presenting **Sympathy,** have clients share personal examples of experiencing sympathy for others. Stress that having sympathy for others is an important part of being prosocial.

▶ When presenting **Empathy,** take time to make the distinction between sympathy and empathy, based on the *Workbook* material. Here are some further guidelines for this section.

◆ Draw upon the material in the introduction to this session, particularly Feshbach's (1984) three-component definition of empathy: ability to see different emotions in others; taking on the role and view of another person; experiencing the emotions of others.

◆ Role model each of the five empathy skills as they are presented. This prepares clients for the exercises in the next section. The provider can role model the skills by thinking out loud. For example, when role modeling **Skill 2, Think and imagine being in another person's place,** the provider can share an experience of having had a conflict with another person. After describing the conflict, the provider talks out loud, or doubles, what the other person might have been thinking and feeling during the conflict. "He must be pretty angry at me." "He is having a hard time seeing my point of view," etc.

▶ When **Practicing Empathy,** have clients apply the five empathy skills when doing each of the exercises. *Worksheets 72* and *73* can stimulate strong emotions in some clients. Have clients list only those persons affected by their AOD abuse and criminal conduct whom they feel comfortable listing. Instruct clients not to give the names of persons, but only who they represent, e.g., son, daughter, victim, etc. Have clients identify whether their statements of how the people were affected represent empathy or sympathy responses.

▶ Clients update their *MSL,* particularly *Skill 28,* their *MP* and update their *MAP.* On their *MP,* have them put EM by those scales requiring empathy to change. In the *MAP,* for their antisocial thinking and behavioral problem areas, have them put the skills of empathy as one tool to resolve these problems.

KEY CONCEPTS

▶ Sympathy and empathy.

▶ Five skills of empathy.

SESSION CLOSURE AND GUIDELINES FOR THERAPEUTIC PROCESSING

Have clients share their character strengths and weaknesses. Debrief clients who had significant emotional responses during the session.

RATIONALE AND OVERVIEW

Summary of Sessions on Anger and Anger Management

Another important component of SRT is the management of anger and the prevention of violence and aggression. *SSC* devotes four sessions to dealing with these topics. *Session 27* focuses on managing anger at the intrapersonal level. This *Guide's* introduction to *Session 27, Managing and Regulating Anger,* discusses: anger as a disorder and anger management treatment; catharsis or "letting go" is not the answer; criminal conduct is angry behavior; and *SSC* is not anger management treatment.

Session 27 helps clients gain a better understanding of the meaning of anger, its clues and signs, and the highly charged events that lead to angry thinking. Clients are given a six-step, two-phase skills approach to regulating anger. The first phase involves mindfulness and awareness of angry thoughts, feelings and triggers. The second phase involves anger-control using mental self-control, expressing constructive anger, problem solving and self-reward. The Yerkes-Dodson Law is used to help clients understand that constructive or optimal levels of productive anger can lead to positive outcomes.

Session 34, Managing Anger in Relationships - The Guilt-Anger Cycle, deals with the relational aspects of anger. This *Guide's* introduction to that session covers the following topics: the *CB Map* for managing anger as an episode or state-condition; trait-condition anger; anger is a social script that is learned. In *Session 34*, the concepts of hostility, anger, aggression, abuse and violence are presented to clients. The causes of relationship anger are discussed. Building on the self-control skills presented in *Session 27,* clients learn and practice specific skills for managing relationship anger. The guilt-anger cycle is presented. The provider is asked to review these topics before presenting *Sessions 38* and *39*. For programs using open groups, some clients in the group may not have had *Sessions 27* or *34*. Thus, it will be important to begin this session with a review of the most important concepts and skills covered in those two sessions.

Overview of *Sessions 38* and *39*

Sessions 38 and *39* are presented in sequence. New clients do not enter at *Session 39*. These sessions move the topic of anger to aggression, abuse and violence. *Session 38* is devoted to providing clients with a basic foundation of understanding aggression, abuse and violence. These are seen as manifestations of anger and represent attacks on people and society. This session also provides clients with the opportunity to do some self-assessment with respect to their risk of future involvement in uncontrolled anger, abuse and violence.

Session 39 represents a departure from the approaches taken in *Sessions 27* and *34*. These two sessions were directed at anger management and focused on changing angry thoughts to get self-control that results in positive outcomes for clients and their relationships. If anger is expressed, it should be constructive in nature, lead to problem solving at a win-win level, and result in prosocial behavior and interactions.

Session 39 is directed at prevention - prevention of aggression and violence. These manifestations of anger do not lead to positive outcomes and result in antisocial, and often, in criminal behaviors. Certainly, one of the best preventive measures for aggression, abuse and violence is the management of angry thoughts, attitudes and emotions. There is a level of acceptable expression of anger, and one way to manage anger is to express it in constructive ways that can lead to positive outcomes.

However, the expression of aggression, abuse and violence is not acceptable and most often, if not always, leads to bad outcomes. The goal is prevention. The Yerkes-Dodson Law shows that excessive levels of anger arousal lead to destructive or impaired performance, e.g. aggression.

Definitions of Nonphysical and Physical Aggression and Abuse

Session 34 provides definitions of hostility, anger, aggression, abuse, and violence, using a number of sources (e.g., Eckhardt & Deffenbacher, 1995; Kassinove & Tafrate, 2002; Novaco, 1994; O'Neill, 1999; Wanberg & Milkman, 1998; Wanberg, Milkman & Timken, 2005). There is common agreement in the literature that aggression is behavior that is directed towards harming or injuring another person or to destroy objects (e.g., Baron, 1977; Eckhardt & Defferbacher, 1995; O'Neill, 1999; Wanberg & Milkman, 1998).

In our original work (Wanberg & Milkman, 1998), aggression and abuse are separated into the two categories of nonphysical and physical, even though there is a tendency in the literature to lump them together (e.g., O'Neill, 1999; Kassinove & Tafrate, 2002; Wexler, 2000). We continue this approach in this work, but provide specific breakdowns within each of these categories. These breakdown definitions in the *Workbook* are based on our original work and on the work of Fall, Howard and Ford (1999), who define four forms of abuse: physical, verbal, emotional, and sexual.

It is more helpful for judicial clients to separate out the physical from the nonphysical. Many judicial clients have engaged in nonphysical abuse and aggression but not physical aggression - violence. Note that we are being very specific in using the term violence - that it is physical aggression and/or abuse. This is fairly congruent with its use in the literature. However, the definitions of violence and aggression tend to overlap in the literature. O'Neill (1999), for example, defines aggression as either physical or verbal, and defines violence as a "deliberate attempt to inflict physical harm" (p. 7).

Anger and Posttraumatic Stress Disorder (PTSD)

There has been an observed relationship between PTSD and anger (Chemtob et al., 1994; Chemtob et. al., 1997; Novaco, 1996). A basic assumption of the *SSC* sessions on anger management is that angry thoughts, beliefs and emotions are strong determinants of criminal conduct. As well, it is safe to say that many judicial clients have been exposed to traumatic events, e.g., violence, death of someone close, and some have identifiable symptoms of PTSD. This is particularly true for female offenders (Milkman & Wanberg, 2008).

Where there is a link between PTSD and exposure to anger and violence, anger management approaches and addressing abuse and violence may stir up PTSD issues for some clients. Providers need to be observant of this and make appropriate treatment referral for such clients. Although *SSC* does not specifically address PTSD, cognitive self-control, social and relationship skills training (SRST) and social responsibility therapy (SRT) approaches offer skills and concepts that can be used in addressing PTSD.

Justification for Sessions on Prevention of Abuse and Violence

The percentage of violent offenders in any judicial system will vary depending on the definition of a violent offense. Serin (2004) notes that in the Canadian system, "based solely on admitting offense, the population in 1995 (10,983 offenders) was comprised of 78 percent violent offenders (robbery, murder, assault, sexual assault)" (p. 12-3). However, by "restricting the definition to persistently violent offenders - those with three or more victims in their criminal history - the prevalence drops to 35.4 percent" (p. 12-3). Rennison (2000) reports that of all of the crimes committed in 1999, about one fourth were violent crimes.

Certainly, these statistics would support the inclusion of sessions for judicial clients that deal with understanding and preventing aggression, abuse and violence. It is probably safe to say that the majority of judicial clients in *SSC* programs do not engage in a physically violent lifestyle. However, all judicial clients (as is true with all individuals) have experienced the emotional state of anger. And, anger is certainly a basis for aggression and violence, even though not all aggression is caused by anger (Howells, 1989).

Some psychologists would conclude that everyone has the potential for aggression and violence. Yet, the literature indicates that the probability of offenders committing an aggressive or violent act is much higher than with persons in the average population. As well, it is difficult to predict who will commit an aggressive or violent act. If the probability is greater among judicial clients, then it makes sense to include aggression and violence prevention as a salient component of the treatment of judicial clients.

Finally, the main purpose of these sessions is to prevent aggressive behavior so as to decrease the probability of bad outcomes and increase the probability of good outcomes for our clients. Certainly, preventing violent crimes is part of the goal. However, violent crimes are a small part of the overall phenomenon of human aggression (Blackburn, 1993, as referenced in Serin, 2004).

SUMMARY OF CONTENT, PRESENTATION SEQUENCE AND GUIDELINES

It is important to reiterate to clients that the *SSC* sessions on anger, anger management, understanding and preventing abuse and violence are not an anger management treatment program per se. Clients with a specific history of anger control problems, abuse and violence will need specific treatment in these areas.

▶ Review *MSL* and *MAP.* Ask members to share *TAP Charting* and review session objectives.

▶ Review the anger self-control skills on page 184 and managing relationship anger skills on page 215.

▶ When presenting **Nonphysical Aggression and Abuse,** have clients share what they see as examples of each of these forms of aggression and abuse. The examples do not have to be personal experiences.

▶ **Physical Aggression and Abuse - Violence** presents three forms of violence. Make sure that clients understand that *SSC* takes the position that violence is any physical expression of aggression. Again, have clients give examples of these forms of violence. They do not have to be personal experiences.

▶ The **Abuse and Violence Focus** helps clients understand that an important part of the aggression response is a perception that needs are being blocked. Not all aggression is perpetrated by an individual who is dominant and controlling. Aggressive behavior is often executed by individuals who feel weak and dominated, and the victim is perceived as in control and powerful.

▶ There are specific **Parts of Abuse and Violence.** The most common model is to see aggression and abuse as involving power and control. However, aggression and violence are also directed at the relationship which controls those involved. Both abusers and victims get involved in another abusive relationship because they fail to solve the problem by being controlled by relationships or by the community. Within this model, violence is directed at not only the person-victim, but also the relationship and the community.

▶ The basic model presented in the section **The Cycle of Violence - Like the Guilt-Anger Cycle,** is based on a variety of sources (e.g., Wanberg & Milkman, 1998; Wexler, 2000).

♦ Although there is a tendency to see this cycle as starting with the tension-building component, the cycle could begin with any of the three components. The release or explosion stage (Wexler, 2000, calls this the acute explosion phase) could be the starting point of the cycle.

- Kassinove and Tafrate (2002) look at this cycle from an episode perspective, involving: Triggers and appraisals, which represent the **build-up stage**; experiences and expressive patterns, which represent the **release or explosion stage**; and outcomes which represent the calm, quiet, **guilt stage**. It is important to note that the quiet or calm outcome may involve the perpetrator of the violence or abuse episode being incarcerated or jailed.

- **Adjunct Exercise:** Have group members discuss whether the cycle of violence is valid with respect to what they have experienced. Make it clear that this sharing should be done within their comfort zone. Providers should not probe, but only use reflective skills.

▶ **Jealousy** is a basic component of aggression and abuse treatment, particularly in domestic violence treatment (e.g., Wexler, 2000). This strong emotion emanates from thoughts of not having what others have or anxiety of losing what one has. At the positive end, it can strengthen relationship bonds. As Wexler (2000) notes, it becomes a problem when individuals spend excessive time worrying about losing a loved one, or when it leads to control of the other person through aggressive behavior, or stifling the relationship by restrictions, to excessive control over others. It is important for clients to learn to discern when jealousy is irrational or even delusional. Jealousy can extend to thoughts and feelings of being short-changed by society and not getting what one deserves, which can lead to aggressive and violent actions.

▶ The purpose of the **Arousal** section is to prepare clients for its management in *Session 39*. Its management is a key to preventing aggression and abuse.

▶ **Self-Assessment of Abuse and Violence** provides clients with an opportunity to evaluate their level of risk for involvement in abuse and violence. The cutoff value of six or more checks is somewhat arbitrary, but does provide clients with an estimate of risk with respect to engaging in uncontrolled abuse and anger. In *Worksheet 74*, we have clients describe episodes of nonphysical and physical abuse and violence that they have witnessed. This avoids putting clients on the spot of listing violence they have been involved in. However, some may choose to give episodes that they have been involved in, either as victim or perpetrator. Providers need to be observant for clients who may have a strong emotional response to this exercise, and use therapeutic skills to debrief these responses while at the same time facilitate the clients' learning from this experience.

▶ Have clients review their *MP* to see how their scores apply to the prevention of aggression and abuse. Should they add these areas to their *MAP* as problems? Update their *MSL*, particularly *Skill 11*.

▶ Using the *SSC Change Scale*, have clients rate their understanding of abuse and violence.

SUMMARY OF KEY CONCEPTS

▶ Nonphysical aggression and abuse.

▶ Physical aggression and abuse - violence.

▶ Power and control over others and the relationship.

▶ Arousal and jealousy.

SESSION CLOSURE AND GUIDELINES FOR THERAPEUTIC PROCESSING

After clients share some of their past experiences related to violence and abuse, do an emotional check with group members to be sure that they have neutralized emotional arousal during the session. For clients who show signs of high levels of stress during these sessions, an individual debriefing session may be indicated.

RATIONALE AND OVERVIEW

The introduction to *Session 38,* a prerequisite to this session, provides background information regarding understanding aggression, abuse and violence. The provider should review that information.

SSC sees uncontrolled angry thoughts and emotions as the basis of aggression and violence. Some authorities do not completely agree with this assumption and hold the view that anger is not a necessary or sufficient condition for aggression (Wexler, 2000) and that not all aggression is caused by anger (Howells, 1989). Yet, it is commonly agreed that anger is often associated with aggression and abuse, that anger and aggression overlap (O'Neill, 1999), and that anger does not necessarily lead to aggression.

If we define anger as only an emotional state, then it is reasonable to conclude that some aggression may occur in the absence of that emotional state. However, in *Sessions 27* and *34,* we define anger as a **cognitive (thoughts, beliefs, attitudes) and emotional state** that varies with different degrees of intensity, and has identifiable physical (tense muscles), mental (agitation and irritability), and behavioral (fly off the handle, restless) signs, often resulting in negative and adverse outcomes. In *Session 38,* we defined aggression and abuse as actions that inflict psychological, emotional, and physical injury on another person.

Using these definitions, we are assuming that angry thinking (and beliefs) and angry affective states underlie **most** actions of aggression, abuse or violence. Prevention of violence would involve identifying the angry cognitive structures, such as expectations or appraisals, associated with or that lead to aggression. As discussed elsewhere, it is often necessary to start with the emotional or physical signs of anger, and then move back to the cognitive structures underlying the anger.

There are some circumstances where anger may not underlie the expression of aggression or violence, such as in war, or self-defense, where physically harmful actions towards others are not determined by angry thoughts or emotions, but rather a set of cognitive structures or affective states such as fear, or performance skills. A soldier most often does not engage in violent conflict based on angry thinking or emotions, rather based on cognitive structures that determine performance skills, developed through repetitive training. Some criminal aggression and violence can also be based on cognitive and affective states that are not anger driven, but on ingrained cognitive structures, such as loyalty to a gang, the Mafia, or a leader.

Outside of these special conditions, angry cognitions and emotional states underlie most aggression and violence, and an important component of preventing aggression and abuse is anger management. However, the prevention of aggression and violence goes beyond anger management and involves specific concepts and skills to change thinking and situations that can lead to aggressive behavior. The purpose of this session is to provide clients with an understanding of some of these concepts and skills. **It is reiterated that the *SSC* sessions in the areas of anger, aggression and violence are not to be seen as independent, stand-alone treatment approaches for these issues. Judicial clients with a significant history of problems in these areas will need to be referred to a separate anger management and violence prevention program.**

Since the 1970s, a number of structured programs in this area have been developed, beginning with the seminal work of Novaco (1975). Most are manual-guided programs that address either the management and control of anger (e.g., Carter & Minirth, 1993; Kassinove & Tafrate, 2002; O'Neill, 1999), or domestic violence and relationship aggression and abuse (e.g., Fall, Howard, & Ford, 1999; Lindsey, McBride, & Platt, 1993; Pence

& Paymar, 1993; Wexler, 2000). Some are specifically designed to work with male abusers (e.g., Wexler, 2000). A good summary of science-based approaches to the treatment of aggression is found in Citrom, Nolan and Volavka (2004). No formal manual-guided program could be found that addresses community or society-oriented aggression, abuse and violence. However, this area is usually addressed through the approaches used in anger management and aggression-violence prevention. *The Resource Guide* (Wanberg & Milkman, 2008) provides a summary of the dynamics of aggression and violence and the most common prevention and treatment approaches.

SUMMARY OF CONTENT, PRESENTATION SEQUENCE AND GUIDELINES

Within the spirit of the *Phase II* focus on positive outcomes, emphasize that the purpose of this session is more than just preventing aggressive and abusive behaviors. It is to develop beliefs and skills that lead to a prosocial and peaceful relationship with others and the community. Present this session using the following guidelines.

▶ Review the *MSL, MAP* and *TAP Charting*. Review the objectives of the session.

▶ Do the *CB Map* around anger and aggression with one client volunteer. Then, before presenting the session content, have clients reflect on the feeling of **power that can come from creating and maintaining harmony and a peaceful relationship with others.** Have clients visualize peaceful interactions with others.

▶ The **Skills in Preventing Violence** are both cognitive and behavioral. The main sources for these skills include: Fall, Howard and Ford, 1999; Kassinove and Tafrate, 2002; O'Neill, 1999; Wanberg and Milkman, 1998; and Wexler, 2000. **Time out** and **escape plan** are considered to be basic action skills in most aggression and abuse prevention programs (e.g., Fall et al., 1999; Kassinove & Tafrate, 2002; Wexler, 2000), and most programs devote one to two sessions to learning and practicing these skills.

　◆ **Time out,** presented in *Session 34*, page 216 of the *Workbook,* should be reviewed with clients. Fall et al. (1999) make it clear that time out is not "walking away." It is part of a relationship agreement that precedes conflictive interaction. The rules are simple: one person communicates the need for time out from the conflict; it always creates a physical distance; specific activities are planned, such as taking a walk but the time is spent reflecting on solutions; and there is the agreement to go back and work at resolution. The key is that, having agreed to a time-out plan, one or all parties in the conflict have to appraise and then communicate that things are getting out of control, and that the attempt to reach a solution has reached a "dead-end." **<u>Adjunct Exercise:</u>** Have clients practice making time out statements. Example: "I just need to take time out from our discussion, it's too upsetting."

　◆ **Escape plan** is another component in most aggression and violence prevention programs (Kassinove & Tafrate, 2002). Parties ahead of time agree that escape may be necessary at times. The rule is that the person leaves the situation with no expected goal other than to stop what appears to be an explosive situation. There is no expectation of re-engagement around the conflict, as in time out. A critical point in the escape plan is when one person blocks the exit of another person. Skills of self-talk ("I am not going to touch her, I will just back up, and let things cool down") and the communication skill of active sharing ("I need just to remove myself - it is me, not you") are the key approaches. **<u>Adjunct Exercise:</u>** Have clients generate and share an escape plan for potential conflict situations. Have clients discuss the dangers of a "path blocking" episode.

　◆ Kassinove and Tafrate talk about **stimulus control** and **avoidance.** These refer to controlling or even avoiding the triggers of anger and, subsequently, aggression, and include: **planned avoidance** (e.g., avoiding heavy traffic); **time-delaying** a response to a situation or question that can provoke anger (a teenager's request to use the family car after having an accident a week before); and using an **alternative response** (instead of responding verbally, write a letter to the person).

- The eight **Rules and Guidelines to Preventing Aggression and Violence** were gleaned from all of the above-cited sources. Have clients share their views of these rules.

- **Jealousy Control** is another component of anger management and violence prevention programs. Wexler (2000) devotes an entire session to this area. Review the material on this topic in the *Workbook,* page 235. Then go over the specific skills to handle jealousy. Relationship issues relevant to jealousy control are: there is always **partial fulfillment** of emotional needs, such as being loved; **balancing dependencies** (Carter & Minirth, 1993); **achieving healthy** cognitive and behavioral **freedom** from relationships.

- **Anger Arousal Control** is a key component of preventing aggression and violence (Kassinove & Tafrate, 2002; Wexler, 2000). Review the **Clues and Signs of Anger,** page 184 in the *Workbook.* One of the most effective methods to manage anger arousal and prevent aggressive behavior, and which has strong empirical support, is relaxation skills (Deffenbacher and associates, 1988, 1992, 1995, 1996; Kassinove & Tafrate, 2002; Wexler, 2000). Review these skills in *Table 7* of the *Workbook,* p. 180. O'Neill's (1999, p. 130) OTSAR (On The Spot Arousal Reduction) approach focuses specifically on relaxation techniques and cognitive skills to reduce anger arousal. OTSAR includes: breathing and other relaxation techniques; self-monitoring by visually measuring the level of anger, thought stopping, distraction techniques, and calming statements. When doing the exercise in this section, have clients use the *Anger Scale, Session 27,* p. 184, to practice self-monitoring of anger levels.

- The **Anger Journal** provides clients with a means to monitor their anger responses and skills management over a two-week period. Again, this approach is used in anger management and aggression prevention programs (O'Neill, 1999). Clients are encouraged to record the anger episodes at their own pace. If they feel it is too difficult or anxiety provoking, have them discontinue journaling and discuss it in group. These clients may be candidates for a formal anger management or violence prevention program.

- **Adjunct Exercise:** Relating the concepts and skills of preventing aggression and violence to interpersonal interactions is not difficult. The real challenge is to have clients see how these concepts and skills are related to anger and violent behavior towards the community and society (e.g., armed robbery). Have clients discuss how they see the concepts and skills in the anger sessions relate to society in general. For example, relate the concept of jealousy and jealousy control to their relationship to the community. Does their anger come from being jealous of not having what others have, e.g., a better car, education, job?

- Have clients update their *MAP.* Have clients review all of the skills in their *MSL,* particularly those related to anger, aggression, abuse and violence.

- Using the *SSC Change Scale,* have clients rate their skill level in preventing abuse and violence.

SUMMARY OF KEY CONCEPTS

- Skills in preventing aggression and violence.

- Aggression and violence prevention rules.

- Jealousy and anger arousal control.

SESSION CLOSURE AND GUIDELINES FOR THERAPEUTIC PROCESSING

Have clients share their level of concerns and confidence in managing anger and preventing aggression and violence.

RATIONALE AND OVERVIEW

Session Purpose

Conflict resolution skills are part of both SRST (Social and Relationship Skills Training) and SRT (*Social Responsibility Therapy*). Settling conflicts in a positive manner helps judicial clients have better outcomes in their relationships with others and the community, and helps prevent relapse and recidivism.

Defining Conflict

We can define conflict in terms of its synonyms - contention, controversy, rivalry, active opposition, friction, clash, competition, struggle, strife. However, it is more helpful to define conflict in contextual terms. For example, Kelley (1987) views conflict as an interpersonal and intrapersonal process. Peterson (1983) provides a process definition of conflict, but sees it involving disruptions or interferences within the interpersonal and social context: conflict is an interpersonal or social process that occurs whenever the actions of one person interfere with the actions of another (p. 365).

Interference with the action of the other person also involves an intrapersonal process (Kelley, 1987). The following example illustrates how the interpersonal interferences also creates an intrapersonal interference.

> A couple begins to argue following the wife's request that her husband help vacuum the house in preparation for the guests coming over for dinner that evening. Husband is in his study pretending that he is reading a book, but really mulling over a problem he had with his boss on Friday. She begins to vacuum which annoys him and interferes with his musing over the problem. He jumps up, grabs the vacuum cleaner and starts to vacuum. She responds in anger and hurt, tells him that he can entertain the guests himself and leaves the house slamming the door behind her.

The conflict between the couple is defined by what Kelley (1987) calls the **interchain interference** (sequence of transactions between the couple), and the **intrachain interference** (sequence of events within the person - the thinking and pondering going on inside the husband. What is also important about Peterson's definition and the above illustration is that feeling, thought and action (the three components of CB focus) interact in producing the intrapersonal and interpersonal interference. This provides the basis for the focus of conflict resolution: the interchain of feeling, thought and action in the interference process.

Conflict With Community and Society

Peterson's (1983) definition of conflict also applies to conflicts with the community or society. Criminal conduct is an example. The actions of one individual (offender) interferes with the actions of others (the community). The interference is with and within the community. However, the actions of the community, or agencies within the community, e.g., law enforcement, the courts, also produce interferences within the offender, much like the husband whose intrapersonal system is interfered with by the wife's vacuuming. The resolution of the offender-community conflict is similar to the resolution of the husband-wife conflict. The first step to resolving this conflict is that the offender takes responsibility for his/her role in this conflict. The community takes responsibility in that it sets up structures to deal with criminal conduct, e.g., treatment programs, court actions, judicial supervision.

Components of Conflict

Kelley (1987) indicates that conflict has three parts: structure, content and process. **Structure** is the situation and persons involved which are relatively stable factors that give rise to the conflict and represent the context of the conflict process - husband, wife, guests coming, vacuuming the house. **Content** is what the conflict is about - wife requesting husband to help vacuum, and husband resisting. **Process** is the conflictive interaction or the interpersonal and intrapersonal interference process - wife asks husband to help with house cleaning and vacuuming, husband resists because he is busy musing about a work situation, wife gets irritated and intentionally vacuums in his presence, husband gets angry and starts vacuuming, wife gets angry and leaves.

Although conflict resolution must include dealing with content, structure and process, we will focus mainly on process as we provide clients with a basis for resolving conflicts and engaging in negotiating as a method of conflict resolution.

Using the *SSC CB Map* to Describe the Conflict Elements and Process

The *CB Map* can be used to illustrate the elements of the conflict process.

- **Situation or event,** or antecedent conditions of the conflict. This is the structure or contextual component and includes a particular situation such as: interaction between two people; economic problems; or persons involved, which could include community.

- **Thoughts, attitudes and beliefs** are activated as a response to the situation, such as: persons perceive (think) their needs are being blocked, their territory being invaded, their rights being threatened, being cheated, short-changed, their domain being interfered with, their social situation being disrupted.

- **Emotional response** or felt conflict resulting from the above cognitions. Could be anger, defeat, elation, hope.

- **Behavioral responses** of those involved to cope with the conflict. There are usually two types of response. Adaptive, which may involve efforts to problem solve, communicate ideas and feelings, bring someone in to help resolve the conflict. Or, the response may be maladaptive, such as getting drunk, arguing, putting each other down, aggression, committing a crime, getting violent, stealing, etc.

- **Outcome of the conflict:** There are four kinds of outcomes. The first is **win-win**, or a positive **outcome,** e.g., mutual agreement, parties are brought closer, all are satisfied, the judicial client receives and responds to treatment and the community feels compensated. The second is a **lose-lose outcome,** e.g., all parties feel suppressed, cheated, short-changed, angry, the person is arrested and there is no compensation for the victim. A third is a **win-lose,** where one party feels positive and satisfied, and the other party is not satisfied, and feels short-changed. The fourth is **no resolution,** nothing is settled, and the conflict continues. The behavioral responses of all parties, maladaptive or adaptive, do not necessarily guarantee the type of outcome. An adaptive response could result in a win-lose, or a lose-lose, or no resolution. Yet, adaptive responses on the part of all involved have higher probabilities of getting to a win-win outcome.

Ross et al. (1986) note that a person engaging in criminal conduct is dealing with internal conflicts, but is also fighting the community or society. Thus, many judicial clients will always perceive the outcome of their legal problems as lose-win - they lose and the community wins. The goal for most judicial clients who enter treatment is that they will eventually see the outcome of their judicial involvement as win-win.

Negotiation

One way that we can approach the resolution of conflicts is through negotiation. Negotiation is working towards compromise and agreement between the parties that allow both to satisfy their needs. What is important to recognize is that "the act of engaging in communication is a process of negotiating our meanings with those of others" (Ruben, 1988, p. 105).

When we communicate, what we really do is negotiate meanings and understandings with other people. Thus, we practice the art of negotiation - because we engage in communication every day. When our meanings match the meanings of others, we can say we are communicating - and we are in fact negotiating.

Judicial clients have not communicated with the community and society. They have not negotiated meanings and understandings with the community. Their meanings and the community meanings are not matching.

It is important for judicial clients to understand that compromise and negotiation are not defeat, but are ways of achieving "no-lose" solutions to problems. Deciding to no longer use substances and be involved in crime is not a lose-win situation. Nor does it mean that the offender is weak.

Living free of AOD problems and criminal conduct is a win-win condition. As Ross and associates note, negotiating is not a show of weakness, but requires social skills and courage to face the conflict in a constructive manner (Ross et al., 1986).

Several sources were used in generating the content for this session. These include Cummings, Long and Lewis (1983), Fisher and Ury (1981), Kelley (1987), King et al. (1994); Ross et al. (1986); Ury (1993); Wanberg and Milkman (1998).

SUMMARY OF CONTENT, PRESENTATION SEQUENCE AND GUIDELINES

Make it clear to the group that the concepts and skills of this session apply not only to their relationship with others but also their relationship with the community and society. The following presentation sequence is recommended for this session.

▶ Review the *MSL* and the *MAP* and invite members to share their *TAP Charting*. Review the objectives of the session.

▶ Have clients review their *Anger Journal*. For clients with whom this is their first session in *Phase II*, give them guidance in doing the *Anger Journal*.

▶ **Opening Discussion:** Have clients define conflict. Then give them the definition above: a conflict takes place in relationships or in a social environment where the actions of one person gets in the way or blocks the actions of another. Have clients share some of the conflicts that they have in their lives. If no client mentioned his or her past criminal behavior, pose this as a question: Did your criminal behavior create a conflict within yourself and with your community?

▶ Discuss **Win-Win Outcomes.** Describe the difference between the adversarial approach - someone is wrong and someone is right - to settling conflicts and the win-win approach. Although **not** stated clearly in the *Workbook*, the underlying theme of this session is that the first step to conflict resolution is for clients to take responsibility for their role in a conflict. Have clients discuss whether they have taken full responsibility to resolve the conflict between themselves and the community.

- Discuss **What Is Involved in Settling Conflicts or Problem Solving. <u>Adjunct Exercise:</u>** Have one or two clients share a recent conflict and then identify the three components of a conflict in those scenarios: 1) the situation or persons involved; 2) what the conflict is about; and 3) the give and take - the interaction among participants.

- Go over the **Guidelines for Working Out a Conflict.** These are time-tested approaches, and found in most work that is done on conflict resolution and negotiation. Review the three non-productive ways of dealing with conflict, presented in *Session 33,* pages 210-211 of the *Workbook* - fight, flight, fake.

- **Working for a Win-Win Outcome** essentially involves five negotiation skills. This model is based on Fisher and Ury's work on conflict resolution and getting a win-win (1981).

  - **<u>Adjunct Exercise:</u>** First, present this scenario. John works for a major package delivery company. He has been on the job for a month. He agreed to take the job if he could be given a route that was fairly close to where he lives. There is a 30-minute time period between when he gets off from work and when his wife goes to work. He has two little children, and he parents them while his wife works. On Friday, his boss, who is new, tells him he is being transferred to a route across town. This will create a major problem for him.

  - **Discussion:** First, have the group do some basic problem solving for John. Then role-play John talking with his boss to see if the decision can be changed. Have those doing the role-play apply the five skills in negotiation. If this doesn't work, what are the other solutions John could consider?

  - **<u>Exercise:</u>** After clients do *Worksheet 76,* have one or two group members share their recent conflict and then have the group analyze the conflict using the five skills to get a win-win outcome.

- In **An Approach for Settling Conflicts,** the Reinhold Niebuhr prayer, or the *Alcoholics Anonymous* serenity prayer, has all of the elements of healthy conflict resolution. Knowing when you cannot change the situation is often the solution. Yet, knowing what you can change is the first step to a solution.

- Have clients update their *MAP* and their *MSL,* particularly *Skills 29* and *30.*

- Using the *SSC Change Scale,* have clients rate their skill level in settling conflicts.

SUMMARY OF KEY CONCEPTS

- Negotiation skills.
- Win-win outcomes.
- Accepting what cannot be changed, and the courage to change what can be changed.

SESSION CLOSURE AND GUIDELINES FOR THERAPEUTIC PROCESSING

Have clients share some of the conflicts that they now face. Then, have them share how they will use the skills they learned in this session to resolve those conflicts. Also use the closure session to process how clients see themselves doing at this time in *SSC.*

RATIONALE AND OVERVIEW

Our values are strong determinants of our actions and thoughts. Throughout *SSC*, we have emphasized values and moral development and responsibility. Many of the concepts and skills that have been imparted to clients have been designed to help clients instill values that underlie living a positive and meaningful life.

A thread that runs through the *SSC* material is the value of moral responsibility. An important part of that value is concern and caring for the welfare and safety of others. The basis for being morally responsible is prosocial attitudes and actions. A strong emphasis of *SSC* and SRT is helping clients change antisocial and criminal thinking and strengthen moral character and prosocial attitudes.

Helping clients change their values and learn prosocial thinking and behavior is a gradual process. This cannot be accomplished by preaching morality, or even stating directly what correct values are. Change is accomplished through the provider role modeling prosocial thinking, talking and acting. It is also accomplished through encouraging clients to look at their belief system, questioning them in ways that they will examine their views and, if they cannot see alternatives, suggesting other ways that they can consider the situations and problems presented. Judicial clients change when they recognize that their antisocial behavior and consequences are in conflict with their values, what is in their best interest and their moral standards.

Session 9 challenged clients to evaluate their level of antisocial behavior and attitudes. They assessed themselves on past and present influences that increase their risk of criminal conduct and recidivism. In that session, prosocial values and moral responsibility were defined as: respecting the rights of others; being accountable to the laws and rules of society; living in harmony with the community; having positive regard and caring for others; and contributing to the good of the community.

Session 36 focused on strengthening character and prosocial attitudes and behaviors. Antisocial, moral character, and prosocial attitudes and behaviors were defined, and clients were given ten ways to strengthen moral character and prosocial behavior.

The purpose of this session is to focus on values and morals and how these impact on thinking and actions. This is part of developing empathy, and helping clients move beyond their egocentric perspectives. Clients work on identifying their personal values, morals, and the standards of conduct expected of people.

SUMMARY OF CONTENT, PRESENTATION SEQUENCE AND GUIDELINES

When introducing this session, review the definition of moral responsibility, as provided in *Session 9*, page 84 in the *Workbook*. Identify moral responsibility and prosocial living as values.

▶ Have clients review their *Master Profile* to see what areas they need to address with respect to values and moral development. Did they identify any particular problems in their *MAP* that relate to the area of moral development and values?

▶ Invite group members to share their *TAP Charting*. Review the objectives of the session.

▶ Have clients review their *Anger Journal*. For clients with whom this is their first session in *Phase II*, give them guidance in doing the *Anger Journal*. This is the last session for doing the journal.

▶ Briefly review the steps in problem solving, *Session 32,* page 205 in the *Workbook.* Problem solving is used in the moral dilemma exercises.

▶ Review the empathy skills presented in *Session 37,* page 229 of the *Workbook.*

▶ When presenting **Values We Have Stressed in *SSC,*** explain that our values and our morals are two of the most important parts of our attitudes and belief system. Also explain that *SSC* has focused on four important values and morals: **Change, freedom, positive relationships, and concern about others.** Clients re-rate themselves on the stages of change scales, *Worksheets 46* and *47,* pages 143-144 in the *Workbook.*

▶ **What Guides Responsible and Prosocial Behavior** has clients list their most important personal values and morals and their view of the important norms and standards of society. Then, clients are challenged to determine whether their criminal conduct and substance abuse sabotage or go against these values. Some clients may have difficulty being honest in these exercises. Encourage honesty about their own feelings. They will not be punished if they list values that deviate from their society. The goal is to identify which prosocial values and morals they adhere to, and if they are important to them, have them struggle with why they would jeopardize these values and morals by committing crimes and using drugs.

Adjunct Exercise: Have clients discuss these questions. What are ways your values go against or conflict with your own set of morals? What are some ways that your values go against or conflict with the set of norms or standards of conduct you listed as most important to the society or community you live in?

▶ The **Value or Moral Dilemma** is one of the most important exercises that judicial clients will do in *SSC.* It is used in a number of judicial treatment programs (e.g., Ross et al., 1986, p. 194; Milkman & Wanberg, 2005; Wanberg & Milkman, 1998; Wanberg et al., 2005). We have expanded this dilemma to include values. The value or moral dilemma is a conflict between the values and morals that one holds, and those held by others. Or, it could be a conflict between one's value and one's moral beliefs, such as the value of having a lot of money, yet living up to the moral of not stealing.

The purpose of the moral dilemma exercises is to get clients to think beyond their egocentric point of view and consider the views of the central character in the dilemma and other group members. This strengthens empathy and reinforces prosocial thinking. This is also an opportunity for clients to practice problem solving and critical reasoning. Providers should reward prosocial and contemplative thinking and any behavior that demonstrates the skills of earlier sessions.

Here are some approaches to the exercises on value and moral dilemmas (adapted from Ross et al., 1986; Wanberg & Milkman, 1998). Clients use personal examples or from newspaper clippings.

◆ **Present the key elements of the moral dilemma:** The event, characters involved, and the circumstances, and all facts around these elements.

◆ **Describe the problem of the central character.** A brief role-play might help, with a group member playing the role of the central character.

◆ **Group members take a position** and state their solution for the central character.

◆ **Divide into groups of three or four** and discuss the reasons for each individual's position, the morality of their positions, and the consequences of the solution. Using the problem-solving approach, have the small groups come to a solution to the dilemma.

◆ **Return to the large group** and have each group report its solution. List the various positions. Use problem-solving skills. Discuss the solutions, and then the **alternative dilemmas** that arise from those solutions. See if the total group can come to one solution. Discuss the various **alternative dilemmas,** e.g., if the dilemma is that the family will be evicted if rent is not paid, the alternative is to borrow money rather than steal it. But this can create a dilemma of not enough money to pay back the loan.

- Get a total consensus (51 percent agree to a solution). Compare the group consensus to those who have a different solution. Have group members reflect on their earlier position considering the arguments that have been presented. Has their position changed? Why or why not? Have group members justify their position.

Do the moral dilemma exercise involving the security guard and the nurse in the emergency room (adapted from Ross et al., 1986; Wanberg & Milkman, 1998). Alternative dilemmas:

- If the group decides the nurse should help the man, give this information: Two weeks earlier a staff member was fired for leaving the emergency room to help victims of a traffic accident.

- If the group decides the nurse should obey hospital rules, tell them this: Based on the symptoms described, the nurse concluded that the man would die if not helped.

Help them see how this exercise helps learn the skills of empathy. Pose these questions for discussion:

- Is there an obligation for the nurse to save the man's life?

- Is the nurse bound to follow the hospital rules?

- What is the nurse's obligation to the mother and child in the waiting room?

- What would the mother in the emergency room think the nurse should do?

- When should rules be broken?

- Would the nurse be responsible if help is not given and the man dies?

- Should the nurse be punished by the hospital if help is given to the man?

- Have clients update their *MAP* and their *MSL,* particularly *Skills 26* through *30.*

- Using the *SSC Change Scale,* clients rate their skill level in handling moral dilemmas so as to get prosocial outcomes.

- Go over the homework, which involves doing a *Thinking Report* on a moral or value dilemma that clients face in the coming week. Review the parts of the *Thinking Report.*

SUMMARY OF KEY CONCEPTS

- Values that are stressed in *SSC.*

- Personal values, personal morals, and community norms.

- The value or moral dilemma.

SESSION CLOSURE AND GUIDELINES FOR THERAPEUTIC PROCESSING

Have clients share some value or moral dilemmas that they think they will be facing in the coming months.

RATIONALE AND OVERVIEW

The sessions in *Module 10* represent the major components of Social Responsibility Therapy (SRT). They focus on learning concepts and skills for developing a prosocial relationship with the community. Fulfillment of responsibility towards others and the community is based on the set of values and moral beliefs one holds. Beyond morals and values, however, is developing and practicing empathy. Through empathy, understanding and sympathy, we demonstrate our values and moral beliefs and our caring for others. Living a prosocial lifestyle involves values and morals based on a willingness to change, valuing our freedom, building positive relationships, showing concern towards others, and contributing to the good of the community.

Responsible living and being prosocial is more than avoiding negative behaviors, e.g., criminal conduct or substance abuse. It also involves making positive responses within relationships and within the community. The last two dimensions of being prosocial and morally responsible, as outlined in *Session 9,* page 84, are most difficult for judicial clients to achieve. They raise the bar with respect to expectations of our clients. They are:

▶ Caring about the welfare and safety of others;

▶ Contributing to the good of the community.

This session focuses on helping clients move in the direction of actualizing these two parts of community responsibility and prosociality. They also are an integral part of developing an empathic and sympathic interaction with others and the community. The first part of this session focuses on ways that judicial clients can contribute to the good of the community. The second part focuses on developing driving behaviors that are concerned about the welfare and safety of others. Driving a motor vehicle is one of the most dangerous activities in our society. It is a high-impact responsibility. It provides a metaphor for clients with respect to responsibility towards others and towards the community.

SUMMARY OF CONTENT, PRESENTATION SEQUENCE AND GUIDELINES

When introducing this session, present the concept that community responsibility and prosocial behavior is more than just living crime- and drug-free. It also involves a proactive and positive response to others and the community. Living crime- and substance abuse-free will bring more meaning and purpose to the lives of our clients.

▶ Invite group members to share their *TAP Charting.* Review the objectives of the session.

▶ Review the five dimensions of being morally responsible and prosocial.

▶ Once again, review the empathy skills presented in *Session 37,* page 229 of the *Workbook.*

▶ Take a few minutes to have clients share the *Thinking Report* homework on a moral or value dilemma they faced this week.

▶ **Reaching Out and Giving to the Community** provides a platform for clients who want to go beyond just staying clean and living crime-free. The key question posted in this section is: "Will the world be a better or worse because of me?" Clients are given five ways to give to the good of the community. They list activities and groups that they can be involved in that reach out to the community and help others.

- **Caring About the Welfare and Safety of Others - Driving With Care** provides the basics of most courses in driving safety. Stress that the most dangerous activity we take part in is driving a car. Some statistics regarding the extent and cost of motor vehicle accidents are provided. An added resource for this session is *Driving With Care: Education and Treatment of the Impaired Driving Offender - Strategies for Responsible Living and Change* (Wanberg et al., 2005).

  There is no one single behavior we engage in that requires more responsibility towards the community and towards others than that of driving a car. Careful driving is a metaphor for demonstrating prosocial behavior and moral responsibility to the community. In addition to what is provided in the *Workbook,* stress that driving a motor vehicle:

  - requires being continually alert;

  - means being at continual risk and danger;

  - provides an opportunity to be concerned and considerate towards others;

  - gives an opportunity to test our good will and patience.

  Worksheet 80 has clients make a list of the driving skills and habits clients need to improve or change.

  Adjunct Exercise: People differ as to their attitudes around driving and their driving behaviors. Have clients share their driving habits, the stress of driving, and feelings that people have when driving. Discuss these questions: What are your attitudes? What kind of driving patterns do you show?

  Exercise: Clients complete the *Driving Assessment Survey* (DAS: Wanberg & Timken, 1991, 2005) and score it in class. The DAS is in *Appendix B* of this *Guide,* along with the scoring procedures. Have the client plot the profile, which is *Worksheet 81.* Encourage clients to be as honest as they can. They should know that the results will only be used for this session and for their own self-awareness. Even when clients are informed of this, they still tend to be defensive around their willingness to disclose information regarding their driving attitudes and behaviors. Then discuss the results in class. The cutoff values for GENRISK provided in the *Workbook* are estimates of risk levels. Clients are the best judge as to level of driving risk. The DAS can provide further clarification regarding this risk. Facilitate discussion around what driving attitudes, thoughts and behaviors they can change.

- Have clients update their *MAP* and their *MSL.*

- Using the *SSC Change Scale,* have clients rate their level of desire to give to the good of their community.

SUMMARY OF KEY CONCEPTS

- Prosocial attitudes and behavior.

- Caring about the welfare and safety of others.

- Giving to the good of the community.

- Driving With Care.

SESSION CLOSURE AND GUIDELINES FOR THERAPEUTIC PROCESSING

Some clients may have one, two or even three impaired driving convictions. Have those clients share their personal experiences in this area. Close the group with a round robin sharing of having clients share one activity or group they plan to get involved in that reaches out and gives to the good of the community.

Clients who finish *Phase I* and *Phase II* should be praised and reinforced for their performance. This is a major accomplishment for judicial clients. Completing *Phase II* is a strong indication that clients are in the *Commitment to Change* (action) stage of change.

For clients in a closed group, *Phase I Closure* will be done in the total group. For the open *SSC* setup, set aside time for clients in their last *Phase II* group to bring closure to *Phase II*. Have clients do the closing reflections and sharing exercise as outlined in the *Workbook* on page 252.

Providers will meet with clients individually or in small groups of two or three persons and review the questionnaires and surveys they completed during *Phase II*. During this session give feedback to clients as to their progress and change, using the results from the *PACE Monitor*. In this closure session, clients are asked to make a decision as to whether they plan to continue into *Phase III*.

This closure session should include a review of the *SSC CB Map* (page 14 in the *Workbook*). Since the focus of *Phase II* has been on skill building and positive actions and outcomes, the *CB STEP Method* should also be reviewed.

The following *PACE* instruments in the *PACE Handbook* are completed by the client and the provider as part of the client's program evaluation process at the end of *Phase II* (see *Table 6.4*, pg. 107)

▶ *Client Program Response - Client* (CPR-C) *Ratings*

▶ *Client Program Response - Provider* (CPR-P) *Ratings*

▶ *Self-Evaluation Questionnaire - SEQ.*

The provider will also score the *CPR-C, CPR-P* and *SEQ* and chart the change process for each client. Clients then receive feedback as to the change profile

and feedback as to how the client did in the overall *SSC* program. Clients rate themselves on the *SSC Change Scales* (page 252 in the *Workbook*) as to their stage of change regarding AOD use patterns and their stage of change for CC thinking and conduct.

Some judicial clients referred to *SSC* will be required by the judicial system to proceed into *Phase III*. Approach these clients with the idea that they do have some choice. An honest discussion should transpire regarding what the client wants to do. Judicial requirements may rule against this "client choice" approach.

Motivational enhancement approaches should be used with clients who are resisting continuing into *Phase III*. Clients make the final decision, and accept the consequences if that decision goes against judicial requirements. They should also be given a choice to enter other comparable programs.

Some judicial clients will have completed their judicial treatment requirements at the end of *Phase II*, and continuing into *Phase III* is optional. These clients should be encouraged to complete all three phases of *SSC*.

Close *Phase II* on a positive note, celebrating the occasion in group and providing a certificate of completion issued by the *SSC* delivery agency. This fits in with the overall spirit of *SSC* that clients have the capacity and have been given the skills to make permanent and positive changes in their lives and to engage in:

▶ Living an AOD-free life;

▶ Living a crime-free life;

▶ Responsible living and a meaningful lifestyle.

PHASE III
ownership of change

Lifestyle Balance and Healthy Living

Change starts with a **challenge.** Establishing change requires a **commitment.** The maintenance of change requires **ownership.** Ownership is the integration phase of *SSC.* Clients put together the meaning of the treatment experience and take consistent action on their own story, goals and desired changes. The change goals, however, may also be those of some external system, such as the family, marriage or the criminal justice system. What is important is that there is consistent demonstration and ownership of living drug- and crime-free.

Phase III of *SSC, Ownership of Change,* puts the "finishing touches" on preparing judicial clients for re-entry and integration into the community, and for the restoration of a positive relationship with society. It builds on the client's increased self-awareness and the coping and change skills learned and practiced in *Phase II.* Providers help clients tie together thoughts, feelings and behaviors that have emerged in the overall treatment experience. Treatment experiences are designed to reinforce and strengthen established changes. *Phase III* strengthens clients' skills to prevent relapse and recidivism through developing strategies for a balanced lifestyle. **Ownership of change** is further strengthened by helping clients develop the skills of critical reasoning. These are advanced skills in the rehabilitation process.

Ownership of Change is also strengthened through the development of concepts and skills for a balanced lifestyle in the areas of work, job, time management, and engaging in healthy play, leisure time, relaxation activities, healthy eating, personal care and physical activity. Ownership of change is further strengthened when clients reach out to receive help and support from peers, family and other community resources.

Finally, a firm grasp on ownership occurs when judicial clients provide support, reinforcement, modeling and mentoring for others who are in a process of change and rehabilitation. Receiving and giving support have great promise for establishing full recovery and live a drug-free and prosocial life. These are the enduring elements of change.

> "No bird soars too high if it soars with its own wings" WILLIAM BLAKE

> "Yet, the wings of birds together give beauty that none alone can create"
> WINSTON ABBOTT

SUMMARY OF *PHASES I* AND *II*

Phase I builds a core knowledge of the areas of change and learning the rules, tools and targets for change with a strong emphasis on self-disclosure and self-awareness. Thoughts and feelings were identified and explored in greater depth. The *CB Map,* skills for changing thinking and beliefs, communication skills, and the pathways to R&R prevention were learned and practiced. A plan for change - the *MAP* - was developed.

Providers in *Phase I* develop a working relationship with clients within the framework of a caring environment so as to maximize self-disclosure and self-discovery. Providers utilize the principles of motivational enhancement and reflective confrontation based on the skills of responding attentiveness, encouragers to share, and feedback clarification.

Phase II, the commitment and action-oriented stage, was based on two important processes: therapeutic and correctional feedback and confrontation; and enhancing self-control and prosocial attitudes and actions towards others and the community.

The **feedback** loop and process are the keys for getting clients to take action on their story. The defensive system opens up and allows greater reception for self-understanding. Clients receive feedback around their change, or lack of change, and their motivation and willingness to change.

Enhancing cognitive self-control, and relationship and community responsibility skills is the second focus of *Phase II.* The goal is for clients to put into practice, on a daily basis, the skills that enhance self-control and responsible living. *Phase II* is structured around strengthening skills in three focal areas:

◗ Cognitive or mental self-control and change;

◗ Skills to enhance positive outcomes in social and interpersonal relationships; and

◗ Skills in enhancing prosocial and community responsibility.

PROVIDER SKILLS AND TREATMENT STRATEGIES FOR *PHASE III*

◗ **Continued assessment and in-depth self-evaluation of the specific treatment needs of clients.** At this point, the provider is more aware of the specific therapeutic needs of clients and should make an effort to match these needs with appropriate services. The *MP* and *MAP,* developed in *Phase I* and continually updated in *Phase II,* continue to become tools for guiding change in *Phase III.*

◗ Continued use of the counseling skills of: **responding attentiveness; invitation to share; reflective feedback clarification; therapeutic and correctional confrontation; and change reinforcement skills.**

◗ **Facilitation of the learning and practice** of mental self-control, relationship, and community responsibility skills through the *CB Map Exercise* and *STEP.* Start most *Phase III* sessions with these methods.

◗ Enhancement of **group facilitation skills** to build a cohesive group through which clients grow and change. *Phase III* involves an increased utilization of group interaction and processing, and greater focus on seeing the group as a vehicle to achieve program objectives.

◗ **Action therapy approaches:** role playing, doubling, actiongrams, action dramas, and role reversals.

◗ Maximize clients' sharing in group experiences and efforts to apply the concepts and skills of *SSC* in their daily living environment. This input can be processed through the use of the *CB Map Exercise* and *STEP.*

PROVIDER GOALS AND OBJECTIVES OF *PHASE III*

▶ Facilitate clients' application of the concepts and skills of mental self-control, relationship building and community responsibility skills learned and practiced in *SSC* in daily living.

▶ Facilitate the strengthening of relapse and recidivism prevention skills through the establishment of a life-style balance.

▶ Facilitate a healthy lifestyle that can lead to meaningful responsible outcomes.

▶ Continue to role model self-control, effective interpersonal interactions, and prosocial attitudes.

▶ Strengthen and reinforce client successes in being prosocial and in maintaining a life free from AOD abuse.

PREPARATION SESSION FOR *PHASE III*

For the closed group structure, the orientation and preparation for *Phase III* can be done in the ongoing *SSC* group. For open group structures, orientation to *Phase III* can be done in a small group of clients who have completed *Phase II,* or on an individual basis.

The outline and content for *Phase III Orientation* is found in the *Workbook,* page 254, *Preparation Session* for *Phase III.* Review the *CB Map Exercise* and the *STEP Method, Figure 23,* page 155, of the *Workbook.* Most *Phase III* sessions start with the CB Map Exercise or with *STEP.* Also, review the overarching goals of *SSC*: 1) preventing relapse; 2) preventing recidivism; and 3) living a comfortable and meaningful life without the use of drugs and criminal involvement. This is also a good time to review the tools for change that *SSC* has used throughout *Phases I* and *II.* We add to the list of nine tools in *Session 2,* the *STEP Method.*

1. *CB Map Exercise.*

2. *Autobiography.*

3. *Master Skills List (MSL), Program Guide 1.*

4. *Master Profile (MP), Program Guide 2.*

5. *Master Assessment Plan (MAP), Program Guide 3.*

6. *Weekly Thinking and Action Patterns (TAP) Charting, Program Guide 4.*

7 *Thinking Report.*

8 *Re-Thinking Report.*

9 *SSC Change Scales,* at the end of each session.

10. *STEP Method:* **S**ituation - **T**hinking Change - **E**motions - **P**ositive Outcome.

The *PACE (Progress and Change Evaluation) Monitor,* which provides the empirical basis for evaluating client progress and change during and at the end of *SSC,* is reviewed in an individual session. The *Preparation Session* for *Phase III* can be done in this individual session or in *Phase III* orientation group. *Phase III* involves two modules and eight two-hour treatment sessions. The time for completion depends on the number of *Phase III* sessions offered each week. It is recommended that no more than two *Phase III* sessions be offered each week.

MODULE 11

Relapse and Recidivism Prevention: Strategies for a Balanced Lifestyle

OVERVIEW

Clients at this point will have met many relapse and recidivism (R&R) challenges and many opportunities to practice their R&R prevention skills. Their R&R goals have been challenged. Some have experienced lapses and even relapses. Many have experienced the process of recidivism - engaging in criminal thinking and behaviors that can lead to full recidivism - committing another crime.

Clients in *Phase II* have met these challenges and applied the concepts and skills learned in *SSC* to prevent a full relapse or full recidivism that would have put them back into the sanctioning process of the judicial system. Those continuing into *Phase III* have demonstrated successful application of the principles and skills of *SSC* which have kept them free of AOD problems and free from involvement in criminal conduct.

The purpose of this module is to strengthen these changes and successes. This module is a review of many of the R&R concepts, and the skills for R&R prevention. Clients review their R&R prevention goals and plan, and the prevention skills that have worked best for them. They gain an understanding of how lifestyle imbalances can lead to R&R and then enhance their R&R prevention plan by developing a better living style balance. Clients look at the high-risk exposures that they have encountered during *SSC*. They learn and practice the skills of critical reasoning which contribute to R&R prevention.

PROVIDER GOALS OF THIS MODULE

- Facilitate the review of the basic concepts of pathways to R&R and pathways to R&R prevention.

- Have clients review their specific R&R prevention goals and their R&R prevention plan.

- Have clients look at the R&R prevention skills that have worked for them.

- Have clients take a candid look at the consequences of the decisions they have made to live drug- and crime-free.

- Using the Marlatt (1985a; Marlatt & Witkiewitz, 2005) global strategies model, have clients look closely at their current lifestyle imbalances and then facilitate their learning strategies and skills to build a balanced lifestyle.

REVIEW OF THE R&R PREVENTION APPROACH IN *SSC*

Before delivering *Module 11*, providers should review the *SSC* R&R prevention concepts and approaches described in *Chapter 5* and in the *Introduction* to *Module 6*. Here are the key concepts:

▶ Overview of the R&R prevention approach used in *SSC*.

▶ The Marlatt model, upon which the *SSC* R&R prevention approach is based, is described in *Chapter 5*.

▶ How the concepts of the Marlatt model are applied to understanding and preventing recidivism. The similarities between relapse and recidivism are also discussed.

▶ The basic goals of R&R treatment.

▶ The common elements that are found in most relapse prevention programs: knowledge base about relapse; identifying high-risk situations and exposures that lead to relapse; and learning skills to manage high-risk exposures. These are applied to understanding and preventing recidivism.

▶ Definitions of relapse and recidivism that are used in *Module 6* and throughout *SSC*. These definitions distinguish between the process of relapse, lapse, and full relapse. For recidivism, we differentiate between "being into recidivism" and "full recidivism" (committing another crime).

▶ Differences between relapse prevention goals for alcohol and for illegal drugs. It is made clear that *SSC* considers total abstinence from the use of illegal drugs, or the illegal use of legal medications as the only acceptable relapse prevention goal. For alcohol, *SSC* identifies two prevention goals of: total abstinence; or preventing problems from the use of alcohol.

▶ Relapse is a process of erosion.

▶ The similarities and differences between relapse and recidivism.

▶ High-risk exposures and triggers.

NEW R&R CONCEPTS AND SKILLS INCLUDED IN THIS MODULE

Two concepts developed in the work of Marlatt (1985a) are utilized in this module: 1) the global self-control model that generates a lifestyle balance; and 2) the decision matrix or window. Marlatt recognized that giving clients a specific set of skills and cognitive strategies was not enough. Helping clients establish global strategies would provide a broader basis for preventing relapse. These global strategies would help to "intervene in the client's overall lifestyle so as to increase overall capacity to deal with stress and to cope with high-risk situations with an increased sense of self-efficacy" (p. 60). These help clients identify early warning signs and situations so as to implement self-control in preventing a lapse or relapse. Global self-control and lifestyle balance strategies are presented in *Session 44*.

The decision matrix or window approach helps identify immediate and delayed gratifications from substance use, and in the case of *SSC*, criminal conduct. It helps the clients weigh the immediate and delayed positive and negative consequences of abstaining from or using substances, or remaining crime-free or engaging in criminal conduct. Using this window, clients take an honest look at these outcome expectancies. This matrix is done in *Phase III* where clients have established a level of self-efficacy and maturity to deal with the recognition that there are benefits to continuing drug use or criminal conduct and to have the self-control to prevent engaging in these behaviors to get immediate rewards. The decision matrix is presented in *Session 44*.

RATIONALE AND OVERVIEW

This session is a review of the concepts and skills presented in *Sessions 15* and *16,* pages 116 to 132 and the worksheets done in *Session 15.* The key concepts to be reviewed are:

▶ R&R - a process of erosion (*Session 15*);

▶ High-risk exposures to and triggers for relapse and recidivism (*Session 15*);

▶ The pathways to relapse and recidivism (*Session 15*);

▶ The pathway to and skills for R&R prevention (*Session 16*); and the R&R prevention plan.

SUMMARY OF CONTENT, PRESENTATION SEQUENCE AND GUIDELINES

Introduce this session with a recognition of the hard work clients have done to prevent R&R, and their efforts in making *SSC* work for them. Although the content of this session is relatively brief, reviewing the material and worksheets clients did in *Session 15* will take considerable time. Maximize interactive processing around this review. Follow the content as presented in the *Workbook,* using the guidelines spelled out below.

▶ Present the session objectives. Apply *STEP* to an event that was high risk for recidivism.

▶ **Updating Your *MP* and *MAP*** zeroing in on the most important problems, since their time in *SSC* is now limited. Have clients review their *MP* and look at the scales that make them vulnerable to R&R.

▶ **Review of the Pathways to Recidivism and Relapse** goes over *Figure 18,* page 121, the pathways to R&R, and updates and reworks *Worksheet 37,* high-risk exposures that could lead to relapse and recidivism, and *Worksheet 39,* their potential pathway to relapse and recidivism.

▶ In **Review of Your R&R Goals,** have clients once again look at the R&R prevention goals they wrote down in *Session 1,* pages 9 and 10, and *Session 16,* pages 126 and 127. Discuss how their goals have changed. Have them update those goals on pages 126 and 127.

▶ In **R&R Prevention Skills That Are Working for You,** carefully review *Figure 19,* page 129, Marlatt's model for R&R prevention, and *Figure 20,* page 130, *SSC* adaptation of this model. *Worksheet 83,* patterned after *Figure 20,* has clients identify those skills they are using to handle high risk exposures.

▶ Have clients update their *MSL.* Remind them to do their *TAP Charting.* Using the *SSC Change Scales,* have clients rate their skill level in preventing relapse and recidivism.

SUMMARY OF KEY CONCEPTS

▶ Pathways to R&R and to R&R prevention.

▶ R&R prevention skills that are working,

SESSION CLOSURE AND GUIDELINES FOR THERAPEUTIC PROCESSING

Use the closure group for unstructured therapeutic processing.

RATIONALE AND OVERVIEW

New clients do not enter at this session since *Session 43* is its prerequisite. Providers may want to use two two-hour blocks of time to deliver this session. The main purpose of this session is to strengthen the progress clients have made in preventing R&R by integrating two strategies into their overall R&R prevention plan: *The Decision Window;* and the *Lifestyle Balance Model.*

The Decision Window

Using the **decision window or matrix strategy** (Marlatt, 1985a, p. 58) can strengthen the R&R prevention plan. This is both an assessment of outcome expectancies and an intervention strategy. It challenges clients to identify the short-term and long-term positive and negative outcomes of abstaining from AOD use and being crime-free or continuing to engage in AOD use and criminal conduct. It provides the basis for knowing the high-risk exposures (expectancy outcomes) that can lead to R&R, and the strengths that support R&R prevention. Clients secure in their R&R prevention journey are appropriate for utilizing this strategy. The Marlatt matrix has been adapted to address relapse **and** recidivism.

Lifestyle Balance Strategy

The **lifestyle balance strategy** also adds to the client's R&R prevention plan. An overview of this strategy will be summarized. The application of the strategy will be described in the *Summary of Content, Presentation Sequence and Guidelines* section below.

A lifestyle imbalance can make clients more vulnerable to high-risk exposures and set in motion the R&R process. Often these high-risk exposures create an internal desire to indulge in a behavior that "I deserve." With relapse, the payoff is quick. It can give immediate gratification. Individuals most vulnerable to what Marlatt (1985a) calls the relapse set-up are those whose lifestyles are **out of balance.** But the set-up is internal. The individual makes conscious choices that lead closer and closer (enhances the erosion process) to a full relapse (going back to a pattern of AOD problems) or recidivism (returning to CC). Yet, people tend to deny responsibility in the set-up process. But responsibility is clearly there. Choices are clearly made.

The choices not only rest in the relapse steps themselves but also in lifestyle imbalance. Marlatt (1985a) sees the degree of balance or imbalance as affecting the desire for indulgence or immediate gratification. He defines balance as "the degree of equilibrium that exists in one's daily life between those activities perceived as external 'hassles' or demands (the 'shoulds'), and those perceived as pleasures or self-fulfillment (the 'wants')" (p. 47).

Persons who operate out of the imbalance of the "shoulds" begin to feel deprived. There is a corresponding desire for gratification that can come through returning to old patterns of use and styles of use (going to the bar every evening after work). The automatic thoughts are: "I deserve more than this"; "I work hard and don't get nowhere"; "They have more than I do. I deserve as much as they do"; "I deserve a good time - a few drinks."

As the desire for indulgence increases, so does the need to "restore balance and equilibrium" (p. 48). This can lead to strong alcohol or other drug-seeking thoughts (cravings) and behaviors (urges). This sequence can lead to what Marlatt calls the cognitive antecedents of relapse: making an excuse to engage in a certain behavior; defensiveness against admission of a drug problem; and decisions or choices associated with the R&R process.

The decision or choice process can present in a benign or unsuspecting manner and certain actions the individual chooses may seem even irrelevant to the possibility of relapse. Marlatt calls these choices *Seemingly Irrelevant Decisions* (SIDS). The individual becomes even more vulnerable when engaging in high-risk thinking ("I'll go down to the bar and chat with a couple of buddies") or high-risk situations (friend drops by with some dope). These decisions to engage in high-risk exposure lead to the end gate of a high probability of relapse or recidivism. This process is illustrated in the boxed components of *Figure 30* in the *Workbook*).

SUMMARY OF CONTENT, PRESENTATION SEQUENCE AND GUIDELINES

The above discussion will help providers prepare for this session. Remind clients that the acceptable relapse prevention goals defined in *SSC* are premised on: 1) **relapsing from the goal of alcohol abstinence or relapsing from a pattern of non-harmful or non-disruptive use of alcohol;** and 2) relapsing from the goal of abstaining from all illegal drugs or the illegal use of legal drugs. Follow the topic sequence in the *Workbook*, using the guidelines outlined below.

▶ Start by reviewing the session objectives. Have them share their *TAP Charting*.

▶ Have one or two clients role-play a situation where they used *SSC* skills to prevent an AOD relapse.

▶ **Reviewing Your Stages of Change** again challenges clients to rate themselves on where they see themselves with respect to AOD use and criminal conduct, using *Worksheets 46* and *47,* pages 143 and 144. Have them use a different mark to distinguish this rating from prior ratings, and date their current rating.

▶ Go over **The Decision Window** or matrix adapted from Marlatt (1985a, p. 58) and modified to fit the substance abusing judicial client. This deals with the rationalization and defensive process that clients develop around consequences of relapse and recidivism.

  ◆ *Worksheet 84* is the relapse decision window and *Worksheet 85* is for recidivism. Clients are to write in their relapse prevention goal and then to identify the immediate and long-term benefits and outcomes of following that goal as well as the immediate and long-term negative outcomes of following that goal. Have clients do the same for recidivism, writing in their recidivism goal of: being crime-free and prosocial; or continue antisocial and criminal conduct.

  ◆ The window changes over time and clients can revise their decision window in such a manner so as to prevent R&R. Early on, clients might have included only minimal immediate and delayed positive outcomes of abstinence or a non-problematic pattern of AOD use. Now clients may see more positive benefits and outcomes from abstinence or a non-problematic use pattern. As clients revise their decision window, they may find that it is difficult for them to find positive benefits for continuing criminal conduct. However, for some clients, one positive consequence of continuing AOD use or criminal conduct is continuing to maintain strong relationships with criminal associates.

  ◆ Help clients with the decision windows by giving examples of short-term and long-term positive and negative outcomes for decisions to use or not use drugs or to live a crime-free life or be involved in crime.

▶ **How Lifestyle Imbalances Lead to Relapse** will help clients understand that living a drug- and crime-free life can create certain imbalances that increase the risk of R&R. Take time to go over the content of this section. Living an AOD and crime free life puts pressure on the judicial client. Clients often say, "it was easier in the old life. I felt more in control." Going back to AOD use and a criminal lifestyle can give immediate resolution to this pressure. The payoff is quick with immediate gratification. The healthy resolution to this pressure and imbalance is for clients to establish a healthy balance between those activities that clients see as causing pressure and activities that bring meaning, pleasure and self-fulfillment into their lives.

- **Adding to Your R&R Plan: Developing a Balance** provides a strategy that goes beyond just managing high-risk exposures. It provides a long-term ownership and maintenance of change and helps clients create a stable and on-going lifestyle balance. As Marlatt has noted, "simply teaching the client to respond mechanically to one high-risk situation after another is not enough" (p. 59). This is the "teaching to fish" metaphor. Providers cannot deal with each and every high-risk situation their clients encounter. Clients need broader and more global strategies and a generalized ability to deal with stress and cope with high-risk thoughts and situations.

Global strategies arm clients with a broad R&R prevention plan. It is a plan for self-control that is ready to go when clients face a high-risk exposure. Clients used this strategy in *Session 23*, page 166, when arming themselves with positive thoughts and having them ready to go when they need them.

Figure 30 in the *Workbook* provides a modification of Marlatt's (1985a, p. 61) *Lifestyle Balance: Global Self-Control Strategies* diagram that clients can utilize to manage or avoid high-risk exposures. These can be cognitive, behavioral or operational. Cognitive would be self-control skills. An operational strategy would be to never associate with individuals who are committing crimes.

Figure 30 will require time for clients to understand. Read carefully the rationale and overview of this session before working with clients around this figure. *Figure 30* is used as a worksheet with clients filling in the blanks in the circles. However, before doing this exercise, carefully go over the elements of this figure. The boxed components of *Figure 30* provide the process and antecedent conditions leading up to relapse or recidivism. The shaded circled components provide the various intervention strategies or activities that address and mitigate the boxed R&R antecedents. In the non-shaded circles, clients put skills that address the R&R boxed antecedents. The circled intervention components will be discussed in relationship to the boxed components which are the targets of intervention.

- **Healthy lifestyle skills** and **positive involvements** counter the **lifestyle imbalances** and create balance. This may be engaging in positive "addictions" that counter the "shoulds" message that tends to lead to feelings of self-deprivation (Marlatt, 1985a). Clients build into their lives healthy activities (strategies) that are part of daily living and that give positive and meaningful gratification to the individual. This daily balance is a process that is ongoing and stable.

- **Self-control skills** and **substituting positive indulgences** counter the desire for **negative indulgences** (criminal acts, drugging). The self-control skills manage the desire for negative indulgences. Positive substitutes are clearly different from the previously "normal" indulging behaviors of drinking or using drugs or a harmful pattern of AOD use. These are activities that clients have at their disposal, they know how to access them, and they provide immediate self-gratification (such as eating a nice meal, healthy sexual activity, etc.).

- **Urge coping skills** and **labeling detachment** counter **cravings and urges.** This involves countering the external cues that precipitate the cravings and urges (e.g., smell of alcohol; seeing people drink; noticing friends on the street; desire to join friends at the bar in the "usual" manner). Sometimes, as Marlatt notes, simply removing oneself from the external cues will do the job. Detaching could involve the client imagining looking down at himself from a cloud and saying: "There's a guy who wants a drink, but he's not going to take one." Labeling involves: "I have this urge to get high, but it's just an urge." Detaching from and labeling the cravings or urges are ways to "ride out" the urge. Just not going to the bar but going home and working on a hobby is enough. The client needs to know that the urge (drug wanting) or craving (drug seeking) will not last forever. It does go away. Labeling and detaching will often speed up the process of "going away."

- Changing the decision window and labeling SIDS (seemingly irrelevant decisions) as warning signs will counter the rationalizations and excuses and SIDS: A powerful component of the relapse process is rationalization - defensiveness (per our previous discussion of denial, we choose to use the term defensiveness) and SIDS. Clients can use several strategies to manage these antecedents to relapse and recidivism. First, labeling SIDS episodes will make them more relevant and increase awareness that these are danger signs; seeing that "just visiting my old drinking buddy" is not irrelevant, but part of the decision process to relapse. Revising the decision window is a skill that counters the rationalizations, which was the exercise done in *Worksheets 84* and *85*. Clients rethink what were perceived, early on, as positive outcomes of criminal conduct, and see them for what they really are. The expectations of AOD use as being positive now change to expectations of negative value and outcomes. The decision not to use drugs is seen to have a benefit of positive relationships with family and friends. A long-term positive outcome might be that the client has more time doing enjoyable activities now that there are no more weekend visits to a friend's house to get high.

- ◆ **Understanding the pathways to R&R** and **Using R&R prevention skills road maps** counters the **high-risk exposures,** as shown in *Figure 18,* page 121, and *Figure 20,* page 130 of the *Workbook.*

▶ The **Highway Map to Responsible Living,** page 136 of the *Workbook,* has clients review the visualization of the R&R prevention path as a highway journey. This has been adapted from Parks and Marlatt (1999) to address the issues of relapse and recidivism for substance abusing judicial clients. This "highway metaphor" is a way of illustrating the choices that clients have at the point leading to high-risk exposures. When confronted with automatic thoughts or thought habits that lead to cravings, urges, or desires for high-risk drinking environments, the client has a choice of routes - city of irresponsible living - regret and crash; or city of responsible living and CARING.

▶ Clients update their *MSL* and reminded to do *TAP Charting.*

▶ Using the *SSC Change Scale,* have clients rate their skill level on making their R&R prevention plans work for them.

SUMMARY OF KEY CONCEPTS

▶ Relapse and recidivism skills-based prevention plan.

▶ The Decision Window.

▶ Lifestyle balance and global prevention strategies.

▶ R&R prevention skills that are working.

SESSION CLOSURE AND GUIDELINES FOR THERAPEUTIC PROCESSING

Give clients an opportunity to process their thoughts and feelings around doing the *Decision Window.* Have clients discuss how looking at the positive benefits of engaging in AOD use and criminal conduct affected their commitment to live a drug-free and crime-free life. Did the positive benefits of staying drug-free and crime-free outweigh the positive benefits of engaging in drug use and CC? Some clients might find that the *Decision Window* increased, at least momentarily, the desire to use drugs or engage in criminal conduct. It is important that clients process these thoughts and feelings.

RATIONALE AND OVERVIEW

Critical Reasoning

We typically see offenders as "tough" and "bullying" and people who "con" others. Often, however, the offender is the one who is easily persuaded and "conned" or gets sold "a bill of goods" by their peers to commit a crime or use drugs. When we look at the many reasons for AOD abuse or criminal behavior, logically and critically, none stands up to the simple scrutiny of making sense.

Critical thinking is the art of thinking logically, rationally, and carefully. The goal is to come to conclusions that are based on adequate and correct information. The logic behind the conclusion is accurate and not based on distorted or biased thinking and incorrect assumptions.

Creative Thinking

Many judicial clients suffer from "cognitive rigidity" or inflexible thinking (Ross et al., 1986, p. 175). They tend to use the same thinking patterns in every situation or problem and often fail to see the inadequacy of the old approaches. They frequently have difficulty considering alternatives, understanding complex situations or adjusting to change. Repetitive behavior is a possible result. This inability to adapt may result in unacceptable, antisocial behavior when the inability to cope is accompanied by a low tolerance for stress. Offenders have difficulty, cognitively, adapting to the demands of the world and conceiving of alternative ways to solve problems. This lack of perspective puts them at risk to engage in criminal conduct. It can become a barrier to engaging in treatment and can make them resistant to the ideas of others.

Creative thinking is an important part of critical reasoning. Creative thinking allows one to break out of the rigid mold of always thinking something must be done in a specific way. It gives people a different perspective of the outside and inside world. It is an important part of problem solving. It is thinking outside of the box. Creative thinking allows one to look at all sides of one's experiences and end up with a product that is new, unique and different. An artistic work is the result of creative thinking.

Session Purpose

The purpose of this session is to help the judicial client develop a logical and critical "eye" for any effort to be persuaded by others to take part in activities that "do not make sense" from the standpoint of being responsible, of being free and healthy. A part of this purpose is to help clients learn to think creatively within the context of critical reasoning.

One approach to achieving the goals of this session is for clients to be exposed to propaganda approaches or being "conned" into thoughts and actions. Critical reasoning is one way to maintain one's sense of separateness and individuality in the face of being exposed to propaganda.

SUMMARY OF CONTENT, PRESENTATION SEQUENCE AND GUIDELINES

Review the key mantra of *SSC:* self-disclosure leads to self-awareness, and through feedback, self-awareness leads to change. Self-disclosure and openness to feedback build self-confidence. To effectively use the skills of critical reasoning and creative thinking, the individual must have a certain level of self-awareness, and thus, self-confidence.

Another important concept to share with clients is that critical reasoning and creative thinking often lead to independent action. This in turn can lead to conflicts with others. However, resolving conflict through the skills of problem solving (*Session 32*) and negotiation (*Session 40*) allows one to be self-confident in engaging in critical and creative thinking while at the same time maintaining a positive relationship with others.

▶ Introduce this session using the above material and ideas, and presenting the session objectives.

▶ Have one or two group members role-play using *SSC* skills which prevent an AOD relapse.

▶ Do a quick **update on the *MP* and *MAP*.** Have clients identify which scales on the *MP* might prevent the use of critical reasoning.

▶ Present the **Skills in Critical and Creative Thinking** using interactive processing and have clients give personal examples of a positive outcome from using each guide. These are really guidelines for engaging in critical and creative thinking. Additional information regarding these skills will be provided.

♦ **Guide 1: Looking at all sides.** This is thinking outside the box. This cuts through rigid thinking. To be creative is to think of new and different ways to get positive outcomes. There are always different ways to deal with the challenges of life other than using drugs or committing a crime.

♦ **Guide 2: Get the facts.** This is seeing and accepting reality as it is, letting the information "flow in," to hear where others are and where we are.

♦ **Guide 3: Stick with thoughts, not emotions.** Let the head control the heart. This is not to say that critical reasoning does not involve sentiment and emotions. Good outcomes depend on being open to one's feelings and having sentiment be part of the process. Emotions are part of the creative response to our world. However, good reasoning and good decision making keep logic in charge.

♦ **Guide 4: Make sense of the facts.** Sometimes it is difficult to connect the dots. We have to stand back and look at the whole picture, bringing in all of the elements. A friend says, "let's break into the house down the street." Ask, "does this make sense? We might see a quick dollar by selling a couple of TVs. But, sitting in jail and missing work will cost me more."

♦ **Guide 5: Am I being conned?** You are conned when you are persuaded to do something before getting the facts or before looking at all sides. This is being subjected to propaganda. Before being conned into using drugs, look at all sides. "Every time I use drugs, I get into trouble with the law. Where will I end up?" Critical thinking will prevent us from being conned or conning ourselves.

♦ **Guide 6: Don't assume.** Help clients learn to get a clear picture, ask questions, learn to recognize what people imply by what they say, and know that people don't always tell what they mean in a clear manner. Assuming without getting the facts and without having good communication often ends up making an ASS out of U and ME. Ask questions if you don't understand. There is no dumb question. Only dumb answers. Pay attention to body language. FIGURE OUT. Listen. Clarify.

♦ **Guide 7: Sort out fact from opinion.** **Adjunct Exercise:** Have clients give examples of a fact, an opinion, and the different kinds of opinions - soft, emotional, extreme.

▶ The content in the section on **Recognizing Propaganda: Being Talked Into Thoughts and Actions** is brief and to the point. Discuss each of the propaganda methods. Then, do the exercise of having the group find examples in newspapers.

- When presenting **Relating Relapse and Recidivism to Propaganda Methods,** do the exercise of taking each propaganda method and discussing how it can lead to AOD use and criminal conduct. Then have them do *Worksheet 86* to see how these methods relate to their own AOD use and CC.

    <u>Adjunct Exercise:</u> Have clients give examples of being "conned" into doing drugs or doing something illegal. Such an example is given below for each of the methods in the *Workbook.* Then, have clients apply *STEP* to one or two of these scenarios to get a positive outcome.

    - **One-sided argument:** Example: Employer to applicant: "This is a great job, it pays well, and you are likely to get promoted to a management position within a year. It does mean you have to move out of town." Friend of applicant: "This would be an awful job. You'll be living in a one-horse town with nothing to do with all the money you are going to be making. Besides that, they aren't really going to give a green kid a job as a manager. And, who am I going to get high with?" In both situations, the applicant is hearing propaganda because each person is giving a ONE-SIDED argument.

    - **The bandwagon approach:** Example: Mark: "Let's get some speed and shoot up." Betty: "I would never do that. I don't believe using drugs is smart." Mark: "Everybody does it."

    - **Repetition:** Example: Within a period of 15 minutes, a friend says to Harry: "Hey, let's get high!" "Be fun to get high tonight!" "I've got a stash in my car!" "Not much doing tonight, getting bored, just as well get wasted."

    - **Testimonial:** Example: Friend attempting to persuade his girlfriend to use cocaine: "Jim's pretty cool. He's going to make all-state. Great quarterback. I was surprised to see him snorting cocaine at the party last week."

    - **Emergency or crisis:** Example: John to his friend who is resisting selling drugs: "This is the one big chance. We won't see this much stuff for a long time, maybe never."

    - **Bargain:** Example: Ben trying to sell a friend a stolen car. "It'll cost you three times this much if you bought it off the lot. And, I'll throw in the computer that was in the back seat."

- Clients update their *MSL.* Remind them to do *TAP Charting.*

- Using the *SSC Change Scale,* have clients rate their skill level in preventing relapse and recidivism.

SUMMARY OF KEY CONCEPTS

- Critical reasoning and creative thinking.

- Propaganda methods.

SESSION CLOSURE AND GUIDELINES FOR THERAPEUTIC PROCESSING

Use the closure group for unstructured therapeutic processing.

MODULE 12

Strengthening Ownership of Change: Skills for a Healthy Lifestyle

OVERVIEW

How do judicial clients firmly fix in their lives the changes they have made? Certainly, it requires continued management of high-risk exposures that lead to relapse and recidivism. Yet, ownership of change also involves achieving the third major goal of *SSC* - living a meaningful and responsible life. This involves tying the changes they have made into a lifestyle of healthy living.

For most judicial clients, AOD use and criminal involvement have been at the center of their lives. Through *SSC*, clients learned skills of self-control and to improve their relationship with others and the community, with the goal of living a drug-free and crime-free life. Learning these skills is not sufficient. *Module 11* provides clients with a global strategy to create a lifestyle balance. Now, we point clients in the direction of lifestyle patterns as alternatives to a lifestyle of drug use and crime.

The purpose of this module is to give substance to the lifestyle balance of clients and look at integrating and strengthening five healthy lifestyle alternatives to AOD use and criminal behavior: meaningful involvement in one's work and job as an expression of healthy productivity; participating in healthy play and leisure time; integrating relaxation into one's daily living; establishing a pattern of healthy eating, personal care and physical activity; and participating in the receiving and giving of help and support in maintaining a healthy and productive lifestyle.

PROVIDER GOALS OF THIS MODULE

▶ Facilitate the learning and practice of lifestyle patterns in clients that strengthen drug-free and crime-free living and lead to meaningful and responsible living.

▶ Help clients develop a balance of these lifestyle patterns within their daily living.

PRESENTATION LOGISTICS

The sessions in this module can stand alone, and new clients can enter at any session. However, it is most effective to present the five sessions in sequence. For open group setups, some clients may get this module before *Module 11*. Thus, it is helpful to provide a summary of *Module 11* for these clients and show how *Modules 11* and *12* are tied together.

RATIONALE AND OVERVIEW

This session has a lot of material and exercises to cover. Providers may find that two two-hour blocks of time are needed for this session.

There is strong evidence to indicate the importance of employment and vocational services in judicial treatment. Being employed and obtaining employment during treatment are all related to reduced involvement in substance use and criminal activity and the prevention of relapse and recidivism (Anglin & Fisher, 1987; Joe, Chastain, & Simpson, 1990; Inciardi et al., 2002; Platt, 1995; Walker & Leukefeld, 2002). Productive and meaningful work is an essential piece to relapse and recidivism prevention and maintaining a balanced lifestyle. Together, it represents one of the main alternatives to AOD use patterns and involvement in criminal conduct.

Even for clients who are on disability, retired, or are unable to be gainfully employed, it is important that they find outlets for being productive. This productivity might be doing volunteer work, working in the garden, maintaining the upkeep of their personal property, etc. It is also important that people feel that they have some kind of vocation or avocation with which to identify. This identity goes beyond just having a job.

However, for many judicial clients, "employment may be very different from their desired lifestyle. Consequently, those delivering employment-rehabilitation services for judicial clients should have a realistic understanding of the difficulties that many drug offenders will have in obtaining, maintaining, and upgrading their employment" (Walker & Leukefeld, 2002, p. 77).

Besides employment representing a significant change in lifestyle, there are other barriers that judicial clients face in finding and maintaining employment. One of the most critical barriers is having a criminal record (Wexler, 2004). This barrier has increased in recent years, particularly with public institutions, large corporations and businesses having policies restricting the employment of felons.

Yet, there are innovative programs that are being developed to manage at least some of the aspects of this barrier (Wexler, 2004). In spite of these barriers, employment and vocational rehabilitation services are critical components of the treatment and aftercare of judicial clients (Inciardi et al., 2002; Wexler, 2004). Too often it is not given enough attention.

Walker and Leukefeld (2002) suggest a phased approach to meeting the work and employment intervention needs of judicial clients:

▶ Obtaining employment;

▶ Managing employment;

▶ Upgrading employment; and

▶ Job placement and coaching.

This session is an introduction to this area of treatment. Its main purposes are for clients to understand their work "tools," learn the skills of finding employment, explore the difference between **work** and **job**, identify their work, take a long-term look at their education and work goals, and learn time and task management. Employed clients in *SSC* can become role models for group members who are looking for a job.

Some clients will need a more extensive or even comprehensive employment and job services program. The provider should evaluate clients in their group with respect to the need for employment and vocational assessment, need for education or training, or employment counseling.

SUMMARY OF CONTENT, PRESENTATION SEQUENCE AND GUIDELINES

Introduce this session with the concept that productive and meaningful work is one of the primary alternatives to AOD use and criminal conduct. Here are some guidelines for presenting this session.

▶ Do a quick **update of the *MP* and *MAP*** relative to areas of work and employment. Review the session's objectives.

▶ Do the *STEP Method* around a situation where a group member has a job problem.

▶ **Know What's in Your "Tool Kit" - The Basics** is part of understanding work. The "took kit" is the work we take to our job.

▶ Introduce **What Is Your Work? Does Your Job Match Your Work?** with a discussion on the difference between work and job. Work is a physical or mental activity and effort that is directed towards accomplishing something. It is the means through which we practice our skills, fulfill our talents and earn our livelihood. Our job is where we go in order to fulfill our work. We take our work to our job. We own our work. It is ours. We don't own our job; it is loaned to us in order to do our work. Work is one way we define our lifestyle.

Exercise: This section is designed to help clients determine if they like their work, if their job matches their work, and whether they should consider seeking different kinds of work.

Adjunct Exercise: Have group members discuss their current work and job goals, using *Worksheet 87* as a platform for this discussion.

▶ **Looking for or Changing Jobs** is just a practice opener for those who are seeking employment. Take the group through these skills and tasks. Some clients will want to work on *Worksheet 88* as homework, or use the worksheet as an ongoing basis in their job-seeking efforts. Judicial clients have a difficult time looking ahead - often feeling discouraged and even hopeless about the future. Providers will need to motivate clients around doing *Worksheet 89*. Additional information is provided for each of the seven skills described in the *Workbook*. An adjunct exercise is provided for each. After presenting and discussing the seven skills, have one or two clients role-play a scene looking for a job.

  ♦ **Developing a resume:** Discuss with clients that a resume describes work history and desire for work. It can be a simple letter or a more detailed document. The resume is the first step in finding a job that matches one's work. Don't leave large periods of time that you can't account for on the resume. Explain such periods by saying: "I was looking for a job that matched my work."

  Adjunct Exercise: Provide clients with a sample resume. Have clients discuss the most difficult part of preparing a resume.

  ♦ **The job application:** Go over a sample of a job application with the group. Most applications emphasize personal strengths and strong job skills. Attend to every question when filling out an application. This will be difficult for some clients, particularly those who have difficulty reading and writing. Sometimes it is hard to answer certain questions such as those requesting applicants to list their legal history. When not understanding certain parts of the application, ask the prospective employer - or a friend. Filling out an application should be viewed as part of the job being applied for.

Adjunct Exercise: Provide the group with a simple sample job application and have them practice filling it out. Hold a discussion around what was most frustrating about filling out the application.

- **Job leads:** Emphasize that job seeking is a full-time job in itself. Encourage clients to go after each potential job until they succeed. Discuss all of the resources that can be used in looking for job leads, e.g., Yellow Pages, internet, newspaper, friends, walking through shopping centers. Clients who get disappointed should be encouraged to talk with friends, family and the group.

  Exercise: Clients complete *Worksheet 88*. The group will need some structure and careful monitoring in this task. Have clients fill in every space in this worksheet.

- **Practice telephone skills** which are important in finding a job. Go through the following steps with the group. *Introduce yourself properly* and ask to *speak to the person in charge of hiring* for the company. When you speak with that person, introduce yourself again. You may say that you have heard that the company is a good employer and that you would like an opportunity to discuss a job with the company. Set up an appointment. If you are unable to speak with the appropriate person the first time you call, ask for his/her name so that you may ask for that person when you call back. Practice your phone skills with a friend or in your group.

  Adjunct Exercise: Have clients rehearse several scenarios and discuss them in the group until clients have the skill necessary to complete the initial phone call.

- **Practice job interviewing:** Talk about being prepared for success and failure. Remind clients that they have work (skills) to sell. They own that work and they sell it.

  Adjunct Exercise: Role-play a job interview. Make some role-play situations result in a failure to get hired. How did the person not hired feel? The judicial client is often sensitive to failure and gets discouraged after being refused a job. Have clients talk about the fact that most people who find a job have many interviews before they are finally hired.

- **Set goals:** Ask clients: Where are they going? What are their short term goals? What are their long-term goals? Using *Worksheet 89*, clients look at their plan for school and/or work for the next three years.

- **Using the Internet:** Discuss using the Internet to look for employment. Demonstrate this in group. As well, many jobs require that the application be submitted through the Internet. For clients who are not computer literate, or who are not comfortable using computers, this may be threatening and uncomfortable. Again, demonstrate this application process in group and have clients practice the process on the computer.

- The **Time and Task Management** section provides seven key approaches to finding meaningful and enjoyable involvement in work and other life tasks. Spell out the difference between **time** and **task-framing.** People get frustrated when they only task frame - devoting all of their time and energies to getting a task done, usually at the last minute. Time-framing involves giving a certain portion of time each day to a task, without the goal of completing the task. This helps avoid the frustration of last-minute efforts. Have incarcerated clients do the exercise by planning their free time or time spent in their room.

- Clients update their *MSL*. Spend some time looking over the *MSL* to see which of these skills are important in maintaining their job or seeking employment.

- Based on the area of employment or vocational needs, have clients update their *MAP*. Do they need to add a problem area to the *MAP* that pertains to job problems or employment.

- Remind clients to do their *TAP Charting.*

- Using the *SSC Change Scales,* have clients rate their skills to do their work and whether they like the job that they have.

SUMMARY OF KEY CONCEPTS

- Work "tool kit."

- Identifying one's work.

- Matching work with job.

- Time and task management.

SESSION CLOSURE AND GUIDELINES FOR THERAPEUTIC PROCESSING

Because of the several tasks in this session, there will be little time for therapeutic processing. Have clients briefly share what they got out of the session. If time permits, have each client share their worries and concerns around how their judicial record will affect their finding employment. Have them use cognitive restructuring skills to change thoughts that lead to those concerns and worries with thoughts that can lead to positive emotions and potential positive behaviors.

RATIONALE AND OVERVIEW

As stated a number of times in this *Guide,* AOD use and criminal conduct have been a large part of the substance abusing judicial client's lifestyle. This involves spending time drinking or doing drugs with friends and engaging in activities related to criminal conduct. Most derived a considerable degree of pleasure from these activities. Once these elements are removed, clients are likely to experience a sense of loss and emptiness. If they are not replaced with other healthy pleasurable activities, they may feel that life is an endless cycle of eating, sleeping, and working. There is an increased probability that clients will experience loneliness, boredom and depression.

Session 46 looks at work and employment as one of the important alternatives to a lifestyle of using drugs and engaging in criminal and antisocial activities. This session focuses on another alternative: healthy play and personal pleasures.

Monti and his colleagues (1989) report "that the number of pleasant activities a person engages in is directly related to the occurrence of positive feelings" (p. 87). People who spend all their time doing required activities, the "shoulds" and "have tos," will most likely have a less fulfilling and rewarding life. *Session 44* addresses this issue with respect to developing a balanced lifestyle. Creating a balanced lifestyle and engaging in positive activities are counters to the "shoulds" message of imbalance that will lead to feeling self-deprivation.

The lifestyle daily balance is a process that is ongoing and stable. It involves built-in activities that are part of daily living and that give positive and meaningful gratification to the individual. Unless this happens, clients become vulnerable to relapse and recidivism. Unless an alternative lifestyle is developed which includes a balance of work and play, clients are likely to feel they deserve to reward themselves with a drink, a hit, a night out with friends, with criminal associates, or even committing a crime. It is important that clients develop a balance in life by devising a schedule that includes healthy play and pleasant activities that they want to do.

An important part of healthy play is to fulfill our pleasures. Milkman and Sunderwirth (1993) conclude that there are four stages we go through when we engage in healthy pleasures. They see these stages as part of the blueprint for fulfillment, and as being important parts of the blueprint for healthy lifestyle alternatives for judicial clients.

▶ **Relaxation:** This is the gateway to what they call natural highs, and is necessary if we are to enjoy healthy pleasures. Healthy play and pleasures are not possible if we are tense, restless, or anxious (p. 27). This is the focus of *Session 48*, one of the lifestyle alternatives.

▶ **Setting healthy boundaries:** This is defining our independent, separate identity while at the same time respecting the rights and boundaries of others.

▶ **Seeking a meaningful engagement of talents:** Engaging healthy pleasures involves fulfilling our inner potential and self-actualization (Maslow, 1954). One of the most meaningful fulfillments and healthy pleasures is receiving support from and giving support to others, our topic for *Session 50*.

▶ **Cultivating body awareness:** Healthy pleasures involve being aware of and caring for our physical being. We cultivate body awareness through healthy eating and physical activity.

SUMMARY OF CONTENT, PRESENTATION SEQUENCE AND GUIDELINES

Introduce this session with the idea that change and recovery from substance abuse and criminal conduct require replacing those activities with healthy alternatives. Healthy play is one of these alternatives. Discuss the dangers of not experiencing enough time for pleasurable activities. Explain the idea that it is possible to have pleasant and "healthy pleasures." These are activities that have mental, physical, or spiritual value for the individual and that are done with others or alone. It may be helpful to present the four stages of engaging in healthy pleasures outlined by Milkman and Sunderwirth (1993).

▶ Start by having a group member use *STEP* to change a negative outcome resulting from a failure to use critical reasoning to a positive outcome. Then review the session objectives.

▶ Discuss **What Is Healthy Play?** Many judicial clients would argue that partying and getting high represent play, and some would argue, healthy play. However, this section makes it clear that healthy play means: moving freely within boundaries; is not harmful to self or others; fulfills pleasures that lead to positive and good outcomes and benefits for self and others; and is prosocial and moral.

The exercise in this section gives providers an opportunity to share or self-disclose healthy play that they have been involved in. This self-disclosure should demonstrate prosocial role modeling. In this section, clients complete only the top part of *Worksheet 90.*

▶ **Fulfilling Our Pleasures - Personal Pleasure Inventory** helps clients understand that healthy play involves fulfilling personal pleasures. The number of pleasant activities a person engages in is directly related to how positive we feel about ourselves. One way for clients to learn healthy play is to know what pleases them. This can provide direction for clients to determine what activities they can engage in to fulfill their personal pleasures and engage in healthy play. The *Personal Pleasure Inventory (PPI*: Milkman & Sunderwirth, 1993; Wanberg, Milkman & Harrison, 1992) can provide clients with this information.

Exercise: Clients will need guidance in completing, scoring and plotting the profile of the *PPI, Worksheet 91.* The scoring instructions are in the worksheet. Take time for clients to examine their findings and share them in group.

▶ Completing **Your List of Healthy Play Activities** involves clients using the *PPI* profile and completing the bottom half of *Worksheet 90.* This worksheet can become part of the client's relapse and recidivism prevention plan. It spells out healthy alternatives to substance use and criminal conduct.

▶ Clients update their *MSL* and are reminded to do *TAP Charting.*

▶ Using the *SSC Change Scales,* have clients rate their skills to do their work and whether they like the job that they have.

SUMMARY OF KEY CONCEPTS

▶ Healthy play.

▶ Fulfilling our pleasures. Matching work with job.

SESSION CLOSURE AND GUIDELINES FOR THERAPEUTIC PROCESSING

Utilize the therapeutic processing based on the needs of the group. If there is time, have clients briefly share one healthy play activity that they plan to use over the next few months.

RATIONALE AND OVERVIEW

The internal disruptive states of stress, and its emotional syndromes of guilt, anger and depression, when experienced at an extreme level of arousal, are considered high-risk exposures for relapse and recidivism. *Session 25* focused on understanding stress, its roots, effects on the body, its signs and symptoms, and its ability to trigger R&R. In *Session 26,* clients measured their stress level, learned and practiced ways to manage stress and looked at the positive faces of anxiety.

There are two approaches to managing stress: 1) managing the stress response and event; and 2) building resilience into the system to prepare for stressful events. The attitude and skills of relaxation go beyond managing a single stress event. The purpose of this session is to provide guidance to clients for building relaxation into their lifestyle - another alternative to involvement in AOD use and criminal conduct. Its purpose is to enhance the meaning and joy in living. In addition to the sources cited in this *Guide's* guidelines to *Sessions 25* and *26,* these were used in developing this session: Barlow, 1988; Lacroix, 1998; Lehrer & Woolfolk, 1993; Maxwell-Hudson, 1996; Smith, 1999; Wanberg & Milkman, 1998; Wanberg et al., 2005).

SUMMARY OF CONTENT, PRESENTATION SEQUENCE AND GUIDELINES

Introduce this session with the concepts presented in the above introduction. Emphasize that, although it is difficult to devote specific time each day to relax, we are talking about a daily program of relaxation. Use these guidelines for session delivery.

▶ Review the session objectives. Do the *STEP Exercise* in the *Workbook.* Clients review their *MAP.*

▶ Review the concepts and skills of *Sessions 25* and *26,* and the relaxation skills in *Table 7,* page 180.

▶ When presenting **The Role of Relaxation in Daily Living,** emphasize that relaxation gives balance in living.

▶ When presenting **Ways That We Relax,** emphasize that the relaxation exercises in *Table 7* are most valuable when they are used on a daily, routine basis, and not just to manage stressful events.

▶ When presenting **Special Activities That Increase Relaxation and Prepare for Stress,** emphasize that healthy relaxation is diverse, and not based only on one activity, such as watching T.V. or only physical exercise. Acknowledge that it is easy to get into a one-activity program of relaxation.

▶ Clients update their *MSL*, do *TAP.* and the *SSC Change Scale* to rate use of relaxation.

SUMMARY OF KEY CONCEPTS

▶ Relaxation gives balance in daily living.

▶ A healthy relaxation program involves diverse activities.

SESSION CLOSURE AND GUIDELINES FOR THERAPEUTIC PROCESSING

Have clients share their daily relaxation activities and how these help in preventing R&R.

RATIONALE AND OVERVIEW

Chapter 2 of this *Guide* provides a summary of health care issues for correctional clients. Before 1970, health care in prison settings was barely on the radar screen. The 1976 landmark case of Estelle v. Gamble (Hegamin, Longshore & Monahan, 2002) established the constitutional right of prisoners to have access to proper health care. However, beginning in the 1980s, the health care systems based on this ruling were seriously challenged by prison overcrowding and a drastic increase in offenders with drug-related crimes due to the implementation of mandatory minimum sentences for drug-related crimes (Hegamin et al., 2002). These were individuals with a history of substance abuse and significant medical problems, not the least of these being chronic and infectious diseases.

The obvious health challenges (Hegamin et al., 2002) were: HIV/AIDS; smoking-related diseases; inmates with age-related health problems; and mental illness. However, with respect to the total population of clients in the judicial system, these problems are only the tip of the iceberg. The lifestyle of the substance abusing judicial client drastically increases the probability of medical-physical problems. Judicial clients tend not to have healthy nutrition; not to attend to their health care needs; and not to engage in physical activity.

Little research can be found as to the level of involvement of judicial clients in meeting their physical health needs. What percent of non-incarcerated judicial clients have had a physical examination, engage in healthy eating habits, exercise daily, attend to their dental hygiene needs, etc.? Whatever the answers, it is safe to assume that most judicial clients need considerable improvement and change in these areas. An obvious conjecture is that there is a positive correlation between the maintenance of physical health and the prevention of R&R.

The purpose of this session is merely to heighten the conscious awareness of judicial clients of the importance of attending to nutrition and physical health and that these needs are much broader than attending to obvious medical problems. These include healthy eating, personal care and physical activity. This represents another lifestyle alternative to AOD use and criminal activity.

This one session only scratches the surface with respect to helping judicial clients establish a healthy physical lifestyle. Providers will want to observe for clients who need more focused services in this area. Intake data should establish the client's medical history and needs and should be part of the client's *MAP* and individual treatment plan. The intake *PACE* instrument, *The Adult Clinical Assessment Profile* (ACAP: Wanberg, 1998, 2006) provides a measure of self-reported medical-physical problems.

SUMMARY OF CONTENT, PRESENTATION SEQUENCE AND GUIDELINES

Introduce this session with the idea that we tend to ignore our health needs until we are faced with significant medical problems. Good health depends on daily attention to our mental and physical needs. One obvious need is for daily, routine exercise, even if that is limited to a 10- to 15-minute walk, or lifestyle exercise such as working in the yard, walking to work, physical work on the job, etc. Also stress that this session focuses only on three aspects of good health care: eating, personal care and physical activity. Here are the guidelines for presenting this session.

▶ Start with reviewing the session objectives and then the *STEP Method Exercise* in the *Workbook*. Have clients share their *TAP Charting*. Have them review their *MAP* to see if they included physical health in their problem list.

- Summarize the five lifestyle alternatives of *Module 12:* Work and job; healthy play; daily relaxation; giving and receiving support; and healthy eating, personal care and physical activity.

- Present the introduction material in the *Workbook* under **Session Content and Focus,** summarizing the benefits of making healthy choices around food, personal care and exercise.

- **Managing Weight and Healthy Eating** provides the bare bones elements of nutrition. Help clients search the Internet for additional information nutrition. When doing *Worksheet 94,* give clients handouts from:

  - MyPyramid Plan: http://www.mypyramid.gov and

  - Dietary Guidelines for Americans 2005: www.healthierus.gov/dietaryguidelines

    These can be downloaded and projected on a screen from the computer. Clients should be encouraged to access these materials on their own. **Adjunct Homework Exercise:** Have clients choose a family member or someone close to share their work on *Worksheet 94.* The key concepts to stress are:

  - Balance calories from foods and beverages with calories burned;

    - Balance portions from each of the Five Basic Food Groups;

    - A vitamin plan worked out with the client's health care provider;

    - Appropriate levels of salt, fats, and sugars;

    - Use moderation and integrate nutrition with exercise.

- **Basic Personal Care** covers some obvious, simple, but often overlooked issues around personal care. Present this in an interactive mode, putting client ideas on good personal care on a flipchart. Providers may want to provide additional information in this area.

- When presenting **Physical Activity,** emphasize: Always consult your health care provider before starting an exercise program or changing your normal level of physical activity. In helping clients do *Worksheet 95,* provide additional information with respect to types of physical activities clients can engage in.

- **Adjunct Homework Exercise:** Recommend that clients get a physical examination or checkup if they have not had one in the past year.

- Clients update their *MSL* and are reminded to do *TAP Charting.*

- Have clients rate their level of healthy eating and level of physical activity, using the *SSC Change Scales.*

SUMMARY OF KEY CONCEPTS

- Balanced portions of healthy foods.

- Personal care habits.

- Appropriate physical exercise and activity based on consultation with the client's health care provider.

SESSION CLOSURE AND GUIDELINES FOR THERAPEUTIC PROCESSING

Have clients share their past attention to their physical health. Can they improve? How do clients see this tied in with their R&R prevention goals?

RATIONALE AND OVERVIEW

This session represents one of the most important lifestyle alternatives to judicial clients - receiving support from and giving support to others. The purpose of this session is to provide guidance in implementing this lifestyle. It is time and research tested - that openness to and receiving support from others in the effort to change is essential. This support goes beyond formal treatment. Community reinforcement approaches are effective in helping clients sustain change ownership (Sisson & Azrin, 1989; Smith & Meyers, 1995). It is one way that clients receive reinforcement for their R&R prevention successes. This session guides clients in utilizing community support groups which strengthen prosocial and community responsibility.

It is also time and research tested that individuals who have made and sustained change also strengthen that change by giving support to others who are attempting to make similar improvements and change. Supporting others who are attempting to stay clean and sober, and prosocial through 12-step work, mentoring, and role modeling are powerful ways to reinforce the client's ownership of change. This is another component of strengthening prosocial behavior and implementing moral and community responsibility.

SUMMARY OF CONTENT, PRESENTATION SEQUENCE AND GUIDELINES

Introduce this session by emphasizing that although all clients in this stage of *SSC* are ready for receiving help and support, not all clients are ready for formal mentoring. Use these guidelines for session delivery.

◗ Present session objectives and do the *STEP Exercise* in the *Workbook*. Clients review their *MAP*.

◗ Facilitate discussion around the question of: What are your thoughts and feelings around how secure you are in the changes you have made in your life?

◗ **Receiving Help and Support: Being Mentored and Supported** identifies two kinds of community support resources: those that provide direct and those that provide indirect support. Clients will need guidance in doing *Worksheet 96*. Again, demonstrate and encourage the use of the Internet.

◗ **Giving Support and Help: Mentoring and Role Modeling** discusses formal and informal mentoring. Discuss the dangers of over-extending and boundary issues in mentoring and helping others. Elaborate on the six guides for mentoring. Have clients identify their strong and weak areas, the latter being important in setting limits when mentoring. Although some *SSC* clients may not be ready for the formal mentoring process, most have the self-control and self-efficacy to engage in the informal mentoring process.

◗ Complete the *SSC Change Scales* on willingness to be helped by a sponsor and willingness to mentor.

SUMMARY OF KEY CONCEPTS

◗ Receiving and giving support.　　◗ Role modeling and mentoring.

SESSION CLOSURE AND GUIDELINES FOR THERAPEUTIC PROCESSING

Have clients openly discuss their readiness to be involved in community support groups and in mentoring and role modeling others.

Clients who finish *Phase III* have taken ownership of change. Give them positive reinforcement and praise for this accomplishment. Close on a positive note, celebrating the occasion with a graduation ceremony and certificate of completion. Strengthen clients' continued journey with the message that they have the capacity and have been given the skills to make permanent the positive changes they have made and to continue to engage in:

▶ Abstinence from the use of illegal drugs and an alcohol-free or alcohol problem-free life;

▶ Living a crime-free life;

▶ Responsible living and a meaningful lifestyle.

For closed groups, *Phase III Closure* is done in the total group. For the open *SSC* groups, make time for clients in their last *SSC* session to do the closing reflection and sharing exercise as outlined in the *Workbook* on page 290.

As part of the closing process, have clients rate themselves once again on the *SSC Change Scales* (page 252 in the *Workbook*) as to their stage of change regarding AOD use patterns and CC thinking and conduct. Have them put a date on their rating check.

Finally, as outlined in the *Program Closure* session on page 290, do an exercise where clients visualize the *SSC Change Scales* that they completed at the end of each session and encourage them to use that visualized scale to rate themselves at the end of each day with a rating of "A good day" or "A great day." This keeps the positive process of STEP - **S**ituation - **T**hinking Change - **E**motion - **P**ositive outcome - foremost in their thinking.

Closure should also involve an individual session scheduled with clients within two weeks of their completing *SSC*. Prior to that session, they complete the final *PACE Instruments*. Clients complete the *Program Closure Inventory (PCI)* and the last *SEQ*. Providers also complete the *PCI* on the client. Providers complete the charting of the *CPR-C* and

CPR-P. The individual closure session covers the following tasks.

▶ Review the client's progress and change, providing feedback from the results of the *PACE* including the following:

◆ *Client Program Response - Client* (CPR-C) *Ratings;*

◆ *Client Program Response - Provider* (CPR-P) *Ratings;*

◆ *Self Evaluation Questionnaire -* (SEQ); and

◆ *Client and provider PCI.*

▶ Complete a continuing care or aftercare plan. This plan motivates and strengthens the continuation of the client's journey of self-improvement and change and responsible living. The importance of continuing care (Inciardi et al., 2002; Peters & Wexler, 2005) and the positive impact of aftercare (McCollister & French, 2002; Wexler, 2004) are discussed in *Chapter 7* of this *Guide.* For clients whose judicial obligations have ended, continuing care will be an option. Thus, motivational enhancement approaches will be necessary to get clients to continue involvement in support services. As noted in *Session 50,* community support groups, e.g., Alcoholics Anonymous, provide the most promising continuing care opportunity for clients.

▶ Review the *SSC CB Map* (page 14 in the *Workbook*) and the *CB STEP Method* (page 155 of the *Workbook*). It is recommended that clients be given a billfold-size laminated display of each of these charts so that they can refer to them from time to time.

Finally, providers are to be congratulated in their successful effort to bring their clients to a positive *SSC* closure. The knowledge, patience, skills, dedication and commitment on the part of providers are recognized as of highest merit and accomplishment.

GOOD THINKING! GOOD DAY! GOOD JOB!

REFERENCES

Abrams, D. B., & Niaura, R. S. (1987). Social learning theory. In H. T. Blane & K. W. Leonard (Eds.), *Psychological theories of drinking and alcoholism* (pp. 131-178). New York: Guilford.

Abramson, M. (1972). The criminalization of mentally disordered behavior: Possible side-effects of a new mental health law. *Hospital and Community Psychiatry, 23*, 101-107.

Ackerman, S. J., & Hilsenroth, M. J. (2001). A review of therapist characteristics and techniques negatively impacting the therapeutic alliance. *Psychotherapy: Theory, Research, Practice, Training, 38*, 171-183.

Ackerman, S. J., & Hilsenroth, M. J. (2003). A review of therapist characteristics and techniques positively impacting the therapeutic alliance. *Clinical Psychology Review, 23*, 1-33.

Acosta, M. C., Haller, D. L., & Schnoll, S. H. (2005). Cocaine and stimulants. In R. J. Frances, S. I. Miller, & A. H. Mack (Eds.), *Clinical textbook of addictive disorders* (pp. 184-218). New York: The Guilford Press.

Agee, V. L. (1979). *Treatment of the violent incorrigible adolescent.* Lexington, MA: Lexington Books.

Agee, V. L. (1986). Institutional treatment programs for the violent juvenile. In S. Apter & A. Goldstein (Eds.), *Youth violence: Program and prospects* (pp. 75-88). New York: Pergamon.

Alberti, R. E., & Emmons, M. L. (1995). *Your perfect right: A guide to assertive living* (7th ed.). San Luis Obispo, CA: Impact Publishers.

Alcoholics Anonymous. (1976). *Alcoholics Anonymous: The story of how many thousands of men and women have recovered from alcoholism* (3rd ed.). New York: Alcoholics Anonymous World Series.

Allport, G. W. (1937). *Personality: A psychological interpretation.* New York: Henry Holt and Company.

Allport, G. W. (1955). *Becoming: Basic considerations for a psychology of personality.* New Haven, CT: Yale University Press, Inc.

American Psychiatric Association. (1994). *Diagnostic and statistical manual of mental disorders* (4th ed.). Washington, DC: Author.

American Psychiatric Association. (2000). *Diagnostic and statistical manual of mental disorders* (4th ed. text revision). Washington, DC: Author.

Anderson, C. M., & Reiss, D. J. (1994). A psychoeducational model for treating the adolescent who is seriously emotionally disturbed. In W. Snyder & T. Ooms (Eds.), *Empowering families, helping adolescents: Family-centered treatment of adolescents with alcohol, drug abuse, and mental health problems* (Series 6, pp. 111-118). Rockville, MD: U.S. Department of Health and Human Services, Center for Substance Abuse Treatment.

Andrews, D. A., & Bonta, J. (1994). *The psychology of criminal conduct* (2nd. ed). Cincinnati, OH: Anderson.

Andrews, D. A., & Bonta, J. (1995). *The Level of Supervision Inventory - Revised.* Toronto: Multi-Health Systems.

Andrews, D. A., & Bonta, J. (1998). *The psychology of criminal conduct* (2nd. ed). Cincinnati, OH: Anderson.

Andrews, D. A., & Bonta, J. (2003). *The psychology of criminal conduct* (3rd ed.). Cincinnati, OH: Anderson.

Anglin, M. D., & Fisher, D. G. (1987). Survival analysis in drug program evaluation: II. Partitioning treatment effects. *International Journal of the Addictions, 22*, 377-387.

Arbuthnot, J., & Gordon, D. A. (1986). Behavioral and cognitive effects of a moral reasoning development intervention for high-risk, behavioral-disordered adolescents. *Journal of Consulting and Clinical Psychology, 54*, 208-216.

Aron, A., Mashek, D., McLaughlin-Volpe, T., Wright, S., Lewandowski, G., & Aron, E. N. (2005). Including close others in the cognitive structure of the self. In M. W. Baldwin (Ed.), *Interpersonal cognition* (pp. 206-232). New York: The Guilford Press.

ASAM: American Society of Addiction Medicine. (2001). *American Society of Addiction Medicine patient placement criteria for the treatment of substance-related disorders - Revised* (ASAM PPC-2-R) (2nd ed.). Chevy Chase, MD: Author.

Bachelor, A. (1991). Comparison and relationship to outcome of diverse dimensions of the helping alliance as seen by client and therapist. *Psychotherapy, 28*, 234-249.

Bachelor, K. A. (1995). Clients' perception of the therapeutic alliance: A qualitative analysis. *Journal of Counseling Psychology, 42*, 322-337.

Baldwin, M. W. (2005). *Interpersonal cognition.* New York: The Guilford Press.

Bandura, A. (1965). Influence of models' reinforcement contingencies on the acquisition of imitated responses. *Journal of Personality and Social Psychology, 1*, 589-595.

Bandura, A. (1969). *Principles of behavior modification*. New York: Holt, Rinehart & Winston.

Bandura, A. (1973). *Aggression: A social learning analysis*. Englewood Cliffs, NJ: Prentice Hall.

Bandura, A. (1977a). *Social learning theory*. Englewood Cliffs, NJ: Prentice-Hall.

Bandura, A. (1977b). Self-efficacy: Towards a unifying theory of behavioral change. *Psychological Review, 84*, 191-215.

Bandura, A. (1978). The self-system in reciprocal determination. *American Psychologist, 33*, 344-358.

Bandura, A. (1981). Self-referent thought: A developmental analysis of self-efficacy. In J. H. Flavell & L. Ross (Eds.), *Social cognitive development: Frontiers and possible futures*. Cambridge: Cambridge University Press.

Bandura, A. (1982). Self efficacy mechanisms in human agency. *American Psychologist, 37*, 122-147.

Bandura, A. (1986). *Social foundations of thought and action*. Englewood Cliffs, NJ: Prentice-Hall.

Bandura, A. (1989). Social cognitive theory. *Annals of Child Development, 6*, 3-58.

Bandura, A. (Ed.). (1995). *Self-efficacy in changing societies*. New York: Cambridge University Press.

Bandura, A. (1997). *Self-efficacy: The exercise of control*. New York: Freeman.

Barber, J. P., Connolly, M. B., Crits-Christoph, P., Gladis, L., & Siqueland, L. (2001). Alliance predicts patients' outcome beyond in-treatment change in symptoms. *Journal of Consulting and Clinical Psychology, 68*, 1027-1032.

Barber, J. P., Luborsky, L., Crits-Christoph, P., Thase, M. E., Weiss, R., Frank, A., et al. (1999). Therapeutic alliance as a predictor of outcome in treatment of cocaine dependence. *Psychotherapy Research, 9*(1), 54-73.

Barlow, D. H. (1988). *Anxiety and its disorders: The nature and treatment of anxiety and panic*. New York: The Guilford Press.

Baron, R. A. (1977). *Human aggression*. New York: Plenum.

Bateman, A., Brown, D., & Pedder, J. (2000). *Introduction to psychotherapy: An outline of psychodynamic principles and practice* (3rd ed.). London: Routledge.

Beck, A. T. (1963). Thinking and depression. *Archives of General Psychiatry, 9*, 324-333.

Beck, A. T. (1964). Thinking and depression II: Theory and therapy. *Archives of General Psychiatry, 10*, 561-571.

Beck, A. T. (1972). *Depression: Causes and treatment*. Philadelphia: University of Pennsylvania Press.

Beck, A. T. (1976). *Cognitive therapy and the emotional disorders*. New York: International Universities Press.

Beck, A. T. (1987). Cognitive models of depression. *Journal of Cognitive Psychotherapy, 1*, 5-37.

Beck, A. (1993). Cognitive approaches to stress. In P. M. Lehrer & R. L. Woolfolk (Eds.), *Principles and practice of stress management* (2nd ed., pp. 333-372). New York: The Guilford Press.

Beck, A. T. (1996). Beyond belief: A theory of modes, personality, and psychopathology. In P. M. Salkovskis (Ed.), *Frontiers of cognitive therapy* (pp. 1-25). New York: Guilford.

Beck, A. T. (1999). *Prisoners of hate: The cognitive basis of anger, hostility, and violence*. New York: HarperCollins.

Beck, A. T. (2006). *Beck Depression Inventory - BDI*. San Antonio, TX: Psychological Corporation.

Beck, A. T., Freeman, A., Davis, D. D., & Associates. (2004). *Cognitive therapy of personality disorders* (2nd ed). New York: The Guilford Press.

Beck, J. S. (1995). *Cognitive therapy: Basics and beyond*. New York: Guilford.

Beck, J. S. (2005). *Cognitive therapy for challenging problems: What to do when the basics don't work*. New York: The Guilford Press.

Benson, H. (1975). *The relaxation response*. New York: Morrow.

Berenson, B. G., & Carkhuff, R. R. (1967). *Sources of gain in counseling and psychotherapy*. New York: Holt, Rinehart & Winston.

Berlo, D. (1960). *The process of communication*. New York: Holt, Rinehart and Winston.

Bernstein, D. A., & Carlson, C. R. (1993). Progressive relaxation: Abbreviated methods. In P. M. Lehrer & R. L. Woolfolk (Eds.), *Principles and practice of stress management* (2nd ed., pp. 53-88). New York: Guilford.

Beutler, L. E., Machado, P. P., & Nuefeldt, S. A. (1994). Therapist variables. In A. E. Bergin & S. L. Garfield (Eds.), *Handbook of psychotherapy and behavioral change* (4th ed., pp. 229-269). New York: Wiley.

Bischof, L. J. (1964). *Interpreting personality theories.* New York: Harper & Row.

Blackburn, R. (1993). *The psychology of criminal conduct.* Chichester, UK: Wiley.

Bloom, B. L. (1985). *Stressful life event theory and research: Implications for primary prevention* (DHHS Publication No. AMD 85-1385). Rockville, MD: National Institute of Mental Health.

Blum, K., Cull, J. G., Braverman, E. R., & Comings, D. E. (1996). Reward deficiency syndrome. *American Scientist, 84*, 132-145.

Boehm, S. L., Valenzuela, C. F., & Harris, R. A. (2005). Alcohol: Neurobiology. In J. H. Lowinson, P. Ruiz, R. B. Millman, & J. G. Langrod (Eds.), *Substance abuse: A comprehensive textbook* (pp. 121-150). Baltimore, MD: Lippincott Williams & Wilkins.

Boeijinga, P. H., Parot P., Soufflet, L., Landron F., Danel, T., Gendre, I., Muzet, M., Demazieres, A., & Luthringer, R. (2004). Pharmacodynamic effects of acamprosate on markers of cerebral function in alcohol-dependent subjects administered at pretreatment and during alcohol abstinence. *Neuropsychobiology, 50*(1), 71-77.

Bohart, A. C., & Greenberg, L. S. (1997). Empathy and psychotherapy: An introductory overview. In A. C. Bohart, & L. S. Greenberg (Eds.), *Empathy reconsidered: New directions in psychotherapy* (pp. 3-31). Washington, DC: American Psychological Association.

Bordin, E. S. (1979). The generalizability of the psychoanalytic concept of the working alliance. *Psychotherapy: Theory, Research and Practice, 16*, 252-260.

Borg, S., Czarnecka, A., Knande, H., Mossberg, D., & Sedvail, G. (1983). Clinical conditions and concentrations of MOPEG in cerebrospinal fluid and urine of male alcoholic patients during withdrawal. *Alcoholism: Clinical and Experimental Research, 7*, 411-415.

Boring, E. (1930). A new ambiguous figure. *American Journal of Psychology, 42*, 444.

Borland, R. (1990). Slip-ups and relapse in attempts to quit smoking. *Addictive Behaviors, 15*, 235-245.

Brickman, P., Rabinowitz, V. C., Karuza, J., Coates, D., Cohn, E., & Kidder, L. (1982). Models of helping and coping. *American Psychologist, 37*, 368-384.

Bruch, H. (1981). Teaching and learning of psychotherapy. *Canadian Journal of Psychiatry, 26*, 86-92.

Brunswig, K. A., Sbraga, T. P., & Harris, C. D. (2003). Relapse prevention. In W. O'Donohue, J. E. Fisher, & S. C. Hayes (Eds.), *Cognitive behavior therapy: Applying empirically supported techniques in your practice* (pp. 321-329). Hoboken, NJ: John Wiley & Sons.

Burgoon, J. K. (1985). Nonverbal signals. In M. L. Knapp & G. R. Miller (Eds.), *Handbook of interpersonal communication* (pp. 344-392). Beverly Hills, CA: Sage Publications, Inc.

Burns, D. D. (1980). *Feeling good: The new mood therapy*. New York: William Morrow.

Burns, D. D. (1989). *Feeling good handbook*. New York: William Morrow.

Burns, D. D. (1999). *Feeling good: The new mood therapy* (revised and updated). New York: Avon Books.

Bush, J. M., & Bilodeau, B. C. (1993). *Options: A cognitive change program* (Prepared by J. M. Bush and B. C. Bilodeau for the National Institute of Corrections and the U.S. Department of the Navy). Washington, DC: National Institute of Corrections.

Caddy, G. R. (1978). Towards a multivariate analysis of alcohol abuse. In P. E. Nathan, G. A. Marlatt, & T. Loberet (Eds.), *Alcoholism: New directions in behavioral research and treatment*. New York: Plenum.

Campbell, D. T., & Fiske, D. W. (1959). Convergent and discriminant validation by the multitrait-multimethod matrix. *Psychological Bulletin, 56*, 81-105.

Cannon, W. B. (1927). The James-Lang theory of emotions: A critical examination and an alternative theory. *American Journal of Psychology, 39*, 106-124.

Cappell, H., & Greeley, J. (1987). Alcohol and tension reduction: An update on research and theory. In H. T. Blane & K. W. Leonard (Eds.), *Psychological theories of drinking and alcoholism* (pp. 15-54). New York: Guilford.

Cappella, J. N. (1985). The management of conversations. In M. L. Knapp & G. R. Miller (Eds.), *Handbook of interpersonal communication* (pp. 393-438). Beverly Hills, CA: Sage.

Carkhuff, R. (1969). *Helping in human relations* (Vols. 1 and 2). New York: Holt, Rinehart & Winston.

Carkhuff, R. (1971). *The development of human resources: Education, psychology and social change*. New York: Holt, Rinehart & Winston.

Carkhuff, R. R., & Berenson, B. G. (1977). *Beyond counseling and therapy* (2nd ed.). New York: Holt, Rinehart & Winston.

Carkhuff, R. R., & Truax, C. (1965). Training in counseling and psychotherapy: An evaluation of an integrated didactic and experimental approach. *Journal of Consulting Psychology, 29*, 333-336.

Carter, L., & Minirth, F. (1993). *The anger workbook: A 13-step interactive plan to help you.* Nashville, TN: Thomas Nelson Publishers.

Castonguay, L. G., Constantino, M. J., & Holtforth, M. G. (2006). The working alliance: Where are we and where should we go. Psychotherapy Theory, Research, Practice, Training, 43, 258-263.

Chandler, M. J., Greenspan, S., & Barenboim, C. (1973). Judgments of intentionality in response to videotaped and verbally presented moral dilemmas: The medium is the message. *Child Development, 44*, 315-320.

Chandler, M. J., Greenspan, S., & Barenboim, C. (1974). The assessment and training of role-taking and referential communication skills in institutionalized emotionally disturbed children. *Developmental Psychology, 10*(4), 546-355.

Chaney, E. F. (1989). Social skills training. In R. K. Hester & W. R. Miller (Eds.), *Handbook of alcoholism treatment approaches: Effective alternatives.* New York: Pergamon.

Chang, G., & Kosten, T. R. (2005). Treatment approaches. In J. H. Lowinson, P. Ruiz, R. B. Millman, & J. G. Langrod (Eds.), *Substance abuse: A comprehensive textbook* (pp. 579-587). Baltimore, MD: Lippincott Williams & Wilkins.

Chemtob, C. M., Hamada, R. S., Roitblat, H. L., & Muraoka, M. (1994). Anger, anger control, and impulsivity in combat-related post-traumatic stress disorder. *Journal of Consulting and Clinical Psychology, 62*, 827-832.

Chemtob, C. M., Novaco, R. W., Hamada, R. S., & Gross, D. M. (1997). Cognitive-behavioral treatment for severe anger in post-traumatic stress disorder. *Journal of Consulting and Clinical Psychology, 65*, 184-189.

Chon, K. K. (2000). Toward an improved understanding of anger: A control theory approach. *Korean Journal of Health Psychology, 5*, 146-170.

Ciraulo, D. A., & Ciraulo, A. M. (1988). Substance abuse. In J. P. Tupin, R. I. Shader, & D. S. Harnett (Eds.), *Handbook of clinical psychopharmacology* (pp. 121-158). Northvale, NJ: Jason Aronson.

Citrome, L., Nolan, K., & Volavka, J. (2004). Science-based treatment of aggression and agitation. In D. H. Fishbein (Ed.), *The science, treatment, and prevention of antisocial behaviors: Evidence-based practice, Volume II* (pp. 11-1 - 11-32). Kingston, NJ: Civic Research Institute, Inc.

Clark, D. A. (2004). Cognitive-behavioral theory and treatment of obsessive-compulsive disorder: Integrating cognitive-behavioral therapy and pharmacotherapy. In R. L. Leahy (Ed.), *Contemporary cognitive therapy* (pp. 161-183). New York: Guilford.

Clark, D. M., & Ehlers, A. (2004). Posttraumatic stress disorder: From cognitive theory to therapy. In R. L. Leahy (Ed.), *Contemporary cognitive therapy* (pp. 141-161). New York: Guilford.

Cloninger, C. R., & Guze, S. B. (1970). Psychiatric illness and female criminality: The role of sociopathy and hysteria in the antisocial woman. *American Journal of Psychiatry, 127*, 79-87.

Cloninger, R., Svrakic, D., & Prybeck, T. (1993). A psychological model of temperament and character. *Archives of General Psychiatry, 44*, 573-588.

Colby, A., & Kohlberg, L. (1987). *The measurement of moral judgement. Vol 1: Theoretical foundations and research validation.* Cambridge: Cambridge University Press.

Collingwood, R. G. (1949). *The idea of nature.* London: Oxford University Press.

Collins, R. L., Blane, H. T., & Leonard, K. E. (1999). Psychological theories of etiology. In P. J. Ott, R. E. Tarter & R. T. Ammerman (Eds.), *Sourcebook on substance abuse: Etiology, epidemiology, assessment and treatment* (pp. 153-165). Boston: Allyn and Bacon.

Connors, G. J., Carroll, K. M., DiClemente, C. C., Longabaugh, R., & Donovan, D. M. (1997). The therapeutic alliance and its relationship to alcoholism treatment participation and outcome. *Journal of Consulting and Clinical Psychology, 65*, 582-598.

Connors, G. J., Donovan, D. M., & DiClemente, C. C. (2001). *Substance abuse treatment and the stages of change.* New York: The Guilford Press.

Copeland, J., Swift, W., Roffman, R., & Stephens, R. (2001). A randomized controlled trial of brief cognitive-behavioral interventions for Cannabis Use Disorder. *Journal of Substance Abuse Treatment, 21*, 55-64.

Costello, C. (Ed.). (1996). *Personality characteristics of the personality disordered.* New York: Wiley.

Cote, G., & Hogins, S. (1990). Co-occurring mental disorders among criminal offenders. *Bulletin of the American Academy of Psychiatry and Law, 18*, 271-281.

Cross, T. L., Bazron, B. J., Dennis, K. W., & Isaacs, M. R. (1989). *Towards a culturally competent system of care* (Monograph Vol. 1). Washington, DC: National Institutes of Mental Health.

Cummings, H. W., Long, L. W., & Lewis, M. L. (1983). *Managing communication in organizations: An introduction.* Dubuque, IA: Gorsuch Scarisbrick Publishers.

Curry, S. G., & Marlatt, G. A. (1987). Building self-confidence, self-efficacy and self control. In W. M. Cox (Ed.), *Treatment and prevention of alcohol problems: A resource manual* (pp. 117-138). New York: Academic Press.

Daley, D. C., & Marlatt, G. A. (1992). Relapse prevention: Cognitive and behavioral interventions. In J. H. Lowinson, P. Ruiz, R. B. Millman, & J. G. Langrod (Eds.), *Substance abuse: A comprehensive textbook* (2nd ed., pp. 533-542). Baltimore, MD: Williams & Wilkins.

Daley, D. C., & Marlatt, G. A. (1997). Relapse prevention: Cognitive and behavioral interventions. In J. H. Lowinson, P. Ruiz, R. B. Millman, & J. G. Langrod (Eds.), *Substance abuse: A comprehensive textbook* (pp. 458-467). Baltimore, MD: Williams & Wilkins.

Daley, D. C., & Marlatt, G. A. (2005). Relapse prevention: Cognitive and behavioral interventions. In J. H. Lowinson, P. Ruiz, R. B. Millman, & J. G. Langrod (Eds.), *Substance abuse: A comprehensive textbook* (4th ed., pp. 772-785). Baltimore, MD: Lippincott Williams & Wilkins.

Dance, F.E.X. (1982). A speech theory of human communication. In F.E.X. Dance (Ed.), *Human communication theory* (pp. 120-146). New York: Harper & Row.

Dance, F.E.X., & Larson, C. E. (1976). *The function of human communication.* New York: Holt, Rinehart and Winston.

Daniel, A. E., Robins, A. J., Reid, J. C., & Wifley, D. E. (1988). Lifetime and six month prevalence of psychiatric disorders among sentenced female offenders. *Bulletin of the American Academy of Psychiatry and the Law, 164,* 333-342.

Dansereau, D. F., Evans, S. H., Czuchry, M., & Sia, T. L. (2004). Readiness and mandated treatment: Development and application of a functional model. In K. Knight & D. Farabee (Eds.), *Treating addicted offenders: A continuum of effective practices* (pp. 29-2 -29-9). Kingston, NJ: Civic Research Institute.

Dees, S. M., Dansereau, D. F., Peer, J. L., Boatler, J. G., & Knight, K. (1991). Using conceptual matrices, knowledge maps, and scripted cooperation to improve personal management strategies. *Journal of Drug Education, 2,* 211-228.

Dees, S. M., Dansereau, D. F., & Simpson, D. D. (2004). Implementing a readiness program for mandated substance abuse treatment. In K. Knight & D. Farabee (Eds.), *Treating addicted offenders: A continuum of effective practices* (pp. 28-2 - 28-11). Kingston, NJ: Civic Research Institute.

Deffenbacher, J. L., Oetting, E. R., Huff, M. E., Cornell, G. R., et al. (1996). Evaluation of two cognitive-behavioral approaches to general anger reduction. *Cognitive Therapy & Research, 20,* 551-573.

Deffenbacher, J. L., Oetting, E. R., Huff, M. E., & Thwaites, G. A. (1995). Fifteen-month follow-up of social skills and cognitive-relaxation approaches to general anger reduction. *Journal of Counseling Psychology, 42,* 400-405.

Deffenbacher, J. L., & Stark, R. S. (1992). Relaxation and cognitive-relaxation treatments of general anger. *Journal of Counseling Psychology, 39,* 158-167.

Deffenbacher, J. L., Story, D. A., Brandon, A. D., Hogg, J. A., & Hazaleus, S. L. (1988). Cognitive and cognitive-relaxation treatments of anger. *Cognitive Therapy and Research, 12,* 167-184.

Delia, J. G., O'Keefe, B. J., & O'Keefe, D. J. (1982). The constructivist approach to communication. In F. E. X. Dance (Ed.), *Human communication theory.* New York: Harper & Row.

DeMuro, S. A. (1997). *Development and validation of an instrument to measure DUI therapeutic educator style: Therapeutic Educator Countermeasures Inventory.* Denver, CO: University of Denver Unpublished Doctoral Dissertation.

Dewey, J. (1910). *How we think.* Washington, DC: Heath & Co.

DiClemente, C. C., & Prochaska, J. O. (1985). Processes and stages of change: Coping and competence in smoking behavior change. In S. Shiffman & T. A. Wills (Eds.), *Coping and substance abuse* (pp. 319-342). New York: Academic Press.

DiClemente, C. C., & Prochaska, J. O. (1998). Toward a comprehensive transtheoretical model of change: Stages of change and addictive behaviors. In W. R. Miller & N. Heather (Eds.), *Treating addictive behaviors* (2nd ed., pp. 3-124). New York: Plenum Press.

DiClemente, C. C., & Velasquez, M. M. (2002). Motivational interviewing and the stages of change. In W. R. Miller & S. Rollnick (Eds.), *Motivational interviewing: Preparing people for change* (2nd ed., pp. 201-216). New York: Guilford Press.

Dilts, S. L., Jr., & Dilts, S. L. (2005). Opioids. In R. J. Frances, S. I. Miller, & A. H. Mack (Eds.), *Clinical textbook of addictive disorders* (pp. 183-156). New York: The Guilford Press.

Dimeff, L. A., & Marlatt, G. A. (1995). Relapse prevention. In R. K. Hester & W. R. Miller (Eds.), *Handbook of alcoholism treatment approaches: Effective alternatives* (2nd ed., pp. 176-194). Boston: Allyn & Bacon.

Ditton, P. M. (1999). *Mental health and treatment of inmates and probationers*. Bureau of Justice Statistics Special Report. Washington, DC: U.S. Department of Justice, Office of Justice Programs.

Dobson, K. S., & Hamilton, K. (2003). Cognitive restructuring: Behavioral tests of negative cognitions. In W. O'Donohue, J. E. Fisher, & S. C. Hayes (Eds.), *Cognitive behavior therapy: Applying empirically supported techniques in your practice* (pp. 84-95). Hoboken, NJ: John Wiley & Sons.

Donohue, B., & Cavenagh, N. (2003). Anger (negative impulse) management. In W. O'Donohue, J. E. Fisher, & S. C. Hayes (Eds.), *Cognitive behavior therapy: Applying empirically supported techniques in your practice* (pp. 10-15). Hoboken, NJ: John Wiley & Sons.

Donovan, D. M. (2005). Assessment for relapse prevention. In D. M. Donovan & G. A. Marlatt (Eds.), *Assessment of addictive behaviors* (2nd ed., pp. 1-48). New York: The Guilford Press.

Douaihy, A., Stowell, K. R., Park, T. W., & Daley, D. C. (2007). Relapse prevention: Clinical strategies for substance use disorders. In K. Witkiewitz & G. A. Marlatt (Eds.), *Therapist's guide to evidence-based relapse prevention* (pp. 37-71). New York: Elsevier Inc.

Drummond, D. C., Litten, R. Z., Lowman, C., & Hunt, W. A. (2000). Craving research: Future directions. *Addiction, 95*(Suppl. 2), 247-255.

Dryden, W., & Mytton, J. (1999). *Four approaches to counseling and psychotherapy*. New York: Routledge.

Duckworth, M. P. (2003). Assertiveness skills and the management of related factors. In W. O'Donohue, J. E. Fisher, & S. C. Hayes (Eds.), *Cognitive behavior therapy: Applying empirically supported techniques in your practice* (pp. 16-27). Hoboken, NJ: John Wiley & Sons.

DuPont, R. L., & DuPont, C. M. (2005). Sedatives/hypnotics and benzodiazepines. In R. J. Frances, S. I. Miller, & A. H. Mack (Eds.), *Clinical textbook of addictive disorders* (pp. 219-244). New York: The Guilford Press.

D'Zurilla, T. J., & Nezu, A. M. (1999). *Problem-solving therapy: A social competence approach to clinical intervention* (2nd ed.). New York: Springer.

D'Zurilla, T. J., & Nezu, A. M. (2001). Problem-solving therapies. In K. S. Dobson (Ed.), *Handbook of cognitive-behavioral therapies* (2nd ed., pp. 211-245). New York: The Guilford Press.

Eckhardt, C., & Deffenbacher, J. (1995). In H. Kassinove (Ed.), *Anger disorders: Definition, diagnosis and treatment*. Bristol: Taylor & Francis.

Efran, J. S., & Clarfield, L. E. (1992). Constructionist theory: Sense and nonsense. In S. McNamee & K. J. Gergen (Eds.), *Therapy as social construction*. London: Sage.

Eisenberg, N., & Miller, P. (1987). Empathy, sympathy, and altruism: Empirical and conceptual links. In N. Eisenberg & J. Strayer (Eds.), *Empathy and development* (pp. 292-316). New York: Cambridge University Press.

Ekman, P. (1973). Cross-cultural studies of facial expression. In P. Ekman (Ed.), *Darwin and facial expression*. New York: Academic Press.

Ekman, P., & Friesen, W. V. (1969). The repertoire of nonverbal behavior: Categories, origins, usage, and coding. *Semiotica, 1*, 49-98.

Ekman, P. V., & Friesen, W. (1975). *Unmasking the face*. Upper Saddle River, NJ: Prentice-Hall.

Ellis, A. (1962). *Reason and emotion in psychotherapy*. New York: Stuart.

Ellis, A. (1975). *A new guide to rational living*. Englewood Cliffs, NJ: Prentice-Hall.

Ellis, A. (2003). Cognitive restructuring of the disputing of irrational beliefs. In W. O'Donohue, J. E. Fisher, & S. C. Hayes (Eds.), *Cognitive behavior therapy: Applying empirically supported techniques in your practice* (pp. 79-83). Hoboken, NJ: John Wiley & Sons.

Ellis, A., & Harper, R. A. (1961). *A guide to rational living*. Englewood Cliffs, NJ: Prentice-Hall.

Emrick, C. D., & Aarons, G. A. (1990). Cognitive-behavioral treatment of problem drinking. In H. B. Milkman & L. I. Sederer (Eds.), *Treatment choices for alcoholism and substance abuse* (pp. 265-286). New York: Lexington Books.

Erikson, E. H. (1959). *Childhood and society* (2nd ed.) New York: Norton.

Erikson, E. H. (1968). *Youth and crisis*. New York: Norton.

Erikson, E. H. (1975). *Life history and the historical moment*. New York: W. W. Norton

Fall, K. A., Howard, S., & Ford, J. E. (1999). *Alternatives to domestic violence: A homework manual for battering intervention groups*. Philadelphia, PA: Taylor & Francis.

Farabee, D., & Leukefeld, C. G. (2002). HIV and AIDS prevention strategies. In C. G. Leukefeld, F. Tims, & D. Farabee (Eds.), *Treatment of drug offenders: Policies and issues* (pp. 172-185). New York: Springer Publishing Company.

Farabee, D. J., Simpson, D. D., Dansereau, D. F., & Knight, K. (1995). Cognitive induction into treatment among drug users on probation. *Journal of Drug Issues, 25*, 669-682.

Ferguson, K. E. (2003). Relaxation. In W. O'Donohue, J. E. Fisher, & S. C. Hayes (Eds.), *Cognitive behavior therapy: Applying empirically supported techniques in your practice* (pp. 330-340). Hoboken, NJ: John Wiley & Sons.

Feshbach, N. D. (1984). Empathy, empathy training and the regulation of aggression in elementary school children. In R. M. Kaplan, V. J. Konecni, & R. W. Novaco (Eds.), *Aggression in children and youth*. The Hague: Martinus Nijhoff.

Feshbach, N. D. (1997). Empathy: The formative years - implications for clinical practice. In A. C. Bohart & L. S. Greenberg (Eds.), *Empathy reconsidered: New directions in psychotherapy* (pp. 33-62). Washington, DC: American Psychological Association.

Field, G. (2004). Continuity of offender treatment: From the institution to the community. In K. Knight & D. Farabee (Eds.), *Treating addicted offenders: A continuum of effective practices* (pp. 33-1 - 33-9). Kingston, NJ: Civic Research Institute.

Fisher, G. L., & Harrison, T. C. (2000). *Substance abuse: Information for school counselors, social workers, therapists, and counselors*. Boston: Allyn and Bacon.

Fisher, R., & Ury, W. (1981). *Getting to YES: Negotiating agreement without giving in*. Boston: Houghton Mifflin.

Fishbein, D. H. (2004). Transdisciplinary and translational approaches to studying and preventing antisocial behavior. In D. H. Fishbein (Ed.), *The science, treatment, and prevention of antisocial behaviors: Evidence-based practice* (pp. 1-1 - 1-15). Kingston, NJ: Civic Research Institute.

Foglia, W. D. (2000). Adding an explicit focus on cognition to criminology theory. In D. H. Fishbein (Ed.), *The science, treatment, and prevention of antisocial behaviors: Evidence-based practice* (pp. 10-1 - 10-25). Kingston, NJ: Civic Research Institute, Inc.

Fox, J. A., & Levin, J. (2003). Serial murder: Popular myths and empirical realities. In A. R. Roberts (Eds.), *Critical issues in crime and justice* (2nd ed., pp. 51-61). Thousand Oaks, CA: Sage Publications.

Frank, J. D. (1963). *Persuasion and healing: A comparative study of psychotherapy*. New York: Schocken Books.

Frank, J. D. (1971). Therapeutic factors in psychotherapy. *American Journal of Psychotherapy, 25*, 350-361.

Frank, J. D. (1974). Psychotherapy: Restoration of morale. *American Journal of Psychiatry, 131*, 271-274.

Frankl, V. E. (1959). *Man's search for meaning*. Boston: Beacon Press.

Frankl, V. E. (1980). *Man's search for meaning: An introduction to logotherapy*. New York: Simon & Schuster.

Franks, C. M., & Barbrack, C. R. (1983). Behavior therapy with adults: An integrative perspective. In M. Hersen, A. E. Kazdin, & A. S. Bellack (Eds.), *Clinical psychology handbook* (pp. 507-524). New York: Pergamon.

Franks, C. M., & Wilson, G. T. (1973-1975). *Annual review of behavior therapy: Theory and practice* (Vols. 1-7). New York: Brunner/Mazel.

Freeman, A., Pretzer, J., Fleming, B., & Simon, K. M. (1990). *Clinical applications of cognitive therapy*. New York: Plenum.

Freud, S. (1893-1895). The psychotherapy of hysteria. *Studies on Hysteria*. S. E., Vol. II.

Freud, S. (1913). *On beginning the treatment (Further Recommendations on the Technique of Psycho-Analysis I)*. S.E. SII.

Fried, R. 0. (1993). The role of respiration in stress and stress control: Toward a theory of stress as a hypoxic phenomenon. In P. M. Lehrer & R. L. Woolfolk (Eds.), *Principles and practice of stress management* (2nd ed., pp. 301-332). New York: Guilford.

Fromme, K., & D'Amico, E. J. (1999). Neurobiological bases of alcohol's psychological effects. In K. E. Leonard & H. T. Blane (Eds.), *Psychological theories of drinking and alcoholism* (2nd ed., pp. 442-455). New York: The Guilford Press.

Frosch, W. A., & Milkman, H. B. (1977), *Ego functions of drug users in the psychodynamics of drug dependence*, National Institute on Drug Abuse Research Monograph 12, pp. 142-156. Rockville, MD: U.S. Department of Health and Human Services, National Institutes of Health.

Fruzzetti, A. E., & Iverson, K. M. (2004). Mindfulness, acceptance, validation, and "individual" psychopathology in couples. In S. C. Hayes, V. M. Follette, & M. M. Linehan (Eds.), *Mindfulness and acceptance: Expanding the cognitive-behavioral tradition* (pp. 168-191). New York: Guilford Press.

Fruzzetti, A. R., & Fruzzetti, A. E. (2003). Dialectics in cognitive and behavior therapy. In W. O'Donohue, J. E. Fisher, & S. C. Hayes (Eds.), *Cognitive behavior therapy: Applying empirically supported techniques in your practice* (pp. 121-129). Hoboken, NJ: John Wiley & Sons.

Gardner, E. L. (2005). Brain reward mechanism. In J. H. Lowinson, P. Ruiz, R. B. Millman, & J. G. Langrod (Eds.), *Substance abuse: A comprehensive textbook* (pp.48-96). Baltimore, MD: Lippincott, Williams & Wilkins.

Garfield, S. L. (1992). Major issues in psychotherapy research. In D. K. Freedheim (Ed.), *History of psychotherapy: A century of change* (pp. 335-359). Washington, DC: American Psychological Association.

Gaston, L. (1990). The concept of the alliance and its role in psychotherapy: Theoretical and empirical considerations. *Psychotherapy, 27*, 143-153.

George, R. L. (1990). *Counseling the chemically dependent: Theory and practice.* Englewood Cliffs, NJ: Prentice-Hall.

George, R. L., & Cristiani, T. S. (1981). *Theory, methods and processes of counseling and psychotherapy.* Englewood Cliffs, NJ: Prentice-Hall.

Gibbs, J. C. (1995). A peer-group treatment program for delinquents. In R. R. Ross, D. H. Antonowicz & G. K. Dhaliwai (Eds.), *Going straight: Effective delinquency prevention and offender rehabilitation* (pp. 179-192). Ottawa: Air Training and Publications.

Gitlow, S. (2001). *Substance use disorders: A practical guide.* New York: Lippincott Williams & Wilkins.

Gitlow, S. F. (1970). The pharmacological approach to alcohol. *Maryland State Medical Journal, 19*, 93-96.

Gitlow, S. F. (1982). The clinical pharmacology and drug interaction of ethanol. In E. M. Pattison & F. Kaufman (Eds.), *Encyclopedic handbook of alcoholism* (pp. 1-18). New York: Gardner.

Gitlow, S. F. (1988). An overview. In S. E. Gitlow & H. S. Peyser (Eds.), *Alcoholism: A practical treatment guide* (2nd ed., pp. 1-18). Philadelphia: W. B. Saunders.

Glass, C. R., & Arnkoff, D. B. (1988). Common and specific factors in client descriptions of and explanations for change. *Journal of Integrative and Eclectic Psychotherapy, 7*, 427-440.

Glass, C. R., & Arnkoff, D. B. (1992). Behavior therapy. In D. K. Freedheim (Ed.), *History of psychotherapy: A century of change* (pp. 587-628). Washington, DC: American Psychological Association.

Glass, C. R., & Arnkoff, D. B. (1997). Questionnaire methods of cognitive self-statement assessment. *Journal of Consulting and Clinical Psychology, 65,* 911-927.

Glassman, S. (1983). In, with, and of the group: A perspective on group psychotherapy. *Small Group Behavior, 14*, 96-106.

Glenn, H. S., & Hockman, R. H. (1977). *Substance abuse.* Unpublished manuscript, NDAC.

Glenn, H. S., & Warner, J. W. (1975). *Understanding substance dependence.* Unpublished manuscript, Social Systems, Inc.

Glenn, H. S., Warner, J. W., & Hockman, R. H. (1977). *Substance dependence.* Unpublished manuscript, NDAC.

Gold, M. S., & Jacobs, W. S. (2005). Cocaine and crack: Clinical aspects. In J. H. Lowinson, P. Ruiz, R. B. Millman, & J. G. Langrod (Eds.), *Substance abuse: A comprehensive textbook* (pp. 218-251). Baltimore, MD: Lippincott Williams & Wilkins.

Goldfried, M. R. (1995). *From cognitive-behavioral therapy to psychotherapy integration: An evolving view.* New York: Springer.

Goldman, M. S., Brown, S. A., & Christiansen, B. A. (1987). Expectancy theory: Thinking about drinking. In H. T. Blane & K. E. Leonard (Eds.), *Psychological theories of drinking and alcoholism* (pp. 181-226). New York: Guilford.

Goldman, M. S., Del Boca, F. K., & Darkes, J. (1999). In H. T. Blane & K. W. Leonard (Eds.), *Psychological theories of drinking and alcoholism* (2nd ed., pp. 203-246). New York: Guilford.

Gorski, T. T. (1993). *Relapse prevention therapy with chemically dependent criminal offenders: The relapse prevention workbook for the criminal offender.* Independence, MO: Herald House/Independence Press.

Gotlib, I. H., & Hammen, C. L. (2002). *Handbook of depression.* New York: The Guilford Press.

Gottfredson, M., & Hirschi, T. (1990). *A general theory of crime.* Palo Alto, CA: Stanford University Press.

Gottman, J., Notarius, C., Gonso, J., & Markman, H. (1976). *A couple's guide to communication.* Champaign, IL: Research Press.

Greeley, J., & Oei, T. (1999). Alcohol and tension reduction. In H. T. Blane & K. W. Leonard (Eds.), *Psychological theories of drinking and alcoholism* (2nd ed., pp. 14-53). New York: Guilford.

Grilly, D. M. (1989). *Drugs and human behavior.* Boston: Allyn & Bacon.

Grinspoon, L., Bakalar, J. B., & Russo, E. (2005). Marihuana: Clinical aspects. In J. H. Lowinson, P. Ruiz, R. B. Millman, & J. G. Langrod (Eds.), *Substance abuse: A comprehensive textbook* (pp. 263-276). Baltimore, MD: Lippincott Williams & Wilkins.

Guajardo-Lucero, M. (2000). *The spirit of culture: Applying cultural competency to strength-based youth development.* Denver: Assets for Colorado Youth.

Gurman, A. S., & Messer, S. B. (2003). Contemporary issues in the theory and practice of psychotherapy. In A. S. Gurman, & S. B. Messer (Eds.), *Essential psychotherapies: Theory and practice* (2nd ed., pp. 1-24). New York: Guilford.

Guy, E., Platt, J., Zwerling, I., & Bullock, S. (1985). Mental health status of prisoners in an urban jail. *Criminal Justice and Behavior, 12*, 29-53.

Ham, H. (1957). *Lecture on the concepts of Kurt Lewin's theory of growth and learning.* Denver, CO: Iliff School of Theology.

Hare, R. D. (1970). *Psychopathy: Theory and research.* New York: Wiley.

Hare, R. D. (1980). A research scale for the assessment of psychopathy in criminal populations. *Personality and Individual Differences, 1*, 111-119.

Hare, R. D. (1986). Twenty years experience with the Cleckley psychopath. In W. H. Reid, D. Door, J. I. Walker, & J. W. Bonner (Eds.), *Unmasking the psychopath.* New York: W. W. Norton.

Hare, R. D. (2003). *Hare Psychopathy Checklist-Revised.* Minneapolis, MN: Pearson Assessments.

Hart, L. (1991). *Training methods that work: A handbook for trainers.* Menlo Park, CA: Crisp Publications.

Hart, L. S., & Stueland, D. S. (1979). An application of the multidimensional model of alcoholism: Differentiation of alcoholics by mode analysis. *Journal of Studies on Alcohol, 40*, 283-290.

Hartley, D., & Strupp, H. (1983). The therapeutic alliance: Its relationship to outcome in brief psychotherapy. In J. Masling (Ed.), *Empirical studies of psychoanalytic theory* (Vol. 1, pp. 1-38). Hillsdale, NJ: Erlbaum.

Hayes, S. C. (2004). Acceptance and commitment therapy and the new behavior therapies. In S. C. Hayes, V. M. Follette, & M. M. Linehan (Eds.), *Mindfulness and acceptance: Expanding the cognitive-behavioral tradition* (pp. 1-29). New York: Guilford Press.

Hayes, S. C., Follette, V. M., & Linehan, M. M. (Eds.). (2004). *Mindfulness and acceptance: Expanding the cognitive-behavioral tradition.* New York: Guilford Press.

Hayes, S. C., & Pankey, J. (2003). Acceptance. In W. O'Donohue, J. E. Fisher, & S. C. Hayes (Eds.), *Cognitive behavior therapy: Applying empirically supported techniques in your practice* (pp. 4-9). Hoboken, NJ: John Wiley & Sons.

Hays, R. D., & Ellickson, P. L. (1990). How generalizable are adolescents' beliefs about pro-drug pressures and resistance self-efficacy? *Journal of Applied Social Psychology, 20*, 321-340.

Hazlett-Stevens, H., & Craske, M. G. (2003). Breathing retraining and diaphragmatic breathing techniques. In W. O'Donohue, J. E. Fisher, & S. C. Hayes (Eds.), *Cognitive behavior therapy: Applying empirically supported techniques in your practice* (pp. 59-64). Hoboken, NJ: John Wiley & Sons.

Hegamin, A., Longshore, D., & Monahan, G. (2002). Health services in correctional settings: Emerging issues and model strategies. In Leukefeld, C. G., Tims, F., & . Farabee, D. (Eds.), *Treatment of drug offenders: Policies and issues* (pp. 335-347). New York: Springer Publishing Company, Inc.

Heider, F. (1958). *The psychology of interpersonal relations.* New York: Wiley.

Heinz, A. (2006). Staying sober. *Scientific American Mind*, April/May, 58-61.

Hester, R. K. (1995). Behavioral self-control training. In R. K. Hester & W. R. Miller (Eds.), *Handbook of alcoholism treatment approaches: Effective alternatives* (2nd ed., pp. 148-159). Boston: Allyn & Bacon.

Hiller, M. L., Knight, K., & Simpson, D. D. (1999). Prison-based substance abuse treatment, residential aftercare, and recidivism. *Addiction, 94*, 833-842.

Hobson, A., & McCarley, R. (1977). The brain as a dream state generator: An activation synthesis hypothesis of the dream process. *American Journal of Psychiatry, 134*(12), 1335-1348.

Hodding, G. C., Jann, M., & Ackerman, I. P. (1980). Drug withdrawal syndromes: A literature review. *The Western Journal of Medicine, 133*, 383-391.

Hodgins, D. C., el Guebaly, N., & Armstrong, S. (1995). Prospective and retrospective reports of mood states before relapse to substance use. *Journal of Consulting and Clinical Psychology, 63*, 400-407.

Hodgins, S., & Cote, G. (1990). Prevalence of mental disorders among penitentiary inmates in Quebec. *Canada's Mental Health, 38*, 1-4.

Hoffman, M. L. (1984). Moral development. In M. H. Bornstein & M. E. Lamb (Eds.), *Developmental psychology: An advanced textbook* (p. 279). Hillsdale, NJ: Lawrence Erlbaum.

Hoffman, M. L. (1987). The contribution of empathy to justice and moral judgment. In N. Eisenberg & J. Strayer (Eds.), *Empathy and its development* (p. 47). New York: Cambridge University Press.

Holden, C. (2001). Behavioral addictions: Do they exist? *Science, 294*, 980-982

Hollander, A. B. (2002). OCD and the brain. http://serendip.brynmawr.edu/bb/neuro/neuroOO/web1/Hollander.html

Hollen, S., & Beck, A. T. (1986). Research on cognitive therapies. In S. L. Garfield & A. E. Bergin (Eds.), *Handbook of psychotherapy and behavior change* (3rd ed., pp. 443-482). New York: Wiley.

Hollin, C. R. (1990). *Cognitive-behavioral interventions with young offenders.* Elmsford, New York: Pergamon.

Horn, J. L., & Wanberg, K. W. (1969). Symptom patterns related to excessive use of alcohol. *Quarterly Journal of Studies on Alcohol, 30,* 35-58.

Horn, J. L., & Wanberg, K. W. (1973). Females are different: On the diagnosis of alcoholism in women. In N. Rosenberg (Ed.), *Contributions to an understanding of alcoholism.* Rockville, Maryland: U. S. Department of Health, Education, Welfare, 332-354.

Horn, J. L., Wanberg, K. W., & Foster, F. M. (1990). *Guide to the Alcohol Use Inventory (AUI).* Minneapolis, MN: National Computer Systems.

Horvath, A. O. (2006). The alliance in context: Accomplishments, challenges, and future directions. *Psychotherapy Theory, Research, Practice, Training, 43,* 258-263.

Horvath, A. O., & Symonds, B. B. (1991). Relation between working alliance and outcome in psychotherapy: A meta-analysis. *Journal of Counseling Psychology, 38,* 139-149.

Howells, K. (1989). Anger management methods in relation to the prevention of violent behavior. In J. Archer & K. Browne (Eds.), *Human aggression: Naturalistic approaches.* London: Routledge.

Hufford, M. H., Witkiewitz, K., Shields, A. L., Kodya, S., & Caruso, J. C. (2003). Applying nonlinear dynamics to the prediction of alcohol use disorder treatment outcomes. *Journal of Abnormal Psychology, 112*(2), 219-227.

Hull, J. G. (1987). Self-awareness model. In H. T. Blane & K. W. Leonard (Eds.), *Psychological theories of drinking and alcoholism* (pp. 272-304). New York: Guilford.

Hull, J., & Bond, C. (1986). Social and behavioral consequences of alcohol consumption and expectancy: A meta-analysis. *Psychological Bulletin, 99,* 347-360.

Hyman, M. M. (1976). Alcoholics 15 years later. *Annals of the New York Academy of Sciences, 273,* 613-623.

Imhoff, J. E. (1995). Overcoming countertransference and other attitudinal barriers in the treatment of substance abuse. In A. M. Washton (Ed.), *Psychotherapy and substance abuse: A practitioner's handbook* (pp. 3-22). New York: Guilford Press.

Inciardi, J. A., Martin, S. S., Butzin, C. A., Hooper, R. M., & Harrison, L. D. (1997). An effective model of prison-based treatment for drug-involved offenders. *Journal of Drug Issues, 27,* 261-278.

Inciardi, J. A., Surratt, H. L., Martin, S. S., & Hooper, R. M. (2002). The importance of aftercare in a corrections-based treatment continuum. In C. G. Leukefeld, F. Tims, & D. Farabee (Eds.), *Treatment of drug offenders: Policies and issues* (pp. 204-216). New York: Springer Publishing Company, Inc.

Ivey, A. E., & Simek-Downing, L. (1980). *Counseling and psychotherapy: Skills, Theories, and Practice.* Englewood Cliffs, NJ: Prentice-Hall, Inc.

Izzo, R. L. & Ross, R. R. (1990). Meta-analysis of rehabilitation programs for juvenile delinquents. *Criminal Justice and Behavior, 17,* 134-142.

Jacobson, E. (1938). *Progressive relaxation* (2nd ed.). Chicago: University of Chicago Press.

Jacobson, N. S., & Margolin, G. (1979). *Marital therapy strategies based on social learning and behavior exchange principles.* New York: Brunner/Mazel.

James, W. (1890). *Principles of psychology.* New York: Henry Holt.

Joe, G. W., Chastain, R. L., & Simpson, D. D. (1990). Relapse. In D. D. Simpson & S. B. Sells (Eds.), *Opioid addiction and treatment: A 12-year follow-up* (pp. 121-136). Malabar, FL: Krieger.

Johnson, B. A., & Ait-Daoud, N. (2005). Alcohol: Clinical aspects. In J. H. Lowinson, P. Ruiz, R. B. Millman, & J. G. Langrod (Eds.), *Substance abuse: A comprehensive textbook* (pp. 151-163). Baltimore, MD: Lippincott Williams & Wilkins.

Jourard, S. M. (1959). Self-disclosure and other cathexis. *Journal of Abnormal and Social Psychology, 59,* 428-431.

Jourard, S. M., & Friedman, R. (1970). Experimenter-subject "distance" and self-disclosure. *Journal of Personality and Social Psychology, 15,* 278-282.

Jourard, S. M., & Resnick, J. L. (1970). The effect of high revealing subjects on self-disclosure of low revealing subjects. *Journal of Humanistic Psychology, 10,* 84-93.

Kadden, R. M. (1999). Cognitive behavior therapy. In P. J. Ott, R. E. Tarter & R. T. Ammerman (Eds.), *Sourcebook on substance abuse: Etiology, epidemiology, assessment and treatment* (pp. 272-292). Boston: Allyn and Bacon.

Kadden, R., Carroll, K., Donovan, D., Cooney, N., Monti, P., Abrams, D., Litt, M., & Hester, R. (1992). *Cognitive-behavioral coping skills therapy manual: A clinical research guide for therapists treating individuals with alcohol abuse and dependence* (Project MATCH Monograph Series, Vol. 3). Rockville, MD: National Institutes on Alcohol Abuse and Alcoholism, U.S. Department of Health and Human Services, National Institutes of Health.

Kadden, R. M., & Cooney, N. L. (2005). Treating alcohol problems. In G. A. Marlatt, & D. M. Donovan (Eds.), *Relapse prevention* (2nd ed., pp. 65-92). New York: Guilford Press.

Kanfer, F. H. (1970). Self-regulation: Research, issues and speculations. In C. Neuringer & J. L. Michael (Eds.), *Behavior modification in clinical psychology* (pp. 178-220). New York: Appleton-Century-Crofts.

Kanfer, F. H. (1975). Self-management methods. In F. H. Kanfer & A. P. Goldstein (Eds.), *Helping people change*. New York: Pergamon.

Kanfer, F. H. (1986). Implications of a self-regulation model of therapy for treatment of addictive behaviors. In W. R. Miller & N. Heather (Eds.), *Treating addictive behaviors: Processes of change*. New York: Plenum.

Kaplan, A., & Laygo, R. (2003). Stress management. In W. O'Donohue, J. E. Fisher, & S. C. Hayes (Eds.), *Cognitive behavior therapy: Applying empirically supported techniques in your practice* (pp. 411-416). Hoboken, NJ: John Wiley & Sons.

Kassinove, H., & Tafrate, R. C. (2002). *Anger management: The complete treatment guidebook for practitioners*. Atascadero, CA: Impact Publishers, Inc.

Kaufman, E. (1994). *Psychotherapy of addicted persons*. New York: Guilford Press.

Kazdin, A. E. (1976). Effects of covert modeling, multiple models, and model reinforcement on assertive behaviors. *Behavior Therapy, 7*, 211-222.

Kazdin, A. E. (1978). Behavior therapy: Evolution and expansion. *The Counseling Psychologist, 7*, 34-37.

Kazdin, A. E. (1979). Imagery elaboration and self-efficacy in the covert modeling of unassertive behavior. *Journal of Consulting and Clinical Psychology, 47*, 725-733.

Kazdin, A. E. (1983). Treatment research: The investigation and evaluation of psychotherapy. In M. Hersen, A. E. Kazdin, & A. S. Bellack (Eds.), *Clinical psychology handbook* (pp. 265-288). New York: Pergamon.

Kelley, H. H. (1987). Toward a taxonomy of interpersonal conflict process. In S. Oskamp & S. Spacapan (Eds.), *Interpersonal processes* (pp. 122-147). Newbury Park, CA: Sage.

Kelly, G. A. (1955). *The psychology of personal constructs* (2 vols.). New York: Norton.

Kendall, P. C., & Bemis, K. M. (1983). Thought and action in psychotherapy: The cognitive-behavioral approaches. In M. Hersen, A. E. Kazdin, & A. S. Bellack (Eds.), *The clinical psychology handbook* (pp. 565-592). New York: Pergamon.

Kennedy, S., & Serin, R. (1999). Examining offender readiness to change and the impact on treatment outcome. In P. M. Harris (Ed.), *Research to results: Effective community corrections: Proceedings of the 1995 and 1996 conference of the International Community Corrections Association (ICCA)* (pp. 215-232). Lanham, MD: Author.

Khantzian, E. J. (1977). The ego, the self, and opiate addiction: Theoretical and treatment considerations. In *The psychodynamics of drug dependence*, National Institute on Drug Abuse Research Monograph 12, pp. 101-118. Rockville, MD: U.S. Department of Health and Human Services, National Institutes of Health.

King, K., Rene, S., Schmidt, J., Stipetich, E., & Woldsweth, N. (1994). *Cognitive intervention program*. Madison, WI: Department of Corrections.

Klosko, J., & Young, J. (2004). Cognitive therapy of borderline personality disorder. In R. L. Leahy (Ed.), *Contemporary cognitive therapy* (pp. 269-298). New York: Guilford.

Knapp, M. L. (1978). *Nonverbal communication in human interaction*. New York: Holt, Rinehart and Winston.

Knapp, M. L., & Daly, J. A. (2002). *Handbook of interpersonal communication* (2nd ed.). Thousand Oaks, CA: Sage Publications, Inc.

Knapp, M. L., & Hall, J. A. (1997). *Nonverbal communication in human interaction*. Orlando, FL: Harcourt Brace College Publishers.

Knight, K., Simpson, D. D., Chatham, L. R., & Camacho, L. M. (1997). An assessment of prison-based drug treatment: Texas' in-prison therapeutic community programs. *Journal of Offender Rehabilitation, 4*(3/4), 75-100.

Knight, K., & Simpson, D. D., & Hiller, M. L. (1999). Three-year reincarceration outcomes for in-prison therapeutic community treatment in Texas. *Prison Journal, 79*(3), 337-351.

Knowles, M. S. (1980). *The modern practice of adult education: From pedagogy to andragogy*. Englewood Cliffs, NJ: Cambridge Adult Education.

Knowles, M. S. (1984). *Andragogy in action: Applying modern principles of adult education*. San Francisco, CA: Jossey-Bass.

Knowles, M. S. (1990). *The adult learner: A neglected species*. Houston, TX: Gulf Publishing Company.

Kohlberg, L. (1964). Development of moral character and moral ideology. In M. L. Hoffman & L. W. Hoffman (Eds.), *Review of child development research, Vol. I* (pp. 383-431). New York: Russell Sage Foundation.

Kohlberg, L. (1981). *The philosophy of moral development*. San Francisco, CA: Harper & Row.

Kosten, T. R., George, T. P., & Kleber, H. D. (2005). The neurobiology of substance dependence: Implications for treatment. In R. J. Frances, S. I. Miller, & A. H. Mack (Eds.), *Clinical textbook of addictive disorders* (pp. 3-15). New York: The Guilford Press.

Kotulak, R., (1996). *Inside the brain: Revolutionary discoveries of how the mind works*. Kansas City, MO: Andrews McMeel.

Krupnick, J. L., Sotsky, S. M., Simmens, S., Moyer, J., Elkin, I., Watkins, J., & Pilkonis, P. A. (1996). The role of therapeutic alliance in psychotherapy and pharmacotherapy outcome: Findings in the National Institute of Mental Health Treatment of Depression Collaborative Research Program. *Journal of Consulting and Clinical Psychology, 64,* 532-539.

Kuhn, T. S. (1970). *The structure of scientific revolutions* (2nd ed.). Chicago: University of Chicago Press.

Lacroix, N. (1998). *Relaxation: 101 essential tips*. New York: DK Publishing, Inc.

Lambert, M. J. (1983). Introduction to assessment of psychotherapy outcome: Historical perspective and current issues. In M. J. Lambert, E. R. Christensen, & S. S. DeJulio (Eds.), *The assessment of psychotherapy outcome* (pp. 3-32). New York: Wiley.

Lambert, M. J., & Bergin, A. E. (1992). Achievements and limitations of psychotherapy research. In D. K. Freedheim (Ed.), *History of psychotherapy: A century of change* (pp. 360-390). Washington, DC: American Psychological Association.

Landenberger, N. A., & Lipsey, M. W. (2005). The positive effects of cognitive-behavioral programs for offenders: A meta-analysis of factors associated with effective treatment. *Journal of Experimental Criminology, 1,* 451-476.

Lang, R. (1990). *Psychotherapy: A basic text*. Northvale, NJ: Jason Aronson Inc.

Lange, A. J., & Jakubowski, P. (1976). *Responsible assertive behavior*. Champaign, IL: Research Press.

Larimer, M. C., Palmer, R. S., & Marlatt, G. A. (1999). Relapse prevention: An overview of Marlatt's cognitive-behavioral model. *Alcohol Research and Health, 23,* 151-160.

Lazarus, A. A. (1971). *Behavior therapy and beyond*. New York: McGraw-Hill.

Lazarus, R. S. (1999). *Stress and emotion: A new synthesis*. New York: Springer.

Lazarus, R. S., & Folkman, S. (1984). *Stress, appraisal and coping*. New York: Springer-Verlag.

Leahy, R. L. (1996). *Cognitive therapy: Basic principles and applications*. Northvale, NJ: Jason Aronson, Inc.

Leahy, R. L. (2003). *Cognitive therapy techniques: A practitioner's guide*. New York: The Guilford Press.

Ledley, D. R., & Heimberg, R. (2005). Social anxiety disorders. In M. M. Antony, D. R. Ledley, & R. G. Heimberg (Eds.), *Improving outcomes and preventing relapse in cognitive-behavioral therapy* (pp. 38-76). New York: Guilford Press.

Lehrer, P. M., & Woolfolk, R. L. (1993). *Principles and practice of stress management* (2nd ed.). New York: The Guilford Press.

Leonard, K. E., & Blane, H. T. (1999). Introduction. In H. T. Blane & K. W. Leonard (Eds.), *Psychological theories of drinking and alcoholism* (2nd ed., pp. 1-13). New York: Guilford.

Leukefeld, C. G., & Tims, F. M. (1982). *Drug treatment in prisons and jails* (NIDA Research Monograph 118). Washington, DC: U.S. Government Printing Office.

Leukefeld, C. G., Tims, F., & Farabee, D. (2002). *Treatment of drug offenders: Policies and issues*. New York: Springer Publishing Company, Inc.

Lewin, K. (1935). *A dynamic theory of personality*. New York: McGraw-Hill.

Lewin, K. (1936). *Principles of topological psychology*. New York: McGraw-Hill.

Lewin, K. (1951). *Field theory in social science: Selected theoretical papers* (D. Cartwright, Ed.). New York: Harper.

Li, T. K. (2000). Clinical perspectives for the study of craving and relapse in animal models. *Addiction, 95*(Suppl. 2), 55-60.

Libet, J., & Lewinsohn, P. M. (1973). The concept of social skill with special reference to the behavior of depressed persons. *Journal of Consulting and Clinical Psychology, 40,* 304-312.

Lin, S. W., & Anthenelli, R. M. (2005). Genetic factors in the risk for substance use disorders. In J. H. Lowinson, P. Ruiz, R. B. Millman, & J. G. Langrod (Eds.), *Substance abuse: A comprehensive textbook* (pp. 33-47). Baltimore, MD: Lippincott Williams & Wilkins.

Linden, W. (1993). The autogenic training method of J. H. Schultz. In P. M. Lehrer & R. L. Woolfolk (Eds.), *Principles and practice of stress management* (2nd ed., pp. 205-230). New York: Guilford.

Lindsey, M., McBride, R. W., & Platt, C. M. (1993). *Amend: Philosophy and curriculum for treating batterers.* Littleton, CO: Gylantic Publishing.

Linehan, M. M. (1993a). *Cognitive-behavioral treatment of borderline personality disorder.* New York: Guilford Press.

Linehan, M. M. (1993b). *Skills training manual for treating borderline personality disorder.* New York: Guilford Press.

Linehan, M. M. (1994). Acceptance and change: The central dialectic in psychotherapy. In S. C. Hayes, N. S. Jacobson, V. M. Follette, & M. J. Dougher (Eds.), *Acceptance and change: Content and context in psychotherapy* (pp. 77-86). Reno, NV: Context Press.

Ling, W., Wesson, D. R., & Smith, D. E. (2005). Prescription opiate abuse. In J. H. Lowinson, P. Ruiz, R. B. Millman, & J. G. Langrod (Eds.), *Substance abuse: A comprehensive textbook* (pp. 459-468). Baltimore, MD: Lippincott Williams & Wilkins.

Lipps, T. (1907). Das wissen von fremden ichen. *Psychol. Untersuchungen, 1,* 694-722.

Lipsey, M. W., Chapman, G., & Landenberger, N. A. (2001). Cognitive-behavioral programs for offenders. *The Annals of the American Academy of Political and Social Science, 578,* 144-157.

Lipsey, M. W., & Landenberger, N. A. (2006). Cognitive-behavioral interventions: A meta-analysis of randomized controlled studies. In B. C. Welsh & D. P. Farrington (Eds.), *Preventing crime: What works for children, offenders, victims, and places.* New York: Springer.

Little, G., & Robinson, K. (1986). *How to escape your prison: A moral reconation therapy workbook.* Memphis, TN: Eagle Wing Books.

Littlejohn, S. W. (1999). *Theories of human communication* (2nd ed.). Belmont, CA: Wadsworth Publishing Company.

Lloyd, A. (2003). Urge surfing. In W. O'Donohue, J. E. Fisher, & S. C. Hayes (Eds.), *Cognitive behavior therapy: Applying empirically supported techniques in your practice* (pp. 451-455). Hoboken, NJ: John Wiley & Sons.

Lowinson, J. H., Ruiz, P., Millman, R. B., & Langrod, J. G. (Eds.). (2005). *Substance abuse: A comprehensive textbook.* Baltimore, MD: Williams & Wilkins.

Luft, J. (1969). *Of human interaction.* Palo Alto, CA: National Press.

Maisto, S. A., Carey, K. B., & Bradizza, C. M. (1999). Social learning theory. In H. T. Blane & K. W. Leonard (Eds.), *Psychological theories of drinking and alcoholism* (pp. 305-345). New York: Guilford.

Margolin, G. (1987). Marital therapy: A cognitive-behavioral-affective approach. In N. S. Jacobson (Ed.), *Psychotherapists in clinical practice: Cognitive and behavioral perspectives* (pp. 232-285). New York: Guilford Press.

Marlatt, G. A. (1978). Craving for alcohol, loss of control, and relapse: A cognitive-behavioral analysis. In P. E. Nathan, G. A. Marlatt, & T. Loberg (Eds.), *Alcoholism: New directions in behavioral research and treatment.* New York: Plenum.

Marlatt, G. A. (1979). Alcohol use and problem drinking: A cognitive-behavioral analysis. In P. C. Kendall & S. D. Hollon (Eds.), *Cognitive-behavioral interventions: Theory, research, and procedures.* New York: Academic Press.

Marlatt, G. A. (1982). Relapse prevention: A self-control program for the treatment of addictive behaviors. In R. B. Stuart (Ed.) *Adherence, compliance, and generalization in behavioral medicine.* New York: Brunner/Mazel.

Marlatt, G. A. (1985a). Relapse prevention: Theoretical rationale and overview of the model. In G. A. Marlatt & J. R. Gordon (Eds.), *Relapse prevention: Maintenance strategies in the treatment of addictive behaviors* (pp. 3-70). New York: Guilford.

Marlatt, G. A. (1985b). Determinants of relapse and skill training interventions. In G. A. Marlatt & J. R. Gordon (Eds.), *Relapse prevention: Maintenance strategies in the treatment of addictive behaviors* (pp. 71-127). New York: Guilford.

Marlatt, G. A. (1985c). Cognitive assessment and intervention procedures for relapse prevention. In G. A. Marlatt & J. R. Gordon (Eds.), *Relapse prevention: Maintenance strategies in the treatment of addictive behaviors* (pp. 201-279). New York: Guilford.

Marlatt, G. A. (1985d). Cognitive factors in the relapse process. In G. A. Marlatt & J. R. Gordon (Eds.), *Relapse prevention: Maintenance strategies in the treatment of addictive behaviors* (pp. 128-200). New York: Guilford.

Marlatt, G. A., Baer, J. S., & Quigley, L. A. (1995). Self-efficacy and addictive behavior. In A. Bandura (Ed.), *Self-efficacy in changing societies.* New York: Cambridge University Press.

Marlatt, G. A., & Barrett, K. B. (1994). Relapse prevention. In M. Galentern & H. Kleber (Eds.), *The textbook of substance abuse treatment*. New York: American Psychiatric Press.

Marlatt, G. A., & George, W. H. (1984). Relapse prevention: Introduction and overview of the model. *British Journal of Addiction, 79*, 261-273.

Marlatt, G. A., & Gordon, J. R. (1980). Determinants of relapse: Implications for the maintenance of behavior change. In P. O. Davidson & S. M. Davidson (Eds.), *Behavior medicine: Changing health lifestyles* (pp. 410-452). New York: Brunner/Mazel.

Marlatt, G. A., & Gordon, J. R. (Eds.). (1985). *Relapse prevention: Maintenance strategies in the treatment of addictive behaviors*. New York: Guilford Press.

Marlatt, G. A., & Witkiewitz, K. (2005). Relapse prevention for alcohol and drug problems. In G. A. Marlatt & D. M. Donovan (Eds.), *Relapse prevention* (2nd ed., pp. 1-44). New York: Guilford Press.

Marmor, J. (1975). Foreword. In B. Sloane, F. Staples, A. Cristol, N. J. Yorkston, & K. Whipple (Eds.), *Psychotherapy versus behavior therapy*. Cambridge, MA: Harvard University Press.

Martin, D. J., Garske, J. P., & Davis, M. K. (2000). Relation of the therapeutic alliance with outcome and other variables: A meta-analytic review. *Journal of Consulting and Clinical Psychology, 68*, 438-450.

Mashek, D. J., Stuewig, J., Furukawa, E., & Tangney, J. (2004). *Connectedness to the criminal community and to the community at large: Psychological and behavioral correlates*. Manuscript under review.

Maslow, A. H. (1954). *Motivation and personality*. New York: Harper.

Masters, R. E. (2004). *Counseling criminal justice offenders* (2nd ed.). Thousand Oaks, CA: Sage Publications, Inc.

Mauck, S. R., & Zagummy, M. J. (2000). Determination of efforts in drunk-driving interventions: A path analysis. *Journal of Alcohol and Drug Education, 45*(2), 23-33.

Maxwell-Hudson, C. (1996). *Massage for stress relief*. New York: DK Publishing, Inc.

McCabe, R. E., & Antony, M. M. (2005). Panic disorder and agoraphobia. In M. M. Antony, D. R. Ledley, & R. G. Heimberg (Eds.), *Improving outcomes and preventing relapse in cognitive-behavioral therapy* (pp. 1-37). New York: Guilford Press.

McCollister, K. E., & French, M. T. (2002). The economic cost of substance-abuse treatment in criminal justice settings. In C. G. Leukefeld, F. Tims, & D. Farabee (Eds.), *Treatment of drug offenders: Policies and issues* (pp. 22-37). New York: Springer Publishing Company, Inc.

McCrady, B. S. (2000). Alcohol use disorders and the Division 12 Task Force of the American Psychological Association. *Psychology of Addictive Behaviors, 14*(3), 267-276.

McDowell, D. (2005). Marijuana, hallucinogens, and club drugs. In R. J. Frances, S. I. Miller, & A. H. Mack (Eds.), *Clinical textbook of addictive disorders* (pp. 157-183). New York: The Guilford Press.

McGregor, I.S, & Gallate, J. E. (2004). Rats on the grog: Novel pharmacotherapies for alcohol craving. *Addictive Behaviors, 29*(7), 1341-1357.

McKay, J. R. (1999). Studies of factors of relapse to alcohol, drug, and nicotine use: A critical review of methodologies and findings. *Journal of Studies on Alcohol, 60*, 566-576.

McKay, M., Rogers, P., & McKay J. (1989). *When anger hurts: Quieting the storm within*. Oakland, CA: New Harbinger Press.

McMasters, E., McMasters, S., Wanberg, K. W., & Milkman, H. B. (2008). *The Automated Progress and Change Evaluation Monitor (A-PACE Monitor)*. Lincoln, NE: Diversion Services, Inc.

McMullin, R. E. (1986). *Handbook of cognitive therapy techniques*. New York: W. W. Norton.

McMullin, R. E. (2000). *The new handbook of cognitive therapy techniques*. New York: W. W. Norton.

McNeece, C. A., & DiNitto, D. M. (1994). *Chemical dependency: A systems approach*. Englewood Cliffs, NJ: Prentice-Hall.

Meichenbaum, D. (1975). A self-instructional approach to stress management: A proposal for stress inoculation training,. In I. Sarason & C. D Spielberger (Eds.), *Stress and anxiety* (Vol. 2). New York: Wiley.

Meichenbaum, D. (1977). *Cognitive-behavior modification: An integrative approach*. New York: Plenum.

Meichenbaum, D. (1985). *Stress inoculation training: A clinical guidebook*. Old Tappan, NJ: Allyn & Bacon.

Meichenbaum, D (1993a). Stress inoculation training: A 20-year update. In P. M. Lehrer & R. L. Woolfolk (Eds.). *Principles and practice of stress management* (2nd ed.). New York: The Guilford Press.

Meichenbaum, D. (1993b). Changing conceptions of cognitive behavior modification: Retrospect and prospect. *Journal of Consulting and Clinical Psychology, 61,* 292-304.

Milkman, H. B., & Frosch, W. A. (1973). On the preferential abuse of heroin and amphetamine. *Journal of Nervous and Mental Disease, 156,* 242-248.

Milkman, H. B., Sunderwirth, S. G. (1987). *Craving for ecstasy: The consciousness and chemistry of escape.* Lexington, MA: D. C. Heath.

Milkman, H. B., & Sunderwirth, S. G. (1993). *Pathways to pleasure: The consciousness and chemistry of optimal experience.* Lexington, MA: Lexington Books.

Milkman, H. B., & Sunderwirth, S. G. (1998). *Craving for ecstasy: The consciousness and chemistry of escape* (2nd ed.). Lexington, MA: D. C. Heath.

Milkman, H. B., & Wanberg, K. W. (2005). *Criminal conduct and substance abuse treatment for adolescents: Pathways to self-discovery and change - The provider's guide.* Thousand Oaks, CA: Sage Publications.

Milkman, H. B., & Wanberg, K. W. (2007). *Cognitive-behavioral treatment: A review and discussion for corrections professionals* (NIC Accession Number 021657). Washington, DC: National Institute of Corrections.

Milkman, H. B., Wanberg, K. W., & Gagliardi (2008). *Criminal conduct and substance abuse treatment for women in correctional settings: Adjunct guide to strategies for self-improvement and change.* Thousand Oaks, CA: Sage Publications.

Miller, P. J., Ross, S. M., Emmerson, R. Y., & Todt, E. H. (1989). Self-efficacy in alcoholics: Clinical validation of the situational confidence questionnaire. *Addictive Behaviors, 14,* 217-224.

Miller, W. R. (1996). What is relapse? Fifty ways to leave the wagon. *Addiction, 91*(Suppl. 12), S15-S27.

Miller, W. R. (2006a). Motivational factors in addictive behaviors. In W. R. Miller & K. M. Carroll (Eds.), *Rethinking substance abuse* (pp. 134-150). New York: The Guilford Press.

Miller, W. R. (2006b). Drawing the science together. In W. R. Miller & K. M. Carroll (Eds.), *Rethinking substance abuse* (pp. 293-312). New York: The Guilford Press.

Miller, W. R., Benefield, R. G., & Tonigan, J. S. (1993). Enhancing motivation for change in problem drinking: A controlled comparison of two therapist styles. *Journal of Consulting and Clinical Psychology, 61,* 455-461.

Miller, W. R., & Carroll, K. M. (Eds.). (2006). *Rethinking substance abuse.* New York: The Guilford Press.

Miller, W. R., & Rollnick, S. (1991). *Motivational interviewing: Preparing people to change addictive behavior.* New York: Guilford.

Miller, W. R., & Rollnick, S. (2002). *Motivational Interviewing: Preparing people to change addictive behavior* (2nd ed.). New York: Guilford.

Miller, W. R., & Tonigan, J. S. (1996). Assessing drinker's motivation for change: The Stages of Change Readiness and Treatment Eagerness Scale (SOCRATES). *Psychology of Addictive Behaviors, 10,* 81-89.

Miller, W. R., Westerberg, V. S., & Waldron, H. B. (1995). Evaluating alcohol problems in adults and adolescents. In R. K. Hester & W. R. Miller (Eds.), *Handbook of alcoholism treatment approaches: Effective alternatives* (2nd ed., pp. 61-88). Boston: Allyn & Bacon.

Miller, W. R., Zweben, A. D., DiClemente, C. C., & Rychtarik, R. G. (1994). *Motivational enhancement therapy manual: A clinical research guide for therapists treating individuals with alcohol abuse and dependence* (Project MATCH Monograph Series, Vol. 2). Rockville, MD: National Institute on Alcohol Abuse and Alcoholism, U.S. Department of Health and Human Services, National Institutes of Health.

Moffitt, T. E. (1993). Adolescent-limited and life-course- persistent antisocial behavior: A developmental taxonomy. *Psychological Review, 100*(4), 674-701.

Monti, P. M., Abrams, D. B., Kadden, R. M., & Cooney, N. L. (1989). *Treating alcohol dependence: A coping skills training guide.* New York: Guilford.

Monti, P. M., Rohsenow, D. J., Colby, S. M., & Abrams, D. B. (1995). Coping and social skills training. In R. K. Hester & W. R. Miller (Eds.), *Handbook of alcoholism treatment approaches: Effective alternatives* (2nd ed., pp. 221-241). Boston: Allyn & Bacon.

Moore, P. J., Turner, R., Park, C. L., & Adler, N. E. (1996). The impact of behavior and addiction on psychological models of cigarette and alcohol use during pregnancy. *Addictive Behaviors, 21,* 645-658.

Moorey, S. (1996). When bad things happen to rational people: Cognitive therapy in adverse life circumstances. In P. M. Salkovskis (Ed.), *Frontiers of cognitive therapy* (pp. 450-469). New York: Guilford.

Moos, R. H., Finney, J. W., & Moos, B. S. (2000). Inpatient substance abuse care and the outcome of subsequent community residential and outpatient care. *Addiction, 95,* 833-846.

Mowrer, O. H. (1963). No guilt, no responsibility. In C. Rolo (Ed.), *Psychiatry in American life* (pp. 156-167). Boston: Little, Brown and Company.

Mowrer, O. H. (1964). *The new group therapy.* Princeton, NJ: D. Van Nostrand Company, Inc.

Mueser, K., Bennett, M., & Kushner, M. (1995). Epidemiology of substance use disorders among persons with chronic mental illnesses. In A. F. Lehman & L. F. Dixon (Eds.), *Double jeopardy: Chronic mental illness and substance use disorders* (pp. 9-25). Chur, Switzerland: Hardwood.

Myers, G. E., & Myers, M. T. (1980). *The dynamics of human communication: A laboratory approach* (2nd ed.). New York: McGraw-Hill Book Company.

Nace, E. P. (2005). Alcohol. In R. J. Frances, S. I. Miller, & A. H. Mack (Eds.), *Clinical textbook of addictive disorders* (pp. 75-104). New York: The Guilford Press.

Najavits, L. (2002). *Seeking safety: A treatment manual for PTSD and substance abuse.* New York: Guilford Press.

Naugle, A. E., & Maher, S. (2003). Modeling and behavioral rehearsal. In W. O'Donohue, J. E. Fisher, & S. C. Hayes (Eds.), *Cognitive behavior therapy: Applying empirically supported techniques in your practice* (pp. 238-246). Hoboken, NJ: John Wiley & Sons.

Nezu, A. M., Nezu, C. M., & Lombardo, E. (2003). Problem-solving therapy. In W. O'Donohue, J. E. Fisher, & S. C. Hayes (Eds.), *Cognitive behavior therapy: Applying empirically supported techniques in your practice* (pp. 301-307). Hoboken, NJ: John Wiley & Sons.

NIDA: National Institute on Drug Abuse. (1993). *Cue extinction: Handbook for program administrators.* Rockville, MD: National Institutes of Health.

Norcross, J. C., Beutler, L. E., & Levant, R. F. (Eds.). (2006). *Evidence-based practices in mental health: Debate and dialogue on the fundamental questions.* Washington, DC: American Psychological Association.

Norris, P. A., & Fahrion, S. L. (1993). Autogenic biofeedback in psychophysiological therapy and stress management. In P. M. Lehrer & R. L. Woolfolk (Eds.), *Principles and practice of stress management* (2nd ed., pp. 231-262). New York: Guilford.

Novaco, R. W. (1975). *Anger control: The development and evaluation of an experimental treatment.* Lexington, MA: Lexington Books.

Novaco, R. W. (1978). Anger and coping with stress. In J. P. Foreyt & D. Rathjen (Eds.), *Cognitive behavior therapy.* Lexington, MA: Heath.

Novaco, R. W. (1986). Anger as a clinical and social problem. In R. Blanchard & C. Blanchard (Eds.), *Advances in the study of aggression, Volume 2.* New York: Academic Press.

Novaco, R. W. (1994). Clinical problems of anger and its assessment and regulation through a stress coping skills approach. In W. O'Donohue & L. Krasner (Eds.), *Handbook of psychological skill training: Clinical techniques and applications.* Boston: Allyn & Bacon.

Novaco, R. W. (1996). Anger treatment and its special challenges. *NCP Clinical Quarterly, 6*(3),

O'Brien, C. P., Childress, A. R., Ehrman, R., et al. (1998). Conditioning factors in drug abuse: Can they explain compulsion? *Psychopharmacology, 12,* 15-22.

O'Farrell, T. J., & Cowles, K. S. (1989). Marital and family therapy. In R. K. Hester & W. R. Miller (Eds.), *Handbook for alcoholism treatment approaches: Effective alternatives* (pp. 183-205). New York: Pergamon Press.

O'Hara, M. (1997). Relational empathy: Beyond modernist egocentrism to postmodern holistic contextualism. In A. C. Bohart & L. S. Greenberg (Eds.), *Empathy reconsidered: New directions in psychotherapy* (pp. 295-320). Washington, DC: American Psychological Association.

Oliver, P. H., & Margolin, G. (2003). Communication/problem-solving skills training. In W. O'Donohue, J. E. Fisher, & S. C. Hayes (Eds.), *Cognitive behavior therapy: Applying empirically supported techniques in your practice* (pp. 96-102). Hoboken, NJ: John Wiley & Sons.

O'Neill, H. (1999). *Managing anger.* London: Whurr Publishers.

Orsillo, S. M., Roemer, L., Lerner, J. B., & Tull, M. T. (2004). Acceptance, mindfulness, and cognitive-behavioral therapy: Comparisons, contrasts, and application to anxiety. In S. C. Hayes, V. M. Follette, & M. M. Linehan (Eds.). *Mindfulness and acceptance: Expanding the cognitive-behavioral tradition* (pp. 66-95). New York: The Guilford Press.

Parks, G. A., & Marlatt, G. A. (1999). Relapse prevention therapy for substance-abusing offenders: A cognitive-behavioral approach. In E. Latessa (Ed.), *What works - strategic solutions: The International Community Corrections Association examines substance abuse.* Maryland: American Correctional Association.

Patterson, C. H. (1966). *Theories of counseling and psychotherapy.* New York: Harper and Row Publishers.

Patterson, C. H., & Hidore, S. C. (1997). *Successful psychotherapy: A caring, loving relationship.* Northvale, NJ: Jason Aronson Inc.

Pattison, E. M., & Kaufman, E. (1982). The alcoholism syndrome: Definitions and models. In E. M. Pattison & E. Kaufman, (Eds.), *Encyclopedic handbook of alcoholism* (pp. 3-30). New York: Gardner Press.

Pattison, E. M., Sobell, M. B., & Sobell, L. C. (1977). *Emerging concepts of alcohol dependence.* New York: Springer.

Patton, B. R., & Giffin, K. (1981). *Interpersonal communication in action: Basic text and readings* (3rd. ed.). New York: Harper & Row.

Peale, N. V. (1952). *The power of positive thinking.* Englewood Cliffs, NJ: Prentice-Hall, Inc.

Pearson, F. S., Lipton, D. S., Cleland, C. M., & Yee, D. S. (2002). The effects of behavioral/cognitive-behavioral programs on recidivism. *Crime and Delinquency, 48*(3), 476-496.

Pelissier, B., Gaes, G., Rhodes, W., Camp, S., O'Neil, J., Wallace, S., & Saylor, W. (1998). *TRIAD drug treatment evaluation project: Six-month report.* Washington, DC: Federal Bureau of Prisons, Office of Research and Evaluation.

Pence, E., & Paymar, M. (1993). *Education groups for men who batter: The Duluth model.* New York: Springer.

Pepper, B., & Massaro, J. (1992). Trans-institutionalization: Substance abuse and mental illness in the criminal justice system. *Ties Lines, 92,* 1-4.

Perkinson, R. R. (1997). *Chemical dependency counseling: A practical guide.* Thousand Oaks, CA: Sage Publications.

Perkinson, R. R. (2002). *Chemical dependency counseling: A practical guide* (2nd ed.). Thousand Oaks, CA: Sage Publications.

Peters, R. H., & Hills, H. (1996). *Dual diagnosis treatment program manual.* Tampa, FL: University of South Florida, Florida Mental Health Institute.

Peters, R. H., & Wexler, H. K. (2005). *Substance abuse treatment for adults in the criminal justice system: A treatment improvement protocol (TIP 44).* Rockville, MD: U. S. Department of Health and Human Services, Substance Abuse and Mental Health Services Administration, Center for Substance Abuse Treatment.

Petersilia, J. (2004). What works in prisoner reentry? Reviewing and questioning the evidence. *Federal Probation, 68*(2), 4-8.

Petersilia, J., & Turner, S. (1993). Evaluating intensive supervision probation and parole: Results of a nationwide experiment. *Research in brief.* Washington, DC: National Instituts of Justice.

Peterson, C., & Seligman, M. E. P. (2004). *Character strengths and virtues: A handbook and classification.* New York: Oxford University Press.

Peterson, D. R. (1983). Conflict. In H. H. Kelley, E. Berscheid, A. Christensen, J. H. Harvey, T. L. Huston, G. Levinger, E. McClintock, L. A. Peplau, & D. R. Peterson (Eds.), *Close relationships.* New York: W. H. Freeman.

Peyser, H. S. (1988). Implications of the disease model for psychotherapy and counseling. In S. E. Gitlow & H. S. Peyser (Eds.), *Alcoholism: A practical treatment guide* (pp. 142-155). Philadelphia: W. B. Saunders.

Piaget, J. (1932). *The moral judgement of the child.* London: Routledge and Kegan Paul.

Platt, J. J. (1995). Vocational rehabilitation of drug abusers. *Psychological Bulletin, 117,* 416-433.

Pomeroy, E. C., Kiam, R., & Green, D. L. (2000). Reducing depression, anxiety, and trauma of male inmates. An HIV/AIDS psychoeducational group intervention. *Social Work Research, 24,* 156-167.

Portenoy, R. K., Payne, R., & Passik, S. D. (2005). Acute and chronic pain. In J. H. Lowinson, P. Ruiz, R. B. Millman, & J. G. Langrod (Eds.), *Substance abuse: A comprehensive textbook* (pp. 863-904). Baltimore, MD: Lippincott Williams & Wilkins.

Prochaska, J. O. (1999). Stages of change approach to treating addictions with special focus on driving while intoxicated (DWI) offenders. In P. M. Harris (Ed.), *Research to results: Effective community corrections: Proceedings of the 1995 and 1996 Conferences of the Internal Community Corrections Association (ICCA)* (pp. 191-213). Lanham, MD: American Correction Association.

Prochaska, J. O., & DiClemente, C. C. (1992). Stages of change in the modification of problem behavior. In M. Hersen, R. Eisler, & P. M. Miller (Eds.), *Progress in behavior modification* (pp. 184-214). Sycamore, IL: Sycamore Publishing.

Prochaska, J. O., DiClemente, C. C., & Norcross, J. C. (1992). In search of how people change: Applications to addictive behaviors. *American Psychologist, 47,* 1102-1114.

Project MATCH Research Group. (1993). Project MATCH: Rationale and methods for a multisite clinical trial matching patients to alcoholism treatment. *Alcoholism: Clinical and Experimental Research, 17,* 1130-1145.

Project MATCH Research Group. (1997). Matching alcoholism treatments to client heterogeneity: Project MATCH posttreatment drinking outcomes. *Journal of Studies on Alcohol, 58,* 7-29.

Raue, P. J., & Goldfried, M. R. (1994). The therapeutic alliance in cognitive-behavior therapy. In A. O. Horvath & L. S. Greenberg (Eds.), *The working alliance: Theory, research and practice* (pp. 131-152). New York: Wiley.

Raue, P. J., Goldfried, M. R., & Barkham, M. (1997). The therapeutic alliance in psychodynamic-interpersonal and cognitive-behavioral therapy. *Journal of Consulting and Clinical Psychology, 65,* 582-587.

Ray, O. S., & Ksir, C. (1996). *Drugs, society, and human behavior* (7th ed.). St. Louis, MO: C. V. Mosby.

Ray, O. S., & Ksir, C. (2002). *Drugs, society, and human behavior* (9th ed.). St. Louis, MO: C. V. Mosby.

Ray, O. S., Ksir, C., & Hart, C. L. (2006). *Drugs, society, and human behavior* (11th ed.). St. Louis, MO: C. V. Mosby.

Rennison, C. M. (2000). *Criminal victimization 1999: Changes 1998-1999 with trends 1993-99.* Washington, DC: Bureau of Justice Statistics.

Repetto, M., & Gold, M. S. (2005). Cocaine and crack: Neurobiology. In J. H. Lowinson, P. Ruiz, R. B. Millman, & J. G. Langrod (Eds.), *Substance abuse: A comprehensive textbook* (pp. 195-218). Baltimore, MD: Lippincott Williams & Wilkins.

Richards, H. J. (2004). How psychopathic? A critical consideration for offender treatment. In K. Knight & D. Farabee (Eds.), *Treating addicted offenders: A continuum of effective practices.* Kingston, NJ: Civic Research Institute.

Robins, C. J., Schmidt III, H., & Linehan, M. M. (2004). Dialectical behavior therapy: Synthesizing radical acceptance with skillful means. In S. C. Hayes, V. M. Follette, & M. M. Linehan (Eds.), *Mindfulness and acceptance: Expanding the cognitive-behavioral tradition* (pp. 30-44). New York: The Guilford Press.

Roehrich, H., Dackis, C. A., & Gold, M. S. (1987). Bromocriptine. *Medical Research Review, 7,* 243-269.

Rogers, C. R. (1942). *Counseling and psychotherapy.* Boston: Houghton Mifflin.

Rogers, C. R. (1951). *Client-centered therapy: Its current practice, implications, and therapy.* Boston: Houghton Mifflin.

Rogers, C. R. (1957). The necessary and sufficient conditions of therapeutic personality change. *Journal of Consulting Psychology, 22,* 95-103.

Rogers, C. R. (1959). A theory of therapy, personality, and interpersonal relationships developed in the client-centered framework. In S. Koch (Ed.), *Psychology: A study of science: Vol. 3. Formulations of the person and the social context.* New York: McGraw-Hill.

Rogers, C. R. (1961). *On becoming a person: A therapist's view of psychotherapy.* Boston: Houghton Mifflin.

Rogers, C. R. (1980). *A way of being.* Boston: Houghton Mifflin Company.

Rogers, C. R., & Dymond, R. (1954). *Psychotherapy and personality change.* Chicago: University of Chicago Press.

Rogers, C. R., Gendlin, E. T., Kiesler, D., & Truax, C. B. (1967). *The therapeutic relationship and its impact: A study of psychotherapy with schizophrenics.* Madison: University of Wisconsin Press.

Rokke, P. D., & Rehm, L. P. (2001). In K. S. Dobson (Ed.), *Handbook of cognitive-behavioral therapies* (2nd ed.). New York: Guilford Press.

Ross, R. R., Fabiano, E. A., & Ross, R. D. (1986). *Reasoning and rehabilitation: A handbook for teaching cognitive skills.* Ottawa, Ontario: University of Ottawa.

Ross, R. R., Fabiano, E. A., & Ross, R. D. (1988). (Re)Habilitation through education: A cognitive model for corrections. *Journal of Correctional Education, 39,* 44-47.

Ross, R. R., & Hilborn, J. (2005). *Reasoning and rehabilitation 2: Short Version for Adults - A handbook for teaching prosocial competence.* Ottawa, Ontario: Cognitive Centre of Canada.

Ross, R. R., & Ross, R. D. (1995). *Thinking straight: The reasoning and rehabilitation program for delinquency prevention and offender rehabilitation.* Ottawa, Ontario: Department of Criminology.

Roth, A., & Fonagy, P. (2005). *What works for whom? A critical review of psychotherapy research* (2nd ed.). New York: The Guilford Press.

Ruben, B. D. (1988). *Communication and human behavior.* New York: Macmillan.

Russell, J., & Fehr, B. (1994). Fuzzy concepts in a fuzzy hierarchy: Varieties of anger. *Journal of Personality and Social Psychology, 67,* 186-205.

Salkovskis, P. M. (1996). The cognitive approach to anxiety: Threat beliefs, safety-seeking behavior, and the special case of health anxiety and obsessions. In P. M. Salkovskis (Ed.), *Frontiers of cognitive therapy* (pp. 48-74). New York: Guilford.

Sarason, I. G., & Sarason, B. R. (1989). *Abnormal psychology: The problem of maladaptive behavior* (6th ed.). Englewood Cliffs, NJ: Prentice-Hall.

Sarason, I. G., & Sarason, B. R. (1995). *Abnormal psychology: The problem of maladaptive behavior* (8th ed.). Englewood Cliffs, NJ: Prentice-Hall.

Sarason, I. G., & Sarason, B. R. (2005). *Abnormal psychology: The problem of maladaptive behavior* (11th ed.). Englewood Cliffs, NJ: Prentice-Hall.

Sayette, M. A. (1999). Cognitive theory and research. In H. T. Blane & K. W. Leonard (Eds.), *Psychological theories of drinking and alcoholism* (2nd ed., pp. 247-291). New York: Guilford.

Sayette, M. A., Shiffman, S., Tiffany, S. T., Niaura, R. S., Martin, C. S., & Shadel, W. G. (2000). The measurement of drug craving. *Addiction, 95*(suppl. 2), 189-210.

Schachter, S., & Singer, J. (1962). Cognitive, social and physiological determinants of emotional state. *Psychological Review, 69,* 379-399.

Scher, C. D., Segal, Z. V., & Ingram, R. E. (2004). Beck's theory of depression: Origins, empirical status, and future directions for cognitive vulnerability. In R. L. Leahy (Ed.), *Contemporary cognitive therapy* (pp. 27-45). New York: Guilford.

Segrin, C. (2003). Social skills training. In W. O'Donohue, J. E. Fisher, & S. C. Hayes (Eds.), *Cognitive behavior therapy: Applying empirically supported techniques in your practice* (pp. 384-390). Hoboken, NJ: John Wiley & Sons.

Seiter, R., & Kadela, K. (2003). Prisoner reentry: What works, what doesn't, and what's promising. *Crime and Delinquency, 49,* 360-368.

Seligman, M. E. P., & Beagley, G. (1975). Learned helplessness in the rat. *Journal of Comparative and Physiological Psychology, 88,* 534-541.

Seligman, M. E. P., & Maier, S. F. (1967). Failure to escape traumatic shock. *Journal of Experimental Psychology, 74,* 1-9.

Seligman, M. E. P., Walker, E. F., & Rosenhan, D. L. (2001). *Abnormal psychology* (4th ed.). New York: W. W. Norton.

Selye, H. (1956). *The stress of life.* New York: McGraw-Hill.

Selye, H. (1974). *Stress without distress.* Philadelphia: J. B. Lippincott.

Selye, H. (1976). *The stress of life* (rev. ed.). New York: McGraw-Hill.

Serin, R. C. (2004). Understanding violent offenders. In D. H. Fishbein (Ed.), *The science, treatment, and prevention of antisocial behaviors: Evidence-based practice, Volume II* (pp. 12-1 - 12-17). Kingston, NJ: Civic Research Institute, Inc.

Sher, K. J. (1987). Stress response dampening. In H. T. Blane & K. W. Leonard (Eds.), *Psychological theories of drinking and alcoholism* (pp. 227-271). New York: Guilford.

Shipley, T. E. (1987). Opponent process theory. In H. T. Blane & K. W. Leonard (Eds.), *Psychological theories of drinking and alcoholism* (pp. 346-387). New York: Guilford.

Shlien, J. (1997). Empathy in psychotherapy: A vital mechanism? Yes. Therapist's conceit? All too often. By itself enough? No. In A. C. Bohart & L. S. Greenberg (Eds.), *Empathy reconsidered: New directions in psychotherapy* (pp. 63-80). Washington, DC: American Psychological Association.

Sims, B. (2005). Treating the substances-addicted offenders: Theory and practice. In B. Sims (Ed.), *Substance abuse treatment with correctional clients: Practical implications for institutional and community settings* (pp. 9-25). New York: Haworth Press.

Sisson, R., & Azrin, N. (1989). The community reinforcement approach. In R. K. Hester & W. R. Miller (Eds.), *Handbook of alcoholism treatment approaches* (pp. 242-258). New York: Pergamon.

Sloane, B., Staples, F., Cristol, A., Yorkston, N. J., & Wipple, K. (1975). *Psychotherapy versus behavior therapy.* Cambridge: Harvard University Press.

Smith, J. C. (1999). *ABC relaxation training: A practical guide for health professionals.* New York: Springer Publishing Company, Inc.

Smith, J. E., & Meyers, R. J. (1995). The community reinforcement approach. In R. K. Hester & W. R. Miller (Eds.), *Handbook of alcoholism treatment approaches: Effective alternatives* (2nd ed., pp. 251-266). Boston: Allyn & Bacon.

Snortum, J., & Berger, D. (1989). Drinking-driving compliance in the United States: Perceptions and behavior in 1983 and 1986. *Journal of Studies on Alcohol, 50,* 306-319.

Solomon, K. E., & Annis, H. M. (1990). Outcome and efficacy expectancy in the prediction of posttreatment drinking behavior. *British Journal of Addictions, 85,* 659-665.

Sovereign, R. G., & Miller, W. R. (1987). *Effects of therapist style on resilience and outcome among problem drinkers.* Paper presented at the Fourth International Conference on Treatment of Addictive Behaviors, Os/bergen, Norway.

Sperry, L. (1999). *Cognitive behavioral therapy of DSM-IV personality disorders: Highly effective interventions for the most common personality disorders.* Philadelphia, PA: Brunner/Mazel.

Sperry, L. (2006). *Cognitive behavioral therapy of DSM-IV personality disorders: Highly effective interventions for the most common personality disorders* (2nd ed.). New York: Routledge.

Spielberger, C. D. (1988). *Manual for the State Trait Anger Expression Inventory.* Odessa, FL: Psychological Assessment Resources.

Spielberger, C. D. (1999). *Manual for the State Trait Anger Expression Inventory - 2.* Odessa, FL: Psychological Assessment Resources.

Springer, D. W., McNeece, C. A., & Arnold, E. M. (2003). *Substance abuse treatment for criminal offenders.* Washington, DC: American Psychological Association.

Staiger, P. K., Greeley, J. D., & Wallace, S. D. (1999). Alcohol exposure therapy: Generalization and changes in responsivity. *Drug and Alcohol Dependence, 57,* 29-40.

Steadman, H. J., Cocozza, J. J., & Melick, M. E. (1987). Explaining the increased arrest rates among mental patients: The changing clientele of state hospitals. *American Journal of Psychiatry, 135,* 816-820.

Steadman, H., Fabisiak, S., Dvoskin, J., & Holohean, E. (1989). A survey of mental disability among state prison inmates. *Hospital and Community Psychiatry, 38,* 1086-1090.

Strupp, H. H. (1978). Psychotherapy research and practice - an overview. In S. L. Garfield & A. E. Bergin (Eds.), *Handbook of psychotherapy and behavioral change* (2nd ed., pp. 3-22). New York: Wiley.

Strupp, H. H., & Howard, K. I. (1992). A brief history of psychotherapy research. In D. K. Freedheim (Ed.), *History of psychotherapy: A century of change* (pp. 309-334). Washington, DC: American Psychological Association.

Tarnas, R. (1991). *The passion of the Western mind.* New York: Ballantine Books.

Taxman, F. S. (2004). Reducing recidivism through a seamless system of care: Components of effective treatment, supervision, and transition services in the community. In K. Knight & D. Farabee (Eds.), *Treating addicted offenders: A continuum of effective practices* (pp. 32-1 - 32-12). Kingston, NJ: Civic Research Institute.

Teplin, L. A. (1990). The prevalence of severe mental disorder among male urban jail detainees: Comparison with the Epidemiologic Catchment Area Program. *American Journal of Public Health, 80,* 663-669.

Teplin, L. A., & Swartz, J. (1989). Screening for severe mental disorders in jails. *Law and Human Behavior, 13,* 1-18.

Thom, R. (1975). *Structural stability and morphogenesis: An outline of a general theory of models.* Reading, MA: Benjamin-Cummings.

Tiffany, S. T. (1990). A cognitive model of drug urges and drug use behavior: Role of automatic and nonautomatic processes. *Psychological Review, 97,* 147-168.

Truax, C. B. (1963). Effective ingredients in psychotherapy. *Journal of Consulting Psychology, 10,* 256-263.

Truax, C. B., & Carkhuff, R. R. (1967). *Toward effective counseling and psychotherapy.* Chicago: Aldine.

Truax, C. B., & Mitchell, K. M. (1971). Research on certain therapist interpersonal skills in relation to process and outcome. In A. E. Bergin & S. L. Garfield (Eds.), *Handbook of psychotherapy and behavioral change: An empirical analysis.* New York: John Wiley.

Ury, W. (1993). *Getting past no: Negotiating your way from confrontation to cooperation.* New York: Bantam Books.

Volkow, N. D., & Fowler, J. S. (2000). Addiction, a disease of compulsion and drive: Involvement of the orbitofrontal cortex. *Cerebral Cortex, 10,* 318-325.

Volkow, N. D., Fowler, J. S., Wang, G., Hitzemann, R., Logan, J., Schlyer, D., Dewey, S., & Wolf, A. P. (1993). Decreased dopamine D2 receptor availability is associated with reduced frontal metabolism in cocaine abusers. *Synapse, 14,* 169-177.

Walker, R., & Leukefeld, C. G. (2002). Employment rehabilitation. In C. G. Leukefeld, F. Tims, & D. Farabee (Eds.), *Treatment of drug offenders: Policies and issues* (pp. 69-79). New York: Springer Publishing Company, Inc.

Wampold, B. E. (2001). *The great psychotherapy debate: Models, methods and findings.* Mahwah, NJ: Erlbaum.

Wanberg, K. W. (1974). *Basic counseling skills manual.* Denver: Alcohol and Drug Abuse Division, Colorado Department of Health.

Wanberg, K. W. (1983). *Advanced counseling skills: The process and structure of therapeutic counseling, a client-oriented, therapist-directed model.* Denver: Alcohol and Drug Abuse Division, Colorado Department of Health.

Wanberg, K. W. (1990). *Basic counseling skills manual.* Denver: Alcohol and Drug Abuse Division, Colorado Department of Health.

Wanberg, K. W. (1992). *A user's guide for the Adolescent Self Assessment Profile.* Arvada, CO: Center for Addictions Research and Evaluation.

Wanberg, K. W. (1997). *The Adult Substance Use Survey (ASUS)*. Arvada, CO: Center for Addictions Research and Evaluation.

Wanberg, K. W. (1998, 2006). *The Adult Clinical Assessment Profile (ACAP): The Adult Self Assessment Profile (ADSAP) and Rating Adult Problems Scale (RAPS)*. Arvada, CO: Center for Addictions Research and Evaluation.

Wanberg, K. W. (2000). *A user's guide to the Adolescent Substance Use Survey - SUS: Differential screening of adolescent alcohol and other drug use problems.* Arvada, CO: Center for Addictions Research and Evaluation.

Wanberg, K. W. (2004). *The Adult Substance Use Survey - Revised (ASUS-R)*. Arvada, CO: Center for Addictions Research and Evaluation.

Wanberg, K. W. (2006). *Gender comparisons among offender populations*. Arvada, CO: Center for Addictions Research and Evaluation.

Wanberg, K. W. (2007). *Personal observations and experiences of the evolution and changes in psychotherapy*. Arvada, CO: Center for Addictions Research and Evaluation.

Wanberg, K. W., & Horn, J. L. (1970). Alcoholism symptom patterns of men and women: A comparative study. *Quarterly Journal of Studies on Alcohol, 31*, 40-61.

Wanberg, K. W., & Horn, J. L. (1983). Assessment of alcohol use with multidimensional concepts and measures. *American Psychologist, 38*, 1055-1069.

Wanberg, K. W., & Horn, J. L. (1987). The assessment of multiple conditions in persons with alcohol problems. In W. M. Cox (Ed.), *Treatment and prevention of alcohol problems* (pp. 27-56). New York: Academic Press.

Wanberg, K. W., & Horn, J. L. (1991). *The Drug Use Self Report: User's guide*. Arvada, CO: Center for Addictions Research and Evaluation.

Wanberg, K. W., & Horn, J. L. (2008). *User's guide to the Alcohol Use Inventory - Revised (AUI-R)*. Arvada, CO: Center for Addictions Research and Evaluation.

Wanberg, K. W., Horn, J. L., & Foster, F. M. (1977). A differential assessment model for alcoholism: The scales of the Alcohol Use Inventory. *Journal of Studies on Alcohol, 38*, 512-534.

Wanberg, K. W., & Knapp, J. (1969). Differences in drinking symptoms and behavior of men and women. *British Journal of the Addictions, 64*, 1-9.

Wanberg, K. W., & Milkman, H. B. (1993, 2004). *The Adult Self Assessment Questionnaire (AdSAQ)*. Arvada, CO: Center for Addictions Research and Evaluation.

Wanberg, K.W. & Milkman, H. B. (1998). *Criminal conduct and substance abuse treatment: Strategies for self-improvement and change.* Thousand Oaks, CA: Sage Publications.

Wanberg, K. W., & Milkman, H. B. (2001). *Criminal conduct and substance abuse treatment: Strategies for self-improvement and change (SSC) - A report on provider training and staff development and client involvement in SSC treatment.* Denver, CO: Center for Interdisciplinary Studies.

Wanberg, K. W., Milkman, H. B., & Harrison, R. (1992). *The Personal Pleasure Inventory*. Denver, CO: The Center for Interdisciplinary Studies, Inc.

Wanberg, K. W. & Milkman, H.B. (2008). *Criminal conduct and substance abuse treatment: History, research and foundational models, a resource guide.* Thousand Oaks, CA: Sage Publications.

Wanberg, K. W., Milkman, H. B., & Timken, D. (2005). *Driving with care: Education and treatment of the impaired driving offender - Strategies for responsible living and change.* Thousand Oaks, CA: Sage Publications.

Wanberg, K. W., & Timken, D. (1991, 2005). *The Driving Assessment Survey (DAS)*. Arvada, CO: Center for Addictions Research and Evaluation.

Washton, A. M., & Zweben, J. E. (2006). *Treating alcohol and drug problems in psychotherapy practice: Doing what works*. New York: The Guilford Press.

Waters, A. M., & Craske, M. G. (2005). Generalized anxiety disorder. In M. M. Antony, D. R. Ledley, & R. G. Heimberg (Eds.), *Improving outcomes and preventing relapse in cognitive-behavioral therapy* (pp. 77-127). New York: Guilford Press.

Watzlawick, P., Beavin, J., & Jackson, D. (1967). *Pragmatics of communication: A study of interactional patterns, pathologies, and paradoxes.* New York: Norton.

Webb, J. A., Baer, P. E., Francis, D. J., & Caid, C. D. (1993). Relationship among social and intrapersonal risks, alcohol expectancies and alcohol usage among early adolescents. *Addictive Behaviors, 18*, 127-134.

Weimer, M. (2002). *Learner centered teaching*. Hoboken, NJ: John Wiley & Sons.

Weissenburger, J. E., & Rush, A. J. (1996). Biology and cognitions in depression: Does the mind know what the brain is doing? In P. M. Salkovskis (Ed.), *Frontiers of cognitive therapy* (pp. 114-134). New York: Guilford.

Welch, S. P. (2005). The neurobiology of marijuana. In J. H. Lowinson, P. Ruiz, R. B. Millman, & J. G. Langrod (Eds.), *Substance abuse: A comprehensive textbook* (pp. 252-262). Baltimore, MD: Lippincott Williams & Wilkins.

Werner, H. (1957). The concept of development from a comparative and organismic point of view. In D. B. Harris (Ed.), *The concept of development*. Minneapolis: University of Minnesota Press.

Wesson, D. R., Smith, D. E., Ling, W., & Seymour, R. B. (2005). Sedative-hypnotics. In J. H. Lowinson, P. Ruiz, R. B. Millman, & J. G. Langrod (Eds.), *Substance abuse: A comprehensive textbook* (pp. 302-313). Baltimore, MD: Lippincott Williams & Wilkins.

Wexler, D. B. (2000). *Domestic violence 2000: An integrated skills program for men.* New York: W. W. Norton & Company.

Wexler, H. K. (1995). Success of therapeutic communities for substance abusers in American prisons. *Journal of Psychoactive Drugs, 27*(1), 57-66.

Wexler, H. K. (2004). An integrated approach to aftercare and employment for criminal justice clients. In K. Knight & D. Farabee (Eds.), *Treating addicted offenders: A continuum of effective practices* (pp. 34-1 - 44-6). Kingston, NJ: Civic Research Institute.

Wexler, H. K., Falkin, G. P., & Lipton, D. S. (1990). Outcome evaluation of a prison therapeutic community for substance abuse treatment. *Criminal Justice and Behavior, 17,* 71-92.

Wexler, H. K., Melnick, G., Lowe, L., & Peters, J. (1999). Three-year reincarceration outcomes for Amity in-prison therapeutic community and aftercare in California. *Prison Journal, 79*(3), 321-336.

Wexler, H. K., Melnick, G., & Chaple, M. (2007). Stigma reduction: The program rehabilitation and restitution initiative. In K. Knight, & D. Farabee (Eds.), *Treating offenders: A continuum of effective practices, Volume II* (pp. 34-1 - 34-13). Kingston, NJ: Civic Research Institute.

Wilson, D. B., Bouffard, L. A., & MacKenzie, D. L. (2005). A quantitative review of structured, group-oriented, cognitive-behavioral programs for offenders. *Journal of Criminal Justice and Behavior, 32*(2), 172-204.

Wilson, G. T., & O'Leary, K. D. (1980). *Principles of behavioral therapy.* Englewood Cliffs, NJ: Prentice-Hall, Inc.

Witkiewitz, K., & Marlatt, G. A. (2007a). Overview of relapse prevention. In K. Witkiewitz & G. A. Marlatt (Eds.), *Therapist's guide to evidence-based relapse prevention* (pp. 3-17). New York: Elsevier Inc.

Witkiewitz, K., & Marlatt, G. A. (2007b). High-risk situations: Relapse as a dynamic process. In K. Witkiewitz & G. A. Marlatt (Eds.), *Therapist's guide to evidence-based relapse prevention* (pp. 19-33). New York: Elsevier Inc.

Wolfe, A. (2001, March 18). The final freedom. *The New York Times Magazine,* pp. 48-51.

Wright, J. H. (2004). Integrating cognitive-behavioral therapy and pharmacotherapy. In R. L. Leahy (Ed.), *Contemporary cognitive therapy* (pp. 341-366). New York: Guilford.

Yerkes, R. M., & Dodson, J. D. (1908). The relation of strength of stimulus to rapidity of habit formation. *Journal of Comparative Neurology of Psychology, 18,* 459-482.

Yochelson, S., & Samenow, S. E. (1976). The criminal personality, Vol. I: A profile for change. New York: Jason Aronson.

Yochelson, S., & Samenow, S. E. (1977). The criminal personality, Vol. II: The change process. New York: Jason Aronson.

Young, J. E. (1994). *Cognitive therapy for personality disorders: A schema-focused approach* (rev. ed.). Sarasota, FL: Professional Resource Press.

Young, J. E., & Flanagan, C. (1998). Schema-focused therapy for narcissistic patients. In E. F. Ronningstam (Ed.), *Disorders of narcissism: Diagnostic, clinical and empirical implications* (pp. 239-262). Washington, DC: American Psychological Association.

Young, R. M., Oei, T. P. S., & Crook, G. M. (1991). Development of drinking self-efficacy questionnaire. *Journal of Psychopathology and Behavioral Assessment, 13,* 1-15.

Zetzel, E. R. (1956). Current concepts of transference. *International Journal of Psychoanalysis, 37,* 369-376.

Zimring, F. M., & Raskin, N. J. (1992). Carl Rogers and client/person-centered therapy. In D. K. Freedheim (Ed.), *History of psychotherapy: A century of change* (pp. 629-657). Washington, DC: American Psychological Association.

Zuroff, D. C., et al. (2000). Relation of therapeutic alliance and perfectionism to outcome in brief outpatient treatment of depression. *Journal of Consulting and Clinical Psychology, 68,* 114-124.

Abuse:
    nonphysical, 289
    physical, 289
    prevention, 292–294
    treatment, 288–291
Acamprosate, 172–173
Accepting process, components in, 71–72
Action therapy, 229
Actiongrams, 136
Actions, thinking/attitudes/beliefs affect on, 159–161 (fig)
Active listening skills, 28, 192–193, 260, 261, 262
Active sharing skills, 186–191, 260, 261, 262
Adjunct provider guide for women in corrections, 5
Adjustment disorder with anger mood, 248
Admission interview, 125
AdSAP/RAPS, 110, 111, 113, 119
Adult Clinical Assessment Profile (ACAP), 112, 115 (fig), 116 (fig), 224
Adult learning model, 36
Adult Self-Assessment Questionnaire (AdSAQ), 106, 109, 110, 111, 113, 117 (fig), 125, 224
Adult Substance Use Survey—Revised (ASUS-R), 110, 111, 112–113, 113, 115 (fig), 119, 125, 224
Aftercare programs, 21
Aggression:
    nonphysical, 289
    physical, 289
Aggression/abuse/violence:
    prevention, 292–294
    treatment, 288–291
    Alcohol, 166–167
    gendered effects of, 167
    genetics and alcohol abuse, 167–168
    health risks of, 167
    metabolism and, 167
    rebound/withdrawal effect, 172, 173
    relapse triggers, 243
    See also AOD treatment; AOD use patterns and outcomes
Alcoholics Anonymous (AA), 32
Amphetamine addiction, and neurochemical process, 174
Anger:
    as learned social script, 271–272
    definition of, 292
    diagnostic classification of anger, 248–249
    guidelines for referral, 250
    guilt-anger (GA) cycle, 273
    managing criticism, 273
    managing/regulating, 74, 248–252, 270–271, 288
    PTSD link with, 289
    relaxation skills and, 274
    trait-condition anger, 271
Anger arousal, 291, 294
Anger Journal, 294
Anger scale, 251
Anticriminal expressions:
    modeling, 38
    punishing client, 38

    vs. procriminal expressions, 38–39
Antisocial behavior, xv
Antisocial behaviors and attitudes, DSM-IV-TR criteria for, 180
Antisocial personality disorder (APD) xv, 103, 180
Antisocial personality pattern (APP), 102 (tab), 103
AOD client, stereotypes about, 32
AOD treatment:
    as client-centered, 19
    counselor-client relationship in, 29–30
    efficacy of motivational enhancement in, 32, 33
AOD use patterns and outcomes, 164–178
    alcohol/other drug use patterns, 169–170
    basic knowledge about alcohol/other drugs, 165–168
    mental-physical pathway to addiction, 171–174
    misuse/abuse patterns, 176–178
    problem/addiction outcomes, 171–175
    Quantity-Frequency-Prediction (QFP) pattern, 169
    social use pattern, 169, 170
    solo use pattern, 169, 170
Appraisal, 67, 70
Arousal, 291, 294
Assertiveness skills development, 74, 267–269
Assessment, 54
    client self-assessment during *SSC,* 119–120
    intake and in-depth, 148
    See also Convergent validation model of assessment; PACE; Screening, for *SCC*
Automated PACE Manager (A-PACE), 110, 113, 120
Attendance/promptness issues, 125
Attributions:
    CBT and, 67, 70
    perceived, 89
Autobiography, 119, 156, 168
Automatic assumptions, 70
Automatic thoughts, 69, 160, 161 (fig), 220, 221
Awareness, 70–71

Balanced/healthy lifestyle strategies, 93
Balanced Relationship Model, 277
Bandwagon approach, 317
Beck Depression Inventory (BDI), 255
Behavior, learning/changing, 162–163
Behavior rehearsal, 74, 258–259
Behavioral intention, 211
Behaviorism, xiii
Beliefs, core, 220, 221
Biological cycle, 244
Biopsyclogical model of stress, 244–245
Biopsyclogical tension and stress, 242–243
Biphasic drugs, 165

Blood alcohol content (BAC), 165, 167
Body language, 189, 190, 193, 214, 261, 316
Brief Therapy. *See* Motivational Enhancement Therapy
Burns Depression Checklist (BDC), 255

Catastrophe theory, 84
CB Map, 52–53, 134, 154 (fig)
    as client self-assessment tool, 119
    STEP component of, 57 (tab), 59 (tab)
CB Map Exercise, 53, 134
Change:
    as natural, 216
    barriers to, 219
    motivation to, 216–217
    plan for, 224
    rules/tools/targets for, 155–157
    self-control affect on, 159–161 (fig)
    stages of, 216
    three-stage approach to, 17
    tools/targets for, 2, 119–120, 156–157
    vs. self-improvement, 8
    See also Change, stages of; Change, transtheoretical model of
Change, stages of, 218–219
    as cyclical, 61–62
    as differential, 60
    as multidimensional, 60
    pace incongruence, 60–61
Change, transtheoretical model of, 17
    action stage, 51–52, 55, 57
    contemplative stage, 51, 53
    determination/preparation stage, 51, 55
    maintenance stage, 52, 57
    precontemplative stage, 51, 53
    relapse stage, 52
Change environment, 217
Change process, 66, 215
Change reinforcement skills, 228
Character pathology. *See* Sociopathy
Classical conditioning, 47
Client-centered model, xiv
Client Program Response—Client (CPR-C), 110, 111, 113, 114, 117 (fig)
Client Program Response—Provider (CPR-P), 110, 113, 114, 118 (fig)
Client Progress Rating, 224
Client-provider relationship, developing effective, 4–5
Client Rights Statement, 124, 336
Cocaine addiction, and neurochemical process, 174
Cognitive analysis training, 28
Cognitive-behavior approach, to change/responsible living, 158–163
Cognitive-behavioral (CB) approach, xiv, 12, 18
Cognitive-behavioral (CB) process of learning/change, 161 (fig)
Cognitive-behavioral (CB) responses, for risk factor/crimonogenic needs reduction,

182 (tab)
Cognitive-behavioral psychology, 18
Cognitive-behavioral therapy (CBT):
    accepting process in, 71–72
    appraisal, 67, 70
    assumptions about AOD misuse and CC, 66
    assumptions/core beliefs, 67
    attitudes role in, 67
    attributions, 67, 70
    automatic assuming process in, 70
    automatic thinking process in, 69
    behavioral therapy roots of, 64
    cognitive distorting process in, 69–70
    cognitive processes of, 69–72
    cognitive structures of, 66–68
    cognitive structures of, model, 68 (fig)
    cognitive therapy roots of, 64
    context of change and, 76
    counselor-client relationship in, 31
    decision making process in, 69
    decisions, 67
    effectiveness of, 65–66
    efficacy and, 25–26, 67
    emotional component of, 76–77
    expectations, 70
    focus of, 64
    goal of, 69
    history of, 64–65
    mediating structures of, 67
    mindfulness/awareness value in, 70–71
    outcome expectancies, 67
    proximal structures of, 66–67
    psychoeducation as shared feature of, 15–16
    rules role in, 67
    self-efficacy and, 75–76
    self-reinforcing feedback process in, 65
    SSC cognitive-behavioral map, 77–79, 78 (fig)
    thought/emotion/behavior interaction process in, 72
    values role in, 67
    See also Cognitive-behavioral therapy (CBT), overview of methods used in
Cognitive-behavioral therapy (CBT), overview of methods used in, 72–75
    anger/emotion management, 74
    assertiveness training, 74
    assessment, 74
    behavior rehearsal, 74
    cognitive restructuring, 72–73
    communication skill building, 74
    follow-up, 74
    interpersonal problem solving, 74
    modeling, 74
    refusal training, 74
    relationship building/maintaining, 74
    role playing, 74
    social or relationship skills training, 73–74
    structured homework, 74
Cognitive change skills, 220
Cognitive distorting process in CBT, 69–70
Cognitive processes of CBT, 69–72
Cognitive restructuring, 65, 72–73
Cognitive self-control, 69
Cognitive structures of CBT, 66–68

model, 68 (fig)
Cognitive/thought restructuring, 18
Collaborative correctional-intervention partnership, 40 (fig)
Communication:
    interpersonal, 186
    other-oriented, 185
    skills building, 74, 187, 285
    verbal, 189–190
Communication skills training (CST), 260–263
Community, giving to, 302
Community-oriented empathy, 286
Compensatory attribution treatment model, 33
Compromise, as skill, 28
Conditioned desire, 243
Conditioned response, 243
Conditioned withdrawal, 243
Confidentiality, 125
Conflict, 295–298
    components of, 296
    defining, 295
    elements of conflict process, 296
    negotiation and, 297
    with community/society, 295
Confrontation, 20, 54
    correctional, 56, 58
    therapeutic, 15, 31–32, 56, 58
Confrontation feedback skills, 228
Conscience, research on, xiii-xiv
Consent for Program Involvement, 124, 334
Consent for Release of Confidential Information, 124, 335
Constructivism, on cognitive system development, 48–49
Continuing care, 21
Continuing care plan (CCP), 139
Convergent validation model of assessment, 15, 98–101
    comprehensive component of, 99
    objectives of, 99–100
    other-report (OR) data in, 100
    outcome component of, 99
    screening component of, 99, 101–105
    self-report (SR) data in, 100
    treatment process and change component of, 99
    value of client self-disclosure in, 100–101
Coping model, 244
Coping response, ineffective, 83
Coping skills, 84, 244
    weak vs. strong, 87–88, 209
Coping skills therapy, 25–26
Correctional confrontation, 56, 58
Correctional counseling, 37–38
Correctional-therapeutic partnership, 37
Counseling and psychotherapy, defining, 13–14
Counselor-client relationship, role in outcomes, 29–34, 35 (fig)
    characteristics of effective, 29
    client as person in, 34
    developing alliance with judicial client, 33–34
    efficacy of, 28–29
    motivational enhancement methods, 32–33
    therapeutic alliance, 30–31

    therapeutic alliance with group, 34
    therapeutic confrontation, effect use of, 31–32
    therapeutic stance, 29–30
Cravings/urges, 84, 126, 243
Creative thinking, 315, 316
Criminal conduct (CC):
    definition of, 180
    life-course sustained (LCS) pattern, 196
    time-limited (TL) pattern, 196
    treatment as client-/society-centered, 19–20, 34
Criminal conduct cycle, and thinking errors, 183–184
Criminal justice supervision, number of children/adults under, xiii
Criminal Thinking and Conduct (CTC) cycle, 183
Critical reasoning, 315, 316
Cue avoidance, 212
Cue extinction, 212
Cultural bias/prejudice, of client, 45
Cultural competence, of provider, 44–45

Decentering, and empathy, 285
Decision making process in CBT, 69
Decision window, 312
Depression, 253–256
    causes of, 255
    components of, 253
    managing, 255–256
    types of, 253
Depression Questionnaire (DQ), 255
Depression Scale, 255
Determinism, xiii
Differential change process, 60
Differentiation response phase of growth, 48, 54
Diversity, 5
    of clients, 44–45
    of judicial settings, 33–34
Dopamine, 166, 167–168, 174
Doubling, 28, 135, 223, 285
Driving Assessment Survey (DAS), 339, 341–343
Driving with care, 303
Dropping out, of treatment, 15, 30
Drug testing, during treatment, 126
Drugs:
    biphasic, 165
    definition of, 166
    direct/indirect effects of, 166
    genetics and drug abuse, 167–168
    health effects of, 168
    how they work, 166
    marijuana, 168
    neurochemical process and, 174
    neurochemical system and, 166
    rebound/withdrawal effect, 172, 173
    system enhances, 166
    system suppressors, 166
    tolerance effect on dependencies, 166
    types of, 166
    See also AOD treatment; AOD use patterns and outcomes
DSM-IV criteria:
    for substance abuse, 104 (tab)

for substance dependence, 105 (tab)
DSM-IV-TR criteria:
  for antisocial behaviors and attitudes, 180
  for antisocial personality disorder, 180
Dynamic cyclical/spiral model to facilitate change, 48 (fig), 49–51
  at macro level, 53
  at micro level, 52–53

Education/therapeutic approaches, integrating, 15–17
  adult learning model, 36
  integrating psychoeducation and therapy, 36–37
  psychoeducational methods/approaches, 36
Efficacy:
  of assertiveness training, 267
  of CBT, 25–26
  of psychosocial therapies, 25–26
  of social/relationship skills training, 257
  of SRST, 73
Egocentric psychotherapy, xiv, xvi
  sociocentric psychotherapy and, 14, 19, 279
Emotional component of CBT, 76–77
Emotional stress, 244
Emotions:
  affective recognition via pictures/video, 28
  management of, 74
  negative emotional state, 72, 84, 256
  positive emotional state, 72, 84
  self-disclosure of, 187
Empathy:
  as interpersonal cognitive construct, 285
  as skill, 27
  decentering and, 285
  defining, 283–284
  interpersonal sensitivity and, 285
  mutual and community-oriented, 286
  prosocial aspects of, 28
  training techniques, 28
  understanding/practicing, 283–287
  vs. sympathy, 283, 286
Empathy training:
  importance in judicial client treatment, 284
  techniques for, 28, 285–286
Encouragers to share skill, 54
Endorphins, 172
Escape plan, 293
Excuse thinking, 219
Existential psychology, xiii, xiv
Expectations:
  CBT and, 70
  outcome, 67, 209
  self-efficacy and, 76

Facilitator interaction, in psychoeducation, 17
Family therapy, xiv
Feedback:
  confrontation feedback skills, 228
  evoking feedback reinforcement, 58

giving/receiving, 135–136
  other-oriented communication and, 192
  provider-directed, 54, 56
  self-discovery, 54, 56
  self-oriented communication and, 190
  self-reinforcing, 65
Flight/fight/fake, 267
Follow-up Assessment Questionnaire (FAQ), 111
Foundational strategy, for treatment. See Client-provider relationship, developing effective; Cognitive-behavioral (CB) approach; Convergent validation model of assessment; Learning/growth and stages of change
FRAMES, 33
Freedom of choice, xiii
Freudian theory, xiii, 30
Full Disclosure Statement, 125, 338
Full recidivism, SCC definition of, 86
Full relapse, SCC definition of, 86
Functional integration response phase of growth, 48

GABA, 172–173
General anger disorder with aggression, 248
General anger disorder without aggression, 248
Global/undifferentiated learning stage, 49, 50
Global/undifferentiated response stage of growth, 48
Group:
  authority transference within, 133
  building cohesive, 20
  therapeutic alliance with, 34
Group facilitation skills, 229
Group leadership, principles of, 137–139
  center authority with group members, 138
  center authority within group, 138
  collaborative relationship, 138
  depersonalizing leadership authority, 137–138
  keep focus on CB change, 138
  keep focus on curriculum themes and concepts, 138
  maximize individual involvement, 138–139
  treatment methods, 137
Growth. See Learning/growth, responses forming basis of; Learning/growth and stages of change; Learning/growth stages
Guilt:
  optimal guilt arousal, 255
  understanding/managing, 253
Guilt-anger (GA) cycle, 273
Guilt Scale, 255

Harm avoidance, 11
Healthy lifestyles skills, 313, 318–329
  eating/personal care/physical activity, 326–327

healthy play/leisure time, 323–324
  job application, 329–330
  job interviewing, 321
  job leads, 321
  relaxation skills, 222–223, 274, 325
  resume development, 329
  telephone skills, 321
  time/task management, 321–322
  work intervention, 319
  work vs. job, 319
Healthy play/leisure time, 323–324
Helping-psychology movement, xiv
High-risk (HR) exposure, 83, 87, 90 (fig)
Highway map, to responsible living, 214, 314
Homework, 74, 125, 259
Humanism, xiv

Identity, in-group, 20
Impaired-control cycle (ICC), 103
Impaired driving, and moral/social responsibility, 19
Incarceration rates, beginning of 21st century, xiii
Individualized Treatment Plan (ITP), 4–5, 98, 125
Initial lapse, 83
Intake and admission forms, 331, 333–338
  Client Rights Statement, 124, 336
  Consent for Program Involvement, 124, 334
  Consent for Release of Confidential Information, 124, 335
  Full Disclosure Statement, 125, 338
  Notice of Federal Requirements Regarding Confidentiality of Alcohol and Drug Abuse Patient Records, 124–125, 337
  Personal Data Questionnaire, 106, 124, 333
Integrative learning stage, 49
Interactive self-assessment, 164
Interpersonal cognition, 186, 285
Interpersonal communication, 186
Interpersonal problem solving, 74
Interpersonal sensitivity, 285
Interpretive schemes, 49
Intrapersonal skill building, 72–73
Invitational skills, 134, 192

Jargon, 44
Jealousy, 291, 293–294
Job application, 329–330
Johari Window, 225
Judicial provider, effective, 41–44, 43 (fig)
  personal dimension of, 41–42
  philosophical perspectives of, 42, 44
  professional dimension of, 42
  profile of, 43 (fig)
Judicial settings, diversity of, 33–34

Lapse, SCC definition of, 86
Learner-centered approach, 131
  vs. information-centered model, 36–37

Learning/growth, responses forming basis of:
    differentiative/sorting out, 17
    global, undifferentiated, 17
    integration/putting together, 17
    Learning/growth and stages of change, 17–18
    assumptions about, 17
    challenge to change treatment phase, 17
    commitment to change treatment phase, 17
    dynamic cyclical/spiral model for facilitating, 48 (fig), 49–51
    dynamic model for learning and growth, 48–51
    external influences on learning/ growth, 60
    internal influences on learning/ growth, 60
    Lewin's response phases of of learning/growth process, 48
    Orthogenetic Principle and, 48–49, 53, 58, 59–60
    ownership treatment phase, 17
    traditional theories of learning and, 47
    treatment phases, 17
Learning/growth stages:
    differentiation, 59
    global/undifferentiated, 49, 59
    integration, 49, 50–51, 53, 58, 59
    sorting out, 49–51, 52–53
    unpacking, 49, 50–51
Learning theory, traditional, 47
    classical conditioning, 47
    model and observational learning, 47
    operant conditioning, 47
Lewin's model of growth, 48, 49, 53, 58
Life-course sustained (LCS) CC pattern, 196
Lifestyle balance, 311–312, 313
Listening skills, active, 192–193
LSI-R Criminal History Scale, 110, 111, 112

Mainstream psychotherapy, as egocentric, xiv
Marijuana, 168
Marlatt Relapse Prevention (RP) model, 200, 201
    erosion concept in, 203
    overview, 82–84, 85 (fig)
Master Assessment Plan (MAP), 54, 55, 93, 110, 119–120, 121 (tab), 224, 225
Master Profile (MP), 54, 55, 119–120, 225
Master Skills List (MSL), 119, 156
Mediation skills, 28
Mental-Behavioral Impaired Control Cycle (MB-ICC), 171–174, 175, 240, 244
Mental change skills. *See* Cognitive change skills
Mental health disorders, 72–73
Mental-Physical Impaired Control Cycle (MP-ICC), 174, 175, 242
Mental self-control, 231–256
Mental self-control/change skills, 233
Mentoring, 328
Mindfulness skills, 71
Minimum symptom criteria approach, 103

Model and observational learning, 47
Modeling:
    empathy, 28
    relationships and, 258
Modernity, worldview in, xiv
Moral behavior. *See* Prosocial behavior
Moral dilemma, 286, 300–301
Moral freedom, xvi
Moral responsibility:
    definition of, 18
    to others/community, 18–19
    value of, 299
    See also Social responsibility theory
Motivation:
    for change, 83–84, 216–217
    for treatment, 16, 17
Motivational enhancement, 15
Motivational Enhancement Therapy (MET), 25–26, 33
Motivational interviewing model, 32
Mowrer, O. H., xiii-xv
Multi-media, use in psychoeducation, 36
Mutual empathy, 286

Naltrexone, 172
Needs, hierarchy of, 276
Negative emotional state, 72, 84, 256
Negative thinking, 234–239
Negotiation, and conflict, 297
Neurosis, xiii
Nonadrenaline (NA), 173
Nonphysical abuse, 289
Nonphysical aggression, 289
Nonverbal communication, 189–190, 262
Notice of Federal Requirements Regarding Confidentiality of Alcohol and Drug Abuse Patient Records, 124–125, 337

Operant conditioning, 47, 162–163
Opoids, 172, 173
Optimal guilt arousal, 255
Orientation Session, 148
Orthogenetic Principle, 48–49, 53, 58
Other-awareness, 192–193, 260
Other-oriented communication, 185
Other-report (OR) data, 100
Outcomes:
    AOD problem/addiction, 171–175, 176, 177–178
    approach/orientation affect on, 25–26
    counselor-client relationship role in, 29–34
    expected, 67, 209
    provider core characteristics affect on, 26–28
    self-efficacy relation to, 76
    therapeutic alliance as predictor of, 15
    win-win, 296, 297, 298

PACE Index, 122
PACE Manager, 110, 120, 121
PACE Monitor, 56, 98, 111, 113, 120, 129
PACE (Progress and Change Evaluation), 98, 105–111, 148, 157

AdSAP/RAPS, 110, 111, 113, 119
Adult Clinical Assessment Profile (ACAP), 112, 116 (fig)
Adult Self-Assessment Questionnaire (AdSAQ), 106, 109, 110, 111, 113, 117 (fig)
Adult Substance Use Survey— Revised (ASUS-R), 110, 111, 112–113, 115 (fig), 119
Client Program Response—Client (CPR-C), 110, 111, 113
Client Program Response—Provider (CPR-P), 110, 113
cognitive-behavioral processing assessment, 109
components of, 105
differential screening and intake, 106, 108
Follow-up Assessment Questionnaire (FAQ), 111
instruments, 105–106, 107 (tab)
LSI-R Criminal History Scale, 110, 111, 112
motivation and readiness for treatment assessment, 109
multiple-factor assessment, 108
outcome assessment, 110–111
Personal Data Questionnaire (PDQ), 106
Phase I Review Guide (PI-RG), 111
post-discharge assessment, 111
Program Attending Record (PAR), 110
program closure assessment, 111
Program Closure Inventory—Client (PCI-C), 111
Program Closure Inventory— Provider (PCI-P), 111
program continuation readiness assessment, 111
Self-Evaluation Questionnaire (SEQ), 106, 108, 110, 111
Status Admission Results (SAQ), 111
strength assessment, 110
treatment progress and change assessment, 110
See also PACE (Progress and Change Evaluation), case example
PACE (Progress and Change Evaluation), case example, 111–119
    ACAP, 112, 116 (fig)
    admission to *SSC,* 111–112
    AdSAQ, 113, 117 (fig)
    ASUS-R, 112, 113, 115 (fig)
    comprehensive assessment, 112–113
    CPR-C, 113, 114, 117 (fig)
    CPR-P, 113, 114, 118 (fig)
    follow-up, 119
    LSI-R Criminal History Scale, 111, 112
    Pace Monitor, 113
    PAR, 113–114, 117 (fig)
    progress/change documentation, 113–119
    retesting on ASUS-R and AdSAP, 119
    SEQ, 114, 118 (fig)–119
    status at discharge, 119
Paradoxical intent, 222
Parole system, and reentry/reintegration

process, 21

Participant's Workbook, overview, 3–4, 147, 151

Partnership, judicial treatment, 39–40

Partnership, provider/client, 39–40

Perceptual shifting, 222

Perceptual training, 28

Personal Data Questionnaire (PDQ), 106, 124, 333

Personal values, 300

Phase I, Challenge to Change, 53–55 (tab), 149–226

    assessment in, 54

    confrontation in, 54

    goal of, 55 (tab)

    introduction to, 150

    methods/techniques for facilitating, 54

    objectives of, 55 (tab)

    program delivery and, 126

    provider goals and objectives, 150

    provider skill structure in, 54

    review/closure session, 129, 226

    therapeutic alliance in, 150

    See also *individual module*

Phase I, Module 1, orientation, 151–157

    goals, 151

    introduction of participant's *Workbook,* 151

    overview, 151

    S1, *SSC* overview/therapeutic relationship, 152–154 (fig)

    S2, rules/tools/targets for change, 155–157

Phase I, Module 2, CB and change/responsible living, 158–163

    goals, 158

    overview, 158

    S3, self-control and change, 159–161 (fig)

    S4, learning/changing behavior, 162–163

Phase I, Module 3, AOD use patterns/outcomes, 164–178

    goals, 164

    overview, 164

    S5, knowledge about alcohol/other drugs, 165–168

    S6, alcohol/other drug use patterns, 169–170

    S7, problem/addiction outcomes, 171–175

    S8, misuse/abuse patterns, 176–178

Phase I, Module 4, understanding/changing criminal thinking/behavior, 179–184

    S9, prosocial/antisocial/criminal thinking and behavior, 180–182

    S10, thinking errors/criminal conduct cycle, 183–184

Phase I, Module 5, self-/other-awareness communication, 185–198

    goals, 185

    overview, 185

    S11, self-awareness, 186–191

    S12, other-awareness, 192–193

    S13, sharing AOD use problems/emotions, 194–195

    S14, CC history sharing, 196–198

Phase I, Module 6, understanding/preventing R&R, 199–214

    applying RP to recidivism, 200–201

basic elements of R&R treatment, 201

empirically supported approaches, 202

goals, 199

goals R&R treatment, 201

high-risk exposure/triggers, 204

Marlatt model, 200

overview, 199

preventing R&R, 204

recidivism definition in module, 203

relapse definition in module, 202–203

R&R erosion process, 203, 205

S15, pathways to R&R, 205–207

S16, pathways to R&R prevention, 208–210

S17, urges/cravings and refusal skills, 211–214

SCC approach, 200

similarities/differences between R&R, 203

Phase I, Module 7, self-improvement/change, 215–226

    change as natural, 216

    change process, 215

    constructing change environment, 217

    enhancing motivation to change, 216–217

    provider goals, 217

    S18, stages/steps/roadblocks to change, 216, 218–219

    S19, thinking/belief change skills, 220–223

    S20, Master Profile/Master Assessment Plan, 224–225

    Phase I Review Guide (PI-RG), 111

Phase II, Commitment to Change, 53, 54, 55–57 (tab), 227–304

    as cyclical, 61–62

    assessment in, 56

    closure session, 129–130, 304

    correctional confrontation in, 56

    goal of, 55, 57 (tab)

    objectives of, 57 (tab)

    Phase I as preparation for, 228

    preparation session, 230

    program delivery and, 126

    provider-directed feedback loop in, 54, 56

    provider goals/objectives, 229

    provider skill structure in, 56

    provider skills/treatment strategies, 228–229

    self-improvement/change/responsible living skills, 227

    skills training in, 56

    STEP approach, 229–230 (fig)

    therapeutic confrontation in, 56

    See also *individual module*

Phase II, Module 8, mental self-control, 231–256

    goals, 231

    optimal cognitive-emotional stimulation, 231–232 (fig)

    overview, 231

    presentation logistics, 231

    S21, mental self-control/change skills, 233

    S22, negative thinking, 234–236

    S23, managing/changing negative

thinking/beliefs, 237–239

    S24, errors in thinking, 240–241

    S25, understanding stress, 242–245

    S26, managing stress/emotions, 246–247

    S27, managing/regulating anger, 248–252

    S28, guilt/depression and positive emotions, 253–256

Phase II, Module 9, social/relationship skills building, 257–277

    background/efficacy of, 257

    defining social skills, 257

    overview, 257

    presentation logistics, 259

    rationale/goals, 259

    S29, strengthening communication skills, 260–261

    S30, starting difficult conversation/keeping it going, 262–263

    S31, giving/receiving praise/positive reinforcement, 264

    S32, problem solving skills, 265–266

    S33, assertiveness skill development, 267–269

    S34, guilt-anger cycle, 270–274

    S35, close/intimate relationships, 275–277

    specific focus areas, 258

    SRST, approaches and methods, 258–259

    SRST, defining, 257

Phase II, Module 10, social/community responsibility skills, 278–303

    character building/strengths focus, 280

    goals, 278

    overview, 278

    presentation logistics, 278

    S36, strengthening character/prosocial attitudes/behavior, 281–282

    S37, understanding/practicing empathy, 283–287

    S38, understanding aggression/abuse/violence, 288–291

    S39, preventing aggression/abuse/violence, 292–294

    S40, settling conflicts/getting to win-win, 295–298

    S41, values/morals for responsible living, 299–301

    S42, giving to community/driving with care, 302–303

    sociocentric approach, implementing, 279–280

    treatment paradigm shift, 278–279

Phase III, Ownership of Change, 53, 57–59 (tab), 304–329

    closure session, 129–130, 329

    correctional confrontation in, 58

    evidence for ownership, 58

    evoking feedback reinforcement, 58

    goal of, 57, 59 (tab)

    internalization of change, 58

    objectives of, 59 (tab)

    overview, 305

    Phases I/II as preparation for, 306

    preparation session, 307

    program delivery and, 126

    provider goals/objectives, 307

    provider skill structure in, 58

provider skills/treatment strategies, 306
    R&R prevention training, 58
    therapeutic confrontation in, 58
    See also *individual module*
Phase III, Module 11, relapse/recidivism prevention, 308–317
    new R&R concepts/skills, 309
    overview, 308
    provider goals, 308
    review of R&R approach, 309
    S44, strengthening R&R prevention skills, 311–314
    S45, strengthening R&R prevention via critical reasoning, 315–317
Phase III, Module 12, healthy lifestyle skills, 318–328
    overview, 318
    presentation logistics, 318
    provider goals, 318
    S46, work/job/time management, 319–322
    S47, healthy play/leisure time, 58, 323–324
    S48, relaxation skills, 325
    S49, eating/personal care/physical activity, 326–327
    S50, receiving/giving support, 328
Physical abuse, 289
Physical aggression, 289
Plan for change, 224
Planned avoidance, 293
Positive emotional state, 72, 84
Positive reinforcement, giving/receiving, 264
Positive thoughts/behavior, reinforcing, 39
Posttraumatic stress disorder (PTSD), 289
Praise, giving/receiving, 264
Precontemplative stage of change, 16
Probation, reentry/reintegration from, 21, 139
Problem of Immediate Gratification (PIG), 240
Problem solving:
    assertiveness skills and, 74, 267–269
    skills for, 16, 265–266
    vicarious, 28
Problem user, abuse/dependence, 93–94, 176
Process of recidivism, *SCC* definition of, 86
Process of relapse, *SCC* definition of, 85, 86
Program Attending Record (PAR), 110, 113–114, 117 (fig)
Program Closure Inventory—Client (PCI-C), 111
Program Closure Inventory—Provider (PCI-P), 111
Program Closure Inventory (PCI), 130
Program delivery, methods/skills for:
    abstinence during treatment, 125–126
    admission interview, 125
    attendance/promptness issues, 125
    confidentiality issues, 125
    continuing care plan, 139
    craving/urges issues, 126
    drug testing during treatment, 126
    expectations of clients, 125–126, 147–148
    expectations of providers/group leaders, 124, 126

individual treatment plan, 125
intake/admission procedures and guidelines, 124–125
participation issues, 125
phase and program closure guidelines, 128–130
Phase I Review and Closure, 129, 130 (tab)
Phases II and *III* Closure, 129–130
recognizing program completion, 130
reentry and reintegration, 139–140
referral information/data, 124
removing client from program, 130–131
screening/intake, 124–125
social responsibility therapy, 136–137
treatment phases, 126
worksheets/homework, 125
    See also Group leadership, principles of; Program delivery, principles for manual-guided; Program delivery, provider knowledge/skills for; Program delivery, structure/strategies for
Program delivery, principles for manual-guided, 131–133
    delivery setting, 132
    focus on concepts/skills, 132
    keep sessions moving, 132
    multi-media/-sensory formats, 131–132
    personalizing curriculum, 131
    psychoeducation-therapy integration, 131
    seating arrangement and work space, 132–133
    sessions as lesson based, 131
    sessions as skill development based, 131
Program delivery, provider knowledge/skills for manual-guided, 133–137
    actiongrams, 136
    adjunct exercises, 136
    basic knowledge areas, 133–134
    CB Map, 134
    CB Map Exercise, 134
    CB STEP method, 134
    continued provider self-evaluation, 140
    core counseling skills, 134
    doubling, 135
    elaboration/personal identification facilitation, 136
    evaluating session delivery efficacy, 140
    for reactive-interactive skills, 136
    for referral, 133
    for reflective-acceptance skills, 136
    for reintegration, 139–140
    for screening/assessment, 133
    giving clinical supervision/training, 140
    giving/receiving feedback, 135–136
    group leadership principles, 137–139
    master knowledge and skills list, 141 (tab)
    maximizing participation/skill development, 135–136
    motivational enhancement skills, 134
    provider qualifications, 140
    receiving clinical supervision, 140

    role-playing, 135
    role reversal, 135
    round robin, 135
    sharing content presentations, 136
    skill practice and rehearsal, 135
    tools for change, 134–135
    updating/review, 136
    various roles of provider, 139
    wagon wheels, 135
Program delivery, structure/strategies for, 126–128
    closed group format, 127, 148
    creativity within fidelity to *SCC* program, 128
    delivery setting and service resources, 128
    delivery strategies, 127–128
    group format, 127
    minimum-maximum time delivery guidelines, 128
    Module I, 126
    no-entry points for open group format, 128
    open group format, 127, 148
    participant *Workbook,* 127
    Phase I as stand-alone in residential setting, 127, 148
    Phase II and *III* delivered in outpatient setting, 127, 148
    treatment phases, 126
Project MATCH, 25–26, 30
Propaganda methods, 316–317
Prosocial behavior, 300
    defining, 28
    value of, 299
Provider:
    adjunct provider guide for women in corrections, 5
    confrontational processes and, 20
    effective judicial, 41–44, 43 (fig)
    overview, 5
    personal characteristics and outcomes, 26–28
    Phase I, goals/objectives, 150, 217
    Phase I, skill structure, 54
    Phase II, goals/objectives, 229
    Phase II, skill structure, 56
    Phase III, goals/objectives, 307, 308, 318
    Phase III, skill structure, 58
    See also Program delivery, provider knowledge/skills for manual-guided
Provider-directed feedback loop, 54, 56
Provider Guide, overview, 3
Psychoeducation, 15–17, 164
    as shared feature of CBT, 15–16
    as stand-alone program, 16
    effectiveness of, 16
    integrating into therapeutic process, 16–17, 131
    support for, in treatment, 15–16
    vs. psychotherapy/counseling, 17
Psychological cycle, 244–245
Psychosocial therapies, efficacy of, 25–26
Psychotherapy and counseling:
    defining, 13–14
    vs. psychoeducation, 17
Punishment/sanctions, ineffectiveness in preventing recidivism, 6, 19, 85, 200
Quantity-Frequency-Prediction (QFP) pattern, 169

Rapport issues, 153
RE-thinking Report, 120, 157
Realistic negative thoughts, 237
Realistic positive thinking, 237
Reasoning skills, acquiring, 16
Recidivism, definition of, 203
Recidivism prevention, 81–82
    See also Relapse and recidivism
    (R&R) prevention
Reentry program, defined, 21
Reentry/reintegration into community,
20–21
    barriers to continuing care, 21
    efficacy of CB approach in, 25
    programs for, 20–21
Referral Evaluation Summary (RES), 124
Referral information/data, 124
Reflective-acceptance feedback approach,
    54, 228
Reflective-acceptance skills, 32, 54, 94
Refusal skills, 74, 211, 213–214, 268
Relapse, definition of, 202–203
Relapse and recidivism (R&R), 199–214
    applying RP to recidivism, 200–201
    as erosion process, 203
    basic elements in treatment, 201
    empirically supported approaches,
    202
    goals of treatment, 201
    high-risk exposure/triggers, 94, 204,
    231, 275
    overview, 199
    pathways to, 205–207
    similarities/differences between R&R,
    203
    urges/cravings and refusal skills,
    211–214
    See also Relapse and recidivism
    (R&R) prevention; Relapse and
    recidivism (R&R) prevention, SSC
    model
Relapse and recidivism (R&R) prevention:
    matching strategy to client, 17–18
    therapy-correction deterrence inte-
    gration and, 19–20
    treatment, core skill strategies in, 18,
    156
Relapse and recidivism (R&R) prevention,
    SSC model, 84–94, 200
    adapting Marlatt model to, 87–89
    as integrated effort for, 93–94
    balanced/healthy lifestyle strategies,
    93
    coping skills, weak vs. strong, 87–88
    expected outcomes, 88
    full recidivism, SCC definition of, 86
    full relapse, SCC definition of, 86
    goals in, 86
    high-risk (HR) exposure, 87, 90 (fig)
    key concepts in, 309
    lapse, SCC definition of, 86
    new concepts/skills, 309
    pathways to R&R prevention, 88–89,
    92 (fig)
    process of recidivism, SCC definition
    of, 86
    process of relapse, SCC definition
    of, 85, 86
    relapse prevention plan develop-
    ment, 93
    rule violation effect, 88–89

self-control and attribution, perceived,
    89
    self-efficacy/self-mastery, 88
    strengthening skills, 311–314
    via critical reasoning, 315–317
Relapse prevention:
    as paradigm shift, 81
    Marlatt Relapse Prevention model,
    82–84, 85 (fig), 200
    using psychoeducation in, 16
Relationships:
    developing effective client-provider,
    4–5
    developing/keeping close/intimate,
    275–277
    therapeutic, 74, 150, 152
Relaxation skills, 222–223, 274, 325
Removing client from program, 130–131
Responding attentiveness skill, 54
Resume development, 329
Retention of treatment, effects on, 15
Risk factor/crimonogenic needs reduction,
    182 (tab)
Role-modeling, 281, 328
Role-playing, 28, 74, 135, 258
Role reversal, 28, 135, 285
Round-robin exercise, 135, 157
RP model. See Marlatt Relapse Prevention
    (RP) model
Rule violation effect (RVE), 83, 88–89, 209,
    240

S-R theory, 47
Sanctioning, within therapeutic context, 39
SAQ, 111
Schema-focused therapy, 220
Screening, for SCC, 101–105
    antisocial behavior level, 102–103
    DSM-IV criteria for substance abuse,
    104 (tab), 106
    DSM-IV criteria for substance depen-
    dence, 105 (tab), 106
    impaired-control cycle, 103
    minimum symptom criteria, 103
    risk determination, 101–102
    self-report using standardized psy-
    chometric instruments, 104–105
    self-selection, 103
    substance abuse problem level,
    103–105
    See also Progress and Change
    Evaluation (PACE)
Seemingly Irrelevant Decisions (SIDs), 240,
    312, 313
Self-assessment, 37, 54
    during SSC, 119–120
    interactive, 164, 179
Self-attribution, 58
Self-awareness, 37, 38, 54, 58, 215
    pathways for, 186–191
    through active sharing, 260
Self-concept, 75–76
Self-control, 53, 56, 58
    affect on change, 159–161 (fig), 220
    anger management and, 251–252,
    273–274
    cognitive, 69
    for negative indulgences, 313
    mental, 73, 231–256, 233

R&R and, 89, 209
Self-determination, 51–52
Self-direction, 51
Self-disclosure, 37, 38, 41–42, 53, 54
    as path to self-awareness, 215
    as self-oriented communication, 190
    barriers to, 187–188
    emotions and, 187
    interactive, 179
    value of, 100–101
Self-discovery feedback, 54, 56
Self-efficacy, 33, 44, 58
    CBT and, 75–76
    core belief of, 68
    decrease in, 83, 209
    relapse and recidivism and, 88, 93
Self-esteem, 75
Self-evaluation, 51
Self-Evaluation Questionnaire (SEQ), 106,
    108, 110, 111, 114, 118 (fig)–119
Self-help groups:
    for reintegration, 22
    in ownership phase, 58
Self-image, 206
Self-importance, 68
Self-improvement vs. change, 8
Self-labeling, 32
Self-liberation, 51
Self-mastery, 44, 58
    R&R and, 88, 205, 209
Self-oriented communication, 185, 190–191
Self-perception, 176
Self-reflection, 51
Self-regulation, 51–52
Self-reinforcement, 65
Self-reinforcing feedback process in CBT,
    65
Self-report, using standardized psychomet-
    ric instruments, 104–105
Self-report (SR) data, 100
Self-selection:
    into AOD problem category, 103
    screening, for SCC, 103
Self-talk methods, 221
Self-value, 68
Situational anger disorder with aggression,
    248
Situational anger disorder without
    aggression, 248
Social and Relationship (interpersonal)
    Skills Training (SRST), 73–74, 257–277,
    280
    approaches/methods, 258–259
    background/efficacy of, 257
    defining, 257
    focus areas, 258
Social-environmental factors, 245
Social/interpersonal skill building, 18
Social learning theory, 271
Social responsibility therapy (SRT), 18–19,
    74, 75, 127, 136–137, 278, 280, 281
Social skills, defining, 257
Social systems theory, xiv
Sociocentric approach, implementing,
    279–280
Sociocentric therapy, xiv, xvi, 14
Sociocultural negativity, 30
Sociopathy, xiv
Sorting out learning stage, 49–50
SRST. See Social and Relationship
    (interpersonal) Skills Training

SSC
    core skill strategies in, 18, 156
    effectiveness/efficacy of, 5–8
    goals/objectives, 145 (fig)
    goals of, 153
    underlying principle of, 65
SSC Change Scales, 120, 157, 163
SSC cognitive-behavioral map in CBT, 77–79, 78 (fig)
State-Trait Anger Expression Inventory, 271
State-Trait Anger Expression Inventory 2, 271
Status Admission Results (SAQ), 111
STEP (Situation—Thinking—Emotional Response—Positive Outcomes), 2, 57 (tab), 59 (tab), 134, 229–230 (fig), 238
Stimulus control, 293
Stimulus-response model, xiii
Stress:
    biopsyclogical model of, 244–245
    biopsyclogical tension and, 242–243
    defining, 243–244
    internal stress response, 247
    major events/triggers for, 242
    managing, 246–247
    positive faces of worry/anxiety, 247
    stress ladder, 247
    stress syndromes, 244
    understanding, 242–245
Structured homework, 74
Subjective desire, 211
Substance abuse counselor, core characteristics of effective, 26, 27, 29
Substance abusing judicial client. *See* Treatment, of substance abusing judicial client
Support group, for reintegration, 22
Sympathy *vs.* empathy, 283, 286

TAP. *See* Thinking and Action Patterns (TAP) Charting
Target groups/delivery setting, 5
Telephone skills, 321
Therapeutic alliance, 15, 30–31, 34, 150, 152
Therapeutic communication methods:
    act on own story, 17
    hearing own story, 17
    telling own story, 17
Therapeutic confrontation, 15, 31–32, 56, 58
Therapeutic relationship, building/maintaining, 74
Therapeutic stance, 15, 20, 29–30, 217
Therapy, integrating with correction deterrence, 19–20
Thinking:
    excuse, 219
    five rules leading to actions/behaviors, 160, 169–170
    mapping pathway to change, 160
Thinking and Action Patterns (TAP) Charting, 120
Thinking/belief change skills, 220–223
Thinking filters, 193
Thinking Report, 120, 157
Thought habits (automatic thoughts), 69, 160, 161 (fig)

Thought stopping/braking, 221
Time-delaying response, 293
Time-limited (TL) CC pattern, 196
Time out, 293
Time/task management, 321–322
Toughing it out, 213
Trait-condition anger, 271
Transtheoretical model of change. *See* Change, transtheoretical model of
Treatment, core strategies in, 4–22
    cognitive-behavioral approach, 18
    cohesive group eliciting prosocial identity, 20
    effective client-provider relationship, 4–5
    facilitating learning/growth and stages of change, 17–18
    integrating education/therapeutic approaches, 15–17
    integrating therapeutic/correctional, 19–20
    moral responsibility to others/community, 18–19
    multidimensional assessment based on validation, 15
    reentry/reintegration into community, 20–21
    relapse and recidivism prevention, 18
    See also Treatment curriculum
Treatment, of substance abusing judicial client:
    conceptual framework for, 22, 23 (fig)
    elimination of symptoms goal of, 11
    growth and change goal of, 11–12
Treatment, overview:
    specific programs, 12–13
    strategies for, 12
    structures of, 12
Treatment, purpose of, 52
Treatment curriculum:
    client progress and change evaluation, 148
    community/society relationship, 146
    developing knowledge base for change, 146
    intake and in-depth assessment, 148
    interpersonal relationships, 146
    key topics of, 145–146
    mental self-control, 146
    orientation session, 148
    participant's workbook, 147
    program agreements/ground rules, 148–149
    relapses/recidivism prevention, 146
    self-assessment/evaluation, 145–146
    service delivery, 148
    treatment alliance development, 145
    See also Phase I, Challenge to Change; Phase II, Commitment to Change; Phase III, Ownership of Change
Treatment paradigm shift, 14, 19, 278–279
Treatment process, interactive components of, 35 (fig)
12-Step Facilitation, 25–26

Urge surfing, 213
Urges/cravings, managing, 211–214, 313

Values:
    in CBT, 67, 70–71
    personal, 300
Verbal communication, 189–190
Vicarious problem solving, 28
Violence:
    prevention, 292–294
    treatment, 288–291

Wagon wheels, 135
Win-win outcomes, 296, 297, 298
Withdrawal, 172, 173, 243
Worksheets/homework, 74, 125, 259

Yerkes-Dodson Law, 232 (fig), 254, 256

Zero-risk, 146, 153, 165, 175
Zero tolerance, 19, 86, 87, 202, 203

Note:

An "s" with a number following denotes a session number.

tab refers to Table

figure refers to Figure

Kenneth W. Wanberg, ThD, PhD, has academic concentrations in biology and mathematics, clinical psychology, psychology of religion, psychometrics and quantitative analysis, interpersonal communication and the psychology of spoken language. He worked as a counselor and clinical psychologist with the Alcoholism Division at the Fort Logan Mental Health Center for 15 years and then as a clinical psychologist with the Division of Youth Corrections, State of Colorado, for 17 years. He has been doing clinical work for 50 years and has had a private practice for 40 years. He has worked as a clinician and researcher in the field of alcohol and drug abuse for over 40 years and in the field of criminal conduct and substance abuse for over 25 years.

Dr. Wanberg has been author, principal investigator and project evaluator of a number of federal and state research and demonstration projects. These include: principle investigator for a six year research project on the identification and analysis of different alcoholism patterns and principle investigator and director of a three year alcoholism counselor training program both funded by the National Institute for Alcoholism and Alcohol Abuse; Author and project co-coordinator for a Colorado statewide training program for alcoholism counselors, funded by the Western Area Alcohol Education Training Program; Senior author and consultant on a three year early detection and intervention system of alcohol and drug problems, funded by the National Institute of Drug Abuse; and Co-author and research director of an extended residential treatment program for the chronic alcoholic, funded by the National Institute of Mental Health's Hospital Improvement Programs. He was also the projector evaluator for the following: a three year Center for Substance Abuse Prevention project for at-risk youth; a three year project that provided substance abuse treatment to Denver's public housing communities, funded by the Center for Substance Abuse Treatment (CSAT); a three year CSAT project for a drug treatment initiative for residential juvenile justice clients; and a seven year residential substance abuse treatment program for committed juvenile offenders, funded by the Colorado Division of Criminal Justice. He has served as a consultant to the Colorado Alcohol and Drug Abuse Division and as a consultant to more than 15 community mental health amd substance abuse agencies, and an adjunct or visiting faculty member of several colleges and universities.

Dr. Wanberg's research focus has been in the area of multivariate studies identifying different patterns and dimensions of substance use and addictive behaviors in adolescence and adult clinical and offender populations and is author and co-author of numerous research articles in this area. Out of this research he and his associates have developed reliable and valid instruments in measuring multiple problem dimensions and conditions related to substance use and abuse.

Dr. Wanberg is senior author with Dr. Harvey Milkman of the 1st (1998) and 2nd (2006, 2008) editions of *Criminal Conduct and Substance Abuse: Strategies for Self-Improvement and Change* (Sage Publications), a treatment manual for offenders with a history of substance abuse. He is senior author of *Driving with Care: Education and Treatment of the Impaired Driving Offender - Strategies for Responsible Living and Change* (2005) and the three participant workbooks that go along with this work (Sage Publications). He is co-author of *Pathways to Self-Discovery and Change: Criminal Conduct and Substance Abuse Treatment for At-Risk Teens* (Sage Publications, 2005).

Dr. Wanberg is a licensed psychologist in private practice, director of the Center for Addictions Research and Evaluation - CARE, Arvada, Colorado, and an evaluation consultant and trainer with a number of juvenile and adult criminal justice agencies and jurisdictions.

Harvey B. Milkman, PhD received his baccalaureate degree from City College of New York and his doctorate from Michigan State University. He is currently professor of psychology at Metropolitan State College of Denver.

His doctoral research was conducted with William Frosch, MD, at Bellevue Psychiatric Hospital in New York City, on the User's Drug of Choice. From 1980–1981, he completed a sabbatical exploration of addictive behavior in Africa, India, and Southeast Asia; in 1985 he was recipient of a Fulbright-Hays Lectureship award at the National University of Malaysia. He has represented the United States Information Agency as a consultant and featured speaker in Australia, Brazil, Iceland, The Netherlands, Peru, Turkey, and Yugoslavia. In March 1998, Dr. Milkman was the keynote speaker at The 21st Annual Treating the Addictions Conference, hosted by The Cambridge Hospital, in affiliation with Harvard Medical School. He is principle author with Stanley Sunderwirth of "The Chemistry of Craving," and author of "Better than Dope," featured articles in Psychology Today, October, 1983 and April, 2001 respectively. From September 1992–June 2002, he was author, principal investigator, and director of Project Self-Discovery: Artistic Alternatives for High-Risk Youth, a national demonstration model funded by The Center for Substance Abuse Prevention and the Edward Byrne Foundation.

In addition to having authored numerous published articles on the personality characteristics of drug abusers and behavioral addiction, Dr. Milkman is principal author of the following books:

- *Craving for Ecstasy: The Consciousness and Chemistry of Escape* (Milkman, H. B., & Sunderwirth, S., 1987, 1998, 2008);
- *Pathways to Pleasure: The Consciousness and Chemistry of Optimal Living* (Milkman, H. B., & Sunderwirth, S. 1993);
- *Project Self-Discovery: Artistic Alternatives for High-Risk Youth* (Milkman, H. B., Wanberg, K. W., & Robinson, C. 1996);
- *Pathways to Self-Discovery and Change: Criminal Conduct and Substance Abuse Treatment for Adolescents* (Milkman, H. B., & Wanberg, K. W. 2005);
- *Criminal Conduct and Substance Abuse Treatment for Women in Correctional Settings: Adjunct Provider's Guide* (Milkman, H. B., Wanberg, K. W., & Gagliardi, B., 2008).

Co-editor of:

- *Addictions: Multidisciplinary Perspectives and Treatments* (winner of the Choice Award for outstanding academic books; Milkman, H. B., & Shaffer, H. 1983)
- *Treatment Choices for Alcoholism and Substance Abuse* (Milkman, H. B., & Sederer, L. 1990)

Co-author of:

- *Criminal Conduct and Substance Abuse Treatment: Strategies for Self-Improvement and Change* (Wanberg, K. W., & Milkman, H. B. 1998/2006);
- *Driving with CARE: Education and Treatment of the Alcohol or Other Drug Driving Offender* (Wanberg, K. W., Milkman, H. B. & Timkin, 2006).

Principle author with Kenneth W. Wanberg of *Cognitive-Behavioral Treatment: A Review and Discussion for Corrections Professionals,* National Institute of Corrections, May 2007.

APPENDIX A
Summary of intake and admission forms

This appendix contains samples of forms that agencies are expected to complete at the time clients are admitted to treatment. Although these forms will vary from state to state, the substance of these forms cover most of the federal and state statutory requirements that govern consent for release of information, consent for participation in treatment, disclosure of program characteristics and elements, provider disclosure about self, and client rights statements.

Providers are expected to be aware of the federal and state laws, statutes and regulatory policies that govern the delivery of assessment and treatment services to alcohol and other drug abuse clients and to those in the juvenile and adult judicial system.

Although summarized in *Chapter 7* of this *Guide*, this appendix contains samples of the following forms that most if not all states or agencies require at the time of admission of a client into an alcohol and other drug and judicial treatment program. These forms are listed below in the order in which they appear in this appendix.

▶ Personal Data Questionnaire (PDQ): An intake form that documents key descriptive information about the client

▶ Consent for Program Involvement

▶ Consent for Release of Confidential Information

▶ Client Rights Statement

▶ Notice of Federal Requirements Regarding Confidentiality

▶ Full Disclosure Statement (disclosure of information about provider and provider's agency)

Providers are encouraged to match the elements of these sample forms with those used in their agencies.

REFERRAL EVALUATION SUMMARY (RES)
STRATEGIES FOR SELF-IMPROVEMENT AND CHANGE - SSC

REFERRAL SOURCE

Name of Referring Individual_____ Phone _____ Date _____

Agency Name and Address _____

CLIENT DATA

Name of Client:_____ Judicial No: _____

Address: _____ Phone: _____

DOB_____ Age _____   Gender: [ ] Male   [ ] Female

Ethnic Group: [ ] Anglo   [ ] Black   [ ] Hispanic   [ ] American Indian   [ ] Asian

Currently Employed: [ ] No   [ ] Yes   In School: [ ] No   [ ] Yes

Criminal Justice Status: [ ] Probation   [ ] Parole   [ ] Community Corrections
                                [ ] Department of Corrections   [ ] other_____

RATING OF CLIENT PROBLEMS

Referring individual is asked to rate the client on each of the following areas as to problem level:

	None	Slight	Moderate	Severe	Very Severe
1. Problems in childhood/adolescence	0	1	2	3	4
2. Family disruption and problems	0	1	2	3	4
3. Marital or relationship problems	0	1	2	3	4
4. Mental health and emotional problems	0	1	2	3	4
5. School adjustment problems	0	1	2	3	4
6. Employment/job adjustment problems	0	1	2	3	4
7. Level of antisocial behavior	0	1	2	3	4
8. Past involvement in criminal conduct	0	1	2	3	4
9. Physical health and medical problems	0	1	2	3	4
10. Involvement with criminal peers	0	1	2	3	4
11. Life disruption due to alcohol use	0	1	2	3	4
12. Life disruption due to other drugs	0	1	2	3	4

TO BE COMPLETED BY SSC PROVIDER

Name of staff handling referral _____ Final screening date _____

Disposition: [ ] No show   [ ] Intake deferred   [ ] Referred _____

                [ ] Client refused admission   [ ] Client admitted to SSC program

Name of provider case Manager _____

PERSONAL DATA QUESTIONNAIRE (PDQ)

NAME: Last_____ First_____ Age:_____ [ ] Male [ ] Female

ETHNIC GROUP: [ ] Anglo [ ] Black [ ] Hispanic [ ] Native Am. [ ] Asian [ ] Other_____

MARITAL STATUS: [ ] Never married [ ] Married [ ] Separated [ ] Divorced [ ] Widowed

    Number of times married_____

DOB: _____ SSN_____ JUDICIAL NUMBER:_____

ADDRESS: _____

    City_____ ZIP_____ Phone_____

LIVING ARRANGEMENT: [ ] Rent   [ ] Own   [ ] Living with family/friends   [ ] House

    [ ] Apartment [ ] Other_____ Months at current residence_____

EDUCATION: Number years_____ Finished: [ ] High School [ ] College [ ] Vocational Tech

EMPLOYMENT: [ ] Full-time [ ] Part-time [ ] Student [ ] Disabled [ ] Homemaker

    [ ] Unemployed: Number of months_____ Number of years_____

MONTHS EMPLOYED: Past year_____ Monthly income $_____ Occupation_____

MEDICAL: General Health [ ] Good [ ] Fair [ ] Poor; Type of medical problems: _____

    Medications: [ ] No [ ] Yes If yes, list: _____

    Physical limitations_____

    Name of medical clinic or doctor_____ Phone_____

    Date of last visit: _____ Date of last physical: _____

LEGAL HISTORY: No. DWI arrests____ Number of Non-DUI Misdemeanors ___ Number of Felonies___

    On probation [ ] No [ ] Yes   On parole [ ] No [ ] Yes

    Months incarcerated _____ Current charges pending [ ] No [ ] Yes

PRIOR AOD TREATMENT: Number of outpatient sessions_____ Number of residential days_____

PRIOR MENTAL HEALTH TREATMENT: Outpatient sessions_____ Residential days_____

PRIOR CORRECTIONAL TREATMENT: Number of sessions_____

SELF-HELP GROUPS: [ ] AA   [ ] NA/CA [ ] Al-Anon/Alateen [ ] Other_____

RELIGIOUS: Church/Synagogue/Mosque: [ ] No [ ] Yes_____

AGENCY: _____STAFF DOING INTAKE: _____ DATE:_____

CONSENT FOR PROGRAM INVOLVEMENT - SAMPLE

I agree to take part in Strategies for Self-Improvement and Change - SSC. I understand that the total program is composed of 50 one and a half to two hour sessions and that I may be offered a part or all of this program. I have been informed that there are three phases of this program, and that the total program could take from six to nine months to complete.

I understand that all programs of this type are not exact sciences, and that not everyone is helped by these programs. It is known that programs set up to help people with substance abuse problems and preventing criminal conduct have a greater chance of being successful when the client is willing to fully take part in the program.

I have been fully informed about my right to confidentiality and the exceptions to that right. I have also been informed of the ground rules and guidelines of this program and I have gone over these with my provider. My signature below is my seal for consent to be part of this program.

_____   _____

Client Signature   Date

_____   _____

Providers Signature   Date

_____

Program Name

CONSENT FOR RELEASE OF CONFIDENTIAL INFORMATION - SAMPLE

I,_____ hereby consent to communication between
    (Name of Client)

_____and
    (Name of agency providing Strategies for Self-Improvement and Change)

_____
    (court, probation, parole, and/or other agency)

Under this consent for release of confidential information, the above client agrees that the following information may be released to the above named agency or agencies:

> information about my assessment, diagnosis, urinalysis, attendance and progress in the program, my cooperation with the program, any violation of the terms of my probation, parole, or court requirements, and if I attend the program while under the influence of alcohol or other drugs.

I also consent to release the following information other than that described to the above agency or agencies:

_____

_____

I understand that this consent will remain in effect and cannot be revoked by me until:

_____ There has been a formal and effective termination or revocation of my release from confinement, probation, or parole, or other proceedings under which I was referred into the program, or

_____ Consent is revoked by me and/or when it expires on the following date_____.

I also understand that my alcohol and/or drug treatment records are protected under Part 2 of Title 42 of the Code of the Federal Regulations governing Confidentiality of Alcohol and Drug Abuse Records and the Health Insurance Portability and Accountability Act of 1996 ("HIPAA"), 45 C.F.R. Pts. 160 & 164. I understand that recipients of this information may redisclose if only in connection with their official duties.

I also release the agency disclosing this information from any and all liability with respect to the release of this information. My signature below provides the authority to release such information.

Name of Client_____

Address of Client_____

Client Signature_____ Date_____

Witness Signature_____ Date_____

CLIENT RIGHTS STATEMENT - SAMPLE

As a client in Strategies for Self-Improvement and Change (SSC), you have certain rights. First, you need to know that a qualified provider may consult with other experts on treatment issues. You are encouraged to discuss your progress in this program at any time with your provider. If you are court ordered to attend this program, you may not be able to end this program without permission of the Probation Department that made the referral.

You are entitled to receive information about the methods, approaches, cost, and length of the program. You will be an active participant in the development of your treatment service plan. You may also seek consultation from another expert regarding the appropriateness of this program for you.

You need to know that the information you give during this program is legally confidential except as required by law. This confidentiality is regulated by state law, and for individuals in substance abuse programs, also by Federal law. Information about your treatment and your case can only be released upon your written request. It may be that you have been ordered to attend this program and it may be a condition of probation, parole or community corrections placement. If this the case, and if there is a condition that a progress report must be sent to your court supervisor (e.g., probation officer) then you still must sign a written consent for such information to be released. Your provider will provide a consent form for you.

There are also exceptions to the law of confidentiality. These exceptions are as follows: if there is a "threat of harm to self or others," the person is of imminent danger to self or others, there is a suspicion of child abuse or if an individual is considered to be gravely mentally disabled. In these cases, a provider, by professional ethics and State Statutes, is obligated to protect the individual or others. In any situation where provider or other professional person suspects child abuse, that suspicion must be reported to the Department of Social Services in the county where the abuse is suspected.

Sexual contact between a client and provider is not a part of any recognized therapy or rehabilitation and is never seen as acceptable under any circumstance or condition. Sexual intimacy between client and provider is illegal and should be reported to the appropriate grievance or professional licensing authority.

I have been informed of my provider's professional credentials, training and experience. I have also read the above information and understand my rights as a client.

_____ _____
        Client Signature   Date

_____ _____
        Provider Signature   Date

NOTICE OF FEDERAL REQUIREMENTS REGARDING
CONFIDENTIALITY OF ALCOHOL AND DRUG ABUSE PATIENT RECORDS

The confidentiality of alcohol and drug abuse patient records maintained by this program is protected by Federal Law and Regulations. Generally, the program may not say to a person outside the program that a client attends the program, or disclose any information identifying a client as an alcohol or drug abuser unless:

- The client consents in writing;

- The disclosure is allowed by a court order, or;

- The disclosure is made to medical personnel in a medical emergency or to qualified personnel for research, audit or program evaluation.

Violation of the federal law and regulations by a program is a crime. Suspected violations may be reported to appropriate authorities in accordance with federal regulations.

Federal law and regulations do not protect any information about a crime committed by a client either at the program or against any person who works for the program or about any threat to commit such a crime.

Federal laws and regulations do not protect any information about suspected child abuse or neglect from being reported under State law to appropriate State or local authorities (See 42 U.S.C. 290dd-3 and 42 U.S.C 290ee-3 for Federal laws and 42 CFR Part 2 for Federal regulations).

Client Name_____

Client Address_____

Client Signature_____ Date_____

Witness Signature_____ Date_____

FULL DISCLOSURE STATEMENT SAMPLE - SAMPLE

D. M. Smith, M.A.
Certified Addictions Counselor

Mr. Smith is an addictions counselor with ABX Treatment Center in Denver, Colorado. He has a Bachelor's Degree in Criminal Justice from the University of Maine and a Master's Degree in Counseling from Northern Colorado University. He has worked in the field of addictions for 17 years. His major fields of interest are criminal conduct and the treatment of clients in the judicial system.

Mr. Smith takes a client centered and cognitive behavioral orientation in counseling. He sees alcoholism and drug addiction as having many causes, including social, psychological and physical. He also holds that social and biological genetics are important factors in the development of a substance abuse problem. He sees the importance of assuming the roles of therapist and correctional specialist in working with clients in the judicial system.

Mr. Smith has special training in the areas of stress management, relaxation therapy, treatment of depression, education and treatment of criminal conduct, substance abuse problems, cognitive behavioral approaches and motivational interviewing. He also has specialized training and experience in working with adult justice clients.

He is a member of the association of Substance Abuse Counselors, the American Corrections Association and the National Association of Alcoholism and Drug Abuse Counselors.

Client Name:_____

Client Signature_____ Date_____

Provider Name:_____

Provider Signature_____ Date_____

APPENDIX B
The Driving Assessment Survey - DAS

The *DAS* is used as an exercise in *Session 41*. Clients complete and score the survey in group. Scoring instructions are provided at the end of the survey. Providers will need to give clients some assistance in scoring. The items in the survey are clustered by scales to make scoring easier. When scoring the GENRISK scale, it is necessary to go through the survey and select those items that are in this scale and then score those items and derive the total GENRISK scale.

After clients score their *DAS*, they put the scores on *Worksheet 82*, page 251 (please note that there are eight scales, and that, on the profile or *Worksheet 82*, RELAX and REBEL were given the same number; REBEL should be number 6, CONVIVIAL number 7, and GENRISK Scale 8).

It is common to find that when comparing *SSC* clients with the impaired driving normative group, *SSC* clients will have higher ranks on the *DAS* scales for three reasons:

▶ Impaired driving offenders are more defensive, even though those in the normative sample completed the *DAS* after they had been sentenced and they were not required to put their names on the instrument;

▶ *SSC* clients are generally more open and self-disclosing;

▶ *SSC* clients will not perceive the results to have an effect on their judicial status or sentence.

Have clients discuss the driving risk patterns that they fit. GENRISK raw scores of greater than 16 puts clients in the moderate to high driving risk range. Also note that responses to the CONVIVIAL items (items 44 through 52) are asked in such a manner to reflect back on past drinking behaviors. This takes into account those *SSC* clients who have stopped AOD use.

Finally, the *DAS* used in this *SSC* edition differs from the one used in the first edition in that items have been renumbered; and those items not scored in the older version of DAS are not included in the one in this appendix.

The DAS is copyrighted and distributed by the Center for Addictions Research and Evaluation - CARE, P. O. Box 1975, Arvada, CO 80001-1975. The *DAS* may be used with *SSC* clients without cost. However, agencies wishing to use the *DAS* with clients not in *SSC* will need to request permission from CARE.

DRIVING ASSESSMENT SURVEY (DAS)

Kenneth W. Wanberg and David Timken
Authors

| NAME: | DATE: | [ ] Female   [ ] Male | Age: |

This survey is made up of questions that describe approaches, attitudes and behaviors that people have towards driving a car. Read each question carefully and then choose the answer that best fits you. Answer each question. The outcome of this survey will be used by you to help you better understand your approach to driving a motor vehicle. To get the most benefit out of this exercise, be as honest and accurate as you can. This will give you an honest picture of yourself and may help you become a safer driver. Your answers will be kept confidential.

1. I like driving in heavy traffic.
   a. Never
   b. Seldom
   c. Often
   d. Very often

2. When driving at high speeds I feel powerful.
   a. Never
   b. Seldom
   c. Often
   d. Very often

3. I have owned vehicles with high horsepower engines.
   a. Never
   b. Seldom
   c. Often
   c. Very often

4. I have chased drivers who annoy me.
   a. Never
   b. Seldom
   c. Often
   d. Very often

5. I feel powerful behind the wheel
   a. Never
   b. Seldom
   c. Often
   d. Very often

6. I have participated in sports such as auto racing, hang gliding, or sky diving.
   a. Never
   b. A few times
   c. Often
   d. Very often

7. High speed driving gives me a sense of power.
   a. Never
   b. Sometimes
   c. Often
   d. Very often

8. I have driven motorcycles at high speed.
   a. Never   1
   b. Sometimes
   c. Often   [   ]
   d. Very often

9. I am a driver who likes to stay ahead of or out in front of traffic.
   a. Not true
   b. Somewhat true
   c. Usually true
   d. Always true

10. I have outrun other drivers.
   a. Never
   b. Seldom
   c. Often
   d. Very often

11. I exceed the speed limit if road conditions are safe.
   a. Not true
   b. Sometimes true
   c. Usually true
   d. Always true

12. I have tried to beat a red light.
   a. Never
   b. Seldom
   c. Often
   d. Very often

13. I have tried to beat trains at crossings.
   a. Never
   b. Seldom
   c. Often
   d. Very often

14. I drive fast and take my chances of getting caught.
   a. Never
   b. Sometimes
   c. Often
   d. Very often

15. I dodge and weave through traffic.
   a. Never.
   b. Seldom
   c. Often
   d. Very often

16. I pass other drivers when not in a hurry.
   a. Never
   b. Seldom
   c. Often
   d. Very often

17. I have taken a risk when driving just for the sake of it.
   a. Never   [   ]
   b. Seldom
   c. Often
   d. Very often   2

18. I honk the horn when I am angry.
   a. Never
   b. Seldom
   c. Often
   d. Very often

1

19. When other drivers do stupid things, I lose my temper.
a. Never
b. Seldom
c. Often
d. Very often

20. I am easily provoked by other drivers when I am driving.
a. Never
b. Seldom
c. Often
d. Very often

21. There are times when I felt like smashing into another driver.
a. Never
b. Seldom
c. Often
d. Very often

22. I swear out loud or cuss under my breath at other drivers.
a. Never
b. Seldom
c. Often
d. Very often

23. It is hard to control my temper when driving.
a. Never
b. Seldom
c. Often
d. Very often

24. I get back at a driver who is behind me and has his bright lights in my rear view mirror.
a. Never
b. Seldom
c. Often
d. Very often

25. When angry, I have flashed my lights at drivers.
a. Never
b. Seldom   3
c. Often   ☐
d. Very often
d. Very often

26. It annoys me when the light turns red just as I get to the intersection.
a. Never
b. Sometimes
c. Often
d. Very often

27. I find myself in a hurry when I drive.
a. Never
b. Seldom
c. Often
d. Very often

28. I have had accidents or received tickets when under stress.
a. Never
b. Once
c. Two or three times
d. More than 3 times

29. I tend to pay less attention to driving when angry or stressed.
a. Incorrect
b. Partly correct
c. Usually correct
d. Always correct

30. When I am upset, I am not as cautious when driving.
a. Never
b. Sometimes
c. Often
d. Very often

31. When mad while driving, I am less cautious.
a. Never
b. Sometimes   4
c. Often   ☐
d. Very often

32. I have found myself driving fast without realizing it.
a. Never
b. Seldom
c. Often
d. Very often

33. It calms me down if I am able to drive when I am upset.
a. Never
b. Seldom
c. Often
d. Very often

34. I am able to relax and reduce tension while driving.
a. Never
b. Sometimes
c. Often
d. Very often

35. I forget about my pressures and problems when I am driving.
a. Never
b. Seldom
c. Often
d. Very often

36. I have driven to "blow off steam" after having an argument.
a. Never
b. Sometimes
c. Often
d. Very often

37. I go driving when I feel depressed.
a. Never
b. Sometimes   ☐
c. Often
d. Very often   5

38. At school or at work I break the rules in order to finish quicker.
a. Never
b. Sometimes
c. Often
d. Very often

39. I don't like police officers.
a. Not true
b. Somewhat true
c. Usually true
d. Always true

40. When it comes to the bottom line, nobody tells me what to do.
a. Not true
b. Somewhat true
c. Usually true
d. Always true

41. I have been in fights or brawls.
a. Never
b. Once or twice
c. Several times
d. Many times

42. I have had trouble because I don't follow the rules.
a. Never
b. Seldom
c. Often
d. Very often

2

43. I have been tattooed.
    a. Never
    b. Once   6
    c. Twice
    d. Three or
       more times

44. I have driven after
    drinking if I really
    had to get home.
    a. Never
    b. Sometimes
    c. Often
    d. Very often

45. I usually drank at bars.
    a. Never
    b. Sometimes
    c. Often
    d. Very often

46. When it came to
    parties, I really liked
    to live it up.
    a. No, not at all
    b. Yes, at times
    c. Usually
    d. Almost always

47. After going to sports
    events, I drank beer
    with my friends.
    a. Never
    b. Sometimes
    c. Often
    d. Very often

48. I enjoyed going to
    parties where no one
    made a big deal about
    heavy drinking.
    a. Never
    b. Sometimes
    c. Often
    d. Very often

49. I stayed out all night
    and drink.
    a. Never
    b. Seldom
    c. Often
    d. Very often

50. I went to parties such
    as keggers on weekends
    a. No, never
    b. Less than one
       weekend a month
    c. One to two weekends
       a month
    d. Three or more
       weekends a month

    7

51. Beating other drivers
    away from intersections
    is fun.
    a. Never
    b. Sometimes
    c. Often
    d. Very often

52. I give the finger to
    other drivers.
    a. Never
    b. Seldom
    c. Often
    d. Very often

53. Better driving training
    and skills would cut
    down on accidents.
    a. Do not agree
    b. Somewhat agree
    c. Mostly agree
    d. Completely agree

54. I could benefit from a
    driving skills and safety
    class.
    a. No, not at all
    b. Maybe a little bit
    c. Yes, most likely
    d. Yes, definitely

    G

SCORING PROCEDURE FOR THE DRIVING ASSESSMENT SURVEY

SCALE NUMBER	SCALE TITLE	ITEMS TO BE SCORED	SCORING WEIGHTS
Scale 1	POWER	1 through 8	a=0, b=1, c=2, d=3
Scale 2	HAZARD	9 through 17	a=0, b=1, c=2, d=3
Scale 3	IMPULSIVE	18 through 25	a=0, b=1, c=2, d=3
Scale 4	STRESS	26 through 31	a=0, b=1, c=2, d=3
Scale 5	RELAXATION	32 through 37	a=0, b=1, c=2, d=3
Scale 6	REBELLIOUSNESS	38 through 43	a=0, b=1, c=2, d=3
Scale 7	CONVIVIAL DRINKING	44 through 52	a=0, b=1, c=2, d=3
G: GENRISK	GENERAL DRIVING RISK	2, 5, 7, 9, 10, 11, 12, 14, 15, 16, 17, 19, 20, 22, 26, 32, 46, 51, 52	a=0, b=1, c=2, d=3

The normative group is a sample of 395 impaired driving offenders evaluated for DWI services